Industry	**Leading Decision-Makers**	
Movie Theaters (Chapter 14) 	Carl Patrick, Sr. (chairman of Carmike) Michael Patrick (president of Carmike) Garth Drabinski (head of Cineplex Odeon)	1. ... cepts to understand and establish a firm's pricing policies. 2. Analyze the effects of market structure on firm behavior and strategic decisions. 3. Incorporate technological change into a firm's strategic planning.
Aircraft (Chapter 17) 	Robert Crandall (CEO of American Airlines) Philip Condit (CEO of Boeing) Jean Pierson (president of Airbus) John McDonnell (chairman of McDonnell Douglas)	1. Apply microeconomics to forecast markets and analyze techniques to reduce costs. 2. Use the net-present-value rule to help guide investment decisions. 3. Analyze the ways in which government policies regarding subsidies, tariffs, and purchasing affect firms' behavior and fortunes.
California water (Chapter 19) 	Bill Bradley (U.S. Senator) Calvin Dooley (Member of Congress) Paul Wellstone (U.S. Senator) Tom Bradley (Los Angeles mayor) Pete Wilson (California governor)	1. Estimate the effects of a government program on economic efficiency, as well as on various segments of the population. 2. Evaluate the nature and size of federal subsidies. 3. Analyze the economic effects of proposed and factual changes in a government program.

APPLIED

Microeconomics

Second Edition

EDWIN MANSFIELD

W·W· Norton & Company   New York   London

Applied Microeconomics

Microeconomics

Second Edition

Copyright © 1997, 1994 by W. W. Norton & Company, Inc.

The text of this book is composed in Granjon.
Composition by New England Typographic Service, Inc.
Manufacturing by Courier Westford
Cover illustration: Credit © Flip Chalfant/The Image Bank

Library of Congress Cataloging-in-Publication Data

Mansfield, Edwin
    Applied microeconomics / Edwin Mansfield.—2nd ed.
        p.   cm.
    Includes bibliographical references and index.
    ISBN 0-393-97032-9
    1. Microeconomics.   I. Title.
HB172.M348   1996
338.5— dc20   96-8232

W. W. Norton & Company, Inc., 500 Fifth Avenue, New York, N.Y. 10110
http://web.wwnorton.com

W. W. Norton & Company Ltd., 10 Coptic Street, London WC1A 1PU

1   2   3   4   5   6   7   8   9   0

To Jared Mansfield,
who got the meridian
lines right.

CONTENTS

PART ONE: INTRODUCTION

1 Demand and Supply 1

2 Applying Microeconomic Theory: Microbreweries, Cocaine, and Spectrum Rights 40

PART TWO: CONSUMER BEHAVIOR AND MARKET DEMAND

3 The Tastes and Preferences of the Consumer 61

4 Consumer Behavior and Individual Demand 97

5 Market Demand 132

6 Applying Microeconomic Theory: The Case of Black Gold 162

PART THREE: THE FIRM: ITS TECHNOLOGY AND COSTS

7 The Firm and Its Technology 187

8 Optimal Input Combinations and Cost Functions 222

9 Applying Microeconomic Theory: The Case of Milk and Dairy Products 273

PART FOUR: MARKET STRUCTURE, PRICE, AND OUTPUT

10 Perfect Competition 297

11 Monopoly 339

12 Monopolistic Competition and Oligopoly 381

13 Game Theory and Strategic Behavior 424

14 Applying Microeconomic Theory: The Case of Carmike Cinemas, Inc. 453

PART FIVE: MARKETS FOR INPUTS

15 Price and Employment of Inputs 479

16 Investment Decisions and Risk 524

17 Applying Microeconomic Theory: The Case of Jetliners 569

PART SIX: ECONOMIC EFFICIENCY

18 Economic Efficiency, Externalities, and Public Goods 595

Applying Microeconomic Theory: The Case of California Water 641

APPENDIX A1

About the Author

Edwin Mansfield is Professor of Economics and Director of the Center for Economics and Technology at the University of Pennsylvania. Prior to joining the Penn faculty, he taught at Carnegie-Mellon, Yale, Harvard, and California Institute of Technology. He has been elected a fellow of the American Academy of Arts and Sciences, of the Econometric Society, of the Center for Advanced Study in the Behavioral Sciences, and he has held Fulbright and Ford Foundation fellowships. He was included on the *Journal of Economic Perspectives'* list of 20 most cited economists in the United States.

Long involved in applied microeconomics, Professor Mansfield has been a consultant to many industrial firms and government agencies, including Exxon, Westinghouse, GTE, Stauffer Chemical, the Rand Corporation, the Small Business Administration, and the Federal Trade Commission, and has given television courses for executives at AT&T, Hewlett-Packard, IBM, and other firms. He has been a member of the board of directors of the American Productivity and Quality Center, the Advisory Committee of the U.S. Bureau of the Census, and the AAAS's Committee on Science, Engineering and Public Policy. He received the Certificate of Appreciation of the U.S. Secretary of Commerce, was appointed to the National Technology Medal Committee, and in 1994 received a special Creativity Award from the National Science Foundation for outstanding scientific/technical progress achieved.

He is the author of 30 books and about 200 articles. His textbooks on economics, microeconomics, managerial economics, and statistics have been adopted at over 1,000 colleges and universities, and have been translated for use abroad. He has been on the editorial board of a number of journals, including the *Journal of the American Statistical Association.* A graduate of

Dartmouth College, he received his M.A. and Ph.D. degrees from Duke University, as well as the Certificate and Diploma of the Royal Statistical Society. He has been chairman of the Visiting Committee at the Rensselaer Polytechnic Institute, U.S. chairman of the U.S.-U.S.S.R. Working Party on the Economics of Science and Technology, and the first U.S. economist to visit and lecture in the People's Republic of China under the 1979 Sino-American agreements. He has received the Publication Award of the Patent Law Association, the Honor Award of the National Technological University for research, teaching, and public service, and the 1996 Kenan Enterprise Award for research and teaching.

Preface

This is a book on applied microeconomics. It has been designed for the many classes given each year for students who want to learn how microeconomic theory can help them become better managers, public officials, lawyers, or members of other such professional groups.

The success of the First Edition of this book was very encouraging, but like any new textbook, use in the classroom has produced lots of good ideas for improvements. While the book's general structure and approach remain much the same in this edition as in the previous one, there are many noteworthy improvements.

A new Chapter 2 has been added, the purpose being to acquaint the student early in the course with the usefulness of microeconomics. This chapter contains three brief cases. The first case looks at the Atlanta Brewing Company, an Atlanta microbrewery, and the market for its products. The second case is concerned with the cocaine epidemic in the United States, with special attention to government policies aimed at dealing with our drug problems. The third case deals with the Federal Communication Commission's auction of spectrum rights. All these cases apply supply-and-demand models and elasticity concepts presented in Chapter 1. They cover material of interest both to business schools and departments of public policy.

Chapter 15 now contains the material on input pricing that formerly occupied two chapters. This combination of the input pricing chapters streamlines the exposition. Further, the addition of the Stackelberg and Bertrand models in Chapter 12, as well as maximin and mixed strategies in Chapter 13, extends the analysis of oligopoly. Also, a brief section on game trees has been added.

Further, many new boxed examples have been included. Specifically, the following are new or updated: (1) "Coffee Bars Invade Manhattan," (2) "The Price of Cotton: Highest since the Civil War," (3) "Calculating a Cost-of-Living Index," (4) "Is a CEO Worth $26 Million per Year?" (5) "Retail Market for Tires," (6) "Increasing the Minimum Wage: Controversy over the Effects," and (7) "Neil Simon Goes Off-Broadway."

My purpose in this book has been to show students *repeatedly* and *in detail* exactly how microeconomic theory can be applied to help solve *real* problems faced by *actual* decision makers in industry and government. Five chapters of this book are devoted entirely to individual industries—petroleum (Chapter 6), milk and dairy products (Chapter 9), movie theaters (Chapter 14), aircraft

(Chapter 17), and California water (Chapter 19). In each of these chapters, after a brief discussion of the industry's structure and problems, the student is asked to use the theory he or she has met in previous chapters to solve ten real multipart problems related to major decisions and issues in this industry. The situation and actual data are given; the decision makers are described in detail and often quoted and pictured. Unlike the snippets currently available, each of these chapters forces the student to become immersed in much of the full complexity of actual industrial and government decisions and to bring a variety of microeconomic tools and concepts to bear on these decisions. For half the problems, answers are provided to guide the student and to provide useful feedback; for the other half, no answers are given. Additional material regarding each of these chapters is printed on the inside front cover of this book.

Further, each of these chapters draws on all preceding parts of the course, and thus helps to prevent the balkanization of knowledge that affects some classes. Too frequently, students forget some of the material presented early in the course by the time they get close to the final examination. Each of these chapters forces the student to use a wide range of analytical tools presented in all previous chapters, and thus encourages a periodic review of previous materials and an integration of various parts of the course. Also, many cases are extended beyond the particular chapters where they appear. Sections of later chapters (as well as end-of-chapter questions) revisit the industries studied in previous cases and show the student how the new techniques taken up in later chapters can be applied to these industries.

How much class time is devoted to each of these chapters will vary, of course, with the nature and length of the course, as well as with the characteristics of the students. To permit instructors to tailor the problems they assign to the needs of their own classes, a wide variety of problems are included, some easy, some challenging. Because each is self-contained, there is no need to take up all of them. Since the answers to the even-numbered problems are not given at the end of the book, these problems may be particularly useful for class discussion or homework assignment. (Answers to the even-numbered problems are available in the *Instructor's Manual*.) Some instructors may prefer to assign many of the problems for homework, but not take them up in class. This can readily be done.

Excluding these five chapters and Chapter 2 (which also is devoted to case studies), this book contains a full treatment of microeconomic theory. Most chapters are almost identical to the corresponding chapters in my *Microeconomics: Theory and Applications,* Ninth Edition. The principal changes in this regard are that the material on uncertainty and investment decisions has been summarized in a single chapter here, and that much of the material on welfare economics, externalities, and public goods has been combined in a single chapter. Like *Microeconomics: Theory and Applications,* a hallmark of this book is the continuous interplay between theory and applications. A list of the over 100 real-world applications (excluding the five chapter-length presentations) contained here is printed on the inside back cover of this book.

A workbook accompanies this text. This supplement (*Study Guide and Casebook for Applied Microeconomics,* Second Edition) contains hundreds of problem sets, problems, and review questions (as well as their answers), which should be helpful to students. The problems and questions have been tested for effectiveness in the classroom. An important feature of this supplement is the inclusion of the following six full-length classroom-tested cases: (1) "The Greatest Auction Ever" (by William Safire), (2) "The Standard Oil Company: British Petroleum Loses Patience" (by J. David Hunger), (3) "The Dairy Industry" (by Richard Fallert, Don Blayney, and James Miller), (4) "Cineplex Odeon Corporation" (by Joseph Wolfe), (5) "Airbus Industries: A Wave of the Future" (by Shaker Zahra, Daniel Hurley, Jr., and John Pearce II), and (6) "California Water Pricing" (by Dorothy Robyn). Each of these cases supplements one of the six chapters of the text dealing with problems and issues in particular industries. Thus, they enable the student to go deeper into these problems and issues and enrich classroom discussion.

An *Instructor's Manual* is available for the text. In addition to teaching suggestions for each chapter, it includes a test bank of multiple-choice questions and problem sets which reflect the decision-making emphasis of the text. Kathryn Nantz, the author of the *Instructor's Manual,* has created a varied menu of teaching materials for this new book.

Test questions are also available to instructors on floppy disks for use with a personal computer. Information on these disks can be obtained from the publisher.

I am indebted to the following instructors and reviewers who have contributed in important ways to this book: Donald C. Cell, Cornell College; Clifford Dobitz, North Dakota State; Tran Dung, Wright State University; Kenneth Hubbell, University of Missouri, Kansas City; Brad Kamp, University of South Florida; Thomas Kniesner, Indiana University; William Lee, St. Mary's College; Annette Levi, California State University, Chico; Mark Machina, University of California, San Diego; Lawrence Martin, Michigan State University; Kathryn Nantz, Fairfield University; James Stephenson, Iowa State University; Charles Strein, University of Northern Iowa; R. Mark Wilson, University of South Florida; and Kurt Zorn, Indiana University. Ed Parsons and W. Drake McFeely of Norton did a fine job. Special thanks go to my wife, who helped in countless ways.

E.M.
Philadelphia, 1997

PART ONE

Introduction

Demand and Supply

1

INTRODUCTION

Paul G. Allen, a cofounder (with William Gates) of Microsoft, the big computer software firm, was worth $6.5 billion in 1995. He was a major investor in dozens of firms, ranging from telecommunications to professional basketball. Clearly, he had to make countless decisions that depended on a knowledge of economics. Economics helps us to understand the nature and organization of our society, the arguments underlying many of the great public issues of the day, and the operation and behavior of business firms and other economic decision-making units. To perform effectively and responsibly as citizens, administrators, workers, or consumers, most people, not just Mr. Allen, need to know some economics.

What does economics deal with? According to one standard definition, economics is concerned with the way in which resources are allocated among alternative uses to satisfy human wants. It is customary to divide economics into two parts: microeconomics and macroeconomics. *Microeconomics* deals with the economic behavior of individual units such as consumers, firms, and resource owners; macroeconomics deals with the behavior of economic aggregates such as gross domestic product and the level of employment. This book is concerned with *applied microeconomics*.

To illustrate the sorts of problems that applied microeconomics can help you solve, consider the largest airline in the United States, American Airlines. How many airplanes should American Airlines buy? And how many workers should be hired to run and service them? And what price should American Airlines charge for a ticket between New York and San Francisco? These are examples of one type of problem that microeconomics is designed to solve. They are questions faced by an individual firm that is trying to maximize its profit or attain some other set of objectives of its owners and managers. Microeconomics serves as the basis for, and is helpful in promoting an understanding of, the powerful modern tools of managerial decision making that help to solve such problems.

But this is not the only function of microeconomics. On the contrary, much of microeconomics is concerned with problems that face us all as citizens. Together we must somehow decide how we want to organize the production and marketing of goods and services in our country. We must also decide how these goods and services are to be distributed among the people. Some of the subtlest and most significant applications of microeconomics are in this area, as we shall see in this and subsequent chapters.[1]

MARKETS

Since applied microeconomics is concerned with the behavior of markets, it is necessary to describe at the outset what we mean by a market. This is not quite as straightforward as it may seem, because most markets are not well defined in a geographical or physical sense. (For example, the New York Stock

---

[1] This chapter provides a brief, initial look at central concepts in microeconomics. Readers familiar with these concepts can use this chapter for review, or go directly to Chapter 2 without loss of continuity.

Exchange is an atypical market in the sense that it is located principally in a particular building.) What is a *market*? A good working definition is that it is a group of firms and individuals in touch with each other in order to buy or sell some good. Of course, not every person in a market has to be in contact with every other person in the market; a person or firm is part of a market even if in contact with only a subset of the other persons or firms in the market.

Markets vary enormously in their size, arrangements, and procedures. For some household goods, all of the consumers west of the Rocky Mountains may be members of the same market. For other goods, like Rembrandt paintings, only a few collectors, dealers, and museums scattered around the world are members of the market. Basically, however, all markets consist primarily of buyers and sellers, although third parties like brokers and agents may be present as well. In most markets, the sellers suggest the price, but this is not always the case. In this chapter, we generally assume that a market contains many small buyers and sellers so that none of them individually exerts a significant influence on the price.[2] We will relax that assumption in later chapters.

Market

THE DEMAND SIDE OF THE MARKET

The Market Demand Curve

The market for every good has a demand side and a supply side. The demand side can be represented by a *market demand schedule,* a table which shows the quantity of the good that would be purchased at each price. (The price of the good is, of course, the amount of money that must be paid for a unit of it.) For example, suppose that the market demand schedule for coal is as shown in Table 1.1.[3] According to this table, 730 million tons of coal will be demanded per year if its price is $40 per ton, 710 million tons of coal will be demanded if

---

[2] More accurately, we generally assume in this chapter that markets are perfectly competitive. A perfectly competitive market exists when no buyer or seller can influence price, output is homogeneous, resources are mobile, and knowledge is perfect. A fuller definition of a perfectly competitive market is given in Chapter 10. (At the end of this chapter, we focus on some cases where information is imperfect.)

[3] These figures are hypothetical, but adequate for present purposes. In subsequent chapters, we shall provide data describing the actual relationship between the price and quantity demanded of various goods. At this point, the emphasis is on the concept of a market demand schedule, not on the detailed accuracy of these figures.

TABLE 1.1 Market Demand Schedule for Coal, 1997	
Price per ton (dollars)	Quantity demanded per year (millions of tons)
40	730
41	710
42	700
43	690
44	680
45	670
46	665

Market demand curve

its price is $41 per ton, and so on. Another way of presenting the data in Table 1.1 is by a *market demand curve,* which is a plot of the market demand schedule on a graph. The vertical axis of the graph measures the price per unit of the good, and the horizontal axis measures the quantity of the good demanded per unit of time. Figure 1.1 shows the market demand curve for coal, based on the figures in Table 1.1.

Two things should be noted concerning Figure 1.1. First, the market demand curve for coal *slopes downward to the right.* In other words, the quantity

FIGURE 1.1 Market Demand Curve for Coal, 1997 The market demand curve for coal shows the quantity of coal that would be purchased at each price.

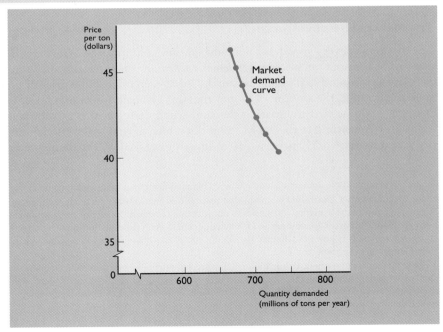

of coal demanded increases as the price falls. This is true of the demand curves for most goods: They almost always slope downward to the right. In subsequent chapters, we shall learn why this is not always the case, but these reasons need not concern us at present. Second, the market demand curve in Figure 1.1 pertains to a *particular period of time:* 1997. It is important to recognize that any demand curve pertains to some period of time, and that its shape and position depend on the length and other characteristics of this period. For example, if we were to estimate the market demand curve for coal for the first week in 1997, it would be a different curve from the one in Figure 1.1, which pertains to the whole year. The difference arises partly because consumers can adapt their purchases more fully to changes in the price of coal in a year than in a week.

Besides the length of the time period, what other factors determine the position and shape of the market demand curve for a good? One important factor is the *tastes of consumers.* If consumers show an increasing preference for a product, the demand curve will shift to the right: That is, at each price, consumers will desire to buy more than previously. On the other hand, if consumers show a decreasing preference for a product, the demand curve will shift to the left, since, at each price, consumers will desire to buy less than previously. For example, if people become more energy-conscious, and begin to take more pride in cutting back on the unnecessary use of energy, the demand curve for coal may shift to the left, as shown in Figure 1.2. The greater the shift in preferences, the larger the shift in the demand curve.

FIGURE 1.2 Effect of Public Emphasis on Energy Conservation on Market Demand Curve for Coal If people take pride in reducing the unnecessary use of energy, the demand curve for coal may shift to the left.

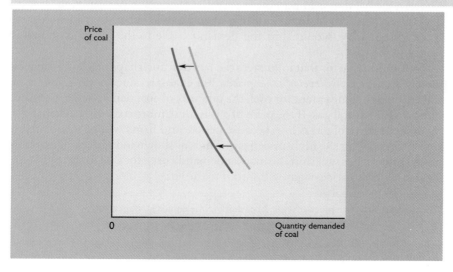

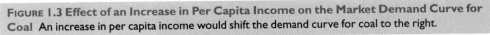

FIGURE 1.3 Effect of an Increase in Per Capita Income on the Market Demand Curve for Coal An increase in per capita income would shift the demand curve for coal to the right.

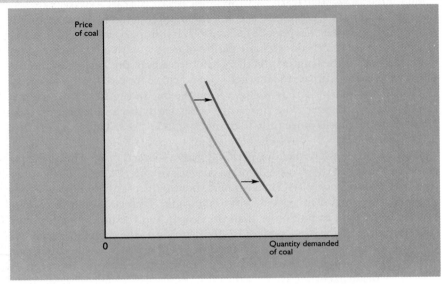

Another factor that influences the position and shape of a good's market demand curve is *the level of consumer incomes.* For some types of products, the demand curve shifts to the right if per capita income increases, whereas for other types of commodities, the demand curve shifts to the left if per capita income rises. In subsequent chapters, we shall analyze why some goods fall into one category and other goods fall into the other, but at present, this need not concern us. All that is important here is that changes in per capita income affect the demand curve. In the case of coal, one would expect that an increase in per capita income would shift the demand curve to the right, as shown in Figure 1.3.

Still another factor that influences the position and shape of a good's market demand curve is the *level of other prices.* For example, since natural gas can be substituted to some extent for coal, the quantity of coal demanded depends on the price of natural gas. If the price of gas is high, more coal will be demanded than if the price of gas is low, because people and firms will be stimulated to substitute coal for the high-priced gas. Thus, as shown in Figure 1.4, increases in the price of gas will shift the market demand curve for coal to the right (and decreases in the price of gas will shift it to the left).[4]

---

[4] Let the quantity demanded of a good per unit of time equal Q_D. In general,

$$Q_D = f(P, T, I, R, N),$$

where P is the price of the good, T stands for the tastes of consumers, I is the level of consumer income, R is the price of related goods, and N is the number of consumers in the market. The

FIGURE 1.4 Effect of an Increase in the Price of Natural Gas on the Market Demand Curve for Coal An increase in the price of natural gas will shift the demand curve for coal to the right.

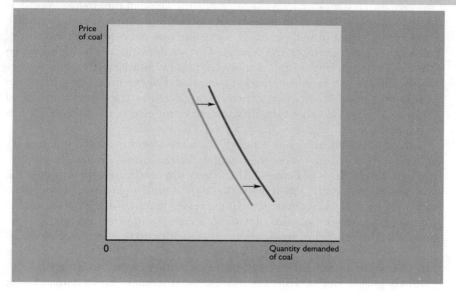

The Price Elasticity of Demand

The shape of a good's market demand curve varies from one good to another and from one market to another. In particular, market demand curves vary in the sensitivity of quantity demanded to price. For some goods, a small change in price results in a large change in quantity demanded; for other goods, a large change in price results in a small change in quantity demanded. To gauge the sensitivity, or responsiveness, of the quantity demanded to changes in price, economists use a measure called the *price elasticity of demand*. The price elasticity of demand is defined as the *percentage change in quantity demanded resulting from a 1 percent change in price.*[5]

Price elasticity of demand

---

demand curve shows the relationship between Q_D and P when the other variables are held constant. In general, changes in the values at which these other variables are held constant will affect the relationship between Q_D and P, which is another way of saying that these other variables will generally influence the position and shape of the market demand curve.

[5] For readers with a knowledge of calculus, it is worth noting that, if Q_D is the quantity demanded and P is the price, a more precise definition of the price elasticity of demand is

$$\eta = \frac{-dQ_D}{dP} \cdot \frac{P}{Q_D}$$

Much more will be said about the measurement, effects, and determinants of the price elasticity of demand in Chapter 5.

For example, suppose that a 1 percent reduction in the price of electricity results in a 1.2 percent increase in the quantity demanded in the United States. If so, the price elasticity of demand for electricity is 1.2. Convention dictates that we give the elasticity a positive sign despite the fact that the change in price is negative and the change in quantity demanded is positive. Clearly, the price elasticity of demand will generally vary from one point to another on a demand curve. For example, the price elasticity of demand may be higher when the price of electricity is high than when it is low. Similarly, the price elasticity of demand will vary from market to market. For example, Japan may have a different price elasticity of demand for electricity than does the United States. (More is said about the demand curve for electricity in Problem 1 in Chapter 5.)

Alfred Marshall, the great English economist who lived about a century ago, was one of the first economists to give a clear formulation of the concept of the price elasticity of demand. It is a very important concept and one that will be used repeatedly throughout this book. One thing to note at the outset is that the price elasticity of demand is expressed in terms of *relative* changes in price and quantity demanded, not *absolute* changes in price and quantity demanded. This is because absolute changes are difficult to interpret. For example, suppose that a price goes up by a dime. This is a lot for a subway ride but little for a house. Similarly, it is a lot for a bottle of beer but little for a 50-gallon keg. A frequent error is to confuse the price elasticity of demand with the slope of the demand curve. They are by no means the same thing.[6]

Suppose that we have a market demand schedule showing the quantity of a commodity demanded in the market at various prices. How can we estimate the price elasticity of market demand? Let ΔP be a change in the price of the good and ΔQ_D be the resulting change in its quantity demanded. If ΔP is very small, we can compute the *point elasticity of demand:*

Point elasticity

$$\eta = -\frac{\Delta Q_D}{Q_D} \div \frac{\Delta P}{P}. \qquad [1.1]$$

Consider Table 1.2 where data are given for very small increments in the price of a commodity. If we want to estimate the price elasticity of demand when the price is between 99.95¢ and $1, we obtain the following result:

$$\eta = -\frac{40,002 - 40,000}{40,000} \div \frac{99.95 - 100}{100} = 0.1.$$

Note that we used $1 as P and 40,000 as Q_D. We could have used 99.95¢ as P and 40,002 as Q_D, but it would have made no real difference to the answer. (Try it and see.)

---

[6] The slope of the demand curve is dP/dQ_D. A glance at footnote 5 will show that this slope is not equal to the price elasticity of demand. Sometimes the price elasticity of demand is also confused with dQ_D/dP. This too is an error since they are by no means the same thing.

TABLE 1.2 Quantity Demanded at Various Prices (Small Increments in Price)	
Price (cents per unit of commodity)	Quantity demanded per unit of time (units of commodity)
99.95	40,002
100.00	40,000
100.05	39,998

However, if we have data concerning only large changes in price (that is, if ΔP and ΔQ_D are large), the answer may vary considerably depending on which value of P and Q_D is used in Equation 1.1. For example, take the case in Table 1.3. Suppose that we want to estimate the price elasticity of demand in the price range between \$4 and \$5. Then, depending on which value of P and Q_D is used, the answer will be

$$\eta = -\frac{20 - 3}{3} \div \frac{4 - 5}{5} = 28.33$$

$$\eta = -\frac{3 - 20}{20} \div \frac{5 - 4}{4} = 3.40.$$

TABLE 1.3 Quantity Demanded at Various Prices (Large Increments in Price)	
Price (dollars per unit of commodity)	Quantity demanded per unit of time (units of commodity)
3	40
4	20
5	3

The difference between these two results is enormous. In a case of this sort, it is advisable to compute the *arc elasticity of demand,* which uses the average value of P and Q_D:

Arc elasticity

$$\eta = -\frac{\Delta Q_D}{(Q_{D1} + Q_{D2})/2} \div \frac{\Delta P}{(P_1 + P_2)/2}$$

$$\eta = -\frac{\Delta Q_D(P_1 + P_2)}{\Delta P(Q_{D1} + Q_{D2})}, \qquad [1.2]$$

where P_1 and Q_{D1} are the first values of price and quantity demanded, and P_2 and Q_{D2} are the second. Thus, in Table 1.3,

$$\eta = -\frac{20 - 3}{(20 + 3)/2} \div \frac{4 - 5}{(4 + 5)/2} = 6.65.$$

This is the arc elasticity of demand when price is between \$4 and \$5.

Price Elasticity and Total Expenditure

The demand for a commodity is said to be *price elastic* if the elasticity of demand exceeds 1. The demand for a commodity is said to be *price inelastic* if the elasticity of demand is less than 1. And the demand for a commodity is said to be **Elastic** of *unitary elasticity* if the price elasticity of demand is equal to 1. Many important **versus** decisions hinge on the price elasticity of demand for a commodity. One reason **inelastic** why this is so is that the price elasticity of demand determines whether a given change in price will increase or decrease the amount of money spent on a commodity — often a matter of basic importance to firms and government agencies.

To illustrate, suppose that the demand for a commodity is elastic; that is, the price elasticity of demand exceeds 1. In this situation, if the price is reduced, the percentage increase in the quantity consumed is greater than the percentage reduction in price. (That this is the case follows from the definition of the price elasticity of demand.) Consequently, a price *reduction* must lead to an *increase* in the expenditure on the product, and a price *increase* must lead to a *decrease* in the expenditure on the product.

On the other hand, suppose that the demand for a commodity is inelastic, that is, the price elasticity of demand is less than 1. In this situation, if the price is reduced, the percentage increase in the quantity consumed is less than the percentage reduction in price. (This follows from the definition of the price elasticity.) Therefore, a price *reduction* must lead to a *decrease* in the expenditure on the product, and a price *increase* must lead to an *increase* in the expenditure on the product. Finally, if the demand for a product is of unitary elasticity, price increases or decreases do not affect the expenditure on the product.

THE SUPPLY SIDE OF THE MARKET

The Market Supply Curve

Each market has a supply side as well as a demand side. The supply side can be represented by a *market supply schedule,* a table which shows the quantity of the good that would be supplied at various prices. For example, suppose that the market supply schedule for coal is shown in Table 1.4.[7] Then 600 million

---

[7] These figures are hypothetical, but adequate for present purposes. In subsequent chapters, we shall provide data describing the actual relationship between the price and quantity supplied of various goods. At this point, the emphasis is on the concept of a market supply schedule, not on the detailed accuracy of these figures.

TABLE 1.4 Market Supply Schedule for Coal, 1997

Price per ton (dollars)	Quantity supplied per year (millions of tons)
40	600
41	650
42	700
43	750
44	775
45	800
46	825

tons of coal will be supplied if its price is $40 per ton, 650 million tons of coal will be supplied if its price is $41 per ton, and so on. Another way of presenting the data in Table 1.4 is by a *supply curve,* which is a plot of the market supply schedule on a graph. The vertical axis of the graph measures the price per unit of the good, and the horizontal axis measures the quantity of the good supplied per unit of time. Figure 1.5 shows the market supply curve for coal, based on the figures in Table 1.4.[8]

FIGURE 1.5 Market Supply Curve for Coal, 1997 The market supply curve for coal shows the quantity of coal that would be supplied at each price.

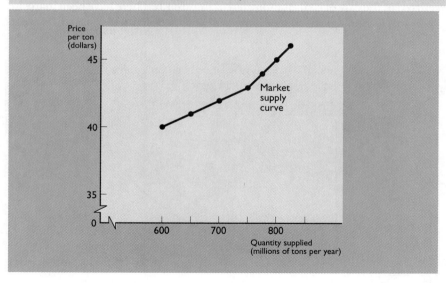

---

[8] Note once more that we assume that the market for coal is perfectly competitive. (See footnote 2.) This simplification is adopted throughout most of this chapter. In subsequent chapters we relax the assumption that markets are perfectly competitive.

Two things should be noted concerning Figure 1.5. First, the market supply curve for coal *slopes upward to the right*. In other words, the quantity of coal supplied increases as the price increases. This is because increases in its price give the makers of coal a greater incentive to produce it and offer it for sale. Empirical studies indicate that the market supply curves for a great many commodities share this characteristic of sloping upward to the right. In subsequent chapters, we will analyze in detail the factors responsible for the shape of a particular good's market supply curve. Second, the market supply curve in Figure 1.5 pertains to a *particular period of time:* 1997. A supply curve pertains to some period of time, and its shape and position depend on the length and other characteristics of this period. For example, if we were to estimate the market supply curve for coal for the first week in 1997, it would be a different curve from the one in Figure 1.5, which pertains to the whole year. In part, the difference arises because coal producers can adapt their output rate more fully to changes in coal's price in a year than in a week.

Besides the length of the time period, what other factors determine the position and shape of the market supply curve for a good? One important factor is *technological change*. Technology is defined as society's pool of knowledge concerning the industrial arts. As technology progresses, it becomes possible to produce commodities more cheaply, so that firms often are willing to supply a given amount at a lower price than formerly. Thus technological change often causes the supply curve to shift to the right. For example, this certainly has occurred in the case of coal, as indicated in Figure 1.6. There have been many important technological changes in coal production in the past fifty years,

FIGURE 1.6 Effect of Technological Change on the Market Supply Curve for Coal
Improvements in technology shift the supply curve to the right.

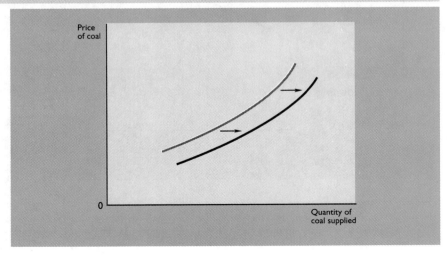

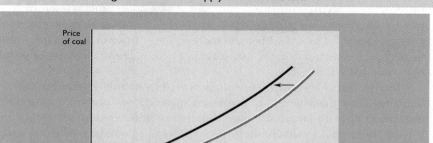

FIGURE 1.7 Effect of Increases in Wages of Coal Miners on the Market Supply Curve for Coal Increases in wage rates shift the supply curve to the left.

including the invention and improvement of continuous mining machinery, trackless mobile loaders, and shuttle cars.

Another factor that influences the position and shape of a good's market supply curve is the *level of input prices*. The supply curve for a commodity is affected by the prices of the resources (labor, capital, and land) used to produce it. Decreases in the prices of these inputs make it possible to produce commodities more cheaply, so that firms may be willing to supply a given amount at a lower price than they formerly would. So decreases in the price of inputs may cause the supply curve to shift to the right. On the other hand, increases in the price of inputs may cause it to shift to the left. For example, if the wage rates of coal miners increase, the supply curve for coal may shift to the left, as shown in Figure 1.7.[9]

The Price Elasticity of Supply

Like market demand curves, market supply curves vary in shape. In particular, they vary with respect to the sensitivity of quantity supplied to price. For some goods, a small change in price results in a large change in quantity sup-

---

[9] Let the quantity supplied of a good per unit of time equal Q_S. In general, $Q_S = g(P, M, V)$, where P is the price of the good, M is the level of input prices, and V stands for the level of technology. The supply curve shows the relationship between Q_S and P when the other variables are held constant. In general, changes in the values at which these other variables are held constant will affect the relationship between Q_S and P; this is another way of saying that these other variables will generally influence the position and shape of the market supply curve.

Price elasticity of supply

plied; for other goods, a large change in price results in a small change in quantity supplied. To gauge the sensitivity of the quantity supplied to changes in price, economists use a measure called the *price elasticity of supply,* which is defined to be *the percentage change in quantity supplied resulting from a 1 percent change in price.*[10] Thus, if a 1 percent increase in the price of natural gas results in a 0.5 percent increase in the quantity supplied, the price elasticity of supply of natural gas is 0.5.

Clearly, the price elasticity of supply is analogous to the price elasticity of demand. Like the latter, it is expressed in terms of relative, not absolute, changes in price and quantity, and it should not be confused with the slope of the supply curve. Its value is likely to vary from one point to another on a supply curve. For example, the price elasticity of supply of natural gas may be higher when the price is low than when it is high. In general, the price elasticity of supply would be expected to increase with the length of the period to which the supply curve pertains. Why? Because, as noted in the previous section, manufacturers of the good will be able to adapt their output rates more fully to changes in its price if the period is long rather than short.

Point and arc elasticities

If we have a market supply schedule showing the quantity of a commodity supplied at various prices, we can readily estimate the price elasticity of supply. Let ΔP be the change in the price of the good and ΔQ_S be the resulting change in its quantity supplied. If ΔP is very small, we can compute the *point elasticity of supply:*

$$\eta_S = \frac{\Delta Q_S}{Q_S} \div \frac{\Delta P}{P}. \tag{1.3}$$

If ΔP is not so small, we can compute the *arc elasticity of supply* by using the average value of Q_S and P in Equation 1.3. These calculations are similar to (but not exactly the same as [11]) those required to compute the price elasticity of demand. To illustrate them, take the case in Table 1.4. Suppose that we want to compute the price elasticity of supply between \$40 and \$41. The arc

---

[10] More accurately, if Q_S is the quantity supplied of the good and P is the price, the price elasticity of supply is

$$\eta_S = \frac{dQ_S}{dP} \cdot \frac{P}{Q_S}.$$

[11] In calculating the price elasticity of demand, we multiply the relative change in quantity demanded resulting from a 1 percent change in price by -1, so that the result will be a positive number. In calculating the price elasticity of supply, we do *not* have to multiply the relative change in quantity supplied resulting from a 1 percent change in price by -1, because it already is positive in the typical case. This is because, as we have already stressed, supply curves generally slope *upward* to the right, whereas demand curves generally slope *downward* to the right.

elasticity of supply is

$$\eta_S = \frac{\Delta Q_S}{(Q_{S1} + Q_{S2})/2} \div \frac{\Delta P}{(P_1 + P_2)/2}$$

$$= \frac{650 - 600}{(650 + 600)/2} \div \frac{41 - 40}{(41 + 40)/2}$$

$$= 3.24.$$

DETERMINANTS OF PRICE

The Equilibrium Price

Prices in a free-enterprise economy are important determinants of what is produced, how it is produced, who receives it, and how rapidly per capita income grows. It behooves us, therefore, to look carefully at how prices themselves are determined in a free-enterprise economy. As a first step toward describing this process, we must define the equilibrium price of a good. At various points in this book, you will encounter the concept of an equilibrium, which is very important in economics, as in many other scientific fields.

An equilibrium *is a situation where there is no tendency for change;* in other words, it is a situation that can persist. Thus *an equilibrium price is a price that can be maintained.* Any price that is not an equilibrium price cannot be maintained for long, since there are basic forces at work to stimulate a change in price. The best way to understand what we mean by an equilibrium price is to take a particular case, such as the market for coal. Let's put both the demand curve for coal (in Figure 1.1) and the supply curve for coal (in Figure 1.5) together in the same diagram. The result, shown in Figure 1.8, will help us determine the equilibrium price of coal.

Equilibrium

We begin by seeing what would happen if various prices are established in the market. For example, if the price were $44 a ton, the demand curve indicates that 680 million tons of coal would be demanded, while the supply curve indicates that 775 million tons would be supplied. Thus, if the price were $44 a ton, there would be a mismatch between the quantity supplied and the quantity demanded per year, since the rate at which coal is supplied would be greater than the rate at which it is demanded. Specifically, as shown in Figure 1.8, there would be an *excess supply* of 95 million tons. Under these circumstances, some of the coal supplied by producers could not be sold, and as in-

FIGURE 1.8 Equilibrium Price and the Quantity of Coal, 1997 The equilibrium price is $42 per ton; the equilibrium quantity is 700 million tons per year.

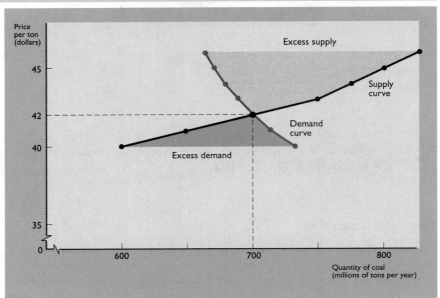

ventories of coal built up, suppliers would tend to cut their prices in order to get rid of unwanted inventories. Thus a price of $44 per ton would not be maintained for long—and for this reason, $44 per ton is not an equilibrium price.

If the price were $40 per ton, on the other hand, the demand curve indicates that 730 million tons of coal would be demanded, while the supply curve indicates that 600 million tons would be supplied. Again we find a mismatch between the quantity supplied and the quantity demanded per year, since the rate at which coal is supplied would be less than the rate at which it is demanded. Specifically, as shown in Figure 1.8, there would be an *excess demand* of 130 million tons. Under these circumstances, some of the consumers who want coal at this price would have to be turned away empty-handed. There would be a shortage. Given this shortage, suppliers would find it profitable to increase the price, and competition among buyers would bid the price up. Thus a price of $40 per ton could not be maintained for long— so $40 per ton is not an equilibrium price.

Equilib-rium price

The equilibrium price must be the price where the quantity demanded equals the quantity supplied. Obviously this is the only price at which there is no mismatch between the quantity demanded and the quantity supplied, and consequently the only price that can be maintained for long. In Figure 1.8, the price at which the quantity supplied equals the quantity demanded is $42 per ton, the price where the demand curve intersects the supply curve. Thus $42 per ton is the equilibrium price of coal under the circumstances visualized in Figure 1.8, and 700 million tons is the equilibrium quantity.[12]

The Actual Price

What we set out to explain was the actual price, not the equilibrium price — since the actual price is all that is observed in the real world. In general, economists simply assume that the actual price will approximate the equilibrium price, which seems reasonable enough, since the basic forces at work tend to push the actual price toward the equilibrium price. Thus, if the demand and supply curves remain fairly stable for a time, the actual price should move toward the equilibrium price.

To see that this is the case, consider the market for coal, as described by Figure 1.8. What if the price somehow is set at $44 per ton? As we saw in the previous section, there is downward pressure on the price of coal under these conditions. Suppose the price, responding to this pressure, falls to $43. Comparing the quantity demanded with the quantity supplied at $43, we find that there is still downward pressure on price, since the quantity supplied exceeds the quantity demanded at $43. The price, responding to this pressure, may fall to $42.50, but comparing the quantity demanded with the quantity supplied at this price, we find that there is still a downward pressure on price, since the quantity supplied exceeds the quantity demanded at $42.50.

So long as the actual price exceeds the equilibrium price, there will be a downward pressure on price. Similarly, so long as the actual price is less than the equilibrium price, there will be an upward pressure on price. Thus there is always a tendency for the actual price to move toward the equilibrium price. But it should not be assumed that this movement is always rapid. Sometimes it takes a long time for the actual price to get close to the equilibrium price. Sometimes the actual price never gets to the equilibrium price because by the time it gets close, the equilibrium price changes. All that safely can be said is that the actual price will move toward the equilibrium price. But of course this information is of great value, both theoretically and practically. For many purposes, all that is required is predicting whether the price will move up or down.

Effects on Price of Shifts in the Demand Curve

We have already seen that demand curves shift in response to changes in tastes, income, and prices of other products. Any supply-and-demand diagram like Figure 1.8 is essentially a snapshot of the situation during a particular period

---

[12] If $P = D(Q)$ is the demand curve and $P = S(Q)$ is the supply curve, we have two equations in two unknowns — price (P) and quantity (Q). To determine the equilibrium price, we can solve these equations simultaneously for P and Q.

of time. The results in Figure 1.8 are limited to a particular period because the demand and supply curves in the figure pertain only to that period. What happens to the equilibrium price of a product (which we shall call good X) when its demand curve changes?

Suppose that consumer tastes shift in favor of good X, causing the demand curve for good X to shift to the right. This state of affairs is shown in Figure 1.9, where the demand curve shifts from D to D_1. It is not hard to see the effect on the equilibrium price of good X. When D is the demand curve, the equilibrium price is OP. But when the demand curve shifts to D_1, a shortage of $(OQ_2 - OQ)$ develops at this price. That is, the quantity demanded exceeds the quantity supplied at this price by $(OQ_2 - OQ)$. Consequently, suppliers raise their prices. After some testing of market reactions and trial-and-error adjustments, the price will tend to settle at OP_1, the new equilibrium price, and quantity will tend to settle at OQ_1.

On the other hand, suppose that consumer demand for good X falls off, perhaps because of a great drop in the price of a product that is an effective substitute for good X. The demand for good X now shifts to the left. Specifically, as shown in Figure 1.9, it shifts from D to D_2. What will be the effect on the equilibrium price of good X? Clearly, the equilibrium price will be OP_2, where the new demand curve intersects the supply curve.

To illustrate the usefulness of this model, consider the market for heating oil. In December 1989, there was an unusual spell of sustained cold weather in the northeastern United States, which caused the demand curve for heating oil to shift markedly to the right. What happened to the price of heating oil?

FIGURE 1.9 Effects of Shifts in the Demand Curve on the Equilibrium Price A rightward shift of the demand curve tends to increase price; a leftward shift tends to reduce price.

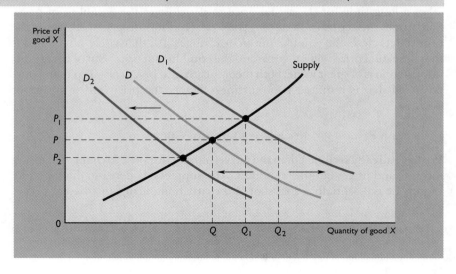

EXAMPLE 1.1

Coffee Bars Invade Manhattan

Coffee bars have been prominent features of the social landscape in European and Middle Eastern cities, but not in the United States. Recently, however, this has begun to change. According to the Specialty Coffee Association, there were about 5,000 coffee bars in the United States in 1993, up from about 200 in 1989, and the figure may hit 10,000 in 1999. This trend began in Portland (Oregon), Seattle, and Chicago, and has begun to hit Manhattan. Whereas there were only about 55 coffee bars in Manhattan in the spring of 1994, the number had doubled 6 months later.

(a) To be successful, a coffee bar must be located where there is heavy pedestrian traffic (since they rely principally on walk-in trade). For simplicity, suppose that there is a fixed number of spaces for rent in Manhattan that are appropriate for a coffee bar. If so, what is the shape of the supply curve for such rental space? (b) Has the entry of coffee bars into Manhattan shifted the demand curve for such rental spaces? If so, has it shifted it to the left or the right? (c) Would this shift in the demand curve for such rental spaces be expected to increase the annual rent for such spaces? (d) According to Benjamin Fox, a partner in the New Spectrum real estate brokerage, "In the last 18 months, the coffee houses have almost single-handedly hiked up New York rents."* Is that what you would have expected? Why or why not?

SOLUTION   (a) This supply curve would be vertical because the quantity supplied would be fixed, regardless of the level of the rent. (b) The entry of coffee bars into Manhattan has shifted the demand curve for such rental space to the right. (c) As shown in the figure below, this rightward shift of the demand curve would be expected to increase the annual rent for such spaces. Before the shift in the demand curve, the equilibrium price (or rent) is OP_0; after the shift, it is OP_1.

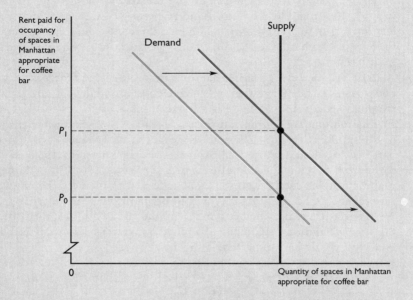

(d) The extent to which rents would be expected to increase depends on the price elasticity of supply and the extent to which the demand curve shifts to the right. If the situation were like that shown in the above figure, one would expect a substantial increase in rents.[†]

*New York Times, November 6, 1994, p. 1 NJR.
[†]For further discussion, see ibid.

In accord with our model, it rose to $1.30 a gallon, which was almost 50 percent higher than in the warmer days a month before.[13]

In general, a shift to the right in the demand curve results in an increase in the equilibrium price, and a shift to the left in the demand curve results in a

[13] "Heating Oil Stockpiles Grow Tight," New York Times, December 23, 1989.

decrease in the equilibrium price. This is the lesson of Figure 1.9. Of course, this conclusion depends on the assumption that the supply curve slopes upward to the right, but, as we noted in a previous section, this is generally the case.

Effects on Price of Shifts in the Supply Curve

Supply curves, like demand curves, shift over time. What happens to the equilibrium price of a good when its supply curve shifts? Suppose that, because of technological advances, producers of good X are willing and able to supply more of good X at a given price than they used to. Specifically, suppose that the supply curve shifts from S to S_1 in Figure 1.10. What will be the effect on the equilibrium price? Clearly, it will fall from OP (where the S supply curve intersects the demand curve) to OP_3 (where the S_1 supply curve intersects the demand curve). On the other hand, suppose that input prices rise, with the result that the supply curve shifts from S to S_2 in Figure 1.10. Clearly, the equilibrium price will increase from OP (where the S supply curve intersects the demand curve) to OP_4 (where the S_2 supply curve intersects the demand curve).

Lovers of turkey were shown in the late 1980s what a shift to the right in the supply curve of a commodity will do. Because of declines in the price of fuel oil, which made turkey coops cheaper to heat, and a drop in the price of the grain that turkeys eat, there was a shift to the right in the supply curve for turkeys. As our theory would predict, the wholesale price of a turkey fell — from 93 cents a pound in 1985 to 88 cents in 1986 to 51 cents in 1987.

FIGURE 1.10 Effects of Shifts in the Supply Curve on the Equilibrium Price A rightward shift of the supply curve tends to reduce price; a leftward shift tends to increase price.

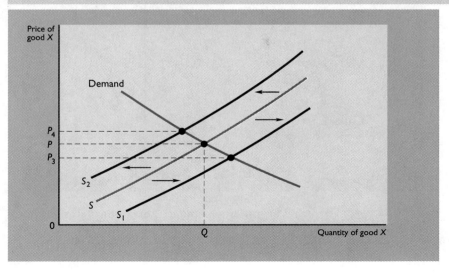

EXAMPLE 1.2

The Price of Cotton: Highest since the Civil War

In March 1995, the price of cotton rose to about $1.10 per pound, the highest level since the Civil War. According to the National Cotton Council in Memphis, Tennessee, cotton clothing has become more popular, increasing its share of fibers used in U.S. manufactured goods from 42 percent in 1985 to 65 percent in 1993. The world's three largest producers of cotton generally have been China, India, and Pakistan, all of which had poor crops in 1994–95. The U.S. crop of almost 20 million bales was expected to be bigger than theirs.

(a) Between October 1994 and March 1995, the price jumped from about 66¢ to about $1.10 a pound. Was this due in part to a shift in the demand curve for cotton? (b) Was it due to a shift in the supply curve for cotton? (c) Will this increase in the price of cotton shift the supply curve for cotton clothing? (d) Will this increase in the price of cotton result in a bigger price hike for cotton clothing if the price elasticity of demand for cotton clothing is low than if it is high?

SOLUTION (a) The growing popularity of cotton clothing probably pushed the demand for cotton to the right, contributing to the price increase. (b) The poor crops in China, India,

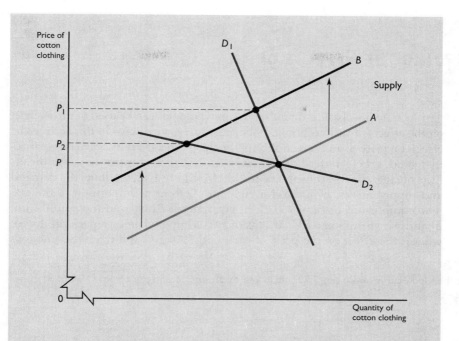

and Pakistan resulted in a big leftward shift of the supply curve for cotton, which was a key factor responsible for the huge run-up in price. (c) Yes. The supply curve for cotton clothing will be shifted upward and to the left. (d) Yes. The increase in the price of cotton will shift the supply curve for cotton clothing from position A to position B in the figure above. If the quantity demanded of cotton clothing is relatively insensitive to an increase in the price of cotton clothing (demand curve D_1), the resulting increase in price is greater than if the quantity demanded is relatively sensitive to price increases (demand curve D_2). In the former case, the price increases from OP to OP_1; in the latter case, it increases from OP to OP_2.*

---

*For further discussion, see *Business Week,* March 13, 1995, and the *Philadelphia Inquirer,* March 11, 1995.

In general, a shift to the right in the supply curve results in a decrease in the equilibrium price, and a shift to the left in the supply curve results in an increase in the equilibrium price. Of course, this conclusion depends on the assumption that the demand curve slopes downward to the right, but, as we noted in a previous section, this is generally the case.

ANALYZING THE EFFECTS OF AN EXCISE TAX

To illustrate how basic demand-and-supply models can be used to throw light on the effects of various public-policy measures, we discuss in this section the effects on price of an excise tax. Suppose that such a tax is imposed on a particular good, say cigarettes.[14] There has been enormous controversy over the effects of cigarettes on consumers' health. In Figure 1.11, we show the demand and supply curves, *D* and *S,* for cigarettes before the imposition of the tax. The equilibrium price of a pack of cigarettes is $1.60, and the equilibrium quantity is 50 million packs. If a tax of $.20 is imposed on each pack produced, what is the effect on the price of each pack? Or to see it from the smoker's

FIGURE 1.11 Effect of an Excise Tax on the Price and Output of Cigarettes A $.20 excise tax shifts the supply curve upward by $.20, and increases the equilibrium price from $1.60 to $1.70 per pack.

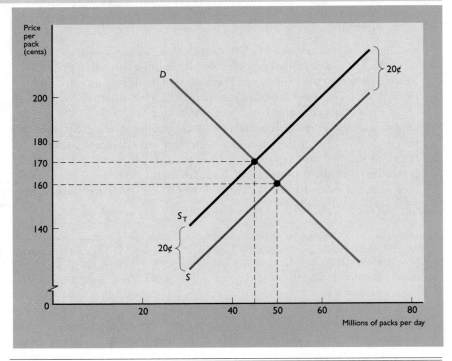

---

[14] For simplicity, we assume that the market for cigarettes is perfectly competitive. In later chapters, we present models that pertain to cases where there are relatively few producers.

perspective, how much of the tax is passed on to the consumer in the form of a higher price?

Since the tax is collected from the sellers, the supply curve is shifted upward by the amount of the tax. In Figure 1.11, the posttax supply curve is S_T. For example, if the pretax price had to be $1.40 a pack to induce sellers to supply 40 million packs of cigarettes, the posttax price would have to be $.20 higher — or $1.60 a pack — to induce the same supply. Similarly, if the pretax price had to be $1.60 a pack to induce sellers to supply 50 million packs of cigarettes, the posttax price would have to be $.20 higher — or $1.80 a pack — to induce the same supply. The reason why the sellers require $.20 more per pack to supply the pretax amount is that they must pay the $.20 per pack to the government. Thus to wind up with the same amount as before (after paying the tax), they require the extra $.20 per pack.

Figure 1.11 shows that, after the tax is imposed, the equilibrium price of cigarettes is $1.70, an increase of $.10 over its pretax level. Consequently, in this case, half of the tax is passed on to consumers, who pay $.10 more for cigarettes. And half of the tax is swallowed by the sellers, who receive (after they pay the tax) $.10 per pack less for cigarettes. But it is not always true that sellers pass half of the tax on to consumers and absorb the rest themselves. On the contrary, in some cases, consumers may bear almost all of the tax (and sellers may bear practically none of it), while in other cases consumers may bear almost none of the tax (and sellers may bear practically all of it). The result will depend on how sensitive the quantity demanded and the quantity supplied are to the price of the good.

Effects of excise tax

In particular, holding the supply curve constant, the less sensitive the quantity demanded is to the price of the good, the bigger the portion of the tax that is shifted to consumers. To illustrate this, consider panel A of Figure 1.12, which shows the effect of a $.20-per-pack tax on cigarettes in two markets, one in which the quantity demanded (D_1) is much more sensitive to price than in the other (D_2). Before the tax, the equilibrium price is OP_0, regardless of whether D_1 or D_2 is the demand curve. After the tax, the equilibrium price is OP_1 if the demand curve is D_1 or OP_2 if the demand curve is D_2. Clearly, the increase in the price to the consumer is greater if the quantity demanded is less sensitive to price (D_2) than if it is more sensitive (D_1).

Also, holding the demand curve constant, the less sensitive the quantity supplied is to the price of the good, the bigger the portion of the tax that is absorbed by producers. To illustrate this, consider panel B of Figure 1.12, which shows the effect of a $.20-per-pack tax on cigarettes in two markets, one where the quantity supplied (S_1) is much more sensitive to price than in the other (S_2). Before the tax, the equilibrium price is OP_3, regardless of whether S_1 or S_2 is the pretax supply curve. After the tax, the equilibrium price is OP_4 if the (pretax) supply curve is S_2, or OP_5 if the (pretax) supply curve is S_1. Clearly, the increase in price to the consumer is greater if the quantity supplied is more sensitive to price (S_1) than if it is less sensitive (S_2).

FIGURE 1.12 Effect of an Excise Tax on the Price of Cigarettes, under Alternative Assumptions Concerning Sensitivity of Quantity Demanded and Quantity Supplied to Price The tax results in a larger increase in price if the quantity demanded is less sensitive to price than if it is more sensitive, and if the quantity supplied is more sensitive to the price than if it is less sensitive.

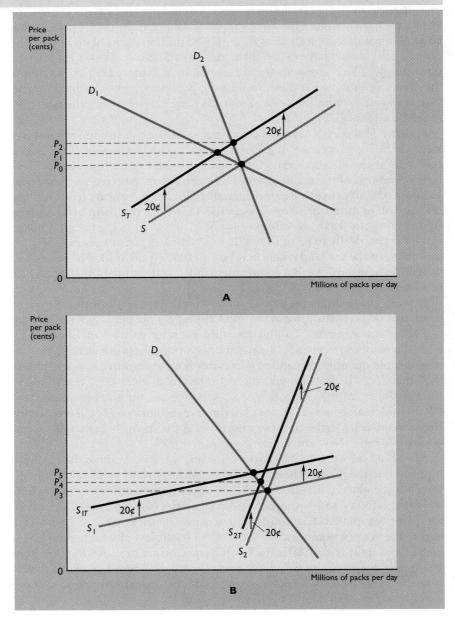

In 1993, President Clinton suggested that he might ask Congress to raise the federal tax on cigarettes by about $2 per pack in order to help finance an overhaul of the U.S. health-care system. Based on a variety of studies, much of the suggested tax increase would be borne by consumers. Experts have estimated that such a tax increase might produce about $100 billion in extra federal revenue over 5 years and reduce the number of people who smoke by more than 7 million—a result that health groups applaud but tobacco producers view with much less enthusiasm. In fact, no such tax was passed.

PRICE FLOORS AND CEILINGS

As a further illustration of how the simple models taken up in this chapter can help to illuminate public-policy issues, consider the case of price floors or price ceilings. As is well known, governments often intervene in markets to prop up the price of a particular good or to see to it that its price does not exceed a certain level. At this point we will sketch only roughly the effects of such price floors or price ceilings. More details on this subject will be added in later chapters.

The effects of a price floor are shown in Figure 1.13. As is evident, the equilibrium price of the good is OP. Nonetheless, because the government feels that this price is not equitable, it sets a minimum price of OP_m. At this minimum price, the quantity supplied (OQ_S) exceeds the quantity demanded (OQ_D), and the government is faced with the problem of disposing of the surplus or of limiting production so that the quantity supplied is no more than OQ_D. One important area where price floors have been adopted in the United States has been agriculture. For major farm commodities like wheat and corn, minimum prices have been established by the government. As our model predicts, a major problem stemming from these price floors has been the disposal and limitation of farm surpluses.[15]

Price floor

The effects of a price ceiling are shown in Figure 1.14. Although the equilibrium price is OP, the government sets a maximum price of OP_n, because it does not want the price of the good to rise to its equilibrium level. At this maximum price, the quantity demanded (OQ_D) exceeds the quantity supplied (OQ_S); in other words, there is a shortage of the good. To allocate the limited supply among the many buyers who want to purchase the good, the govern-

Price ceiling

---

[15] In Chapters 9 and 10, we discuss these agricultural price floors and their effects in much more detail. In March 1996, President Clinton signed legislation to end most government controls over planting decisions, but many members of Congress said that they would reconsider the matter in subsequent years.

FIGURE 1.13 Effects of a Price Floor If the government sets a minimum price of OP_m, the quantity supplied exceeds the quantity demanded, and there is the problem of disposing of the surplus.

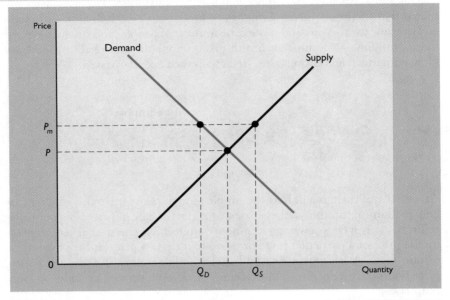

FIGURE 1.14 Effects of a Price Ceiling If the government sets a ceiling price of OP_n, the quantity demanded exceeds the quantity supplied, and there is a shortage of the good.

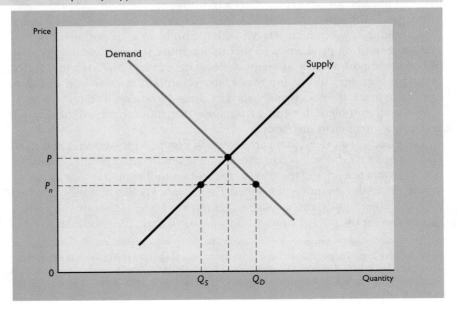

ment may resort to some form of rationing. For example, in World War II when price controls were in effect, families were issued ration coupons which determined how much they could buy of various commodities. Frequently, *black markets* develop under these circumstances, where the good is sold illegally at a price higher than the legal maximum. As our model predicts, a major problem stemming from price ceilings has been the resolution of the shortages that ensue.

Rent Control in New York City: Illustration of a Price Ceiling

Price floors and ceilings can and do affect our everyday lives. Since 1943, New York City has had a system of rent control which imposes ceilings on rents. The purpose is, of course, to establish a rent (that is, the price of using an apartment for a month) that is below the equilibrium level. One important justification that proponents of rent control give for such price ceilings is that they help the poor. In the short run, rent control is likely to transfer income from landlords to tenants. According to the *New York Times*, "For almost half a century, rent regulation, which has provided virtual lifetime guarantees of inexpensive or below-market-price apartments to hundreds of thousands of families, regardless of means, has been politically untouchable in New York City."[16]

But as time goes on, rent control can have some very undesirable effects. As shown in Figure 1.14, a price ceiling results in a shortage. That is, the quantity demanded of apartments will exceed the quantity supplied. According to some observers, New York City has a shortage of about $3 billion worth of new rental housing despite a loss in population of about 1 million people in the 1970s and the nation's largest government-assisted middle-income and low-rent public housing programs. In 1986, it was reported that some people had to look for a year or more to obtain an apartment.

Because the quantity demanded exceeds the quantity supplied, the available apartments have to be rationed by some device other than price. This, of course, may allow landlords to engage in many forms of subtle and not-so-subtle discrimination in choosing tenants. Also, landlords will have an incentive to accept side payments or bribes from those looking for housing. They will curtail maintenance of their properties in many cases; because there is a shortage, renters are willing to accept poorer service and do more things for themselves. To the extent possible, landlords may try to subdivide apartments, since the sum of the ceilings on the rents from the subdivisions may exceed the ceiling on the rent from the original apartment. In all these ways, landlords may try to adjust to, and to some extent evade, the price ceilings.

In New York, according to the RAND Corporation, rent increases have fallen far short of cost increases because of the rent-control laws. For housing units built before 1943, the average increase in rents was about 2 percent per

---

[16] *New York Times,* March 22, 1992.

EXAMPLE 1.3

Rent Control California Style: Mobile Home Owners versus Park Owners

Rent control laws covering mobile home parks are common in California. A mobile home park is a tract of land on which there are pads which are rented to residents who live in mobile homes that they own, but which are placed on pads that they rent. Once placed on a pad, very few mobile homes are ever moved. The rent control laws have prevented the owners of mobile home parks from raising rents in accord with the increases in their costs. In a case involving the city of Santa Barbara, the U.S. Court of Appeals expressed its concern that these laws have "eviscerated" the property rights of the park owners, and have given "a windfall to current park tenants at the expense of current mobile park owners."*

(a) Do you think that these laws have had an effect on the price of a mobile home? (b) If so, is this due to their effect on the demand curve for mobile homes, the supply curve for them, or both? (c) Why have they had this effect on the demand and/or supply curve? (d) In what sense, if any, have they given a windfall to current park tenants at the expense of current mobile park owners?

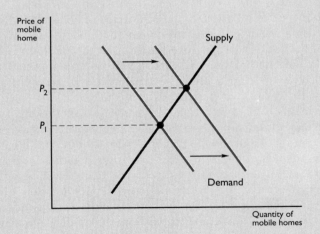

SOLUTION   (a) Yes. According to studies by UCLA's Werner Hirsch, the price of a mobile home tends to be about 32 percent higher in communities that have enacted these laws than in those without them. (b) As shown above, this price increase (from OP_1 to OP_2) is due to a rightward shift in the demand for mobile homes in communities with these laws. (c) The demand curve for mobile homes has been pushed to the right by these laws because they lower the costs of mobile home owners, thus raising the value of a mobile home. All other things being equal, a potential buyer is willing to pay more for a mobile home located in an area where rents paid to park owners are lower than elsewhere. (d) Mobile home owners in rent-controlled areas have seen the value of their mobile homes rise. This is due to the reduction in the rents (current and prospective) they must pay to the park owners.[†]

---

* *Hall v. City of Santa Barbara,* U. S. Court of Appeals, 9th Circuit, no. 85-5838, August 22 (1986).

[†] For further discussion, see Werner Hirsch, "An Inquiry into Effects of Mobile Home Park Rent Control," *Journal of Urban Economics,* September 1988.

year, whereas the average increase in costs to the landlords was about 6 percent per year. Thus it is not surprising that more new housing has not been built, and that existing housing often has been poorly maintained.

The *New York Times* has argued that the city should end "rent regulation for apartments as they become vacant. . . . It would increase housing supply for the benefit of most people." Most economists certainly would agree that the continuation of a price ceiling is not a policy that is likely to resolve a serious shortage. But our purpose here is not to decide whether the opponents of rent controls are right or wrong; instead, it is to indicate the central role played by the microeconomic concepts discussed in this chapter in understanding the issue. Even though this chapter deals only with the basic concepts of demand and supply, the results are of importance in illuminating this and many other major policy issues.

IMPERFECT INFORMATION, AUCTIONS, AND THE WINNER'S CURSE

Throughout this chapter we have assumed that both buyers and sellers have reliable information concerning the nature and quality of the goods traded in the markets under consideration, as well as the prices at which they are sold.

For many purposes, this is a reasonable first approximation to reality. But in some cases, it misses the essence of the situation. For example, suppose that a piece of land is auctioned off. This piece of land appears to have valuable oil and mineral deposits, but no one knows exactly what they are worth. (Until a variety of complex and expensive tests are performed, it is impossible to tell whether oil is present, and if so, in what amount.) *If each bidder bids what he or she thinks the land is worth,* how much will the highest bidder be willing to pay for this land?

Without knowing more about the particular piece of land, it is impossible to provide a numerical answer to this question. Nonetheless, economists have shown that the following remarkable proposition is true: If each bidder behaves in the assumed way, *the highest bidder is likely to pay more for the land than it is worth.* To see why, suppose that each bidder makes an estimate of what the land is worth, and that *on the average, the bidders' estimates are approximately correct.* Since each bidder is assumed to submit a bid that equals his or her estimate of the land's worth, the highest bidder is likely to pay more for the land than it is worth because his or her estimate of the land's value must exceed the average estimate, which is approximately equal to the land's true value. (If his or her estimate did not exceed the average estimate, he or she would not be the highest bidder.)[17]

Winner's curse

To illustrate this so-called "winner's curse," suppose that ten oil firms make bids for a particular piece of land, and that each firm's estimate of its value is shown in Table 1.5. Because each firm is assumed to bid what it thinks the land is worth, the winning bid ($20,000) is made by Exxon. But if, on the average, the firms' evaluations are approximately correct, then the true value of the piece of land is about $17,000, since this was their average estimate. Thus Exxon is likely to have paid too much for it.

TABLE 1.5 Estimates of Value of a Piece of Land, Ten Oil Firms

Firm	Estimate of value of land	Firm	Estimate of value of land
American Petrofina	$15,000	Exxon	$20,000
Amoco	16,000	Occidental	17,000
Ashland	17,000	Phillips	16,000
Atlantic Richfield	18,000	Texaco	19,000
Chevron	16,000	Unocal	16,000
		Average	$17,000

[17] For discussions of this and related points, see P. Milgrom, "Auctions and Bidding: A Primer," *Journal of Economic Perspectives,* Summer 1989; J. Kagel and D. Levin, "The Winner's Curse and Public Information in Common Value Auctions," *American Economic Review,* December 1986; and S. Thiel, "Some Evidence on the Winner's Curse," *American Economic Review,* 1988.

Can the winner's curse be avoided? The answer is yes. To avoid it, sophisticated bidders make bids that are *below* their estimates of what the land is really worth. Thus the ten oil firms, recognizing the existence of the winner's curse, may submit bids that are several thousand dollars less than their estimates of the land's true value. In this way, they try to insure that, if they are the highest bidder, they will not have paid too much for the land.

Much more will be said about auctions in Chapter 2, where we take up the Federal Communications Commission's auction of spectrum licenses. An important point to note is that, if buyers are able and willing to collude, the outcome of an auction may be quite different than if they act independently. For example, suppose that the oil firms in Table 1.5 are able and willing to get together before the auction and decide among themselves which firm will get the piece of land, after which they submit bids that look independent but really are formulated so that the designated firm is the highest bidder. In such a case, the price received by the seller may be significantly less than if the buyers act independently. Why? Because it is in the buyers' interest to keep the price low.

ASYMMETRIC INFORMATION AND THE MARKET FOR USED CARS

In some markets, buyers and sellers do not have the same information. For example, consider the market for used cars. The seller of a used car generally knows a great deal more about its performance and weaknesses than does the buyer. This *asymmetry of information* will influence how the market works. To see why, suppose that all new cars are good or defective; that after a person buys a new car, he or she finds out whether it is good or defective; and that, if this car is offered for sale (as a used car), a potential buyer will not be able to determine (before buying it) whether it is good or defective.

Asymmetric information

Under these circumstances, the equilibrium price of a used car will be less than the price of a new car. Since the buyer of a used car cannot tell the difference between a good and a defective car, both good and defective used cars must sell for the same price. Clearly, this price must be less than the price of a new car. Otherwise, it would pay to buy a new car, determine whether it is defective, and (if it proves to be defective) sell it and buy another new car. Unless the price of a used car is less than the price of a new one, there would be no demand for used cars.

"Lemons" — that is, defective cars — are likely to constitute a large number of the used cars offered for sale. Owners of good used cars are likely to find the

Lemons

equilibrium price of a used car so low that they are not motivated to offer many of their cars for sale. On the other hand, defective used cars may constitute a large number of the used cars offered for sale, and this makes potential buyers even more inclined to offer relatively low prices for used cars.

The buyer of a used car would be willing to pay more than the equilibrium price if he or she were sure of getting a good one, and the seller of a good used car would be delighted to agree to such a transaction. However, the asymmetry of information—the fact that the seller knows whether the used car is good or defective, but the buyer does not—makes it difficult for such trades to occur. Faced with this situation, sellers of used cars try in various ways to *signal* buyers that their car is good. They cite relevant facts concerning the car, they encourage the buyer to have his or her experts inspect it before purchase, and they offer money-back guarantees or free service contracts.[18]

In subsequent chapters, we will discuss other cases of asymmetric information. For example, Chapter 13 considers cases where firms do not know their rivals' costs as well as they know their own costs, and Chapter 16 discusses cases where insurance companies cannot monitor the behavior of people they insure, with the result that the latter may not take reasonable precautions to avoid the catastrophes that trigger payment of the insurance. In recent years, economists have devoted considerable attention to the effects of asymmetric information on markets.

SUMMARY

1. The market demand curve for a good almost always slopes downward to the right; that is, the quantity demanded increases as the price falls. The position and shape of the market demand curve for a good depend on the tastes of consumers, on the level of consumer incomes, on the prices of other goods, and on the length of the time period to which the demand curve pertains.

2. The price elasticity of demand, defined as the percentage change in the quantity demanded resulting from a 1 percent change in price, is a mea-

---

[18] For a seminal article in this area, see G. Akerlof, "The Market for Lemons," *Quarterly Journal of Economics,* August 1970, reprinted in E. Mansfield, *Microeconomics: Selected Readings,* 5th ed. (New York: Norton, 1985), pp. 55–66.

sure of the responsiveness of quantity demanded to changes in price. The price elasticity of demand will generally vary from one point to another on a demand curve. Estimated price elasticities are of two different types: point elasticities and arc elasticities.

3. The market supply curve for a good generally slopes upward to the right; that is, the quantity supplied increases as the price rises. The position and shape of the market supply curve for a good depends on the state of technology, input prices, and the length of the time interval to which the market supply curve pertains.

4. The price elasticity of supply, defined as the percentage change in the quantity supplied resulting from a 1 percent change in price, is a measure of the responsiveness of quantity supplied to changes in price. The price elasticity of supply will generally vary from one point to another on a supply curve.

5. An equilibrium price is a price that can be maintained. In a competitive market, it is the price where the quantity demanded equals the quantity supplied. In other words, it is the price where the demand curve intersects the supply curve. If the actual price exceeds the equilibrium price, there will be an excess supply of the good, and the actual price will tend to fall. If the actual price is less than the equilibrium price, there will be an excess demand for the good, and the actual price will tend to rise.

6. In general, a shift to the right in the demand curve results in an increase in the equilibrium price, and a shift to the left in the demand curve results in a decrease in the equilibrium price. In general, a shift to the right in the supply curve results in a decrease in the equilibrium price, and a shift to the left in the supply curve results in an increase in the equilibrium price.

7. Demand-and-supply analysis can be used to predict the effect of an excise tax. Since the tax is collected from the sellers, the supply curve of the good on which the tax is imposed is shifted upward by the amount of the tax. How much the price of the good is increased by the tax depends on how sensitive the quantity demanded and quantity supplied are to changes in the price of the good.

8. Models of this type can also be used to analyze the effects of price floors and price ceilings imposed by government. Price floors tend to result in surpluses, and price ceilings tend to result in shortages.

9. In some markets, it is important to recognize that buyers and sellers have imperfect information. Under certain circumstances, the winning bid in an auction is likely to be too high if it equals what the bidder believes to be the value of the auctioned item. This is the "winner's curse."

10. Buyers and sellers sometimes do not have the same information. For example, the seller of a used car generally knows far more about its performance and weaknesses than does the buyer. This asymmetry of information can have an important influence on how a market functions.

QUESTIONS/PROBLEMS

1. When the Democratic National Convention was held in New York City in 1992, Tim Zagat, publisher of a well-known restaurant guide, helped to organize an unusual treat for the convention delegates and others: about 100 of New York's leading restaurants would offer a three-course lunch for $19.92. While this is hardly a cheap meal, the price was well below that ordinarily charged by such restaurants. The result was a considerable increase in their business, and most maintained the $19.92 price after the end of the convention. As Mr. Zagat said, "The reaction surprised all of us." (a) Le Perigord, a French restaurant on East 52 Street, ordinarily served lunch for about 40 people each day before the price reduction; afterward, it served about 150 people per day. Its preconvention price for a lunch was $29. What was the price elasticity of demand for a lunch at Le Perigord? (b) According to the *New York Times*, "The pricier a restaurant, the more its business has tended to grow with the promotion." If another restaurant's preconvention price was $5 less than Le Perigord's, but the price elasticity of demand was the same, can we be sure that the percentage increase in the number of lunches at this restaurant will be less than at Le Perigord? (c) Did the daily expenditure on lunches at Le Perigord increase due to the price reduction? Is this consistent with your answer to part (a)? (d) According to Jerry Kretchmer of Gotham Bar and Grill, "We think we're making a little money, but we don't know." Is it possible that this price reduction could reduce the restaurants' profits? How could this occur?

2. In late 1992, the U.S. government announced that in 30 days it would begin collecting a very substantial tax on all still white wine imported from Europe. This import tax (or tariff) was announced in an effort to get European governments to reduce the subsidies they pay their farmers. According to the U.S. government, these subsidies have unfairly reduced the demand for U.S. exports of agricultural goods. White wine was singled out because France, the staunchest opponent of compromise in this dispute with the United States, is Europe's chief exporter of white wine to the United States (1991 sales: $125 million). (a) According to Banfi Products Corporation, a large wine importer, the retail price of a typical bottle of French white wine was likely to rise from $9.50 to $28.25 if this import tax went into effect. Was this because of a rightward shift of the demand curve for French white wine? Or was it because of a leftward shift of the supply curve for French white wine? (b) Harry F. Mariani, president of Banfi Products Corporation, said the price of French white wines that retailers acquired before the tax would probably rise after the imposition of the tax:

"Whoever has some white wine left will probably raise the price at the end, even if they didn't pay the tax." Is such behavior legal? Why should a consumer pay a retailer for a tax that the retailer did not pay? (c) If the demand for French white wine is price elastic, would this tax reduce the amount spent by U.S. consumers on French white wine? (d) Would this tax affect the demand curve for California wine? If so, how? (e) A few weeks after the U.S. government announced this new tax on European white wine, a compromise was reached with European governments on how to reduce farm subsidies, and the new tax was dropped. French farmers marched to protest in Paris. Was this because they favored the tax?

3. There is a considerable amount of air travel between Los Angeles and New York City; it is one of the most intensively traveled routes in the country. According to P. Verleger, the price elasticity of demand for air travel between Los Angeles and New York City is about 0.67. (a) Suppose that an economic consultant says that the demand curve for air travel between Los Angeles and New York City is as shown below.

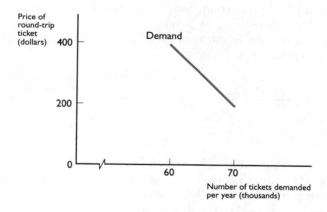

Is this graph in accord with Verleger's findings? Why or why not? (b) Suppose that the airlines double the price of a ticket between Los Angeles and New York City. Will this price increase affect the demand curve for air travel between these two cities? If so, in what way? (c) Suppose that a severe recession occurs. Will this affect the demand curve for air travel between these two cities? If so, in what way? (d) Because of the marked increase in the price of jet fuel (and other things), the cost of providing air transportation between Los Angeles and New York City has changed appreciably in recent decades. Does such a change in cost affect the demand curve for air travel between these two cities? If so, in what way?

4. The demand curve for a product is $P = 100 - 2Q_D$, where P is the product's price (in dollars per pound) and Q_D is quantity demanded (in millions

of pounds per year). The actual price of the product is $70 per pound. If the supply curve for the product is $P = 50 + 3Q_S$, where Q_S is quantity supplied (in millions of pounds per year), would you expect the price to rise or fall? If so, by how much? Why?

5. Suppose that the demand curve for cantaloupes is

$$P = 120 - 3Q_D,$$

where P is the price per pound (in cents) of a cantaloupe and Q_D is the quantity demanded per year (in millions of pounds). Suppose that the supply curve for cantaloupes is

$$P = 5Q_S,$$

where Q_S is the quantity supplied per year (in millions of pounds). What is the equilibrium price per pound of a cantaloupe? What is the equilibrium quantity of cantaloupes produced?

6. In July 1986, there was a major drought in the southeastern United States. As a result, beef prices fell by 5 percent. Why? (Hint: The drought reduced hay and feed production, and farmers moved their cattle much earlier to slaughterhouses.)

7. Suppose that the numbers of cameras demanded in the United States at various prices are as follows:

Price of a camera (dollars)	Quantity demanded per year (millions of cameras)
80	20
100	18
120	16

Draw three points on the demand curve for cameras. Calculate the arc price elasticity of demand when (a) the price is between $80 and $100, and (b) the price is between $100 and $120.

8. Suppose that the relationship between the quantity of cameras supplied per year in the United States and the price per camera is as follows:

Price of a camera (dollars)	Quantity supplied per year (millions of cameras)
60	14
80	16
100	18
120	19

Draw four points on the supply curve for cameras, and estimate the price elasticity of supply when the price is between $80 and $100.

9. Based on the data presented in Questions 7 and 8, what is the equilibrium price of a camera in the United States? If the price is $80, will there be an

excess demand? An excess supply? If the price is $120, will there be an excess demand? An excess supply?

10. Suppose that an excise tax of $40 is imposed on each camera. What will be the posttax equilibrium price of a camera? What will be the posttax equilibrium quantity? How does it compare with the pretax equilibrium quantity?

11. After the government imposes the tax in Question 10, it decides to set a price ceiling of $100 on the price of a camera. Will there be a surplus of cameras? A shortage? If so, how big a surplus or shortage?

12. According to Richard Titmuss of the London School of Economics, no Englishman pays even a shilling for all the blood his physicians prescribe for him, and no blood donor is paid for his blood. Yet blood is more readily available for patients there than in the United States where we pay for the donation of blood. What hypotheses can be advanced to account for this?

13. Suppose that the government puts a price floor of 80 cents per pound on cantaloupes. How big will be the resulting surplus of cantaloupes, based on the data in Question 5? What measures can the government adopt to cut down on this surplus?

14. Indicate whether each of the following will shift the demand curve for cantaloupes to the left or to the right, or have no effect on it: (a) a report by the U.S. Surgeon-General that cantaloupes cause cancer, (b) a 10 percent increase in the price of honeydew melons, (c) a 20 percent increase in per capita income, (d) a 10 percent increase in the wages of workers producing cantaloupes.

15. The market supply curve for good Y is a straight line through the origin. Does the price elasticity of supply vary with good Y's price? What is good Y's price elasticity of supply?

16. In March 1995, severe floods, the worst of this century, occurred in California's Salinas and Pajaro Valleys. Extensive damage was done to the lettuce, strawberry, broccoli, celery, and artichoke crops. The Salinas Valley produces half the country's lettuce. At the Philadelphia Wholesale Market, lettuce prices (for cartons of 24) were as follows on March 1, 1995 and April 4, 1995:

Type of lettuce	March 1	April 4
Iceberg	$7.50–$9.00	$45–$55
Green leaf	$7.50–$8.00	$25–$28
Romaine	$10	$30–$35

(a) Were the price changes due to changes in the demand or supply curve for lettuce? (b) Restaurants subsequently began to replace lettuce-based salads with pasta salads. Why? (c) Were lettuce producers outside the Salinas and Pajaro Valleys helped or hurt by these floods? Why?

Applying Micro-economic Theory: Microbreweries, Cocaine, and Spectrum Rights

INTRODUCTION

This is a book on applied microeconomics. Thus, before going any further, let's consider several illustrations of how the simple concepts presented in the previous chapter can be applied. Specifically, we take up in this chapter (1) the growth of microbreweries, (2) the cocaine epidemic, and (3) the Federal Communications Commission's auction of spectrum rights. It is hard to imagine a more diverse set of topics. Yet they have at least one thing in common: all of them can be understood only if you know some simple microeconomic theory. To help develop your capacity to apply the concepts in the previous chapter, nine multipart problems are presented, after very brief introductions to each of these topics.

THE BIRTH OF RED BRICK ALE

To begin with, let's consider Gregory Kelly, founder and president of the Atlanta Brewing Company, which first produced beer in July 1994. Prior to establishing this firm, he spent 10 years at Guinness, the large British maker of spirits and beer. When he was 38 years old, he invested nearly all his life savings of $150,000 in the fledgling company. An additional $1.2 million was obtained from investors who bought the firm's stock.

The Atlanta Brewing Company is a microbrewery, one that produces less than 15,000 barrels annually. After first appearing in northern California and the Pacific Northwest, microbreweries have begun to appear in more and more parts of the country. The first microbrewery in Atlanta, Georgia, Atlanta Brewing is dedicated to the production of traditionally brewed, high-quality "craft" beers. After obtaining the necessary financing, he rented and renovated an old warehouse, and hired an 80-year-old brewmaster, Karl Strauss, as a consultant to formulate recipes for his beers. Pumps, cold tanks, and pine-sided tanks were imported from England.

Mr. Kelly used market research to help decide what to name his ale, and eventually settled on "Red Brick Ale." Recognizing the importance of getting Red Brick Ale into stores, bars, and restaurants, he succeeded in getting the largest local distributor to handle his new product even before he approached potential investors. Starting up a new venture of this kind is a risky business, as indicated in his business plan to potential investors, which cautioned that

Gregory Kelly (right)
with William Campbell,
mayor of Atlanta

"no assurance can be given that the company will achieve profitable operations in the future."[1]

Red Brick Ale received an enthusiastic reception. In November 1994, Mr. Kelly said, "I can't keep up with the demand. We're going to sell in the first 12 months about 100,000 cases of beer, 7,246 barrels."[2] The beer sold for $5.99 for six bottles. These sales occurred without any advertising because "I can't afford to put Red Brick on billboards around Atlanta."[3] Given its apparent success, the new beer began to be sold outside Georgia in 1995.

THE U.S. BEER INDUSTRY

Red Brick Ale is not typical of the U.S. beer industry, which has experienced little or no growth in sales in recent years (Table 2.1). One reason for this lack of growth is that consumers, concerned about their health and appearance, have become more calorie-conscious. Many people have turned from beer to other beverages that have fewer calories and less alcohol. Also, the increase in the national drinking age to 21 (which President Reagan signed into law in 1984) and the increased number and more-rigorous enforcement of drunk-driving laws probably reduced beer consumption in the United States.

---

[1] *New York Times,* November 20, 1994, p. 12F.
[2] Ibid.
[3] Ibid.

TABLE 2.1 Production of Malt Beverages in the United States (millions of barrels)

Year	Production	Year	Production
1981	195	1988	197
1982	194	1989	197
1983	196	1990	202
1984	193	1991	204
1985	194	1992	201
1986	194	1993	202
1987	196	1994	203

SOURCE: *Brewers Almanac.*

The largest brewer in the United States is Anheuser-Busch, which has almost half the market. Its biggest seller is Budweiser (with 52 percent of the firm's shipments in 1992). The most profitable firm in the brewing industry, its after-tax annual earnings were about $900 million in the early 1990s (Table 2.2). Since the equity of its shareholders was about $4 billion, the return on the owners' investment was over 20 percent per year. Anheuser-Busch has diversified into other fields, such as food products and real estate (and the St. Louis Cardinals baseball club), but it's primary business continues to be beer.

Anheuser-Busch's principal rival is Miller Brewing Company, purchased by Philip Morris in 1970. Miller rose from seventh place in the industry in 1972 to second in 1977, due in part to the phenomenal success of its Lite Beer, one of the first low-calorie beers. According to its president, William Howell, "We have built our success by doing our homework, finding out what beer consumers want and then delivering it.... We have been innovators in product, merchandising, and advertising.[4]

TABLE 2.2 Income Statement, Anheuser-Busch, 1990–1994 (billions of dollars)

	1994	1993	1992	1991	1990
Net sales	12.0	11.5	11.4	11.0	10.7
Cost of goods sold	7.8	7.4	7.3	7.1	7.1
Selling and administrative expenses	2.4	2.3	2.3	2.1	2.1
Interest and other costs	0.2	0.7	0.3	0.3	0.2
Income taxes	0.7	0.5	0.6	0.6	0.5
Net income	1.0	0.6	0.9	0.9	0.8

[4] L. Byars and T. Neil, "Miller Brewing Company", in H. Bartlett (ed.), *Cases in Strategic Management for Business* (New York: Dryden Press, 1988), p. 260.

MICROBREWERIES: CAN YOU APPLY THE THEORY?

The following three problems are concerned with the market for microbrews (the beer produced by microbreweries), the entry of the major brewers into the microbreweries' markets, and the effects of the taxes imposed by the government on beer.

PROBLEM 2.1 To many consumers, particularly the more affluent and sophisticated, microbrews are much different from, and more appealing than, mass-produced beer. Although specialty beers (which include microbrews or craft beers) sold only about a half million barrels in 1990, their sales grew to almost 2.5 million barrels in 1994 (Figure 2.1). During 1994, microbreweries produced only about 1 percent of the beer brewed in the United States, but some analysts forecast that eventually they may account for 10 percent of production. According to Frank Walters, director of research for Impact International, a trade

FIGURE 2.1 ANNUAL SALES OF SPECIALTY BEERS

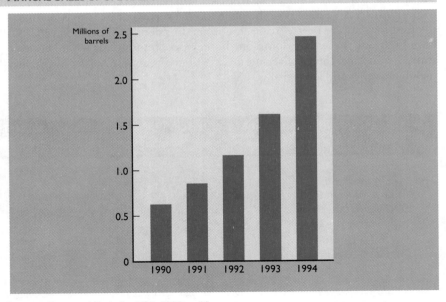

SOURCE: *Business Week,* April 24, 1995, p. 66.

newspaper, demand for the more flavorful microbrews is expected to grow by 30 percent per year or more.[5]

(a) In 1994, was the market for Red Brick Ale a national market or a regional market? (Were practically all of the potential buyers located in Georgia?)

(b) According to Mr. Kelly, about 100,000 cases of Red Brick Ale were sold in the first year, at $5.99 for six bottles. If the (arc) price elasticity of demand for Red Brick Ale was 0.8, how many cases would have been sold if the price had been $6.50 for six bottles?

(c) Is the demand curve for Red Brick Ale the same as the demand curve for all microbrews in Georgia? Why or why not?

(d) If there is a fall in the price of mass-produced beer, is the demand curve for microbrews likely to shift to the left or the right? Why?

(e) According to *Business Week*, microbrews "have several ingredients in common: high price, deeper flavoring, and, to the cognoscenti, a far hipper image than that conjured up by a six-pack of Bud."[6] If the supply curve for microbrews is to the left of the supply curve for mass-produced beer, can this help to explain the higher price of microbrews than mass-produced beer?

PROBLEM 2.2 Attracted by the growing market for microbrews, the big beer producers have begun to introduce specialty beers of their own. At a recently converted test brewery in St. Louis, Anheuser-Busch has formulated Elk Mountain Amber Ale, Red Dog, and Icehouse, its new entries into this market. Like the microbrews, these specialty beers are aimed at consumers who find the mass-produced beers like Budweiser or Miller Lite relatively uninteresting. The big brewers are touting the richness of flavor and high quality of their new specialty beers.

(a) Assuming that the microbrews produced by the big beer producers are of the same quality as those produced by the microbreweries, will the entry of the big producers into this market result in a shift of the supply curve for microbrews? If so, will this curve shift to the left or the right? Why?

(b) If the microbrews produced by the big beer producers are of the same quality as those produced by the microbreweries, will the entry of the big producers tend to lower the price for microbrews? If so, why?

(c) Does the entry of the big producers threaten the financial viability of the microbreweries? If you owned stock in the Atlanta Brewing Company, would you be concerned? Why or why not?

[5] Ibid.
[6] *Business Week,* April 24, 1995.

(d) Some observers feel that the specialty beers introduced by the big beer producers are not of the same quality as those produced by the microbreweries. For example, Christopher Finch, coauthor of *America's Best Beers,* has been reported to have doubts on this score.[7] If these doubts are correct, should the specialty beers produced by the big producers be lumped together with those produced by microbreweries, and regarded as a single product in a supply-and-demand analysis? Why or why not?

(e) Whether or not specialty beers produced by big producers are as good as the output of microbreweries, there is a widespread feeling that consumers have a negative reaction to a craft beer with a big brewer's name on the label. As one executive put it, "We heard loud and clear that the consumer doesn't want a craft beer coming from a large beer."[8] If so, should the specialty beers produced by large producers and microbreweries be lumped together and regarded as a single product? Why or why not?

PROBLEM 2.3   Beer is one of the most highly taxed consumer products. Taxes are the largest individual element in the price of beer. In 1995, the federal excise tax was $18 a barrel (except for very small breweries), and the state excise tax was about $9 per barrel. In 1994, the U.S. government received $3.4 billion from taxes on malt beverages. Combined federal, state, and local taxes totaled about $5.25 billion.[9]

(a) Why is beer one of the most highly taxed consumer products?

(b) Suppose that the demand and supply curves for beer are as follows:

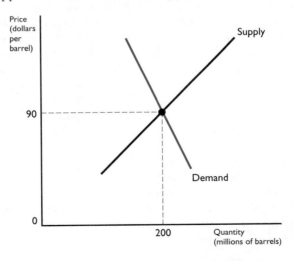

[7] Ibid.
[8] Ibid.
[9] These figures were provided by an executive at Anheuser-Busch.

If a tax of $30 per barrel is imposed on beer, what will be the effect on the price of beer? What will be the effect on the quantity of beer consumed?

(c) A television commentator says that this tax will be paid for entirely by consumers. Is this true?

(d) Does this tax increase or decrease the amount consumers spend on beer? How big is the increase or decrease?

(e) If the government subsequently raises the tax on beer, with the result that the price of beer goes up to $120 per barrel, how big must the increase in the beer tax have been? (Assume that the demand and supply curves for beer remain as shown above.)

(f) The U.S. government imposes a tax of only $7 per barrel on the first 60,000 barrels of beer produced per year by a firm, and $18 per barrel on any amount produced above that amount. According to the business plan submitted by the Atlanta Brewing Company to potential investors, "This is a considerable cost advantage over the major brewers..." Does this give the microbreweries a competitive edge over the big brewers? Does this mean that they can sell their beer profitably at a lower price than the big brewers can?

THE COCAINE EPIDEMIC

It is a big jump from beer to cocaine, but microeconomic theory can be applied effectively to either one. The United States has experienced a cocaine epidemic in recent years, and it is not over. Beginning in the 1960s, cocaine use grew until in the early 1980s about 9 million people were users (Figure 2.2). While this number has declined since then, total cocaine consumption has not fallen because the percentage using cocaine at least weekly (heavy users) has increased (Figure 2.3). This is not the first such epidemic. Between 1885 and 1915, when cocaine was legal, druggists sold "toothache drops" containing cocaine, and Coca-Cola contained very small amounts of cocaine. But after 1915, the epidemic subsided as the public became more and more concerned about crimes committed by cocaine users and other undesirable consequences of the drug.

Total expenditure on cocaine control in the United States—including local, state, and federal funds and the cost of private as well as public treatment—was about $13 billion in 1992. These expenditures are for four types of programs: (1) domestic enforcement programs, which result in the arrest and imprisonment of drug dealers and the seizure of their assets (including co-

FIGURE 2.2 **Number of Cocaine Users, by Intensity of Use** The number of cocaine users declined between 1982 and the early 1990s.

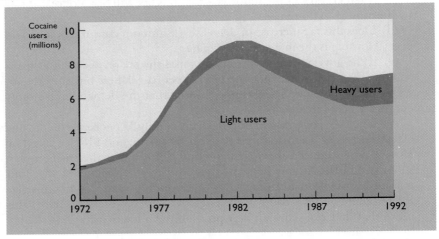

SOURCE: C. Peter Rydell and Susan Everingham, *Controlling Cocaine: Supply versus Demand Programs* (Santa Monica, Calif.: Rand Corporation, 1994).

FIGURE 2.3 **Cocaine Consumption, by Type of User** Because of increased consumption by heavy users, total cocaine consumption did not decline between 1985 and 1992.

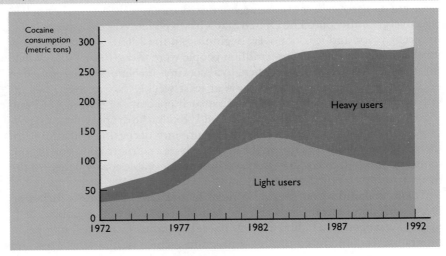

SOURCE: Rydell and Everingham, *Controlling Cocaine.*

Customs agents seizing
cocaine

caine); (2) interdiction at the U.S. border by the Coast Guard, the Army, and
the Customs Service, all of which seize cocaine; (3) source-country programs,
which destroy coca leaf and seize intermediate and final cocaine products in
South and Central America; and (4) outpatient and residential treatment of
users aimed at getting them off cocaine.

The lion's share of the expenditures on cocaine control goes for domestic
enforcement programs. In 1992, about 73 percent went for such programs,
while 13 percent was devoted to interdiction, and source-country control and
treatment programs each received 7 percent. The domestic enforcement programs are carried out by a variety of federal agencies, the most prominent
being the Drug Enforcement Administration, and state and local police
forces.[10]

CONTROVERSIES OVER DRUG POLICY

There has been a public debate over drug policy in the United States. On the
one hand, the so-called hawks in the drug war, led by former National Drug
Control Director William Bennett, favor expansion of activities aimed at the
imprisonment of drug sellers and the discouragement of drug users. Pointing
to the crime associated with drug distribution, they question whether drug

[10] This section is based on C. Peter Rydell and Susan Everingham, *Controlling Cocaine: Supply
versus Demand Programs* (Santa Monica, Calif.: Rand Corporation, 1994).

treatment or efforts at prevention can make any real dent in the problem. (Many treatment programs have relapse rates exceeding 60 percent). Moreover, they feel that strict enforcement of existing laws is needed to make treatment and prevention programs effective.

The "doves," led by Senator Joseph Biden of Delaware, feel differently. In their view, while vigorous enforcement is important, treatment and prevention programs are being neglected and should be expanded considerably, even if this means a cut in enforcement activities. Some doves argue that drugs should be legalized. In some Western European countries, such as Holland, Italy, Spain, and Switzerland, governments have been reluctant to apply the criminal law against users. In other countries, such as Germany, Norway, and Sweden, the criminal law has been applied, but not as aggressively as in the United States.

According to leading experts like Peter Reuter of the University of Maryland, the hawks "have been in soaring ascendance. Though they grumble about the lack of severity in punishment of drug users and dealers, they have managed to massively increase funding for such punishment, to expand the scope of efforts to detect drug users in many settings and to intensify the severity of penalties imposed on those convicted of selling or using drugs."[11] For example, in 1988, Congress increased the mandatory sentence for selling 50 grams of crack cocaine to 5 years.

THE COCAINE EPIDEMIC: CAN YOU APPLY THE THEORY?

The following three problems are concerned with the demand and supply of cocaine and the effects of government programs to control cocaine use.

PROBLEM 2.4   A wide variety of people consume cocaine. Following Everingham and Rydell, we define *heavy users* as people who use cocaine at least weekly. (Other people who use cocaine at least once a year are *light users*). The percentage of users that are heavy users is particularly high—about 50 percent—among the homeless and the incarcerated. There is a decline in cocaine use as people get older; only about 30 percent of users still use cocaine 10 years after they begin. As shown in

---

[11] Peter Reuter, "Hawks Ascendant: The Punitive Trend of American Drug Policy," *Daedalus,* 1992, p. 20. This section is based largely on Reuter's work.

Figures 2.2 and 2.3, the proportion of users that are heavy users has increased considerably in recent years, and heavy users account for a much larger proportion of total cocaine consumption than in 1972.

On the average, treatment programs are about 80 percent effective at keeping cocaine users off the drug while they are in the program, but many people who start such programs leave before completion and many return to cocaine after such programs. About 6 percent of heavy users leave heavy use each year, about two-thirds of them due apparently to treatment programs. However, many who leave heavy use do not give up the drug entirely.

(a) According to Peter Reuter, "Drug abuse or dependence is increasingly concentrated in inner-city populations...."[12] If the demand curve for drugs outside the inner cities has shifted to the left, would this help to account for this trend?

(b) Cocaine use now tends to be inversely related to the level of education of a person. If the average number of years of education in one area is double that of another area (of the same population), would you expect the demand curve for cocaine in the former area to be to the left or the right of that in the latter area?

(c) Are treatment programs meant to shift the demand curve for cocaine? If so, are they meant to shift it to the left or the right? Why?

(d) Some observers raise the following question regarding treatment programs: "Why should we be putting tax dollars into treating something that people have brought on themselves?"[13] Do you agree? Why or why not?

(e) Studies by the Rand Corporation, a California think tank, have recommended that more resources be devoted to treatment programs because they result in a greater reduction in cocaine consumption per dollar spent than other types of programs. Why should you care about how much cocaine consumption is reduced per dollar spent?

PROBLEM 2.5 Cocaine is produced in South America, chiefly in Peru, Bolivia, and Colombia. Coca leaf, the raw agricultural product, must be transported before it can be marketed in New York or Washington, D.C. Government programs aimed at the arrest and imprisonment of drug dealers (and the seizure of their assets), interdiction of cocaine at the U.S. border, and destruction of coca leaf and intermediate and final cocaine products in South and Central America are all meant to raise the costs of cocaine suppliers. At each stage of the production and distribution process, the suppliers of cocaine incur costs because of seizures of

---

[12] Reuter, "Hawks Ascendant," p. 28.
[13] *New York Times,* June 19, 1994, p. 19.

their product by government agencies, because of the seizure of their assets, and because they must compensate their workers for the risk of arrest and incarceration. Also, suppliers must pay to prevent government agencies from finding out about their activities and employees.

(a) Whereas the price of cocaine is about $4,000 per kilogram at the airstrip in South America, it is over $100,000 on the street in the United States.[14] Why such a big difference?

(b) It has been estimated that the retail price of cocaine would fall by 80 or 90 percent if cocaine were legal. For example, in 1988 the price would have been about $15 or $20 per pure gram rather than $143.[15] Is this due, at least in part, to the effect of legalization on the supply curve for cocaine? If so, why?

(c) Are government programs aimed at arresting and imprisoning drug dealers, intercepting cocaine at the U.S. border, and destroying coca leaf and cocaine in South and Central America designed to shift the supply curve for cocaine? If so, are they designed to shift it to the left or the right?

(d) C. Peter Rydell and Susan Everingham of the Rand Corporation estimate that a $246 million extra annual expenditure on cocaine seizures, asset seizures, and arrest and imprisonment of drug dealers in the United States would push up the price of cocaine in the United States by about 2 percent. Will the effect on cocaine consumption depend on the price elasticity of demand for cocaine? Why or why not?

(e) According to Rydell and Everingham, the price elasticity of demand for cocaine is about 0.5. If so, what will be the effect of the $246 million extra annual expenditure in part (d) on annual cocaine consumption?

PROBLEM 2.6   A cocaine habit is expensive to maintain and risky to boot. To users, the risk of arrest may not be trivial; it has been estimated that the probability of arrest in a 10-year using career may be as high as .60 (and higher for African-Americans and males than for others). To drug dealers, the risks may also be substantial; a study of drug dealers in Washington, D.C., has concluded that "street sellers of drugs faced about a 22 percent probability of imprisonment in the course of a year's selling and that, given expected time served, they spend one-third of their selling careers in prison."[16]

---

[14] Rydell and Everingham, *Controlling Cocaine,* p. 11.

[15] Mark Moor, "Supply Reduction and Drug Law Enforcement," in Michael Tonry and James Wilson (eds.), *Drugs and Crime* (Chicago: University of Chicago Press, 1990).

[16] Reuter, "Hawks Ascendant," p. 27. Also see Peter Reuter, Robert MacCoun, and Patrick

FIGURE 2.4 Price of Cocaine: 1977–1992 During 1977 to 1992, there was a spectacular decrease in the price of cocaine.

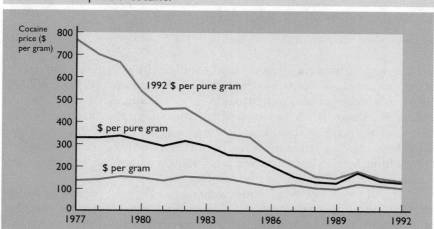

SOURCE: Rydell and Everingham, *Controlling Cocaine.*

(a) During 1977 to 1992, there was a spectacular decrease in the retail price of cocaine in the United States; in 1992 dollars, the price fell from about $750 to about $120 per pure gram (Figure 2.4). Was this what policymakers in the United States were trying to achieve?

(b) Consumption of cocaine increased during 1977 to 1992 (Figure 2.3), while its price fell (Figure 2.4). Rydell and Everingham suggest that one possible explanation is that: "Cocaine suppliers have learned how to run their business more efficiently over time, improving their techniques of avoiding law enforcement by trial-and-error experimentation."[17] Why is this a possible explanation?

(c) There seems to be a general agreement that the demand curve for cocaine shifted to the right during 1972 to 1985. Would this shift in the demand curve help to explain the decrease in price? Why or why not?

(d) During 1985 to 1992, there is some evidence that the demand curve for cocaine may have shifted to the left. Would this shift in the demand curve help to explain the decrease in price? Why or why not?

Murphy, *Money from Crime: A Study of the Economics of Drug Dealing in Washington, D.C.* (Santa Monica, Calif.: Rand Corporation, 1990).
[17] Rydell and Everingham, *Controlling Cocaine,* p. 59.

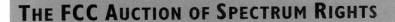

THE FCC AUCTION OF SPECTRUM RIGHTS

Let's move now from the shadowy world of illicit drugs to the raucous world of the airwaves. In his column in the *New York Times,* March 16, 1995, William Safire, a leading political pundit, said, "They all laughed at the economist Milton Friedman when he suggested a generation ago that the Federal Government auction off broadcast licenses, instead of giving them away to political favorites. The last laugh is his; last week, in the greatest auction in history, bidding for wireless places on a tiny fragment of the broadband spectrum committed nearly $8 billion to the U.S. Treasury."[18]

For many years, spectrum licenses were assigned by the Federal Communications Commission (FCC), which held hearings to decide which of a number of applicants were most suitable. But the procedure was so cumbersome and time-consuming that it eventually was replaced with lotteries which awarded licenses at random among the applicants. In 1993, Congress gave the FCC the authority to auction off licenses. Each license remains in effect for up to a decade, but if it is being used effectively, its renewal is almost automatic.

In 1994, the FCC auctioned off a variety of wavelengths, formerly reserved for the military, which were to be devoted to personal communications services (PCS) like pocket telephones, portable fax machines, and wireless computer networks. The auction continued from December 5, 1994 to March 13,

---

[18] *New York Times,* March 16, 1995. For an early suggestion of this idea, see R. H. Coase, "The Federal Communications Commission," *Journal of Law and Economics,* October 1959.

TABLE 2.3 Highest Bids (per Person) for U.S. Licenses for Broadband Personal Communications Services

Market	Winning bidder	Winning bid ($ millions)	Price per person (dollars)
1. Chicago	PCS Primeco, L.P.[a]	$385	32
2. Chicago	AT&T Wireless PCS Inc.	373	31
3. Atlanta	AT&T Wireless PCS Inc.	198	29
4. Seattle	GTE Macro Communications	106	28
5. Seattle	Wireless Co. L.P.[b]	105	27
6. Washington/Baltimore	AT&T Wireless PCS Inc.	212	27
7. Atlanta	GTE Macro Communications	185	27
8. Los Angeles/San Diego	Pacific Telesis	494	27
9. Miami/Fort Lauderdale	Wireless Co., L.P.[b]	132	27
10. St. Louis	AT&T Wireless PCS Inc.	119	26

[a] Bell Atlantic, Nynex, U.S. West, Air Touch Communications

[b] Sprint, Comcast, Tele-Communications, Inc., Cox Cable.

SOURCE: *Philadelphia Inquirer,* March 17, 1995.

1995. Ninety-nine licenses to provide PCS across the United States were auctioned off. The bidders included telephone companies (long distance, local, and cellular) and cable television firms.

The biggest winner was Wireless Co., L.P., a partnership of Sprint, Tele-Communications, Inc., Cox Cable, and Comcast Telephony, which placed winning bids in 29 markets; in all, its bids totaled about $2.1 billion. The second biggest winner was AT&T Wireless PCS Inc., a wholly owned subsidiary of AT&T Corporation, which was the winning bidder in 21 markets, with bids totaling about $1.7 billion (For the ten highest bids per person in the market, see Table 2.3.)

THE ROLE OF ECONOMICS IN THE DESIGN AND OPERATION OF THE AUCTION

After the auction, FCC Chairman Reed Hundt said, "It is a wonderful honor for us to be able to introduce competition in a robust, vigorous way in the wireless communications business of the future. The auctions today represent what our country is capable of achieving when all decide to pull in the same di-

Reed Hundt

rection.... I am very pleased with how smoothly this auction—the biggest in the known universe—ran. The FCC auction team worked around-the-clock for over a year to get the job done. What they accomplished is nothing short of historic."[19]

It is important to recognize that the FCC auction team included economists and that economic theorists played a central role in the design and operation of this auction. Paul Milgrom and Robert Wilson of Stanford University did seminal work on the theory of auctions, which was useful in designing this auction. The FCC hired John McMillan of the University of California at San Diego as a consultant, and the National Telecommunications and Information Administration hired John Ledyard of California Institute of Technology as a consultant. Together with economists who were employees of these agencies, these economists provided advice that government officials relied on.

In addition, the major telephone companies used a platoon of economic theorists as consultants. Among them were Pacific Bell (Paul Milgrom, Charles Plott, and Robert Wilson), Bell Atlantic (Jeremy Bulow and Barry Nalebuff), Air Touch Communications (Preston McAfee), Telephone and Data Systems (Robert Weber), Cellular Telecommunications Industry Association (Mark Isaac), Nynex (Robert Harris and Michael Katz), MCI (Peter Cramton), and American Personal Communications (Daniel Vincent).

---

[19] Federal Communications Commission, *Auctions,* March 13, 1995.

Economists have been pleased with the results of this and other auctions."[20] As Peter Cramton of the University of Maryland put it, "After decades of lobbying for auctions, economists finally got their way and witness the wisdom in their recommendations.... Taxpayers, consumers, and firms are all better-off with auctions. The only losers are politicians—who lose the ability to bestow gifts on those parties that support their election campaigns.... So long as budget deficits remain a problem, it is hard to imagine that Congress would be able to reverse the... decision [to rely on auctions] without setting off a grass-roots rebellion among taxpayers."[21]

THE FEDERAL COMMUNICATIONS COMMISSION: CAN YOU APPLY THE THEORY?

The following three problems are concerned with the design and operation of the FCC's auction of spectrum rights, as well as its approval of new radio stations.

PROBLEM 2.7 Not all auctions follow the same rules or operate in the same way. Economists have studied how an auction's design influences the likely outcomes. Following the recommendation of economic theorists, the FCC decided to hold an open auction rather than a sealed-bid auction. In an open auction, buyers raise their bids until only one (the winner) is left. In a sealed-bid auction, each bidder submits a sealed bid; the highest bidder wins.

(a) Was the winner's curse likely to be present in this auction? Why or why not?

(b) If the winner's curse is present, will bidders tend to make bids that are well below their estimates of what a license is worth? Why or why not?

(c) According to economic theorists, bidders are likely to be more confident and more inclined to bid higher in an open auction than in a sealed-bid auction. Why?

---

[20] Prior to the big auction, a much smaller auction of 11 narrowband PCS licenses was carried out by the FCC in July 1994.

[21] Peter Cramton, "Money Out of Thin Air: The Nationwide Narrowband PCS Auction," unpublished, September 1994, p. 43.

(d) Many participants in the auction seemed proud that a great deal of money was raised. For example, Wayne Perry, vice chairman of McCaw Cellular Communications, Inc. said, "For once, the government is doing a great job dragging money out of people."[22] And FCC Chairman Reed Hundt said, "We're happy the [federal budget] deficit issue is being addressed so successfully."[23] Would the amount of money raised be likely to be greater if buyers colluded or if they acted independently? Why?

(e) One advantage of sealed-bid auctions over open auctions, according to economists, is that collusion among buyers is deterred. Why?

PROBLEM 2.8   In April 1993, two licenses for satellite-television service were auctioned off in a sealed-bid auction in Australia. The winners were Hi Vision Ltd. and Ucom, Pry. Ltd.; their winning bids were about $140 million and $120 million, respectively. Because these bids were larger than expected, and because these firms were not among the major players in the Australian television industry, the Australian government announced that the auction ushered in "a whole new era."

To the consternation of the government, both Hi Vision and Ucom defaulted on their highest bids. Thus, the licenses had to be re-awarded at the next highest levels, which were also theirs. It soon became clear that each firm had submitted a large number of bids, each about $5 million higher than the next. After defaulting on a number of its highest bids, Ucom eventually paid about $80 million for one license and $50 million for the other. One of Australia's politicians called it "one of the world's great media license fiascos," and Bob Collins, Australia's communications minister, almost was sacked."[24]

(a) What was the fundamental flaw in the design of this auction?

(b) Can this flaw be eliminated? If so, how?

(c) When the FCC auctioned off spectrum rights, it stipulated that firms had to make down payments to the FCC based on how many people were in the geographical areas for which they wanted to bid. Thus, Wireless Co, L.P. made down payments of about $120 million, and AT&T Wireless PCS Inc. made down payments of about $80 million. Was this designed to help avoid the sorts of problems encountered in Australia?

(d) The FCC also stipulated that a high bidder withdrawing its bid during the auction would be liable for the difference between its bid and the price ultimately obtained for the license. For bids withdrawn after the auction, there would be a supplementary penalty of 3 percent. Would this help to avoid the difficulties encountered in Australia? Why or why not?

---

[22] *Wall Street Journal,* July 28, 1994.

[23] *Washington Post,* July 30, 1994, p. A1.

[24] John McMillan, "Selling Spectrum Rights," *Journal of Economic Perspectives,* Summer 1994.

PROBLEM 2.9 The FCC is a major federal regulatory agency with responsibilities extending far beyond the auction of spectrum rights. From the mid-1980s to the early 1990s, the FCC, which regulates the nation's airwaves, approved over a thousand new radio stations. According to Paul Kagan Associates, a market research firm in Carmel, California, the average price of a combined AM/FM radio station fell from abut $6.2 million in 1987 to about $1.8 million in 1990.[25]

(a) Is there a market for radio stations, just as there is a market for wheat, corn, or lamb chops?

(b) Did the FCC contribute to the fall in the price of radio stations? If so, how?

(c) If the FCC had mandated that the price of a radio station should remain at about $6.2 million in 1990, would there have been a shortage of radio stations? Why or why not?

(d) Under the conditions described in part (c), would there have been a surplus of radio stations? Why or why not?

CONCLUSION

To illustrate the wide variety of areas where the simple concepts presented in the previous chapter can be applied, we have taken up three quite different topics. The first topic, the growth and impact of microbreweries, is of great importance to brewing executives like Gregory Kelly. In addition, it is of interest to investors (who must decide whether to put money in microbreweries like the Atlanta Brewing Company) and to consumers (who have shown a remarkable taste for microbrews). The second topic, the cocaine epidemic, is a key challenge for public policy in the United States and other countries. All citizens must have at least rudimentary knowledge of the factors influencing cocaine consumption and the effectiveness of various approaches to reducing its deleterious effects. The third topic, the activities of the Federal Communications Commission, with special emphasis on its auction of spectrum rights, is an important illustration of how government agencies work, a central concern of both firms and individual citizens and taxpayers. Although these three topics seem at first glance to have essentially nothing in common, they all can be analyzed effectively with the simple concepts taken up in the previous chapter. This illustrates the power and adaptability of microeconomic theory, to which we now return in the next several chapters.

---

[25] *New York Times,* June 30, 1991.

SELECTED SUPPLEMENTARY READINGS

1. *The Brewers Almanac,* Beer Institute (Washington, DC, annual).
2. D. Greer, "Beer: Causes of Structural Change," in L. Deutsch (ed.), *Industry Studies* (Englewood Cliffs, N.J.: Prentice-Hall, 1993).
3. L. Byars and T. Neil, "Miller Brewing Company," in H. Bartlett (ed.), *Cases in Strategic Management for Business* (New York: Dryden Press, 1988).
4. *Business Week,* April 24, 1995, p. 66.
5. F. Fabricant, "Finally, New York Takes to Brew Pubs," *New York Times,* April 17, 1996, p. C1.
6. C. Peter Rydell and Susan Everingham, *Controlling Cocaine: Supply versus Demand Programs* (Santa Monica, Calif.: Rand Corporation, 1994).
7. P. Reuter, "Hawks Ascendant: The Punitive Trend of American Drug Policy," *Daedalus,* 1992.
8. M. Moor, "Supply Reduction and Drug Law Enforcement," in Michael Tonry and James Wilson (eds.), *Drugs and Crime* (Chicago: University of Chicago Press, 1990).
9. *New York Times,* June 19, 1994, p. 19.
10. Federal Communications Commission, *Auctions,* March 13, 1995.
11. R. H. Coase, "The Federal Communications Commission," *Journal of Law and Economics,* October 1959.
12. *Washington Post,* July 30, 1994, p. A1.
13. J. McMillan, "Selling Spectrum Rights," *Journal of Economic Perspectives,* Summer 1994.

PART TWO

Consumer Behavior and Market Demand

The Tastes and Preferences of the Consumer

3

INTRODUCTION

Economists have devoted a considerable amount of study to consumer behavior; this is understandable since the U.S. consumer spends trillions of dollars per year on final goods and services. About 70 percent of the final goods and services produced by the U.S. economy go directly to consumers. (The rest are sold to business firms, to the government, and in export markets.) Moreover, the importance of consumers is not a purely U.S. phenomenon. For example, in our neighbor to the north, Canada, about two-thirds of the final goods and services produced by the Canadian economy go directly to consumers. Similar figures could be cited for many other countries.

In this chapter we present a simple model to represent the consumer's tastes and to help predict how much of various commodities he or she will buy. Besides being of interest for its own sake, this model is a first step toward analyzing the forces underlying the market demand curve, the importance of which was stressed in Chapter 1. Some of the major concepts that are introduced in this model are indifference curves, the marginal rate of substitution, utility, and the budget line. Finally, we show how this body of theory has been applied to help solve very important practical problems of budget allocation by government agencies.

THE NATURE OF THE CONSUMER'S PREFERENCES

Our purpose in this chapter is to present a simple model of consumer behavior that will enable us to predict how much of a particular commodity — hot dogs, paint, housing — a consumer buys during a particular period of time. Clearly, one of the most important determinants of a consumer's behavior is his or her tastes or preferences. After all, some consumers like Sherlock Holmes and others like comic books; some like Verdi and others like the Rolling Stones. And it is obvious that these differences in tastes result in quite different decisions by consumers as to what commodities they buy. In this section we present several basic assumptions that the economist makes about the nature of the consumer's tastes.

To begin with, suppose that the consumer is confronted with any two market baskets, each containing various quantities of commodities. For example, one market basket might contain 1 ticket to a basketball game and 3 chocolate bars, while the other might contain 4 bottles of soda and 1 bus ticket. The first assumption that the economist makes is that consumers can decide whether they prefer the first market basket to the second, whether they prefer the second to the first, or whether they are indifferent between them.[1] This certainly seems to be a plausible assumption.

**Transi-
tivity** Second, we assume that the consumer's preferences are transitive. For example, if a man prefers Budweiser to Heineken and Heineken to Coors, he must also prefer Budweiser to Coors. Otherwise his preferences would not be transitive, which would mean that his preferences would be contradictory or

---

[1] One way of telling whether the consumer prefers one market basket to another is to set equivalent prices for them and ask which one the consumer wants.

inconsistent. Similarly, if he is indifferent between mince pie and pumpkin pie and between pumpkin pie and apple pie, he must also be indifferent between mince pie and apple pie. His tastes may be judged to be shallow or deep, lofty or mean, selfish or generous. This makes no difference to the theory. But his preferences must be transitive. Although not all consumers may exhibit preferences that are transitive, this assumption certainly seems to be a plausible basis for a model of consumer behavior.

Third, we assume that the consumer always prefers more of a commodity to less. For example, if one market basket (a very big one) contains 15 harmonicas and 2 gallons of gasoline, whereas another market basket (also big) contains 15 harmonicas and 1 gallon of gasoline, we assume that the first market basket, which unambiguously contains more commodities, is preferred. Also, we assume that, by adding a certain amount of harmonicas to the second market basket, we can make it equally desirable in the eyes of the consumer to the first market basket; that is, we can make the consumer indifferent between them. These assumptions, like the previous two, seem quite plausible.

INDIFFERENCE CURVES

If the assumptions in the previous section hold, we can represent the consumer's tastes or preferences by a set of indifference curves. *An indifference curve is the locus of points representing market baskets among which the consumer is indifferent.* For example, suppose we confine our attention to the ten market baskets in Table 3.1, in which the first market basket contains 1 pound of meat and 4 pounds of potatoes, the second market basket contains 1 pound of meat and 6 pounds of potatoes, and so on. Suppose the consumer is asked to choose between various pairs of these market baskets and that he or she is indifferent between some of these market baskets. For example, the consumer may not care whether he or she consumes 4 pounds of meat plus 2 pounds of potatoes or 2 pounds of meat plus 3 pounds of potatoes. Suppose that we enlarge the number of market baskets (containing various quantities of meat and potatoes) under consideration, so that we include all market baskets in which from 1 to 8 pounds of meat are combined with from 1 to 8 pounds of potatoes. Then suppose we plot each of the market baskets on a diagram like Figure 3.1 and that *curve A is the set of points representing market baskets among which the consumer is indifferent.* For example, this curve includes all the market baskets that the consumer regards as being equivalent (in terms of his or her satisfaction) to 4 pounds of meat plus 2 pounds of potatoes.

*Indif-
ference
curve*

TABLE 3.1 Alternative Market Baskets

Market basket	Meat (pounds per unit of time)	Potatoes (pounds per unit of time)
1	1	4
2	1	6
3	2	3
4	2	4
5	3	2
6	3	3
7	4	1
8	4	2
9	5	0
10	5	1

Curve *A* is an *indifference curve*. Of course there are many such indifference curves, each pertaining to a different level of satisfaction. For example, indifference curve *B* in Figure 3.1 represents a higher level of satisfaction than indifference curve *A*, since it includes market baskets with more of both meat and potatoes than the market baskets represented by indifference curve *A*. One can visualize a series of indifference curves — one showing all market baskets that are equivalent (in the eyes — or belly — of the consumer) to 1

FIGURE 3.1 Indifference Curves The consumer is indifferent among the market baskets represented by points on indifference curve *A*. Market baskets represented by points on indifference curve *B* are preferred over those represented by points on indifference curve *A*.

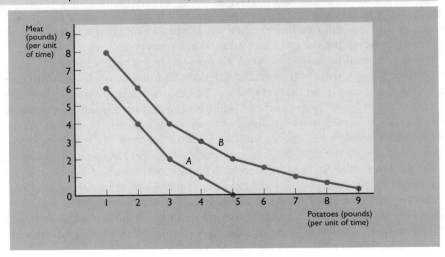

FIGURE 3.2 Indifference Maps of Various Consumers The shape of a consumer's indifference curves may vary greatly, depending on his or her tastes. However, consumer *D*'s positively sloped indifference curves are ruled out by the assumption that the consumer prefers more of a commodity to less.

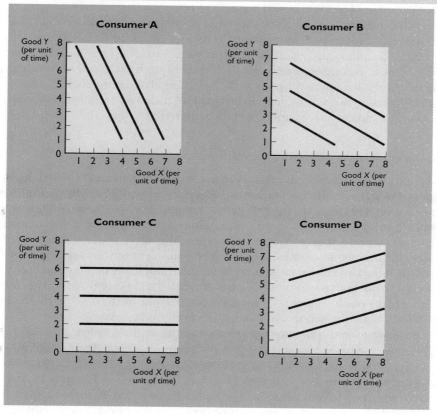

pound of potatoes and 2 pounds of meat, one showing all market baskets that are equivalent to 2 pounds of potatoes and 2 pounds of meat, and so on. The resulting series of indifference curves is called an *indifference map*.

A consumer's indifference map lies at the heart of the theory of consumer behavior, since such a map provides a representation of the consumer's tastes. To illustrate how a consumer's indifference map mirrors his or her tastes, consider the various indifference maps in Figure 3.2. Consumer *A*'s indifference curves are relatively steep, whereas consumer *B*'s indifference curves are relatively flat. What does this mean? Apparently consumer *A* needs several extra units of good *Y* to compensate for the loss of a single unit of good *X*. Thus, in this sense, good Y is less important (relative to good X) to consumer A than to consumer B.

What about consumers C and D in Figure 3.2? Apparently consumer C regards good X as useless, since he does not care whether he has more or less of it. Consumer D seems to regard good X as a nuisance, since she is willing to reduce the amount of good Y she consumes in order to get rid of some good X. But situations of this sort are ruled out by the assumption (discussed on page 63) that the consumer prefers more of a commodity to less. This does not mean that some things are not a nuisance. It means only that in the case of consumer D we would define a commodity as the lack of good X, not the consumption of good X. Using this simple, legitimate trick, we no longer violate this assumption, since more of all commodities is now preferred to less.

Characteristics of Indifference Curves

All indifference curves have certain characteristics that should be noted. First, given the fact (noted in the last section) that every commodity is defined so that more of it is preferred to less, it follows that indifference curves must have a negative slope. If more of both commodities is desirable, and if one market basket has more of good Y, it must have less of good X than another market basket if the two market baskets are to be equivalent in the eyes of the consumer. If the two market baskets are equivalent, and if one market basket contains more of both commodities — which would be the case if an indifference curve had a positive slope — it would mean that one or the other of the commodities is not defined so that more of it is preferred to less.

Second, given the fact that every commodity is defined so that more of it is preferred to less, it also follows that indifference curves that are higher in graphs like Figure 3.1 represent greater levels of consumer satisfaction than indifference curves that are lower. For example, curve B in Figure 3.1 is preferred to curve A. Why? Because the higher curve, curve B, includes market baskets with as much of one good and more of the other (or as much of the second good and more of the first) than the lower curve A. This is what we mean when we say that a curve is higher or lower.

Third, indifference curves cannot intersect. To prove this statement, let's show that a contradiction arises if we assume two indifference curves intersect. For example, take the case of two intersecting indifference curves in Figure 3.3. On indifference curve A, market basket 1 is equivalent to market basket 2. On indifference curve B, market basket 1 is equivalent to market basket 3. Hence, if the indifference curves intersect, market basket 2 must be equivalent to market basket 3. But this cannot be, since market basket 3 contains more of both commodities than market basket 2, and commodities are defined so that more of them is preferred to less. If the consumer's tastes are transitive, as we assume in this model, there cannot be an intersection of indifference curves.

FIGURE 3.3 **Intersecting Indifference Curves: A Contradiction of the Assumptions** If indifference curves A and B were to intersect, the consumer would be indifferent between market baskets 2 and 3, which is impossible since market basket 3 contains more of both commodities than market basket 2.

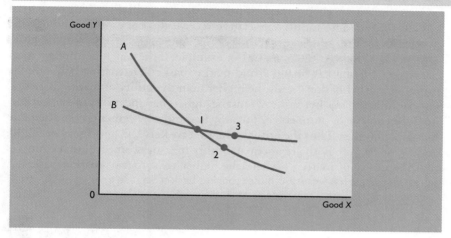

THE CONCEPT OF UTILITY

In previous sections, we have stressed that the consumer's indifference map is a representation of his or her tastes. This certainly is true, since the consumer's indifference map shows each and every one of his or her indifference curves. Given the indifference map of a particular consumer, we can attach a number, a *utility,* to each of the market baskets that might confront this consumer. *This utility indicates the level of enjoyment or preference attached by this consumer to this market basket.* Since all market baskets on a given indifference curve yield the same amount of satisfaction, they would have the same utility. Market baskets on higher indifference curves would have higher utilities than market baskets on lower indifference curves.

Utility

The purpose of attaching these utilities to market baskets is that, once this is done, we can tell at a glance which market baskets the consumer would prefer over other market baskets. If the utility attached to one market basket is higher than that attached to another market basket, he or she will prefer the first over the second market basket. If the utility attached to the first market basket is lower than the second, he or she will prefer the second over the first market basket. If the utility attached to the first market basket equals the second, he or she will be indifferent between the two market baskets.

How should we choose these utilities? Any way will do as long as market baskets on the same indifference curve receive the same utility and market baskets on higher indifference curves receive higher utilities than market baskets on lower indifference curves. For example, if the consumer prefers market basket 1 to market basket 2, and market basket 2 to market basket 3, the utility of market basket 1 must be higher than the utility of market basket 2, and the utility of market basket 2 must be higher than the utility of market basket 3. But any set of numbers conforming to these requirements is an adequate measure of utility. Thus the utility of market baskets 1, 2, and 3 may be 50, 40, and 30, or 10, 9, 8. Both are adequate utility measures, since all that counts is that the utility of market basket 1 be higher than that of market basket 2, which in turn is higher than that of market basket 3.[2]

THE MARGINAL RATE OF SUBSTITUTION

Marginal rate of substitution

In a previous section, we pointed out that consumers differ in the importance that they attach to an extra unit of a particular good. Of course, this is hardly news. For example, it is well known that an alcoholic will sometimes trade a valuable item like a watch for an extra drink of whiskey, whereas the president of the Temperance Union will not give a cent for an extra (presumably the first) dose of Demon Rum. However, news or not, it is useful to have a measure of the relative importance attached by the consumer to the acquisition of another unit of a particular good. The measure that economists have devised is called the *marginal rate of substitution,* a term indicative of the economist's talent for elegant and graceful phrasemaking.

---

[2] Let U represent the consumer's utility, and let the consumer consume x_1 units of good 1, x_2 units of good 2, and so on. The *utility function* is the relationship between U and $x_1, x_2, \ldots, x_n$:

$$U = U(x_1, x_2, \ldots, x_n).$$

Using this utility function, one can define an indifference curve very simply. An indifference curve is given by the equation

$$U(x_1, x_2, \ldots, x_n) = a,$$

where a is a constant.

EXAMPLE 3.1

The Experimental Determination of Indifference Curves

K. MacCrimmon and M. Toda published an experimental study in which they asked a group of college students to choose among market baskets containing various amounts of money and pens. One of the students said she was indifferent among market baskets *A* to *E* below. MacCrimmon and Toda also asked the students to choose among market baskets containing various quantities of money and French pastries (to be eaten on the spot). The same student said she was indifferent among market baskets *F* to *J* below.

Market basket	Number of pens	Amount of money (dollars)	Market basket	Number of French pastries	Amount of money (dollars)
A	0	20.00	F	0	6.00
B	50	17.50	G	3	5.50
C	100	15.00	H	6	5.00
D	130	14.00	I	8	6.00
E	160	13.00	J	10	7.00

(a) Draw the student's indifference curve for money and pens. (Assume that the points given in the table can be connected with straight lines.) (b) Draw her indifference curve for money and French pastries. (c) Do these indifference curves represent the same level of utility? (d) Are French pastries always a good? (e) If the French pastries could be taken home and eaten later, would the indifference curve for money and French pastries be the same as that given above?

SOLUTION (a) and (b) The indifference curves are shown below.

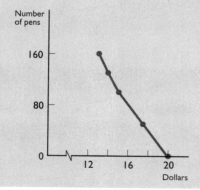

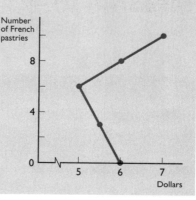

(c) No, since one indifference curve includes market basket *A*, which contains $20 alone, while the other indifference curve includes market basket *F*, which contains $6 alone. So long as more money is preferred to less, the former indifference curve must represent a higher level of utility than the latter. (d) No. For more than 6 French pastries, the indifference curve is upward sloped to the right because the student was willing to consume more French pastries only if she received more money. (e) No. The student would probably have not required more money to make her willing to consume more than 6 French pastries, if she did not have to eat them on the spot.*

---

*For further discussion, see K. MacCrimmon and M. Toda, "The Experimental Determination of Indifference Curves," *Review of Economic Studies,* October 1969.

The *marginal rate of substitution* is defined as the number of units of good Y that must be given up if the consumer, after receiving an extra unit of good X, is to maintain a constant level of satisfaction. For example, in Figure 3.4, the consumer can give up $(OY_2 - OY_1)$ units of good Y to receive $(OX_2 - OX_1)$ extra units of good X, and this trade will leave him or her no better or no worse

FIGURE 3.4 Marginal Rate of Substitution The marginal rate of substitution of good X for good Y is $(OY_2 - OY_1)/(OX_2 - OX_1)$, which is the number of units of good Y that must be given up—per unit of good X received—to maintain a constant level of satisfaction.

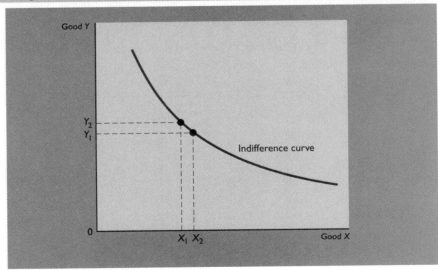

off. Thus the marginal rate of substitution of good X for good Y is $(OY_2 - OY_1)/(OX_2 - OX_1)$. This is the number of units of good Y that must be given up—per unit of good X received—to maintain a constant level of satisfaction.

FIGURE 3.5 Indifference Curves: Convexity The economist's model of consumer behavior assumes that indifference curves are convex, as shown in panel A. In other words, it is assumed that an indifference curve lies above its tangent.

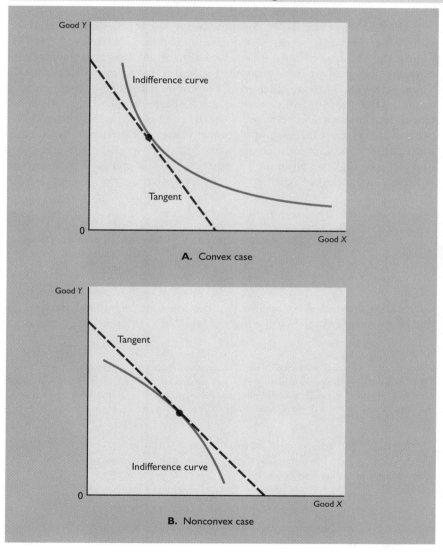

More precisely, the marginal rate of substitution is equal to −1 times the slope of the indifference curve. Thus the marginal rate of substitution of good X for good Y is higher for consumer A (whose indifference curve on page 65 is steeper) than for consumer B (whose indifference curve is flatter). In general, the marginal rate of substitution will vary from point to point on a given indifference curve,[3] since the indifference curve's slope will vary from point to point. For example, on indifference curve A (or curve B) in Figure 3.1, the marginal rate of substitution of potatoes for meat gets smaller as the consumer has more potatoes and less meat.

In the economist's model of consumer behavior it is generally assumed that indifference curves have the sort of shape exhibited by curves A and B in Figure 3.1. More specifically, it is assumed that they show that the more the consumer has of a particular good, the less will be the marginal rate of substitution of this good for any other good. Put somewhat crudely, this amounts to assuming that the more the consumer has of a particular good, the less important to him or her (relative to other goods) is an extra unit of this good. In mathematical terms, this assumption means that indifference curves are *convex*. In other words, an indifference curve lies above its tangent, as illustrated in panel A of Figure 3.5 (on the previous page). This contrasts with the case presented in panel B of Figure 3.5 where the indifference curve is not convex.[4]

Con-
vexity

THE BUDGET LINE

Given his or her tastes, we assume that the consumer is rational, in the sense that he or she tries to get on the highest possible indifference curve. In other

---

[3] The definition in the previous paragraph is an approximation that is quite adequate when good X is measured in small units. Suppose that there are only two commodities and that an indifference curve is $U(x_1, x_2) = a$. (Recall the discussion in footnote 2.) Taking the total differential, we obtain

$$\frac{\partial U}{\partial x_1} dx_1 + \frac{\partial U}{\partial x_2} dx_2 = 0.$$

Thus the slope of the indifference curve is

$$\frac{dx_2}{dx_1} = -\frac{\partial U}{\partial x_1} \div \frac{\partial U}{\partial x_2},$$

which equals −1 times the marginal rate of substitution of the first good for the second good.

[4] The assumption of convexity may not always hold, but a discussion of cases where it fails belongs in a more advanced book.

words, the consumer tries to maximize his or her utility. To do so, the consumer must consider factors other than his or her own tastes. Account must be taken of the prices of various commodities and the level of the consumer's income, since both of these factors limit, or constrain, the nature and size of the market basket that he or she can buy.

The consumer's money income is the amount of money that he or she can spend per unit of time.[5] If William Smith had an infinite money income, he would not have to worry about certain market baskets' being too expensive for him to purchase. He could simply buy the market basket he liked best — the market basket on his highest indifference curve. But no one has an unlimited money income. Even the Rockefellers and Mellons cannot get on their highest indifference curve, since this would mean the expenditure of more than even they have. For us poorer folk, the problem is more difficult still, since our incomes are much smaller. What we can buy is much more severely constrained by our incomes.

> **Money income**

Besides his or her money income, the consumer must also take account of the prices of all relevant commodities. The price of a commodity is the amount of money that the consumer must pay for a unit of the commodity. The higher prices are, the fewer units of a commodity can be bought with a given money income. For example, an income of $50,000 went a lot further when movies were 50¢ and sodas were 5¢ a bottle than it does now when movies are often $7 and sodas are 60¢ or more a can.

To show how the consumer's money income and the level of commodity prices influence the nature and size of the market baskets available to the consumer, it simplifies matters without distorting the essentials of the situation if we assume that there are only two commodities that the consumer can buy, good X and good Y. Since the consumer must spend all his or her money income on one or the other of these two commodities, it is evident that

$$Q_X P_X + Q_Y P_Y = I, \qquad [3.1]$$

where Q_X is the amount the consumer buys of good X, Q_Y is the amount the consumer buys of good Y, P_X is the price of good X, P_Y is the price of good Y, and I is the consumer's money income.[6] For example, if the price of good X is $1 a unit and the price of good Y is $2 a unit and the consumer's income is $100, it must be true that $Q_X + 2Q_Y = 100$. Note that we assume that the consumer takes prices as given. This, of course, is generally quite realistic.

It is possible to plot the combinations of quantities of goods X and Y that the

---

[5] To the extent that the consumer can borrow, the amount he or she can borrow can, for some purposes, also be included as income, since it increases the amount the consumer can spend during the period.

[6] Of course, the consumer can also save some of his or her income, but from the point of view of this model, savings can be viewed as a commodity like any other. Thus, with this amendment, Equation 3.1 can easily encompass savings.

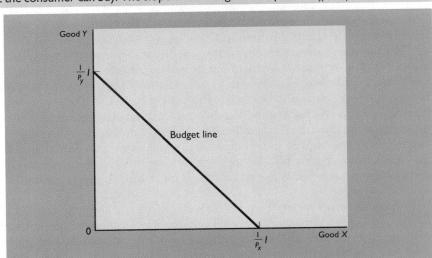

consumer can buy on the same sort of graph as the indifference map. Solving Equation 3.1 for Q_Y, we have

$$Q_Y = \frac{1}{P_Y} I - \frac{P_X}{P_Y} Q_X. \qquad [3.2]$$

Equation 3.2, which is a straight line, is plotted in Figure 3.6. The first term on the right-hand side of Equation 3.2 is the intercept of the line on the vertical axis: It is the amount of good Y that could be bought by the consumer if he or she spent all his or her income on good Y. The slope of the line is equal to the negative of the price ratio, P_X/P_Y.

The straight line in Equation 3.2 is called the *budget line*. It shows all the combinations of quantities of good X and good Y that the consumer can buy. In subsequent sections, we shall be interested in the effects of changes in product prices and money income on consumer behavior. These changes are reflected by changes in the budget line. Equation 3.2 shows that increases in money income increase the intercept of the budget line, but leave unaffected the slope of the budget line. For example, Figure 3.7 shows the effect of an increase in income, with C the original budget line and D the budget line after the increase in income. Conversely, decreases in income lower the intercept of the budget line. In Figure 3.7, E is the budget line after a decrease in income, with C once again the original budget line.

Equation 3.2 also shows what happens to the budget line if the price of good X changes. Increases in P_X increase the absolute value of the slope of the bud-

Budget line

FIGURE 3.7 Effect of a Change in Income on the Budget Line Increases in money income increase the intercept of the budget line, but do not affect its slope.

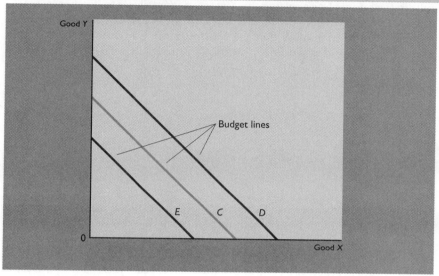

FIGURE 3.8 Effect of a Change in the Price of Good X on Budget Line If the original budget line is F, an increase in the price of good X changes the budget line to G; a decrease in the price of good X changes it to H.

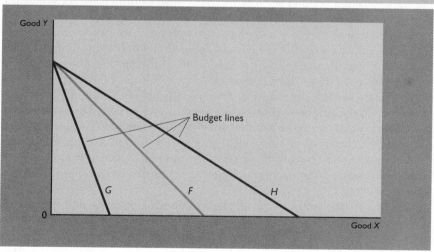

get line; decreases in P_X decrease the absolute value of the slope. The vertical intercept of the line is unaffected. Figure 3.8 shows the effect of changes in P_X on the budget line. Suppose that the original budget line is F. If P_X increases, the budget line becomes G. If P_X decreases, the budget line becomes H. Intuitively, it is easy to see why an increase (decrease) in the price of good X results in the budget line's cutting the X axis at a point closer to (farther from) the origin. The point where the budget line cuts the X axis equals the maximum number of units of good X that the consumer can buy with his or her fixed money income, and this number obviously is inversely related to the price of good X.

THE EQUILIBRIUM OF THE CONSUMER

Given that the consumer is constrained to purchase one of the market baskets that lies on the budget line, which one will he or she choose? To answer this question, we assume, as noted in the previous section, that the consumer tries to maximize utility. This assumption is so general and so reasonable that most people would accept it as a good approximation to reality. Of course, this is not to deny that some acts are irrational. However, by and large, people's actions seem to be such that they promote, not frustrate, the achievement of their goals. Even the ascetic, although his or her actions may seem irrational at first glance, can be regarded as attempting to maximize utility if we recognize the very peculiar nature of his or her tastes.

Going a step further, we note that, although the consumer may attempt to maximize utility, he or she may not succeed in doing so because of miscalculation or for other reasons. The problem of maximizing utility may not be as simple as it looks. For example, how many people know how much their cars really cost them? It is not that they do not know how to do the arithmetic, although even the brightest people have been known to have lapses in this regard. More important is the fact that what should or should not be regarded as a cost in a particular situation is not always straightforward. More will be said on this score in subsequent chapters. For the moment, all we want to point out is that consumers may not be able to achieve the maximization of utility, at least right away.

However, if the consumer is allowed some time to adapt and to learn, it seems likely that he or she will eventually find the market basket that maximizes his or her utility. Let us define the consumer's equilibrium behavior as a course of action that will not be changed by him or her in favor of some other course of action if the consumer's money income, tastes, and the prices he or she faces remain the same. Then the consumer's equilibrium behavior will be to choose the market basket that maximizes his or her utility. And eventually

FIGURE 3.9 Equilibrium of the Consumer The market basket that will maximize the consumer's utility is V, the one on the budget line that is on his or her highest indifference curve.

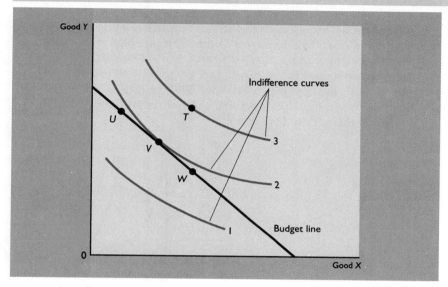

FIGURE 3.9 Equilibrium of the Consumer The market basket that will maximize the consumer's utility is V, the one on the budget line that is on his or her highest indifference curve.

one would expect the consumer to come very close to acting in accord with this equilibrium behavior.

More precisely, what market basket will maximize the consumer's utility? Figure 3.9 brings together the consumer's indifference map and his or her budget line. All the relevant information needed to answer this question is contained in Figure 3.9. *The indifference map shows what the consumer's preferences are.* For example, any market basket on indifference curve 3 is preferred to any on indifference curve 2, and any market basket on indifference curve 2 is preferred to any on indifference curve 1. The consumer would like to choose a market basket on the highest possible indifference curve. This is the way to maximize his or her utility.

But not all market baskets are within reach. *The budget line shows what the consumer can do.* He or she can choose any market basket such as U, V, or W on the budget line, but he or she cannot obtain a market basket like T which is above the budget line. (Of course, the consumer can also buy any market basket below the budget line, but any such market basket lies on a lower indifference curve than a market basket on the budget line.) Since this is the case, *the market basket that will maximize the consumer's utility is the one on the budget line that is on his or her highest indifference curve*—which is V in Figure 3.9. It can readily be seen that this market basket is at a point where the budget line is tangent to an indifference curve. This market basket, V, is the one that the ra-

Maximizing utility

EXAMPLE 3.2

Sickness and Health Insurance

John Jones, a Chicago stockbroker, was very sick last year, but is in good health this year. He belongs to a health insurance plan which stipulates that the patient must pay the first $200 of medical expenses that he or she incurs per year and that the insurance company will pay 80 percent of the patient's medical expenses above $200 (which is called the "deductible"). Mr. Jones's budget line and indifference curves are shown below, for this year and last year:

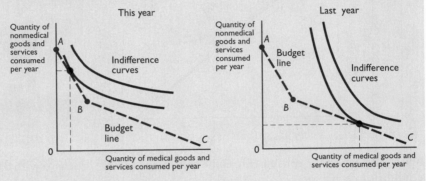

(a) Why are his indifference curves so much flatter this year than last year? (b) His budget line is *ABC*. Why isn't it a straight line? (c) Suppose that Mr. Jones could pay a fixed fee of $800 per year for health insurance, and that the insurance company would reimburse him for any and all health expenses. What would be the shape of his budget line? (d) Under the circumstances described in part (c), what incentive would Mr. Jones have to restrict his consumption of medical goods and services? (For example, why not waste medicine?) (e) If his budget line is *ABC,* does he have any incentive to restrict his consumption of medical goods and services?

SOLUTION   (a) Last year, he was very sick; thus, if the amount of medical goods and services he received went down by 1 unit, it took a considerable extra amount of nonmedical goods and services to offset the loss. This year, he is in good health; thus, if the amount of medical goods and services he receives goes down by 1 unit, it takes only a relatively small extra amount of nonmedical goods and services to offset the loss. (b) The budget line is not a straight line because, if he spends less than $200 on medical goods and services, he pays the full amount, whereas for expenses above $200, he pays only 20 cents for each dollar's worth of medical goods and services. (The insurance company pays the remaining 80 cents.) (c) His budget line would be a horizontal line because, once he pays the fixed fee, the price of an extra unit of medical goods and services is zero. (d) There is little or no incentive to restrict consumption, since he pays nothing (at least in money) for extra medical goods and services. (e) Yes, since even for expenses above $200, he must pay 20 cents for every extra dollar of medical goods and services.*

---

*For further discussion, see the *Economic Report of the President* (Washington, D.C.: Government Printing Office, 1993).

tional consumer would, according to our model, be predicted to buy in equilibrium.[7]

---

[7] Mathematically, one can state the conditions for equilibrium as follows: Suppose that the consumer's utility function is

$$U = U(x_1, x_2, \ldots, x_n).$$

Then he or she maximizes U subject to the constraint that

$$x_1 p_1 + x_2 p_2 + \cdots + x_n p_n = I,$$

where p_i is the price of the ith good. To maximize U subject to the constraint, we construct the function

$$L = U(x_1, x_2, \ldots, x_n) - \lambda(x_1 p_1 + \cdots + x_n p_n - I),$$

where λ is a Lagrangian multiplier. The first-order conditions for a maximum are

$$\frac{\partial L}{\partial x_1} = \frac{\partial U}{\partial x_1} - \lambda p_1 = 0$$

$$\frac{\partial L}{\partial x_2} = \frac{\partial U}{\partial x_2} - \lambda p_2 = 0$$

$$\ldots \ldots \ldots \ldots \ldots$$

$$\frac{\partial L}{\partial x_n} = \frac{\partial U}{\partial x_n} - \lambda p_n = 0$$

$$\frac{\partial L}{\partial \lambda} = x_1 p_1 + x_2 p_2 + \cdots + x_n P_n - I = 0.$$

From these equations it follows that

$$\frac{\partial L}{\partial x_1} \div p_1 = \frac{\partial U}{\partial x_2} \div p_2 = \cdots = \frac{\partial U}{\partial x_n} \div p_n$$

$$x_1 p_1 + x_2 p_2 + \cdots + x_n p_n - I = 0. \qquad \text{(Cont.)}$$

CORNER SOLUTIONS

Although we have just stated that the consumer will choose the market basket where the budget line is tangent to an indifference curve (market basket V in Figure 3.9), there are exceptions. In particular, the consumer may consume *none* of some goods because even tiny amounts of them (or the minimum amount of them that can be bought) are worth less to the consumer than they cost. For example, although your money income may permit you to buy some Dom Perignon champagne (which you would enjoy), you may not purchase any because even a swallow would be worth less to you than it would cost.

Figure 3.10 shows the situation graphically. For simplicity, we suppose that there are only two goods, Dom Perignon champagne and good Y. Given the position of the consumer's indifference curves, he or she will maximize utility by choosing market basket M, which contains all good Y and no Dom

FIGURE 3.10 Corner Solution The market basket that maximizes the consumer's utility is M, which lies on the vertical axis.

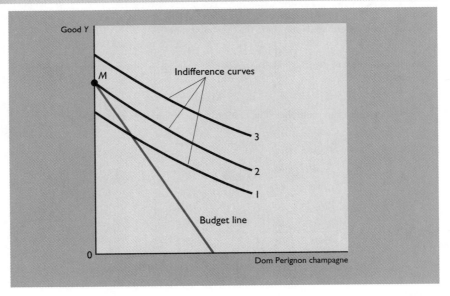

If utility is cardinally measurable, this result is equivalent to the budget allocation rule in Equation 3.3 in the chapter appendix. We ignore the possibility of corner solutions where the optimal value of $x_1, x_2, \ldots,$ or x_n is zero, but take it up in our discussion of Figure 3.10.

EXAMPLE 3.3

The Food-Stamp Program

In 1992 the food-stamp program in the United States included about 27 million individuals, and cost about $25 billion. Suppose that if a family is eligible for food stamps, it pays $80 per month to obtain $150 worth of food.

(a) If the family's cash income is $250 and it is not eligible for food stamps, draw its budget line on a graph where the quantity of food consumed per month is measured along the horizontal axis and the quantity of nonfood items consumed per month is measured along the vertical axis. (b) Draw the family's budget line on this graph if it is eligible for food stamps. (c) Show that if the family were given $70 in cash (rather than in food), it might achieve a higher level of satisfaction.

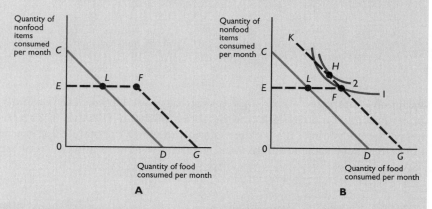

SOLUTION

(a) Without food stamps, the family's budget line is *CD* in panel A. In this panel, *OC* is the quantity of nonfood items the family can obtain with its entire income ($250) and *OD* is the quantity of food it can obtain with it. (b) With food stamps, the family's budget line is *CLFG* in panel A. *EC* is the quantity of nonfood items the family can buy with $80. If the family buys food stamps, *OE* is the maximum quantity of nonfood items it can obtain once it pays for the food stamps. *EF* is the $150 worth of food it receives with the food stamps, and *DG* (=*LF*) is the $70 worth of food that it can obtain with food stamps that it couldn't otherwise obtain when the quantity of nonfood items is held constant. If the quantity of nonfood items consumed by the family exceeds *OE*, it does not have enough money left for food to buy food stamps, so the budget line is the same as without food stamps. (That is, it is *CL*.) If the quantity of nonfood items consumed by the family does not exceed *OE,* it can buy food stamps, and consume an extra amount of food equal to *DG,* so the budget line is *FG.* (c) If the family were given $70 in cash (rather than in food), its budget line would be *GK* in panel B. Because its money income increases by $70, the budget line is higher than, but parallel to, the old budget line, *CD.* With this budget line, the family can reach point *H* on indifference curve 2, whereas with budget line *CLFG,* the best it can do is reach point *F* on indifference curve 1. Since indifference curve 2 is higher than indifference curve 1, the family achieves a higher level of satisfaction if it receives the cash rather than the food. Of course, not all families have indifference curves of this sort; some have indifference curves such that they achieve as high a level of satisfaction with the food as with the cash. This is the case for families with indifference curves tangent to the budget line between *F* and *G.**

*For further discussion, see K. Clarkson, "Welfare Benefits of the Food Stamp Program," *Southern Economic Journal,* July 1976, and M. MacDonald, *Food, Stamps, and Income Maintenance* (New York: Academic Press, 1977).

Perignon champagne at all. This market basket maximizes the consumer's utility because it is on a higher indifference curve than any other market basket on the budget line. It is a *corner solution,* in which the budget line reaches the highest achievable indifference curve along an axis (in this case, the vertical axis).

REVEALED PREFERENCE AND THE MEASUREMENT OF INDIFFERENCE CURVES

Thus far we have assumed that the consumer's indifference curves were measured by asking him or her to choose between various market baskets. However, after thinking about this procedure for a short while, one might object that people cannot, or will not, provide trustworthy answers to direct questions concerning their preferences. The man who surreptitiously visits an erotic stage show (and repeatedly buys the best seats in the house) may claim that such shows are sinful and repugnant to him. Is there any way to measure a person's indifference curves other than by asking direct questions concerning the person's tastes? Is there any way to deduce a consumer's indifference curves from his or her actual behavior rather than from his or her professed preferences?

The theory of revealed preference is an attempt to do just that. We assume that we can vary the consumer's money income and the prices he or she faces, changing these factors in accord with the experiment. Then assuming that the consumer's tastes remain fixed during the course of the experiment, we see how he or she reacts to the various levels of money income and prices. The basic idea behind the formulation and interpretation of the experiments is as follows: The consumer may choose one market basket over a second market basket either because he or she prefers the first to the second or because the first is cheaper than the second. Thus, if we vary prices so that the first market basket is not cheaper than the second and if the first is still chosen over the second, we can be sure that the first market basket is preferred over the second.

Consider the case of two commodities, good X and good Y. Let A in Figure 3.11 represent the market basket (Oa of good X and Oa' of good Y) that the consumer purchases when his or her budget line is QQ'. From this it follows that every point (each representing a market basket) on or below QQ' is re-

FIGURE 3.11 **Revealed Preference** By varying the budget line (from QQ' to SS' to WW'), and by observing which market basket the consumer chooses when confronted with each budget line, we can obtain information concerning the location and shape of the indifference curve running through point A.

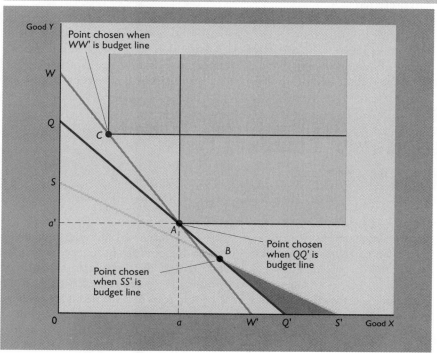

vealed to be inferior to A in the eyes of this consumer, since all these points were available to the consumer and he or she chose A. Moreover, every point in the darkened area above and to the right of A is preferred to A because each such point represents a market basket with at least as much of both commodities as A. Thus, since a commodity is defined so that more of it is preferred to less, each such point must be preferred to A. Therefore the indifference curve running through point A must lie in between the budget line and the darkened area.

To get a better idea of the location and shape of this indifference curve, consider any other point on QQ'—for example, B. This point is inferior to A but there is some budget line that will make the consumer purchase it. Suppose that this budget line is SS'. Then we can deduce that the colored area is inferior to A in the eyes of the consumer, since it is inferior to B, and B is inferior to A. This procedure can be used to narrow the zone of ignorance — the zone where we are unsure whether the included points are inferior or superior to A—that is below and to the right of A. To narrow the zone of ignorance above and to the left of A, we adopt the following procedure. We establish a new budget line, WW', which includes point A. Let C be the market basket the consumer chooses when he or she has the new money income and prices represented by this new budget line. Since C is no more expensive than A under these conditions, C is shown to be preferred to A. Moreover, all points above and to the right of C are also preferred to A, since they are preferred to C, and C is preferred to A.

If these procedures were repeated over and over again, one would eventually derive an indifference curve. Obviously, however, this would be a long and laborious process. The theory of revealed preference is more important as a means of demonstrating that indifference curves can, in principle, be derived in this way, than as a means of actually deriving indifference curves.

DETERMINANTS OF CONSUMER TASTES AND PREFERENCES

In previous sections of this chapter, we have discussed how the consumer's tastes can be represented and the way his or her tastes influence the market basket that is chosen. But we have said nothing about the factors that determine his or her tastes. Clearly, the consumer's tastes can be changed by various forms of experience. The child whose widest grins of satisfaction are reserved for candy and other sweets grows into the woman who politely declines a sweet drink in favor of dry white wine. The boy who regards the ballet as sissy stuff grows to be the man who pays $100 for a ticket to the Royal Ballet and gives away complimentary ringside tickets to the fights. Age has a great effect on a person's tastes; so does education. Indeed, one of the benefits of education is that it allows people to appreciate and enjoy various forms of experience more keenly than they otherwise would.

Another factor influencing a consumer's tastes is his or her observation of what other consumers have. These effects are sometimes called demonstration effects. For example, if the Joneses have a Mercedes, their neighbors, the Smiths, may feel that they should have one, too. Or if the Joneses' daughter can buy expensive clothes, the Smiths may feel that their daughter should have them, too. (Whether their daughter feels this way is another matter—which shows the importance of asking in each case what individuals are regarded as the "consumer," and how decisions are made.) Sometimes an opposite kind of effect is at work: If many consumers have a certain commodity, others may not want it. For example, the snobbish Crandalls may take pride in having tastes that are different from those of the common herd of mankind.

Demonstration effects

Another important determinant of a consumer's tastes is the advertising and selling expenses incurred by manufacturers and sellers of various goods and services. There can be no doubt that advertising influences consumers, although the extent of its influence varies greatly from one product to another, and from one consumer to another. For goods where quality is hard for the consumer to measure, and where the relative advantages of a particular good or brand are not very great, advertising may play a very important role. Of course, advertising also plays a significant role merely by informing the consumer of the existence and characteristics of new products. Much more will be said about the effects of advertising in subsequent chapters.

Advertising

Finally, we have assumed in previous sections that a consumer's tastes (that is, his or her indifference map) are independent of the structure of prices. For example, changes in the prices of meat and potatoes are not supposed to affect the indifference map in Figure 3.1. This rules out cases in which goods are consumed because they are expensive—conspicuous consumption—and cases in which quality is judged by price. This assumption is a reasonable first approximation but it obviously does not hold for all cases. It is possible to extend our model to allow for violations of this assumption; however, a discussion of such extensions properly belongs in a more-advanced text.

BUDGET ALLOCATION BY NEW YORK STATE: AN APPLICATION

In Chapter 1 we said that microeconomics has turned out to be useful in helping to solve many important practical problems; yet in this chapter we have provided no evidence so far to support that statement. The material provided in previous sections of the present chapter must be understood if the reader is to understand the theory of consumer behavior. But it is by no means obvious how it would enable anyone to solve any kind of practical problem. Appearances, however, can be deceiving. The kind of analysis discussed in this chapter can be useful in many contexts. The purpose of this section is to show how the model described in previous sections has been used to solve problems of budget allocation by government agencies.

Highways versus mass transit

For concreteness' sake, let's consider the case of New York State, which received in 1993 about $3 billion per year (from federal sources and a state petroleum tax) to be spent during the mid-1990s on highways and/or mass transit (subways, buses, and urban rail lines), both of which could be used to meet the transportation needs of the state's population.[8] How should it allocate this sum between them? In other words, how much should it spend on highways, and how much should it spend on mass transit? This is an important decision, one that involves huge sums of money and the time, comfort, and convenience of many people.

What has this problem got to do with the theory of consumer preferences we discussed in previous sections of this chapter? Strange as it may seem, economists have used the theory discussed above to help solve this kind of problem. The way in which they have dealt with the problem is instructive in many respects, one being that it illustrates how simple models can be adapted to throw light on very complicated problems.

In effect, the economists have said, "Let's view the government of New York State as a consumer. Let's regard highways and mass transit as two goods that the state government can buy, with each good having a price and the total amount that can be spent on them both being fixed. Assuming that the state government is interested in maximizing the effectiveness of the state's transportation system, let's use as indifference curves for the state government the combinations of extra miles of highway and extra miles of mass transit that will result in a certain expected addition to the state's total transportation capability. Clearly, the bigger the expected addition to this capability, the higher the indifference curve. Then let's find the point on the budget line (which can be derived from the price of a mile of highway, the price of a mile of mass transit, and the total budget to be allocated) that lies on the highest indifference curve. This point will indicate the optimal allocation of the budget."

To actually attack the problem in this way, the first step, of course, is to determine various "indifference curves" of the "consumer," the state government. Figure 3.12 shows what they might look like. As in Figure 3.4, each indifference curve slopes downward, since highways can be substituted for mass transit, and vice versa. Moreover, they are likely to be convex. What ex-

---

[8] For relevant discussion, see the *New York Times,* May 25, 1992.

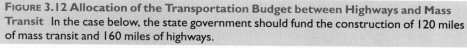

FIGURE 3.12 Allocation of the Transportation Budget between Highways and Mass Transit In the case below, the state government should fund the construction of 120 miles of mass transit and 160 miles of highways.

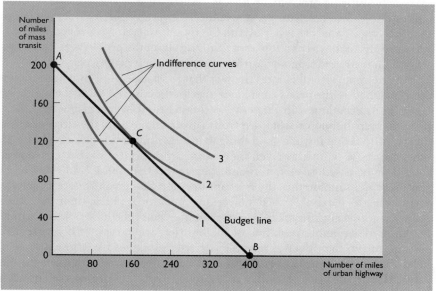

actly does each of these indifference curves mean? Consider indifference curve 1. Each point on this indifference curve represents a combination of highways and mass transit that results in the same addition to transportation capability, that is, the same expected addition to the state's ability to transport people quickly and safely. The state government is viewed as being interested in maximizing the state's transportation capability. In other words, transportation capability (measured in this way) is a measure of this consumer's "utility." Thus the consumer is indifferent among all the points on indifference curve 1. And the consumer clearly prefers indifference curve 2 to indifference curve 1, because points on indifference curve 2 result in more transportation capability than those on indifference curve 1.

Having constructed the indifference curves, the next step is to construct the appropriate budget line. If the State of New York has $3 billion to spend in the year under consideration, if each mile of mass transit costs $15 million, and if each mile of highway costs $7.5 million, the budget line is *AB* in Figure 3.12. Based on our discussion on pages 72 to 76, this should be clear enough. Given this budget line and the indifference map, the problem boils down to finding the point on the budget line that lies on the highest indifference curve. A careful inspection of Figure 3.12 shows that this optimal point is point *C,* where the state government funds the construction of 120 miles of mass transit and 160 miles of highways.

Optimal allocation

In recent years, economic analysis of this kind has played an important role in policymaking in many government agencies. In practice, of course, the measurement of "transportation capability" or "social worth" often presents extremely difficult problems, with the result that it is not possible to draw curves like 1, 2, and 3 with great accuracy. Nevertheless, this does not mean that this type of analysis is not useful. On the contrary, it has proved very useful, since it provides a correct way of thinking about the problem. It focuses attention on the relevant factors, and puts them in their proper place.[9]

This example also illustrates the fact that most aspects of microeconomics are concerned with means to achieve specified ends, not with the choice of ends. Thus economists in this case were interested in increasing the transportation capability to be obtained from a given budget. But they took as given the hypothesis that it was a good thing to increase transportation capability. In other words, they took as given the fact that the "utility" of the "consumer" should be increased. In certain circumstances, this hypothesis could be wrong. For example, suppose that the relevant decision makers in the state government want to maximize their power and influence, rather than the state's transportation capability. The same techniques could be used; all that would be required is a reinterpretation of the indifference curves.[10] Of course, this does not mean that it is not valuable to have techniques like those discussed here. They are obviously of great value. What it does mean is that one cannot expect them to do more than they are designed to do. They cannot tell us what our goals or ends should be.

SUMMARY

1. We assume that, when confronted with two market baskets, a consumer can say which one is preferred, or whether he or she is indifferent between

---

[9] It should be emphasized, however, that the particular example presented in this section is highly simplified, and that the solution in Figure 3.12 is based on arbitrarily chosen assumptions (and is entirely illustrative). Note that costs incurred by parties other than the state government are ignored. Also, the indifference curves may not always have the shape shown in Figure 3.12. Further, miles of highway or mass transit are rather crude units of measurement, and the estimates of highway and mass transit costs per mile are only illustrative. Despite these and other limitations, this example communicates the spirit of this sort of analysis.

[10] Under these circumstances, each indifference curve would show the combinations of highways and mass transit that result in the same level of power and influence for the relevant decision makers in the state government.

them. Also, we assume that the consumer's tastes are transitive and that a commodity is defined in such a way that more is preferred to less.

2. An indifference curve is the locus of points representing market baskets among which the consumer is indifferent. A consumer's tastes can be represented by a set of indifference curves. An indifference curve must have a negative slope, and two indifference curves cannot intersect. Market baskets on higher indifference curves provide more satisfaction than those on lower indifference curves.

3. Utility is a number that indexes the level of satisfaction derived from a particular market basket. Market baskets with higher utilities are preferred over market baskets with lower utilities. The consumer is assumed to be rational in the sense that he or she tries to maximize utility.

4. The slope of an indifference curve (multiplied by -1) is called the marginal rate of substitution. The marginal rate of substitution shows approximately how many units of one good must be given up if the consumer, after receiving an extra unit of another good, is to maintain a constant level of satisfaction.

5. The budget line indicates all the combinations of quantities of goods — all the market baskets — that the consumer can buy, given his or her money income and the level of each price. In equilibrium, we would expect the consumer to attain the highest level of satisfaction that is compatible with the budget line; this means that the consumer will choose the market basket on the budget line that is on the highest indifference curve. This market basket is at a point where the budget line is tangent to an indifference curve (unless there is a corner solution).

6. The model of consumer behavior presented in this chapter has been used to solve problems of budget allocation by government agencies. To illustrate its use, we took up a case study involving expenditures on urban transportation.

QUESTIONS/PROBLEMS

1. In the diagram on the next page, we show one of Ellen White's indifference curves and her budget line. If the price of good A is $50, what is Ms. White's income? What is the equation for her budget line? What is the slope of the budget line? What is the price of good B? What is her marginal rate of substitution in equilibrium?

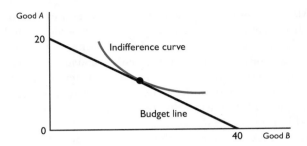

2. "A survey shows that most people prefer Cadillacs to Chevrolets." What exactly does this mean? If this is true, why do more people drive Chevrolets than Cadillacs?

3. One of Ms. Jones's indifference curves includes the following market baskets. Each of these market baskets gives her equal satisfaction.

Market basket	Meat (pounds)	Potatoes (pounds)
1	2	8
2	3	7
3	4	6
4	5	5
5	6	4
6	7	3
7	8	2
8	9	1

In her case, what is the marginal rate of substitution of potatoes for meat? How does the marginal rate of substitution vary as she consumes more meat and less potatoes? Is this realistic?

4. "As a society becomes increasingly affluent, wants are increasingly created by the process by which they are satisfied." Do you agree? Why or why not? Assuming that this is true, what would be the implications of this for the theory of consumer behavior?

5. Martin Cole purchases 100 loaves of bread per year when the price is $1 per loaf. The price increases to $1.50. To offset the harm to Martin, his father gives him $50 a year. Will Martin be better or worse off after the price increase plus the gift than he was before? Will his consumption of bread increase or decrease?

*6. "Whether or not utility is some kind of glow or warmth, or happiness, is

* This question pertains to the chapter appendix.

here irrelevant; all that counts is that we can assign numbers to entities or conditions which a person can strive to realize." Comment on this statement. Do you agree with it? Why or why not?

7. Suppose that consumers in San Francisco pay twice as much for apples as for pears, whereas consumers in Los Angeles pay 50 percent more for apples than for pears. If consumers in both cities maximize utility, will the marginal rate of substitution of pears for apples be the same in San Francisco as in Los Angeles? If not, in which city will it be higher?

8. A consumer is willing to trade 1 pound of steak for 3 pounds of hamburger. He currently is purchasing as much steak as hamburger per month. The price of steak is twice that of hamburger. Should he increase his consumption of hamburger and reduce his consumption of steak? Or should he reduce his consumption of hamburger and increase his consumption of steak?

*9. Suppose that James Gray spends his entire income on goods X and Y. The marginal utility of each good is independent of the amount consumed of the other good. The price of X is $100 and the price of Y is $500.

Number of units of good consumed	Mr. Gray's marginal utility (utils)	
	Good X	Good Y
1	20	50
2	18	45
3	16	40
4	13	35
5	10	30
6	6	25
7	4	20
8	2	15

If Mr. Gray has an income of $1,000 per month, how many units of each good should he purchase?

10. Steve Walcott spends a total of $4,000 per month on goods A and B. The price of A is $200 per unit, and the price of B is $800 per unit. Draw Mr. Walcott's budget line. At what point does it cut the axis along which the quantity of A is measured? At what point does it cut the axis along which the quantity of B is measured? What is its slope?

---

* This question pertains to the chapter appendix.

APPENDIX

ORDINAL AND CARDINAL UTILITY

Economists, as we have seen, assume that the amount of satisfaction a consumer gets from a particular market basket can be measured by its utility. Following the lead of E. Slutsky, Vilfredo Pareto, John Hicks, and others, they generally assume that utility is measurable in an *ordinal* sense; this means that a consumer can only *rank* market baskets with regard to the satisfaction they give him or her.[11] For example, you may be able to say with assurance that you prefer two tickets to the Super Bowl to two tickets to the San Francisco Opera, but you may not be able to say how much more satisfaction you get from the former than from the latter. For an ordinal measurement of utility, this is adequate, since all that is needed is a ranking.

Ordinal utility

In contrast, according to such great nineteenth-century economists as William Stanley Jevons of England, Karl Menger of Austria, and Leon Walras of France, utility was measurable in a *cardinal* sense, which means that the difference between two measurements is itself numerically significant. For example, if I weigh 185 pounds and you weigh 170 pounds, the difference between these measurements has numerical significance: It says that I weigh 15 pounds more than you do. Moreover, if the difference between Bill Cosby's weight and Dolly Parton's weight is 70 pounds, it follows that the difference between my weight and yours is less than the difference between Bill Cosby's weight and Dolly Parton's. According to most nineteenth-century economists, utility was measurable in the same sense.

Cardinal utility

Our discussion in this chapter was based on the modern assumption that utility is ordinally measurable, which is less restrictive than the older assumption that utility is cardinally measurable. That is, we need not assume that a consumer can answer questions like: How much extra satisfaction will you get from a second helping of mashed potatoes? However, if one is willing to assume that the consumer is able to characterize his or her preferences by attaching a cardinal utility to each market basket, it is possible to obtain some additional results, presented in this appendix. In order to focus on the important factors at work here, let's assume that there are only two goods, food and medicine.

---

[11] For example, see J. Hicks, *Value and Capital* (New York: Oxford University Press, 1946); H. Hotelling, "Demand Functions with Limited Budgets," *Econometrica,* 1935, and P. Samuelson, *Foundations of Economic Analysis* (Cambridge, Mass: Harvard University Press, 1947).

Consider a consumer making choices concerning how much of each good to buy. In contrast to our earlier discussion in this chapter, suppose that it is possible to measure the amount of satisfaction that the consumer gets from each market basket by its cardinal utility. For example, the utility attached to the market basket containing 2 pounds of food and 1 ounce of medicine may be 13 utils, and the utility attached to the market basket containing 1 pound of food and 1 ounce of medicine may be 8 utils. (A util is the traditional unit in which utility is expressed.)

MARGINAL UTILITY

It is important to distinguish between total utility and marginal utility. The total utility of a market basket is the number described in the previous paragraph, whereas *the* marginal utility *measures the additional satisfaction derived from an additional unit of a commodity (when the levels of consumption of all other commodities are held constant).* To see how marginal utility is obtained, let's take a close look at Table 3.2. The total utility the consumer derives from the consumption of various amounts of food is given in the middle column of this table. (For simplicity, we assume for the moment that only food is consumed.) The marginal utility, shown in the right-hand column, is the extra utility derived from each amount of food over and above the utility derived from 1 less pound of food. Thus it equals the difference between the total utility of a certain amount of food and the total utility of 1 less pound of food.

Marginal utility

For example, as shown in Table 3.2, the *total* utility of 3 pounds of food is 13 utils, which is a measure of the total amount of satisfaction that the consumer gets from this much food. In contrast, the *marginal* utility of 3 pounds of food is the extra utility obtained from the third pound of food—that is, the total utility of 3 pounds of food less the total utility of 2 pounds of food. Specifically, as shown in Table 3.2, it is 4 utils. Similarly, the *total* utility of 2 pounds of food

TABLE 3.2 Consumer's Total and Marginal Utilities from Consuming Various Amounts of Food per Day

Pounds of food	Total utility	Marginal utility[a]
0	0	—
1	4	4 (= 4 − 0)
2	9	5 (= 9 − 4)
3	13	4 (= 13 − 9)
4	16	3 (= 16 − 13)
5	18	2 (= 18 − 16)

[a]These figures pertain to the interval between the indicated number of pounds of food and 1 pound less than the indicated number. This table assumes that no medicine is consumed.

is 9 utils, which is a measure of the total amount of satisfaction that the consumer gets from this much food. In contrast, the *marginal* utility of 2 pounds of food is the extra utility from the second pound of food — that is, the total utility of 2 pounds of food less the total utility of 1 pound of food. Specifically, as shown in Table 3.2, it is 5 utils.

The Law of Diminishing Marginal Utility

It seems reasonable to believe that, as a person consumes more and more of a particular commodity, there is, beyond some point, a decline in the extra satisfaction derived from the last unit of the commodity consumed. For example, if a person consumes 2 pounds of food in a particular period of time, it may be just what the doctor ordered. If he or she consumes 3 pounds of food in the same period of time, the third pound of food is likely to yield less satisfaction than the second. If he or she consumes 4 pounds of food in the same period of time, the fourth pound of food is likely to yield less satisfaction than the third. And so on.

Law of diminishing marginal utility

This assumption or hypothesis is often called the law of diminishing marginal utility. This law states that, *as a person consumes more and more of a given commodity (the consumption of other commodities being held constant), the marginal utility of the commodity eventually will tend to decline.* In other words, it states that the relationship between the marginal utility of a commodity and the amount consumed will be like that shown in Table 3.2. Beyond some point (2 pounds of food in Table 3.2), the marginal utility declines as the amount consumed increases.

THE BUDGET ALLOCATION RULE

If the law of diminishing marginal utility holds true, *the consumer, if he or she maximizes utility, will allocate his or her expenditures among commodities so that, for every commodity purchased, the marginal utility of the commodity is proportional to its price.* Thus, in the case of the consumer whose choices are limited to food and medicine, the optimal market basket is the one where

$$\frac{MU_F}{P_F} = \frac{MU_M}{P_M},$$ [3.3]

where MU_F is the marginal utility of food, MU_M is the marginal utility of medicine, P_F is the price of a pound of food, and P_M is the price of an ounce of medicine. This is a famous result. In the rest of this appendix, we will explain why it is true.

Budget allocation rule

To understand why the budget allocation rule in Equation 3.3 is correct, it is convenient to begin by pointing out that MU_F/P_F is the marginal utility of the *last dollar's worth* of food and that MU_M/P_M is the marginal utility of the *last dollar's worth* of medicine. To see why this is so, take the case of food. Since MU_F is the extra utility of the *last pound* of food bought, and since P_F is the price of this *last pound,* the extra utility of the *last dollar's worth* of food must be MU_F/P_F. For example, if the last pound of food results in an extra utility of 4 utils and this pound costs \$2, then the extra utility from the last dollar's worth of food must be $4 \div 2$, or 2 utils. In other words, the marginal utility of the last dollar's worth of food is 2 utils.

Since MU_F/P_F is the marginal utility of the last dollar's worth of food and MU_M/P_M is the marginal utility of the last dollar's worth of medicine, what Equation 3.3 really says is that *the rational consumer will choose a market basket where the marginal utility of the last dollar spent on all commodities purchased is the same.* To see why this must be so, consider the numerical example in Table 3.3, which shows the marginal utility the consumer derives from various amounts of food and medicine. Rather than measuring food and medicine in physical units, we measure them in Table 3.3 in terms of the amount of money spent on them.

TABLE 3.3 Consumer's Marginal Utilities from Consuming Various Amounts of Food and Medicine per Day

Dollars worth of each commodity	Food	Medicine
1	9	4
2	7	3
3	4	2
4	3	1
5	2	0

Given the information in Table 3.3, how much of each commodity should the consumer buy if his or her money income is only \$4 (a ridiculous assumption but one that will help to make our point)? Clearly, the first dollar the consumer spends should be on food since it will yield him or her a marginal utility of 9. The second dollar he or she spends should also be on food since a second dollar's worth of food has a marginal utility of 7. (Thus the total utility derived from the \$2 of expenditure is $9 + 7 = 16$.[12]) The marginal utility of the third dollar is 4 if it is spent on more food—and 4 too if it is spent on medicine. Suppose that he or she chooses more food. (The total utility derived from the \$3 of expenditure is $9 + 7 + 4 = 20$.) What about the final dollar? Its mar-

---

[12] Since the marginal utility is the extra utility obtained from each dollar spent, the total utility from the total expenditure must be the sum of the marginal utilities of the individual dollars of expenditure.

ginal utility is 3 if it is spent on more food and 4 if it is spent on medicine; thus he or she will spend it on medicine. (The total utility derived from all $4 of expenditure is $9 + 7 + 4 + 4 = 24$.)

Clearly, the consumer, if rational, will allocate $3 of his or her income to food and $1 to medicine. This is the equilibrium market basket, the market basket that maximizes consumer satisfaction. The important thing to note is that this market basket conforms to the budget allocation rule in Equation 3.3. As shown in Table 3.3, the marginal utility derived from the last dollar spent on food is equal to the marginal utility derived from the last dollar spent on medicine. (Both are 4.) Thus the market basket has the characteristic described in the paragraph before last: The marginal utility of the last dollar spent on all commodities is the same.

In general, one can prove mathematically that the budget allocation rule in Equation 3.3 is correct. (Such proof is given in footnote 7 on page 79.) Since this rule provides valuable insight into rational decision making, it should be understood. However, its applicability is limited by the fact that utility ordinarily is not cardinally measurable.

Consumer Behavior and Individual Demand

4

THE EQUILIBRIUM OF THE CONSUMER: REVIEW AND ANOTHER VIEWPOINT

In this chapter, we proceed further with the development of a model of consumer behavior. Building on the results of the previous chapter, we show how the consumer responds to changes in his or her money income and to changes in the prices of commodities. In addition, we present some illustrations of how this theory has been applied to help solve important problems of public policy. Specifically, we describe how it has been applied to the evaluation of the effects of sugar import quotas and to the interpretation and construction of price indexes.

To begin with, it is useful to review briefly the conditions under which the consumer is in equilibrium. However, rather than merely parrot what has already been said in the previous chapter, we look at these conditions from a somewhat different point of view. We said in the previous chapter that the consumer's equilibrium market basket is at a point where the budget line is tangent to an indifference curve: This is the market basket that maximizes the consumer's utility.[1] Since the slope of the indifference curve equals -1 times the marginal rate of substitution of good X for good Y (see page 72) and since the slope of the budget line is $-P_X/P_Y$ (see page 74), it follows that the rational consumer will choose in equilibrium to allocate his or her income between good X and good Y so that the marginal rate of substitution of good X for good Y equals P_X/P_Y.

This is a famous result—and a very useful one that should be understood fully. It is easier to agree that it is true than it is to see what it really means and why it is true. Perhaps the best way to understand this result is to define once

Marginal rate of substitution

again the marginal rate of substitution: The marginal rate of substitution is the rate at which the consumer is *willing* to substitute good X for good Y, holding his or her total level of satisfaction constant. Thus, if the marginal rate of substitution is 3, the consumer is willing to give up 3 units of good Y in order to get 1 more unit of good X.

Price ratio

On the other hand, the price ratio, P_X/P_Y, is the rate at which the consumer is *able* to substitute good X for good Y. Thus, if P_X/P_Y is 2, he or she *must* give up 2 units of good Y to get 1 more unit of good X. What the result described in this section is really saying is: The rate at which the consumer is willing to substitute good X for good Y (holding satisfaction constant) must equal the rate at which he or she is able to substitute good X for good Y. Otherwise it is always possible to find another market basket that will increase the consumer's satisfaction. And this means, of course, that the present market basket is not the equilibrium one that maximizes consumer satisfaction.

To see that this must be the case, suppose that the consumer has chosen a market basket in which the marginal rate of substitution of good X for good Y is 3. Suppose that the ratio P_X/P_Y is 2. If this is the case, the consumer can trade 2 units of good Y for an extra unit of good X in the market, since the price ratio is 2. But this extra unit of good X is worth 3 units of good Y to the consumer, since the marginal rate of substitution is 3. Consequently, he or she can increase satisfaction by trading good Y for good X—and this will continue to be the case as long as the marginal rate of substitution exceeds the price ratio. Conversely, if the marginal rate of substitution is less than the price ratio, the consumer can increase satisfaction by trading good X for good Y. Only when the marginal rate of substitution equals the price ratio does the consumer's market basket maximize his or her utility.

---

[1] For simplicity, we assume here that the optimal market basket is not a corner solution. (See pages 80 to 82.)

EFFECTS OF CHANGES IN CONSUMER MONEY INCOME

With this review in mind, let us turn to new territory and consider the effect of changes in money income on the amounts of good X and good Y purchased by the consumer. For example, suppose that the consumer is a student and that the amount of money he earns and receives from home increases from \$7,000 to \$10,000 a year. What effect will this have on his purchases? How much of the extra money will he spend on books? Entertainment? Clothes? Food?

In the previous chapter, we saw that an increase in money income results in an increase in the intercept of the budget line, but leaves unaffected the slope of the budget line (as long as the prices of commodities remain constant). Similarly, a decrease in money income results in a decrease in the intercept of the budget line, but leaves unaffected the slope of the budget line (as long as the prices of commodities remain constant). To determine the effect of a change in money income on the market basket chosen by the consumer, one can compare the equilibrium position based on the budget line corresponding to the old level of money income with the equilibrium position based on the budget line corresponding to the new level of money income.

For example, suppose that the budget line corresponding to the old level of income—\$7,000 in the case of the student—is A in Figure 4.1. Given the consumer's indifference map, the market basket that maximizes his utility is comprised of Oa units of good X and Ob units of good Y if his income is at the old level. Now suppose that his income rises—to \$10,000 in the case of the student—and that the new budget line is B in Figure 4.1. With these new conditions, the market basket that maximizes his utility is comprised of Oc units of good X and Od units of good Y.

Clearly, the way in which an increase in money income influences a consumer's purchases depends on his or her tastes. In other words, the nature of the market basket chosen at the old income, the nature of the market basket chosen at the new income, and consequently the nature of the difference between these two market baskets is influenced by the shape of the consumer's indifference curves. Also, the way in which an increase in money income influences a consumer's purchases depends on the price ratio, P_X/P_Y. Of course, this price ratio is held constant when we analyze the effects of changes in money income on consumer behavior, but the level at which the price ratio is held constant will influence the results.

FIGURE 4.1 Effects of Changes in Money Income on Consumer Equilibrium The income-consumption curve connects points (like U, V, and W) representing equilibrium market baskets corresponding to all possible levels of money income.

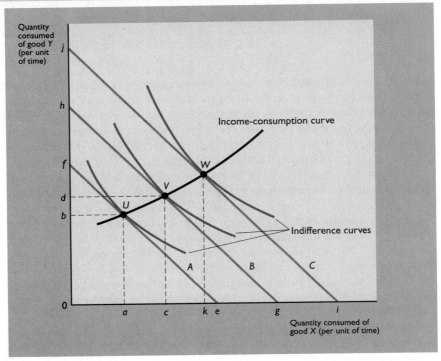

Income-Consumption and Engel Curves

Holding commodity prices constant, we find that each level of money income results in an equilibrium market basket for the consumer. That is, corresponding to each level of money income is an equilibrium market basket for a particular consumer. For example, the equilibrium market baskets corresponding to three income levels are represented by points *U, V,* and *W* in Figure 4.1. If we connect all the points representing equilibrium market baskets corresponding to all possible levels of money income, the resulting curve is called the *income-consumption curve*. Figure 4.1 shows such a curve.

The income-consumption curve can be used to derive Engel curves, which are important for studies of family expenditure patterns. An *Engel curve* is the relationship between the equilibrium quantity purchased of a good and the level of income.[2] Ernst Engel was a nineteenth-century German statistician

Income-consumption curve

Engel curve

---

[2] Often an Engel curve is defined to be the relationship between the consumer's *expenditure* on a commodity and his or her money income. But since the commodity prices are held constant,

who did pioneering work related to such curves, named after him by economists.

It is easy for us to see how an Engel curve can be derived from the income-consumption curve. Take the case in Figure 4.1 as an example. When money income equals P_X times Oe (or P_Y times Of, since they are equal), the income-consumption curve shows that the consumer buys Oa units of good X. When money income equals P_X times Og (or P_Y times Oh), the income-consumption curve shows that the consumer buys Oc units of good X. When money income is P_X times Oi (or P_Y times Oj), the income-consumption curve shows that the consumer buys Ok units of good X. These are three points on the Engel curve for good X for this consumer. Each of these points shows the equilibrium amount of good X that he or she purchases at a certain level of money income. As more and more points are included, all the points on the Engel curve for good X for this consumer are traced out. The result is shown in Figure 4.2.

Of course, the shape of a consumer's Engel curve for a particular good will depend on the nature of the good, the nature of the consumer's tastes, and the

FIGURE 4.2 Engel Curve for Good X An Engel curve is the relationship between the equilibrium quantity purchased of a good and the level of income.

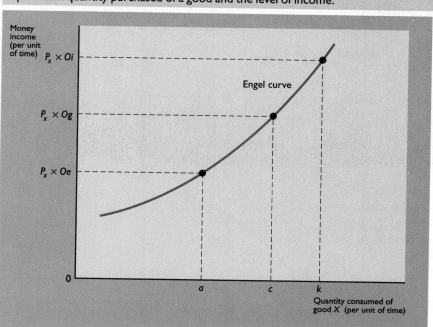

the consumer's expenditure on the product is proportional to the number of units of the commodity that he or she consumes. So it makes no real difference for present purposes whether we use expenditure or quantity demanded of the commodity as the relevant variable.

Shape of Engel curve

level at which commodity prices are held constant. For example, Engel curves with quite different shapes are shown in panels A and B of Figure 4.3. According to the Engel curve in panel A, the quantity consumed of the good increases with income, but at a *decreasing* rate. According to the Engel curve in panel B the quantity consumed of the good increases with income, but at an *increasing* rate. A comparison of panel A with panel B shows that a change in income from *Ou* to *Ov* does not have as great an effect on consumption of the good in panel B as on consumption of the good in panel A.

FIGURE 4.3 **Engel Curves: Various Shapes** As shown in panel A, the quantity consumed of the good increases with income, but at a decreasing rate. In panel B, the quantity consumed of the good increases with income, but at an increasing rate.

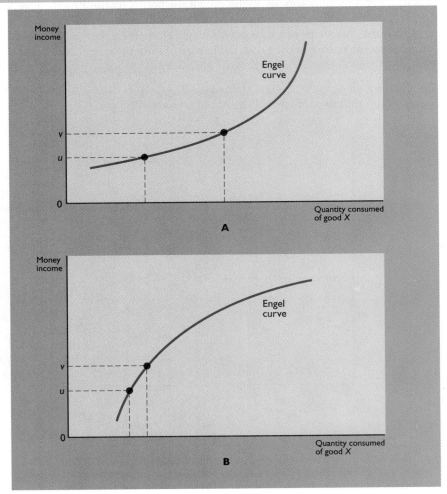

In general, one would expect that Engel curves for goods like salt and shoelaces would show that the consumption of these commodities does not change very much in response to changes in income. For example, only a rather unusual type of person would respond to a large increase in income by gorging himself or herself with salt and shoelaces — singly or in combination. On the other hand, goods like caviar and filet mignon might be expected to have Engel curves showing that their consumption increases considerably with increases in income. In general, this is probably so. But one should be careful about such generalizations. For example, if the consumer were a vegetarian, this would not hold true for filet mignon.

EFFECTS OF CHANGES IN COMMODITY PRICE

In the previous two sections we have been concerned with the effect of changes in money income on the market basket that, in equilibrium, will be chosen by the consumer. Another important question is: Holding the consumer's money income constant, what will be the effect of a change in the price of a certain commodity on the amount of this commodity that the consumer will purchase? For example, take the case of the college student mentioned in the section before last. Suppose that his income remains constant at $7,000 and that the prices of all commodities other than food are held constant. Further, suppose that the price of food is allowed to vary and that we watch how the quantity of food that he consumes (per unit of time) varies in response to changes in the price of food. What sort of relationship exists between the price of food and the quantity of food that he consumes (per unit of time)?

This case is unnecessarily specific. Let's pose the question more generally. Let's assume that there are only two commodities, good X and good Y. Suppose that the price of good Y and the money income of the consumer are held constant, but the price of good X is allowed to vary from one level to another. Suppose that the budget line corresponding to the original price of good X is B in Figure 4.4. If the price of good X is increased and the new budget line is C, the new equilibrium market basket for the consumer will be T, rather than the original equilibrium market basket of S. (In the previous chapter, we saw that an increase in the price of good X increases the absolute value of the slope of the budget line but does not affect the vertical intercept of the line.) Thus the increase in the price of good X will result in the consumer's buying Ou units of good X and Ov units of good Y, rather than the original market basket composed of Or units of good X and Os units of good Y.

FIGURE 4.4 Effects of Changes in the Price of Good *X* on Consumer Equilibrium The price-consumption curve connects points (like *R, S,* and *T*) representing equilibrium market baskets corresponding to all possible levels of the price of good *X.*

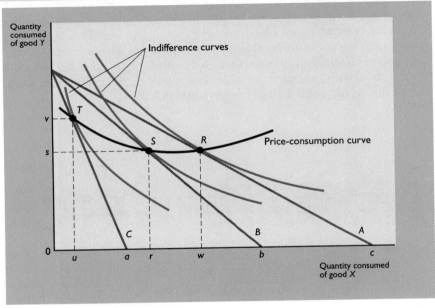

Price-
consump-
tion
curve

Corresponding to each price of good *X* is an equilibrium market basket that can be determined in this way. The curve that connects the various equilibrium points is called the *price-consumption curve.* Figure 4.4 shows the price-consumption curve for this consumer, given the level of his or her money income and the price of good Y. One reason why the price-consumption curve is of interest is that it can be used to derive the consumer's individual demand curve for the commodity in question. The individual demand curve shows how much of a given commodity the consumer would purchase (per unit of time) at various prices of the commodity, holding constant the consumer's money income, his or her tastes, and the prices of other commodities. The individual demand curve is a central concept in the theory of consumer behavior.

How can the individual demand curve be derived from the price-consumption curve? To illustrate the procedure, consider the case in Figure 4.4. When the price of good *X* is *I/Oa* (where *I* is the money income of the consumer), the price-consumption curve shows that the consumer buys *Ou* units of good *X.*[3]

---

[3] From Figure 4.4, we know that the price of good *X* must be *I/Oa* when the budget line is *C* because, if the consumer devotes all his or her money income, *I,* to good *X,* he or she can get *Oa* units of good *X.*

FIGURE 4.5 **Individual Demand Curve for Good** X The individual demand curve shows how much good X the consumer would purchase at various prices of good X. The location of the individual demand curve (such as D, E, or F) depends on the consumer's income and tastes, as well as on the prices of other goods.

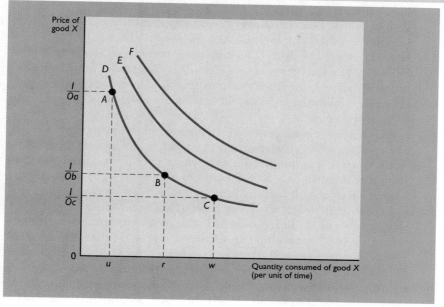

When the price of good X is I/Ob, the price-consumption curve shows that the consumer buys Or units of good X. When the price of good X is I/Oc, the price-consumption curve shows that the consumer buys Ow units of good X. These are three points on the individual demand curve. By deriving more and more points in this way, one can obtain the entire individual demand curve for good X. The result, curve D, is shown in Figure 4.5.

The Individual Demand Curve: Location and Shape

The location and shape of an individual demand curve will depend on the level of money income and the level at which the prices of other goods are held constant, as well as on the nature of the commodity and the tastes of the consumer. For example, suppose that we consider the demand curve for good X of the consumer represented in Figure 4.5. If his or her income were to be held constant at a level higher than I, a different demand curve would result. Rather than D it might be E in Figure 4.5. Also, if the price of good Y were higher than that assumed in Figure 4.4, a different demand curve would result. Rather than D, it might be F in Figure 4.5. An important point to remember about a demand curve is that it is always drawn with certain

EXAMPLE 4.1

Medical Insurance and the Demand for Medical Care

Medical insurance plays a key role in the system of health care in the United States. Many employees receive medical insurance as a fringe benefit from their employers. Since employees have not had to pay income taxes on this fringe benefit, some economists, such as Martin Feldstein (former chairman of President Reagan's Council of Economic Advisers), argue that too much medical insurance has been provided by employers, and that the resulting economic waste runs into billions of dollars.

(a) Why would an employee (who pays 30 cents in taxes for every extra dollar earned) prefer an additional dollar of nontaxed medical insurance rather than another dollar of wages, even if the dollar's worth of insurance is worth only 80 or 90 cents to him or her? (b) Why are employers led to provide medical insurance which is worth less to their employees than it costs? (c) If less medical insurance were provided tax free, what would be the effect on the price paid by an employee for medical care? (d) Suppose that an employee's demand curve for medical care is as shown below. If the cost of a patient-day of care is OP_0, but if (because of the insurance) the employee pays a price of only OP_2, will the employee demand some medical care that is worth less to him or her than it costs? (e) In 1989, the *New York Times* proposed that the federal government "tax health benefits that exceed a certain basic level . . . ." Why might this help reduce excess health costs?

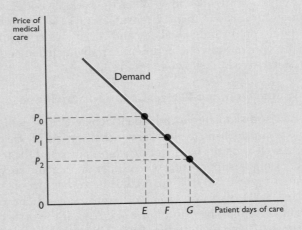

SOLUTION (a) Another dollar of wages, if the tax rate is 30 percent, is worth 70 cents. Thus, even if a dollar's worth of medical insurance is worth only 80 or 90 cents, it is worth more than an extra dollar of wages. (b) Employers are competing among themselves to obtain and keep good workers. If workers prefer a dollar's worth of medical insurance to an extra dollar's worth of wages, employers will act accordingly. (c) If less medical insurance were provided tax free, this employee would have to pay more of the full costs of medical care. In other words, the price to him or her of medical care would increase. (d) Yes. The maximum amount that the employee would pay for an extra unit of medical care can be determined from the demand curve. For example, the maximum amount that the employee would pay for the OFth day of care is OP_1. (Why? Because if the price were any higher than OP_1, the employee would demand less than OF days of care.) If the employee pays a price of only OP_2, he or she demands OG days of care. But the maximum amount that the employee would pay exceeds the cost (OP_0) only for the first OE days of care. (This is obvious because the demand curve lies above OP_0 only for quantities demanded that are less than OE.) For the remaining EG days of care, the maximum amount that the employee would pay is less than the cost. (e) It would give the worker more incentive to restrict his or her health costs.*

* For further discussion, see Martin Feldstein, "The Welfare Loss of Excess Health Insurance," *Journal of Political Economy,* March 1973, and "The Health Crisis and Baby Bells," *New York Times,* August 10, 1989.

assumptions about the level of the consumer's money income and the level of other prices in mind. In general it is only valid if these assumptions are correct.

It is important to differentiate between shifts in a consumer's demand curve for a particular commodity and changes in the amount of the commodity that he or she consumes. As we have seen, a consumer's demand curve may shift because of changes in his or her income or tastes, as well as because of changes in the prices of other goods. Such shifts in the consumer's demand curve are likely to result in changes in the amount of the commodity that he or she consumes, but they are not the only reason for such changes. In addition, changes in the price of the good will result in changes in the amount of the commodity that he or she consumes. We must be careful to distinguish between cases where the demand curve remains the same and changes in the consumption of the commodity occur because of changes in the commodity's price, and cases where the demand curve shifts. The movement from point A to B in Figure 4.5 is an example of the former; the shift of the demand curve from D to E is an example of the latter.

SUBSTITUTION AND INCOME EFFECTS

When the price of a good changes, the consumer is affected in two ways: First, he or she attains a different level of satisfaction, and second, he or she is likely to substitute now-cheaper goods for more-expensive goods. The total effect of a price change is illustrated in Figure 4.6. The original price ratio is given by the slope of the budget line A. Given this price ratio, the consumer chooses point U on indifference curve 1, and consumes Ox_1 units of good X. Now suppose that the price of good X is increased and B is the new budget line. Given the new price ratio, the consumer chooses point V on indifference curve 2, and consumes Ox_2 units of good X. The total effect of the price change on the quantity demanded of good X is a reduction of $Ox_1 - Ox_2$ units.

FIGURE 4.6 Substitution and Income Effects for a Normal Good If the price of good X increases (and the budget line shifts from A to B), the total effect of this price change on the quantity demanded of good X is a reduction of $Ox_1 - Ox_2$ units. This total effect can be divided into two parts: the substitution effect (a reduction of the quantity consumed from Ox_1 to Ox_3 units) and the income effect (a reduction of the quantity consumed from Ox_3 to Ox_2 units).

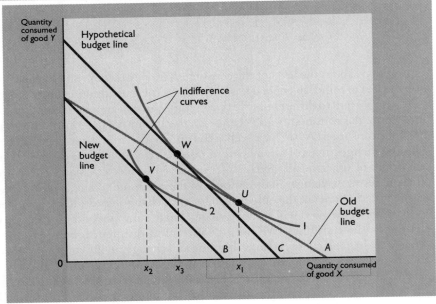

The total effect of this — or any — price change can be divided conceptually into two parts: the substitution effect and the income effect. First, consider the substitution effect. In Figure 4.6, when the price of good X increases, it is clear that a decrease occurs in the consumer's level of satisfaction: He or she winds up on indifference curve 2 rather than indifference curve 1. Suppose that, when the price goes up, we could increase the consumer's money income by an amount sufficient to keep him or her on the old indifference curve. If this could be done, it would mean that the budget line would be parallel to the budget line B, but that it would be tangent to indifference curve 1. This hypothetical budget line is labeled C in Figure 4.6. The *substitution effect* is defined to be the movement from the original equilibrium point U to the imaginary equilibrium point W, which corresponds to the hypothetical budget line C. The substitution effect is the reduction of the quantity consumed from Ox_1 to Ox_3 units of good X. Or put differently, it is the change in quantity demanded of good X resulting from a price change when the level of satisfaction is held constant.

Substitution effect

Next, consider the income effect. The movement from the imaginary equilibrium point W to the actual new equilibrium point V is the income effect. This movement does not involve any change in prices; the price ratio is the same in budget line C as in budget line B. It is due to a change in total satisfaction; such a change is a movement from one indifference curve to another. If we define the consumer's real income as his or her level of satisfaction (or utility), the *income effect* is the change in quantity demanded of good X due entirely to a change in real income, *all prices being held constant*. In Figure 4.6, it is the reduction from Ox_3 to Ox_2 units. The total effect of a change in price is obviously the sum of the income effect and the substitution effect.[4]

Income effect

Normal and Inferior Goods

The substitution effect is always negative. That is, if the price of good X increases and real income is held constant, there will always be a decrease in the consumption of good X; and if the price of good X decreases and real income is held constant, there will always be an increase in the consumption of good X. This result follows from the fact that indifference curves are convex (see Chapter 3). However, the income effect is not predictable from the theory alone. In most cases, one would expect that increases in real income will result in increases in consumption of a good and that decreases in real income will result in decreases in consumption of a good. This is the case for so-called *normal goods*. But not all goods are normal. Some goods are called *inferior goods* be-

Normal versus inferior goods

---

[4] For an explanation of substitution and income effects in elementary mathematical terms, see J. Henderson and R. Quandt, *Microeconomic Theory*, (3d ed.; New York: McGraw-Hill, 1980), and H. Varian, *Microeconomic Analysis* (3d ed.; New York: Norton, 1992).

cause the income effect is the opposite (of that of a normal good) for them. An illustration of an inferior good is given in Figure 4.7, where real income is assumed to increase from indifference curve 1 to indifference curve 2. Prices are assumed to be the same before and after the increase in real income; the original budget line is A and the subsequent budget line is B. Figure 4.7 shows that, because of the shapes of the indifference curves, the consumer purchases $(OX_2 - OX_3)$ fewer units of good X after the increase in real income than he or she originally did.

Ordinarily, the substitution effect of a price change is strong enough to offset an inferior good's income effect, with the consequence that the quantity demanded of a good is inversely related to its price. However, it is possible for an inferior good to have an income effect that is so strong that it offsets the substitution effect, with the result that the quantity demanded is directly related to the price, at least over some range of variation of price. A case of this sort is known as *Giffen's paradox*. For Giffen's paradox to occur, a good must be an inferior good, but not all inferior goods exhibit Giffen's paradox.

Margarine is an inferior good for some consumers. Increases in their real income will lead them to substitute butter for margarine. Many other examples

FIGURE 4.7 Inferior Good With an increase in real income, the consumer reduces his or her consumption of good X from OX_2 to OX_3 units. For this consumer, good X is an inferior good.

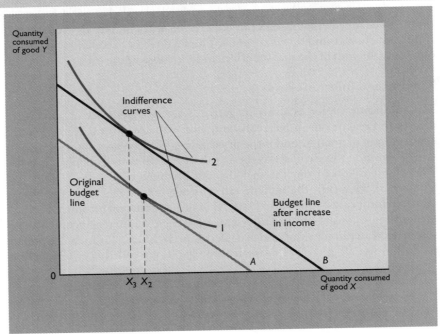

of inferior goods could be put forth, although, as stated above, inferior goods are in the minority. Giffen's paradox is a much, much rarer phenomenon. In the rest of this book, we shall assume that goods do not exhibit Giffen's paradox. That is, all demand curves are assumed to have a negative slope.

CONSUMER SURPLUS

Previous sections have presented a model of how consumers respond to changes in price and money income. But no attempt has been made to indicate how this model can be used to help solve practical problems. In the balance of this chapter, we discuss some applications of this model. Let's start with the very simple case where a consumer receives an additional amount of some good. For example, suppose that the consumer receives 3 pounds of sugar from a kindly (and not particularly calorie-conscious) neighbor. How much is this sugar worth to the consumer? This example, while trivial and homely in the extreme, will enable us to derive some results that will be used in the next section to throw light on an important problem of public policy.

To determine how much the additional 3 pounds of sugar are worth to this consumer, the proper question to ask is: What is the maximum amount that he or she would be willing to pay for the extra sugar? The consumer's demand curve for sugar provides the answer to this question. Suppose that the consumer's demand curve for sugar is as shown in the left-hand panel of Figure 4.8, and that he or she is presently consuming no sugar. For simplicity, suppose that sugar can only be purchased in units of a pound; in other words, fractions of a pound cannot be purchased. (This assumption will be relaxed later.)

The maximum amount that the consumer will pay for the first pound of sugar is 60 cents. As shown by the demand curve in the left-hand panel of Figure 4.8, the consumer would not buy any sugar at all if the price were above 60 cents per pound, but at a price of 60 cents he or she will buy 1 pound. The maximum amount that the consumer will pay for the second pound of sugar is 45 cents. As shown in Figure 4.8, the price must be lowered to 45 cents to induce the consumer to buy a second pound. Finally, the maximum amount that the consumer will pay for the third pound of sugar is 30 cents. As shown in Figure 4.8, the price must be lowered to 30 cents to induce the consumer to buy a third pound.

Adding up the maximum amounts that the consumer would pay for each pound of sugar, we find that the total maximum amount that he or she would be willing to pay for all 3 additional pounds of sugar is 60 + 45 + 30 = 135

FIGURE 4.8 Consumer Surplus from 3 Pounds of Sugar Whereas the consumer would be willing to pay up to 135 cents (the shaded area in the left-hand panel) for 3 extra pounds of sugar, he or she only has to pay 90 cents (the shaded area in the middle panel) for them. Thus the consumer surplus—the net benefit to the consumer—is 135 − 90 = 45 cents (the shaded area in the right-hand panel).

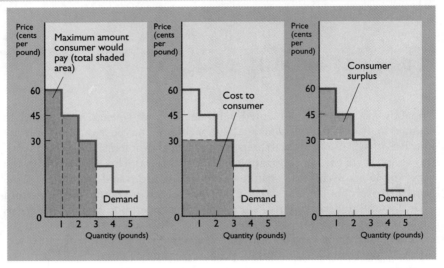

cents. The important thing to note is that this total maximum amount equals the area under the demand curve from 0 to 3 pounds of sugar. In other words, it equals the shaded area in the left-hand panel of Figure 4.8. To see this, note that this shaded area equals the sum of three rectangles shown in this panel. The area of the tallest shaded rectangle equals 60 cents, the area of the next tallest rectangle equals 45 cents, and the area of the shortest rectangle equals 30 cents; thus the total shaded area equals 60 + 45 + 30 = 135 cents.

Having determined the value of the additional 3 pounds of sugar to the consumer, let's suppose that he or she no longer receives sugar from a kindly neighbor. Instead, the consumer must pay 30 cents per pound for sugar. At this price, the consumer's demand curve in Figure 4.8 shows that he or she will buy 3 pounds of sugar, and pay 3 × 30 = 90 cents for them. Since the total cost of the 3 pounds of sugar equals the price per pound (30 cents) times the quantity purchased (3 pounds), it equals the shaded area in the middle panel of Figure 4.8. (This shaded area is a rectangle with length equal to the price per pound and width equal to the quantity purchased.)

Whereas the 3 pounds of sugar are worth 135 cents to the consumer, he or she only has to pay 90 cents for them. The difference between what the consumer would be willing to pay (135 cents) and what the consumer actually has

Con-
sumer
surplus

to pay (90 cents) is called *consumer surplus*. Consumer surplus is a measure of the net benefit received by the consumer. Since the consumer receives sugar worth 135 cents (to him or her) for 90 cents, he or she receives a net benefit of 45 cents. Geometrically, consumer surplus can be represented by the shaded area in the right-hand panel of Figure 4.8. To see why this is the case, note that, to obtain consumer surplus, we must deduct the shaded area in the middle panel (which equals the cost of the sugar) from the shaded area in the left-hand panel (which equals the maximum amount the consumer would pay for the sugar). The result is, of course, the shaded area in the right-hand panel.

Finally, we must relax the assumption that sugar can only be purchased in units of a pound. If fractions of a pound can be purchased, the demand curve is a smooth line, as in Figure 4.9 (rather than a series of steps, as in Figure 4.8). But regardless of whether the demand curve is smooth or a series of steps, the maximum amount that the consumer will pay for 3 pounds of sugar is the area under the demand curve from 0 to 3 pounds of sugar. In Figure 4.9, this area equals *OABC*. Since the price of a pound of sugar is *OP* in Figure 4.9, the amount that the consumer actually pays for 3 pounds of sugar is equal to the area of rectangle *OPBC*. Since consumer surplus equals the maximum amount that the consumer would pay (area *OABC*) minus the amount he or she actually pays (area *OPBC*), the shaded area in Figure 4.9 equals consumer surplus.

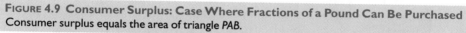

FIGURE 4.9 Consumer Surplus: Case Where Fractions of a Pound Can Be Purchased
Consumer surplus equals the area of triangle *PAB*.

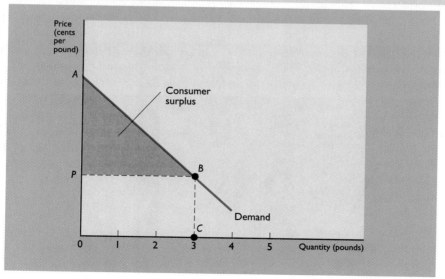

Consumer Surplus and Restrictions on Sugar Imports

The concept of consumer surplus is of practical importance. To illustrate how it has been used, let's consider U.S. restrictions on sugar imports, a subject that has stimulated plenty of controversy. Because their costs are relatively high, U.S. sugar producers find it difficult to compete with Central American and other foreign producers. To protect the U.S. sugar industry from foreign competition, the U.S. government has imposed restrictions on how much foreign-produced sugar can be imported into the United States. (In 1995, only 1.3 million tons could be imported.) One of the major questions concerning such restrictions is: How much of a loss do they impose on U.S. consumers?

To see how the theory introduced in the previous section can be of use in dealing with this question, suppose that, in the absence of government restrictions on sugar imports, the price of sugar in the United States would be OP_0 in Figure 4.10. Based on the consumer's demand curve in the left-hand panel of this graph, the consumer would purchase OQ_0 pounds of sugar per year, the total cost of the sugar being $OP_0 \times OQ_0$. However, this total cost is an underestimate of what the sugar is really worth to the consumer. As stressed in the previous section, the consumer receives a consumer surplus equal to the shaded area in the left-hand panel of Figure 4.10.

If the government imposes restrictions on sugar imports into the United States, the price of sugar will rise (because the import restrictions push the supply curve for sugar upward and to the left). Suppose that the price goes up to OP_1, as shown in the middle panel of Figure 4.10. Because of the higher price, the consumer will purchase somewhat less sugar (OQ_1 rather than OQ_0 pounds per year). The total amount spent on sugar will increase from $OP_0 \times OQ_0$ to

FIGURE 4.10 Reduction in Consumer Surplus Due to an Increase in the Price of Sugar
If the price of sugar increases from OP_0 to OP_1, there will be a reduction in consumer surplus equal to area $P_0 P_1 LM$.

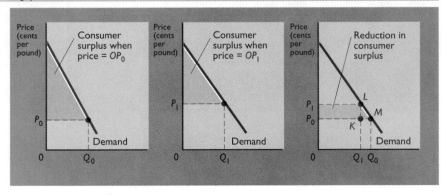

$OP_1 \times OQ_1$. More important, the price increase results in a reduction in consumer surplus. If price equals OP_1, the consumer surplus equals the shaded area in the middle panel of Figure 4.10. Thus the increase in price from OP_0 to OP_1 results in a reduction in consumer surplus equal to the shaded area in the right-hand panel of Figure 4.10. (Clearly, this shaded area equals the shaded area in the left-hand panel minus that in the middle panel.) As shown there, the loss in consumer surplus equals the area to the left of the demand curve from the original price to the increased price.[5]

The loss to the consumer from the price increase can be measured by the shaded area in the right-hand panel of Figure 4.10. To understand more clearly why this measure is a sensible one, note that this shaded area is composed of two parts: rectangle P_0P_1LK and triangle KLM. The first part (rectangle P_0P_1LK) shows the extra amount that the consumer has to pay for the amount of sugar he or she consumes (after the price increase). Clearly, this extra amount equals $(OP_1 - OP_0)OQ_1$, and is equal to the area of rectangle P_0P_1LK. The second part (triangle KLM) shows the net loss to the consumer because he or she consumes less sugar (OQ_1 rather than OQ_0 pounds) due to the higher price. As we saw in the previous section, the value to the consumer of the forgone ($OQ_0 - OQ_1$) pounds of sugar (that is, the maximum amount that he or she would pay for them) is equal to area Q_1LMQ_0. If we subtract area Q_1KMQ_0, which equals the amount that the consumer would have had to pay for these ($OQ_0 - OQ_1$) pounds, the net loss to the consumer is triangle KLM.

Ilse Mintz, in a study published by the American Enterprise Institute, applied this technique to estimate the loss to consumers due to the restrictions on sugar imports.[6] According to her estimates, the demand curve for sugar in the United States was as shown in Figure 4.11. The restrictions raised the price of sugar by 2.57 cents, as shown in Figure 4.11. Without the restrictions, U.S. consumers would have purchased 23.2 billion pounds of sugar; with them, they purchased 22.4 billion pounds. As indicated in the right-hand panel of Figure 4.10, the reduction in consumer surplus due to the price increase equals the area to the left of the demand curve from the original price to the increased price. This area, which is shaded in Figure 4.11, equals $\frac{1}{2}$ (2.57¢) (22.4 billion + 23.2 billion) = $586 million per year.

Thus Mintz's results indicated that U.S. consumers were worse off by about $586 million per year because of restrictions on sugar imports. Subsequent studies, based on the same technique, have borne out her conclusion that these restrictions have imposed considerable losses on U.S. con-

---

[5] The shaded area in the right-hand panel of Figure 4.10 also measures the *gain* in consumer surplus if price is *lowered* from OP_1 to OP_0. Based on our discussion in this and the previous section, the reader should be able to demonstrate that this is true.

[6] I. Mintz, *U.S. Import Quotas, Costs and Consequences* (Washington, D.C.: American Enterprise Institute, February 1973).

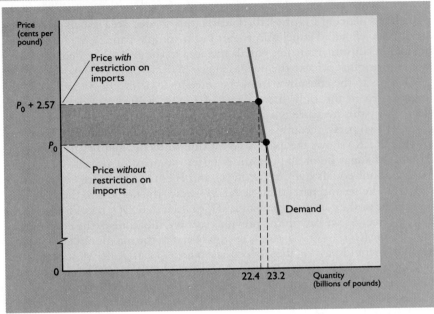

FIGURE 4.11 Reduction in Consumer Surplus Due to Restrictions on Sugar Imports
Because of restrictions on sugar imports, the price of sugar was increased by 2.57¢ per pound. The reduction in consumer surplus equaled $586 million per year, the shaded area in the graph.

sumers.[7] (According to some estimates, these losses have reached about $1 billion per year.) It is not our intention to take up the pros and cons of such restrictions at this point. (Much more will be said on this score in Chapter 6.) For present purposes, all that we want to do is illustrate how the concept of consumer surplus has been used to shed light on important questions of public policy.[8]

---

[7] For example, see M. Morkre and D. Tarr, *Staff Report on Effects of Restrictions on U.S. Imports,* Federal Trade Commission, June 1980. According to the 1987 Annual Report of the Council of Economic Advisers, the import quota is imposed to maintain price supports for sugar at three to four times the world price. See the *Economic Report of the President* (Washington, D.C.: Government Printing Office, 1987).

[8] One further point needs to be made concerning the concept of consumer surplus. When we use this concept, we assume that the consumer's indifference curves are of a particular type. Suppose that we plot the consumer's indifference curves where the amount of sugar consumed per day is the good on the horizontal axis and the amount of money that the consumer can spend on all goods other than sugar is the good on the vertical axis. (See Problem 1 on page 126 for a discussion of goods of the latter kind.) When we use the concept of consumer surplus, we assume that these indifference curves are parallel; that is, the vertical distance between any two indifference curves is the same regardless of where along the horizontal axis one measures this

INDEXES OF THE COST OF LIVING

Another area where the theory described in previous sections has proved useful is in the construction of index numbers of the cost of living. The phrase *cost of living* means the cost of living at a constant level of satisfaction. Cost-of-living indexes have always been closely associated with the issue of inflation. For example, labor unions want to know whether wages are keeping pace with the cost of living. Automatic adjustments in wages based on changes in cost-of-living indexes have been incorporated in many wage contracts. And cost-of-living indexes are used to measure changes in the purchasing power of the dollar for a variety of purposes, including the adjustment of pensions and welfare payments (and even alimony payments).

The most famous index of the cost of living is the Consumer Price Index, which the Bureau of Labor Statistics has been calculating for over fifty years. This index includes the prices of practically everything people buy for living—food, clothing, homes, automobiles, household supplies, house furnishings, fuel, drugs, doctors' fees, rent, transportation, and so forth. It pertains to urban consumers, and is based on data concerning the spending habits and prices paid by such consumers. Prices are obtained by personal visits to a sample of about 25,000 retail stores and service establishments in the United States. Prices are collected at intervals ranging from once every month to once every 3 months. Based on these data, the Bureau of Labor Statistics publishes each month the Consumer Price Index for the urban population as a whole and for each of 28 metropolitan areas.

In the following sections, we describe briefly how the Consumer Price Index is constructed, and point out that it is not an ideal price index. Ideally, a cost-of-living index is constructed so that, if the index goes up more rapidly than a family's money income, we can be sure that the family is worse off, whereas if the index goes up less rapidly than the family's money income, we can be sure that the family is better-off. Thus, if the ideal price index increases by 15 percent between 1996 and 1999, we can be sure that a family is worse off in 1999 than in 1996 if its money income increases by less than 15 percent, and that it is better-off if its money income increases by more than 15 percent. As you might expect, ideal price indexes are not easy to come by in the real world.

---

distance. This is a very restrictive assumption, but according to some economists, it may be a reasonable approximation for commodities, like sugar, on which the consumer spends only a small amount of his or her income. Fortunately, for many applications, this approximation is good enough for practical purposes. See R. Willig, "Consumer Surplus Without Apology," *American Economic Review,* September 1976.

THE CONSUMER PRICE INDEX

To see how the Consumer Price Index is constructed, suppose for simplicity that there are only two goods, hamburgers and coffee, and that in 1996 the typical household bought 500 units of hamburger and 400 units of coffee per month. Since the price in 1996 was $3 per unit for hamburger and $1.25 per unit for coffee, the total amount that this household spent in 1996 on this market basket of goods and services—500 units of hamburger and 400 units of coffee—was 500($3) + 400($1.25) = $2,000 per month.

In 1999, suppose that the price of hamburger rises to $4 per unit and that the price of coffee rises to $2 per unit. The Consumer Price Index attempts to summarize or describe these price increases from 1996 to 1999 in a single number. The first step in calculating this index is to determine what the 1996 market basket—500 units of hamburger and 400 units of coffee—would cost in 1999. Since the 1999 price of hamburger is $4 per unit and the 1999 price of coffee is $2 per unit, the answer is 500($4) + 400($2) = $2,800. The next step is to divide this figure ($2,800) by the 1996 cost of this market basket ($2,000), the result being 1.40; this means that the cost increased by 40 percent from 1996 to 1999. Thus the Consumer Price Index rose by 40 percent during this period; if it was 100 in 1996, it was 140 in 1999.

More generally, suppose that the typical household buys H_1 units of hamburger and C_1 units of coffee in year 1, the price of hamburger then being P_1^H per unit and the price of coffee being P_1^C per unit. The money income, I, required to buy this market basket is

$$I = H_1 P_1^H + C_1 P_1^C.$$
[4.1]

Thus, since the typical household buys this market basket in year 1, its money income must equal I. In year 2 (subsequent to year 1), the money income, I', required to buy this market basket is

$$I' = H_1 P_2^H + C_1 P_2^C,$$
[4.2]

where P_2^H is the price per unit of hamburger and P_2^C is the price per unit of coffee in year 2. Thus, if the price index is 100 in year 1, its value in year 2 equals

$$p^* = 100 \frac{I'}{I} = 100 \frac{H_1 P_2^H + C_1 P_2^C}{H_1 P_1^H + C_1 P_1^C}.$$
[4.3]

EXAMPLE 4.2

New York City's Water Crisis

On January 7, 1986, Mayor Edward Koch of New York City proposed that water meters be installed in all buildings in the city. This was not a new idea. When New York City experienced a water crisis a number of years ago (because the average rate of use of water exceeded the yield of the water system), the mayor's Committee on Management Survey recommended the use of universal metering. Many consumers paid only a flat fee for water and were not metered. With metering, consumers would be charged 2¢ per hundred gallons of water. The cost of installing and operating the meters was estimated to be about $50 per million gallons of water saved per day. But this was only part of the cost of metering, since it did not include the loss to consumers arising from the fact that they would be led to consume less water. To make a fair comparison of the cost of metering with the cost of other ways of meeting the crisis, it was obvious that such losses should be taken into account.

(a) If a consumer's demand curve for water was approximately linear, as shown below, how large was the monetary value of his or her loss due to the consumption of less water? (b) How much was the monetary value of such losses per million gallons of water saved? (c) Including such losses as well as the cost of installing and operating the meters, what was the total cost of each million gallons of water saved by metering? (d) The cost of providing water with a new dam was estimated to be about $1,000 per million gallons per day. Was building a new dam (which in fact was done) the right solution?

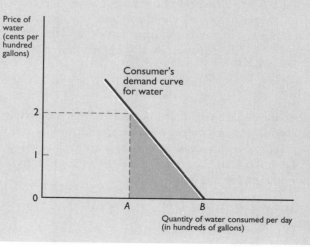

SOLUTION   (a) Without metering, the consumer would consume *OB* hundreds of gallons of water per day (since the price of an extra hundred gallons was zero). With metering, the consumer would consume *OA* hundreds of gallons of water per day (since the price of an extra hundred gallons was 2¢). The consumer would be willing to pay an amount equal to the shaded area under the demand curve for the *(OB − OA)* hundreds of gallons per day that he or she forgoes because of metering. Since the demand curve is assumed to be linear, this equals $\frac{1}{2}$ × 2¢ × the quantity of water saved per day (in hundreds of gallons). In other words, it equals 1¢ per hundred gallons saved per day. (b) Since 1¢ per hundred gallons is equivalent to $100 per million gallons, the monetary value of such losses was $100 per million gallons saved. (c) $100 + $50 = $150. (d) It appears that metering would have been cheaper than building the dam. (However, it should be recognized that this kind of analysis is subject to limitations described in Chapter 19.)*

---

* For further discussion of this case, see J. Hirschleifer, J. Milliman, and J. DeHaven, *Water Supply* (Chicago: University of Chicago Press, 1970).

Graphical Representation of the Price Index

To relate our discussion of the Consumer Price Index to the previous material on consumer behavior, let's consider three different budget lines for the average household. *The first budget line is the one that describes this household's situation in year 1.* Because this household had a money income of *I* in year 1, and because the price of a unit of hamburger was P_1^H and the price of a unit of coffee was P_1^C in year 1, the equation for this budget line is

$$H = \frac{I}{P_1^H} - \frac{P_1^C}{P_1^H} C \qquad [4.4]$$

This budget line — labeled "Year 1 budget line" — is shown in Figure 4.12.

The second budget line is the one that describes this household's situation in year 2, assuming that its money income is the same in year 2 as in year 1. Recalling that the price of a unit of hamburger is P_2^H and the price of a unit of coffee is P_2^C in year 2, the equation for this budget line is

$$H = \frac{I}{P_2^H} - \frac{P_2^C}{P_2^H} C. \qquad [4.5]$$

This budget line — labeled "Year 2 budget line" — is shown in Figure 4.12.

The third budget line is a hypothetical budget line that describes this household's Hypo-
situation in year 2 if it had just enough money income (no more, no less) to buy the thetical
market basket it bought in year 1. Given that this household purchased H_1 units budget
of hamburger and C_1 units of coffee in year 1, the market basket it purchased line
in year 1 can be represented by point A in Figure 4.12. And since this hypothetical budget line assumes that this household has just enough income to
purchase this market basket, it follows that this hypothetical budget line must
pass through point A. Moreover, because this hypothetical budget line assumes that the prices of hamburger and coffee are at their year 2 levels, it must
have the same slope as the actual budget line in year 2. (Why? Because the
slope of a budget line equals the price ratio, as emphasized on page 74.) Thus
this hypothetical budget line must be parallel to the actual budget line in year
2—and it must pass through point A. In other words, it must be the
"Hypothetical year 2 budget line" shown in Figure 4.12.

Assuming for simplicity that the price index in year 1 equals 100, it is easy to
calculate the price index in year 2. The first step is to divide the vertical intercept of the "Hypothetical year 2 budget line" by the vertical intercept of the

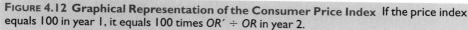

FIGURE 4.12 Graphical Representation of the Consumer Price Index If the price index
equals 100 in year 1, it equals 100 times $OR' \div OR$ in year 2.

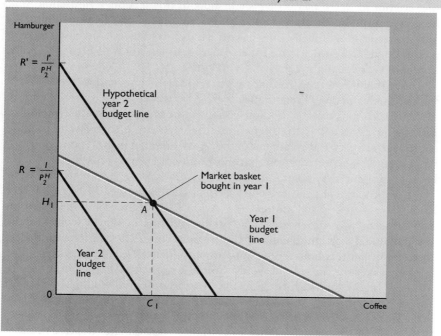

"Year 2 budget line." That is, we divide OR' by OR in Figure 4.12. The reason why we divide OR' by OR is that the result equals $I' \div I$. To see why, note that OR' equals I'/P_2^H and that $OR = I/P_2^H$, as indicated in Figure 4.12. (Of course, this follows from the fact that the vertical intercept of a budget line equals money income divided by the price of the good on the vertical axis.) The second step is to multiply $OR' \div OR$ by 100. Since $OR' \div OR$ equals $I' \div I$, it follows from Equation 4.3 that if the price index is 100 in year 1, its value in year 2 is 100 times $OR' \div OR$. In this way, we can represent the price index graphically.

PROBLEMS WITH THE PRICE INDEX

As pointed out in a previous section, an ideal price index would tell us the extent to which a family's money income would have to increase (or decrease) in a certain period of time to offset price changes and maintain the family's well-being at a constant level. In practice, cost-of-living indexes, like most things in life, are not ideal. In fact, as we shall show in this section, a household that bought H_1 units of hamburger and C_1 units of coffee in year 1 would not maintain the same level of well-being in year 2 if its income were increased to keep pace with the Consumer Price Index. Instead, its level of well-being would be higher in year 2 than in year 1.

To see that this is true, consider Figure 4.13, which reproduces the "Year 1 budget line" and the "Hypothetical year 2 budget line" we drew in Figure 4.12. In addition, two of the household's indifference curves are included. Indifference curve 1 is the highest indifference curve that this household could reach in year 1. It is tangent to the "Year 1 budget line" at point A; this is what would be expected given that this household in fact bought the market basket represented by point A in year 1.

As we know from the previous section, the Consumer Price Index rose from 100 in year 1 to 100 times $I' \div I$ in year 2. If this household's money income rose by this same percentage, its budget line in year 2 would be the "Hypothetical year 2 budget line." Indifference curve 2 is the highest indifference curve that this household could attain under these circumstances. (The market basket the household would choose is at point B.) Since indifference curve 2 is higher than indifference curve 1, this household would be better-off in year 2 than in year 1 if its money income increased by the same percentage as the Consumer Price Index.

In other words, the Consumer Price Index overestimates the rate of inflation. To understand why, it is important to recognize that this index takes no

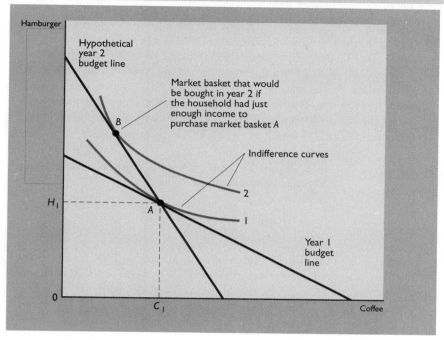

FIGURE 4.13 Bias in the Consumer Price Index If the household's money income goes up by the same percentage as the price index, the household can attain a higher indifference curve (2 rather than 1). Thus the price index overestimates the true rate of inflation.

account of the fact that households adapt their purchases to changes in prices. For example, if the price of coffee goes up a lot more than the price of hamburger, households are likely to cut back on their consumption of coffee and beef up their consumption of hamburger. The Consumer Price Index ignores such changes in the household's market basket. It compares the household's cost of purchasing a *fixed* market basket (the market basket purchased in year 1) in year 2 with that in year 1.[9]

Upward bias

In addition, there are other problems in the Consumer Price Index. For one thing, the quality of a product often changes over time, and it is difficult to know how to adjust the change in the product's price for the quality change. For example, suppose that the price of a refrigerator goes up by 10 percent between 1996 and 1999, but the quality of the refrigerator also increases. How

---

[9] A price index of this sort (that is, one calculated according to Equation 4.3) is often called a *Laspeyres price index.* If C_2 were substituted for C_1 and if H_2 were substituted for H_1 in Equation 4.3, the result would be a so-called *Paasche price index.* In other words, a Paasche index is based on the market basket purchased in year 2. (C_2 and H_2 are the numbers of units of coffee and hamburger bought in year 2.)

EXAMPLE 4.3

Calculating a Cost-of-Living Index

According to the Bureau of Labor Statistics, the price of food was 2.8 percent higher in the United States in 1995 than in 1994, and the price of shelter was 3.2 percent higher in 1995 than in 1994.* Suppose that a family spent half of its 1994 money income on food and half on shelter. (a) For this family, calculate a price index for 1995, given that the index's value in 1994 was 100. (b) If prices increased more rapidly in the city where this family lives than in the country as a whole, is the result in part (a) correct? (c) Is there likely to be a bias in this price index?

SOLUTION   (a) From Equation 4.3, we see that the value of the price index in 1995 is

$$100\left(\frac{F_1 P_2^F + S_1 P_2^S}{F_1 P_1^F + S_1 P_1^S}\right),$$

where F_1 is the number of units of food bought in 1994 and S_1 is the number of units of shelter bought in 1994. The price of a unit of food is P_1^F in 1994 and P_2^F in 1995, and the price of a unit of shelter is P_1^S in 1994 and P_2^S in 1995. The above formula is exactly the same as the expression in Equation 4.3. However, since the goods now are food and shelter rather than hamburgers and coffee, F_1 and S_1 are used in place of H_1 and C_1 — and P_1^F, P_2^F, P_1^S, and P_2^S are used in place of P_1^H, P_2^H, P_1^C, and P_2^C, respectively. We can rewrite the above formula as

$$100 \times \frac{F_1 P_1^F\left(\dfrac{P_2^F}{P_1^F}\right) + S_1 P_1^S\left(\dfrac{P_2^S}{P_1^S}\right)}{F_1 P_1^F + S_1 P_1^S}$$

$$= 100\left(\frac{F_1 P_1^F}{F_1 P_1^F + S_1 P_1^S}\right)\left(\frac{P_2^F}{P_1^F}\right) + 100\left(\frac{S_1 P_1^S}{F_1 P_1^F + S_1 P_1^S}\right)\left(\frac{P_2^S}{P_1^S}\right).$$

Since $F_1 P_1^F + S_1 P_1^S$ equals the family's money income in 1994, $F_1 P_1^F \div (F_1 P_1^F + S_1 P_1^S)$ equals the proportion of its 1994 money income spent on food, which equals $1/2$. Similarly, $S_1 P_1^S \div (F_1 P_1^F + S_1 P_1^S)$ equals the proportion of its 1994 money income spent on shelter, which equals $1/2$. Thus since $P_2^F/P_1^F = 1.028$ and $P_2^S/P_1^S = 1.032$, the above formula equals

$$100\left(\tfrac{1}{2}\right)(1.028) + 100\left(\tfrac{1}{2}\right)(1.032) = 103.0.$$

> The value of the price index in 1995 is 103.0; this indicates that the price level rose by 3.0 percent from 1994 to 1995. (b) No. The calculations in part (a) assume that the prices paid by the family increased at the same rate as in the country as a whole. If they increased more rapidly, the price index for the family exceeded 103.0. (c) This price index may overestimate the true rate of inflation for reasons cited on pages 122 to 123.
>
> ---
>
> * The figures for both 1995 and 1994 pertain to November, and come from the *1996 Annual Report of the Council of Economic Advisers.*

much of the 10 percent price increase is offset by the quality increase? This is a very tricky question. Although the Bureau of Labor Statistics tries to adjust price changes for changes in quality, the available evidence seems to indicate that the adjustments sometimes are crude at best.[10]

SUMMARY

1. Another way of expressing the conditions for consumer equilibrium is as follows: The rational consumer will choose in equilibrium to allocate his or her income between good X and good Y in such a way that the marginal rate of substitution of good X for good Y equals the ratio of the price of good X to the price of good Y.

2. If we hold commodity prices constant, each level of money income results in an equilibrium market basket for the consumer, and the curve that connects the points representing all these equilibrium market baskets is called the income-consumption curve. The income-consumption curve can be used to derive the Engel curve, which is the relationship between the equilibrium amount of a good purchased by a consumer and the level of the consumer's money income. Engel curves play an important role in family expenditure studies.

---

[10] This discussion of the Consumer Price Index is simplified in many regards. For more complete accounts, see R. Pollak, *The Theory of the Cost-of-Living Index* (New York: Oxford University Press, 1989); W. E. Diewert, "The Economic Theory of Index Numbers: A Survey," Discussion paper 79–09, Department of Economics, University of British Columbia, March 1979; S. Braithwait, "The Substitution Bias of the Laspeyres Price Index: An Analysis Using Estimated Cost of Living Indexes," *American Economic Review,* March 1980; and R. Gordon, "The Consumer Price Index: Measuring Inflation and Causing It," *Public Interest,* 1981.

3. Holding constant the consumer's money income as well as the prices of other goods, we can determine the relationship between the price of a good and the amount of this good that a consumer will consume. This relationship is called the consumer's individual demand curve for the good in question. The individual demand curve, one of the central concepts in the theory of consumer behavior, can be derived from the price-consumption curve, which includes all the equilibrium market baskets corresponding to various prices of the good.

4. The location and shape of an individual demand curve will depend on the level of money income and the level at which the prices of other goods are held constant, as well as on the nature of the good and the tastes of the consumer. It is important to differentiate between shifts in a consumer's demand curve for a particular commodity and changes in the amount of the commodity that he or she consumes.

5. The total effect of a price change on the quantity demanded can be divided into two parts: the substitution effect and the income effect. The substitution effect is the change in quantity demanded of a good resulting from a price change when the level of satisfaction, or real income, is held constant. The income effect shows the effect of the change in real income that is due to the price change. The substitution effect is always negative. The income effect is not predictable from the theory alone: Its sign is different for normal goods than for inferior goods.

6. An illustration of how this model of consumer behavior has been used to help solve practical problems is provided by the study of the effects of sugar import quotas. An important question in this case was: How can one estimate the monetary value of the loss to consumers arising from the fact that import quotas raise the price of sugar and lower sugar consumption? If certain assumptions are made, this question can be answered, at least approximately, based on the concept of consumer surplus.

7. Another type of problem where this sort of model has proved useful is in the construction of index numbers of the cost of living. The methods used to calculate the Consumer Price Index, as well as its limitations, have been discussed.

QUESTIONS/PROBLEMS

1. As shown on the following page, the price-consumption curve for good X is upward sloping when good Y is the money spent by the consumer on goods other than good X. Of course, good Y is a peculiar sort of good, but

there is nothing to prevent us from defining a good in this way. In weighing every purchase the consumer must decide whether to give up money he or she can spend on goods other than good X in exchange for good X. Since good Y is money, its price is always 1. (For example, it takes a quarter to buy a quarter.)

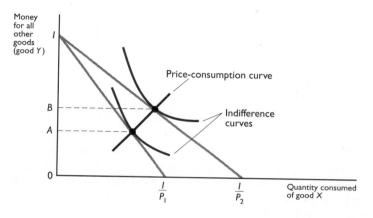

(a) Prove that the consumer's demand curve for good X is price inelastic. (Hint: Recall from Chapter 1 that, if the demand for a good is price inelastic, a decrease in its price results in a decrease in the amount spent on it.) (b) Prove that, if this price-consumption curve were downward sloping, the consumer's demand curve for good X would be price elastic.

2. In late 1985, New York City's Department of Consumer Affairs published the results of an 11-month study of prescription drug prices charged by 92 pharmacies in New York. The survey reported that 30 tablets of Dyazide (prescribed for high blood pressure) cost $16.95 at one pharmacy and $6.95 at another pharmacy about 3 miles away.[11] (a) If a person bought Dyazide at the former pharmacy, would his or her consumer surplus have been the same as if he or she bought it at the latter pharmacy? Why or why not? (b) Does a pharmacy always have an incentive to increase a customer's consumer surplus? Why or why not?

3. Lewis and Clark Lake is a large reservoir in South Dakota created on the Missouri River by the Gavins Point Dam. It is located in an area where there are few natural bodies of water, and it has become very popular as a recreational area. Suppose that 10,000 families are potential users of the lake for recreational purposes and that each family's demand curve for recreational trips to the lake is as follows on the next page:

[11] *New York Times,* December 28, 1985, p. 48.

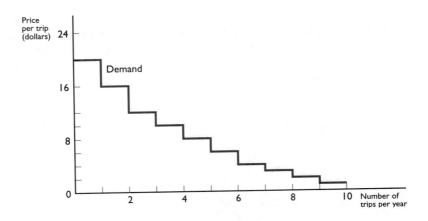

(a) If an ordinance were passed which limited each family to no more than five trips per year to the lake, what is the loss (in money terms) to each family? (b) If an ordinance were passed which allowed a family to use the lake for recreational purposes only if it purchased a permit for $75 a year, would it be worthwhile for each family to buy the permit if it could not use the lake without the permit (and it could use the lake as much as it liked with one)? (c) Suppose that we consider two goods: trips to the lake and money that can be spent on things other than trips to the lake. In answering parts (a) and (b), what assumption are you making regarding each family's indifference curves concerning these two goods?

4. In the previous question, how much is the consumer surplus from each family's utilization of the lake if there is a charge of $8 for each trip to the lake?

5. Suppose that all consumers pay 25 cents for a telephone call and 25 cents for a newspaper (and that all consumers purchase some of both goods). (a) If all consumers are maximizing utility, is it possible to determine each consumer's marginal rate of substitution of telephone calls for newspapers? (b) Suppose that a local economist applies for a grant to estimate this marginal rate of substitution; his proposed procedure is to ask a sample of consumers. Can you suggest a simpler procedure? (c) Based on these facts alone, can you estimate this marginal rate of substitution? If so, what is it?

6. A representative of the dairy industry asserts that, as income increases, the proportion of income spent on food tends to rise. (a) Do you think this proposition is true? Why or why not? (b) Indicate the general shape of the Engel curve for food, based on this proposition.

7. According to some observers, the typical Irish peasant in the nineteenth century was so poor he spent almost all his income for potatoes. When the

price of potatoes fell, he could get the same amount of nutrition for a smaller expenditure on potatoes, so some of his income was diverted to vegetables and meat. Since the latter also provided calories, he could even reduce his consumption of potatoes under these circumstances. If this is true, were potatoes (a) a normal good? (b) an inferior good? (c) a good exhibiting Giffen's paradox?

8. Suppose that a family consumes a quite different set of commodities in a later period than in an earlier one, and that many of the goods it consumes in the later period were not available in the earlier one. What difficulties does this cause the economist who would like to construct a cost-of-living index?

9. Suppose that a 1 percent increase in the price of pork chops results in Ms. Smith's buying 3 percent fewer pork chops per week. (a) What is the price elasticity of demand for pork chops on the part of Ms. Smith? (b) Is her demand for pork chops price elastic or price inelastic? (c) Will an increase in the price of pork chops result in an increase, or a decrease, in the total amount of money that she spends on pork chops?

10. Calculate a cost-of-living index for a family that consumes the following amounts of bread and clothing (and no other goods) in 1993 and 1996:

	1993	1996
Amount consumed of bread	100	140
Amount consumed of clothing	120	130
Price of bread (dollars)	0.30	0.50
Price of clothing (dollars)	30.00	40.00

APPENDIX

ORDINAL AND CARDINAL UTILITY

Besides the ordinary demand curve discussed in this chapter, economists are interested in income-compensated demand curves. In Figure 4.6, we showed how (in principle) the effects of a price change can be divided into a substitution effect and a price effect. To carry out this decomposition, when the price of a good changes, we adjust the consumer's money income so that he or she remains on the same indifference curve. This is not the only procedure that could be adopted. Instead, we could change the consumer's money income so

FIGURE 4.14 Income-Compensated and Ordinary Demand Curves for Good X **For** normal goods, the ordinary demand curve is flatter than the income-compensated demand curve.

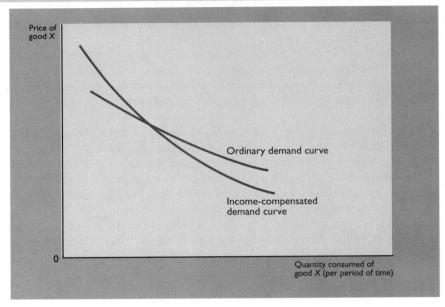

that he or she could still buy the market basket (no more, no less) that was purchased before the price change.[12]

Income-compensated demand curve

If this latter procedure is used, we can construct an income-compensated demand curve for the good in question (say good X) by seeing how much the consumer demands of good X at each level of price, *when his or her money income is adjusted so that, regardless of the price of good* X, *the original market basket can be purchased.* The results are shown in Figure 4.14, together with the ordinary demand curve for good X. Both the income-compensated demand curve and the ordinary demand curve show the relationship between the price of good X and the amount of this good demanded by the consumer. The difference between them reflects the fact that the ordinary demand curve assumes that the consumer's money income is *held constant,* whereas the income-compensated demand curve assumes the consumer's money income is *adjusted to allow him or her to purchase the original market basket.*

---

[12] The procedure used in Figure 4.6 to carry out the decomposition is due to Sir John Hicks; the alternative procedure discussed in this appendix is due to the Russian economist Eugen Slutsky.

In Figure 4.14, note that the ordinary demand curve is flatter than the income-compensated demand curve. This will always be the case for a normal good. When price falls, the income effect is positive for a normal good. Whereas the ordinary demand curve includes this income effect, the income-compensated demand curve does not. Thus, when price falls, the quantity demanded increases by a greater amount based on the ordinary demand curve than it does based on the income-compensated demand curve.

Income-compensated demand curves are of practical importance because the empirical relationships between price and quantity obtained in statistical investigations are often really demand curves of this type. In their calculations, statisticians and econometricians generally hold constant the effects of real income; this means that the results often approximate income-compensated demand curves. More will be said about these empirical relationships in Chapter 5.

Market Demand

5

INTRODUCTION

Robert Eaton, who has been chairman of the Chrysler Corporation, is much more concerned with the quantity of cars that will be demanded by the entire national market than with the quantity of cars that you or I will purchase next year. Economists, too, when confronted with many problems, are much more interested in the quantity of a good demanded in a market than in the quantity of a good demanded by a particular individual. For example, as we saw in Chapter 1, it is the market demand curve, not the individual demand curve, that (together with the market supply curve) determines the equilibrium price of a good. Thus, at this point we must turn from individual demand (the topic of the previous chapter) to market demand.

In this chapter, after showing how the market demand curve is related to the demand curves of the individual consumers in the market, we discuss some major determinants of the price elasticity of market demand. Then we take up the effects of two other factors, besides the good's price, on the quantity of the good that is demanded in the market—aggregate money income and the prices of other commodities. Next, we look at market demand from the seller's side of the market, placing emphasis on the concept of marginal revenue and the differences between the demand curve for the industry and the demand curve for the firm. Finally, we discuss the measurement of market demand curves, and we describe two cases where such measurements were used to help guide public and private decision makers.

DERIVATION OF THE MARKET DEMAND CURVE

In Chapter 4, we showed how an individual demand curve can be derived from a consumer's indifference map. This demand curve is of course the relationship between the quantity of the good demanded by the consumer (per unit of time) and the good's price, when the money income of the consumer and the prices of other goods are held constant. The shape and level of the individual demand curve obviously depend on the consumer's tastes, as reflected in his or her indifference map. They also depend on the level of the consumer's money income and the level of the prices of other goods.

The *market demand curve* for a commodity is simply the *horizontal* summation of the individual demand curves of all the consumers in the market. Put differently, to find the market quantity demanded at each price, we add up the individual quantities demanded at that price. For example, Table 5.1 shows the individual demand schedules for four consumers.[1] If these four consumers comprise the entire market, the market demand schedule is given in the last column of Table 5.1. Figure 5.1 shows the individual demand curves based on these same data, as well as the resulting market demand curve.

Market demand curve

The market demand curve for a commodity is one of the most important concepts in microeconomics. The market demand curve shows how much of the commodity will be purchased (per unit of time) by the consumers in the market at each possible price (given that the level of money income of the con-

---

[1] Recall from Chapter 1 that a demand schedule is a table showing the quantity demanded at various prices.

sumers and the prices of other commodities are held constant). Information regarding the market demand curve is of the utmost importance to producers of the commodity. Obviously, they need to know how much of the commodity

TABLE 5.1 Individual and Market Demand Schedules

Price (cents per unit of the commodity)	Quantity demanded (per unit of time)				Quantity demanded in market (per unit of time)
	Individual *A*	Individual *B*	Individual *C*	Individual *D*	
	(units of the commodity)				
1	50	40	30	20	140
2	40	30	25	19	114
3	30	20	18	18	86
4	25	15	13	17	70
5	20	14	13	16	63
6	15	13	11	15	54
7	10	12	9	14	45
8	8	11	7	13	39
9	6	10	5	12	33
10	5	9	3	11	28

Figure 5.1 Individual and Market Demand Curves The market demand curve is the horizontal summation of the individual demand curves.

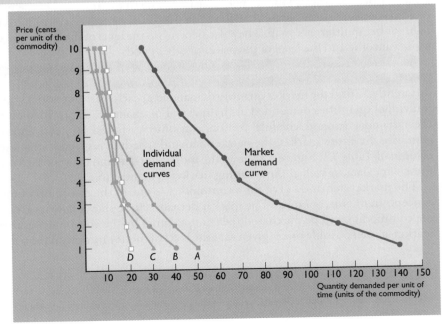

can be sold at various prices. The market demand curve is also of great importance to economists because, as pointed out in Chapter 1, it plays an important role in determining the price of the commodity.

THE PRICE ELASTICITY OF DEMAND

At each point on the market demand curve, the price elasticity of demand, defined as the percentage change in the quantity demanded resulting from a 1 percent change in price, gauges the sensitivity of the quantity demanded to changes in price. Chapter 1 pointed out the significance of the price elasticity of demand, but nothing has been said about its determinants. What determines whether the demand for a commodity is price elastic or price inelastic in a certain price range? Why does the price elasticity of demand for one commodity equal 3.0 and the price elasticity of demand for another commodity equal 1.5? This is a very important question, and the one to which we turn our attention in this section.

First, and foremost, the price elasticity of demand for a commodity depends on the number and closeness of the *substitutes* that are available. If a commodity has many close substitutes, its demand is likely to be price elastic. If increases occur in the price of the product, a large proportion of its buyers will turn to the close substitutes that are available; if decreases occur in its price, a great many buyers of substitutes will switch to this product.

Role of substitutes

Of course, the extent to which a commodity has close substitutes depends on how narrowly it is defined. In general, one would expect that, as the definition of the product becomes narrower and more specific, the product has more close substitutes and its demand becomes more price elastic. Thus the demand for a particular brand of shirts is likely to be more price elastic than the overall demand for shirts and the demand for shirts is likely to be more price elastic than the demand for clothing as a whole. If a commodity is defined so that it has perfect substitutes, its price elasticity of demand is infinite. Thus, if the cotton produced by Farmer Jones is exactly the same as the cotton produced by other farmers and if he increases his price slightly (to a point above the market level), his sales would be reduced to nothing.

Second, it is sometimes asserted that the price elasticity of demand for a commodity is likely to depend on the importance of the commodity in consumers' budgets. For example, the demand for commodities like thumbtacks, pepper, and salt may be quite inelastic. The typical consumer spends only a very small fraction of his or her income on such goods. On the other hand, for commodities that bulk larger in the typical consumer's budget, like major ap-

EXAMPLE 5.1

Residential Demand for Water

Water is obviously of fundamental importance to human beings, no matter where they live. However, this does not mean that the residential demand for water is the same in one region as in another. Henry Foster and Bruce Beattie have estimated the demand curve for water in six regions of the United States. The results, shown below, pertain to New England and the Northern Atlantic region, the Midwest, the Southeast, the Plains and Rocky Mountain region, the Southwest, and the Pacific Northwest.

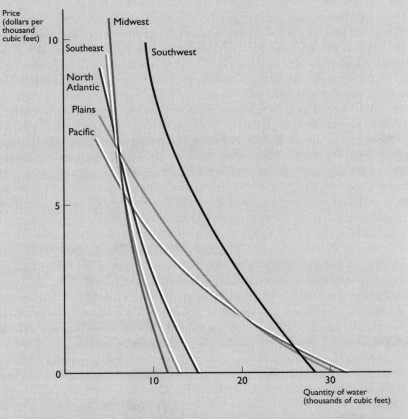

(a) If the price of water is $5 per thousand cubic feet, in which region is the consumption of water highest? (b) According to their findings, the price elasticity of demand for water in all regions is between 0.39 and 0.69. Why do you think the demand for water is price inelastic? (c) In those regions where outdoor use comprises a relatively large fraction of total water use, the price elasticity of demand tends to be relatively high. Why? (d) The demand curve for water in the summer tends to be to the right of the demand curve in the winter, and it tends to be more price elastic than the demand curve in the winter. Why?

SOLUTION (a) Southwest. (b) Because there are few good substitutes for water. (c) Outdoor use of water is less essential than the use of water for drinking, cooking, and bathing purposes. Thus the quantity of water demanded for outdoor use is more sensitive to price than is the quantity of water demanded for drinking, cooking, and bathing purposes. (d) Because more water for outdoor use is demanded in the summer, and because this demand is relatively price elastic for the reason given in the answer to part (c).*

---

* For further discussion, see D. Gibbons, *The Economic Value of Water* (Washington, D.C.: Resources for the Future, 1986).

pliances, the elasticity of demand may tend to be higher. Consumers may be more conscious of, and influenced by, price changes in the case of goods that require larger outlays. However, although a tendency of this sort is sometimes hypothesized, there is no guarantee that it exists. As some economists have pointed out, the link between a commodity's price elasticity of demand and its importance in consumers' budgets may in fact be much weaker than that which is implied by this hypothesis.

Third, the price elasticity of demand for a commodity is likely to depend on the length of the period to which the demand curve pertains. (Every market demand curve — like every individual demand curve — pertains, of course, to a certain time interval.) In many cases, demand is likely to be more elastic, or less inelastic, over a long period of time than over a short period of time. The longer the period of time, the easier it is for consumers and business firms to substitute one good for another. If, for example, the price of natural gas should decline relative to other fuels, the consumption of natural gas in the week after the price decline would probably increase very little. But over a period of several years, people would have had an opportunity to take account of the price decline in choosing the type of fuel to be used in new houses and renovated old houses. In the longer period of several years, the price decline would have a greater effect on the consumption of natural gas than it would have in the shorter period of 1 week.[2]

THE INCOME ELASTICITY OF DEMAND

Up to this point, we have been concerned solely with the effect of price on the quantity of the commodity demanded in the market. Yet price is not the only factor that influences the quantity demanded in the market. Another important factor is the level of money income among the consumers in the market. For example, if consumers have plenty of money to spend, the quantity demanded of beef is likely to be greater than if they are poverty stricken. Or if incomes in a particular community are high, the quantity demanded of caviar is likely to be greater than if incomes are low.

Income elasticity of demand   For an individual consumer, we saw in Chapter 4 that the relationship between money income (per period of time) and the amount consumed of a particular commodity (per period of time) can be represented by an Engel curve. Recall that this curve is based on the condition that the prices of all commodities remain constant. At any point on the Engel curve, one can characterize the sensitivity of the amount consumed to changes in the consumer's money income by the *income elasticity of demand,* which is defined as

$$\eta_I = \frac{\Delta Q}{Q} \div \frac{\Delta I}{I},$$ [5.1]

where ΔQ is the change in quantity consumed that results from a small change in the consumer's money income ΔI, Q is the original quantity consumed, and I is the original money income of the consumer.[3]

Some goods have positive income elasticities, indicating that increases in the consumer's money income result in increases in the amount of the good consumed. For example, one would generally expect steak and caviar to have

---

[2] For durable goods like cars, the price elasticity of demand may be lower in the long run than in the short run. If the price of cars increases, the quantity demanded is likely to go down considerably because many potential buyers will put off purchasing a new automobile. However, with the passage of time, the quantity of cars demanded will tend to go up as old cars wear out.

[3] More precisely, the income elasticity of demand is

$$\frac{dQ}{dI} \div \frac{Q}{I}.$$

The text definition is the same except that finite differences are substituted for derivatives.

positive income elasticities. Other goods have negative income elasticities, indicating that increases in the consumer's money income result in decreases in the amount of the good consumed. For example, margarine and poor grades of vegetables and other types of food might have negative income elasticities.[4] However, one must be careful to point out that the income elasticity of demand for a good is likely to vary considerably, depending on the level of the consumer's money income. Thus, in some ranges of income, the income elasticity may be positive; in other ranges of income, it may be negative.

The concept of income elasticity of demand can be applied to an entire market as well as to a single consumer; the only change required in Equation 5.1 is that we interpret Q as the total quantity demanded in the market, I as the aggregate money income of all consumers in the market, and ΔQ and ΔI as the changes in the total quantity demanded and in the aggregate money income. As in the case of the individual consumer, it is assumed that the prices of all commodities are held constant. Figure 5.2 shows a variety of possible relationships between the total quantity demanded in the market and the aggregate money income of the consumers. In one case, the income elasticity is greater than 1; this means that a 1 percent increase in money income results in more

FIGURE 5.2 Various Types of Relationships between the Quantity Demanded and Aggregate Income The quantity demanded of a good may be related in a variety of quite different ways to aggregate income.

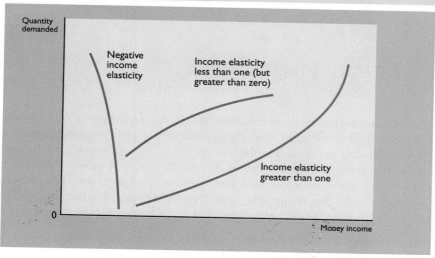

---

[4] The similarity between goods with a negative income elasticity and inferior goods should be obvious.

than a 1 percent increase in the total quantity demanded. In another case, the income elasticity is less than 1 (but greater than 0); this means that a 1 percent increase in money income results in less than a 1 percent increase in the total quantity demanded. In still another case, the income elasticity is negative, indicating that increases in aggregate money income result in decreases in the total quantity demanded.[5]

There are, of course, enormous differences among goods with respect to their income elasticity of demand. No refined statistical surveys are needed to tell us that the income elasticities of demand for high-quality food and clothes are generally higher than the income elasticities of demand for salt and Kleenex. Luxury items are generally assumed to have high income elasticities of demand. Indeed, one way to define *luxuries* and *necessities* is to say that luxuries are goods with high income elasticities of demand, and necessities are goods with low income elasticities of demand.

Luxuries and necessities

Engel's law

An empirical law of consumption, *Engel's law,* was developed in the nineteenth century by Ernst Engel (whose work was noted in Chapter 4). Based on data concerning the budgets and expenditures of a large number of families, Engel found that the income elasticity of demand for food was quite low. He concluded from this result that the proportion of its income spent on food by a country (or a family) was a good index of its welfare, with the better-off countries spending a smaller proportion on food than the poorer ones. This generalization is crude, but still serviceable within limits.[6]

CROSS ELASTICITIES OF DEMAND

In previous sections we have discussed the effects of two factors—the price of the commodity and the level of aggregate money income—on the quantity of the commodity demanded in the market. These two factors are not the only important ones; another important factor is the price of other commodities. Holding constant the commodity's own price (as well as the level of money incomes) and allowing the price of another commodity to vary, there may be important effects on the quantity demanded in the market for the commodity in

---

[5] Of course, the quantity demanded may be influenced by the distribution of money income among consumers as well as the aggregate money income. We assume that the income distribution is held constant.

[6] A number of economists, including H. Houthakker, have made excellent empirical studies of Engel's law and its validity.

question. By observing these effects, we can classify pairs of commodities as *substitutes* or *complements,* and we can measure how close the relationship (either substitute or complementary) is.

Consider two commodities, good X and good Y. Suppose that good Y's price goes up. What is the effect on the quantity of good X that is bought (per unit of time)? The *cross elasticity of demand* is defined as

Cross
elasticity
of de-
mand

$$\eta_{XY} = \frac{\Delta Q_X}{Q_X} \div \frac{\Delta P_Y}{P_Y}, \qquad [5.2]$$

where ΔP_Y is the change in the price of good Y, P_Y is the original price of good Y, ΔQ_X is the resulting change in the quantity demanded of good X, and Q_X is the original quantity demanded of good X. Thus the cross elasticity of demand is the relative change in the quantity of good X resulting from a 1 percent change in the price of good Y.[7]

Whether goods X and Y are classified as *substitutes* or *complements* depends on whether the cross elasticity of demand is positive or negative. For example, an increase in the price of lamb, when the price of pork remains constant, will tend to increase the quantity of pork demanded; thus η_{XY} is positive, and lamb and pork are classified as substitutes. On the other hand, an increase in the price of fishing licenses may tend to decrease the purchase of fishing poles when the price of fishing poles remains constant; thus η_{XY} is negative, and fishing licenses and fishing poles are classified as complements. Figure 5.3 shows the relationship between the consumption of good X and the price of good Y, given that they are substitutes or complements.

Substi-
tutes and
comple-
ments

The cross elasticity of demand looks at the change in quantity demanded that results from a change in price *without* compensating for the change in the level of real income. This is the only feasible procedure because we seldom have data concerning the indifference maps of individual consumers. Also, we are generally interested in the relationship between commodities in the whole market rather than the relationship for a particular consumer.[8]

---

[7] More precisely, the cross elasticity of demand is

$$\frac{dQ_X}{dP_Y} \div \frac{Q_X}{P_Y}.$$

Note that the definition in the text is the same except that finite differences are substituted for derivatives.

In subsequent discussions of marginal revenue, marginal product, marginal cost, and other such terms, we shall use finite differences and not bother to repeat each time the alternate definition based on the use of derivatives (since the alternative definition is obvious in each case).

[8] For a single individual, goods can be classified as substitutes or complements more accurately on the basis of his or her utility function. Good Y is a substitute (complement) for good X if the marginal rate of substitution of good Y for money is reduced (increased) when good X is substituted for money in such a way as to leave the consumer no better or worse off than before.

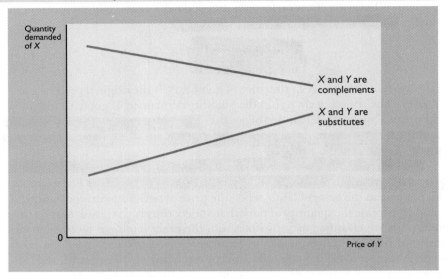

FIGURE 5.3 Relationship between the Consumption of Good *X* and the Price of Good *Y*, Given That They Are Substitutes or Complements If goods *X* and *Y* are substitutes, the quantity demanded of *X* is directly related to the price of good *Y*. If they are complements, the relationship is inverse.

Finally, one other point should be noted. Whether goods X and Y are substitutes or complements can be determined by looking at the relative change in the quantity demanded of good X divided by the relative change in the price of good Y, that is, η_{XY}. It can also be determined by looking at the relative change in the quantity demanded of good Y divided by the relative change in the price of good X, η_{YX}. However, it should not be expected that the two elasticities will have the same numerical value. For example, goods X and Y may be substitutes, but the consumption of good X may be more sensitive to changes in the price of good Y than the consumption of good Y is to price changes of good X.

THE SELLERS' SIDE OF THE MARKET AND MARGINAL REVENUE

Up to this point, we have looked at the subject of demand chiefly from the point of view of consumers. But, as we have already noted, the expenditures of

EXAMPLE 5.2

Fur Sales Take a Hit

From 1972 to 1986, retail sales of fur garments in the United States rose continually, from about $.4 billion to about $1.8 billion, after which there was no growth until 1989, when sales increased slightly to $1.9 billion. Subsequently, there was a sickening thud in the fur industry as sales dropped almost 40 percent in 1990 and almost 20 percent in 1991. As shown below, sales in 1991 were no higher than a decade before.

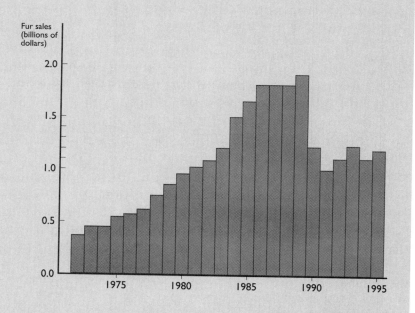

(a) In 1992, Bill Outlaw, a spokesman for the Fur Information Council of America, blamed the sales decline on the recession, saying "We're facing the same problem other luxury industries are." If the income elasticity of demand for furs was 3, how much of the decrease in fur sales in 1990 and 1991 could be attributed to changes in consumers' incomes? (Adjusted for inflation, total income increased by about 1 percent in 1990 and fell by about 1 percent in 1991.) (b) In 1990, the federal government imposed a 10 percent tax on expensive furs. If the price elasticity of demand for furs was 1.5, how much of the decrease in fur sales could be attributed to this tax? (Assume for simplicity that the tax resulted in a 10 percent price increase.) (c) Animal-rights activists claimed that, because of their efforts, the public was less interested in buying furs. Furriers, on the other hand, maintained that a more important factor was that the winters of the early 1990s were relatively mild. How might you estimate the relative importance of these factors?

SOLUTION (a) If the income elasticity of demand for furs was 3, the 1 percent increase in total income in 1990 would have increased the quantity of furs demanded by 3 percent, and the 1 percent decrease in total income in 1991 would have decreased the quantity demanded by 3 percent. (b) If the price of furs increased by 10 percent, this would have reduced the quantity demanded by about 15 percent. (Subsequently, this tax was lifted.) (c) To see how much effect the average temperature has on fur sales, you might estimate the relationship between fur sales and average temperature when price and income are held constant. On the basis of such a statistical study of historical data, you might estimate how much of a drop in fur sales, if any, would have been expected during the early 1990s because of this factor. The effects of animal-rights activists are harder to estimate, but they seem to have had some effect. For example, some leading clothes designers like Calvin Klein, Donna Karan, Giorgio Armani, and Bill Blass have announced they no longer will use furs.*

* For further discussion, see the *Philadelphia Inquirer,* June 17, 1992, and the *New York Times,* May 1, 1994. Sales data for 1992 to 1995 were obtained from the Fur Information Council.

the consumers are the receipts of the sellers. In the next three sections, we look at demand from the other side of the market—the seller's side. We begin by defining marginal revenue. Then, in the following section, we show how marginal revenue can be estimated from the demand curve. Next, we discuss the differences between the demand curve for the industry and the demand curve for the firm. Finally, we discuss the relationship between marginal revenue and the price elasticity of demand. These results are of great importance and they form a bridge to the theory of the firm, which is presented in later chapters.

Total revenue   The sellers of a commodity are interested, of course, in the total amount of money spent by consumers on the commodity. This amount is called *total revenue* by economists. From the market demand curve, one can easily determine the total revenue of the sellers at each price, since total revenue is, by definition, price times quantity. Thus, in Table 5.2, total revenue is $36 at a price of

TABLE 5.2 Quantity Demanded, Total Revenue, and Marginal Revenue

Price (dollars per unit of the commodity)	Quantity demanded (units of the commodity)	Total revenue (dollars)	Marginal revenue (dollars per unit of the commodity)
13	0	0	
12	1	12	12
11	2	22	10
10	3	30	8
9	4	36	6
8	5	40	4
7	6	42	2
6	7	42	0
5	8	40	−2
4	9	36	−4
3	10	30	−6

$9. The value of total revenue at various prices is shown in the third column of Table 5.2.

Economists and firms are also concerned with *marginal revenue,* which is defined as the addition to total revenue attributable to the addition of 1 unit to sales. Thus, if $R(q)$ is total revenue when q units are sold and $R(q - 1)$ is total revenue when $(q - 1)$ units are sold, the marginal revenue between q units and $(q - 1)$ units is $R(q) - R(q - 1)$. This is illustrated in Table 5.2. For example, when only 1 unit is sold, it is possible to charge a price of $12 and the total revenue is $12. The marginal revenue between 1 unit of output and 0 units of output is total revenue at 1 unit of output minus total revenue at 0 units of output. Since the latter is 0, the marginal revenue between 1 unit of output and 0 units of output is $12.

It is evident from Table 5.2 that total revenue from a given number of units of output — say n units — is equal to the sum of marginal revenue between 0 and 1 unit of output, marginal revenue between 1 and 2 units of output, and so on up to marginal revenue between $(n - 1)$ and n units of output. For example, total revenue for 2 units of output is $22, which equals the sum of marginal revenue between 0 and 1 unit of output ($12) and marginal revenue between 1 and 2 units of output ($10). It is easy to prove that this will always be true. By the definition of marginal revenue, the sum of the marginal revenue between 0 and 1 unit of output, 1 and 2 units of output, and so on up to $(n - 1)$ and n units of output is

$$[R(1) - R(0)] + [R(2) - R(1)] + [R3) - R(2)] + \cdots + [R(n) - R(n - 1)].$$

Since $R(1), R(2), \ldots, R(n - 1)$ appear with both positive and negative signs, they cancel out; and since $R(0) = 0$, this sum must equal $R(n)$.

Marginal revenue

Marginal revenue curve

The *marginal revenue curve* shows marginal revenue at various levels of output of a commodity. For example, panel A of Figure 5.4 shows the marginal revenue curve for the situation in Table 5.2. Note that the marginal revenue curve lies above zero when total revenue is increasing, that it lies below zero when total revenue is decreasing, and that it equals zero when total revenue is at a maximum. For example, in panel A of Figure 5.4, the marginal revenue curve is zero between 6 and 7 units of output, and inspection of Table 5.2 confirms that they are the output levels where total revenue is maximized. Also, marginal revenue is shown to be positive for output levels of less than 6 units and negative for output levels of greater than 7 units; inspection of Table 5.2 confirms that total revenue is increasing up to 6 units of output and is decreasing beyond 7 units of output.

The marginal revenue curve consists of a number of "steps" when the demand curve is defined for only a relatively few points. For example, this is the case in panel A of Figure 5.4. However, as the demand curve is defined for more and more points, the "teeth" of the saw-toothed marginal revenue curve become finer and finer. For example, they are finer in panel B than in panel A.

FIGURE 5.4 Demand and Marginal Revenue Curves As the demand curve is defined for more and more points, the "teeth" of the saw-toothed marginal revenue curve become finer and finer. When the demand curve is continuous, so is the marginal revenue curve.

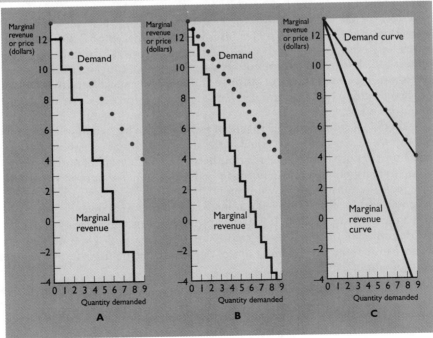

Finally, when the demand curve is continuous, as in panel C, the marginal revenue curve becomes continuous, too.[9]

INDUSTRY AND FIRM DEMAND CURVES

Throughout this chapter we have been concerned with the market demand curve for a commodity. It is important to distinguish between the market demand curve for a commodity and the market demand curve for the output of a single firm producing the commodity. Of course, if only one firm produces the commodity (in which case the industry in question is a *monopoly*), there is no difference between these demand curves. But if there is more than one firm producing the commodity, as is usually the case, the demand curve for the output of each firm will generally be quite different from the demand curve for the commodity. In particular, the firm's demand curve will generally be more price elastic than that facing the industry as a whole, since the products of other firms are close substitutes for the products of any one firm.

Suppose that there are a great many sellers of the product in question, say 50,000 sellers of the same size, and that the conditions in the industry are close to *perfectly competitive*. (In perfect competition, the number of firms is large and their products are homogeneous, and for simplicity it is assumed that the firms have full knowledge of the market. Much more will be said about perfect competition in subsequent chapters.) In a case of this sort, if any one firm were to triple its output and sales, the total industry output would increase by only 0.004 percent. Since this change in total output is too small to have any noticeable effect on the price of the commodity, each seller can act as if variations in its own output will have no real effect on market price. Put differently, it ap-

Perfectly competitive firm's demand curve

---

[9] Let the demand curve be

$$P = a - bQ.$$

Then the total revenue curve is

$$R = PQ = aQ - bQ^2,$$

and the marginal revenue curve is

$$\frac{dR}{dQ} = \frac{d(PQ)}{dQ} = a - 2bQ.$$

Thus the marginal revenue curve is a straight line and it has the same intercept on the y axis (that is, a) as the demand curve. (P is price, and Q is quantity demanded.)

FIGURE 5.5 Demand Curve for the Output of a Firm in a Perfectly Competitive Industry For a firm in a perfectly competitive industry, the demand curve is horizontal.

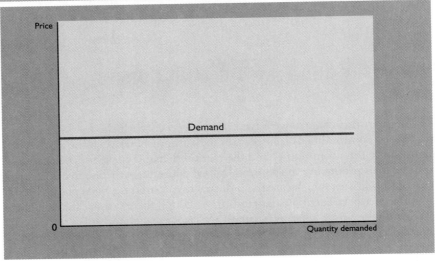

pears to each firm that it can sell all it wants —within the range that is within its capabilities —without influencing the price. Thus the demand curve facing the individual firm in perfect competition is *horizontal.*

The firm in a perfectly competitive market can increase its sales rate without shading its price to get the extra business. Its demand curve, shown in Figure 5.5, is infinitely elastic: A very small decrease in price would result in an indefinitely large increase in the quantity it could sell, and a very small increase in price would result in its selling nothing. Moreover, since price remains constant, each additional unit sold increases total revenue by the amount of the price, the consequence being that price and marginal revenue are always equal. Thus, in the case of perfect competition, the demand curve facing a particular firm and the marginal revenue curve facing that firm are one and the same.

In a situation where the industry is not perfectly competitive, the demand curve for the output of a particular firm will not be horizontal, but it is likely to be more elastic than the demand curve for the commodity. If competition is not perfect, marginal revenue will not equal price, as it does in perfect competition. Instead, it will be less than price because demand is less than infinitely elastic.

Finally, it is important to note that marginal revenue at a certain output level is related in the following way to price and the price elasticity of demand

EXAMPLE 5.3

Animal Experiments and the Theory of Demand

Experimental psychologists like B. F. Skinner have long studied the behavior of rats and other animals. During the early 1980s, some microeconomists began to carry out similar sorts of research. In one well-known experiment, white rats were put in cages containing levers to activate dipper cups. When its lever was pushed down by a rat, one dipper cup provided a certain amount of collins mix; the other provided a certain amount of root beer. A rat was allotted a fixed "income" of so many pushes per day on the levers, and the experimental economists established the "price" per unit of collins mix and root beer as the number of pushes the rat had to "spend" to procure a unit.

(a) One rat was given an income of 300 pushes per day, and both liquids were priced at 20 pushes per day, with the result that the rat drank about 11 units of root beer and about 4 units of collins mix per day. Then the experimenters increased the price of root beer to 40 pushes and reduced the price of collins mix to 10 pushes, while adjusting the rat's income so that it could purchase its old "market basket" if it wanted. Did this mean that the rat's budget line was unchanged? (b) After the changes in prices and income described in part (a), the rat changed its "market basket" to 17 units of collins mix and 8 units of root beer per day. Was this in accord with the theory of consumer behavior? (c) In another experiment, a rat was able to obtain either standard laboratory food or water by pushing down the levers. No alternative food or liquid was available. Based on the rat's behavior when the "prices" of food and water were varied, its price elasticity of demand for food was 0.20. Why is this price elasticity so low? (d) In the same experiment, the cross elasticities of demand were:

Commodity	Cross elasticity of demand (percentage change in quantity demanded of this good due to a 1 percent change in the price of the other good)
Food	−0.55
Water	−0.32

Why are the cross elasticities of demand negative?

SOLUTION   (a) No. The slope of the budget line is −1 times the price ratio. When both liquids were priced at 20 pushes per day, the slope was –1. After the price changes, the ratio of the price of root beer to the price of collins mix was 4; thus, the slope was –4. Since its slope changed, it is obvious that the budget line must have changed. (b) Yes. Since root beer became more expensive relative to collins mix, one would expect anyone (rat or human being) to reduce the consumption of root beer and to increase the consumption of collins mix. (c) Goods that have few good substitutes tend to have low price elasticities of demand. There obviously are few, if any, good substitutes for food. (d) Food and water are complements because there are physiological limits on the amount that animals can increase their food consumption without increasing their fluid intake.*

* For further discussion, see J. Kagel, R. Battalio, H. Rachlin, and L. Green, "Demand Curves for Animal Consumers," *Quarterly Journal of Economics,* February 1981, and J. Kagel, R. Battalio, H. Rachlin, L. Green, R. Basmann, and W. Klemm, "Experimental Studies of Consumer Demand Behavior," *Economic Inquiry,* March 1975.

at that output level:

$$MR = P\left(1 - \frac{1}{\eta}\right), \tag{5.3}$$

where *MR* is marginal revenue, *P* is price, and η is the price elasticity of demand.[10] For example, if the price of a good is $10 and if its price elasticity of demand is 2, marginal revenue equals $10[1 − 1/2] = $5. Equation 5.3 is a very famous result which will be discussed further in subsequent chapters.

---

[10] Let *P* be price and *Q* be quantity demanded. If the demand curve is $P = f(Q)$, marginal revenue is

$$MR = \frac{d(PQ)}{dQ} = f(Q) + Q\frac{df(Q)}{dQ} = P + Q\frac{dP}{dQ}.$$

Thus marginal revenue must be less than price as long as $dP/dQ < 0$. It follows from this equation that

$$MR = P\left(1 + \frac{QdP}{PdQ}\right)$$

$$= P\left(1 - \frac{1}{\eta}\right).$$

MEASUREMENT OF DEMAND CURVES

The market demand curve plays a very important role in microeconomics, and there have been literally hundreds of published studies — and many more unpublished ones — that attempt to measure the market demand curves for particular commodities. This section describes briefly various ways in which such empirical studies have been carried out. The following two sections provide examples of the ways in which the results of such studies have been used to help solve important practical problems.

One technique that is frequently used to estimate the demand curve for a particular commodity is the direct market experiment. The idea is to vary the price of the product while attempting to keep other market conditions fairly stable (or to take changes in other market conditions into account). For example, the Parker Pen Company conducted an experiment some years ago to determine the price elasticity of demand for its product Quink. They raised the price from 15 cents to 25 cents in four cities and found that demand was quite inelastic. Also, in some stores, the old package selling at 15 cents was put next to a package marked "New Quink, 25 cents"; the heavy sales of New Quink also indicated that demand was quite inelastic. Attempts were made to estimate the cross elasticity of demand with other brands as well. *Market experiments*

Another technique that is sometimes employed is to interview consumers and administer questionnaires concerning their buying habits, motives, and intentions. Unfortunately, the direct approach of simply asking people how much they would buy of a particular commodity at particular prices does not seem to work very well in most cases. The snap judgments of consumers in response to such a hypothetical question do not seem to be very accurate. However, more subtle approaches can be of value. For example, interviews carried out at Campbell Soup led it to introduce a new line of low-salt soups. And interviews carried out by a maker of baby food indicated that most buyers of its product selected it on their doctor's recommendation, and that most of them knew very little about prices or substitutes. This information, together with other data, led the manufacturer to the conclusion that the price elasticity of demand was quite low. *Consumer interviews*

Still another very popular technique is the use of statistical methods to extract information from data regarding sales, prices, incomes, and other variables in the past. Basically, what is involved is a comparison of various points in time or various sectors of the market; the point of this comparison is to see what effect the observed variation in price, income, and other relevant variables, had on the quantity demanded. For example, to estimate the price elasticity of demand, one might plot the quantity demanded in 1997 versus the 1997 price, the quantity demanded in 1996 versus the 1996 price, and so on. If *Statistical techniques*

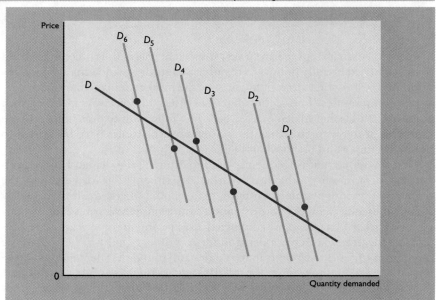

FIGURE 5.6 Illustration of Identification Problem The estimated demand curve *D* is a hybrid that resembles none of the true demand curves ($D_1, \ldots, D_6$).

the results were as shown by the points in Figure 5.6, one might construct a curve like *D* as an estimate of the demand curve.

Although this example provides some understanding of the type of analysis that is involved, it makes the naive assumption that the demand curve has remained constant over the period. Suppose that the 1997 demand curve was D_1, that the 1996 demand curve was D_2, and so on. Then the estimated demand curve *D* is a hybrid that resembles none of the true demand curves. Sophisticated econometric techniques have been developed for dealing with this so-called *identification problem.* Econometric techniques have also been devised to measure at the same time the effect of money income and the prices of other commodities on the quantity demanded; thus estimates can be made of the relationship between a commodity's price and the quantity demanded when these other factors are held constant. However, even an elementary description of these econometric techniques lies outside the scope of this book.[11]

---

[11] For a description of these techniques, see J. Johnston, *Econometric Methods* (3d ed.; New York: McGraw-Hill, 1984); J. Kmenta, *Elements of Econometrics* (2d ed.; New York: Macmillan Co., 1986); or E. Berndt, *The Practice of Econometrics* (Reading, Mass.: Addison-Wesley, 1991).

TABLE 5.3 Estimated Price Elasticity of Demand for Selected Commodities, United States

Commodity	Price elasticity	Commodity	Price elasticity
Electricity	1.20	Potatoes	0.31
Beef	0.92	Oats	0.56
Women's hats	3.00	Barley	0.39
Sugar	0.31	Buckwheat	0.99
Corn	0.49	Haddock	2.20
Cotton	0.12	Tires	1.20
Wheat	0.08	Movies	3.70

SOURCES: H. Schultz, *Theory and Measurement of Demand,* (Chicago: University of Chicago Press, 1938); M. Spencer and L. Siegelman, *Managerial Economics* (Homewood, Ill.: Irwin, 1959); F. Bell, "The Pope and the Price of Fish," *American Economic Review,* December 1968; L. Taylor, "The Demand for Electricity: A Survey," *Bell Journal of Economics,* Spring 1975; and H. Houthakker and L. Taylor, *Consumer Demand in the United States* (Cambridge, Mass.: Harvard University Press, 1970).

TABLE 5.4 Estimated Cross Elasticities of Demand for Selected Commodities

Commodity	Cross elasticity with respect to price of:	Cross elasticity
Beef	Pork	+0.28
Butter	Margarine	+0.67
Margarine	Butter	+0.81
Pork	Beef	+0.14
Electricity	Natural gas	+0.20
Natural gas	Fuel oil	+0.44

SOURCE: Wold, *Demand Analysis;* R. Halvorsen, "Energy Substitution in U.S. Manufacturing," *Review of Economics and Statistics,* November 1977.

TABLE 5.5 Estimated Income Elasticities of Demand for Selected Commodities

Commodity	Income elasticity	Commodity	Income elasticity
Butter	0.42	Meat	0.35
Cheese	0.34	Milk	0.07
Cream	0.56	Restaurant	
Eggs	0.37	consumption	1.48
Fruits and berries	0.70	Tobacco	1.02
Flour	−0.36	Haddock	0.46
Electricity	0.20	Dentists' services	1.41
Liquor	1.00	Furniture	1.48
Margarine	−0.20	Books	1.44

SOURCES: Wold, *Demand Analysis,* p. 265; Bell, "The Pope and the Price of Fish"; Houthakker and Taylor, *Consumer Demand in the United States;* and Taylor, "The Demand for Electricity."

Each of the approaches to the measurement of demand curves has its disadvantages. Direct experimentation can be expensive or risky because customers may be lost and profits cut by the experiment. Also, since they are seldom really controlled experiments and since they are often of relatively brief duration and the number of observations is small, experiments often cannot produce all the information that is needed. Interviews and questionnaires suffer from a great many disadvantages, some of which are noted above. So do consumer clinics where consumers are placed in simulated market conditions and changes in their behavior are observed as the conditions of the experiment are changed; consumer clinics are expensive and they cannot avoid the distortion due to the consumers' realizing that they are in an experimental situation.[12]

The difficulties involved in the application of statistical and econometric techniques are also very considerable. Unreliable and biased results can be obtained if important variables are unwittingly (or wittingly) omitted from the analysis. If some of the variables influencing the quantity demanded are highly correlated among themselves, it may not be possible to obtain reliable estimates of the separate effects of each of them. Also, the demand function is likely to be only one of a number of equations that connect the relevant variables, and it may be difficult to unscramble these equations adequately from the available statistics.

There are no easy remedies for these problems. Nevertheless, these problems, although sometimes formidable, are not insolvable. Many interesting and important studies have been made of the demand curves for particular commodities. And many interesting estimates have been made of the price elasticity, the income elasticity, and the cross elasticity of demand of various commodities. A sample of the results is presented in Tables 5.3, 5.4, and 5.5 (on the preceding page). The reader should study these tables carefully.

APPLICATIONS

Free Public Transit

The concepts of price elasticity, income elasticity, and cross elasticity of demand have many practical uses. For example, consider the proposals that have

---

[12] W. Baumol, "The Empirical Determination of Demand Relationships," reprinted in Mansfield, *Microeconomics: Selected Readings,* 5th ed.

been made to provide free public transit service in our metropolitan areas. Proponents of free public transit point out that there is considerable concern in our cities over traffic congestion, and they argue that, if public transit were free, many commuters would use public transit rather than their cars, alleviating traffic problems, decreasing air pollution, and reducing the demand for parking facilities.

Whether public transit should be free is an important and complex issue of public policy. To evaluate this proposal, decision makers have to consider a host of questions, including how the public transit agencies would be financed in the absence of fares. Two of the most fundamental questions are: To what extent would free transit fares increase the use of public transit? To what extent would it reduce the use of automobiles in the city? Clearly, these questions must be answered if one is to forecast the consequences of free public transit.

Faced with these questions, the U.S. Department of Transportation asked a team of economists at Charles River Associates to study them.[13] With respect to the effect of free fares on the use of public transit, the economists pointed out that the answer depends on the price elasticity of demand for public transit service. If this price elasticity is high, the reduction of the price of public transit from its current level to zero will result in a considerable increase in the number of trips made on public transit. On the other hand, if it is very low, such a price reduction will result in little increase in the number of such trips. In fact, according to estimates made by the economists, this price elasticity is about 0.17. Thus free transit fares would result in about a 40 percent increase in the number of trips made on public transit.[14]

With respect to the effects of free public transit on the use of automobiles in the city, the economists pointed out that the answer depends on the cross elasticity of demand for auto travel (in the city) with respect to transit fares. This cross elasticity is positive because auto travel and public transit are substitutes. If this cross elasticity is high, the reduction of transit fares to zero will result in a considerable drop in the use of autos in the city. On the other hand, if this cross elasticity is low, such a fare reduction would have little effect on the num-

---

[13] T. Domencich and G. Kraft, *Free Transit* (Lexington, Mass.: Heath, 1970).

[14] To obtain this figure, note that it follows from Equation 1.2 that, if P_2 equals zero (and thus if $\Delta P = P_2 - P_1 = -P_1$),

$$\eta = \frac{\Delta Q_D}{(Q_{D1} + Q_{D2})}$$

$$= \frac{Q_{D2}/Q_{D1} - 1}{(1 + Q_{D2}/Q_{D1})}.$$

Thus $Q_{D2}/Q_{D1} = (1 + \eta) \div (1 - \eta)$. Since η is approximately 0.17, Q_{D2}/Q_{D1} is approximately $(1 + .17) \div (1 - .17) = 1.41$.

The elasticity figure used here pertains to work travel. For a more complete discussion, see ibid.

ber of auto trips in the city. In fact, according to the economists' estimates, the value of this cross elasticity is such that free transit would reduce auto trips in the city by only about 7 percent.[15]

These results have been of use to federal, local, and other officials, as well as to other groups, in their treatment of this important issue. Based on these results, it appears that free transit would not stimulate huge increases in transit usage, and "that it will be very difficult to divert auto travelers to transit by lowering fares. . . ."[16] Although these facts alone cannot resolve the issue, they certainly are of great relevance. Without question, the concepts of the price elasticity and cross elasticity of demand have played an important role in illuminating this major policy issue.

Not a Cough in a Carload?

The concepts discussed in this chapter are obviously of fundamental importance in the formulation of business policy, as well as public policy. To illustrate the use of the concept of price elasticity by business, let's consider the U.S. cigarette industry, which has been dominated by six firms (Reynolds, Philip Morris, Brown and Williamson, American Brands, Lorrilard, and Liggett). In its home market, this industry has been on the defensive in recent decades because of warnings by the Surgeon General (and others) that cigarette smoking is hazardous to human health. Since January 1, 1971, there has been a ban on cigarette advertising on radio and television in the United States. In June 1992, the Supreme Court opened the door for damage suits by smokers against the cigarette industry.

Despite the attacks by physicians and others on cigarette smoking, the price of cigarettes has gone up at a spectacular rate. During the 1980s and early 1990s, no major item purchased by U.S. consumers experienced as rapid a price increase. According to Patrick Jackman of the Bureau of Labor Statistics, "Like clockwork, the industry raises prices twice a year, in the November–December period and in May–June."[17] In 1991, cigarettes averaged $1.74 per pack, up from $.63 in 1980. (On the average, a smoker puffs 19.1 cigarettes, just under a pack, a day.) These price increases have resulted in handsome profits for the cigarette companies. For example, about two-thirds of Philip Morris's profits have stemmed from cigarettes; only about one-third has come from its food and beer products.

Why were cigarette firms able to get away with such hefty price increases? The answer lies in the low price elasticity of demand for cigarettes—about 0.3 or 0.4, according to many studies. Whereas big price increases would be a big

---

[15] Ibid., p. 102.

[16] Ibid., p. 98.

[17] *New York Times,* July 30, 1991, and May 22, 1992.

mistake in many industries, since the quantity demanded would plummet, this is not the case in the cigarette industry. A 10 percent increase in cigarette prices is likely to reduce the quantity demanded by only 3 or 4 percent; this reflects the fact that many consumers find it difficult to kick the smoking habit. Knowing this, the cigarette industry raised its prices without having to worry about a mass exodus of its customers.

But in accord with our discussion on page 147, the price elasticity of demand for the cigarettes produced by a particular firm is likely to exceed the price elasticity of demand for cigarettes as a whole. On April 3, 1993, Philip Morris cut the price of its Marlboro cigarettes, the world's most popular brand, from about $2.20 to $1.80 per pack. This unexpected price reduction, which was front-page news, was due to a fall in Marlboro's market share from 24.3 to 22.2 percent, as smokers shifted their purchases toward discount and generic brands costing as little as $.89 per pack. Philip Morris initiated this 20 percent price cut to stem the movement of consumers away from Marlboro (which has been described as the world's best-selling consumer product[18]). A few weeks later, Reynolds announced comparable price reductions for its leading premium brands, Winston and Camel. The upward march of cigarette prices seemed to be over, at least temporarily.

SUMMARY

1. The market demand curve for a commodity is simply the horizontal summation of the individual demand curves of all the consumers in the market. Since individual demand curves almost always slope downward to the right, it follows that market demand curves will do so, too.
2. The price elasticity of demand for a commodity depends on the number and closeness of substitutes that are available. If a commodity has many close substitutes, its demand is likely to be elastic. The extent to which a commodity has close substitutes depends on how narrowly it is defined.
3. The income elasticity of demand is the percentage change in quantity demanded resulting from a 1 percent change in money income. Commodities differ greatly in their income elasticities. Goods that people regard as luxuries are generally assumed to have high income elasticities of demand. Indeed, one way to define luxuries and necessities is to say that

---

[18] *New York Times,* April 3, 1993.

luxuries are goods with high income elasticities of demand, and necessities are goods with low income elasticities of demand.

4. The cross elasticity of demand is the relative change in the quantity demanded of good X divided by the relative change in the price of good Y. Whether commodities are classified as substitutes or complements depends on whether the cross elasticity is positive or negative.

5. Marginal revenue is the addition to total revenue attributable to the addition of the last unit of sales. Obviously, total revenue from *n* units of output is equal to the sum of marginal revenue in the intervals between 0 and 1 unit of output, 1 and 2 units of output, and so on up to $(n - 1)$ to *n* units of output.

6. It is important to distinguish between the market demand curve for a commodity and the market demand curve for the output of a single firm producing the commodity. In a perfectly competitive industry, the firm's demand curve will be horizontal. If the industry contains more than one firm but is not perfectly competitive, the firm's demand curve will not be horizontal, but it is likely to be more elastic than the demand curve for the commodity.

7. One technique used to estimate the market demand curve is direct market experimentation. Another technique is to interview consumers and administer questionnaires concerning their habits, motives, and intentions. Still another technique is the use of statistical and econometric techniques to extract information from data regarding sales, prices, incomes, and other variables in the past.

8. Each of these approaches has its disadvantages, and there is no easy remedy to the estimation problem. Nevertheless, the difficulties generally are not insurmountable. Many interesting and important estimates have been made of the demand curves for various goods.

QUESTIONS/PROBLEMS

1. D. Chapman, T. Tyrell, and T. Mount estimated that the long-run price elasticity of demand for electricity by all U.S. residential consumers is 1.2, that the income elasticity of demand for electricity by such consumers is 0.2, and that the cross elasticity of demand for electricity with respect to the price of natural gas is 0.2. (a) If the price of electricity is expected to rise by 1 percent in the long run, by how much would the price of natural gas have to change to offset the effect of this increase in electricity's price on the

quantity of electricity consumed? (b) Among residential consumers in a Chicago suburb, holding other factors constant, there was the following relationship between their aggregate money income and the amount of electricity they consumed:

Aggregate income (millions of dollars)	Quantity of electricity consumed
100	300
110	303
121	306

Is this evidence consistent with the results presented by Chapman, Tyrell, and Mount? If not, what factors might account for the discrepancy? (c) Would you expect the income elasticity of demand and the cross elasticity of demand to be higher or lower in the short run than in the long run? Why?

2. A business analyst who works for a New York investment firm tells her clients that the demand curve for videocassette recorders has shifted to the right, and that at the same time the price elasticity of demand for videocassette recorders has increased from 3 to 4. Is this possible? Can the new demand curve be entirely above and to the right of the old demand curve if the new price elasticity is 4 whereas the old price elasticity was 3?

3. The steel industry has long maintained that the demand for steel is price inelastic. According to a well-known study by T. Yntema, the price elasticity of demand for steel is no more than 0.4. (a) Are there any major substitutes for steel? If so, what are some of them? (b) Some years ago the chief executive officer of Bethlehem Steel testified before a Senate committee that the price elasticity of demand for steel was much less than 1. If so, can we deduce that the demand for Bethlehem's steel is price inelastic? (c) If the demand for Bethlehem's steel is inelastic at the price it is charging, is it maximizing its profits? (d) Is the cross elasticity of demand between Bethlehem's steel and imported Japanese steel positive or negative? Why?

4. The cross elasticity of demand can be used to determine which products belong to the same market. For example, in a famous antitrust case, the U.S. Department of Justice brought suit against the Du Pont Company for having monopolized the sale of cellophane. In its defense, Du Pont claimed that cellophane had many close substitutes, such as aluminum foil, waxed paper, and polyethylene. Can you guess how Du Pont used cross elasticities of demand in this case? (Incidentally, the Supreme Court accepted Du Pont's argument in its landmark decision handed down in 1953.)

5. Suppose that a consumer considers Geritol of supreme importance and that he spends all his income on Geritol. To this consumer, what is the

price elasticity of demand for Geritol? What is the income elasticity of demand for Geritol? What is the cross elasticity of demand between Geritol and any other good?

6. In the aluminum industry, is the demand curve for the output of each firm horizontal? (Why or why not?) Is it less elastic than the demand curve for aluminum as a whole? (Why or why not?) Is the price of aluminum less than, equal to, or greater than marginal revenue?

7. Which of the following are likely to have a positive cross elasticity of demand: (a) automobiles and oil, (b) graphite tennis rackets and aluminum tennis rackets, (c) gin and tonic, (d) fishing poles and fishing licenses, (e) a Harvard education and a Stanford education?

8. The demand for refined sugar in the United States has declined greatly since 1975, due in part to reports that it causes tooth decay, reduces the nutritional value of the diet, and leads to obesity. Given that per capita consumption of refined sugar has declined, can we be sure that the price elasticity of demand for refined sugar is (a) less than 1, (b) greater than 1, (c) greater than 0?

9. Suppose the mayor of New York asked you to advise him concerning the proper fare that should be charged by the New York City subway. How might information concerning the price elasticity of demand be useful?

10. According to the Senate Subcommittee on Antitrust and Monopoly, the income elasticity of demand for automobiles in the United States is between 2.5 and 3.9. What does this mean? If incomes rise by 5 percent, what effect will this have on the quantity of autos demanded? How might this fact be used by General Motors?

11. Suppose you are a trustee of a major university. At a meeting of the board of trustees, one university official argues that the demand for places at this university is completely inelastic. As evidence, he cites the fact that, although the university has doubled its tuition in the last decade, there has been no appreciable decrease in the number of students enrolled. Do you agree? Comment on his argument.

12. According to William Baumol, "Some mail-order houses have employed systematic programs in which a few experimental pages were bound inconspicuously into the catalogues distributed to customers within restricted geographical regions, thus permitting observation of the effects of price, product, or even catalogue display variations." Comment on the accuracy of this technique. What might be some of the problems in estimating a product's price elasticity of demand in this way? What techniques might be better than this one?

13. Show that, if the Engel curve for a good is a straight line through the origin, the income elasticity of demand for the good is 1.

14. E. Lewit and D. Coate estimated the price elasticity of demand for cigarettes among adults to be about 0.42 and the income elasticity to be about

0.08. (a) Among adults in a Texas community, holding other factors constant, there is the following relationship between their aggregate money income and the amount of cigarettes they consume:

Aggregate income (millions of dollars)	Quantity of cigarettes consumed
100	1,000
110	1,001
121	1,002

Is this evidence consistent with the results presented by Lewit and Coate? (b) Does your answer to part (a) depend on the units in which the quantity of cigarettes consumed is measured in the table above? (c) During 1967 to 1970, the Federal Communications Commission required that one anti-smoking television commercial be aired for every four prosmoking advertisements, under the Fairness Doctrine. What effect did this have on the demand curve for cigarettes? (d) Would you expect changes in price to have as much effect on how many cigarettes existing smokers consume as on whether people begin to smoke?

15. Studies by John DiNardo of the University of California at Irvine, Thomas Lemieux of Princeton University, and Karen Model of Harvard University indicate that for teenagers, alcohol and marijuana are substitutes. Does this imply that tough marijuana enforcement is likely to increase teenage drinking?

Applying Microeconomic Theory: The Case of Black Gold

INTRODUCTION

Oil is often called black gold, and for good reason, since countries and companies possessing oil have been propelled into enormous wealth and power. Saudi Arabia, Iran, Iraq, and other oil-rich countries have in recent decades become significant players on the world stage. Judged in purely economic terms, oil is of central importance to the industrial economies of the world. As shown in Table 6.1, oil is the source of over 40 percent of the energy consumed in the United States; it far outdistances natural gas, coal, nuclear power, or hydroelectric power. One of the most significant products made from crude oil is gasoline, which powers the bulk of the world's automobiles. Other important

Year	Petroleum	Natural gas	Coal	Nuclear	Hydro and others	Total
1974	46.1	30.0	17.5	1.8	4.6	100.0
1976	47.3	27.4	18.3	2.8	4.2	100.0
1978	48.6	25.6	17.6	3.9	4.3	100.0
1980	45.0	26.9	20.3	3.6	4.2	100.0
1982	42.7	26.1	21.6	4.4	5.2	100.0
1984	41.9	25.0	23.0	4.8	5.3	100.0
1986	43.4	22.5	23.3	6.0	4.8	100.0
1988	42.7	23.1	23.5	7.1	3.6	100.0
1990	41.2	23.8	23.5	7.6	3.9	100.0

TABLE 6.1 Percent of U.S. Energy Consumption by Energy Source, 1974–1990

SOURCE: R. Beck, *Oil Industry Outlook* (Tulsa, Okla.: Penn Well, 1991).

products made from it are heating oil, diesel fuel, jet fuel, and a host of petro-chemicals.

In the United States, oil production dates back to Edwin Drake's well at Titusville, Pennsylvania, in 1859. Before World War II, a notable development was the discovery of the East Texas field, described below. The oil industry is composed of firms involved in exploring for oil, drilling oil wells, transporting oil to refineries, refining oil, and transporting and marketing the refined oil products to millions of farflung consumers. But the most visible of these firms are the huge multinational oil firms like Exxon, Phillips, ARCO, Sohio (now part of British Petroleum), and a variety of others taken up in this case.

During the past 20 years, the world has witnessed one oil crisis after another. This chapter presents ten multipart problems that analyze selected aspects of many of these crises. To provide the background information required to understand and do these problems, we begin with a very brief thumbnail sketch of some major developments in the oil industry, beginning in 1930.

OIL EXPLORATION AND THE PRICE OF OIL

On October 4, 1930, the headline of the *Henderson (Texas) Daily News* was, "Joiner's Wildcat a Gusher." Columbus ("Dad") Joiner, a threadbare promoter who drilled a well on an East Texas farm, had found the great East Texas oil field, a reservoir of oil 45 miles long and 5 to 10 miles wide. Most geologists had rejected the idea that there was oil in East Texas, but Doc Lloyd, a bogus geologist, had sold Joiner on the idea, and although his geological description of

the East Texas region was quackery, the amazing fact was that he specified exactly where Joiner should drill. The result was the discovery of what was then the biggest oil field in the United States.[1]

In early 1930, the price of crude oil was about a dollar a barrel. About 6 months after the discovery of the East Texas field, the price was as low as 15 cents a barrel. The slogan in the oil states like Texas and Oklahoma became "A dollar a barrel," which is the price the oil producers in these states wanted to restore.[2] On August 17, 1931, Texas Governor Ross Sterling, a founder of the Humble Oil Company, stated that East Texas was in "open rebellion" and sent Texas Rangers and the National Guard to shut down oil production there, which they did.

Eventually, the Texas Railroad Commission (with help from other states and the federal government) controlled production levels for oil by limiting the number of days that oil wells could produce. For example, the number of days of permitted production was 261 in 1952, but fell to 194 in 1954 (a recession year).[3] One of the reasons given for these limitations was that they promoted the conservation of oil and the adoption of less-wasteful rates of production from oil wells, but it was undeniable that they also had the effect, not unforeseen by the powerful oil industry and its allies and dependents, of pushing up the price of oil. The central point to recognize is that, although the U.S. price of oil was not fixed directly by government (federal or state), the

---

[1] D. Yergin, *The Prize* (New York: Simon & Schuster, 1991), p. 665.

[2] Ibid.

[3] J. Blair, *The Control of Oil* (New York: Pantheons, 1976), p. 165.

commission's control over production levels resulted in substantial indirect control over price.

THE WORLD OIL MARKET AND THE CRISIS OF 1973

Even during the 1930s, when the East Texas field was discovered, the market for crude oil was a world market, not just a U.S. market. And that is certainly true today. On the supply side, the Middle East is now the leading region for crude-oil production, with Saudi Arabia, Iran, the United Arab Emirates, Iraq, and Kuwait being particularly important. Other noteworthy oil producers are Russia, the United States, Canada, China, Indonesia, Mexico, Nigeria, the United Kingdom, and Venezuela. On the demand side, all the major industrial countries have a great thirst for oil, which has come to provide over 40 percent of the world's energy, up from about 10 percent in 1925.[4]

The big oil firms (often called the Seven Sisters)—Exxon, Mobil, Chevron, Texaco, Gulf (now part of Chevron), Shell, and British Petroleum—played a major role in oil exploration and production in the Middle East and many other parts of the world for decades. Inevitably, there were tensions between them and the countries where the oil was located over the division of revenues. During the 1970s and 1980s, many of those countries nationalized their foreign-dominated oil industries. For example, Exxon's operations in Venezuela and British Petroleum's operations in Kuwait, Iraq, Libya, and Nigeria were nationalized.

---

[4] J. Griffin and H. Steele, *Energy Economics and Policy* (New York: Academic Press, 1980).

The Organization of Petroleum Exporting Countries (OPEC), now a group of 12 major oil-producing countries including Saudi Arabia, Iran, Venezuela, and Libya, was formed in 1960. In late 1973 and 1974, in an effort to punish Israel's allies in its war with Egypt and Syria and to increase their own revenues, OPEC's members cut back their oil production and thus fired a still-famous shot heard around the oil-using world. The result was a huge increase in the price of oil; Saudi oil went from $2.48 a barrel in 1972 to $11.25 in 1974 (Table 6.2). It is no exaggeration to say that the world was stunned by this bold (and from a petroleum consumer's perspective, unwelcome) move.

TABLE 6.2 U.S. and Saudi Crude-Oil Prices, 1970–1991, in Current and 1982 Dollars

Year	Average U.S. Price		Saudi Price[a]	
	Current dollars per barrel	1982 dollars per barrel	Current dollars per barrel	1982 dollars per barrel
1970	3.18	8.62	1.80	4.88
1971	3.39	8.90	2.18	5.72
1972	3.39	8.52	2.48	6.23
1973	3.89	8.64	5.12	11.38
1974	6.74	12.60	11.25	21.03
1975	7.56	12.95	12.38	21.20
1976	8.14	13.32	12.38	20.26
1977	8.57	13.20	13.66	21.05
1978	8.96	12.82	13.66	19.54
1979	12.51	15.90	14.34[b]	18.22[b]
1980	21.59	24.04	27.00	30.07
1981	31.77	32.42	33.00	33.67
1982	28.52	28.52	34.00	34.00
1983	26.19	25.85	29.00	28.63
1984	25.88	24.94	28.00	27.00
1985	24.09	23.34	28.00	27.13
1986	12.51	12.49	17.52	17.49
1987	15.40	14.98	—	—
1988	12.58	11.77	—	—
1989	15.86	14.14	—	—
1990	20.03	17.22	—	—
1991	16.50	14.16	—	—

[a]Posted price of Saudi Arab Light oil for 1970 to 1979 and official government selling price for 1980 to 1986.

[b]These figures do not reflect the price increases in 1979.

SOURCE: *Basic Petroleum Data Book* (Washington, D.C.: American Petroleum Institute, 1992).

Faced with the quadrupling of the world oil price, the U.S. government decided to keep the price of domestically produced crude oil below the world level. In early 1974, for example, the average price of domestic oil was about $7 per barrel, well under the world price of over $11. Some members of the Nixon Administration—for example, William Simon, then head of the Federal Energy Office—seemed to favor decontrolling the U.S. price of oil and letting it rise to the world level. But the general feeling was that this would exacerbate inflationary pressures, hurt consumers, and be regarded as a windfall benefit to the big oil companies.[5]

In 1974, U.S. motorists wanted to purchase more gasoline than was available at existing prices, the result being that some form of rationing had to be adopted. Economists within the Nixon Administration such as Herbert Stein, chairman of the Council of Economic Advisers, were opposed to the issuance of ration coupons (like those used in World War II).[6] As it turned out, the rationing system that developed was based on how long people were willing to wait at gas pumps. Lines of cars would form at gas stations, and those people who were willing to wait eventually got the gasoline they desired. Those who were unwilling to spend their time in this way did not get gasoline, at least while this temporary rationing occurred.

THE 1979 OIL CRISIS AND THE REACTION OF THE 1980S

In 1979, about five years after the first jump in oil prices in 1973–74, another massive price increase occurred because of the revolution in oil-rich Iran. This revolution succeeded both in deposing the shah of Iran and in temporarily stopping oil production there. Although the loss of Iranian production was partly offset by stepped-up production elsewhere, the price of crude oil leaped from 13 to over 30 dollars per barrel, the result being another period of temporary gas lines which were used to ration gasoline—and big increases in gasoline prices (Table 6.3).

However, it should not be assumed that gasoline was the only product that was affected in a major way. To illustrate, consider heating oil, another important product made from crude oil. The price elasticity of demand for heating

---

[5] C. Goodwin (ed.), *Energy Policy in Perspective* (Washington, D.C.: Brookings Institution, 1981), p. 461.

[6] Ibid., p. 449.

TABLE 6.3 Regular Motor Gasoline Pump Price, 1972–1990 (cents per gallon)

Year	Price
1972	36
1973	40
1974	52
1975	57
1976	59
1977	62
1978	63
1979	86
1980	119
1981	131
1982	122
1983	116
1984	113
1985	112
1986	86
1987	90
1988	90
1989	100
1990	115

SOURCES: U.S. Bureau of the Census, *Statistical Abstract of the United States* (Washington, D.C.: Government Printing Office, 1986); Beck, *Oil Industry Outlook*; and *Basic Petroleum Data Book*.

oil has been roughly estimated to be about 0.12 in the short run.[7] Because it takes time for new houses to be built and for old houses to be renovated so that one fuel can be substituted for another, it is not surprising that the estimated short-run price elasticity is quite low.

In the long run, the cross elasticity of demand between heating oil and natural gas has been estimated as about 1.5, and the cross elasticity of demand between heating oil and electricity seems to be about 0.7.[8] These high cross elasticities indicate that the quantity of heating oil demanded is very sensitive to changes in the price of natural gas and electricity (relative to oil's price). Both cross elasticities are positive; this would be expected since both natural gas and electricity are major substitutes for heating oil.

Returning to the events of 1979, one consequence of the Iranian revolution was a huge run-up in the price of heating oil. Between 1978 and 1981 the price

---

[7] Beck, *Oil Industry Outlook*.
[8] G. Lakshmanan and W. Anderson, "Residential Energy Demand in the United States," *Regional Science and Urban Economics*, August 1980. These are very tentative estimates, as the authors stress, but adequate for present purposes.

Sheikh Ahmed Yamani

of home heating oil rose from about $.39 to $1.03 per gallon. This enormous increase accelerated a shift to natural gas and electricity for heating, more emphasis by home owners on fuel conservation, and a substantial reduction in heating oil used.[9]

By the late 1970s and early 1980s, Sheikh Ahmed Yamani, the oil minister of Saudi Arabia, had become a symbol of OPEC. Educated at the University of Cairo, the New York University Law School, and the Harvard Law School, he had been appointed oil minister at the age of 32, 11 years before the 1973 cutback of oil by OPEC. According to Henry Kissinger, "His watchful eyes and little VanDyke beard made him look like a priggish young don playing at oil policy but not really meaning the apocalyptic message he was bringing, especially as it was put forward with a gentle voice and a self-deprecatory smile at variance with the implications of his actions."[10]

In June of 1978, Sheikh Yamani said that: "From our own studies and from all the reliable studies I have read, there are very strong indications that there will be a shortage of supply of oil sometime around the mid–1980s if not before. . . . No matter what we do, that date is coming."[11] But Sheikh Yamani apparently did not recognize that the United States and other major nations were becoming much more energy efficient. For example, the 1975 federal laws calling for a doubling of the efficiency of new cars to 27.5 miles per gallon by 1985 reduced U.S. oil consumption considerably. Moreover, new sources of oil were developed and expanded. Mexico, Alaska, and the North Sea experienced major increases in production, and countries like Egypt and Malaysia became significant exporters. (Between 1977 and 1982, OPEC's share of the non-Communist world's total oil output fell from two-thirds to less than one-half, a remarkable decline.)

[9] Beck, *Oil Industry Outlook.*
[10] Yergin, *The Prize,* p. 672.
[11] Ibid., p. 641.

Contrary to Sheikh Yamani's prediction, in 1986 the bottom fell out of the oil market; the price of Texas oil fell by about 70 percent, and shock waves reverberated through the executive suites of the oil companies. Among the major reasons for this price drop was a substitution of other fuels (like coal and nuclear power) for oil, as well as the buildup of non-OPEC oil supply and increases in energy efficiency.

THE PROFITABILITY OF OIL FIRMS

All but one of the topics that must be understood to do the problems presented in this chapter have now been covered. The remaining topic is the profitability of the oil firms, which was a major political issue during the 1970s and 1980s. In 1974, Senator Henry Jackson of Washington accused the largest oil companies of making "obscene profits." They denied this, but it certainly was true that their 1973 earnings were considerably higher than 1972's. In 1979, when President Jimmy Carter announced a phased decontrol of oil prices, he proposed a "windfall profits tax" on oil firms, which he felt would capture part of their "huge and undeserved" profits for the U.S. people.

As a percentage of stockholder equity, the profits of the oil industry were much higher than those of all manufacturing industries in the period 1979 to 1983 (Table 6.4). But in the middle and late 1980s, when the price of oil fell,

TABLE 6.4 Profits as a Percent of Stockholders' Equity, Petroleum Industry and All Manufacturing Industries, 1965–1986

Year	Petroleum	All manufacturing	Year	Petroleum	All manufacturing
1965	11.9	13.8	1976	14.8	15.0
1966	12.6	14.1	1977	14.2	15.0
1967	12.9	12.6	1978	19.8	15.0
1968	12.9	13.2	1979	30.0	16.4
1969	12.1	12.7	1980	30.7	13.9
1970	10.9	10.3	1981	25.6	13.6
1971	11.2	10.9	1982	18.7	9.2
1972	10.8	12.1	1983	17.8	10.6
1973	15.6	14.5	1984	14.3	12.5
1974	19.6	15.2	1985	11.7	10.1
1975	13.9	12.6	1986	3.7	9.5

SOURCES: J. Griffin and H. Steele, *Energy Economics and Policy*; *Economic Report of the President* (Washington, D.C.: Government Printing Office, 1992), and source of Table 6.3.

there was little talk of excess profits. For example, Robert Horton, chairman of the Standard Oil Company of Ohio, sent a letter in 1987 to stockholders saying 1986 "was a terrible year; we reported a net loss of $345 million . . . [O]ur average oil price was only $13.83 per barrel in 1986, compared with $26.43 in the previous year."[12]

Moreover, in early 1992, major oil companies like Exxon, Chevron, Mobil, and Texaco reported lackluster profits which they attributed partly to weak demand for their products due to the sluggish world economy.[13]

OPEC'S OUTPUT CURTAILMENT IN 1973: CAN YOU APPLY THE THEORY?

The following three problems are concerned with the events immediately before and after OPEC's 1973 reduction in oil production.

PROBLEM 6.1 Prior to OPEC's cutback of output, there was an oil import quota in the United States. A quota is a limit on how much can be imported. First established by President Dwight D. Eisenhower in 1959, the Mandatory Oil Import Quota permitted firms to import only a certain amount of oil. Supporters of the quota argued that we could not afford to depend on foreigners for our oil because foreign sources might be cut off in war or other emergencies. Opponents argued that the cost to the consumer of this quota was high and that the oil requirements for national security were overstated.

In 1973, when government officials became increasingly concerned about impending fuel shortages, opposition to the oil import quota mounted. Finally, in April 1973, President Richard M. Nixon announced that he was suspending direct control over the quantity of crude oil that could be imported. The oil import quota was dead.

(a) The graph on the next page shows the 1968 supply curve for domestically produced petroleum, the supply curve for foreign produced petroleum, and the demand curve for petroleum in the United States.[14]

---

[12] J. D. Hunger, "The Standard Oil Company: British Petroleum Loses Patience," in E. Mansfield, *Study Guide and Casebook in Applied Microeconomics,* 2nd edition (New York: Norton, 1997).
[13] *New York Times,* July 24, 1992, and July 28, 1992.
[14] The data are only approximate. For further discussion, see J. Burroughs and T. Domencich, *An Analysis of the United States Oil Import Quota* (Lexington, Mass.: Heath, 1970).

On the basis of this graph, was foreign oil (much of it from the Middle East) cheaper to produce than U.S. oil?

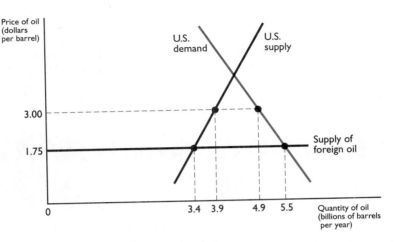

(b) If there had been no oil import quota, what would the U.S. price of petroleum have been? How much oil would the United States have imported?

(c) With an oil import quota of 1 billion barrels per year, what was the U.S. price?

(d) In dollar terms, how great was the annual loss to U.S. consumers due to the oil import quota?

PROBLEM 6.2 Before the output curtailment by OPEC, many oil analysts viewed the world oil market as being reasonably competitive, the supply curve for crude oil being

$$Q_S = 17 + 0.25P,$$

where Q_S is the quantity of crude oil supplied (in billions of barrels) and P is the price of crude oil (in dollars per barrel)[15]. After this output curtailment, this supply curve was

$$Q_S = 14 + 0.25P.$$

Both before and after this output curtailment, the demand curve for crude oil was

$$Q_D = 19 - 0.25P.$$

---

[15] The supply and demand curves presented here are only rough approximations, but they are accurate enough for present purposes.

(a) Holding constant the price of crude oil, by how much did OPEC reduce the quantity of crude oil it supplied? At the equilibrium price before the output curtailment, what was the percentage reduction in total quantity supplied?

(b) What was the equilibrium price of crude oil before OPEC curtailed its output? What was it afterward?

(c) What was the equilibrium quantity of crude oil demanded and supplied before OPEC curtailed its output? What was it afterward?

(d) The above equations represent the short-run effects of OPEC's action, not the long-run effects. In the long run, the price elasticity of demand for crude oil was about 0.4. Was this greater or less than the price elasticity of demand for crude oil in the short run if the price was $10 per barrel? Why?

(e) In the long run, would you expect OPEC's output curtailment to have as big an effect on the price of crude oil as in the short run? Why or why not?

PROBLEM 6.3 After OPEC announced its cutback in exports of oil to the United States in late 1973, the first official estimates by U.S. policymakers were that U.S. consumers would have to reduce their consumption of gasoline by 20 to 30 percent. William Simon, the newly appointed federal "energy czar," stated repeatedly that he wanted to avoid issuing ration coupons for gasoline if possible. So did other government officials, on the grounds that rationing of this sort would lead to black markets and create a large bureaucracy. For example, as noted above, Herbert Stein, chairman of the Council of Economic Advisers, argued against such a rationing scheme.

Herbert Stein

(a) How could gasoline consumption be cut by 20 to 30 percent without rationing?

(b) Many leading economists pointed out to Simon and other government policymakers that the short-run demand for gasoline is quite inelastic. Specifically, the short-run price elasticity of demand for gasoline was estimated to be 0.3 by Harvard's Hendrik Houthakker, 0.4 by Alan Greenspan (later chairman of the Federal Reserve), and 0.2 by the U.S. Department of Transportation. If the arc elasticity of demand for gasoline equaled 0.3, how big a price increase was required to cut consumption by 25 percent? (Be careful: Note that the *arc* elasticity of demand is 0.3.)

(c) In fact, did the price of gasoline rise in the next few years as much as indicated in your answer to part (b)? (For relevant data, see Table 6.3.) If not, why not?

GAS LINES, TAXES, AND OIL EXPLORATION: CAN YOU APPLY THE THEORY?

The following three problems deal with some major consequences of the oil crisis of 1973, as well as a proposal to help reduce major U.S. dependence on OPEC oil.

PROBLEM 6.4   As pointed out above, gasoline was rationed in 1974 based on how long people were willing to wait at gas pumps. Suppose that the following diagram shows the indifference curves and budget line of Katherine Muller, a consumer with an income of $25,000 per year. Ms. Muller had to allocate her income between gasoline and goods other than gasoline. The price of gasoline is assumed to have been 50¢ per gallon in 1974, and her budget line was *BD,* as shown below:

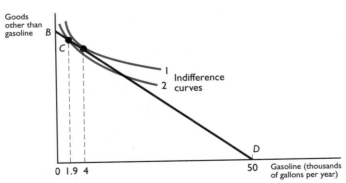

(a) How many gallons of gasoline would Ms. Muller have liked to purchase per year?

(b) Because she could not spend time waiting in line at the gas pumps, Ms. Muller could obtain only 1,900 gallons of gasoline (no more) per year once rationing began, although she still only had to pay 50¢ per gallon. After the onset of rationing, did her budget line continue to be BD in the above diagram? If not, draw her new budget line.

(c) After rationing began, what was the highest indifference curve that Ms. Muller could reach? Was this a higher or lower indifference curve than the one she could have reached before rationing began? Thus, was she better or worse off because of rationing?

(d) According to studies carried out at that time, rural motorists tended to wait in line longer than urban motorists. What does this suggest about the price (including the value of time spent waiting in line) elasticity of demand for gasoline in rural areas as compared with that in urban areas? Why might this be the case?

(e) Losses in consumer surplus due to gasoline rationing of this sort during the period December 1973 to March 1974 were estimated to have been about $.5 billion in California alone.[16] Explain how a loss of consumer surplus can arise for this reason.

PROBLEM 6.5 After OPEC cut back its production and drove up the price of oil, both the Nixon administration and many of its critics agreed that the United States should reduce its consumption of gasoline and thus decrease its dependence on OPEC oil (which in 1973 satisfied 65 percent of non-Communist oil consumption).[17] Within the federal government, there were repeated suggestions that the tax on gasoline should be raised, but a major objection to this proposal was that it would hurt the poor. In 1980, presidential candidate John Anderson suggested that the revenues from the tax be returned to the public in the form of a tax rebate. One question that he was asked frequently by newspaper reporters was: If the tax revenues were returned to consumers in the form of a tax rebate, why should gasoline consumption fall?

(a) Suppose that in 1980 the tax on gasoline had been raised, the result being an increase in the price of gasoline from $1 to $1.25 per gallon. If the market demand and supply curves for gasoline were as shown on the next page, how big a tax increase would have been required in 1980 to raise the price of gasoline this much?

---

[16] H. Frech and W. Lee, "The Welfare Cost of Rationing-by-Queuing Across Markets: Theory and Estimates from the U.S. Gasoline Crisis," *Quarterly Journal of Economics,* 1987.

[17] Yergin, *The Prize.*

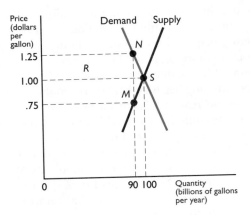

(b) If the revenues from the tax were not returned to the public in the form of a tax rebate, what would have been the loss, in dollar terms, to consumers of gasoline?

(c) After paying the increased tax to the government, would sellers of gasoline have received less for a gallon of their gasoline? If so, how much less?

(d) How much revenue would the government have received from this tax increase?

(e) Returning to Ms. Muller, when gasoline cost $1 per gallon (and no rationing occurred), her budget line was *KL* in the graph below. (Note that her income differed from that in Problem 6.4.) If the price had risen to $1.25 per gallon, what would her budget line have been? Why?

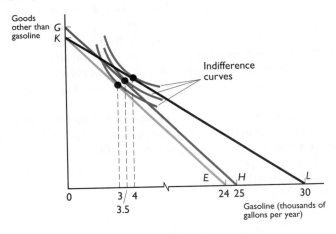

(f) Before the increase in the gasoline tax (and with no rationing), how much gasoline did Ms. Muller consume? After the increase in the gasoline tax, how much would she have consumed? Taken by itself, would the increase in the gasoline tax have reduced her gasoline consumption? If so, by how much?

(g) If the revenue from the gasoline tax increase had been rebated to Ms. Muller, her budget line would have shifted to *GH* in the graph above. Why is this budget line parallel to line *KE*?

(h) How much would have been the tax rebate to Ms. Muller, according to the preceding graph?

(i) After both the gasoline tax increase and the receipt of the tax rebate, would Ms. Muller reduce her consumption of gasoline? If so, by how much?

(j) Was John Anderson correct in believing that an increase in the gasoline tax together with a rebate of the tax revenues to the public would reduce gasoline consumption?

Robert Anderson

Prudhoe Bay Oil Field

PROBLEM 6.6 In 1966, a joint venture of the Atlantic Richfield Company (ARCO) and the Exxon Corporation drilled a costly well about 60 miles south of Alaska's north coast, which turned out to be dry. Robert Anderson, ARCO's chairman, had to decide whether to drill another well 60 miles away, at Prudhoe Bay. He said yes, but as he later recalled, "It was more a decision not to cancel a well already scheduled than to go ahead."[18] The result was the largest oil field ever discovered in North America.

Three years later, Phillips Petroleum, after a string of dry holes, found oil 10,000 feet beneath the North Sea. When asked at a technical meeting what techniques Phillips had used to analyze the geology of the field, a

[18] Ibid., p. 571. Also see M. E. Barrett, "Atlantic Richfield Company," *Case Research Journal,* Autumn 1990.

Phillips official replied "Luck." To obtain the oil, drilling rigs had to work through water depths much greater than attempted before, and go on to drill another 4 miles under the seabed (while sometimes coping with 50-foot waves and 70-mile-per-hour winds).[19]

(a) In 1986, the price of crude oil fell precipitously, as we saw on page 170. The price of West Texas Intermediate, the barometer of U.S. oil prices, sank from $30 per barrel in October 1985 to $10 per barrel in March 1986 and remained under $18 for the rest of the year.[20] There was panic and pandemonium in the oil patch. Was this due in part to rightward shifts of the supply curve for oil caused by oil discoveries like Prudhoe Bay and the North Sea? If so, why didn't the price fall in the late sixties and early seventies? (These two major oil fields were discovered in the late 1960s.)

(b) Table 6.1 shows that, whereas petroleum accounted for 49 percent of U.S. energy consumption in 1978, its share had fallen to 42 percent in 1984. Is this partly attributable to the differences between the long run and the short run in the price elasticity of demand for crude oil? (Recall Problem 6.2.) Is this fact symptomatic of changes on the demand side of the oil market that helped to cause the 1986 price drop? If so, what were these changes?

(c) British Petroleum had bought a substantial number of leases to drill at Prudhoe Bay before the Atlantic Richfield Company discovered oil there. In 1970, it traded its share of the Prudhoe Bay oil field to Standard Oil of Ohio (Sohio) for 53 percent of Sohio's equity. Sohio became British Petroleum's U.S. arm, and in 1978 Alton Whitehouse, Jr.,

British Petroleum Building

Alton Whitehouse, Jr.

[19] Ibid., p. 669.

[20] Hunger, "The Standard Oil Company."

the lawyer (trained at the University of Virginia) who represented Sohio in the negotiations with British Petroleum, became Sohio's CEO. Acknowledging his lack of technical knowledge of the oil industry, he divided the firm into business groups and delegated most operating responsibility to the heads of these groups. One result was an increase in Sohio's exploration staff from 60 people in 1977 to almost 1,000 in 1983, but a substantial reduction in late 1985, 1986, and 1987.[21] Explain why the size of Sohio's exploration staff behaved in this way.

COMIC RELIEF FROM THE NATION'S CAPITOL: CAN YOU APPLY THE THEORY?

While the nation wrestled during the 1980s with serious oil-related problems, the public and the oil industry were not denied some comical moments, as illustrated by the fact that the city government of Washington, D.C., decided in 1980 to levy a 6 percent excise tax on gasoline sold within the city limits. The following problem deals with this extraordinary exercise in local public finance.

PROBLEM 6.7 Washington's city fathers expected this tax to increase the price of gasoline by about 6 percent, which it did. Apparently, they also felt that gasoline sales within the city would not be influenced substantially by the price increase. According to various studies, the price elasticity of demand for gasoline tends to be only about 0.1 in the very short run of a year or so. But in a period of 3 years, it increases to about 0.3 (the figure used in Problem 6.3); in 5 years it is about 0.5; and in a period of 10 to 20 years, it is about 1.0. This seems reasonable. If the price of gasoline goes up, it takes time for drivers to change their habits and replace less fuel efficient cars with more fuel efficient ones. Certainly, in a year or two, one would not expect many people to drive appreciably less in response to an increase in the price of gasoline.[22]

(a) As pointed out above, the price elasticity of demand for gasoline in the very short run (of about a year or so) is approximately 0.1. Does this

---

[21] Ibid. and J. D. Hunger, "The Standard Oil Company of Ohio: Growing Pains in the Eighties," in T. Wheelen and J. D. Hunger (eds.), *Cases in Strategic Management and Business Policy* (Reading, Mass.: Addison-Wesley, 1987).

[22] R. Pindyk, *The Structure of World Energy Demand* (Cambridge, Mass.: MIT Press, 1979).

mean that, if gas stations in Washington, D.C. increase their prices by 6 percent, they will experience a 0.6 percent reduction in quantity of gasoline sold? Why or why not?

(b) A study (carried out many years ago) found that the price elasticity of demand was 0.7 to 1.1 for gasoline in Tennessee when prices in neighboring states were held constant.[23] Does this mean that, if gas stations in Washington, D.C., increase their prices by 6 percent, they will experience about a 4.2 to 6.6 percent reduction in quantity of gasoline sold? Why or why not?

(c) In fact, the quantity of gasoline sold within Washington, D.C. fell by about 33 percent within a few months of the 6 percent price increase. Based on this fact, what seems to have been the approximate value of the arc price elasticity of demand?

(d) Why was the price elasticity of demand so much higher than the figure of 0.1 cited earlier in this problem?

(e) Five months after it was enacted, Washington's gasoline tax was repealed on the grounds that it had not increased tax revenues and that it hurt both local motorists and local gas stations. Who benefited from the city's gasoline tax? Why?

PROFITABILITY OF THE OIL FIRMS: CAN YOU APPLY THE THEORY?

The next two problems deal with the oil firms' bids for leases to drill oil and with the profitability of one major oil firm, the Standard Oil Company of Ohio.

PROBLEM 6.8   In 1971, E. Capen, R. Clapp, and W. Campbell, three ARCO engineers, wrote as follows in the *Journal of Petroleum Technology:*

In recent years, several major [oil] companies have taken a rather careful look at their record and those of the [oil] industry in areas where sealed competitive bidding is the method of acquiring leases [to drill for oil]. The most notable of these areas, and perhaps the

---

[23] L. Clark, "The Elasticity of Demand for Tennessee Gasoline," *Journal of Marketing,* April 1951.

most interesting, is the Gulf of Mexico. Most analysts turn up the rather shocking result that, while there seems to be a lot of oil and gas in the region, the [oil] industry is not making as much return on its investment as it intended. In fact, if one ignores the era before 1950, when land was a good deal cheaper, he or she finds that the Gulf has paid off at something less than the local credit union.[24]

(a) In the 1969 sale of leases for tracts of land on Alaska's North Slope, the sum of the winning bids was $900 million; the sum of the second-highest bids was $370 million. A 1983 study of the profitability of over 1,000 leases in the Gulf of Mexico indicated that only about 22 percent of the leases were profitable and that these leases yielded only about a 19 percent rate of return.[25] Does this evidence suggest that the firms making the winning bids were excessively optimistic about the amount of oil likely to be found?

(b) According to Capen, Clapp, and Campbell, "If [you] win a tract against two or three others, [you] may feel fine about [your] good fortune. But how should [you] feel if [you] won against 50 others? Ill."[26] If you were in charge of an oil company's exploration activities, how would you avoid bidding too much for leases?

PROBLEM 6.9 Based on its large share of the Prudhoe Bay oil field, Standard Oil of Ohio (Sohio) prospered handsomely in the 1970s and early 1980s. In 1978, it suddenly found itself the ninth largest oil firm in terms of assets, with Prudhoe Bay accounting for 80 percent of its assets. By 1987, Sohio's annual profits of almost $2 billion were almost 50 times its profits a decade earlier. Since Alton Whitehouse, Sohio's chairman, knew that Prudhoe Bay's oil production was likely to go down in the late 1980s, he and his colleagues decided to do two things: (1) invest heavily in oil exploration to maintain the level of the firm's oil reserve and (2) diversify into other industries.

In 1981, Sohio bought Kennecott Corporation, the nation's biggest copper producer, for about $1.8 billion. Subsequently, copper prices fell and Kennecott, with much higher costs than copper producers in Chile and

[24] E. Capen, R. Clapp, and W. Campbell, "Competitive Bidding in High-Risk Situations," *Journal of Petroleum Technology,* June 1971, p. 641.

[25] W. Mead, A. Moseidjord, and P. Sorensen, "The Rate of Return Earned by Lessees under Cash Bonus Bidding of OCS Oil and Gas Leases," *Energy Journal,* 1983, and K. Hendricks, R. Porter, and B. Boudreau, "Information, Returns, and Bidding Behavior in OCS Auctions: 1954–69," *Journal of Industrial Economics,* 1987, p. 529.

[26] Capen, Clapp, and Campbell, "Competitive Bidding in High-Risk Situations," p. 645.

other countries, lost about $700 million between 1981 and the end of 1985. Between 1980 and 1985, Sohio spent nearly $5 billion on oil exploration and leases, its biggest investment being at Mukluk, 14 miles off the north coast of Alaska, a place that geologists regarded as being quite possibly the site of an oil field as big as Prudhoe Bay. After spending about $1.7 billion for leases and drilling, it turned out to be the most expensive dry hole in history, although there was clear evidence that oil had once been trapped there. As Richard Bray, president of Sohio's production company put it, "We drilled in the right place. We were simply 30 million years too late."[27]

Besides exploration, another way that an oil company can increase its oil reserves is to buy up another oil company. In fact, this is what a number of firms did in the 1980s. (For example, Chevron bought Gulf for about $13 billion.) Commenting on Sohio, Lawrence Tween, an oil analyst for Kidder Peabody, said in 1986, "If they had gone out three or four years ago (1982–1983) and bought an independent oil company, they would have been in a substantially better position."[28]

Robert Horton

British Petroleum, which held a majority interest in Sohio, had allowed Sohio's management great freedom to set its own course. In 1986, British Petroleum's top management announced that there had been a number of disappointments and that it intended to intervene more directly. Alton Whitehouse reluctantly resigned as Sohio's chairman and was replaced by Robert Horton, a British Petroleum executive who was a member of Sohio's board of directors. In May 1986, Horton volunteered that "If I have somewhat of a reputation as a hatchet man, it's perhaps because I've never

---

[27] Yergin, *The Prize,* p. 733.

[28] G. Putka, R. Winter, and G. Stricharchuk, "How and Why BP Put Its Own Commanders at Standard Oil Helm," *Wall Street Journal,* March 7, 1986, p. 8.

been reluctant to admit it when I made a mistake."[29] (In early 1989 he rose to chairman of British Petroleum, and in 1992 reportedly resigned under pressure.[30])

In 1987, British Petroleum, which owned 55 percent of Sohio's stock, offered to pay $7.4 billion to the other stockholders to obtain full control of the company. The First Boston Corporation, hired by Sohio's minority stockholders to evaluate British Petroleum's offer, said it was about $1.6 billion too low. Whereas British Petroleum forecasted that the price of crude oil would be $18 per barrel in 1988, First Boston forecasted it would be about $20 per barrel.[31] In 1986, Sohio's oil reserves were estimated to be about 2.4 billion barrels, so the minority stockholders' 45 percent interest amounted to about .45 × 2.4 = 1.08 billion barrels.[32] Regardless of which of the above forecasts one uses, the value of over a billion barrels of oil would seem to be at least $18 billion, since the lower of the two price forecasts was $18 per barrel. Wasn't British Petroleum's offer far more than $1.6 billion too low?

THE OIL MARKET IN THE 1990S: CAN YOU APPLY THE THEORY?

The final problem is concerned with the oil market in the 1990s, with particular emphasis on demand, supply, and oil prices.

PROBLEM 6.10   The early 1990s saw a brief, but serious, international conflict over oil. In late 1990 and early 1991, the United States and its allies were engaged in a full-scale war against Iraq, which had invaded its neighbor Kuwait, with the intention of seizing Kuwait's rich oil fields. After Iraq's defeat, it was prohibited by the United Nations from exporting crude oil. The mid-1990s were a period of relative calm in the oil markets. Experts tried hard to forecast what the next crisis might be.

[29] Business Week, May 23, 1986, p. 79.

[30] New York Times, August 7, 1992, p. D1.

[31] Hunger, "The Standard Oil Company."

[32] Value Line Investment Survey, Part 3: Ratings and Reports, 3d ed., Vol. 42, No. 29 (April 10, 1987), p. 402.

(a) In 1990, the price of oil rose to $40 a barrel, but it fell substantially after the war.[33] Why?

(b) During the mid-1990s, Iraq tried to get this ban lifted. Sheikh Yamani, addressing a London conference in 1994, said that if this ban were lifted and if OPEC did not cut output to make way for Iraq's oil exports, oil prices "could plunge below $10 a barrel."[34] Do you agree? Why or why not?

(c) According to the International Energy Agency, which studies energy trends, as developing countries increase their demand for automobiles, air conditioning, and other staples of modern urban living, they will raise their energy consumption by 4 percent per year through the year 2010. In Asia alone, oil consumption has been predicted to rise in the next decade by 8 million barrels per day, as much oil as was produced by Saudi Arabia in 1994.[35] Will this tend to push up oil prices? Why or why not?

(d) In November 1994, the OPEC oil ministers froze the level of their total oil output at its current level. Specifically, they agreed to maintain OPEC's total production constant at 24.5 million barrels per day. "Taken all together, it seems to mean higher prices," said Cyrus Tahmassebi, chief economist for Ashland, Inc.[36] Why did he say this?

(e) Some experts believe that new technology, improved efficiency, and the opening of vast foreign areas to exploration may increase non-OPEC oil production by about 6.5 percent by the year 2000.[37] Would this tend to offset the factors pushing up oil prices? Why or why not?

CONCLUSION

Sheikh Yamani was one of the movers and shakers of the international community, and Alton Whitehouse and Robert Horton were the leaders of one of the world's largest and most powerful firms. To understand their actions and motives, as well as the events that influenced their behavior, it is essential to have at least a basic knowledge of demand and supply curves, price elasticities of demand and supply, the theory of consumer behavior, and other such topics.

---

[33] *New York Times,* July 13, 1995.

[34] *New York Times,* April 12, 1994.

[35] *New York Times,* June 23, 1994.

[36] *New York Times,* November 24, 1994.

[37] *New York Times,* December 27, 1994.

One of the morals of this chapter is that simple microeconomic tools can be surprisingly powerful and profitable. Take, for example, the fall of oil prices in the mid-1980s. Given the fundamental changes in demand and supply that took place in response to OPEC's actions, the application of simple microeconomic models should have made you very skeptical of the prevailing forecasts during the late 1970s and early 1980s that oil prices were going only one way — up. And such skepticism, if acted on, could have enhanced your performance as a manager, investor, and citizen.

SELECTED SUPPLEMENTARY READINGS

1. D. Yergin, *The Prize* (New York: Simon & Schuster, 1991).
2. J. Griffin and H. Steele, *Energy Economics and Policy* (New York: Academic Press, 1980).
3. *Basic Petroleum Data Book* (Washington, D.C.: American Petroleum Institute, 1995).
4. H. Frech and W. Lee, "The Welfare Cost of Rationing-by-Queuing Across Markets: Theory and Estimates from the U.S. Gasoline Crisis," *Quarterly Journal of Economics,* 1987.
5. G. Putka, R. Winter, and G. Stricharchuk, "How and Why BP Put Its Own Commanders at Standard Oil Helm," *Wall Street Journal,* March 7, 1986.
6. K. Hendricks, R. Porter, and B. Boudreau, "Information, Returns, and Bidding Behavior in OCS Auctions," *Journal of Industrial Economics,* 1987.

PART THREE

The Firm: Its Technology and Costs

The Firm and Its Technology

7

THE ASSUMPTION OF PROFIT MAXIMIZATION

Philip Condit is the head of a firm (Boeing, of airliner fame); so are Lee Raymond and John Reed (heads of Exxon and Citibank, respectively.) What is a firm? Put briefly, it is a unit that produces a good or service for sale. In contrast to not-for-profit institutions like the Ford Foundation, firms attempt to make a profit. There are literally millions of firms in the United States: Some are proprietorships (owned by a single person), some partnerships (owned by two or more people), and some corporations (which are fictitious legal persons). About six-sevenths of the goods and services produced in the United States are produced by firms; the rest are provided by government and not-for-profit institutions. It is obvious that an economy like ours revolves around the activities of firms.

As a first approximation, economists generally assume that firms attempt to maximize profits. However, the economist's definition of profits does not coincide with the accountant's. The economist does not assume that the firm attempts to maximize the current, short-run profits measured by the accountant. Instead he or she assumes that the firm will attempt to maximize the sum of profits over a long period of time, these profits being properly discounted to the present. Also, when the economist speaks of profits, he or she means profit after taking account of the capital and labor provided by the owners. More will be said on this score in the next chapter.

Economic Profit

Although the assumption of profit maximization serves as a reasonable first approximation, it has obvious limitations. For one thing, the making of profits generally requires time and energy, and if the owners of the firm are the managers as well, they may decide that it is preferable to sacrifice profits for leisure. (Profit maximizers in Miami Beach and the Virgin Islands encourage this type of thinking.) In a case of this sort, it is more accurate to assume that the owner-manager, like the consumer, is maximizing utility, since utility is a function of his or her profits and the amount of leisure he or she enjoys. Using the kind of analysis described in Chapter 3, we can determine how much money the owner-manager will give up for leisure (see Question 1 on page 218).

It should also be noted that, in an uncertain world, the concept of maximum profit is not clearly defined. Since any particular course of action will not result in a unique, certain level of profit, but in a variety of possible levels of profit, each with a certain probability of occurrence, it makes no sense to speak about the maximization of profits. However, if the firm is able, explicitly or implicitly, to attach a probability to each level of profit that could result from each course of action, it is meaningful to assume that the firm attempts to maximize expected profits.[1] For simplicity, we shall assume in the following pages that the firm has full knowledge of the relevant variables, and that there is no uncertainty.

Observers of the modern corporation often state that profits are not the sole objective of these firms. Industry spokespersons often claim that the following objectives are also of importance: achieving better social conditions in the firm's community, increasing (or at least maintaining) its market share, creating an image as a good employer and a useful part of the community, and so forth. For example, oil firms, studied at length in the previous chapter, often stress their concern over the environment and over the reduction of wasteful

---

[1] Expected profit is defined as the long-term average value of profit—the sum of the various possible levels of profit, after each level is weighted by the probability of its occurrence. The firm may be interested in the riskiness, as well as the expected value of profits, in which case it will maximize expected utility. See Chapter 16.

uses of fuel. Besides the question of how seriously one should take such self-proclaimed goals, the important issue is how distinct these goals are from the goal of profit maximization. To the extent that many of these goals are simply means to achieve profits *in the long run,* there may be less inaccuracy in the profit maximization assumption than might appear at first glance.

In addition, economists are interested in the theory of the profit-maximizing firm because it provides rules of behavior for firms that do want to maximize profits. The theory of the profit-maximizing firm suggests how a firm should operate if it wants to make as much money as possible. Even if a firm does not want to maximize profit, the theory can be useful. For example, it can show how much the firm is losing by taking certain courses of action. In recent years the theory of the profit-maximizing firm has been studied more and more for the sake of determining rules of business behavior.

FIRM OWNERS AND MANAGERS: A PRINCIPAL-AGENT PROBLEM

In the previous section, we pointed out that economists generally regard the assumption of profit maximization as only a first approximation.[2] One factor that can stand in the way of the maximization of profit is the separation of ownership from control in the large corporation. The owners of the firm — the stockholders — usually have little detailed knowledge of the firm's operations. Even if the board of directors is made up largely of people other than top management, top management usually has a great deal of freedom as long as it seems to be performing reasonably well. Under the circumstances, one might suppose that the behavior of the firm often will be dictated in part by the interests of the management group, the result being larger salaries, more perquisites, and a bigger staff than otherwise would be the case.

This is a so-called *principal-agent problem.* An *agency relationship* exists between the firm's owners and its managers: the managers are *agents* who work for the owners, who are the *principals.* The principal-agent problem is that the

---

[2] For discussions of models of the firm based on assumptions other than profit maximization, see H. Simon, "Theories of Decision-Making in Economics and Behavioral Science," reprinted in Mansfield, *Microeconomics: Selected Readings,* 5th ed.; R. Cyert and J. March, *A Behavioral Theory of the Firm* (Englewood Cliffs; N.J.: Prentice-Hall, 1963); and H. Leibenstein, "Allocative Efficiency vs. X-Efficiency," reprinted in Mansfield, *Microeconomics: Selected Readings,* 5th ed.

managers may pursue their own objectives, even though this reduces the profits of the owners.[3] Consider Joan Johnson, a manager (and part owner) who gets satisfaction both from her profits from the firm she manages and from the benefits (large staff, company-paid travel, and so on) that she receives from this firm. If she were the sole owner of her firm, an extra dollar of benefits she receives would reduce her profits by 1 dollar. In other words, the cost of these benefits would come entirely out of her own pocket. On the other hand, if she were to own only one-quarter of her firm (and if Japanese investors own the rest), an extra dollar of benefits would reduce her profits by only 25 cents. Thus only one-quarter of the cost of these benefits would come out of her pocket.

Clearly, Joan Johnson is likely to increase the amount of benefits she receives if the cost to her of a dollar's worth of benefits is 25 cents rather than a dollar. Since the other owners pick up three-quarters of the tab, why not take an extra "business" trip to Paris (and get a good meal at Tour D'Argent)? If she had to pay the full cost, she would forgo the Paris trip (and eat at McDonald's); but since she only pays 25 percent of the full cost, she finds it worthwhile to go to Paris.

If a manager like Joan Johnson is not an owner of the firm, this problem becomes even more severe. Since the cost of the benefits she receives is borne entirely by the owners, she has an incentive to increase these benefits very substantially. Because the owners of the firm find it difficult to distinguish between those benefits that promote profits and those that do not do so, she has a certain amount of leeway. But the owners are unlikely to put up with this kind of behavior if it becomes too serious or blatant. After all, the cost of these additional benefits comes entirely out of their pockets!

What can the owners do? To begin with, they can avoid investing in a firm where the managers behave in this way. If no owners are willing to invest, and if the managers have to put up their own funds to finance the business, the situation is the same as when Joan Johnson was the sole owner of her firm. As we saw above, the benefits she received were constrained by her having to pay their full costs. If the managers do not finance the business themselves, they must formulate a contractual agreement that would be attractive to potential owners. One possibility might be to establish a contract making the managers

[3] See M. Jensen and W. Meckling, "Theory of the Firm: Managerial Behavior, Agency Costs, and Ownership Structure," *Journal of Financial Economics,* 1976; J. Pratt and R. Zeckhauser (eds.), *Principals and Agents: The Structure of Business* (Boston: Harvard Business School, 1985); and E. Fama, "Agency Problems and the Theory of the Firm," *Journal of Political Economy,* 1980. Also, see O. Williamson, *The Economics of Discretionary Behavior* (Englewood Cliffs, N.J.: Prentice-Hall, 1964), as well as his *Markets and Hierarchies: Analysis and Antitrust Implications* (New York: Free Press, 1975) and *The Economic Institutions of Capitalism* (New York: Free Press, 1985).

EXAMPLE 7.1

Is a CEO Really Worth $26 Million per Year?

During the 1990s there has been considerable controversy over the compensation of chief executive officers (CEOs) of major corporations. The compensation in 1994 of the ten highest-paid CEOs in the United States was as follows:

Name	Company	Compensation ($ millions)
Charles Locke	Morton	26
James Donald	DSC	24
Carl Reichardt	Wells Fargo	17
Reuben Mark	Colgate-Palmolive	16
Eckhard Pfeiffer	Compaq	15
James Caynes	Bear Sterns	15
Hugh McColl	Nationsbank	14
Laurence Bossidy	Allied Signal	12
Louis Gerstner	IBM	12
Sanford Weill	Travelers	12

According to many critics, top corporate managers in the United States are overpaid, their compensation being 2 to 3 times bigger than those of their counterparts in Britain, France, Germany, and Japan.

(a) In many instances, a CEO's compensation is set by members of the firm's board of directors, who are friendly with (and perhaps beholden to) the CEO. Can this contribute to a principal-agent problem? If so, how? (b) According to some (but not all) studies, the compensation of a firm's chief executive officer is directly related to the profitability of the firm. If true, does this prove that higher pay leads to better performance? (c) In 1992, the New York City Employees Retirement System, which owned about 260,000 shares of Reebok stock, wanted to present to shareholders a proposal that the firm create a committee of independent directors to determine compensation for the firm's top executives. In 1990, the firm, which makes athletic shoes, paid its CEO $33 million in cash and stock options. Why do you think the New York retirement system made this proposal? What do you think it hoped to achieve?

SOLUTION (a) Yes. The members of a board who set the CEO's compensation may set it at a high level because of friendship (and the expectation that they may be rewarded in return).

(b) Not necessarily. Higher profitability may result in higher compensation, not the other way around. It is very difficult to tell whether the huge amounts paid top executives induce them to do a significantly better job than if they were paid less. Some experts say yes; some say no. (c) According to Elizabeth Holtzman, a trustee of the New York City Retirement System, "We want to see compensation of executives tied more closely to performance, and the best way to do that is to have an independent compensation committee." In her view, executive compensation seemed excessive in 1990, since Reebok's profits had been stagnant for several years.*

---

* For further discussion, see *Business Week,* April 24, 1995, and May 4, 1992; the *New York Times,* March 20, 1992; G. Crystal, *In Search of Excess* (New York: Norton, 1991); P. Milgrom and J. Roberts, *Economics, Organization, and Management* (Englewood Cliffs, N.J.: Prentice-Hall, 1992); S. Rosen, "Contracts and the Market for Executives," National Bureau of Economic Research, 1990; and N. Rose, "Executive Compensation," National Bureau of Economics Research, Cambridge, Mass., 1994–95.

---

responsible for paying for the benefits that they receive; but such a contract would be very difficult, if not impossible, to enforce, since the owners would have to monitor the managers' activities in minute detail.

A more feasible procedure might be to establish a contract that gives the managers an incentive to reduce benefits and to pursue objectives that are reasonably close to profit maximization. For example, the firm's owners might give the managers a financial stake in the success of the firm. Many corporations have stock purchase plans, whereby managers can purchase shares of common stock at less than market price. These plans provide managers with an incentive to promote the firm's profits and to act in accord with the interests of the firm's owners. Recent empirical research suggests that, if managers own between 5 and 20 percent of a firm, the firm is likely to perform better (in terms of profitability) than if they own less than 5 percent.[4]

If the firm is poorly managed and if its owners are unable to exert proper control over its management, it may be taken over by other owners who are tougher and more adept in this regard. Sometimes the takeover is relatively cut-and-dried; the old owners are happy to sell out to the new owners. But in other cases, the old management may go to great lengths to avoid being taken over by new owners. The firms that are targets of hostile takeovers tend to be

---

[4] R. Morck, A. Shleifer, and R. Vishny, "Management Ownership and Corporate Performance: An Empirical Analysis," *Journal of Financial Economics,* March 1988.

poorly performing companies; one way that the performance of such companies may be improved is through takeovers.[5]

TECHNOLOGY AND INPUTS

One of the fundamental determinants of a firm's behavior is the state of technology. Whether a firm produces textiles or locomotives, whether a firm is big or small, whether a firm is run by a genius or a moron (or even your brother-in-law), the firm cannot do more than is permitted by existing technology. Technology, as we defined it in Chapter 1, is the sum total of society's pool of knowledge concerning the industrial and agricultural arts. Although this definition is accurate, it is not very useful in indicating how we can represent the state of technology in a model of the firm. The purpose of the rest of this chapter is to show how economists represent the state of technology.

To begin with, an *input* is defined as anything that a firm uses in its production process. Most firms require a wide variety of inputs. For example, some of the inputs used by major steel firms like Bethlehem Steel or Nucor are iron ore, coal, oxygen, and the services of skilled labor of various types, blast furnaces, open hearths, electric furnaces, and rolling mills, as well as the services of the people managing the companies. To give a more humble example, the inputs in the production and sale of hot dogs by a street vendor are the hot dogs, the rolls, the stove, the truck, and the services of the vendor.

In representing and analyzing production processes, we assume that all inputs can be divided into two categories: fixed inputs and variable inputs. A *fixed input* is an input whose quantity cannot be changed during the period of time under consideration. This period will vary from problem to problem. Of course, the amount of most inputs can be varied to some extent, no matter how brief the time interval. But for some inputs, the cost of quick variation in their amount is so large as to make such variation impractical. For simplicity, we regard these inputs as being fixed. The firm's plant and equipment are examples of inputs that often are included in this category.

On the other hand, a *variable input* is an input whose quantity can be changed during the relevant period. For example, the number of workers hired to perform a job like construction can often be increased or decreased on

Fixed input

Variable Input

[5] R. Morck, A. Shleifer, and R. Vishny, "Characteristics of Hostile and Friendly Takeover Targets," in A. Auerbach (ed.), *Takeovers: Causes and Consequences* (Chicago: University of Chicago Press, 1988).

short notice. The amount of raw material used in the production of a commodity like dresses can often be increased or decreased by using up or building up the firm's inventories. The amount of water used in the production of a service like a car wash can sometimes be varied within limits simply by turning the relevant knobs.

THE SHORT RUN AND THE LONG RUN

Whether an input is regarded as variable or fixed depends on the length of the period under consideration. The longer the period, the more inputs are variable, not fixed. Although the length of the relevant period varies from problem to problem, economists have found it useful to focus special attention on two time periods: the short run and the long run. The *short run* is defined to be that period of time in which some of the firm's inputs are fixed. More specifically, since the firm's plant and equipment are among the most difficult inputs to change quickly, the short run is generally understood to mean the length of time during which the firm's plant and equipment are fixed. On the other hand, the *long run* is that period of time in which all inputs are variable. In the long run, the firm can make a complete adjustment to any change in its environment.

Short run versus long run

In both the short run and the long run, a firm's productive processes ordinarily permit substantial variation in the proportions in which inputs are used. In the long run, there can be no question but that input proportions can be varied considerably. For example, at General Motors, an automobile die can be made on conventional machine tools with more labor and less expensive equipment, or it can be made on numerically controlled machine tools with less labor and more expensive equipment. Similarly, at Boeing, an airplane can be almost handmade or it can be made using much equipment and relatively little labor. In the short run, there are also considerable opportunities for changes in input proportions. For one thing, the ratio between fixed and variable inputs can vary greatly.

Production processes with fixed, not variable, proportions are ones where there is one, and only one, ratio of inputs that can be used. For example, to produce a certain product, 2 hours of labor must be combined with a certain amount of capital. Consequently, if output is increased or decreased, the quantity of all inputs must be varied in proportion to output. There seem to be very few cases where all inputs must be combined in fixed proportions. However, there are cases where the amount of a *certain* input can be varied only within narrow limits. For example, a particular drug produced by Merck or Pfizer may have to contain a certain amount of aspirin per ounce of the drug. Thus it is not unusual for some inputs to be required in relatively fixed proportions but it is very unusual for this to be the case for all or most inputs.

THE PRODUCTION FUNCTION

For any commodity, the *production function* is the relationship between the quantities of various inputs used per period of time and the maximum quantity of the commodity that can be produced per period of time. More specifically, the production function is a table, a graph, or an equation showing the maximum output rate that can be achieved from any specified set of usage rates of inputs. The production function summarizes the characteristics of existing technology at a given point in time; it shows the technological constraints that the firm must reckon with.

Production function

To illustrate the production function, consider the simplest case—when there is one fixed input and one variable input. Suppose that the fixed input is the service of an acre of land, the variable input is labor (in units per year), and the output is corn (in bushels). Suppose that a scientifically inclined farmer decides to find out what the effect on annual output will be if he or she applies various numbers of units of labor during the year to the acre of land. (The farmer can vary the number of units of labor by hiring fewer or more laborers.) If he or she obtains the results in Table 7.1, then these results might be regarded as the production function in this situation. Alternatively, the curve in

TABLE 7.1 Output of Corn When Various Amounts of Labor Are Applied to 1 Acre of Land

Amount of labor (units per year)	Output of corn (bushels per year)
1	6
2	13.5
3	21
4	28
5	34
6	38
7	38
8	37

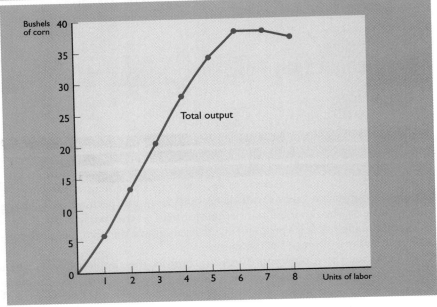

Figure 7.1, which presents exactly the same results, might be regarded as the production function.

The production function is an important starting point for the analysis of the firm's technology: It gives us the maximum *total output* that can be realized by using each combination of quantities of inputs. But there is more that we need to know about the production process. In particular, two other important concepts are the average product and the marginal product of an input.

The *average product* of an input is total product (that is, total output) divided by the amount of the input used to produce this amount of output. The *marginal product* of an input is the addition to total output due to the addition of the last unit of the input, when the amounts of other inputs used are held constant.

To illustrate these concepts, let us go back to the farmer in Table 7.1. On the basis of the production function shown in this table, we can compute the average product and marginal product of labor. Both the average product and the marginal product of labor will vary, of course, depending on how much labor is used. If $Q(L)$ is the total output rate when L units of labor are used per year, the average product of labor when L units of labor are used per year is $Q(L)/L$.

TABLE 7.2 Average and Marginal Products of Labor

Amount of labor	Total output	Average product of labor	Marginal product of labor[a]
0	0	—	—
1	6.0	6.00	6.0
2	13.5	6.75	7.5
3	21.0	7.00	7.5
4	28.0	7.00	7.0
5	34.0	6.80	6.0
6	38.0	6.33	4.0
7	38.0	5.43	0.0
8	37.0	4.62	−1.0

[a] These figures pertain to the interval between the indicated amount of labor and 1 unit less than the indicated amount of labor.

And the marginal product of labor when between L and $(L - 1)$ units of labor are used per year is

$$Q(L) - Q(L - 1).$$

Thus the average product of labor is 6 bushels of corn per unit of labor when 1 unit of labor is used, and the marginal product of labor is 7.5 bushels of corn per unit of labor when between 1 and 2 units of labor are used. The results for other levels of utilization of labor are shown in Table 7.2.

Panel A of Figure 7.2 shows the average product curve for labor. The numbers are taken from Table 7.2. As is typically the case for production processes, the average product of labor (which is the only variable input in this case) rises, reaches a maximum, and then falls. Panel B of Figure 7.2 shows the marginal product curve for labor. (These numbers also are taken from Table 7.2.) The marginal product of labor also rises, reaches a maximum, and then falls. This, too, is typical of many production processes.[6] Finally, panel C of Figure 7.2 shows both the average product curve and the marginal product curve for labor. As is always the case, marginal product exceeds average product when the latter is increasing, equals average product when the latter reaches a maximum, and is less than average product when the latter is decreasing. This is simply a matter of arithmetic: If the addition to a total is greater (less) than the average, the average is bound to increase (decrease).[7]

---

[6] Sometimes, however, an input's marginal product decreases throughout the entire range of its utilization.

[7] If x is the amount of the variable input that is used and

$$Q = f(x),$$

(Cont.)

FIGURE 7.2 Average and Marginal Product Curves for Labor Marginal product exceeds average product when the latter is increasing, and is less than average product when the latter is decreasing.

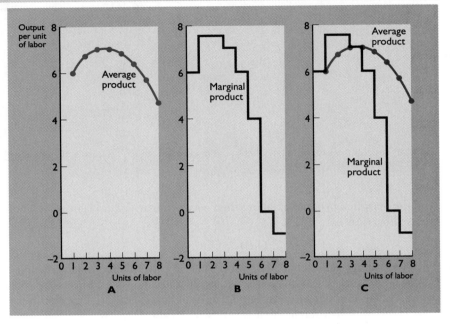

Tables 7.1 and 7.2 are constructed on the assumption that land, the fixed input, is equal to one acre. Suppose that we could increase the amount of land to two acres. What effect would this have on total output and on the average and marginal products of labor? Generally, over the relevant range of production, an increase in the fixed input will result in an increase in all of them. For example, the result might be like that shown in Figure 7.3.

---

where Q is the output rate, then the average product of the variable input is $Q/x = f(x)/x$, and the marginal product of the variable input is $dQ/dx = df(x)/dx$.

Thus average product is a maximum when

$$\frac{d(Q/x)}{dx} = \left(\frac{dQ}{dx} - \frac{Q}{x}\right)\frac{1}{x} = 0;$$

this means that dQ/dx must equal Q/x when the average product is a maximum. But since dQ/dx is the marginal product and Q/x is the average product, this proves the proposition in the text: When the average product is a maximum, the average product equals the marginal product.

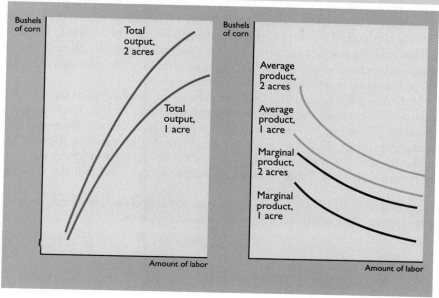

FIGURE 7.3 Total Output, Average Product, and Marginal Product Curves for Labor, with 1 and 2 Acres of Land An increase in the amount of land results in a shift in all three of these curves. (Note that only part of each of these curves is shown; the region where average or marginal product is increasing is omitted.)

THE LAW OF DIMINISHING MARGINAL RETURNS AND THE GEOMETRY OF AVERAGE AND MARGINAL PRODUCT CURVES

Previous sections have defined the production function and the average and marginal products of an input. We are now in a position to discuss one of the most famous laws of microeconomics — the law of diminishing marginal returns. The law of diminishing marginal returns, like the Scriptures, is often quoted and frequently misinterpreted. Put very briefly, this law states that *if equal increments of an input are added, the quantities of other inputs held constant, the resulting increments of product will decrease beyond some point; that is, the marginal product of the input will diminish.* This law is illustrated by Table 7.2; beyond 3 units of labor, the marginal product of labor decreases.

Several things should be noted concerning this law. First, the law of diminishing marginal returns is an empirical generalization, not a deduction from physical or biological laws. In fact, it seems to hold for most production functions in the real world. Second, it is assumed that technology remains fixed. The law of diminishing marginal returns cannot predict the effect of an additional unit of input when technology is allowed to change. Third, it is assumed that there is at least one input whose quantity is being held constant. The law of diminishing marginal returns does not apply to cases where there is a proportional increase in all inputs. Fourth, it must be possible, of course, to vary the proportions in which the various inputs are used.

If there is a fixed input and only one variable input, the typical form of the relationship between the amount of the variable input and the total output is given by OT in Figure 7.4.[8] Given such a graph, how can we determine the average product and the marginal product of the variable input? To make the analysis more concrete, suppose that Figure 7.4 refers to another farm like the one in Table 7.1, that the output is corn, and that the variable

Figure 7.4 Measurement of the Average Product When *OA* units of the variable input are used, the average product of the variable input equals the slope of the line *OB*.

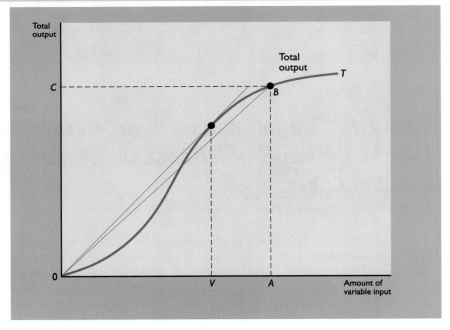

---

[8] In Figure 7.4, we assume that the amount of the variable input is varied continuously; the result is that the total output, the average product, and the marginal product curves are continuous.

FIGURE 7.5 Measurement of the Marginal Product The marginal product of the variable input equals the slope of line *NN'* when *OG* units of variable input are used.

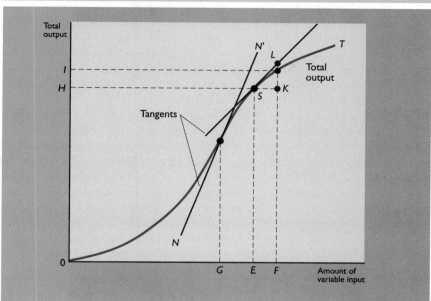

input is labor. First, consider the average product of the variable input, labor. Since average product equals total output divided by the amount of variable input, the average product of any amount of variable input, *OA,* equals *AB* (= *OC*) divided by *OA.* And *AB/OA* is obviously the slope of the line *OB,* which joins the origin and the point on the total output curve corresponding to this amount of variable input. Thus the slope of the line joining the origin and the relevant point on the total output curve is equal to the average product of the variable input, labor.

Second, consider the marginal product of the variable input, labor. Given the total output curve in Figure 7.5 (which is the same as that in Figure 7.4), how can we determine the marginal product? If the amount of variable input increases from *OE* to *OF,* total output increases from *OH* to *OI.* Clearly, as the increment in the amount of variable input becomes smaller and smaller, the extra output divided by the extra variable input, *HI/EF,* approaches the slope of the total output curve at *S.* (Even if the increment is *EF,* the approximation is not too bad: The slope of the total output curve is *KL/SK = KL/EF,* which is fairly close to *HI/EF.*) Thus, since the slope of a curve at any point equals the slope of its tangent at that point, we can determine the marginal product of any amount of variable input by drawing the tangent to the total output curve at that amount of variable input and measuring its slope. For example, the slope of NN' is the marginal product of the variable input when OG units of the variable input are used.

Using these results, it is possible to prove a number of interesting results concerning the average product curve (the curve showing the relationship between average product and the amount of variable input used) and the marginal product curve (the curve showing the relationship between marginal product and the amount of variable input used). To begin with, in Figure 7.4, since a line joining the origin and a point on the total output curve is bound to be steepest (that is, have the maximum slope) when the line is tangent to the total output curve, it follows that the average product must be a maximum if OV units of variable input are used. Moreover, since the tangent to the total output curve is exactly the same as the line joining the origin and the total output curve when OV units of the variable input are used, the slope of the tangent must equal the slope of this line, and marginal product must equal average product. Thus *marginal product must equal average product when the latter is a maximum.*[9] Also, since the marginal product is a maximum at OG (Figure 7.5), where the slope of the tangent to the total output curve is greatest, and since OG is less than OV, it follows that *the maximum marginal product occurs at a lower level of variable input than the maximum average product.*

THE PRODUCTION FUNCTION: TWO VARIABLE INPUTS

In the previous sections, we were concerned with the case in which there is only one variable input. In the next four sections, we take up the more general case in which there are two variable inputs. These variable inputs can be thought of as working with one or more fixed inputs, or they may be thought of as the only two inputs (in which case the situation is the long run). In either case, it is easy to extend the results to as many inputs as one likes. This section takes up the production function; the next two sections are concerned with its representation by a system of geometric constructs called isoquants.

If we increase the number of variable inputs from one to two, the production function becomes slightly more complicated, but it is still the relationship between various combinations of inputs and the maximum amount of output that can be obtained from them. Really, the only change is that the output is a function of two variables rather than one. For example, suppose in our agri-

---

[9] Of course this is precisely the same result as that stated on page 197.

TABLE 7.3 Hypothetical Production Function for Corn, Two Variable Inputs

Amount of labor (units)	Number of acres			
	1	2	3	4
	(bushels of corn produced per year)			
1	5	11	18	24
2	14	30	50	72
3	22	60	80	99
4	29	80	115	125
5	34	84	140	145

cultural example that we allow both land and labor to vary; the results might be as given by Table 7.3. This is the production function in tabular form. Note that we can obtain the marginal product of each input by holding the other input constant. For example, the marginal product of land when 4 units of labor are used and when between 1 and 2 acres of land are used is 51 bushels per acre; the marginal product of labor when 2 acres are used and when between 3 and 4 units of labor are used is 20 bushels per unit. Similarly, the average product of either land or labor can be computed simply by dividing the total output by the amount of either land or labor that is used.[10]

Another way to present the production function is by a surface, like that in Figure 7.6. The production surface is $OAQB$.[11] The height of a point on this surface denotes the quantity of output. Dropping a perpendicular down from a point on the production surface to the "floor" and seeing how far the resulting point is from the labor and land axes indicates how much of each input is required to produce this much output. For example, to produce $U'U$ units of output requires $OB_1 (= A_1U')$ units of labor and $OA_1 (= B_1U')$ acres of land. Conversely, one can take any amounts of land and labor, say OA_2 acres of land and OB_2 units of labor, and find out how much output they will produce by measuring the height of the production surface at D', the point where labor input is OB_2 and land input is OA_2. According to Figure 7.6, the answer is $D'D$.

Note that this hypothetical production function illustrates the fact that a given amount of output can be produced in quite different ways. For example, in Table 7.3, 80 bushels of corn can be produced with either 4 units of labor and

---

[10] If x_1 is the amount of the first input and x_2 is the amount of the second input, the production function is

$$Q = f(x_1, x_2),$$

where Q is the output rate. The marginal product of the first input is $\partial Q/\partial x_1$; the marginal product of the second input is $\partial Q/\partial x_2$.

[11] Note that this surface is not meant to represent the numerical values in Table 7.3 but is a general representation of how a production surface of this sort is likely to appear.

2 acres of land or with 3 units of labor and 3 acres of land. (Moreover, the production function does not include many of the different ways in which a given output can be produced because it includes only efficient combinations of inputs.)[12] Generally there is a variety of ways to produce a given output and a variety of efficient input combinations; thus it is possible for the firm to substitute one input for another in producing a specified amount of output.

ISOQUANTS

Isoquant An *isoquant* is a curve showing all possible (efficient) combinations of inputs that are capable of producing a certain quantity of output. Given the production function, one can readily derive the isoquant pertaining to any level of output. For example, in Figure 7.6, suppose that we want to find the isoquant corresponding to an output of $U'U$. All that we need to do is to cut the production surface at the height of $U'U$ parallel to the base plane, the result being EUF, and to drop perpendiculars from EUF to the base. Clearly, this results in a curve that includes all efficient combinations of land and labor that can produce $U'U$ bushels of corn.[13]

Several isoquants, each pertaining to a different output rate, are shown in Figure 7.7. The two axes measure the quantities of inputs that are used. In contrast to the previous diagrams, we assume that labor and capital—not labor and land—are the relevant inputs in this case. The curves show the various combinations of inputs that can produce 50, 100, and 150 units of output. For example, consider the isoquant pertaining to 50 units of output per period of time. According to this isoquant, it is possible to attain this output rate if OL_0 units of labor and OK_0 units of capital are used per period of time. Alternatively, this output rate can be attained if OL_1 units of labor and OK_1 units of capital—or OL_2 units of labor and OK_2 units of capital—are used per period of time.

---

[12] For example, if 2 units of labor and 3 units of capital can produce 1 unit of output, this combination of inputs and output will not be included in the production function if it is also possible to produce 1 unit of output with 2 units of labor and 2 units of capital. The former input combination is clearly inefficient, since it is possible to obtain the result with the same amount of labor and less capital.

[13] Using the notation in footnote 10, an isoquant shows all combinations of x_1 and x_2 such that $f(x_1, x_2)$ equals a certain output rate.

FIGURE 7.6 **Production Function, Two Variable Inputs** The production surface, *OAQB*, shows the amount of total output that can be obtained from various combinations of quantities of land and labor.

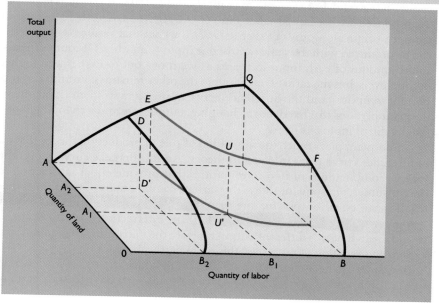

FIGURE 7.7 **Isoquants** These three isoquants show the various combinations of capital and labor that can produce 50, 100, and 150 units of output.

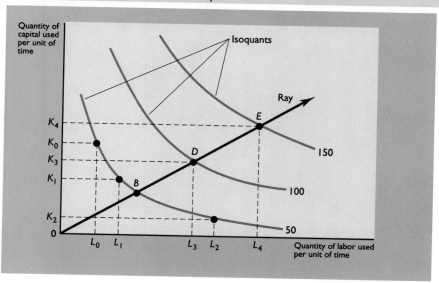

A *ray* is a line that starts from some point and goes off into space. A ray from the origin, such as *OBDE,* describes all input combinations where the capital-labor ratio is constant, with the slope of the ray being equal to the constant capital-labor ratio. For example, at points *D* and *E,* 100 and 150 units of output are produced with a capital-labor ratio of $OK_3/OL_3 = OK_4/OL_4$. Moving out from the origin along any ray, such as *OBDE,* we see that various output levels can be produced with the same ratio of one input to another. Of course, the absolute amount of each input increases as we move out to higher and higher output levels, but the ratio of one input to the other remains constant. It is important to understand the difference between such a ray and an isoquant; an isoquant pertains to a fixed, not a changing, output rate and a changing, not a fixed, ratio of inputs.

An isoquant plays much the same kind of role in production theory that an indifference curve plays in demand theory. An indifference curve shows the various combinations of two commodities that provide equal satisfaction to the consumer; an isoquant shows the various combinations of two inputs that result in an equal output for the firm. It is obvious that, like indifference curves, two isoquants cannot intersect. If an intersection were to occur, it would mean that two different output rates are the maximum obtainable from a given combination of resources; this is obviously absurd.

Isoquants can be used to illustrate the case in which inputs must be used in fixed proportions. Figure 7.8 shows a case of this sort; the necessary ratio of

FIGURE 7.8 Isoquants in the Case of Fixed Proportions If inputs must be used in fixed proportions, the isoquants are right angles.

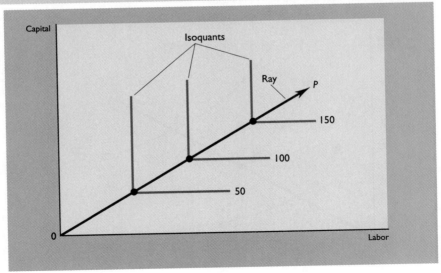

capital to labor is the slope of the ray *OP*. The isoquants are right angles, indicating that, if one input is changed while the other input is held constant, there is no increase in the output rate. In other words, the marginal product of either input is zero if the other input is held constant.

The Economic Region of Production

In some cases, isoquants may have positively sloped segments, or bend back on themselves, as shown in Figure 7.9. Above *OA* and below *OB,* the slope of the isoquants is positive; this implies that increases in both capital and labor are required to maintain a certain output rate. If this is the case, the marginal product of one or the other input must be negative. Above *OA,* the marginal product of capital is negative; thus output will increase if less capital is used while the amount of labor is held constant. Below *OB,* the marginal product of labor is negative; thus output will increase if less labor is used while the amount of capital is held constant. The lines *OA* and *OB* are called *ridge lines.*

Ridge lines

Clearly, no profit-maximizing firm will operate at a point outside the ridge lines, since it can produce the same output with less of both inputs, and this must be cheaper. To illustrate this, consider point *C* in Figure 7.9. Because this is a point where the isoquant is positively sloped—and thus outside the ridge lines—it requires a greater amount of both labor and capital than some other point (for example, point *D*) on the same isoquant. Since both capital and labor

FIGURE 7.9 The Economic Region of Production No profit-maximizing firm will operate at a point outside the ridge lines, *OA* and *OB*.

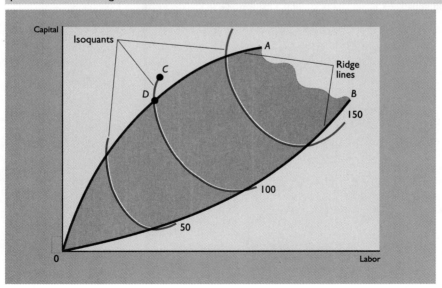

have positive prices, it must be cheaper to operate at point D than at point C. In general, it is always possible to find a cheaper way to produce a given quantity of output than to operate at a point outside the ridge lines. Thus the shaded area between the ridge lines is often called the *economic region of production*. For example, in Figure 7.9, the economic region of production is the area between OA and OB. No rational firm will venture outside this region.

Substitution among Inputs

From both a practical and a theoretical point of view, it is important to study the rate at which one input must be substituted for another to maintain a constant output rate. Consider the isoquant Z in Figure 7.10. The relevant output rate can be produced with OL_0 units of labor and OK_0 units of capital. However, if the amount of labor is increased to OL_1, the same output rate can be attained with less capital: OK_1 units rather than OK_0. Thus, in the relevant range, the rate at which labor can be substituted for capital is $-(OK_0 - OK_1)/(OL_0 - OL_1) = BA/BC$; the minus sign is added to make the result a positive number. If we consider a very small increase in labor (OL_1 being very close to OL_0), BA/BC equals -1 times the slope of the tangent, G, to the isoquant at A, which is called the *marginal rate of technical substitution*. It measures, for small changes in labor, the change in capital required per unit change in labor. The reader will note that, as its name indicates, it is analogous to the marginal rate of substitution in demand theory. (Economists, having found an elegant and

Marginal rate of technical substitution

FIGURE 7.10 The Marginal Rate of Technical Substitution The marginal rate of technical substitution equals -1 times the slope of the tangent, G, to the isoquant.

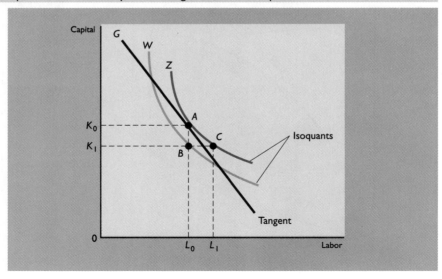

EXAMPLE 7.2

How to Produce Broilers

Over 8 billion dollars worth of broiler chickens are produced in the United States per year. Broilers are fed corn and soybean oilmeal. According to data published by the Organization for Economic Cooperation and Development, a 1-pound weight gain can be achieved for a broiler during a specified period if the broiler is fed any one of the following combinations of quantities of corn and soybean oilmeal.

Quantity of corn (pounds)	Quantity of soybean oilmeal (pounds)
1.0	0.95
1.1	0.76
1.2	0.60
1.3	0.50
1.4	0.42

(a) Plot these data as an isoquant. (b) Calculate the marginal rate of technical substitution at all points along this isoquant. (c) Is this isoquant convex? (d) If the price of a pound of corn equals the price of a pound of soybean oilmeal, should a broiler be fed 1.1 pounds of corn and 0.76 pounds of soybean oilmeal?

SOLUTION

(a) The isoquant is as follows:

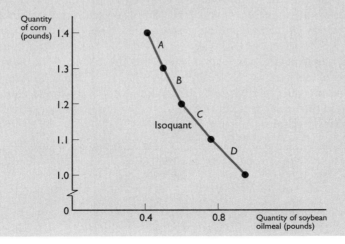

(b) For each segment (A, B, C, D) of the isoquant, the marginal rate of technical substitution is as follows:

Segment	Marginal rate of technical substitution
A	$-(1.4 - 1.3) \div (.42 - .50) = 1.25$
B	$-(1.3 - 1.2) \div (.50 - .60) = 1.00$
C	$-(1.2 - 1.1) \div (.60 - .76) = 0.63$
D	$-(1.1 - 1.0) \div (.76 - .95) = 0.53$

(c) Yes, since the marginal rate of technical substitution falls as more soybean oilmeal is substituted for corn. (d) No, because other combinations of corn and soybean oilmeal are cheaper. If P equals the price of a pound of either corn or soybean oilmeal, the cost of 1.1 pounds of corn and 0.76 pounds of soybean oilmeal is $1.86P$. In contrast, the cost of 1.2 pounds of corn and 0.60 pounds of soybean oilmeal is $1.80P$, which is lower.*

---

* For further discussion, see Organization for Economic Cooperation and Development, *Interdisciplinary Research in Input/Output Relationships and Production Functions to Improve Decisions and Efficiency for Poultry Production* (Paris: OECD, 1966).

felicitous phrase like the marginal rate of substitution, did not want to abandon it for anything cumbersome.)

Using the diagram in Figure 7.10, it is easy to demonstrate that the marginal rate of technical substitution of labor for capital is equal to the ratio of the marginal product of labor to the marginal product of capital. Suppose that labor input is held at the OL_0 level, while capital is increased from OK_1 to OK_0. Output would increase from the level (say Q_1) corresponding to isoquant W to the level (say Q_0) corresponding to isoquant Z. The marginal product of capital is $(Q_0 - Q_1)/(OK_0 - OK_1) = (Q_0 - Q_1)/BA$. On the other hand, suppose that capital is held at OK_1 while labor is increased from OL_0 to OL_1. The marginal product of labor is $(Q_0 - Q_1)/(OL_1 - OL_0) = (Q_0 - Q_1)/BC$. Thus the ratio of the marginal product of labor to the marginal product of capital equals BA/BC, which (in the limit for small changes in the amount of labor) equals the marginal rate of technical substitution.[14]

---

[14] Using the notation of footnote 10, the total differential of the production function is

$$dQ = \frac{\partial f}{\partial x_1} dx_1 + \frac{\partial f}{\partial x_2} dx_2.$$

Since output remains constant along an isoquant, $dQ = 0$ along an isoquant. Thus

$$\frac{\partial f}{\partial x_1} dx_1 + \frac{\partial f}{\partial x_2} dx_2 = 0,$$

(*Cont.*)

It is also easy to show that the marginal rate of technical substitution of labor for capital tends to decrease as an increasing amount of labor is substituted for capital. As labor is substituted for capital, the marginal product of labor tends to fall. Increases in labor, holding capital constant, result in a decrease in the marginal product of labor in the economic region of production. When capital is decreased, even more of a decrease occurs in the marginal product of labor, since a decrease in capital results in a downward shift in the marginal product curve for labor. At the same time, the marginal product of capital rises (for the same kinds of reasons) as more labor is substituted for capital. Thus, since the marginal rate of technical substitution equals the marginal product of labor (which is falling) divided by the marginal product of capital (which is rising), it must be falling as labor is substituted for capital.

Since the marginal rate of technical substitution falls as labor is substituted for capital, it follows that isoquants must be convex. (See page 71.) Because the marginal rate of technical substitution equals -1 times the slope of the isoquant and because the marginal rate of technical substitution falls as we move to the right along an isoquant, the absolute value of the slope of the isoquant must be getting smaller as we move to the right along an isoquant. But if the absolute value of the slope is getting smaller as we move to the right, the isoquant must be convex.

THE LONG RUN AND RETURNS TO SCALE

Previous sections have shown how a firm's technology can be represented by a production function and have described the characteristics of production functions (and of related concepts like the marginal and average product) that seem to hold in general for production processes. However, one important characteristic of production functions has not been described: how output responds in the long run to changes in the *scale* of the firm. In other words, suppose that we consider a long-run situation in which all inputs are variable, and suppose that the firm increases the amount of all inputs by the same proportion. What will happen to output? This is an important question, the answer

---

and the marginal rate of technical substitution, defined as $-dx_2/dx_1$, is

$$\frac{\partial f}{\partial x_1} \div \frac{\partial f}{\partial x_2},$$

which is the ratio of the marginal product of the first input to the marginal product of the second input. This is another proof of the proposition in the text.

to which (as we shall see in subsequent chapters) helps to determine whether firms of certain sizes can survive in an industry.

To repeat, what will happen to output under the assumed conditions? Clearly, there are three possibilities: First, output may increase by a larger proportion than each of the inputs. For example, a doubling of all inputs may lead to more than a doubling of output. This is the case of *increasing returns to scale.* Second, output may increase by a smaller proportion than each of the inputs. For example, a doubling of all inputs may lead to less than a doubling of output. This is the case of *decreasing returns to scale.* Third, output may increase by exactly the same proportion as the inputs. For example, a doubling of all inputs may lead to a doubling of output. This is the case of *constant returns to scale.*

Increasing, decreasing, and constant returns to scale

At first glance it may seem that production functions must necessarily exhibit constant returns to scale. After all, if two factories are built with the same plant and the same type of workers, it would seem obvious that twice as much output will result. Unfortunately (or fortunately, depending on your point of view), it is not as simple as that. For instance, if a firm doubles its scale, it may be able to use techniques that could not be used at the smaller scale. Thus, although one could double a firm's size by simply building two small factories, this may be inefficient. One large factory may be more efficient than two smaller factories of the same total capacity because it is large enough to use certain techniques that the smaller factories cannot use.

Another reason for increasing returns to scale stems from certain geometrical relations. For example, since the volume of a box that is 4×4×4 feet is 64 times as great as the volume of a box that is 1×1×1 foot, the former box can carry 64 times as much as the latter box. But since the area of the six sides of the 4×4×4 foot box is 96 square feet and the area of the six sides of the 1×1×1 foot box is 6 square feet, the former box only requires 16 times as much wood as the latter. Greater specialization also can result in increasing returns to scale: As more men and machines are used, it is possible to subdivide tasks and allow various inputs to specialize. Also economies of scale may arise because of probabilistic considerations: For example, because the aggregate behavior of a bigger number of customers tends to be more stable, a firm's inventory may not have to increase in proportion to its sales.

Decreasing returns to scale can also occur; the most frequently cited reason is the difficulty of coordinating a large enterprise. It can be difficult even in a small firm to obtain the information required to make important decisions; in a large firm the difficulties tend to be greater. It can be difficult even in a small firm to be certain that management's wishes are being carried out; in a larger firm these difficulties too tend to be greater. Although the advantages of a large organization seem to have captured the public fancy, there are often very great disadvantages. For example, in certain kinds of research and development, there is evidence that large engineering teams tend to be less effective than smaller ones and that large firms tend to be less effective than small ones.

FIGURE 7.11 Constant, Increasing, and Decreasing Returns to Scale Panel A shows constant returns to scale, panel B shows increasing returns to scale, and panel C shows decreasing returns to scale.

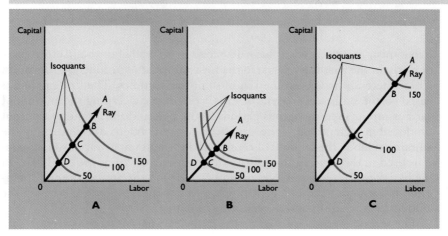

Diagrams like those in Figure 7.11 can be used to analyze and describe the situation in a particular firm. Panel A describes a case in which there are constant returns to scale. Examination of the isoquants for outputs of 50, 100, and 150 units shows that they intersect any ray from the origin, like *OA,* at equal distances. (That is, $OD = DC = CB$.) In other words, twice as much of both inputs are needed to produce 100 units of output than to produce 50 units of output, and three times as much of both inputs are needed to produce 150 units of output than to produce 50 units of output. Panel B describes a case in which there are increasing returns to scale. In this case, successive isoquants, as one moves out from the origin, become closer and closer together. For example, OD > DC > CB. Panel C describes a case in which there are decreasing returns to scale. In this case, successive isoquants become farther and farther apart as we move out from the origin. For example, $OD < DC < CB$.

Whether there are constant, increasing, or decreasing returns to scale in a particular situation is an empirical question that must be settled case by case. There is no simple, all-encompassing answer.[15] In some industries the available evidence may indicate that increasing returns are present over a certain range of output. In other industries, decreasing or constant returns may be present. In the next section, we turn to a discussion of empirical studies.

---

[15] Also, it is important to note that the answer is likely to depend on the level of output that is considered. There may be increasing returns to scale at small output levels and constant or decreasing returns to scale at larger output levels.

MEASUREMENT OF PRODUCTION FUNCTIONS

Economists and statisticians have devoted a great deal of time and effort, particularly in the past forty years, to the measurement of production functions. Three methods have been used in most of these studies. The first method is **Time series data** based on the statistical analysis of time series data concerning the amount of various inputs used in various periods in the past and the amount of output produced in each period. For example, one might obtain data concerning the amount of labor, the amount of capital, and the amount of various raw materials used in the aluminum industry during each year from 1961 to 1997. On the basis of such data and information concerning the annual output of aluminum during 1961 to 1997, one might estimate the relationship between the amounts of the inputs and the resulting output.

Cross-section data The second method is based on the statistical analysis of cross-section data concerning the amount of various inputs used and output produced in various firms or sectors of the industry at a given point in time. For example, one might obtain data concerning the amount of labor, the amount of capital, and the amount of various raw materials used in various firms in the aluminum industry in 1997. On the basis of such data and information concerning the 1997 output of each firm, one might estimate the relationship between the amounts of the inputs and the resulting output.

Engineering data The third method is based on technical information supplied by the engineer or the agricultural scientist. This information is collected by experiment or from experience with the day-to-day workings of the technical process. There are considerable advantages to be gained from approaching the measurement of the production function from this angle because the range of applicability of the data is known, and, unlike time series and cross-section studies, we are not restricted to the narrow range of actual observations. However, there are also some difficult problems in this approach, which are discussed in the following paragraphs.

All three approaches are handicapped by the fact that the data may not always represent technically efficient combinations of inputs and output. For example, because of errors or constraints, the amount of inputs used by the aluminum industry in 1997 may not have been the minimum required to produce the 1997 output of the aluminum industry. Since the production function theoretically includes only efficient input combinations, a case of this sort should be excluded if our measurements are to be pristine pure. In practice, however, such cases are not always excluded (or recognized) and the resulting estimate of the production function is in error for this reason.

Another important problem is the measurement of capital input. The principal difficulty stems from the fact that the stock of capital is composed of various types and ages of machines, buildings, and inventories. Combining them into a single measure—or a few measures—is a formidable problem. In addition, errors can arise in the first two techniques because various data points, which are assumed to be on the same production function, are in fact on different ones. Moreover, biases can occur because of identification problems somewhat similar to those discussed on page 152.

With regard to the third method, it is difficult to combine the results for the processes for which engineers have data into an overall plant or firm production function. Since engineering data generally pertain to only a part of the firm's activities, this is often a very hard job. For example, engineering data tell us little or nothing about the firm's marketing or financial activities. Moreover, engineering data are generally available for only parts of the firm's fabricating activities.

Despite these difficulties, estimates of production functions have proved of considerable interest and value. Many of these estimates have been based on the assumption that the production function is a so-called Cobb-Douglas function, which is

Cobb-Douglas function

$$Q = AL^{\alpha_1}K^{\alpha_2}M^{\alpha_3}, \qquad [7.1]$$

where Q is the output rate; L is the quantity of labor; K is the quantity of capital; and M is the quantity of raw materials; and A, α_1, α_2 and α_3 are parameters that vary from case to case. Ordinarily it is assumed that the value of each α is less than 1, which ensures that the marginal product of each input (which equals its α times its average product) decreases with increases in its utilization. Increasing returns to scale occur if $\alpha_1 + \alpha_2 + \alpha_3 > 1$; decreasing returns to scale occur if $\alpha_1 + \alpha_2 + \alpha_3 < 1$.[16]

Table 7.4 shows the estimates of α_1, α_2, and α_3 for a number of industries in the United States and abroad. They provide interesting information concerning production relations in these industries. To see more clearly the implications of these results, note that α_1 is the percentage increase in output resulting from a 1 percent increase in labor, holding the quantities of the other inputs constant. For example, in the Canadian telephone industry in about 1972, a 1 percent increase in labor would have resulted in a 0.70 percent increase in output. Similarly, α_2 is the percentage increase in output resulting from a 1 percent increase in capital, holding the quantities of other inputs constant.

The results also cast light on returns to scale. In 6 of the 18 cases, there seem to be decreasing returns; in 12 of the 18 cases there seem to be increasing re-

---

[16] In Equation 7.1, there are three inputs. In other Cobb-Douglas production functions, there may be more or less than three inputs.

TABLE 7.4 Estimates of α_1, α_2, and α_3, for Selected Industries

Industry	Country	α_1	α_2	α_3	$\alpha_1 + \alpha_2 + \alpha_3$
Gas	France	.83	.10	—	0.93
Railroads	United States	.89	.12	.28	1.29
Coal	United Kingdom	.79	.29	—	1.08
Food	United States	.72	.35	—	1.07
Metals and machinery	United States	.71	.26	—	0.97
Communications	Russia	.80	.38	—	1.18
Cotton	India	.92	.12	—	1.04
Jute	India	.84	.14	—	0.98
Sugar	India	.59	.33	—	0.92
Coal	India	.71	.44	—	1.15
Paper	India	.64	.45	—	1.09
Chemicals	India	.80	.37	—	1.17
Electricity	India	.20	.67	—	0.87
Food[a]	United States	.63	.44	—	1.07
Paper[a]	United States	.62	.37	—	0.98
Telephone	Canada	.70	.41	—	1.11
Chemicals[b]	United States	.54	.38	.11	1.03
Aircraft[b]	United States	.79	.18	.04	1.01

[a] The figure for α_1 is the sum of the figures given for production workers and nonproduction workers.

[b] In these cases, M is cumulated past expenditure on research and development, not the quantity of raw materials, and K is the quantity of capital services.

SOURCES: A. A. Walters, "Production and Cost Functions," *Econometrica*, January 1963; J. Moroney, "Cobb-Douglas Production Functions and Returns to Scale in U.S. Manufacturing," *Western Economic Journal*, 1967; A. Dobell, L. Taylor, L. Waverman, T. Liu, and M. Copeland, "Communications in Canada," *Bell Journal of Economic and Management Science,* 1972; J. P. Lewis, "Postwar Economic Growth and Productivity in the Soviet Communications Industry," *Bell Journal of Economics and Management Sciences.* Autumn 1975; and Z. Griliches, "Returns to Research and Development Expenditures in the Private Sector," in J. Kendrick and B. Vaccara (eds.), *New Developments in Productivity Measurement and Analysis* (Chicago: National Bureau of Economic Research, 1980).

turns to scale. Finally, it is possible to construct isoquants from the results in Table 7.4. For example, Figure 7.12 shows some isoquants for the French gas industry. Note that these isoquants (*A, B,* and *C*) are similar in shape to the hypothetical isoquants introduced earlier in this chapter.[17]

---

[17] There has also been much use made of the transcendental logarithmic production function described in L. Christenson, D. Jorgenson, and L. Lau, "Conjugate Duality and the Transcendental Logarithmic Production Function," *Econometrica*, July 1971. The French data in Figure 7.12 come from studies by M. Verhulst of the gas industry.

FIGURE 7.12 **Isoquants for the French Gas Industry** These estimates of actual isoquants for the French gas industry are similar in shape to what microeconomic theory predicts.

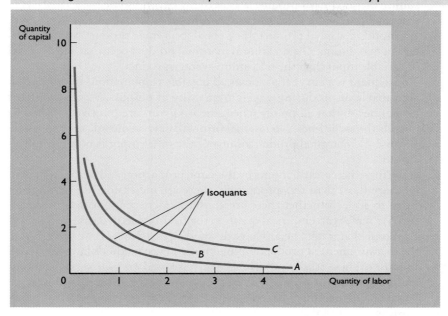

SUMMARY

1. As a first approximation, economists generally assume that firms attempt to maximize profits. This is the standard assumption in economics, because it is a close enough approximation for many important purposes and because it provides rules of behavior for firms that do want to make as much money as possible.
2. The production function is used by economists to represent the technology available to the firm. For any commodity, the production function is the relationship between the quantities of various inputs used per period of time and the maximum quantity of the commodity produced per period of time.
3. In analyzing production processes, we generally assume that all inputs can be divided into two categories: fixed and variable. In the short run, the firm's plant and equipment are fixed; in the long run, all inputs are variable. Both in the short run and in the long run, a firm's production processes ordinarily permit substantial variation in input proportions.

4. The law of diminishing marginal returns states that as equal increments of one input are added, the quantities of other inputs held constant, the resulting increments of product will decrease beyond some point; that is, the marginal product of the input will diminish.

5. An input's marginal product must equal its average product when the latter is a maximum. The maximum marginal product occurs at a lower level of variable input than the maximum average product.

6. An isoquant is a curve that shows all possible combinations of inputs that are capable of producing a certain quantity of output. We can construct ridge lines so that all points where the isoquants are positively sloped lie outside the ridge lines. No rational firm will operate outside the ridge lines because the marginal product of one or the other input is negative in this region.

7. If the firm increases all inputs by the same proportion and output increases by more (less) than this proportion, there are increasing (decreasing) returns to scale. Whether there are constant, increasing, or decreasing returns to scale is an empirical question that must be settled case by case.

8. Economists and statisticians have devoted a great deal of time and effort to the measurement of production functions. Three methods have been used in most of these studies: statistical analysis based on time series of inputs and output, statistical analysis based on cross-section data, and analysis based on engineering data. Although there are a great many difficulties in existing measurement techniques, estimates of production functions have proved of considerable interest and value.

QUESTIONS/PROBLEMS

1. Economists have suggested that the entrepreneur (the owner-manager of the firm) maximizes utility, which is a function of the firm's profits and the amount of leisure the entrepreneur enjoys. Suppose that a particular

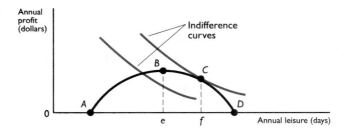

entrepreneur's indifference curves between profit and leisure are as shown in the preceding graph. Also, suppose that the amount of work that the entrepreneur must do is proportional to his or her firm's output. If this is the case, the relationship between leisure and profit is given by the curved line *ABCD*.

(a) Why does the relationship between leisure and profit have the shape indicated by *ABCD*? (b) Will the entrepreneur maximize profit? (c) If the entrepreneur's indifference curves were horizontal lines, would he or she maximize profit?

2. Suppose that an entrepreneur's utility depends on the size of his or or her firm (as measured by its output) and its profits. In particular, the indifference curves are as follows:

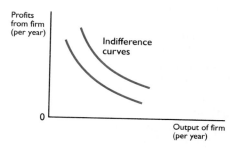

(a) Will the entrepreneur maximize profit? (b) If not, will he or she produce more or less than the profit-maximizing output? (c) Draw a graph to indicate the point he or she will choose.

3. Fill in the blanks in the following table:

Number of units of variable input	Total output (number of units)	Marginal product[a] of variable input	Average product of variable input
3	—	Unknown	30
4	—	20	
5	130	—	—
6	—	5	—
7	—	—	$19\frac{1}{2}$

[a] These figures pertain to the interval between the indicated amount of the variable input and 1 unit less than the indicated amount of the variable input.

4. In Question 3, does the production function exhibit diminishing marginal returns? If so, at what number of units of variable input do diminishing marginal returns begin to set in? Can you tell on the basis of the table in Question 3?

5. As the quantity of a variable input increases, explain why the point where *marginal* product begins to decline is encountered before the point where *average* product begins to decline. Explain, too, why the point where *aver-*

age product begins to decline is encountered before the point where *total* output begins to decline.

6. Suppose that a good is produced with two inputs, labor and capital, and that the production function is

$$Q = 10\sqrt{L}\sqrt{K},$$

where Q is the quantity of output, L is the quantity of labor, and K is the quantity of capital. Does this production function exhibit increasing returns to scale? Decreasing returns to scale? Constant returns to scale? Explain.

7. Econometric studies of the cotton industry in India indicate that the Cobb-Douglas production function can be applied, and that the exponent of labor is .92 and the exponent of capital is .12. Suppose that both capital and labor were increased by 1 percent. By what percent would output increase?

8. In an article published by the Federal Reserve Bank of Philadelphia in 1989, it is suggested that bank managers "be encouraged to own stock in the companies they manage. In this way, they would directly benefit from the decisions they make that increase the market value of the bank."[18] Is this suggestion aimed at solving the principal-agent problem? If so, how effective do you think it would be?

9. (Advanced) Suppose you are assured by the owner of an aircraft factory that his firm is subject to constant returns to scale, with labor and capital the only inputs. He claims that output per worker is a function of capital per worker only. Is he right?

10. Laserex, a manufacturer of lasers, reports that the marginal product of labor is 10 units of output per hour of labor and that the marginal rate of technical substitution of labor for capital is 5. What is the marginal product of capital?

11. The following graph shows the combinations of quantities of grain and protein that must be used to produce 150 pounds of pork. Curve A assumes that no Aureomycin is added, while curve B assumes that some of it is added.

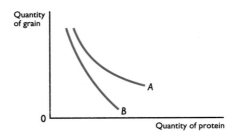

[18] L. Mester, "Owners Versus Managers: Who Controls the Bank?" *Business Review,* May 1989.

(a) If Aureomycin can be obtained free, should pork producers add it?

(b) Does the addition of Aureomycin affect the marginal rate of technical substitution? If so, how?

12. The Conway Company, which produces steel, hires a consultant to estimate its production function. The consultant reports that the firm's production fuction is

$$Q = 3A + 4L$$

where Q is the number of tons of steel produced by Conway per year, A is the number of acres of land used by Conway, and L is the number of hours of labor used per year.

(a) Do you think that this production function includes all the relevant inputs? Explain.

(b) If this production function is applied to all possible values of L, do the results seem reasonable? Why or why not?

(c) Does this firm conform to the law of diminishing marginal returns? Explain.

13. The executive vice president of the Sarafian Corporation has concluded that $Q = AL^{\alpha}K^{\beta}$, where Q is the output rate, L is the rate of labor input, and K is the rate of capital input. The firm's statisticians say that $\alpha = 0.7$ and $\beta = 0.4$. Based on these figures, the executive vice president claims that there are increasing returns to scale in this firm.

(a) Is the executive vice president correct?

(b) If α were 0.6 rather than 0.7, would she be correct?

Optimal Input Combinations and Cost Functions

DECISIONS REGARDING INPUT COMBINATIONS

In the previous chapter we were concerned with the motivation of the firm and the way in which the technology available to the firm can be represented. We decided to assume, as a first approximation, that firms attempt to maximize profit. We also decided that the technology available to the firm can be represented by a production function, which conforms to certain rules like the law of diminishing marginal returns. These decisions take us part way—but only part way—toward a model of the firm. The next step is to determine how a profit-maximizing firm will combine inputs to produce a given quantity of output. That is the purpose of this chapter.

To be specific, suppose that Eckhard Pfeiffer, head of Compaq Computer, and his colleagues decide for some reason that Compaq should produce 500 computers of a particular type next year. Suppose that, in accord with the conclusions of the previous chapter, we assume that Compaq is an out-and-out profit maximizer, and that we are given its production function, derived largely through engineering studies and statistical analysis. On the basis of this information, can we predict what combination of inputs Compaq will use to produce these 500 computers next year and how much it will cost to produce them? Or putting the problem somewhat differently, suppose that we are hired by Compaq to help with this decision. Can we tell Compaq what combination of inputs it *should* use and how much it *should* cost to produce this amount?

In this chapter, we begin by determining which combination of inputs a firm will choose if it minimizes the cost of producing a given amount of output. Then we discuss the nature of costs—what is meant by a cost and how various concepts of cost differ from one another. Finally, we show how the short-run and long-run cost functions of the firm can be derived theoretically, and we provide a brief discussion of the measurement of cost functions.

THE OPTIMAL COMBINATION OF INPUTS

For the sake of generality, let's consider a firm of any sort, not just Compaq Computer. If the firm maximizes profit, it will minimize the cost of producing a given output or maximize the output derived from a given level of cost.[1] This seems obvious. Suppose that the firm is a perfect competitor in the input markets; this means that it takes input prices as given. (The case in which the firm can influence input prices is taken up in Chapter 15.) Suppose that there are two inputs, capital and labor, that are variable in the relevant time period. What combination of capital and labor should the firm choose if it wants to maximize the quantity of output derived from the given level of cost?

As a first step toward answering this question, let's determine the various combinations of inputs that the firm can obtain for a given expenditure. For example, if capital and labor are the inputs and the price of labor is P_L per unit and the price of capital is P_K per unit, the input combinations that can be ob-

---

[1] The conditions for minimizing the cost of producing a given output are the same as those for maximizing the output from a given cost. This is shown in the present section. Thus we can view the firm's problem in either way.

tained for a total outlay of R are such that

$$P_L L + P_K K = R,$$ [8.1]

where L is the amount of the labor input and K is the amount of the capital input. Given P_L, P_K, and R, it follows that

$$K = \frac{R}{P_K} - \frac{P_L}{P_K} L.$$ [8.2]

Thus the various combinations of capital and labor that can be purchased, given P_L, P_K, and R, can be represented by a straight line like that shown in Figure 8.1. (Capital is plotted on the vertical axis, labor is plotted on the horizontal.) This line, which has an intercept on the vertical axis equal to R/P_K and **Isocost** a slope of $-P_L/P_K$, is called an *isocost curve*.
curve
    If we superimpose the relevant isocost curve on the firm's isoquant map, we can readily determine graphically which combination of inputs will maximize the output for the given expenditure. Obviously, the firm should pick that point on the isocost curve that is on the highest isoquant, for example, P in Figure 8.2. This clearly is a point where the isocost curve is tangent to the isoquant. Thus, since the slope of the isocost curve is the negative of P_L/P_K and

FIGURE 8.1 Isocost Curve The isocost curve shows the combinations of inputs that can be obtained for a total outlay of R.

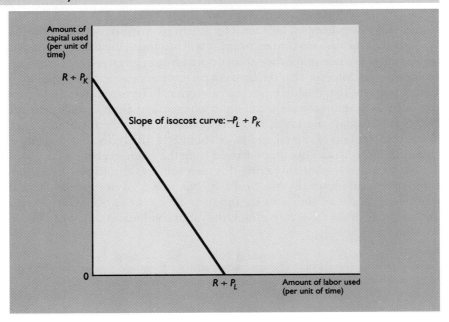

FIGURE 8.2 Maximization of Output for Given Cost FIGURE 8.2 **Maximization of Output for Given Cost** To maximize output for a given cost, the firm should choose the input combination at point P.

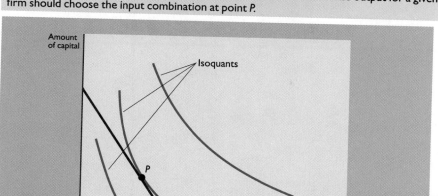

the slope of the isoquant is the negative of the marginal rate of technical substitution, it follows that the optimal combination of inputs must be such that the ratio of input prices, P_L/P_K, equals the marginal rate of technical substitution. Since it will be recalled that the marginal rate of technical substitution of labor for capital is MP_L/MP_K, it follows that the optimal combination of inputs is one where $MP_L/MP_K = P_L/P_K$. Or, put differently, the firm should choose an input combination where $MP_L/P_L = MP_K/P_K$.

In general, the firm will maximize output by distributing its expenditures among various inputs in such a way that the marginal product of a dollar's worth of any one input is equal to the marginal product of a dollar's worth of any other input used. The firm will choose an input combination such that

$$\frac{MP_a}{P_a} = \frac{MP_b}{P_b} = \cdots = \frac{MP_m}{P_m}, \qquad [8.3]$$

where $MP_a, MP_b, \ldots, MP_m$ are the marginal products of inputs $a, b, \ldots, m$, and $P_a, P_b, \ldots, P_m$ are the prices of inputs $a, b, \ldots, m$.

Returning to the case where labor and capital are the only two inputs, suppose that a firm decides to spend $200 on these inputs and that the price of labor is $10 per unit and the price of capital is $20 per unit. Table 8.1 shows the marginal product of each input when various combinations of inputs (the total

TABLE 8.1 Marginal Products of Capital and Labor

Amount of input used		Marginal product[a]	
Labor	Capital	Labor	Capital
2	9	20	4
4	8	18	6
6	7	16	8
8	6	14	10
10	5	12	12
12	4	10	14
14	3	8	16
16	2	6	18
18	1	4	20

[a]The marginal products are defined for the interval between the indicated amount of labor or capital and 1 unit (capital) or 2 units (labor) less than this amount.

cost of each combination being $200) are used. What combination is best? According to Equation 8.3, the marginal product of capital should be set at twice the marginal product of labor, since the price of a unit of capital is twice the price of a unit of labor. This occurs at 14 units of labor and 3 units of capital; thus this is the optimal combination.

To prove that this allocation of cost ($140 to labor and $60 to capital) is optimal, suppose that we shift $20 from labor to capital (with the result that $120 is devoted to labor and $80 to capital). Since the marginal product of the extra unit of capital that is gained is 14 units of output and the marginal product of the 2 units of labor given up is 2 times 8 units of product, this change will reduce output by 2 units.[2] Similarly, the transfer of $20 from capital to labor will reduce output.

Optimal input combination

A graph similar to Figure 8.2 can be used to determine the input combination that will minimize the cost of producing a given output. Moving along the isoquant corresponding to the stipulated output level, we must find that point on the isoquant that lies on the lowest isocost curve, for example, W in Figure 8.3. Input combinations on isocost curves like C_0 that lie below W are cheaper than W, but they cannot produce the desired output. Input combinations on isocost curves like C_2 that lie above W will produce the desired output but at a higher cost than W. It is obvious that the optimal point, W, is a point where the isocost curve is tangent to the isoquant. Thus, to minimize the cost of producing a given output or to maximize the output from a given cost out-

[2] The marginal product of labor between 12 and 14 units of labor is 8 units of output per unit of labor. The marginal product of capital between 3 and 4 units of capital is 14 units of output per unit of capital.

FIGURE 8.3 Minimization of Cost for Given Output To minimize the cost of producing the amount of output corresponding to this isoquant, the firm should choose the input combination at point W.

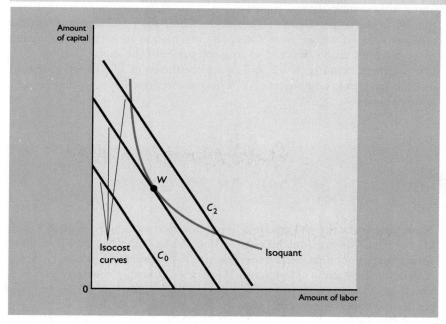

lay, the firm must equate the marginal rate of technical substitution and the input-price ratio.[3]

---

[3] Suppose that Q is the output rate and that the production function is $Q = f(x_1, x_2)$, where x_1 and x_2 are the amounts of the two inputs used. If we want to find the values of x_1 and x_2 that maximize Q for the given cost C_0, we set up the Lagrangian function:

$$L = f(x_1, x_2) - \lambda(P_1 x_1 + P_2 x_2 - C_0),$$

where P_1 is the price of the first input, P_2 is the price of the second input, and λ is the Lagrangian multiplier. Some first-order conditions are

$$\frac{\partial L}{\partial x_1} = \frac{\partial f}{\partial x_1} - \lambda P_1 = 0 \quad \text{and} \quad \frac{\partial L}{\partial x_2} = \frac{\partial f}{\partial x_2} - \lambda P_2 = 0,$$

which imply that $\partial f / \partial x_1 \div P_1 = \partial f / \partial x_2 \div P_2 = \lambda$, the condition in Equation 8.3.

If we want to minimize the cost for the given output Q_0, we set up the Lagrangian function:

$$P_1 x_1 + P_2 x_2 - M[f(x_1, x_2) - Q_0],$$

where M is the Lagrangian multiplier. Some first-order conditions are

$$P_1 - \frac{M \partial f}{\partial x_1} = 0 \quad \text{and} \quad P_2 - \frac{M \partial f}{\partial x_2} = 0, \qquad \textit{(Cont.)}$$

Note that this tells us how to solve the problem posed at the beginning of the chapter—the problem of a computer firm (Compaq) that decides for some reason to produce 500 computers of a particular type next year and wants to know what combination of inputs to use. All that we need to do is to estimate the isoquant that pertains to an output by Compaq of 500 computers of this type per year. (If we are given Compaq's production function, this is simple enough.) Then using data concerning the prices of the inputs, we can draw isocost curves, as in Figure 8.3, and determine the point, like W, where the isoquant is tangent to an isocost curve. This point represents the optimal combination of inputs.

THE PRODUCTION OF CORN: AN APPLICATION

To show how the theory presented in previous sections can be applied to help improve decision making, this section describes how Earl Heady, a prominent agricultural economist, helped to determine the optimal combination of fertilizers in the production of Iowa corn.[4] He carried out experiments to determine the effect of various quantities of nitrogen (N) and phosphate (P) on corn yield per acre (Y), and found that

$$Y = -5.682 - .316N - .417P$$
$$+6.3512 \sqrt{N} + 8.5155 \sqrt{P} + .3410 \sqrt{PN}, \qquad [8.4]$$

where P and N are measured in pounds per acre and Y is measured in bushels per acre. This equation is a production function: It shows the amount of output (Y) that can be derived from various amounts of the inputs (N and P). Various isoquants (for yields of 40, 60, 80, 104, and 120 bushels per acre) are shown in Figure 8.4.

What is the optimal combination of nitrogen and phosphate fertilizers? This is an important question, both to farm managers and to the general public. Corn is a very large and valuable crop, and it is important that it be produced as economically as possible. Suppose that a farm manager is thinking of

---

which imply that $\partial f / \partial x_1 \div P_1 = \partial f / \partial x_2 \div P_2 = 1/M$, the condition in Equation 8.3. If the output level is the same, the values of x_1 and x_2 that are chosen must be the same, regardless of whether the output is maximized for the given cost or the cost is minimized for the given output.

[4] See E. Heady, "An Econometric Investigation of the Technology of Agricultural Production Functions," *Econometrica,* April 1957.

FIGURE 8.4 **Optimal Combination of Nitrogen and Phosphate** Based on these actual isoquants for Iowa corn, the optimal point is *G*, where about 91 pounds of nitrogen and about 113 pounds of phosphate are used per acre.

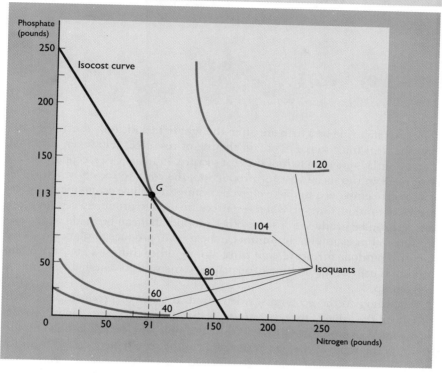

spending $30 per acre on fertilizer and that he wants to know how this expenditure should be allocated between nitrogen and phosphate. At the time of Heady's study, the price of nitrogen was 18¢ per pound and the price of phosphate was 12¢ per pound. Thus, since he is going to spend $30,

$$18N + 12P = 3,000.$$

Solving for *P*, we find that

$$P = 250 - 1.5N. \qquad [8.5]$$

This is the formula for the isocost curve in this case, which is plotted in Figure 8.4.

To maximize the amount of corn that can be produced with this $30 expenditure on fertilizer, the farm manager should find the point on this isocost curve that is on the highest isoquant. As shown in Figure 8.4, this optimal point is *G*, where about 91 pounds of nitrogen per acre and about 113 pounds of phosphate per acre are used. This is the optimal input combination. Of course, the figure of $30 was chosen arbitrarily, but regardless of the total expenditure that is chosen, this method will provide the optimal allocation.

THE NATURE OF COSTS

The costs incurred by a firm are often thought to include only the money outlays the firm must make to obtain the use of resources. However, the firm's money outlays are only part of the cost picture. In many cases, economists are interested in the social costs of production, the costs to society when its resources are employed to make a given commodity. Since economic resources are, by definition, limited, when resources are used to produce a certain product, less can be produced of some other product that can be made with those resources. For example, aluminum can be used to produce airplanes, cooking utensils, outdoor furniture, and cans, among other things. Thus, when aluminum is used in the making of airplanes, some value of alternative products is given up.

Alternative cost, or opportunity cost   According to the economist's definition, the *cost* of producing a certain product is the value of the other products that the resources used in its production could have produced instead. For example, the cost of producing airplanes is the value of the goods and services that could be obtained from the manpower, equipment, and materials used currently in aircraft production. The costs of inputs to a firm are their values in their most valuable alternative uses. These costs, together with the firm's production function (which indicates how much of each input is required to produce various amounts of the product), determine the cost of producing the product. This is called the *alternative cost doctrine* or the *opportunity cost doctrine*.

Historical cost   It is important to note that the alternative cost of an input may not equal its *historical cost,* which is defined to be the amount the firm actually paid for it. For example, if some gullible soul buys the Brooklyn Bridge for $1,000, this does not mean that its value, either to the buyer or to society, is $1,000. Similarly, if a firm invests $1 million in a piece of equipment that is quickly outmoded and is too inefficient relative to new equipment to be worth operating, its value is clearly not $1 million. Although conventional accounting rules place great emphasis on historical costs, the economist—and the sophisticated accountant and manager—stresses that historical costs should not necessarily be accepted uncritically.

Of course, the alternative cost of an input depends on the use for which the cost is being determined. For example, the cost of a pound of aluminum to

EXAMPLE 8.1

Rice Milling in Indonesia

Indonesia had a study performed by a team of U.S. engineers to determine what sorts of facilities it should adopt for the milling of rice. Four types of facilities were evaluated: (1) husker-polishers, (2) integrated rice mills, (3) bulk satellites, and (4) bulk terminals. In its initial report, the team recommended that Indonesia devote the bulk of its funds to the last three types. Soon after this report was submitted, C. Peter Timmer, a Harvard economist, constructed an isoquant for milling rice (corresponding to the relevant quantity of rice to be produced), the inputs being labor and capital.

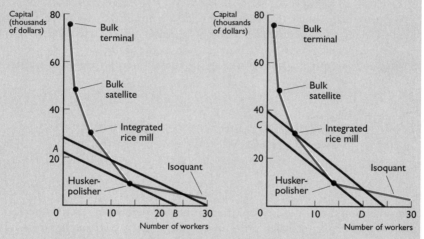

This isoquant is shown in both of the panels above. The point on the isoquant corresponding to each type of facility is indicated. For example, the bulk terminal requires about $78,000 in capital inputs and about one worker to produce this amount of output.

(a) If the isocost curves were straight lines parallel to *AB* (as in the left-hand panel of the figure), what type of facility was optimal? (b) If the isocost curves were straight lines parallel to *CD* (as in the right-hand panel of the figure), what type of facility was optimal? (c) Timmer was not sure what the ratio of the price of labor to the price of capital would be, but he was reasonably sure that it would be between that underlying isocost curve *AB* and that underlying isocost curve *CD*. If this is true, can we be reasonably certain of what type of facility was optimal? (d) Was the set of isocost curves that was parallel to *AB* based on a higher or a lower ratio of the price of labor to the price of capital than that underlying isocost curve *CD?* (e) The engineering team recommended the use of bulk terminals and bulk satellites because they were necessary to *modernize* (their term) Indonesian rice marketing. Is this a persuasive argument?

SOLUTION   (a) Husker-polishers, since the point on the isoquant corresponding to this type of facility was on the lowest isocost curve (this curve being *AB*). (b) Husker-polishers, since the point on the isoquant corresponding to this type of facility was on the lowest isocost curve (this curve being *CD*). (c) Yes. Husker-polishers will be optimal. (d) It was based on a lower ratio. We know that this is true because the slope of *AB* is closer to zero than the slope of *CD*. (*AB* is closer to being horizontal than *CD*.) As pointed out previously, the slope of an isocost curve equals $-P_L/P_K$. Thus, if *AB*'s slope is closer to zero than *CD*'s, it must be based on a lower ratio of P_L to P_K. (e) No. Policymakers generally are interested in minimizing the cost of producing a given output, not obtaining the most modern type of equipment (for its own sake).*

---

*See C. P. Timmer, J. Thomas, L. Wells, and D. Morawetz, *The Choice of Technology in Developing Countries* (Cambridge, Mass.: Harvard University Press, 1975).

transportation uses is the amount the aluminum is worth in nontransportation uses; the cost of a pound of aluminum to the aircraft industry is the amount the aluminum is worth to other transportation industries as well as in nontransportation uses; and the cost of a pound of aluminum to Boeing is the amount the aluminum is worth to other aircraft manufacturers as well as in all nonaircraft uses. If all aluminum were homogeneous in all relevant respects, all three of these alternative costs would tend to be the same, because aluminum would be transferred from low-value uses to high-value uses until the yields in all uses were the same. However, if aluminum is not homogeneous, it is not necessary that these alternative costs be equal.

The alternative uses of a resource will often be different in the long run than in the short run. For example, in the short run, a plumber generally cannot enter fields requiring specialized skills unrelated to plumbing. But given time he or she can acquire other skills and become a programmer or a machinist. In the long run, alternatives tend to be greater and more varied than in the short run. Frequently, the alternative cost of an input is underestimated because people look only at its alternative uses in the short run.

The Enforcement of the Laws: An Application

Many of the concepts of microeconomics are useful for the formulation of public policy, as well as for business decision making. To illustrate this point, let's consider how the concept of alternative costs can be used to shed light on the optimal enforcement of the laws. The question here is: What proportion of the people who commit crimes of a certain kind should society try to apprehend and convict? Your first reaction may be that they all should be caught and convicted; but, if so, it is easy to show that you ought to reconsider.

To answer this question properly, let's begin by looking at how the costs to society from crime depend on the level of law enforcement. Clearly, the damage to the victims will tend to increase as the laws are enforced more leniently because people will be encouraged to engage in criminal activities. In other words, as the chance of getting caught decreases, more people will be willing to take the chance, with the result that criminal activity will increase, and the damage to crime victims will increase. Thus, as illustrated in Figure 8.5, the costs to society from crime will increase if society permits a decrease in the probability that a criminal will be apprehended and convicted. For example, in Figure 8.5, these costs will be OC_1 if the probability is .4, but OC_2 if the probability is .6. **Costs from crime**

Looking only at the costs to society from crime, it appears that the optimal level of this probability is 1, that is, that the optimal policy is to catch and convict all criminals. But this ignores another important type of cost—the cost to society of apprehending and convicting criminals. After all, the services of police officers, detectives, prosecutors, judges, and wardens, as well as other resources used to apprehend and convict criminals, are not free. On the contrary, these resources all have alternative costs—since they can be used in other activities. For example, the police officer who tries to nail a purse snatcher could be working in industry or in some other part of government.[5] **Costs of apprehension**

How do the social costs of apprehending and convicting criminals depend on the level of law enforcement? Clearly, they go up as the laws are enforced more stringently because more people and nonhuman resources are required to ferret out and convict criminals. Thus, as shown in Figure 8.5, the costs to society of apprehending and convicting criminals will increase with increases in the probability that a criminal will be apprehended and convicted. For example, these costs will be OC_4 if the probability is .4, but OC_3 if it is .6.

Recognizing that both of these costs must be taken into account, it is clear that the optimal level of law enforcement is at the point where the sum of both costs is a minimum. Thus, under the circumstances shown in Figure 8.5, the optimal value of the probability of apprehension and conviction is .6. To increase it beyond .6 would not be socially desirable because the extra cost of ap-

---

[5] Even the conscription of juries results in social costs, since the jurors could be performing other services.

FIGURE 8.5 Optimal Level of Law Enforcement Taking account of both the costs to society from crime and the costs of apprehending and convicting criminals, the optimal value of the probability of apprehension and conviction of a criminal is .6.

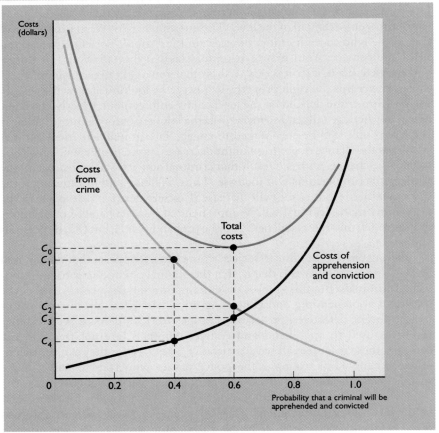

prehension and conviction would exceed the resulting reduction in the cost to society from crime. Among others, Nobel laureates Gary Becker and George Stigler have carried out a number of illuminating studies of the economics of crime and punishment. Of course, economics is only one of many disciplines that have a role to play here. But as illustrated by Figure 8.5, relatively simple microeconomic concepts can throw a great deal of light on many fundamental questions in this area.[6]

---

[6] See G. Becker, "Crime and Punishment: An Economic Approach," *Journal of Political Economy,* March 1968; S. Rottenberg, "The Clandestine Distribution of Heroin, Its Discovery and Suppression," *Journal of Political Economy,* January 1968; and G. Stigler, "The Optimum Enforcement of Laws," *Journal of Political Economy,* May 1970.   *(Cont.)*

SOCIAL VERSUS PRIVATE COSTS AND EXPLICIT VERSUS IMPLICIT COSTS

The social costs of producing a given commodity do not always equal the private costs, which are defined to be the costs to the individual producer. For example, a steel plant may discharge waste products into a river located near the plant. To the plant, the cost of disposing of the wastes is simply the amount paid to pump the wastes to the river. However, if the river becomes polluted and if its recreational uses are destroyed and the water becomes unfit for drinking, additional costs are incurred by other people. Differences of this sort between private and social costs occur frequently; in Chapter 18 we shall see that such differences may call for remedial public policy measures.

Turning to the private costs of production, it is important to recognize that there are two types of costs, both of which are generally important. The first type is *explicit costs*, which are the ordinary expenses that accountants include as the firm's expenses. They are the firm's payroll, payments for raw materials, and so. The second type is *implicit costs*, which include the costs of resources owned and used by the firm's owner. The second type of costs is often omitted in calculating the costs of the firm.

Explicit costs

Implicit costs

Implicit costs arise because the alternative cost doctrine must be applied to the firm as well as to society as a whole. Consider Martin Moran, the proprietor of a firm who invests his own labor and capital in the business. These inputs should be valued at the amount he would have received if he had used these inputs in another way. For example, if he could have received a salary of $50,000 if he worked for someone else, and if he could have received dividends of $10,000 if he invested his money in someone else's firm, he should value his labor and his capital at these rates. It is important that these implicit costs be included in a firm's total costs. Their exclusion can result in serious error.

THE PROPER COMPARISON OF ALTERNATIVES

It is also important to note that, in making decisions, costs incurred in the past often are irrelevant. Suppose that you are going to make a trip and that you

---

Note that the kind of model utilized in this section will be discussed further and in more detail when we discuss environmental pollution in Chapter 18.

want to determine whether it will be cheaper to drive your car or to go by bus. What costs should be included if you drive your car? Since the only *extra* costs that will be incurred will be the gas and oil (and a certain amount of wear and tear on tires, engine, and so on), they are the only costs that should be included. Costs incurred in the past, such as the original price of the car, and costs that will be the same regardless of whether you make the trip by car or bus, such as your auto insurance, should not be included. On the other hand, if you are thinking about buying a car to make this and many other trips, these costs should be included.[7]

As an illustration, consider the case of a major airline, which deliberately runs extra flights that do no more than return a little more than its out-of-pocket costs. Suppose this airline is faced with the decision of whether to run an extra flight between city *X* and city *Y*. Suppose the fully allocated costs — the out-of-pocket costs plus a certain percent of overhead, depreciation, insurance, and other such costs — is $4,500 for the flight. Suppose the out-of-pocket costs — the actual sum that this airline has to disburse to run the flight — are $2,000 and the expected revenue from the flight is $3,100. In a case of this sort, this airline will run the flight. This is the correct decision, since the flight will add $1,100 to profit. It will increase revenue by $3,100 and costs by $2,000. Overhead, depreciation, and insurance will be the same whether the flight is run or not. In this decision, the correct concept of cost is out-of-pocket, not fully allocated costs. Fully allocated costs are irrelevant and misleading here. The importance of this way of looking at costs cannot be overemphasized.[8]

COST FUNCTIONS IN THE SHORT RUN

At the beginning of this chapter, we showed how the profit-maximizing firm will choose the combination of inputs to produce any given level of output. (Recall that this input combination is the one that minimizes the firm's cost of producing this level of output.) Given this optimal input combination, it is a simple matter to determine the profit-maximizing firm's cost of producing any

---

[7] This example is worked out in more detail in the paper by E. Grant and W. Ireson in E. Mansfield, *Managerial Economics and Operations Research* (5th ed.; New York: Norton, 1987)

[8] It is very important in applied work to recognize what are the relevant alternatives and their effects. In this connection, it may be worthwhile to cite the case of the well-known actor Maurice Chevalier, who, when asked how it felt to have reached his advanced age, is said to have replied, "Fine, relative to the alternative."

level of output, since this cost is the sum of the amount of each input used by the firm multiplied by the price of the input. Given the firm's cost of producing each level of output, we can define the firm's cost functions, which play a very important role in the theory of the firm. A firm's cost functions show various relationships between its costs and its output rate. The firm's production function and the prices it pays for inputs determine the firm's cost functions. Since the production function can pertain to the short run or the long run, it follows that the cost functions can also pertain to the short run or the long run. In the next four sections, we discuss the short-run cost functions; then we turn to the long-run cost functions.

The short run is a time period so brief that the firm cannot change the quantity of some of its inputs. However, as the length of the time period increases, the quantities of more and more inputs become variable. Any time interval between one where the quantity of no input is variable and one where the quantities of all inputs are variable could reasonably be called the short run. However, as we pointed out in Chapter 7, we use a more restrictive definition: We say that the short run is the time period so brief that the firm cannot vary the quantities of plant and equipment. These are the firm's fixed inputs, and they determine the firm's scale of plant. Inputs like labor, which the firm can vary in quantity in the short run, are the firm's variable inputs.

The amount of calendar time corresponding to the short run will be longer in some industries than in others. In industries where the amount of fixed inputs is small and relatively easily modified, the short run may be very short. For example, this may be the case in cotton textiles. On the other hand, in other industries the short run may be measured in years. For example, in the steel industry, it takes a long time to expand a firm's basic productive capacity.

Three concepts of total cost in the short run are important: total fixed cost, total variable cost, and total cost. *Total fixed costs* are the total obligations per period of time incurred by the firm for fixed inputs. Since the quantity of the fixed inputs is fixed (by definition), the total fixed cost will be the same regardless of the firm's output rate. Examples of fixed costs are depreciation of buildings and equipment and property taxes. In Table 8.2, the firm's total fixed costs are assumed to be $1,000; the firm's total fixed cost function is shown graphically in Figure 8.6.

Total variable costs are the total costs incurred by the firm for variable inputs. They increase as the firm's output rate increases, since larger output rates require larger variable input rates, which mean higher variable costs. For example, the larger the product of a cotton mill, the larger the quantity of cotton that must be used, and the higher the total cost of the cotton. A hypothetical total variable cost schedule is shown in Table 8.2; Figure 8.6 shows the corresponding total variable cost function. Up to a certain output rate (2 units of output), total variable costs are shown to increase at a decreasing rate; beyond that output level, total variable costs increase at an increasing rate. *This latter characteristic of the total variable cost function follows from the law of diminishing*

Total fixed costs

Total variable costs

Units of output	Total fixed cost (dollars)	Total variable cost (dollars)	Total cost (dollars)
0	1,000	0	1,000
1	1,000	50	1,050
2	1,000	90	1,090
3	1,000	140	1,140
4	1,000	196	1,196
5	1,000	255	1,255
6	1,000	325	1,325
7	1,000	400	1,400
8	1,000	480	1,480
9	1,000	570	1,570
10	1,000	670	1,670
11	1,000	780	1,780
12	1,000	1,080	2,080

TABLE 8.2 Fixed, Variable, and Total Costs

FIGURE 8.6 Fixed, Variable, and Total Costs The total cost function and the total variable cost function have the same shape, since they differ by only a constant amount, which is total fixed cost.

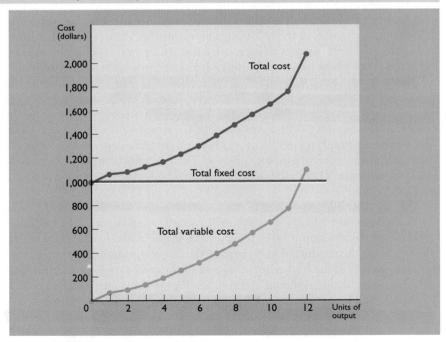

marginal returns. At small levels of output, increases in the variable inputs may result in increases in their productivity, with the result that total variable costs increase with output, but at a decreasing rate. More will be said on this score in the next section.

Finally, *total costs* are the sum of total fixed costs and total variable costs. To derive the total cost column in Table 8.2, add total fixed cost and total variable cost at each output. The corresponding total cost function is shown in Figure 8.6. The total cost function and the total variable cost function have the same shape, since they differ by only a constant amount.

Total costs

Average and Marginal Costs

The total cost functions are of great importance, but it is possible to get a better understanding of the behavior of cost by looking at the average cost functions and the marginal cost function as well. There are three average cost functions, corresponding to the three total cost functions. The *average fixed cost* is total fixed cost divided by output. Table 8.3 and Figure 8.7 show the average fixed cost function in the example given in the previous section. The average fixed cost declines with increases in output; mathematically, the average fixed cost function is a rectangular hyperbola.

Average fixed cost

The *average variable cost* is total variable cost divided by output. For the example in the previous section, the average variable cost function is shown in Table 8.3 and Figure 8.8. At first, increases in output result in decreases in average variable cost, but beyond a point, they result in higher average variable cost. The results of the theory of production in Chapter 7 lead us to expect this

Average variable cost

TABLE 8.3 Average and Marginal Costs

Units of output	Average fixed cost (dollars)	Average variable cost (dollars)	Average total cost (dollars)	Marginal cost[a] (dollars)
1	1,000.00(=1,000÷1)	50.00(=50÷1)	1,050.00(=1,050÷1)	50(=1,050−1,000)
2	500.00(=1,000÷2)	45.00(=90÷2)	545.00(=1,090÷2)	40(=1,090−1,050)
3	333.33(=1,000÷3)	46.67(=140÷3)	380.00(=1,140÷3)	50(=1,140−1,090)
4	250.00(=1,000÷4)	49.00(=196÷4)	299.00(=1,196÷4)	56(=1,196−1,140)
5	200.00(=1,000÷5)	51.00(=255÷5)	251.00(=1,255÷5)	59(=1,255−1,196)
6	166.67(=1,000÷6)	54.17(=325÷6)	220.83(=1,325÷6)	70(=1,325−1,255)
7	142.86(=1,000÷7)	57.14(=400÷7)	200.00(=1,400÷7)	75(=1,400−1,325)
8	125.00(=1,000÷8)	60.00(=480÷8)	185.00(=1,480÷8)	80(=1,480−1,400)
9	111.11(=1,000÷9)	63.33(=570÷9)	174.44(=1,570÷9)	90(=1,570−1,480)
10	100.00(=1,000÷10)	67.00(=670÷10)	167.00(=1,670÷10)	100(=1,670−1,570)
11	90.91(=1,000÷11)	70.91(=780÷11)	161.82(=1,780÷11)	110(=1,780−1,670)
12	83.33(=1,000÷12)	90.00(=1,080÷12)	173.33(=2,080÷12)	300(=2,080−1,780)

[a]Note that marginal cost pertains to the interval between the indicated output level and 1 unit less than this output level.

FIGURE 8.7 Average Fixed Cost Average fixed cost declines with increases in output, since it equals total fixed cost divided by output.

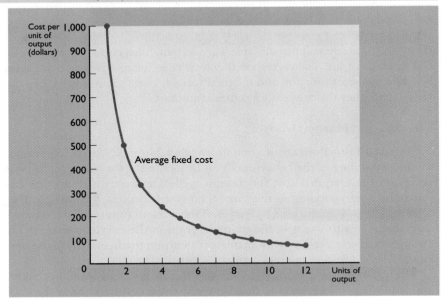

FIGURE 8.8 Average Variable Cost Because the average product of the variable input generally rises and then falls with increases in output, average variable cost decreases and then rises with increases in output.

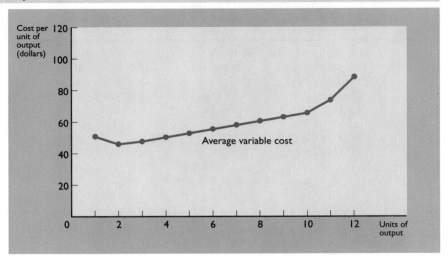

curvature of the average variable cost function. If AVC is the average variable cost, TVC is the total variable cost, Q is the quantity of output, V is the quantity of the variable input, and W is the price of the variable input, it is obvious that

$$AVC = \frac{TVC}{Q} = W\frac{V}{Q}.$$

Thus, since Q/V is the average product of the variable input (AVP),

$$AVC = W\frac{1}{AVP}. \qquad [8.6]$$

Consequently, since AVP generally rises and then falls with increases in output (see Figure 7.2, page 198) and since W is constant, AVC must decrease and then rise with increases in output. The fact that the shape of the average variable cost curve follows in this way from the characteristics of the production function is important and should be fully understood.

The *average total cost* is total cost divided by output. For the example in the previous section, the average total cost function is shown in Table 8.3 and Figure 8.9. The average total cost equals the sum of average fixed cost and average variable cost; this helps to explain the shape of the average total cost func-

Average total cost

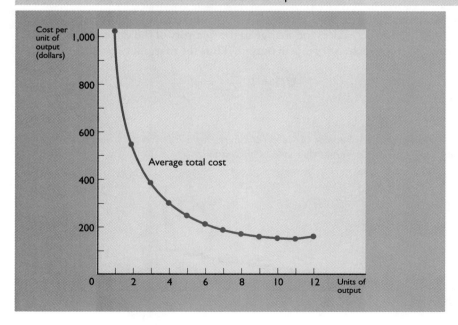

FIGURE 8.9 Average Total Cost Average total cost equals average fixed cost plus average variable cost. It falls and then rises with increases in output.

tion. For those levels of output where both average fixed cost and average variable cost decrease, average total cost must decrease too. However, average total cost achieves its minimum after average variable cost, because the increases in average variable cost are for a time more than offset by decreases in average fixed cost. (All the average cost curves are shown in Figure 8.11.)

Marginal cost   The *marginal cost* is the addition to total cost resulting from the addition of the last unit of output. That is, if $C(Q)$ is the total cost of producing Q units of output, the marginal cost between Q and $(Q - 1)$ units of output is $C(Q) - C(Q - 1)$. For the example in the previous section, the marginal cost function is shown in Table 8.3 and Figure 8.10. At low output levels, marginal cost may decrease (as it does in Figure 8.10) with increases in output, but after reaching a minimum, it increases with further increases in output. The reason for this behavior is found in the law of diminishing marginal returns. If ΔTVC is the change in total variable costs resulting from a change in output of ΔQ and if ΔTFC is the change in total fixed costs resulting from a change in output of ΔQ, marginal cost equals

$$\frac{\Delta TVC + \Delta TFC}{\Delta Q}.$$

But since ΔTFC is zero (fixed costs being fixed), marginal cost equals

$$\frac{\Delta TVC}{\Delta Q}.$$

Moreover, if the price of the variable input is taken as given by the firm, $\Delta TVC = W(\Delta V)$, where ΔV is the change in the quantity of the variable input resulting from the increase of ΔQ in output. Thus the marginal cost equals

$$MC = W\frac{\Delta V}{\Delta Q} = W\frac{1}{MP}, \qquad [8.7]$$

FIGURE 8.10 Marginal Cost   Because of the law of diminishing marginal returns, marginal cost, after reaching a minimum, rises with further increases in output.

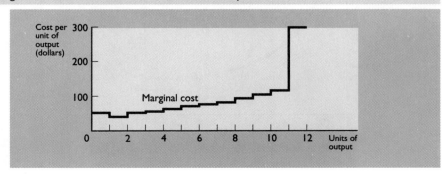

FIGURE 8.11 Average and Marginal Cost Curves Average total cost achieves its minimum at a higher output rate than average variable cost, because the increases in average variable cost are up to a point more than offset by decreases in average fixed cost.

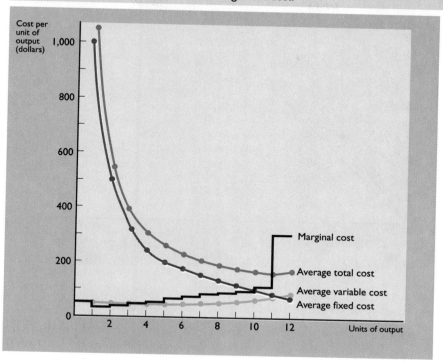

where MP is the marginal product of the variable input. Since MP generally increases, attains a maximum, and declines with increases in output (see Figure 7.2, page 198), marginal cost normally decreases, attains a minimum, and then increases.[9] The fact that the shape of the marginal cost function depends in this way on the law of diminishing marginal returns is important and should be fully understood.

---

[9] If C is total cost, $C = F + V(Q)$, where F is the total fixed costs and $V(Q)$ is total variable costs. Thus average fixed cost is F/Q, average variable cost is $V(Q)/Q$, and average total cost is $F/Q + V(Q)/Q$. The marginal cost equals $dC/dQ = dV(Q)/dQ$.

It is easy to show that marginal cost equals average variable cost when average variable cost is a minimum. If average variable cost is a minimum,

$$\frac{d[V(Q)/Q]}{dQ} = \left[\frac{dV(Q)}{dQ} - \frac{V(Q)}{Q}\right]\frac{1}{Q} = 0;$$

this means that $dV(Q)/dQ = V(Q)/Q$, which means that marginal cost equals average variable cost. It is also easy to show that marginal cost equals average total cost when average total cost is

FIGURE 8.12 **Construction of the Average Cost Function** The average cost at output OQ_0 is OZ, which is the slope of OR. The average cost at output OQ_1 is OE, which is the slope of OS.

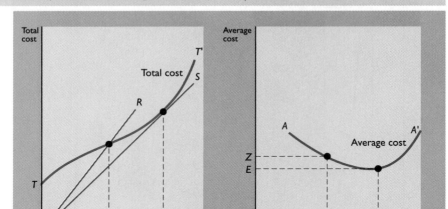

Geometry of Average and Marginal Cost Functions

Given the total cost function, we frequently want to derive the average and marginal cost functions. The purpose of this section is to show how this can be done graphically. The procedures are quite similar to those used in Chapter 7 to derive average and marginal product curves. Figure 8.12 shows how the average cost function can be derived from the total cost function, OTT', which is shown in panel A. (Note that, when we refer to average cost, we mean average *total* cost.) The average cost at any output level is given by the slope of the ray from the origin to the relevant point on the total cost function. For example, the average cost at an output OQ_0 is the slope of OR. We plot this slope, which equals OZ, against OQ_0 in panel B. For each output, we plot in panel B the slope of the ray (from the origin to the relevant point on the total cost function) against the output, which results in AA', the average cost function. Beginning with a very small output, it is clear from Figure 8.12 that increases in output

---

a minimum. When average total cost is a minimum,

$$\frac{d[F/Q + V(Q)/Q]}{dQ} = \left\{\frac{dV(Q)}{dQ} - \left[\frac{F}{Q} + \frac{V(Q)}{Q}\right]\right\}\frac{1}{Q} = 0;$$

this means that $dV(Q)/dQ = F/Q + V(Q)/Q$, which means that marginal cost equals average total cost.

result in decreases in average cost, since the slope of such rays decreases with increases in output. However, it is also clear that average cost reaches a minimum at OQ_1, since beyond OQ_1 the slope of these rays increases with increases in output.

Figure 8.13 illustrates the derivation of the marginal cost function. As output increases from OQ_2 to OQ_3, total cost (OTT' in panel A) increases from OC_2 to OC_3. Thus the extra cost per unit of output is

$$\frac{OC_3 - OC_2}{OQ_3 - OQ_2} = \frac{BA}{CB}.$$

If we increase OQ_2 until the distance between OQ_2 and OQ_3 is extremely small, the slope of the tangent (UU') at A becomes a very good estimate of BA/CB. In the limit, for changes in output in a very small neighborhood around OQ_3, the slope of the tangent to the total cost function at OQ_3 is marginal cost. In panel B, MM' shows the slope of the tangent to the total cost curve at each output; this is the marginal cost function. It is evident from Figure 8.13 that, at small output rates, marginal cost decreases with increases in output, since the slope of the tangent to the total cost function decreases with increases in output. However, it is also evident that marginal cost reaches a minimum, OV, at OQ_4

FIGURE 8.13 Construction of the Marginal Cost Function The marginal cost at output OQ_3 is the slope of the tangent, UU'. When average cost is a minimum (at output OQ_1), marginal cost equals average cost (OE).

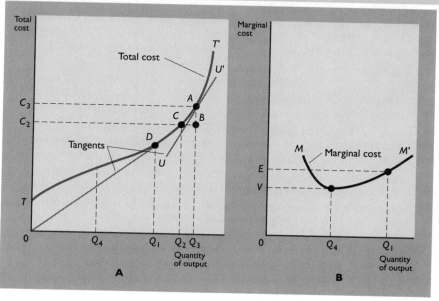

EXAMPLE 8.2

Short-Run Costs of a Boeing 747

The Boeing 747 is an airplane that carries many of the world's travelers. According to data provided by Boeing to a Senate committee in 1975, the cost (in cents) per passenger-mile of operating such an airplane on a flight of 1,200 and 2,500 miles with 250, 300, and 350 passengers aboard was as follows:

Number of passengers	Number of miles	
	1,200	2,500
	(cents per passenger mile)	
250	4.3	3.4
300	3.8	3.0
350	3.5	2.7

(a) If the number of passengers is between 250 and 300, what is the marginal cost of carrying an extra passenger on a 1,200-mile flight? (b) If the number of passengers is 300 and if the flight is between 1,200 and 2,500 miles, what is the marginal cost of flying an additional mile? (c) In 1975, the economy fare for a 2,500-mile flight was $156.60. If a Boeing 747 carried 300 passengers on such a flight, would it cover its operating costs? (d) Do you think that the above table can be applied to 1997? Why or why not? (Much more will be said about the economic characteristics of the Boeing 747 and other jetliners in Chapter 17.)

SOLUTION (a) If 250 passengers were carried, total operating costs were 1,200 × 250 × 4.3¢, or $12,900. If 300 passengers were carried, total operating costs were 1,200 × 300 × 3.8¢, or $13,680. Thus, since 50 extra passengers cost an extra $13,680 − $12,900, or $780, one extra passenger costs (approximately) an extra $780 ÷ 50, or $15.60. (b) For a 1,200-mile flight, total operating costs were 1,200 × 300 × 3.8¢, or $13,680. For a 2,500-mile flight, total operating costs were 2,500 × 300 × 3.0¢, or $22,500. Since 1,300 extra miles cost an extra $22,500 − $13,680, or $8,820, one extra mile cost (approximately) an extra $8,820 ÷ 1,300, or $6.78. (c) Yes. The total operating cost per passenger equaled 2,500 × 3.0¢, or $75, which is less than $156.60. (d) No. Input prices are different in 1997 than in 1975. For example, fuel prices increased greatly in the late 1970s. Also, wage rates of airline personnel are different in 1997 than in 1975.*

---

*See S. Breyer, *Regulation and Its Reform* (Cambridge, Mass.: Harvard University Press, 1982), and U.S. Senate Committee on the Judiciary, *Civil Aeronautics Board Practices and Procedures*, 1975. Note that these data pertain only to an airplane's operating costs.

and increases thereafter, since the slope of the tangent to the total cost function is a minimum at OQ_4 and increases thereafter.

It should also be noted that when average cost is a minimum (at output OQ_1), the slope of the ray OD equals the slope of the tangent to the total cost function, since OD is the tangent to the total cost function. Thus, since average cost equals the slope of the ray OD and marginal cost equals the slope of the tangent to the total cost function, it follows that *average cost must equal marginal cost at the output level where average cost is a minimum.* In Figures 8.12 and 8.13, both equal OE.

The Break-even Chart: An Application

A standard tool used by economists to help solve certain kinds of managerial problems is the break-even chart, which is an important practical application of cost functions. Typically, a break-even chart assumes that the firm's average variable costs are constant in the relevant output range. Thus the firm's total cost function is assumed to be a straight line, as shown in Figure 8.14. In Figure 8.14, we assume that the firm's fixed costs are $300 per month and that its variable costs are $1 per unit of output per month. Since average variable cost is constant, the extra cost of an extra unit—marginal cost—must be constant, too, and equal to average variable cost.

To construct a break-even chart, the firm's total revenue curve must be plotted on the same chart with its total cost function. It is generally assumed that the price the firm receives for its product will not be affected by the amount it sells, with the result that total revenue is proportional to output and the total revenue curve is a straight line through the origin. Figure 8.14 shows the total revenue curve, assuming that the price of the product will be $1.50 per unit. The break-even chart, which combines the total cost function and the total revenue curve, shows the monthly profit or loss resulting from each sales level. For example, Figure 8.14 shows that, if the firm sells 300 units per month, it will make a loss of $150 per month. The chart also shows the break-even point, the output (and sales) level that must be reached if the firm is to avoid losses; in Figure 8.14, the break-even point is 600 units of output per month.

FIGURE 8.14 Break-even Chart The break-even point, the output (and sales) level that the firm must reach to avoid losses, is 600 units of output per month.

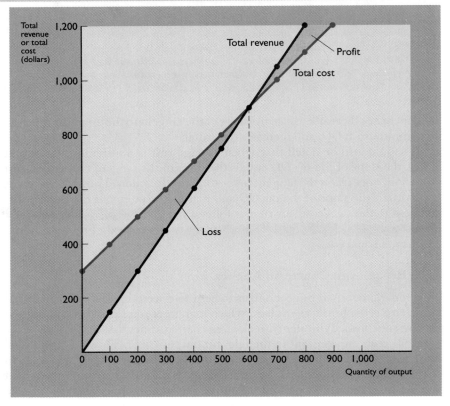

In recent years, break-even charts have been used extensively by company executives, government agencies, and other groups. Under the proper circumstances, break-even charts can produce useful projections of the effect of the output (and sales) rate on costs, receipts, and profits. For example, a firm may use a break-even chart to determine the effect of a projected decline in sales on profits. Or it may use it to determine how many units of a particular product it must sell in order to break even. However, break-even charts must be used with caution, since the assumptions underlying them may be inappropriate. If the product price is highly variable or costs are difficult to predict, the estimated total cost function and the estimated total revenue curve may be subject to considerable error.

Although the total cost function generally is assumed to be a straight line in break-even charts, this assumption can easily be dropped and a curvilinear total cost function can be used instead. However, for fairly small changes in

EXAMPLE 8.3

The Effects of Biotechnology on an Antibiotic's Production Costs

One of the most exciting areas of technology in the 1990s is biotechnology. The following actual comparison has been made of the cost per pound of producing an antibiotic drug using conventional methods and using new methods based on biotechnology:*

	Conventional	Biotechnology
Raw materials	$ 5.12	$2.47
Labor	1.24	0.95
Utilities	2.73	0.71
Plant and equipment	3.49	1.44
Overhead	.75	0.56
Total	$13.32	$6.14

This comparison assumes that 5.9 million pounds per period are produced with each method. Suppose that a conventional plant and a plant based on biotechnology are in existence, and that a major chemical firm would like to know what the cost per pound would be if each plant produced 5.5 (rather than 5.9) million pounds per period. It hires you as an adviser. What's the answer?

SOLUTION Assuming that overhead and plant and equipment costs are fixed costs, the total fixed costs are $5.9 \times (3.49 + 0.75) = 25.0$ million dollars at the conventional plant and $5.9 \times (1.44 + 0.56) = 11.8$ million dollars at the plant based on biotechnology. If average variable cost for each plant is constant for outputs ranging from 5.5 to 5.9 million pounds, and if output equals Q million pounds per period, the total variable costs (in millions of dollars) are $(5.12 + 1.24 + 2.73)Q = 9.09Q$ at the conventional plant and $(2.47 + 0.95 + 0.71)Q = 4.13Q$ at the plant based on biotechnology.

Adding the total fixed and total variable costs, we get the total costs, which equal (in millions of dollars)

$$TC_c = 25.0 + 9.09Q$$

at the conventional plant. Thus, if $Q = 5.5$, total costs are $25.0 + 9.09(5.5) = 75.0$ million dollars, and cost per pound is $75 million divided by 5.5 million pounds, or $13.64. At the plant based on biotechnology, total costs (in millions of dollars) are

$$TC_b = 11.8 + 4.13Q,$$

so, if $Q = 5.5$, total costs are $11.8 + 4.13(5.5) = 34.5$ million dollars, and cost per pound is \$34.5 million divided by 5.5 million pounds, or \$6.27.

To sum up, if each plant produced 5.5 (rather than 5.9) million pounds per period, it appears that cost per pound would be \$6.27 at the plant based on biotechnology, as compared to \$13.64 at the conventional plant. However, before accepting these results, you should make sure that overhead and plant and equipment costs are fixed costs, while the costs of raw materials, labor, and utilities are variable costs. Further, you should see whether average variable cost really is close to constant for outputs ranging from 5.5 to 5.9 million pounds.

*A Hacking, *Economic Aspects of Biotechnology* (Cambridge: Cambridge University Press, 1986), p. 267. Because of rounding errors, the figures in the table do not sum to the totals.

output, a linear approximation is probably good enough in many cases. As we shall see (later in this chapter), empirical studies suggest that the total cost function is often close to linear, as long as the firm is not operating at capacity.[10]

COST FUNCTIONS IN THE LONG RUN

In the long run, the firm can build any scale or type of plant that it wants. All inputs are variable; the firm can alter the amounts of land, buildings, equipment, and other inputs per period of time. There are no fixed cost functions (total or average) in the long run, since no inputs are fixed. A useful way to look at the long run is to consider it a *planning horizon.* While operating in the short run, the firm must continually be planning ahead and deciding its strategy in the long run. Its decisions concerning the long run determine the sort of short-run position the firm will occupy in the future. For example, before a firm makes the decision to add a new type of product to its line, the firm is in a long-run situation, since it can choose among a wide variety of types and sizes of equipment to produce the new product. But once the investment is made,

[10] Note, however, that the results of some of these studies have been subjected to criticism of various sorts. See page 262.

FIGURE 8.15 Short-Run Average Cost Functions for Various Scales of Plant The long-run average cost function is the solid portion of the short-run average cost functions, $S_1DES'_3$.

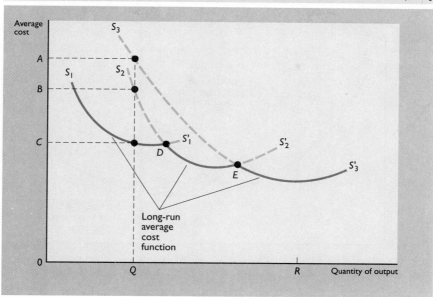

the firm is confronted with a short-run situation, since the type and size of equipment is, to a considerable extent, frozen.

Suppose that it is possible for a firm to construct only three alternative scales of plant; the short-run average cost function for each scale of plant is represented by $S_1S'_1$, $S_2S'_2$, and $S_3S'_3$, in Figure 8.15. In the long run, the firm can build (or convert to) any one of these possible scales of plant. Which scale is most profitable? Obviously, the answer depends on the long-run output rate to be produced, since the firm will want to produce this output at a minimum average cost. For example, if the anticipated output rate is OQ, the firm should choose the smallest plant, since it will produce OQ units of output per period of time at a cost per unit, OC, which is smaller than what the medium-sized plant (its cost per unit being OB) or the large plant (its cost per unit being OA) can do. However, if the anticipated output rate is OR, the firm should choose the largest plant.

The *long-run average cost function* shows the minimum cost per unit of producing each output level when any desired scale of plant can be built. In Figure 8.15, the long-run average cost function is the solid portion of the short-run average cost functions, $S_1DES'_3$. The broken-line segments of the short-run functions are not included because they are not the lowest average costs, as is evident from the figure.

Long-run average cost function

FIGURE 8.16 Long-Run Average Cost Function The long-run average cost function, which shows the minimum long-run cost per unit of producing each output level, is the envelope of the short-run functions.

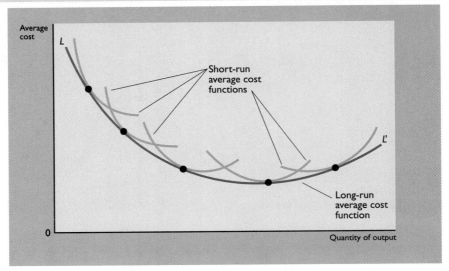

At this point, we must abandon the simplifying assumption that there are only three alternative scales of plant. In fact, there are a great many alternative scales, with the result that the firm is confronted with a host of short-run average cost functions, as shown in Figure 8.16. The minimum cost per unit of producing each output level is given by the long-run average cost function LL'. The long-run average cost function is tangent to each of the short-run average cost functions at the output where the plant corresponding to the short-run average cost function is optimal. Mathematically, the long-run average cost function is the envelope of the short-run functions.

Note, however, that the long-run average cost function (LL') is not tangent to the short-run functions at their minimum points, unless the LL' curve is horizontal. When the LL' curve is decreasing, it is tangent to the short-run functions to the left of their minimum points. When the LL' curve is increasing, it is tangent to the short-run functions to the right of their minimum points. A famous mistake was made by the well-known Princeton economist, Jacob Viner, in his pathbreaking 1931 article regarding cost functions. He tried to get the LL' curve to be tangent to the short-run functions at their minimum points. As noted above, this in general cannot be done.

In terms of least-cost input combinations, the long-run average cost function can be interpreted in the following way: For any specified output, the total cost—and the average cost—is the smallest in the long run when all inputs (not just those that were variable in the short run) are combined in such a way

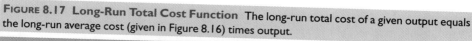

FIGURE 8.17 Long-Run Total Cost Function The long-run total cost of a given output equals the long-run average cost (given in Figure 8.16) times output.

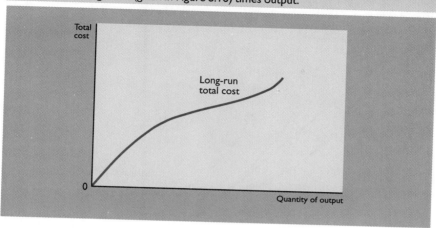

that the marginal product of a dollar's worth of one input equals the marginal product of a dollar's worth of any other input used. Only if the firm uses the least-cost combination of all inputs to produce each level of output can the levels of cost shown by the long-run average cost function be reached.

Given the long-run average cost of producing a given output, it is easy to derive the long-run total cost of the output, since the latter is simply the product of long-run average cost and output. Figure 8.17 shows the relationship between long-run total cost and output; this relationship is called the *long-run total cost function*. Given the long-run total cost function, it is easy to derive the *long-run marginal cost function,* which shows the relationship between output and the cost resulting from the production of the last unit of output if the firm has plenty of time to make the optimal changes in the quantities of all inputs used. Of course, long-run marginal cost must be less than long-run average cost when the latter is decreasing, equal to long-run average cost when the latter is a minimum, and greater than long-run average cost when the latter is increasing. It can also be shown that, when the firm has built the optimal scale of plant for producing a given level of output, long-run marginal cost and short-run marginal cost will be equal at that output.[11]

Long-run total cost function

Long-run marginal cost function

---

[11] Suppose that the long-run average cost of producing an output rate Q is $L(Q)$ and that the short-run average cost of producing this output with the ith scale of plant is $A_i(Q)$. Let $M(Q)$ be the long-run marginal cost and $R_i(Q)$ be the short-run marginal cost with the ith scale of plant. If the firm is maximizing profit, it is operating where short-run and long-run average costs are equal; in other words, $L(Q) = A_i(Q)$. Also, the long-run average cost function is tangent to the

FIGURE 8.18 **The Expansion Path** The expansion path indicates how, as output changes from 50 to 100 to 150 units (but input prices remain fixed), the quantity that is used of each input changes.

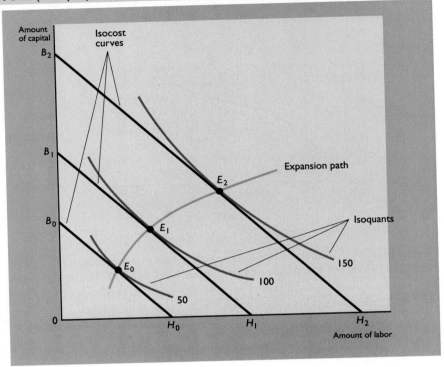

The Expansion Path and Long-Run Total Costs

At this point, it is also worthwhile to show how a firm's long-run total cost function can be derived from its isoquants. Figure 8.18 shows a firm's iso-

---

short-run average cost function, this means that

$$\frac{dL(Q)}{dQ} = \frac{dA_i(Q)}{dQ} \quad \text{and} \quad Q\frac{dL(Q)}{dQ} = Q\frac{dA_i(Q)}{dQ}.$$

From these conditions, it is easy to prove that the long-run marginal cost, $M(Q)$, equals the short-run marginal cost, $R_i(Q)$:

$$M(Q) = \frac{d[QL(Q)]}{dQ} = L(Q) + Q\frac{dL(Q)}{dQ}.$$

$$R_i(Q) = \frac{d[QA_i(Q)]}{dQ} = A_i(Q) + Q\frac{dA_i(Q)}{dQ}.$$

Since we know from the previous paragraph that $L(Q) = A_i(Q)$ and that $QdL(Q)/dQ = Q\,dA_i(Q)/dQ$, it follows that $R_i(Q)$ must equal $M(Q)$.

quants corresponding to output levels of 50, 100, and 150. The least-cost combination of inputs to produce 50 units of output is represented by point E_0, where the isoquant is tangent to the relevant isocost curve. Similarly, the least-cost combination of inputs to produce 100 units of output is represented by point E_1, and the least-cost combination of inputs to produce 150 units of output is represented by point E_2. These tangency points (E_0, E_1, and E_2), as well as those representing the least-cost combinations of inputs to produce other quantities of output, lie along a curve known as the *expansion path,* shown in Figure 8.18. The expansion path indicates how, as the output rate changes (but input prices remain fixed), the quantity of each input changes.

Expansion path

If capital and labor are the only inputs, it is a simple matter to derive the long-run total cost function from the expansion path. Each point on the expansion path represents the least-cost combination of inputs to produce a certain output in the long run (since neither input is fixed). Consider point E_0, which corresponds to an output of 50 units. The total cost of the combination of inputs represented by E_0 is OH_0 times P_L, the price of a unit of labor. Why? Because point E_0 is on isocost curve B_0H_0; this means that the input combination at point E_0 costs the same as that at point H_0. And the cost of the input combination at point H_0 equals OH_0 times P_L.

Consequently, to obtain one point on the long-run total cost function, we plot OH_0 times P_L against 50 units of output, as shown in Figure 8.19. To ob-

FIGURE 8.19 Derivation of the Long-Run Total Cost Function The total cost of input combinations E_0, E_1, and E_2 in Figure 8.18 are $OH_0 \times P_L$, $OH_1 \times P_L$, and $OH_2 \times P_L$, respectively. Thus the minimum cost of producing 50 units is $OH_0 \times P_L$, the minimum cost of producing 100 units is $OH_1 \times P_L$, and the minimum cost of producing 150 units is $OH_2 \times P_L$.

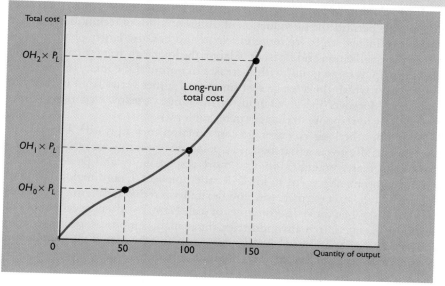

tain a second such point, consider point E_1 on the expansion path, which corresponds to an output of 100 units. Using the same reasoning as in the previous paragraph, the total cost of the combination of inputs represented by E_1 is OH_1 times P_L. Thus the minimum cost of producing 100 units of output in the long run is OH_1 times P_L; this means that the point on the long-run total cost function corresponding to an output of 100 units is OH_1 times P_L. Consequently, OH_1 times P_L is plotted against 100 units of output in Figure 8.19. Repeating this procedure for each of a number of different output levels, we obtain the long-run total cost function shown in Figure 8.19.

The Shape of the Long-Run Average Cost Function

The long-run average cost function in Figure 8.16 is drawn with much the same sort of shape as the short-run average cost function. Both decrease with increases in output up to a certain point, reach a minimum, and increase with further increases in output. However, the factors responsible for this shape are not the same in the two cases. In the case of the short-run average cost function, the theory of diminishing marginal returns is operating behind the scenes. The short-run average cost function turns upward because decreases in average fixed costs are eventually counterbalanced by increases in average variable costs due to decreases in the average product of the variable input. However, the law of diminishing marginal returns is not responsible for the shape of the long-run average cost function, since there are no fixed inputs in the long run.

The shape of the long-run average cost function is determined in part by economies and diseconomies of scale. As pointed out in Chapter 7, increases in scale often result in important economies, at least up to some point. Because larger scale permits the introduction of different kinds of techniques, because larger productive units are more efficient, and because larger plants permit greater specialization and division of labor, the long-run average cost function declines, up to some point, with increases in output. Of course, the range of output over which the average cost function declines varies from industry to industry. (Moreover, in a given industry, this range varies over a period of time, particularly in response to changes in technology.)

Why does the long-run average cost function turn upward? The answer that is generally given is that, beyond a point, increases in scale result in inefficiencies in management. More and more responsibility and power must be given by top management to lower-level employees. Coordination becomes more difficult, red tape increases, and flexibility is reduced. It is not easy to determine just when these diseconomies of scale begin to offset the economies of scale already cited. In many industries, the available empirical studies seem to indicate that after an initial decline, long-run average cost is constant over a considerable range of output. The situation is like that shown in Figure 8.20.

EXAMPLE 8.4

Long-Run Costs at IBM

The IBM Corporation is a leading manufacturer of electronic computers. Based on its internal memoranda, IBM's long-run total cost of producing various quantities of its Pisces (370/168) machines was as shown below.

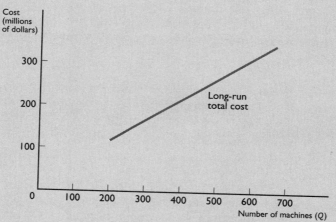

For output levels in the relevant range, the equation for this total cost function is

$$C = 28{,}303{,}800 + 460{,}800\,Q,$$

where C is total cost (in dollars) and Q is the number of machines.
   (a) If the entire market for this type of machine is 1,000 machines, and if all firms have the same long-run total cost function, to what extent would a firm with 50 percent of the market have a cost advantage over a firm with 20 percent of the market? (b) What is the long-run marginal cost of producing such a machine? Does marginal cost depend on output? (c) Do there appear to be economies of scale? (d) The data presented above are forecasts of costs based largely on engineering data, not an historical record of actual costs. Why would IBM make such forecasts? What factors might result in errors in these forecasts?

SOLUTION   (a) If Q equals 500, average cost equals $[28{,}303{,}800 + 460{,}800(500)] \div 500 = \$517{,}408$. If Q equals 200, average cost equals $[28{,}303{,}800 + 460{,}800(200)] \div 200 = \$602{,}319$. Thus a firm with 50 percent of the market has an average cost that is about 14 percent below that of a firm with 20 percent of the market. (b) $460,800. (It is clear from the above equation that, if Q increases by 1, C increases by $460,800.) In the output range covered by the data (about 200 to 700 units, according to the graph above), marginal cost does not vary. (c) Yes. Since long-run average cost equals 460,800 + 28,303,800/Q, long-run average cost declines with increases in Q. (d) Since profits equal revenues minus costs, such forecasts are very useful in estimating the profits (or losses) that will accrue to the firm if it sells various quantities of output. However, such forecasts can be in error if input prices (such as wage rates) differ from the assumptions on which the forecasts are based, or if the productivity of inputs differs from what is expected.*

---

*See G. Brock, *The U.S. Computer Industry* (Cambridge, Mass.: Ballinger, 1975), and IBM, "Poughkeepsie SDD Cost Estimating," *Telex v. IBM,* Plaintiff's Exhibit 213.

Eventually, however, one would expect the long-run average cost function to rise.

It is important to note that the shape of the long-run average cost function is of great significance from the viewpoint of public policy. If the long-run average cost function decreases markedly up to a level of output that corre-

FIGURE 8.20 Apparent Shape of Many Long-Run Average Cost Functions In many industries, after an initial decline, long-run average cost seems to be constant over a considerable range of output.

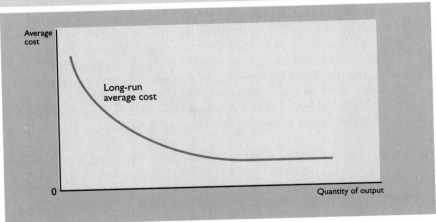

sponds to all, or practically all, that the market demands of the commodity, it makes little sense to force competition in this industry, since costs would be higher if the output were divided among a number of firms than if it were produced by only one firm. In this case, the industry is a natural monopoly, and government agencies like the Federal Energy Regulatory Commission and the Federal Communications Commission, rather than competition, often are relied on to regulate the industry's performance. (This topic will be discussed further in Chapter 11.)

ECONOMIES OF SCOPE

In our discussion of cost functions, we generally have focused attention on the costs of producing a single product, without reference to whatever other products the firm may be making at the same time. Some firms like DuPont or Exxon turn out hundreds of different products. If a firm produces more than one product, it may experience *economies* or *diseconomies of scope.*

Economies of scope exist when a single firm producing various products jointly can produce them more cheaply than if each product is produced by a separate firm. For example, suppose that the Monarch Manufacturing Company produces 1,000 tons of lumber and 2,000 tons of paper, the total cost being $120,000. If a firm producing 1,000 tons of lumber would incur costs of $50,000, and if a firm producing 2,000 tons of paper would incur costs of $90,000, Monarch experiences economies of scope because its cost of producing both lumber and paper ($120,000) is less than the cost of producing them separately ($50,000 + $90,000 = $140,000).

A measure of the degree of economies of scope is the following:

$$\frac{TC(Q_1) + TC(Q_2) - TC(Q_1 + Q_2)}{TC(Q_1 + Q_2)}, \qquad [8.8]$$

where $TC(Q_1)$ is the total cost of producing Q_1 units of the first good only, $TC(Q_2)$ is the total cost of producing Q_2 units of the second good only, and $TC(Q_1 + Q_2)$ is the cost of jointly producing Q_1 units of the first good and Q_2 units of the second good. Thus, in the case of Monarch, this measure of the degree of economies of scope equals

$$\frac{\$50,000 + \$90,000 - \$120,000}{\$120,000} = 0.17.$$

If this measure is negative, there are diseconomies of scope, which means that the cost of jointly producing the goods is greater than if they are produced separately.

Economies of scope often occur because the production of various products uses common production facilities or other inputs. For example, the production of cars and trucks may use the same sheet metal or engine assembly facilities. In other cases, economies of scope occur because the production of one product produces by-products that the producer can sell. For example, a cattle producer may sell the hides of its cattle which are raised for beef. Regardless of the reason for their existence, it is important to recognize that economies of scope can be important.[12]

MEASUREMENT OF COST FUNCTIONS

Economists have made a great many studies to estimate cost functions—or *cost curves,* as they are often called—in particular firms and industries. Typically, these studies have been based on the statistical analysis of historical data regarding cost and output. Some studies have relied primarily on time series data, in which the output level of a firm is related to its costs. For example, Figure 8.21 plots the output level of a hypothetical firm against its costs in various years in the past. Other studies have relied primarily on cross-section data, in which the output levels of various firms at a given point in time are related to their costs. For example, Figure 8.22 plots the 1997 output of eight firms in a given industry against their 1997 costs. Using data of this sort, as well as engineering data, economists have attempted to estimate the relationship between cost and output.

There are a number of important difficulties in estimating cost functions in this way. First, accounting data, which are generally the only cost data available, suffer from a number of deficiencies when used for this purpose. The time period used for accounting purposes generally is longer than the economist's short run. The depreciation of an asset over a period of time is determined largely by the tax laws rather than by economic criteria. Many inputs

---

[12] For further discussion, see J. Panzar and R. Willig, "Economies of Scope," *American Economic Review,* 1981, and E. Bailey and A. Friedlander, "Market Structure and Multiproduct Industries: A Review Article," *Journal of Economic Literature,* September 1982.

FIGURE 8.21 Relationship between Total Cost and Output: Time Series for a Given Firm
Each year's level of total cost is plotted against the firm's output level during the year. Ordinarily, such a relationship is only a very crude approximation to the firm's total cost function.

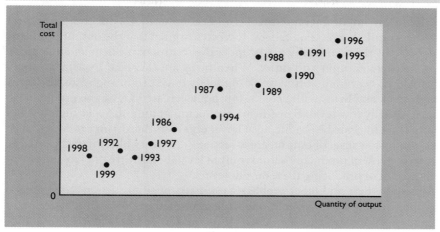

are valued at historical, rather than alternative, cost. Moreover, accountants often use arbitrary allocations of overhead and joint costs.

Second, engineering data also suffer from important limitations. Engineering data, like cost accounting data, relate to processes within the firm. One difficulty in using them to estimate cost functions for an entire firm is that the

FIGURE 8.22 Relationship between Total Cost and Output: Cross Section Each firm's level of cost during 1997 is plotted against the firm's output level during that year. Such a relationship generally is only a very rough approximation of the relevant cost function.

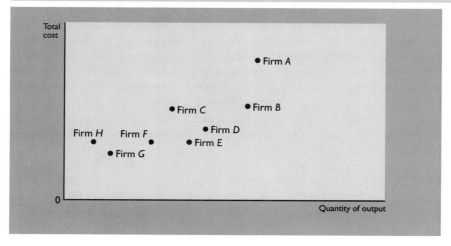

costs of various processes may affect one another and may not be additive. Also, there is the inevitable arbitrariness involved in allocating costs that are jointly attached to the production of more than one commodity in multi-product firms.

Third, an important criticism of cross-section studies is that they are subject to the so-called regression fallacy. It is often argued that the output produced and sold by the firm is only partly under the control of the firm and that actual and expected output will differ. When firms are classified by actual output, firms with very high output levels are likely to be producing at an unusually high level, and firms with very low output levels are likely to be producing at an unusually low level. Since firms producing at an unusually high level of output are likely to be producing at lower unit costs than firms producing at an unusually low level of output, cross-section studies are likely to be biased, the observed cost of producing various output levels being different from the minimum cost of producing these output levels.

Despite these and other problems, estimates of cost functions have proved of considerable use, both to economists interested in promoting better managerial decisions and to economists interested in testing and extending economic theory. From the latter point of view, one of the most interesting conclusions of the empirical studies is that the long-run average cost function in most industries seems to be L-shaped (as in Figure 8.20), not U-shaped. That is, there is no evidence that it turns upward, rather than remaining horizontal, at high output levels (in the range of observed data). A summary of the results of some of the major studies carried out in recent years is presented in Tables 8.4 and 8.5. The reader should study these tables carefully, since they summarize a great many interesting results.

Another interesting conclusion of the empirical studies is that marginal cost in the short run tends to be constant in the relevant output range. As shown in Tables 8.4 and 8.5, this is a frequent result of these studies. This result seems to be at variance with the theory presented earlier (pages 242 to 243), which says that marginal cost curves should be U-shaped. To explain this variance, critics have asserted that the empirical studies are biased toward constant marginal cost by the nature of accounting data and the statistical methods used. Another reason why marginal costs appear constant is that the data used in these studies often do not cover periods when the firm was operating at the peak of its capacity. Although marginal costs may well be relatively constant over a wide range, it is inconceivable that they do not eventually increase with increases in output.

An illustration of the sort of empirical work that has been done in this area is Joel Dean's pioneering study of the short-run cost functions in a hosiery mill. This study, published in 1941, was one of the first attempts by an economist to measure a firm's cost function. Dean found that the total cost function was lin-

L-shaped long-run average cost function

TABLE 8.4 Results of Studies of Cost Functions: General Industry[a]

Author	Industry	Type	Period	Result
Johnston	Multiple product	TS	S	"Direct" cost is linearly related to output. MC is constant.
Dean	Leather belts	TS	S	Significantly increasing MC rejected by Dean.
Dean	Hosiery	TS	S	MC constant. SRAC "failed to rise."
Dean and James	Shoe stores	CS	L	LRAC is U-shaped (interpreted as not due to diseconomies of scale).
Holton	Retailing (Puerto Rico)	E	L	LRAC is L-shaped. But Holton argues that inputs of management may be undervalued at high outputs.
Ezekiel and Wylie	Steel	TS	S	MC declining, but large sampling errors.
Yntema	Steel	TS	S	MC constant.
Ehrke	Cement	TS	S	Ehrke interprets as constant MC. Apel argues that MC is increasing.
Nordin	Light plant	TS	S	MC is increasing.
Gupta	29 manufacturing industries (India)	CS	L	LRAC is L-shaped in 18 industries, U-shaped in 5, and linear in the rest.
Jansson and Schneerson	Shipping	CS	L	Economies of scale in hauling, but not in handling.
Norman	Cement	CS,E	L	Substantial economies of scale.
Zagouris, Caouris, and Kantsos	Solar desalinization	E	L	Economies of scale.
Allen and Liu	Motor Carriers	CS	S	Scale economies.

[a]The following abbreviations are used: MC = marginal cost, AC = average cost, SRAC = short-run average cost, LRAC = long-run average cost, S = short run, L = long run, Q = questionnaire, E = engineering data, CS = cross section, and TS = time series.

SOURCES: A. A. Walters, "Production and Cost Functions," *Econometrica*, January 1963; V. Gupta, "Cost Functions, Concentration, and Barriers to Entry in 29 Manufacturing Industries in India," *Journal of Industrial Economics*, 1968; J. Jansson and D. Schneerson, "Economies of Scale of General Cargo Ships," *Review of Economies and Statistics*, May 1978; G. Norman, "Economies of Scale in the Cement Industry," *Journal of Industrial Economics*, June 1979; N. Zagouris, Y. Caouris, and E. Kantsos, "Production and Cost Functions of Water Low-Temperature Solar Desalinization," *Applied Economics*, September 1989; and W. B. Allen and D. Liu, "Service Quality and Motor Carrier Costs," *Review of Economics and Statistics*, August 1995.

TABLE 8.5 Results of Studies of Cost Functions: Public Utilities

Author	Industry	Type[a]	Result[b]
Nerlove	Electricity (U.S.A.)	CS	LRAC excluding transmission costs declines, then shows signs of increasing.
Johnston	Coal (U.K.)	CS	Wide dispersion of costs per ton.
Johnston	Road passenger) transport (U.K.)	CS	LRAC either falling or constant.
Johnston	Life assurance	CS	LRAC declines.
McNulty	Electricity (U.S.A.)	CS	Average costs of administration are constant.
Dhrymes and Kurz	Electricity (U.S.A.)	CS,TS	Substantial economies of scale.
Eads, Nerlove, and Raduchel	Airlines (U.S.A.)	CS,TS	No evidence of substantial economies of scale.
Knapp	Sewage purification (U.K.)	CS	Significant economies of scale up to 10 million gallons daily.
Stevens	Refuse collection (U.S.A.)	CS	Considerable economies of scale in cities up to 20,000 population.
Railways			
Borts	U.S.A.	CS	LRAC increasing in East, decreasing in South and West.
Broster	U.K.	TS	Operating cost per unit of output falls.
Mansfield and Wein	U.S.A.	TS	MC is constant.
Griliches	U.S.A.	CS	No significant economies of scale to an indiscriminate expansion of traffic.
Caves, Christensen, and Swanson	U.S.A.	CS	Economies of scale.
Friedlander and Spady	U.S.A.	CS	Economies of scale.
Harmatuck	U.S.A.	CS	Economies of scale.
Harris	U.S.A.	CS	Economies of scale.
Keeler	U.S.A.	CS	Economies of scale.
Sidhu, Charney, and Due	U.S.A.	CS	Economies of scale.

[a] CS means cross section and TS means time series.

[b] LRAC means long-run average cost, and MC means marginal cost.

SOURCES: A. A. Walters, "Production and Cost Functions," *Econometrica*, January 1963; P. Dhrymes and M. Kurz, "Technology and Scale in Electricity Generation," *Econometrica*, July 1964; G. Eads, M. Nerlove, and W. Raduchel, "A Long-Run Cost Function for the Local Service Airline Industry," *Review of Economics and Statistics*, August 1969; Z. Griliches, "Railroad Cost Analysis," *Bell Journal of Economics and*

Management Science, 1972; M. Knapp, "Economies of Scale in Sewage Purification and Disposal," *Journal of Industrial Economics*, December 1978; B. Stevens, "Scale, Market Structure, and the Cost of Refuse Collection," *Review of Economics and Statistics*, August 1978; D. Caves, L. Christensen, and J. Swanson, "Productivity Growth, Scale Economies and Capacity Utilization in U.S. Railroads, 1955–74," *American Economic Review*, December 1981; A. Friedlander and R. Spady, *Freight Transport Regulation* (Cambridge, Mass.: MIT Press, 1981); D. Harmatuck, "A Policy-Sensitive Railway Cost Function," *Logistics and Transportation Review*, May 1979; R. Harris, "Rationalizing the Rail Freight Industry," University of California, Berkeley, 1977; T. Keeler, "Railroad Costs, Returns to Scale, and Excess Capacity," *Review of Economics and Statistics*, May 1974; N. Sidhu, A. Charney, and J. Due, "Cost Functions of Class II Railroads and the Viability of Light Traffic Density Railway Lines," *Quarterly Review of Economics and Business*, Autumn 1977; R. Braeutigam, A. Daughety, and M. Turnquist, "The Estimation of a Hybrid Cost Function for a Railroad Firm," *Review of Economics and Statistics*, August 1982; S. Jara-Diaz and C. Winston, "Multiproduct Transportation Cost Functions: Scale and Scope in Railroad Operations," Massachusetts Institute of Technology, 1981; and T. Keeler, *Railroads, Freight, and Public Policy* (Washington, D.C.: Brookings Institution, 1983).

ear within the range of observation, marginal cost being constant. His estimate of the total cost function is shown in Figure 8.23.

Another illustration of studies of this kind is Martin Feldstein's study of cost functions in British hospitals. Among other things, he found that the long-run average cost function "is a shallow U-shaped curve with a minimum at the current average size (310 beds), [which indicates] . . . that the medium size hospital of 300 to 500 beds is at least as efficient at providing general ward care as are larger hospitals."[13] Figure 8.24 shows the average cost function he esti-

FIGURE 8.23 Total Cost Curve: Hosiery Mill (Monthly Costs) According to a very early, classic study, the total cost function for a hosiery mill was as shown here.

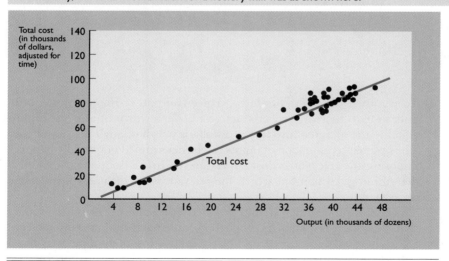

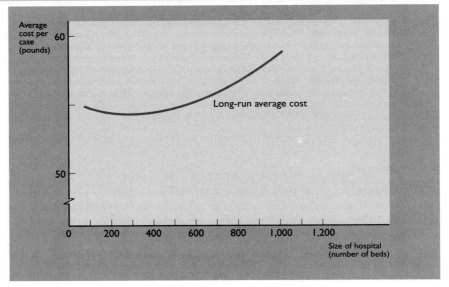

FIGURE 8.24 Long-Run Average Cost Function: British Hospitals Based on this estimated long-run cost function, hospitals of about 300 to 500 beds have lower long-run average costs than larger hospitals.

mated. His study illustrates the fact that microeconomic concepts are useful for nonprofit (and government) organizations as well as for firms.

SUMMARY

1. To minimize the cost of producing a given output, a firm must combine inputs so that the marginal product of a dollar's worth of any one input is equal to the marginal product of a dollar's worth of any other input used. The optimal combination of inputs can be determined graphically by superimposing the relevant isocost curves on the firm's isoquant map, and by determining the point at which the relevant isoquant touches the lowest isocost curve.
2. The cost of producing a certain product is the value of the other products that the resources used in its production could have produced instead. This is the alternative cost doctrine. The alternative cost of an input may not be equal to its historical cost, and it is likely to be smaller in the short run than in the long run. (Opportunity cost is another name for alternative cost.)

3. The social costs of producing a given commodity do not always equal the private costs, as in the case of a steel mill that discharges wastes into a river. In making decisions, costs incurred in the past and costs that are the same for all alternative courses of action are irrelevant.

4. A cost function is a relation between a firm's costs and its output rate. The firm's production function and the prices it pays for inputs determine a firm's cost function.

5. Three concepts of total cost are important in the short run: total fixed costs, total variable costs, and total costs. The average fixed costs, average variable costs, average costs, and marginal costs are also important.

6. The short-run average cost function decreases at first, but eventually it turns up because of the law of diminishing marginal returns. Similarly, the marginal cost curve eventually turns up for the same reason.

7. A useful way to look at the long run is to view it as a planning horizon. Economies and diseconomies of scale affect the shape of the long-run average cost function. Because of economies of scale, the long-run average cost curve is likely to decrease, up to some point, with increases in output. As output becomes greater and greater, it is often stated that diseconomies of scale will result, with the consequence that the long-run average cost curve will turn upward. The shape of the long-run average cost curve in a particular industry is of great importance from the viewpoint of public policy.

8. Economists have made a great many studies to estimate the cost functions of particular firms and industries. Typically, these studies have been based on historical data regarding cost and output, although accounting data, which are generally the only cost data available, suffer from a number of deficiencies when used for this purpose.

9. One of the most interesting conclusions of these studies is that the long-run average cost curve seems to be L-shaped. However, the evidence is limited. Another interesting conclusion is that the short-run marginal cost function often seems to be horizontal, not U-shaped. But this may be due in considerable part to the limited range of the observations.

QUESTIONS/PROBLEMS

1. In October 1986, about 9 months after the crash of the space shuttle *Challenger,* the Congressional Budget Office published a study indicating that the marginal cost of a 1989 flight by a space shuttle would be about $48 million. (a) What kinds of expenses are included in this figure? (b) Should the entire cost of the shuttle be included? Why or why not? (c) According to

the study, the "Challenger accident will increase the marginal cost of shuttle operations. . . ."[14] Why was this likely?

2. According to the National Academy of Engineering, the long-run average total cost of producing an aircraft increases by about 35 percent if 350, rather than 700, of the aircraft are produced. Since the end of World War II, the number of prime free-world manufacturers of large commercial air transports has decreased from 22 to only a few.[15] Are these two facts related? If so, how?

3. Fill in the blanks in the table below.

Output	Total cost (dollars)	Total fixed cost (dollars)	Total variable cost (dollars)	Average fixed cost (dollars)	Average variable cost (dollars)
0	50	50	0	—	—
1	70	50	20	50	—
2	100	50	50	25	—
3	120	50	70	17	—
4	150	50	100	—	—
5	200	50	150	—	—

Suppose that the price of an important input increases greatly, with the result that each of the above figures concerning total cost rises by 50 percent. What effect would this have on the value of marginal cost?

4. As we saw in Example 7.2, a 1-pound weight gain can be achieved for a broiler during a specified period if the broiler is fed any of the following combinations of quantities of corn and soybean oilmeal.

Quantity of corn (pounds)	Quantity of soybean oilmeal (pounds)
1.0	0.95
1.1	0.76
1.2	0.60
1.3	0.50
1.4	0.42

(a) If the price of a pound of corn (which is P) equals the price of a pound of soybean oilmeal, what is the cost of each combination? What is the minimum-cost combination (of those shown above)? (b) Plot the isocost curves

---

[14] Congressional Budget Office, *Setting Space Transportation Policy for the 1990s* (Washington, D.C.: Government Printing Office, 1986), p. 25.

[15] National Academy of Engineering, *The Competitive Status of the U.S. Civil Aviation Manufacturing Industry* (Washington, D.C.: National Academy Press, 1985).

and the isoquant. Use this graph to determine the minimum-cost combination. Compare your results with those obtained in part (a).

5. Economist T. Yntema estimated the short-run total cost function of the United States Steel Corporation (now USX Corporation) in the 1930s to be as follows:

$$C = 182.1 + 55.73Q,$$

where C is total annual cost (in millions of dollars) and Q is millions of tons of steel produced. (a) What was U.S. Steel's fixed cost? (b) If U.S. Steel made 10 million tons of steel, what was its average variable cost? (c) What was U.S. Steel's marginal cost? (d) Do you think that this equation provided a faithful representation of U.S. Steel's short-run total cost function, regardless of the value of Q? (e) If you needed to estimate this firm's marginal cost in 1995, would you use this equation? (f) In recent years, there have been charges that Japanese steel makers have been "dumping" steel in the United States — that is, selling here below cost. Can this equation be used to tell whether this is so?

6. According to Frederick Moore, "The '.6 rule' derived by engineers is a rough method of measuring increases in capital cost as capacity is expanded. Briefly stated the rule says that the increase in cost is given by the increase in capacity raised to the .6 power." Give some reasons why this rule holds for tanks, columns, compressors, and similar types of equipment. (Hint: Capacity of a container is related to volume, whereas cost is related to surface area.)

7. The graph below shows the average total cost of producing a ton of ammonia using the partial oxidation process and the steam reforming process, with plants of various sizes (as measured by daily capacities). In particular, curve C pertains to the partial oxidation process when naptha is used as a

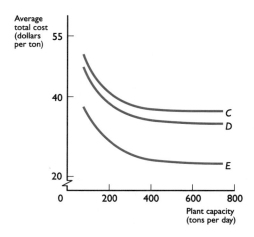

raw material, curve D pertains to the steam reforming process when naptha is used as a raw material, and curve E pertains to the steam reforming process when natural gas is used as a raw material. (a) Can the short-run cost function for ammonia be derived from this graph? (b) This graph assumes that naptha costs $.008 per pound and natural gas costs $.20 per mcf; if this assumption is true, which process should be used? (c) Does this graph suggest that there are economies of scale in ammonia production? (d) The graph on the preceding page pertains to conditions in the early 1960s. In the late 1960s, a new process for producing ammonia was introduced. Using this new process, a plant with a capacity of 1,400 tons per day had an average cost of about $16 per ton. Did the long-run cost function for the production of ammonia shift between the early and late 1960s?

8. A plant producing a component of the space shuttle can produce any number of these components (up to 100 per week) at a total cost of $100, but it cannot produce more than 100 per week, regardless of how much its costs are. Graph its marginal cost curve. Indicate why few (if any) plants in the real world have a marginal cost curve of this sort.

9. Suppose that you are a consultant to a firm that publishes books. Suppose that the firm is about to publish a book that will sell for $10 a copy. The fixed costs of publishing the book are $5,000; the variable cost is $5 a copy. What is the break-even point for this book?

10. Suppose that a semiconductor plant's production function is $Q = 5LK$, where Q is its output rate, L is the amount of labor it uses per period of time, and K is the amount of capital it uses per period of time. Suppose that the price of labor is $1 a unit and the price of capital is $2 a unit. The firm's vice president for manufacturing hires you to figure out what combination of inputs the plant should use to produce 20 units of output per period. What advice would you give?

APPENDIX

THE LEARNING CURVE

In many industries like aircraft, electronics, and machine tools, technological change is due in considerable part to learning and on-the-job experience that occurs as a firm produces more and more of a given item. Thus, holding the firm's output rate constant, its average cost declines with increases in its *cumulative* total output (that is, the total number of items of this sort that it has produced in the past). For example, production of the first thousand C-46 transport planes required about 75 percent more hours of labor than production of the second thousand aircraft of this type, even though the number of aircraft produced per month remained about the same. Thus the average cost of this airplane fell substantially as cumulative total output grew.

It is important to distinguish between cost reductions due to *learning* and   Learning
cost reductions due to *economies of scale*. Holding constant the number of C-46 transport planes produced by this firm in the past, if the average cost of producing such a plane during the current period declines as more of them are produced, the decline is due to economies of scale. Holding constant the number of such planes produced per period of time, if the average cost falls (as in the previous paragraph) when the firm's cumulative total output of this plane increases, this is due to learning.

Economists often use the *learning curve* to represent the extent to which the average cost of producing an item falls in response to increases in its cumulative total output. Figure 8.25 shows the learning curves for two products, a machine tool and a semiconductor chip. (A semiconductor chip is a key component employed to store information in computers and other electronic products.) As you can see, learning results in bigger reductions in average cost for the semiconductor chip than for the machine tool. Of course, these cost re-

FIGURE 8.25 Learning Curve for Semiconductor Chip and Machine Tool* For both products, average cost falls as cumulative total output increases.

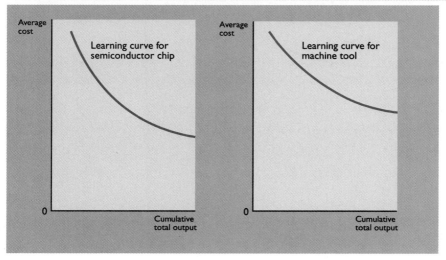

*The horizontal and vertical scales are different in the left-hand figure than in the right-hand figure, but it is clear that a doubling of cumulative output results in a greater percentage reduction in average cost in the left-hand figure than the right-hand figure.

ductions are not automatic: They occur only if workers and managers strive for increased efficiency. But for many products of this sort, a doubling of cumulative output tends to produce about a 20 to 30 percent reduction in average cost. As would be expected, this implies that learning results in more dramatic cost reductions (in absolute terms) when cumulative total output is small than when it is large.

The learning curve has played an important role in decision making in both government and industry. As an illustration, consider the case of Texas Instruments, a major producer of semiconductor chips and other electronic products. When the semiconductor industry was relatively young, Texas Instruments priced its product at less than its then-current average costs in order to increase its output rate and its cumulative total output. Believing that the learning curve was relatively steep, it hoped that this would reduce its average costs to such an extent that it would be profitable to produce and sell at this low price. This strategy was extremely successful. As Texas Instruments continued to cut price, its rivals started to withdraw from the market, its output continued to increase, its costs fell further, and its profits increased.[16]

---

[16] For a classic paper concerning learning curves, see K. Arrow, "The Economic Implications of Learning by Doing," *Review of Economic Studies,* June 1962. The Boston Consulting Group was a leading advocate of their application to corporate planning. Also see A. Michael Spence, "Competition, Entry, and Antitrust Policy," in Mansfield, *Microeconomics: Selected Readings,* 5th ed., and L. Argote and D. Epple, "Learning Curves in Manufacturing," *Science,* February 23, 1990.

Applying Microeconomic Theory: The Case of Milk and Dairy Products

INTRODUCTION

The milk and dairy products industry is big and economically (and politically) important. In recent years, cash receipts from U.S. milk and dairy products have been about $20 billion, well over 10 percent of the cash receipts from all farm commodities. While milk is produced and processed in every state, over half the country's milk production has occurred in Wisconsin, California, New York, Minnesota, and Pennsylvania.[1] Furthermore, the milk industry is

---

[1] R. Fallert, D. Blayney, and J. Miller, *Dairy: Background for 1990 Farm Legislation* (Washington, D.C.: U.S. Department of Agriculture, 1990), part of which is reprinted in E. Mansfield, *Study Guide and Casebook in Applied Microeconomics, 2d ed.* (New York: Norton, 1997).

unconcentrated, there being over 100,000 dairy farms in the United States. If the government did not intervene in the milk market, which it does, this market might be reasonably close to perfectly competitive, as there are very large numbers of buyers and sellers and the product is reasonably standardized.[2]

At present, the milk industry is in a state of turmoil and faces fundamental problems and opportunities in the future. In particular, recent decades have seen massive revisions in consumers' perceptions of the desirability and dietary safety of some milk products, bold new technologies that have stirred enormous controversies within and outside the industry itself, keen economic and cultural rivalries between the traditional farmers of Wisconsin and New York and the comparative newcomers of California and Texas, and continual arguments over the role of the federal government in regulating the price of milk and other dairy products.

In this chapter, we present ten multipart problems, which analyze selected aspects of many of these trends and issues. To provide the background information required to understand and do these problems, we begin with a thumbnail sketch of the costs, returns to scale, demand, regulation, and prospective changes in technology of dairy farms. Our principal focus is on Dennis and Sue McGraw, owners of an actual Wisconsin dairy farm.

THE COSTS OF PRODUCING MILK

Dennis and Sue McGraw have a dairy farm with 60 cows on the outskirts of Dodgeville, Wisconsin, a town of about 3,500 people. They live in a farmhouse built in 1929, close to a large white barn. In the summer, "the sweet smell of blossoms mingles with fresh-cut grass, manure, and sour molasses-smelling silage."[3] All members of the McGraw family — Dennis, Sue, and their children, as well as Dennis's father, who has grown the cows' feed — have worked on the 370-acre farm. Even their two dogs have earned their keep by rounding up the cows.

Dairy farmers like the McGraws use many types of labor, materials, services, capital, and land as inputs. For the country as a whole, the breakdown of the average total cost of producing a pound of milk in 1989 is given in Table 9.1. As you can see, the average total cost was 14.03 cents, of which 6.55 cents

---

[2] Dairy farming has been the least concentrated of all animal products enterprises. A. Manchester, *The Public Role in the Dairy Economy* (Boulder, Colo.: Westview, 1983).

[3] *Philadelphia Inquirer,* June 14, 1992, p. C2.

The McGraw dairy farm

The McGraw family

(or almost 50 percent) went for feed for the cows. Another 2.92 cents went for hired labor, milk hauling and marketing, and miscellaneous items; and 2.98 cents went for general farm overhead, taxes, insurance, and capital replacement. Finally, 1.58 cents were the estimated costs of using the owner's capital and labor, as well as the cost of unpaid labor (like that of the McGraw family).

TABLE 9.1 Average Cost of Producing a Pound of Milk, United States, 1989[a]	
	Cents per pound
Feed	6.55
Hired labor	1.05
Milk hauling and marketing	0.61
Miscellaneous[b]	1.26
General farm overhead	0.87
Taxes and insurance	0.40
Capital replacement[c]	1.71
Return to owner's capital and land	1.00
Unpaid labor	0.58
	14.03

[a] Besides milk, dairy farms sell breeding or culled livestock, which in 1989 brought in receipts of 1.26 cents per pound of milk.

[b] Includes artificial insemination (0.13); veterinary and medicine (0.21); livestock hauling (0.03); fuel, lube, and electricity (0.25); repairs (0.38); fees (0.06); and supplies (0.20).

[c] Replacement costs are an imputed charge sufficient to maintain average equipment, machinery, and purchased breeding livestock investment and production capacity through time. They are based on current prices of capital assets.

SOURCE: Fallert, Blayney, and Miller, *Dairy: Background for 1990 Legislation.*

Take a close look at the last two cost items in Table 9.1. Are they the ordinary sorts of costs on which any accountant focuses? No, they are implicit costs. Specifically, they are the estimated alternative cost (or opportunity cost) of the capital and land owned by the farmer and used on his or her farm, and the estimated alternative cost (or opportunity cost) of the unpaid labor of the people who work on the farm. The U.S. Department of Agriculture, which gathers and publishes these cost figures, is sophisticated enough to recognize the distinction between explicit and implicit costs and the importance of including both.

RETURNS TO SCALE IN MILK PRODUCTION

Whereas the farm operated by Dennis and Sue McGraw is representative of the traditional type of farm that has been the bulwark of the great dairy states like Wisconsin, Minnesota, New York, and Pennsylvania, there is considerable evidence that the nature of dairy farming is changing. Between 1980 and 1989, the share of United States milk production in the Pacific, Mountain, and Southern Plains states increased by 6.1 percentage points, while the share of the long-time dairy regions fell. In the early 1990s, California produced more milk than Wisconsin.[4] (For changes in national milk production from 1971 to 1994, see Table 9.2.)

One reason why California has overtaken Wisconsin is that it has lower costs. In 1988, the average total cost of a pound of milk in the Pacific states was 11.17 cents, as contrasted with 13.89 cents in the Upper Midwest. This cost differential is due in part to economies of scale. Dairy farms on the Pacific coast and in Florida lead the country with herd sizes typically in the range of 500 to 1,500 cows. In traditional milk producing areas of the Upper Midwest and Northeast, dairy farms generally have 50 to 150 cows. The big dairy farms in California and elsewhere are essentially milk factories where herds of about 1,000 cows (or more) are constantly being fed and milked, with their output being monitored by computers.[5]

---

[4] U.S. Congress, Office of Technology Assessment, *U.S. Dairy Industry At a Crossroad* (Washington, D.C.: U.S. Government Printing Office, May 1991), *Philadelphia Inquirer,* June 14, 1991, p. C2, and U.S. Department of Agriculture, *Milk Production,* February 16, 1995.

[5] U.S. Congress, Office of Technology Assessment, *U.S. Dairy Industry At a Crossroad.*

TABLE 9.2 Milk Production, United States, 1971–1994

Year	Billions of pounds	Year	Billions of pounds
1994	154	1982	136
1993	151	1981	133
1992	151	1980	128
1991	148	1979	123
1990	148	1978	121
1989	144	1977	122
1988	145	1976	120
1987	143	1975	115
1986	143	1974	116
1985	143	1973	115
1984	135	1972	120
1983	140	1971	119

SOURCES: U.S. Bureau of the Census, *Statistical Abstract of the United States* (Washington, D.C.: Government Printing Office, 1987, 1991), Economic Research Service, U.S. Department of Agriculture, *Dairy Situation and Outlook Yearbook,* August 1991, and National Agricultural Statistics Service, Washington, D.C., February 1995.

To illustrate, consider the Ron Quinn dairy of Tulare County, California, the leading county for milk production in the United States. This dairy hires

Ron Quinn

a work force of 22 people, and cows are milked 18 hours a day. The dairy's 1,200 cows, protected by sunshades, live in corrals and are fed eight times a day by machines that push high-protein feed toward them. During the summer, they are sprayed with water by misters. Because exercise cuts their milk production, they never walk more than 200 yards to be milked. The farm contains 1,200 acres on which alfalfa is grown year-round for the cows. Computers on the dairy's feed trucks enable its managers to get the best available price on the feed that the dairy purchases.[6]

---

[6] *Philadelphia Inquirer,* June 14, 1992, p. C2.

THE ENORMOUS CONTROVERSY OVER bST

The McGraws, like other dairy farmers, are currently enmeshed in a nationwide controversy over the application of biotechnology. Based on research conducted at Cornell University, the National Institute for Research in Dairying in England, and elsewhere, it was found that somatotropin, sometimes called growth hormone, could increase the amount of milk produced by cows. Somatotropin is produced by the anterior pituitary gland, a small gland located at the base of the brain. Artificially introduced somatotropin must be injected to be biologically active.

According to the U.S. Office of Technology Assessment,

> The impact of bST [bovine somatotropin] on milk production will vary according to the quality of management on individual farms, but a reasonable expectation is that successful adopters would experience, on average, a 12 percent boost in production. However, the increase in output per cow tends to be absolute (in number of pounds) rather than proportional to normal production. Thus, approximately the same increase in pounds of milk produced might be expected (in comparably managed herds) from all cows. . . . Because bST is rapidly cleared from the bloodstream and is not

FDA Building

stored in the body, . . . bST is needed every day to sustain the increase in milk yield. This requires daily injections or use of a prolonged release formulation of bST.[7]

In November 1993, the Food and Drug Administration (FDA) approved the marketing of bST. In its view, milk produced with the genetically engineered hormone is indistinguishable from milk that is not. Nonetheless, a variety of concerns have been raised about the safety of bST for humans and animals, as well as its economic effects. Critics claim that bST increases the incidence of udder infections in treated cows and taints the milk supply with pus and bacteria.[8] During its first year on the market, Monsanto, the firm which developed and marketed it, reported that about 11 percent of the country's dairy farmers were using it, a figure that critics challenged.[9]

THE DEMAND FOR MILK AND DAIRY PRODUCTS

Dairy farmers like the McGraws know that changes in consumer tastes, as well as new techniques like bST, can affect their industry significantly. Table 9.3 shows the per capita consumption of milk from 1960 to 1990. As you can see, the consumption of plain whole milk fell during this period by over 50 percent, while the consumption of low-fat milk increased markedly, and the consump-

---

[7] U.S. Congress, Office of Technology Assessment, *U.S. Dairy Industry At a Crossroad,* p. 4.

[8] *Science,* October 21, 1994, and *New York Times,* October 30, 1994.

[9] *New York Times,* February 1, 1995, and March 12, 1995.

TABLE 9.3 Per Capita Consumption of Milk and Dairy Products, United States, 1960–1990 (pounds per year)

Year	Plain whole milk	Low-fat milk	Skim milk	Yogurt	Cream	Condensed and evaporated milk	Butter	Cheese	Ice cream
1990	88	98	23	4	5	3	4	25	16
1985	120	83	13	4	4	4	5	22	18
1980	141	72	12	3	3	4	4	18	18
1975	175	55	12	2	3	5	5	14	19
1970	207	31	12	1	4	7	5	11	18
1960	251	2	11	a	b	14	8	8	18

[a] Less than 0.5 pound per year.
[b] Published figures include specialties as well.
SOURCE: See Table 9.2.

tion of skim milk more than doubled. Adding all types of milk together, per capita milk consumption declined by about 20 percent. Turning to products made from milk, the average U.S. consumer purchased more and more cheese and yogurt, but less butter and condensed milk, as shown in Table 9.3. (Ice cream consumption has remained fairly steady.)

These dramatic changes have been due in part to the altered views of what is a healthy diet. Consumers have become much more concerned about calories, fat, and cholesterol intake. Gone are the days when mothers encouraged their families to slather butter on their toast and drink plenty of whole milk. Instead, the emphasis now is on few calories and the avoidance of fats and cholesterol. However, not all is gloom on the nation's dairy farms: the big bright spot is the increase in the per capita consumption of cheese, shown in Table 9.3.

GOVERNMENT REGULATION OF MILK PRICES

The McGraws and other milk suppliers have been subject to a host of regulations. In part, this reflects people's concerns about health hazards. Early in this century, the U.S. Public Health Service became interested in the problem of milk-borne diseases; in 1924, it developed a model regulation — the Standard Milk Ordinance — which was adopted by many states and municipalities. But in recent years, much of the controversy over milk regulation has been concerned with pricing, not health hazards. Federal and state regulations put floors under the price of milk. As pointed out in Chapter 1, these price floors have been established to bolster the incomes of farmers, who benefit from higher prices. Consumers, in contrast, have been hurt by them.[10]

For milk eligible for fluid consumption, milk processors have paid minimum prices based on how the milk is used. The lowest prices have been for milk used to make butter, cheese, and nonfat dry milk; a somewhat higher price has had to be paid for milk used to make ice cream and yogurt; a still higher price has had to be paid for milk used for fluid consumption. For the last type of milk, the minimum price has gone up with increasing distance from Eau Claire, Wisconsin. In other words, the price floor has gotten higher as one moves away from Eau Claire — a facet of the regulations that has angered dairy farmers in Wisconsin and Minnesota. (This regulation dates back to the 1930s when Eau Claire had a great deal of surplus milk, and the federal government established higher minimum prices elsewhere to reimburse Wisconsin farmers for their shipping costs.) In addition, the federal government has bought butter, cheese, and nonfat dry milk in whatever quantities have been needed to keep their market price from falling below the floors which the government itself has set.[11] (Prices of milk and cheese in recent years are shown in Table 9.4.)

These price floors for milk and dairy products have aroused widespread and intense controversy for many years. Editorials in urban newspapers have regularly attacked government milk programs as complex devices enabling dairy farmers to perform legal economic muggings on consumers. In response, politicians from dairy states portray the farmers as deserving and unappreci-

---

[10] Manchester, *The Public Role in the Dairy Economy.*

[11] U.S. Congress, Office of Technology Assessment, *U.S. Dairy Industry At a Crossroad.* Also, see U.S. General Accounting Office, *Milk Pricing* (Washington, D.C.: Government Printing Office, November 1989), and U.S. General Accounting Office, *Milk Marketing Orders: Options for Change* (Washington, D.C.: Government Printing Office, March 1988).

TABLE 9.4 Price of Milk and Cheese, 1970–1990 (cents per pound)		
	Price received by farmers for whole milk	Wholesale price of American cheese (Wisconsin assembly points)
1990	13.73	137
1988	12.26	124
1986	12.51	127
1984	13.46	138
1982	13.61	138
1980	13.05	133
1975	8.75	87
1970	5.71	55

SOURCE: See Table 9.2.

ated; for example, William Proxmire, former senator from Wisconsin, has said, "The No. 1 victim of economic injustice in this country today is the farmer and especially the dairy farmer."[12] In 1996, Congress phased out price supports for butter, powdered milk, and cheese over four years, and reduced the number of regional price supports for milk.

MILK PRODUCTION: CAN YOU APPLY THE THEORY?

The following four problems take up various aspects of a dairy farm's market, technology, and costs, now and in the past.

PROBLEM 9.1   George and Gloria Wilber owned a dairy farm in Colebrook, Connecticut. They were the last dairy farmers in this town where there were more than a dozen a generation ago. They owned 60 Brown Swiss cows, which they said were worth about $2,000 apiece, and they sold their milk to Agri-Mark, a marketing cooperative. In early 1992, they received about $4,500 per month for their milk which, after deducting other expenses, did not cover half their $3,000-a-month feed bill. After five years of losing money, the Wilbers were trying in 1992 to sell their herd and leave dairy farming.

[12] J. Grant, "Milk and Honey," *Barron's,* May 30, 1977, p. 7.

(a) According to Mr. Wilber, one of the principal reasons for his losses was that fuel and labor costs, as well as taxes, were relatively high in Connecticut. Some dairy farmers believe that Connecticut's state government should support the price of milk at a higher level than in other states in order to offset these disadvantages, which they regard as unfair. Evaluate this proposal.

(b) Mr. Wilber has said, "In the town of Colebrook, our soil is very stony. You're not going to be able to set strawberry beds or plant sweet corn."[13] Does this imply that the alternative (or opportunity) cost of using Mr. Wilber's land for dairy farming is low? Why or why not?

(c) The area surrounding the Wilber farm, once dotted with many grazing cows, now contains the weekend homes of many New Yorkers. Do you think that the alternative (or opportunity) cost of using Mr. Wilber's land for dairy farming has increased over the past 20 years? Why or why not? What signals does the price system use to inform the Wilbers whether their land can be used more efficiently for purposes other than dairy farming?

(d) Did the fact that the Wilbers' land was used for dairy farming bring satisfaction and enjoyment to other people in the area? (Hint: Were there environmental effects?)

Department of Agriculture

PROBLEM 9.2 Many years ago, the U.S Department of Agriculture carried out experiments to determine how a cow's milk production during a particular period was related to how much she was fed.[14]

---

[13] *New York Times,* June 2, 1992, p. B6.

[14] See L. Weiss, *Case Studies in American Industry* (2d ed.; New York: Wiley, 1971)

A cow must be fed a certain amount just to maintain herself; beyond that point, more feed resulted in more milk, as shown below:

Pounds of feed consumed by a cow	Pounds of milk produced by a cow
5,700	7,600
6,100	8,200
6,600	8,800
7,100	9,400
7,500	9,800
7,900	10,000

(a) What is the marginal product of a pound of feed if between 5,700 and 6,100 pounds of feed are consumed? If between 7,500 and 7,900 pounds of feed are consumed?

(b) What is the average product of a pound of feed if 5,700 pounds of feed are consumed? If 7,900 pounds of feed are consumed?

(c) Does milk production seem to conform to the law of diminishing marginal returns? Why or why not?

(d) If a farmer increases the quantity of feed consumed from 5,700 pounds to 6,100 pounds, does this raise the average product of a pound of feed? If so, would you expect the marginal product of a pound of feed to be more than the average product? Why or why not?

(e) At which of the above quantities of feed consumed is the average product of a pound of feed greatest?

(f) A dairy farmer hires you as a consultant to determine whether the optimal amount to feed a cow is the amount at which the average product of feed is highest. The farmer says that he has been told that the smart thing to do is maximize the amount of milk produced per pound of feed, and that this seems reasonable to him. Is he right? Why or why not?

PROBLEM 9.3 At the Cox Dairy Farm, which has 50 cows, suppose that the relationship between the milk output of a cow and the amount she is fed is as shown in Problem 9.2. For simplicity, suppose that this farm's only variable cost is the amount it spends for feed, which costs 6¢ per pound, and that its fixed costs total $40,000 during the relevant period. The farmer, Robert Cox, and his family do all the work on this farm, and hold no other jobs. Their time is fully occupied (dawn to dusk) by the farm work, regardless of how much milk their cows produce.

(a) Why is the cost of labor on this farm a fixed cost, not a variable cost?

(b) Since all of the labor is performed by family members, how can one attach a monetary value to the farm's labor cost?

(c) What is the farm's total cost if each of its cows produces 7,600 pounds of milk during this period? If each cow produces 10,000 pounds of milk?

(d) What is the farm's average variable cost if each cow produces 7,600 pounds of milk during this period? If each cow produces 10,000 pounds of milk?

(e) What is the farm's average fixed cost if each cow produces 7,600 pounds of milk during this period? If each cow produces 10,000 pounds of milk?

(f) What is the farm's marginal cost if each cow produces between 9,800 and 10,000 pounds of milk during this period?

(g) Robert Cox asks his accountant how much he should feed his cows. His accountant replies that he should choose the amount of feed per cow that minimizes the farm's average total cost. According to his accountant, if each cow consumes 7,500 pounds of feed, the farm's average total cost is 13.0¢ per pound of milk, and this is the minimum value of the farm's average total cost. Is this really the amount of feed (according to Problem 9.2) that would minimize the farm's average total cost? Is this really the optimal amount to feed each cow? Why or why not?

PROBLEM 9.4   According to an early study conducted by the U.S. Department of Agriculture, 8,500 pounds of milk can be produced during a specified time period by a cow fed the following combinations of hay and grain:[15]

Quantity of hay (pounds)	Quantity of grain (pounds)
5,000	6,154
5,500	5,454
6,000	4,892
6,500	4,423
7,000	4,029
7,500	3,694

(a) Plot these data as an isoquant. Is this isoquant convex?

(b) What is the marginal rate of technical substitution when between 5,000 and 5,500 pounds of hay are used? What is it when between 5,500 and 6,000 pounds of hay are used?

(c) If the price of a pound of hay equals the price of a pound of grain,

---

[15] For further discussion, see E. Heady's classic work, *Economics of Agricultural Production and Resource Use* (New York: Prentice-Hall, 1952).

should a cow be fed 5,000 pounds of hay and 6,154 pounds of grain? Why or why not?

(d) If the price of a pound of hay equals 1.05 times the price of a pound of grain, what is the least-cost combination of inputs to produce 8,500 pounds of milk?

(e) Dairy farms produce both milk and cows. If the cost of producing 100,000 pounds of milk and 4 cows is 60 percent of the cost of producing them separately, what is the degree of economies of scope?

ECONOMIES OF SCALE: CAN YOU APPLY THE THEORY?

The following two problems pertain to economies of scale, a very important topic to dairy farmers.

PROBLEM 9.5   According to the U.S. Office of Technology Assessment, the relationship between the long-run average cost of milk production and the size of a dairy farm (as measured by its number of cows) in California and New York in 1985 were as shown below:[16]

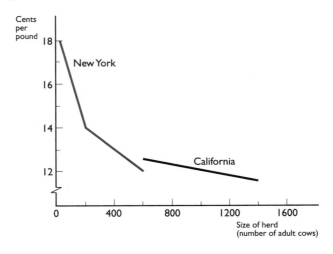

---

[16] U.S. Congress, Office of Technology Assessment, *U.S. Dairy Industry At a Crossroad.*

(a) What is the average total cost of a pound of milk produced by a New York farm with 50 cows? By a New York farm with 400 cows? Based on these data, do there appear to be economies of scale in milk production in New York?

(b) What is the average total cost of a pound of milk produced by a California farm with 600 cows? By a California farm with 1,200 cows? Based on these data, do there appear to be economies of scale in milk production in California?

(c) The climate is much milder in California than in New York or Wisconsin. Thus, as Kent Cheeseborough, manager of the Ron Quinn dairy in Tulare County, California, has pointed out, "We get 9 or 10 cuttings [of alfalfa, which is fed to cows] a year. In Wisconsin, they're lucky if they can get three."[17] A consultant prepares a study for the dairy industry in which he assumes that the production function for milk is the same in California as in Wisconsin. He attributes California's lower costs to the availability of relatively inexpensive immigrant labor. Evaluate the assumptions and findings of this study.

(d) When asked whether he was planning to expand his Wisconsin farm to match the size of those in California, Dennis McGraw said, "Right now I have no desire to get that big. Why should we? We're making a go of it right now."[18] One reason why Mr. McGraw is reluctant to expand his farm is that it would mean becoming a full-time manager. As he put it, "I'd fall asleep sitting behind a desk."[19] Does it appear that Mr. McGraw wants to maximize profit? How would you characterize his objectives?

| **PROBLEM 9.6** | Agricultural economists have estimated the production functions for dairy farms. Suppose that a study came up |

with the following result for a particular type of Minnesota dairy farm:

$$Q = KA^{.05}L^{.05}E^{.10}N^{.80}F^{.60},$$

where Q is the output of milk per period, A is the amount of land used, L is the amount of labor used, E is the amount of equipment used, N is the number of cows on the farm, F is the amount of feed used, and K is a constant.[20]

The owner of a Minnesota dairy farm of this type is concerned that her farm may be too small to compete effectively with larger dairy farms. Her

---

[17] *Philadelphia Inquirer,* June 14, 1992, p. C2.

[18] Ibid.

[19] Ibid.

[20] The formula shown above is illustrative, not the result of a careful statistical study. But for present purposes, this makes no real difference.

farm is of below-average size, and she is troubled by the possibility that larger farms may be more efficient than farms like hers. She is considering the merger of her farm with a neighboring farm that is essentially the same (in size and other characteristics) as her own.

(a) If the amount of every input is doubled, in accord with the merger under consideration, what will be the percentage change in output, according to the above equation?

(b) Are there economies of scale, according to this equation?

(c) For many years, there has been considerable technological change in dairy farming. For example, whereas milking used to be largely a hand operation, milking machines are now found almost everywhere, and with the general use of artificial insemination, bulls have become as rare on dairy farms as calls to the Maytag repairman. Does the above equation recognize that technological change of this sort occurs? If so, how? Can a merger influence how rapidly new technologies are adopted?

EFFECTS OF bST: CAN YOU APPLY THE THEORY?

The following two problems take up some of the economic effects of bST from the points of view of both an individual farm and the industry as a whole.

PROBLEM 9.7 If the Cox Dairy Farm, discussed in Problem 9.3, were to adopt bST, output per cow would increase by 1,200 pounds during the relevant period. For simplicity, suppose that this increase would be the same (that is, 1,200 pounds) regardless of how much feed a cow consumes.

(a) Would the marginal product of a pound of feed (when between 5,700 and 6,100 pounds of feed are consumed) be increased by the use of bST? Why or why not? Would the marginal product curve for feed shift to the right? Why or why not?

(b) After the adoption of bST, what would be the average product of a pound of feed when 7,500 pounds of feed are consumed per cow? Would it be higher than before bST was used? (Use the data in Problems 9.2 and 9.3 to answer this and subsequent parts of this problem.)

(c) If this farm adopts bST, what would be the total cost of producing 10,000 pounds of milk per cow? (Assume that the cost of using bST is $60 per cow during the relevant period.) Would it be lower than if bST is not adopted? If so, how much lower?

(d) After the adoption of bST, what would be the average total cost, average variable cost, and average fixed cost of producing 10,000 pounds of milk per cow? Would all of them be lower than before the introduction of bST? Why or why not?

(e) If bST is adopted, what would be the marginal cost of a pound of milk if each of this farm's cows is producing between 11,000 and 11,200 pounds of milk? Would the adoption of bST result in the movement of the farm's marginal cost curve to the right by 50 times 1,200 pounds? Why or why not?

(f) If the price of a pound of milk was 12.132 cents, what would be the break-even point for this farm after the adoption of bST? Should you assume that the total cost function is linear as in Figure 8.14?

(g) If you were asked to provide Mr. Cox with advice as to whether he should use bST, what would your advice to him be?

PROBLEM 9.8   In the early 1990s, there was a bitter battle waged over the acceptance of bST. On the one side, the National Farmers Union (with 300,000 members) and other farm groups fought hard to convince state legislators and other organizations to ban its use, even though the Food and Drug Administration had decided that it posed no health hazard to people. On the other side, farmers like William Morris of Chatham, Pennsylvania, who has 500 cows on 1,000 acres, believe that, "The question is do consumers want high-quality milk for less money, or do they want us to produce it the way we always have?"[21] Of course, the firms that developed and produced bST — American

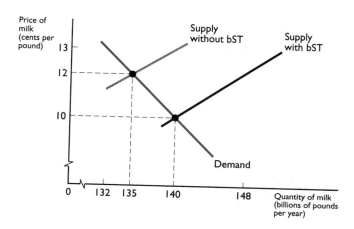

[21] *West Chester Daily Local News,* August 11, 1992, p. C5.

Cyanamid, Eli Lilly, Monsanto, and Upjohn — fought hard to get it approved and marketed.[22]

(a) If the situation is as shown in the graph on the preceding page, how big an effect would the adoption of bST have on the price of milk if the government did not intervene in the milk market?

(b) Why would the adoption of bST shift the supply curve for milk to the right?

(c) In dollar terms, how large would the benefits to consumers be if bST were adopted (and if the government did not intervene)?

(d) If consumers can be convinced by those fighting against bST that milk from bST-supplemented cows is dangerous, what will be the effect on the demand curve for such milk?

(e) According to the *New York Times,* "Lower milk prices will . . . benefit consumers . . . [But as] many as 10 percent of the country's dairy farmers might be forced out of business."[23] Why might they be forced out of business?

(f) Some states, like Wisconsin and Minnesota, have banned the use of bST, although these bans were later rescinded. Do you think that its use should be banned by the states? Why or why not?

(g) In April 1996, *Business Week* said that bST had not caught on. "Monsanto has had difficulty persuading farmers to use the product, which requires complicated training. Continued consumer resistance has also hurt. Analysts estimate that bST is losing about $10 million annually."[24] If you were president of Monsanto, what factors would you consider in determining whether to continue marketing this product?

THE DEMAND FOR DAIRY PRODUCTS: CAN YOU APPLY THE THEORY?

The following problem pertains to what we previously singled out as a bright spot in the dairy industry: the big increase in the consumption of cheese.

PROBLEM 9.9 Between 1980 and 1990, the per capita consumption of cheese rose from 18 to 25 pounds per year, a big boost for the milk and dairy products industry. Suppose that you were an analyst of

---

[22] "Market Sours on Milk Hormones," *Science,* November 17, 1989.
[23] "Hiding Behind Hormones in Milk," *New York Times,* May 15, 1989.
[24] "So Shall Monsanto Reap?" *Business Week,* April 1, 1996.

this industry, and that a client asked you to explain why this increase in cheese consumption occurred. Looking at publications of the U.S. Department of Agriculture, you find that the price elasticity of demand for cheese is about 0.30, and the income elasticity of demand for cheese is about 0.45.[25]

(a) Between 1980 and 1990, the retail price of cheese increased by about 48 percent, but it is important to correct for inflation when comparing prices at various points in time. During this same period, the Consumer Price Index rose by about 59 percent. When corrected for inflation, did the price of cheese go up or down between 1980 and 1990? When the price of cheese in both 1990 and 1980 is measured in 1980 dollars, what was the percentage change in the price of cheese during this period?

(b) Based on the change in its price alone, how big a percentage change would have been expected in the quantity of cheese demanded between 1980 and 1990?

(c) Per capita disposable personal income went up by 18 percent (adjusted for inflation) during 1980 to 1990. Based on this fact, how big a percentage change in the quantity of cheese demanded would have been expected between 1980 and 1990?

(d) Taken together, do changes in price and income account for the entire growth from 1980 to 1990 in the quantity of cheese demanded? If not, how much of this growth is unaccounted for?

(e) The per capita consumption of Italian-style cheese more than doubled between 1980 and 1990. Why did this occur? Does this suggest one of the factors explaining the growth in cheese consumption unaccounted for by price and income changes?

---

[25] See Economic Research Service, U.S. Department of Agriculture, *Dairy Situation and Outlook Yearbook,* August 1991, and R. Haidacher, J. Blaylock, and L. Myers, *Consumer Demand for Dairy Products* (Washington, D.C.: U.S. Department of Agriculture, 1988). The income elasticity of demand for cheese in Table 5.5 is somewhat different from the figure given by the Department of Agriculture because it pertains to a different time and area.

(f) Recent studies show that the cross elasticity of demand for cheese with respect to the price of beef is about –0.30.[26] Can you think of any reason why this cross elasticity is negative?

(g) George Lee's indifference curves and price-consumption curve for cheese are as shown below:

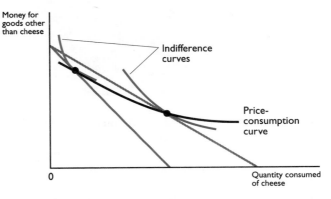

Is he a typical consumer, on the basis of the data given in this problem? If not, in what respect is he atypical, and why?

GOVERNMENT REGULATION: CAN YOU APPLY THE THEORY?

The remaining problem is concerned with the price floors established by the federal government; much more will be said on this score in Chapter 10.

John R. Block

---

[26] Ibid.

PROBLEM 9.10 In 1983, a new federal milk program was established. According to *Business Week,* "Agriculture Secretary John R. Block struck a secret deal with the powerful dairy lobby. He agreed to support a new milk program proposed by the dairy industry. . . . In return, the dairy lobby agreed to throw its weight behind a bill that would cut subsidies to grain and cotton farmers."[27] But this strategy didn't work, since Congress rejected the cuts in other farm programs but adopted the dairy bill and President Ronald Reagan signed it.

(a) The problem that the new program was designed to solve was a mounting oversupply of milk. U.S. output rose in 1983 to a record 140 billion pounds, and as shown in Table 9.5, the Agriculture Department's Commodity Credit Corporation, which was obligated by law to purchase surplus dairy products so as to maintain the price floor set by the government, accumulated a huge amount of butter, cheese, and nonfat dry milk — about 10 percent of annual consumption. (And this was after the federal government made massive donations of these products to the poor.) Some critics of the new program within the Reagan administration claimed that, if the price floor of about 13 cents per pound had been reduced, the dairy industry would have been healthier. But according to Irvin Elkin, president of the Associated Milk Producers, Inc., "Major cuts in support prices run the risk of driving many dairy farm families out of business, which would mean higher milk prices."[28] If the situation was as shown in the graph on page 294, is this true? (Warning: To provide some

TABLE 9.5 Dairy Products Removed from the Commercial Market by the U.S. Department of Agriculture, 1970–1990

Year	Removals		Nonfat dry milk	Percent of amount marketed
	Butter	Cheese		
	(millions of pounds)			
1990	400	22	118	1.1
1988	313	238	268	3.8
1986	288	468	827	10.1
1984	202	447	678	9.4
1982	382	642	948	13.1
1980	257	350	634	8.6
1975	63	68	395	4.7
1970	246	49	452	5.1

SOURCE: *Dairy Situation and Outlook Yearbook.*

[27] "Why the New Milk Law Won't Cure the Dairy Glut," *Business Week,* December 12, 1983.
[28] Ibid.

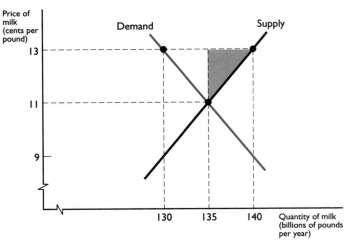

variety, the situation in the graph above differs from that in the graph in Problem 9.8.)

(b) In dollar terms, how big was the reduction in consumer surplus because the government supported the milk price at 13 cents per pound? (Your answers to this and subsequent parts of this problem should be based on the graph above.)

(c) Farmers would have produced 135 billion pounds of milk per year if the government had abandoned its price support. Without the price support, how much less would the farmers' profits have been from these 135 billion pounds of milk?

(d) If the price support had been abandoned, farmers would have produced 135 billion pounds of milk; with the price support, they produced 140 billion pounds of milk. In Chapter 10, we shall see that their profit from the extra 5 billion pounds of milk equals the shaded area in the graph above.[29] Adding this area to your answer to part (c), you can obtain the total amount of extra profit farmers received because of the government price support. What is this amount?

(e) How much did taxpayers pay farmers for the milk bought up by the Department of Agriculture?

---

[29] More accurately, this is the increase in producer surplus due to the production of the extra 5 billion pounds of milk. Producer surplus includes both the aggregate profits of the farmers and the amount that owners of inputs (used to make milk) are compensated above and beyond the minimum they would insist on. The concept of producer surplus is taken up in Chapter 10. For now, we assume that the increase in producer surplus in this case equals the increased profits of the farmers.

(f) Because taxpayers are consumers in another guise, if you add your answer to part (b) to your answer to part (e), you can obtain the total losses to consumers because of this government price support. What is this amount? Does it exceed the farmers' gains?

(g) If the aim of the price support program was to bolster farmers' incomes, can you think of a less costly (to consumers) way of increasing farmers' profits by the amount they receive from this price support program? (Hint: What if direct payments were made by consumers to producers, but the milk price supports were abolished?)

CONCLUSION

It is time now to return from the dairy farms of Dennis and Sue McGraw, Ron Quinn, and George and Gloria Wilber to the classroom. Clearly, their industry is in a state of dramatic change, both because of alterations in consumer tastes and because of regional shifts and technological upheavals. Also, government price regulation (which will be discussed further in Chapter 10) is a major issue affecting the general public as well as the milk industry. But the most important point for present purposes is that the microeconomic concepts and models you learned in previous chapters are essential to understand how to manage a dairy farm, or how the milk industry is evolving. Such simple concepts as alternative (or opportunity) cost, production function, average and marginal cost, and returns to scale are enormously useful, and help sophisticated managers and investors (and sometimes even observers) to earn their bread and butter. As you can see from this case, it would be hopeless to try to understand what is going on in this industry without them.

SELECTED SUPPLEMENTARY READINGS

1. U.S. Congress, Office of Technology Assessment, *U.S. Dairy Industry at a Crossroad* (Washington, D.C.: U.S. Government Printing Office, May 1991).
2. J. Grant, "Milk and Honey," *Barron's,* May 30, 1977.

3. R. Haidacher, J. Blaylock, and L. Myers, *Consumer Demand for Dairy Products* (Washington, D.C.: U.S. Department of Agriculture, 1988).

4. "Milking Consumers," *New York Times,* July 22, 1995.

5. "Monsanto Has Its Wonder Hormone. Can It Sell It?" *New York Times,* March 12, 1995.

6. "Analysis Questions BST's Safety to Cows," *Science,* October 21, 1994.

7. "So Shall Monsanto Reap?" *Business Week,* April 1, 1996.

8. "House-Senate Committee Agrees on Overhaul of Farm Programs," *New York Times,* March 22, 1996.

PART FOUR

Market Structure, Price, and Output

10

Perfect Competition

Previous chapters have provided models of the behavior of consumers and firms. In Chapters 10 to 13 we turn to the analysis of markets; our principal purpose is to explain the behavior of price and output. We will be concerned with questions of the following sort: What determines the price of a product? What determines how much of a product is produced? How are resources allocated among alternative uses? These are some of the most basic—and most important—questions in economics. In Chapter 1, we provided some preliminary answers to these questions. In Chapters 10 to 13, we discuss them in much more detail.

To begin with, we must distinguish between various types of markets. Economists have found it useful to classify markets into four general types: perfect competition, monopoly, monopolistic competition, and oligopoly. This classification is based largely on the number of firms in the industry that supplies the product. In perfect competition and monopolistic competition, there are many sellers, each of which produces only a small part of the industry's output. In monopoly, on the other hand, the industry consists of only a single firm. Oligopoly is an intermediate case where there are few sellers.

In this chapter we investigate how price and output are determined in perfectly competitive markets. Monopoly, monopolistic competition, and oligopoly are taken up in subsequent chapters. The analysis in this chapter brings together, and builds on, the topics discussed in previous chapters. In Chapter 1, we emphasized the important role played by the market demand and market supply curves. In Chapter 5, we used the tools devised in Chapters 3 and 4 to show how a product's market demand curve can be derived. In the present chapter, we use the tools devised in Chapters 7 and 8 to show how a product's market supply curve can be derived. Then we discuss in detail the way in which the demand and supply sides of the market interact to determine the equilibrium price and output of the firm and the industry in the short run and the long run.

PERFECT COMPETITION

What do economists mean by perfect competition? When first exposed to this concept, students sometimes find it difficult to grasp because it is quite different from the concept of competition used by their relatives and friends in the business world. When business executives speak of a highly competitive market, they generally mean a market where each firm is keenly aware of its rivalry with a few others and where advertising, packaging, styling, and other competitive weapons are used to attract business away from them. In contrast, the basic feature of the economist's definition of perfect competition is its impersonality. Because there are so many firms in the industry, no firm views another as a competitor, any more than one small wheat farmer views another small wheat farmer as a competitor.

Perfect competition

More specifically, *perfect competition* is defined by four conditions. First, perfect competition requires that the product of any one seller be the same as the product of any other seller. This is an important condition because it makes sure that buyers do not care whether they purchase the product from one seller or another, as long as the price is the same. Note that the *product* may be defined by a great deal more than the physical characteristics of the good. Although the various English pubs may serve the same beer, their products may not be identical because the atmosphere may be friendlier in one place than another, the location may be better, and so forth.

Second, perfect competition requires each participant in the market, whether buyer or seller, to be so small, in relation to the entire market, that he or she cannot affect the product's price. No buyer can be large enough to wangle a better price from the sellers than some other buyer. No seller can be large enough to influence the price by altering his or her output rate. Of course, if all producers act together, changes in output will certainly affect price, but any producer acting alone cannot do so. It will be recalled from Chapter 5 that this means that the firm's demand curve is horizontal.

Third, perfect competition requires that all resources be completely mobile. In other words, each resource must be able to enter or leave the market, and switch from one use to another, very readily.[1] More specifically, it means that labor must be able to move from region to region and from job to job, it means that raw materials must not be monopolized, and it means that new firms can enter and leave an industry. Needless to say, this condition is often not fulfilled in a world where considerable retraining is required to allow a worker to move from one job to another and where patents, large investment requirements, and economies of scale make difficult the entry of new firms.

Fourth, perfect competition requires that consumers, firms, and resource owners have perfect knowledge of the relevant economic and technological data. Consumers must be aware of all prices. Laborers and owners of capital must be aware of how much their resources will bring in all possible uses. Firms must know the prices of all inputs and the characteristics of all relevant technologies. Moreover, in its purest sense, perfect competition requires that all these economic decision-making units have accurate knowledge of the future together with the past and present.

Having described these four requirements, it is obvious that no industry is perfectly competitive. Some agricultural markets may be reasonably close, since the first three requirements are frequently met; but even they do not meet all of the requirements.[2] Nevertheless, this does not mean that the study of the behavior of perfectly competitive markets is useless. A model may be quite useful even though some of its assumptions are unrealistic. The conclusions derived from the model of perfect competition have proved very useful in explaining and predicting behavior in the real world. They have permitted a reasonably accurate view of resource allocation in important segments of our economy.

---

[1] Of course, this does not mean that such movements of resources do not take time. In the short run, many resources cannot be transferred from one use to another.

[2] Some agricultural markets in which the conditions would otherwise be reasonably close to perfect competition are heavily affected by government programs. See pages 326 to 331.

PRICE DETERMINATION IN THE SHORT RUN

The Output of the Firm

Having described perfect competition, we proceed to the determination of price and output. The first question we take up is: How much output will the firm produce in the short run? In the short run, the firm can expand or contract its output rate by increasing or decreasing the rate at which it employs variable inputs. Since the market is perfectly competitive, the firm cannot affect the price of its product and, like any perfectly competitive firm, it can sell any amount of its product that it wants at the prevailing price. Also, assume, as in previous chapters, that the firm maximizes its profits. To illustrate the firm's situation, consider the example in Table 10.1. The market price is $10 a unit, and the firm can produce as much as it chooses. Thus the firm's total revenue at various output rates is given in column 3 of Table 10.1. The firm's total fixed cost, total variable cost, and total cost are given in columns 4, 5, and 6 of Table 10.1. Finally, the last column shows the firm's total profit, the difference between total revenue and total cost, at various output rates.

TABLE 10.1	Cost and Revenue of a Firm: Prices Taken as Given by the Firm					
Output per period	Price (dollars)	Total revenue (dollars)	Total fixed cost (dollars)	Total variable cost (dollars)	Total cost (dollars)	Total profit (dollars)
0	10	0	12	0	12	−12
1	10	10	12	2	14	− 4
2	10	20	12	3	15	5
3	10	30	12	5	17	13
4	10	40	12	8	20	20
5	10	50	12	13	25	25
6	10	60	12	23	35	25
7	10	70	12	38	50	20
8	10	80	12	69	81	− 1

Figure 10.1 provides a graphical description of the relationship between total revenue and total cost, on the one hand, and output, on the other. Of course, the vertical distance between the total revenue curve and the total cost curve is the profit at the corresponding output rate. (Note once again that cost curves are another name for cost functions. Both terms are in common use.) Below 2 units of output and above 7 units of output, this distance is negative.

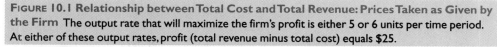

FIGURE 10.1 Relationship between Total Cost and Total Revenue: Prices Taken as Given by the Firm The output rate that will maximize the firm's profit is either 5 or 6 units per time period. At either of these output rates, profit (total revenue minus total cost) equals $25.

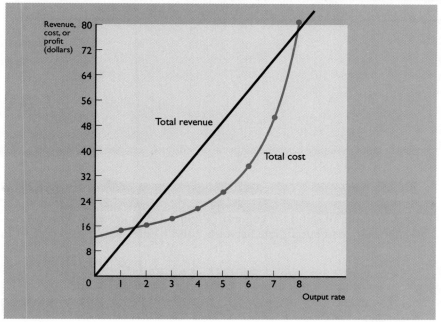

Since the firm can sell either large or small volumes of output at the same price per unit, the total revenue curve will be a straight line through the origin. This is always the case when the firm takes the price as given. The total cost curve has the kind of shape we would expect, on the basis of Chapter 8, of a short-run total cost curve.

Based on an examination of either Table 10.1 or Figure 10.1, the output rate that will maximize the firm's profit is either 5 or 6 units per time period. These are the output rates where the profit figure in the last column of Table 10.1 is the largest and where the vertical distance between the total revenue and total cost curves in Figure 10.1 is the greatest.

For many purposes it is convenient to present the marginal revenue and marginal cost curves, as well as the total revenue and total cost curves. Table 10.2 shows marginal revenue and marginal cost at each output rate. These figures were derived in the way shown in Chapters 5 and 8. Figure 10.2 shows the resulting marginal revenue and marginal cost curves. Since the firm takes the price as given, marginal revenue equals price, since the change in total revenue resulting from a 1-unit change in sales necessarily equals the price.

Optimal output rate

TABLE 10.2 Marginal Revenue and Marginal Cost: Prices Taken as Given by the Firm

Output per period	Marginal revenue (dollars)	Marginal cost[a] (dollars)
1	10	2
2	10	1
3	10	2
4	10	3
5	10	5
6	10	10
7	10	15
8	10	31

[a] This is the marginal cost between the indicated output level and 1 unit less than this output level.

PERFECT COMPETITION

P=MR=MC The important thing to note is that the maximum profit is achieved at the output rate where price (= marginal revenue) equals marginal cost. Both the figures in Table 10.2 and the curves in Figure 10.2 indicate that price equals marginal cost at an output rate between 5 and 6 units, which we know from

FIGURE 10.2 Marginal Revenue and Marginal Cost: Prices Taken as Given by the Firm
When output is at the profit-maximizing level of 5 or 6 units, price equals marginal cost.

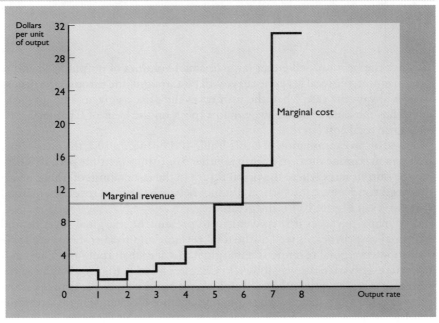

Table 10.1 or Figure 10.1 to be the profit-maximizing output. Is this merely a chance occurrence, or will it usually be true that price will equal marginal cost at the profit-maximizing output rate?

Price Equals Marginal Cost

The fact that price equals marginal cost at the optimal output rate is not merely a chance occurrence; it will usually be true if the firm takes as given the price of the product. To prove that this is the case, consider Figure 10.3, which shows a typical short-run marginal cost curve. Suppose that the price is OP_0. At any output rate (after perhaps an irrelevant range in which marginal cost is falling) less than OX, price exceeds marginal cost; thus increases in output will increase profit, since they will add more to total revenues than to total costs. At any output rate above OX, price is less than marginal cost; thus decreases in output will increase profit, since they will reduce total cost more than total revenue. Since increases in output up to OX result in increases in profit and further increases in output result in decreases in profit, OX must be the profit-maximizing output.

Even if the firm is doing the best it can, it may not be able to earn a profit. For example, if the price is OP_2 in Figure 10.3, short-run average costs exceed the price at all possible outputs. Since the short run is too short to allow the

FIGURE 10.3 Short-Run Average and Marginal Cost Curves If price is OP_0, the firm will produce an output of OX; if price is OP_2, it will produce an output of OY; and if price is less than OP_3, it will produce nothing.

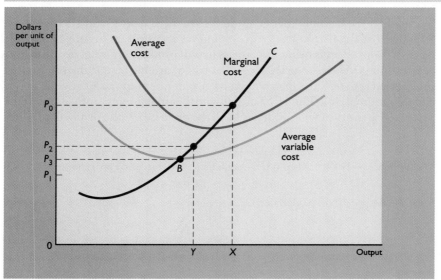

firm to alter the scale of its plant, it cannot liquidate its plant in the short run. All that the firm can do is to produce at a loss or discontinue production. The firm's decision will depend on whether the price of the product will cover average variable costs. If there exists an output rate where price exceeds average variable costs, it will pay the firm to produce, even though price does not cover average total costs. If there does not exist an output rate where price exceeds average variable costs, the firm is better-off to produce nothing at all. Thus, if the average variable cost curve is as shown in Figure 10.3, the firm will produce if the price is OP_2, but not if it is OP_1.

Discontinuing production

The reasoning behind this conclusion is as follows: If the firm produces nothing, it must still pay its fixed costs. Consequently, if the loss resulting from production is less than the firm's fixed costs, it is more profitable (in the sense that losses are smaller) to produce than not to produce. On a per unit basis, this means that it is better to produce than to discontinue production if the loss per unit of production is less than average fixed costs, that is, if $ATC - P < AFC$, where ATC is average total costs, P is price, and AFC is average fixed cost. But this will be so if $ATC < AFC + P$, since P has merely been added to both sides of the inequality. Subtracting AFC from both sides, this will be so if $ATC - AFC < P$. But $ATC - AFC$ is average variable costs. This means that we have proved what we set out to prove: that it is better to produce than to discontinue production if price exceeds average variable costs.

Thus, if the firm maximizes profit or minimizes losses, it sets its output rate so that short-run marginal cost equals price.[3] But this rule, like most others, has an exception: If the market price is too low to cover the firm's average variable costs at any conceivable output rate, the firm will minimize losses by discontinuing production.

Finally, it is a simple matter to derive the firm's short-run supply curve. Suppose that the firm's short-run cost curves are those in Figure 10.3. If the price of the product is below OP_3, the firm will produce nothing, because there is no output level where price exceeds average variable cost. If the price of the product exceeds OP_3, the firm will set its output rate at the point at which price equals marginal cost. This is the output rate that maximizes profit. Thus, if the price is OP_0, the firm will produce OX; if the price is OP_2, the firm will produce

---

[3] Let the total cost be $C(Q)$, where Q is the output rate. The total profit per period is

$$\pi = PQ - C(Q),$$

where P is the price of the product. If π is a maximum,

$$P - \frac{dC(Q)}{dQ} = 0,$$

or price must equal marginal cost. The second-order condition for a maximum is

$$\frac{d^2C(Q)}{dQ^2} > 0.$$

FIGURE 10.4 The Supply Curve of the Perfectly Competitive Firm The supply curve of the perfectly competitive firm equals OP_3BC.

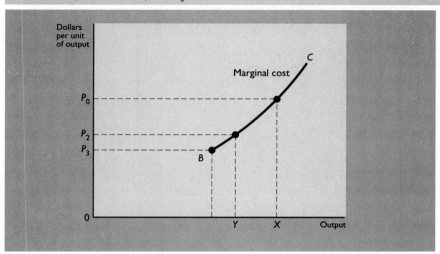

OY, and so forth. The resulting supply curve is that shown in Figure 10.4 as OP_3BC. *Given the way it was constructed, this curve is exactly the same as the firm's short-run marginal cost curve for prices above* OP_3; *at or below* OP_3, *the supply curve coincides with the price axis.*

Short-Run Supply Curve of the Industry

The price of the industry's product in the short run was given to us in the previous section. What we want to do is to see how it is determined. This price is influenced both by the consumers that demand the good and the firms that supply it. The determinants of the industry demand curve (that is, the market demand curve) have been discussed in previous chapters, particularly in Chapter 5. In this section, we discuss the determinants of the short-run industry supply curve (that is, the short-run market supply curve), and in the next section, we combine the demand and supply curves to determine the industry's price and output in the short run.

As a rough approximation, the industry's short-run supply curve can be regarded as the horizontal summation of the short-run supply curves of all the firms in the industry. For example, if there were three firms in the industry and if their supply curves were OSS_1S_1', OSS_2S_2', OSS_3S_3' in Figure 10.5, the industry's supply curve would be $OSS'S''$, since $OSS'S''$ shows the amounts of the product that all the firms together would supply at various prices. Of course, if there were only three firms, the industry would not be perfectly competitive, but we can ignore this inconsistency. The point of Figure 10.5 is to il-

Rough approximation

FIGURE 10.5 Horizontal Summation of Short-Run Supply Curves of Firms If increases or decreases in output by all firms simultaneously do not affect input prices, the industry supply curve is $OSS'S''$, the horizontal summation of the firms' supply curves.

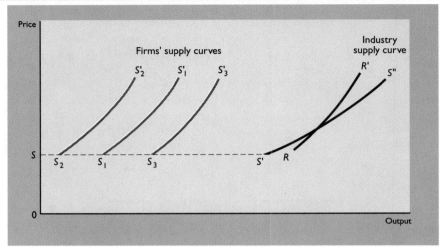

lustrate the fact that the industry supply curve is the horizontal summation of the firm supply curves, at least under one important assumption.

The assumption underlying this construction of the short-run industry supply curve is that supplies of inputs to the industry as a whole are perfectly elastic. In other words, it is assumed that increases or decreases in output by all firms simultaneously do not affect input prices. This is a strong assumption. Although changes in the output of one firm alone often cannot affect input prices, the simultaneous expansion or contraction of output by all firms may well alter input prices, with the result that the individual firm's cost curves—and supply curve—will shift. For example, an expansion of the whole industry may bid up the price of certain inputs, with the result that the cost curves of the firms in the industry will be pushed upward.[4]

If, contrary to the assumption underlying Figure 10.5, input prices are influenced in this way by expansion of the industry, what will be the effect on the short-run industry supply curve? It will make the short-run industry supply curve less elastic than $OSS'S''$. In the relevant price range, the curve might be more like RR'. To see this, note that expansion of the industry causes the short-run average cost curve and the short-run marginal cost curve to move upward, because of the resulting increase in input prices. But if the marginal cost curve

---

[4] More will be said about the effect of industry output on individual cost curves in subsequent sections of this chapter.

EXAMPLE 10.1

Auctions and Experimental Economics

In the 1980s and 1990s, Charles Plott of Caltech, Vernon Smith of the University of Arizona, and others have carried out a variety of interesting experiments to study how markets work in relatively simple situations. The subjects (often college students) trade a commodity with no intrinsic value. Buyers make a profit by purchasing the commodity from sellers and reselling it to the experimenter. Sellers make a profit by buying units from the experimenter and selling them to buyers. The terms on which the experimenter will buy or sell the commodity are spelled out to the subjects (and determine the demand and supply curves).

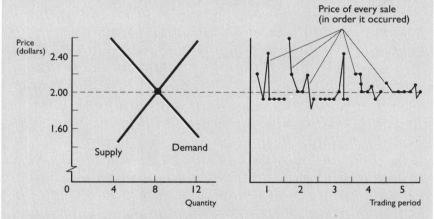

In one of Smith's experiments, an auction occurred in which public bids or offers were made to buy or sell units of the good in question. There were five trading periods. Each participant was free to accept whatever terms he or she chose. The market demand and supply curves were as shown in the left-hand panel in the above figure. The right-hand panel shows the price of every sale in the order in which it occurred.

(a) In this experiment, did the actual price converge on the competitive equilibrium price? (b) How many trading periods were required before the actual prices all were within about 10 percent of the competitive equilibrium price? (c) Did this experiment incorporate all the characteristics of perfect competition? (d) Did this experiment prove that actual price always converges on the competitive equilibrium price?

SOLUTION   (a) Yes. The competitive equilibrium price is $2, and it is clear from the right-hand panel of the graph that the actual price tended to converge on it as time went on. (b) By the fourth trading period, all the actual prices at which sales were made were within about 10 percent of $2, the competitive equilibrium price. (c) No. According to the customary definition, a perfectly competitive market contains a great many buyers and sellers, whereas only a few existed in this experiment. It is noteworthy that the competitive equilibrium price is a good approximation to the outcome of this auction even though the number of buyers and sellers is not very large. (d) No. The results of experiments vary depending on the number of buyers and sellers and the way the market is organized. For example, if there is only one seller, the price tends to depart from the competitive equilibrium price. (More will be said on this score in Chapter 11.)*

*For further discussion, see C. Plott, "Theories of Industrial Organization as Explanation of Experimental Market Behavior," reprinted in Mansfield, *Microeconomics: Selected Readings,* 5th ed., and V. Smith, A. Williams, W. K. Bratton, and M. Vannoni, "Competitive Market Institutions: Double Auctions vs. Sealed Bid-Offer Auctions," *American Economic Review,* March 1982.

moves upward, price will equal marginal cost at a lower output than would have been the case if the marginal cost curve had not moved.

In summary, the shape of the short-run supply curve is determined by the number of firms in the industry, the size of the plant and other factors determining the shape of the marginal cost curve of each firm, and the effect of changes in industry output on input prices.

Short-Run Equilibrium Price and Output for the Industry

Equilibrium price and output

As we know from Chapter 1, the short-run equilibrium price level is the price at which the quantity demanded and the quantity supplied of the product in the short run are equal. For example, if the demand curve is D and the supply curve is as shown in Figure 10.6, the equilibrium price is OP and the equilibrium industry output is OQ, this point being the intersection of the demand and supply curves. Once enough time has elapsed for firms to adjust their utilization of the variable inputs, the price will tend to equal this equilibrium level. If the price is above this equilibrium level, the quantity supplied will tend to exceed the quantity demanded, with the result that the price will tend to fall. If the price is below this equilibrium level, the quantity demanded will tend to exceed the quantity supplied, with the result that the price will tend to rise. There is no tendency for the price to move in one direction or the other if and only if it is at the equilibrium level.

FIGURE 10.6 Determination of Price and Output in the Short Run If the demand curve shifts from D to E, the price will eventually rise to OP_1, and each firm (that produces) will adjust its output rate upward so its marginal cost equals the higher price.

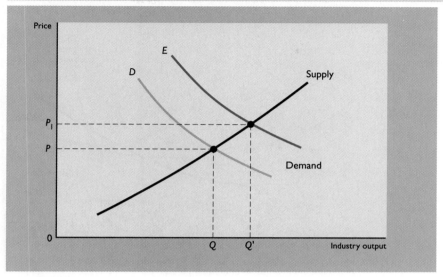

At the equilibrium price, price will equal marginal cost for all firms that choose to produce, rather than shut down their plants. Price may be above or below average total cost, since there is no necessity that profits be zero or that fixed costs be covered in the short run. An increase in demand will increase equilibrium price and output in the short run. For example, suppose that demand shifts from D to E in Figure 10.6. The shift in the demand curve will cause a shortage at the old price, OP, with the result that the price will eventually be pushed up to OP_1. At the same time, each firm will adjust its output rate upward so that its marginal cost will equal the higher price, with the result that industry output will grow to OQ'.

PRICE DETERMINATION IN THE LONG RUN

The Long-Run Adjustment Process

In the long run, the firm can change its plant size. This means that established firms may leave an industry if the industry has below-average profits, or that new firms may enter an industry if the industry has above-average profits. The

FIGURE 10.7 Initial Change of Plant Size in the Long Run To maximize profit in the long run, the firm will choose an output level (OQ_2) and plant size so that the long-run marginal cost is equal to price (OP) at the point where the short-run marginal cost (M_2M_2') of the plant is equal to price.

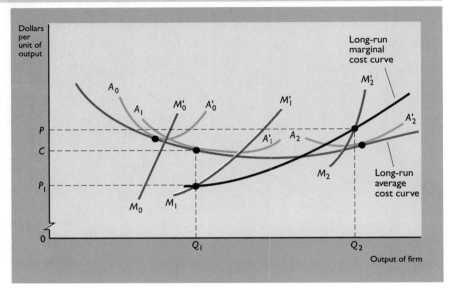

next two sections are concerned with the long-run equilibrium of a perfectly competitive industry. We begin in this section by describing the adjustment process for an established firm.

Suppose that the firm has a plant with short-run average and marginal cost curves of A_0A_0' and M_0M_0', shown in Figure 10.7. Suppose that the price of the product is OP. With its existing plant the firm makes a small profit on each unit of output. However, in the long run, the firm is not limited to this plant. The firm could build a plant corresponding to any of the short-run cost curves in Figure 10.7. For example, it could build a medium-sized plant corresponding to the short-run cost curves of A_1A_1' and M_1M_1', or it could build a large plant corresponding to the short-run cost curves of A_2A_2' and M_2M_2'. What will the firm do in the long run? If it attempts to maximize profit it will choose to build the plant corresponding to short-run cost curves of A_2A_2' and M_2M_2'. The maximum attainable profit under the postulated circumstances will be earned by using this plant and producing OQ_2 units of output per period of time.

In general, maximum profit will be obtained by producing at an output rate and with a plant such that the *long-run marginal cost is equal to price at the point where the short-run marginal cost of the plant is equal to price*. This, of course, is true at the output of OQ_2 units and with the plant corresponding to short-run cost curves A_2A_2' and M_2M_2' in Figure 10.7. The plant will be chosen so that long-run marginal cost equals price, since this clearly is a condition for profit maximization in the long run. To maximize profit, the firm will operate this plant at the point where short-run marginal cost equals price. Thus the equality of long-run marginal cost, short-run marginal cost, and price follows from the assumption of profit maximization. (See footnote 11, Chapter 8.)

If all firms in the industry except this one had plants of optimal size, the expansion of this one firm would have no significant influence on price. Consequently, since OP is greater than the average cost of producing OQ_2 units, all firms would be earning a profit. Recall from Chapter 8 that costs, as reckoned by economists (but not accountants), include the returns that could be gotten from the most lucrative alternative use of the firm's resources. Consequently, an *economic profit* means that the firm is making more than it could make with its resources in other industries. Of course, the existence of above-average profits in this industry attracts new entrants; when these new firms enter the industry, the adjustment process must go on.

Economic profit

The arrival of new entrants shifts the industry supply curve to the right. That is, more will be supplied at a given price than before. For example, suppose that the industry supply curve shifts from S to S_1 in Figure 10.8, with the result that the price drops from OP to OP_1 and industry output increases from OQ to OQ_3. Although total industry output increases (because of the new entrants), the output of each of the firms is smaller. Given that the price is now OP_1, the optimal output of each firm is OQ_1, rather than OQ_2 (see Figure 10.7). And the optimal plant is the one corresponding to the short-run cost curves A_1A_1' and M_1M_1'. Firms that have built plants corresponding to the short-run cost curves A_2A_2' and M_2M_2' will lose a great deal of money. But even those

FIGURE 10.8 Effects of the Entry of New Firms Because of the entry of firms, the industry supply curve shifts to the right, and equilibrium price falls from OP to OP_1.

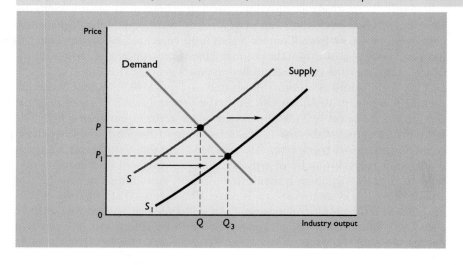

firms that have plants of optimal size (corresponding to the short-run curves A_1A_1' and M_1M_1') will lose P_1C dollars per unit.

This does not mean that firms with plants of optimal size are not maximizing profits. On the contrary, it is evident from Figure 10.7 that, with the price at OP_1, long-run marginal cost equals short-run marginal cost equals price when the firm produces OQ_1 units of output with the plant corresponding to the short-run cost curves A_1A_1' and M_1M_1'. Thus this is the profit-maximizing solution for the firm. The trouble is that, even if the firm does the best it can, it cannot make an economic profit. The result will be an out-migration of firms from the industry. Since the returns that could be obtained from the firm's resources are greater in other industries, entrepreneurs will transfer these resources to other industries. In this way, the adjustment process will go on, since the exit of firms will shift the industry's supply curve to the left.

Long-Run Equilibrium of the Firm

When and where will this adjustment process end? Eventually, enough firms will leave the industry so that economic losses are eliminated, but profits are avoided, too. At this point the remaining firms will be in equilibrium. In other words, the long-run equilibrium position of the firm is at the point at which its long-run average total costs equal price. If price is in excess of average total costs for any firm, economic profits are being earned and new firms will enter the industry. If price is less than average total costs for any firm, that firm will eventually leave the industry.

Going a step further, we can show that price must be equal to the *lowest value* of long-run average total costs. In other words, firms must be producing at the minimum point on their long-run average cost curves. The reason for this is as follows: To maximize their profits, firms must operate where price equals long-run marginal cost. Also, we have just seen that they must operate where price equals long-run average cost. But if both of these conditions are satisfied, it follows that long-run marginal cost must equal long-run average cost. And we know from Chapter 8 that long-run marginal cost is equal to long-run average cost only at the point at which long-run average cost is a minimum. Thus this must be the equilibrium position of the firm.

Price = marginal cost = average cost

This equilibrium position is illustrated in Figure 10.9. When all adjustments are made, price equals OB. Since the demand curve is horizontal, the marginal revenue curve is the same as the demand curve, both being BB'. The equilibrium output of the firm is OV, and its plant corresponds to short-run average and marginal cost curves AA' and MM'. At this output and with this plant, long-run marginal cost equals short-run marginal cost equals price: This insures that the firm is maximizing profit. Also, long-run average cost equals short-run average cost equals price. This insures that economic profits are zero. Since the long-run marginal cost and long-run average cost must be equal, the equilibrium point is at the bottom of the long-run average cost curve.

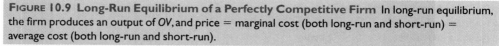

FIGURE 10.9 **Long-Run Equilibrium of a Perfectly Competitive Firm** In long-run equilibrium, the firm produces an output of *OV*, and price = marginal cost (both long-run and short-run) = average cost (both long-run and short-run).

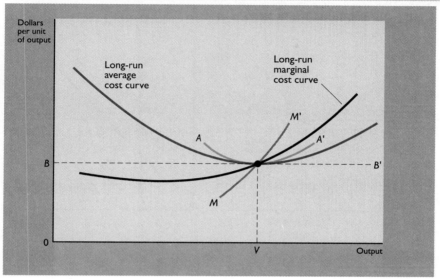

Since price must be the same for all firms in the industry, this implies that the minimum of the long-run average cost curve must be the same for all firms. However, this is not as unrealistic as it appears at first glance. Firms that appear to have lower costs than others in the industry often have unusually good resources or particularly able managements. The owners of superior resources (including management ability) can obtain a higher price for them if they are put to alternative uses than more ordinary resources. Consequently, the alternative costs, or implicit costs, of one's using superior resources are higher than those of using ordinary resources. If this is taken into account, and if these superior resources are costed properly, the firms with apparently lower costs have no lower costs at all.

Constant-Cost Industries

In the previous two sections, it was assumed implicitly that the industry exhibited constant costs; this means that expansion of the industry does not result in an increase in input prices. Figure 10.10 shows long-run equilibrium under conditions of constant cost. The left-hand panel shows the short- and long-run cost curves of a typical firm in the industry. The right-hand panel shows the demand and supply curves in the market as a whole, *D* being the original demand curve and *S* being the original short-run supply curve. It is

FIGURE 10.10 **Long-Run Equilibrium: Constant-Cost Industry** A constant-cost industry has a horizontal long-run supply curve, as shown in panel B. If demand shifts upward from D to D_1, the resulting increase in price (to OP_1) results in the entry of firms, which shifts the supply curve to the right (to S_1), pushing the price back to its original level (OP).

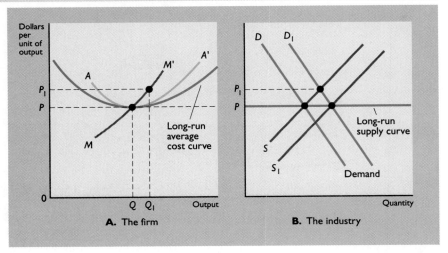

A. The firm   **B.** The industry

assumed that the industry is in long-run equilibrium, with the result that the price line is tangent to the long-run (and short-run) average cost curve at its minimum point. (OP is the price.)

Assume now that the demand curve shifts to D_1. In the short run, with the number of firms fixed, the price of the product will rise from OP to OP_1, each firm will expand output from OQ to OQ_1, and each firm will be making economic profits since OP_1 exceeds the short-run average costs of the firm at OQ_1. The consequence is that firms will enter the industry and shift the supply curve to the right. In the case of a constant-cost industry, the entrance of the new firms does not affect the costs of the existing firms. The inputs used by this industry are used by many other industries as well, and the appearance of the new firms in this industry does not bid up the price of inputs and consequently raise the costs of existing firms. Neither does the appearance of the new firms lower the costs of existing firms.

Constant-cost industry   Consequently, *a constant-cost industry has a horizontal long-run supply curve.* Since output can be expanded by increasing the number of firms producing OQ units at an average cost of OP, the long-run supply curve is horizontal at OP. So long as the industry remains in a state of constant costs, its output can be expanded indefinitely. If price exceeds OP, firms would enter the industry; if price were less than OP, firms would leave the industry. Thus long-run equilibrium can only occur in this industry when price is OP. And industry output can be expanded or contracted, in accord with demand conditions, without altering this long-run equilibrium price.

Increasing- and Decreasing-Cost Industries

An increasing-cost industry is shown in Figure 10.11. The original conditions are the same as in Figure 10.10, the original demand curve being D, the original supply curve being S, the equilibrium price being OP, and the long-run and short-run average cost curves of each firm being LL' and AA' in the left panel. As in Figure 10.10, the original position is one of long-run equilibrium, since the price line is tangent to the average cost curves at their minima.

Now suppose that the demand curve shifts to D_1, with the result that the price of the product increases and firms earn economic profits, and thus attract new entrants. More and more inputs are required by the industry, and in an increasing-cost industry, the price of inputs increases with the amount used by the industry. Consequently, the cost of inputs increases for the established firms as well as the new entrants and the average cost curves are pushed up to $L_1L'_1$ and $A_1A'_1$.

If the marginal cost curve of each firm is shifted to the left by the increase in input prices, the industry supply curve will tend to shift to the left. However, this tendency is more than counterbalanced by the effect of the increase in the number of firms, which shifts the industry supply curve to the right. The latter effect must more than offset the former effect because otherwise there

FIGURE 10.11 Long-Run Equilibrium: Increasing-Cost Industry An increasing-cost industry has a positively sloped long-run supply curve, as shown in panel B. After long-run equilibrium is achieved, increases in output require increases in the price of the product.

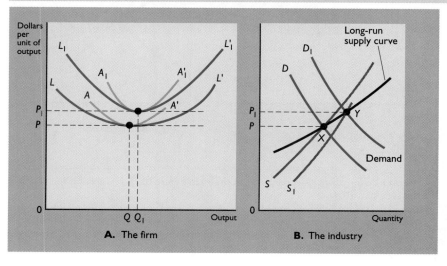

A. The firm **B. The industry**

would be no expansion in total industry output. (No new resources would
have been attracted to the industry.) The process of adjustment must go on
until a new point of long-run equilibrium is reached. In Figure 10.11, this
point is where the price of the product is OP_1 and each firm produces OQ_1
units; the new short-run supply curve is S_1.[5]

**Increas-
ing-cost
industry**
    An increasing-cost industry *has a positively sloped long-run supply curve.*
That is , after long-run equilibrium is achieved, increases in output require increases in the price of the product. For example, points X and Y in Figure
10.11 are both on the long-run supply curve for the industry. So the difference between constant-cost and increasing-cost industries is as follows: In
constant-cost industries, new firms enter in response to an increase in demand
until price returns to its original level; whereas in increasing-cost industries,
new firms enter until the minimum point on the long-run average cost curve
has increased to the point where it equals the new price.[6]

    A decreasing-cost industry is shown in Figure 10.12. Once again, we begin
with an industry in long-run equilibrium, the demand curve being D, the

FIGURE 10.12 Long-Run Equilibrium: Decreasing-Cost Industry A decreasing-cost industry
has a negatively sloped long-run supply curve, as shown in panel B. After long-run equilibrium is
achieved, increases in output are accompanied by decreases in price.

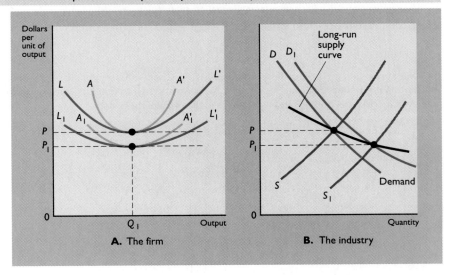

A. The firm   **B.** The industry

[5] We cannot be sure that OQ_1 exceeds OQ, as shown in Figure 10.11. It is possible for OQ_1 to be
less than or equal to OQ.

[6] This is only one way in which equilibrium can be achieved in increasing-cost industries. It is
also possible that the increase in input prices (due to the expansion of industry output) raises average cost more than the increase in demand raises average revenue. Thus firms may experience
losses, some may leave the industry, and the remaining firms may produce at a larger scale.

EXAMPLE 10.2

What Would Be the Effects of National Dental Insurance?

Many countries, such as Sweden and the United Kingdom, have national health insurance covering dental services. In the United States,
there have been proposals for such dental insurance. A number of questions arise concerning the effects of these proposed insurance schemes,
one of the most important being: How much more dental care would be
demanded if these plans were implemented? Economists at the Rand
Corporation have estimated that the demand curves for dental care
for adult males, adult females, and children in the United States are as
follows:*

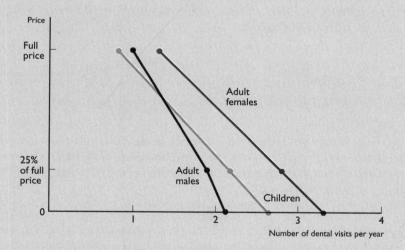

(a) According to some proposals, national dental insurance would
pay for three-quarters of the price of dental care. About how much of an
increase in the quantity demanded of dental care would result if these
proposals were adopted? (b) Based on the above diagram, can you determine whether it would be possible to meet the resulting increase in
demand with the current number of dentists? If not, what additional
curve do you need? (c) Do you think that the quantity of dental services
supplied would be the same, regardless of the price of dental care? Why
or why not? (d) What would be the effect of the above proposals on the
market demand curve for dental care? Why? (e) Would the price of
dental care tend to rise? (f) Many economists suggest that, if the above
proposals for a national dental insurance plan were adopted, they should
be phased in slowly and gradually, as in Sweden in 1974. Why?

| SOLUTION | (a) Based on the demand curves shown on page 317, the quantity demanded of dental care would more |

SOLUTION (a) Based on the demand curves shown on page 317, the quantity demanded of dental care would more than double if people were to pay 25 percent of the full price. (b) No. If the market for dental services were perfectly competitive, the supply curve for dental care would be needed to tell us how much dental care would be supplied at each price. (c) No. As the price of dental care increases (at least up to some point), it seems likely that more dental services will be supplied. (d) The market demand curve for dental care would tend to shift to the right. At a particular price, people would demand more dental care than in the past because they would have to pay only 25 percent of this price. (e) If the demand curve for dental services were to shift to the right, and if the supply curve were not to shift (and if it were to slope upward to the right), the price would tend to rise. (f) It would take considerable time for the supply of dental services to adjust to the increase in demand.†

---

*W. Manning and C. Phelps, "The Demand for Dental Care," *Bell Journal of Economics,* Autumn 1979.

†For further discussion, see ibid. and the *New York Times,* May 26, 1993.

short-run supply curve being S, the price being OP, and the long-run and short-run average cost curves of each firm being LL' and AA'. As before, we postulate an increase in demand to D_1, the result being economic profit for established firms and the entry of new firms. However, in the case of a decreasing-cost industry, the expansion of the industry results in a decrease in the costs of the established firms. Thus the new long-run equilibrium is at a price of OP_1, the equilibrium output of each firm being OQ_1, and the new long-run and short-run average cost curves being L_1L_1' and A_1A_1'.

**Decreas-
ing-cost
industry**
　　A decreasing-cost industry *has a negatively sloped long-run supply curve.* That is, after long-run equilibrium is reached, increases in output are accompanied by decreases in price. *External economies,* which are cost reductions that occur when the industry expands, may be responsible for the existence of decreasing-cost industries. An example of an external economy is an improvement in transportation that is due to the expansion of an industry and that reduces the costs of each firm in the industry. If there are important external economies, an industry may be subject to decreasing costs. Note that the external economies are quite different from economies of scale: The individual firm has no control over external economies.

　　Most economists seem to regard increasing-cost industries as being the most frequently encountered of the three types. Decreasing-cost industries are the most unusual situation, although quite young industries may fall into this category.

THE ALLOCATION PROCESS: SHORT AND LONG RUNS

At this point, it is instructive to describe the process by which a perfectly competitive economy—an economy composed of perfectly competitive industries—would allocate resources. The allocation of resources among alternative uses is one of the major functions of an economic system. Equipped with the concepts of this and previous chapters, we can now describe how a perfectly competitive economy goes about shifting resources in accord with changes in consumer demand.

To be specific, suppose that a change occurs in tastes, with the result that consumers are more favorably disposed toward corn and less favorably disposed toward potatoes than in the past. What will happen in the short run? **Shift in** The increase in the demand for corn increases the price of corn, and results in **tastes** some increase in the output of corn. However, the output of corn cannot be increased very substantially because the capacity of the industry cannot be expanded in the short run. Similarly, the fall in the demand for potatoes reduces the price of potatoes, and results in some reduction in the output of potatoes. But the output of potatoes will not be curtailed greatly because firms will continue to produce as long as they can cover variable costs.

The change in the relative prices of corn and potatoes tells producers that a reallocation of resources is called for. Because of the increase in the price of corn and the decrease in the price of potatoes, corn producers are earning economic profits and potato producers are showing economic losses. This will trigger a redeployment of resources. If some variable inputs in the production of potatoes can be used as effectively in the production of corn, these variable inputs may be withdrawn from potato production and switched to corn production. Even if there are no variable inputs that are used in both corn and potato production, adjustment can occur in various interrelated markets, with the result that corn production gains resources and potato production loses resources.

When short-run equilibrium is attained in both the corn and potato industries, the reallocation of resources is not yet complete since there has not been enough time for producers to build new capacity or liquidate old capacity. In **Short-run** particular, neither industry is operating at minimum average cost. The corn **effects** producers may be operating at greater than the output level where average cost is a minimum; and the potato producers may be operating at less than the output level where average cost is a minimum.

What will happen in the long run? The shift in consumer demand from potatoes to corn will result in greater adjustments in production and smaller adjustments in price than in the short run. In the long run, existing firms can leave potato production and new firms can enter corn production. Because of short-run economic losses in potato production, some potato land and related equipment will be allowed to run down, and some firms engaged in potato production will be liquidated. As firms leave potato production, the supply curve shifts to the left, causing the price to rise above its short-run level. The transfer of resources out of potato production will stop when the price has increased, and costs have decreased, to the point where losses are avoided.

While potato production is losing resources, corn production is gaining them. The short-run economic profits in corn production will result in the entry of new firms. The increased demand for inputs will raise input prices and cost curves in corn production, and the price of corn will be depressed by the movement to the right of the supply curve because of the entry of new firms. Entry ceases when economic profits are no longer being earned. At that point, when long-run equilibrium is achieved, there will be more firms and more resources used in the corn industry than in the short run.

Long-run effects
Finally, long-run equilibrium is established in both industries, and the reallocation of resources is complete. It is important to note that this reallocation can affect industries other than corn and potatoes. If potato land and equipment can be easily adapted to the production of corn, which seems unlikely, potato producers can simply change to the production of corn. If not, the resources used in potato production are converted to some use other than corn, and the resources that enter corn production come from some use other than potato production. The full repercussions can be analyzed by general equilibrium analysis, which is discussed in Chapter 18.

PRODUCER SURPLUS, TOTAL SURPLUS, AND EFFICIENT OUTPUT

The Nature of Producer Surplus and Total Surplus

Having described the process by which a perfectly competitive economy would allocate resources, we now turn to the efficiency of a competitive market. As we shall see, many economists believe that a competitive market maximizes the aggregate economic welfare of consumers and producers. To understand their arguments, it is useful to begin by defining *producer surplus,* a concept that is analogous to consumer surplus, but relates to producers, not consumers. Recall that consumer surplus was defined in Chapter 4 as the net benefit that consumers receive above and beyond what they have to pay for a

FIGURE 10.13 **Producer Surplus** The producer surplus from the production and sale of the equilibrium output of this good (3,300 units) equals the shaded area—the area above the supply curve and below the price.

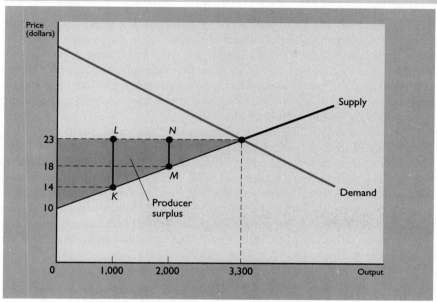

good. Producer surplus is the analogous measure for producers: It shows how much producers receive above and beyond the minimum price that would be required to get them to produce and sell their goods.

Producer surplus

For example, consider Figure 10.13, which shows the demand and supply curves for a particular good. The equilibrium price is $23. According to the supply curve, producers would be willing to supply the 1,000th unit of this good (that they produce and sell) for $14. Thus, because they receive the equilibrium price of $23 for this unit, they receive a bonus or surplus of $23−$14 =$9 from its production and sale. Similarly, they receive a bonus or surplus of $23−$18=$5 from the 2,000th unit of this good that they produce and sell, since the supply curve shows that they would be willing to supply this unit if its price were $18. As shown in Figure 10.13, the bonus or surplus received by producers from the production and sale of a particular unit of output is the vertical distance from the horizontal line at the equilibrium price ($23) down to the supply curve at this output. For example, the surplus is $KL = \$9$ from the 1,000th unit and $MN = \$5$ from the 2,000th unit. Adding up these vertical distances for all 3,300 units of output produced and sold, we find that the producer surplus from *all* the 3,300 units equals the total shaded area in Figure 10.13— the area above the supply curve and below the price. In Figure 10.13, this area equals $\frac{1}{2}$ ($23 − $10) (3,300) = $21,450.

Producer surplus includes (1) the aggregate profits of firms producing the good, plus (2) the amount that owners of inputs (used to make the good) are compensated above and beyond the minimum they would insist on. Just as consumer surplus measures the net benefit to consumers, so producer surplus measures the net benefit to producers. (When referring to producer surplus, "producers" refers both to the owners of the producing firms and to the owners of inputs used by these firms.) Consumers would like to increase consumer surplus; producers would like to increase producer surplus. Since both consumer surplus and producer surplus are dollar amounts, they can be added together, the result being *total surplus,* which is a measure of aggregate net benefit to both consumers and producers.

Total surplus

The shaded area in Figure 10.14 shows the total surplus if the perfectly competitive output of 3,300 units is produced and sold. The top shaded area shows the consumer surplus, the amount that consumers would be willing to pay for these units above and beyond the $23 per unit that they have to pay. The bottom shaded area shows the producer surplus, the amount that producers receive above and beyond the minimum required to get them to produce and sell these 3,300 units. Since total surplus is defined as the sum of consumer and producer surplus, it equals the sum of the top shaded area and the bottom shaded area in Figure 10.14.

FIGURE 10.14 Perfect Competition Maximizes Total Surplus, the Sum of Consumer and Producer Surplus Up to the perfectly competitive output, here 3,300 units, every extra unit of output increases total surplus, which is the shaded area.

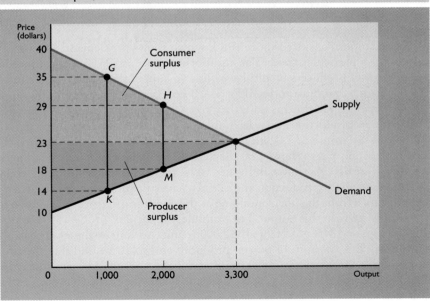

Total surplus is a measure of the total net gain to consumers and producers from the production and sale of a particular number of units of the good. For example, consider the 1,000th unit. As shown in Figure 10.14, consumers are willing to pay up to $35 for this unit, and the minimum amount that producers would take for producing and selling this unit is $14; thus, the total net gain—the difference between the most that consumers will pay for this unit and the least that it can be produced and sold for—is $35−$14 = $21, which is the vertical distance KG in Figure 10.14. Similarly, the total net gain from the production and sale of the 2,000th unit is $29−$18=$11, the vertical distance MH in Figure 10.14. If we add the vertical distances for all the 3,300 units produced and sold, we get the total shaded area in Figure 10.14, which equals $49,500. [Consumer surplus equals $\frac{1}{2}$ ($40−$23) (3,300) = $28,050, and as we already know, producer surplus equals $21,450, so the sum equals $28,050 + $21,450=$49,500.]

Perfect Competition and the Maximization of Total Surplus

Total surplus varies with how many units are produced. If the maximum amount that consumers are willing to pay for an extra unit exceeds the minimum amount that producers would accept for producing and selling it, the production and sale of this extra unit increases total surplus. Up to the perfectly competitive output of 3,300 units, every extra unit increases total surplus because the demand curve (which shows the maximum amount that consumers would pay for an extra unit of the good) lies *above* the supply curve (which shows the minimum amount that producers would accept for producing and selling it). Beyond the perfectly competitive output of 3,300 units, every extra unit reduces total surplus because the demand curve (which shows the maximum amount that consumers would pay for an extra unit of the good) lies *below* the supply curve (which shows the minimum amount that producers would accept for producing and selling it). Thus, since total surplus rises as output increases up to the perfectly competitive level and decreases beyond that point, it follows that total surplus is maximized when output is at the perfectly competitive level.

Maximizing total surplus

This result—that the perfectly competitive output maximizes the total net gain to consumers and producers—is important. As we shall see, it is a major reason why economists tend to prefer perfect competition over other market structures like monopoly. But it should be recognized that the present analysis makes a number of implicit assumptions which will be discussed at length in subsequent chapters. For one thing, it is assumed that private and social costs (and benefits) are equal. If this is not the case, there may be social advantages in government intervention leading to an output different from that which would occur under perfect competition. For example, in cases where the social costs of polluting the air or water exceed the private costs to the firms doing the polluting, society may be better-off if output, and hence pollution, is less than would occur under perfect competition.

EXAMPLE 10.3

Rent Control and Total Surplus

Rent control, as we know from previous chapters, exists in many cities, including New York. Suppose that the demand and supply curves for rental housing in a particular city are as shown in the graph below and that rent control is instituted. In particular, landlords are no longer allowed to charge rents exceeding $600 per month. For simplicity, assume that all the city's apartments are basically the same in size and desirability and that no landlord can evade the $600 price ceiling.

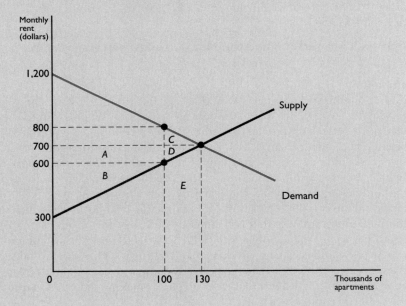

(a) According to the above graph, rent control will result in fewer apartments (100,000 rather than 130,000) being offered for rent. What will be the effect of rent control on the consumer surplus of those people who get apartments? (b) What will be the effect on the consumer surplus of those who no longer can obtain apartments? (Assume that those who are willing to pay most for apartments are the ones who get them.) (c) What will be the effect of rent control on producer surplus? (d) What will be the effect on total surplus, and why is this of significance in judging the social desirability of rent control?

SOLUTION (a) Those consumers who are fortunate enough to occupy apartments under rent control will gain $700 −$600=$100 per month. Since there are 100,000 such apartments, the gain in consumer surplus to these consumers will equal area *A*, which is 100,000×$100, or $10 million per month. (b) The consumers who can no longer obtain apartments would have been willing to pay an amount equal to areas *C* + *D* + *E* for these 30,000 apartments, but had to pay only an amount equal to areas *D* + *E*. Thus, there was a consumer surplus equal to area *C*, which is $\frac{1}{2}$ ($800−$700) (130,000 − 100,000) = $1.5 million per month. Because these consumers can no longer obtain this surplus, they will lose $1.5 million per month. (c) Without rent control, producer surplus would equal areas *A* + *B* + *D*, since this is the area above the supply curve and below $700, the rent (price) that would have prevailed. With rent control, producer surplus equals area *B*, since this is the area above the supply curve and below the new rent (price)— $600. Thus, producer surplus will go down by area *A* + *D*, which is $11.5 million. (d) According to the answers to parts (a) to (c), consumer surplus will rise by $10 million−$1.5 million=$8.5 million, and producer surplus will fall by $11.5 million. Since the gain in consumer surplus is less than the fall in producer surplus, total surplus will go down by $11.5 million−$8.5 million=$3 million. This is of significance because, if consumers are judged to be no more (or less) deserving than producers, it indicates that rent control will reduce total welfare. However, the limitations of this sort of analysis should be borne in mind. (See below, page 323, and Chapter 18.)

Also, the use of total surplus as a measure of how well a market is functioning from society's point of view entails a number of assumptions. In particular, it is assumed that a dollar gained or lost by every person should be given the same weight, regardless of whether he or she is rich or poor, deserving or undeserving, or a consumer or producer. For example, suppose that the price of a particular good is pushed downward because the government imposes a price ceiling on this good, the result being that consumer surplus rises by $1 million, producer surplus falls by $1 million, and total surplus is unchanged. (In other words, consumers gain $1 million from the price reduction, and producers lose the same amount.) If total surplus is used as a measure of economic performance, the imposition of this price ceiling would be said to neither increase nor decrease social welfare. But this is true only if consumers are regarded as no more or less deserving than producers, which may or may not be true, depending on the circumstances (and on one's point of view). More will be said on this score in Chapter 18.

AGRICULTURAL PRICES AND OUTPUT: AN APPLICATION

Perhaps the most important sector of the U.S. economy that contains industries that are reasonably close to perfect competition is agriculture. Farming is still our most important single industry, although it includes a much smaller percentage of our people than it once did. One of the most important points to note about U.S. agriculture is that agricultural prices generally fell, relative to other prices, from World War I to the early 1970s. That is, if we correct for changes in the general price level resulting from overall inflation, there was a declining trend in farm prices. Another important fact is that farm incomes vary between good times and bad to a much greater extent than nonfarm incomes, whereas farm output is more stable than industrial output.

The theory presented in this and previous chapters is useful in explaining the reasons for these characteristics of U.S. agriculture. Figure 10.15 shows the demand and supply curves for farm products at various points in time. Since we know from Chapter 5 that the demand for food does not grow very rapidly in this country, we would expect the demand curve to shift relatively slowly to the right, from D in the first period to D_1 in the second period to D_2 in the third period. On the other hand, because of very great technological improvements in agriculture, the supply curve has been shifting relatively rapidly to the right, from S in the first period to S_1 in the second period to S_2 in the third period. The consequence is that agricultural prices fell (relative to other prices) from OP to OP_1 to OP_2.

It is also easy to see why farm incomes are so unstable. We know from Chapter 5 that the demand curve for basic farm products is relatively inelastic. Also, the supply curve for basic farm products is relatively inelastic in the short run. Since both the demand curve and the supply curve are inelastic, a small shift (to the right or left) in either curve, or both, results in a large change in price. To illustrate, consider Figure 10.16. In panel A, the demand and supply curves are much less elastic than in panel B, with the result that a small shift in the demand curve results in a much bigger change in price in panel A than in panel B.[7]

---

[7] For simplicity, suppose that the demand and supply curves exhibit the same elasticity at each point, in which case

$$Q_D = \alpha_0 P^{-\beta_0} \qquad\qquad [10.1]$$

and $\qquad\qquad Q_S = \alpha_1 P^{\beta_1}, \qquad\qquad [10.2]$

(Cont. on page 328)

FIGURE 10.15 Shifts in Demand and Supply: Agriculture Agricultural prices have fallen (relative to other prices) because the demand curve has shifted slowly to the right, whereas the supply curve has shifted rapidly to the right.

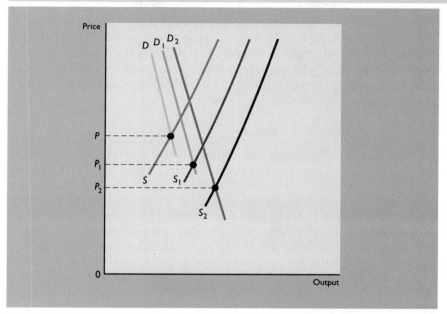

FIGURE 10.16 Relationship between Elasticity of Supply and Demand and Instability of Price Because the demand and supply curves are much less elastic in panel A than in panel B, a small shift in the demand curve (from D to D_1) results in a much bigger change in price in panel A than in panel B.

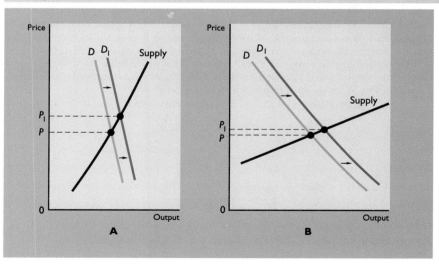

Although agricultural prices have generally fallen (relative to industrial prices) over the past 60 years, this trend was reversed sharply in 1973 and 1974, when farm prices rose at an astonishing rate. Due to poor harvests in other countries and the devaluation of the dollar, as well as trade with the Communist world, there was a marked upward shift to the right of the demand curve for U.S. farm products. As would be predicted by our theory, farm prices rose rapidly in response to this shift in the demand curve. For example, the price of wheat rose from under $2 to over $5 per bushel. Anyone who witnessed the proceedings would have been quick to agree that farm prices behaved in accord with our model.

Government Subsidy Programs

Another important fact about U.S. agriculture that must be added to this picture is government intervention and aid. Both Figures 10.15 and 10.16 are based on the supposition that agricultural markets are free. For about half of all farm products, the government has established price support programs of one sort or another. (The price supports for milk were described in some detail in the previous chapter.) These programs vary in many respects, but the general idea behind them is that the federal government has tried to increase farm prices in various ways. For products where such programs exist, the perfectly competitive model is clearly an inappropriate device to predict price and output. But, as we shall see in this section, the basic elements of the theory remain useful in analyzing the effects of these programs.

More specifically, the programs in operation can be described in terms of Figure 10.17. As pointed out in Chapter 9, a support price, OP', is set which is

where P is price, Q_D the quantity demanded, and Q_S the quantity supplied. Equation 10.1 is the demand function in which β_0 is the price elasticity of demand. Equation 10.2 is the supply function in which β_1 is the price elasticity of supply. Suppose that the demand curve shifted slightly, with α_0 increasing or decreasing by a small amount. What would be the effect on the equilibrium price? Suppose that the supply curve shifted slightly, with α_1 increasing or decreasing by a small amount. What would be the effect on the equilibrium price?

Since $Q_D = Q_S \, (=Q)$ in equilibrium, it follows from Equations 10.1 and 10.2 that

$$\log P = \frac{\log \alpha_0 - \log \alpha_1}{\beta_0 + \beta_1}.$$

Thus
$$\frac{dP}{P} \div \frac{d\alpha_0}{\alpha_0} = \frac{1}{\beta_0 + \beta_1}$$

and
$$\frac{dP}{P} \div \frac{d\alpha_1}{\alpha_1} = \frac{-1}{\beta_0 + \beta_1}$$

Consequently, as stated in the text, the relative change in price resulting from a small relative change in α_0 or α_1 is bigger if β_0 and β_1 are small than if β_0 or β_1 is large.

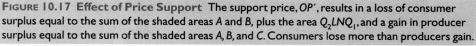

FIGURE 10.17 **Effect of Price Support** The support price, *OP'*, results in a loss of consumer surplus equal to the sum of the shaded areas *A* and *B*, plus the area Q_2LNQ_1, and a gain in producer surplus equal to the sum of the shaded areas *A*, *B*, and *C*. Consumers lose more than producers gain.

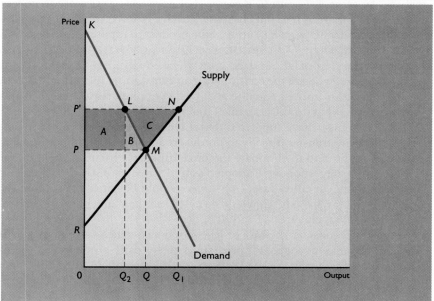

above the equilibrium price, *OP,* with the consequence that output equals OQ_1, consumers buy OQ_2, and the rest (which equals $OQ_1 - OQ_2$) has to be purchased by the government. The imposition of the support price means, of course, that farmers receive more for their crop than they otherwise would, and the difference in their receipts is $OP' \times OQ_1 - OP \times OQ$.

One important question is whether producers of farm products gain more from these programs than consumers of farm products lose. How much do consumers lose? Without the price support, consumer surplus would equal the area of triangle *PMK*. (Recall that consumer surplus is the area under the demand curve and above the price, here *OP.*) With the price support, consumer surplus equals the area of triangle *P'LK* (the area under the demand curve and above *OP',* the support price). Thus, the price support results in a loss of consumer surplus equal to the shaded areas *A* and *B*. How much did producers gain? Without the price support, producer surplus would equal the area of triangle *PMR*. (Recall that producer surplus is the area above the supply curve and below the price, here *OP.*) With the price support, producer surplus equals the area of triangle *P'NR* (the area above the supply curve and below OP', the support price). Thus, the price support results in a gain of producer surplus equal to the shaded areas A, B, and C.

Since consumer surplus falls by areas A and B, and since producer surplus increases by areas A, B, and C, it seems that producers gain more than consumers lose. But this is true only because we have ignored the cost to the government of buying $(OQ_1 - OQ_2)$ units of the product to support its price at OP'. That cost is $OP'(OQ_1 - OQ_2)$, since the government buys $(OQ_1 - OQ_2)$ units of the product at a price of OP', and this cost, which equals area Q_2LNQ_1, is borne by the taxpayers, who are the consumers in another guise. Including this cost, consumers lose an amount equal to area Q_2LNQ_1, plus areas A and B, which greatly exceeds what producers gain. Thus, total surplus falls.

Many economists have suggested that it would be more efficient for consumers simply to transfer directly to producers an amount of money equal to areas A, B, and C and to eliminate the price support. Producers would be as well-off if this suggestion were adopted as under the price support: they gain areas A, B, and C in either case. Consumers would be better-off because the cost to them (areas A, B, and C) would be much less than under the present system (area Q_2LNQ_1 plus areas A and B).

To illustrate, consider the case of dairy products, which were discussed at length in the previous chapter. If price supports for dairy products were eliminated, producers during the late 1980s would have lost about \$1.44 billion per year (since areas A, B, and C totaled about \$1.44 billion). If consumers had simply paid them this amount, they would have saved about \$2.22 billion per year (since area Q_2LNQ_1 plus areas A and B totaled about \$3.66 billion, which was about \$2.22 billion more than consumers would have paid the producers of dairy products.)[8] Note that, if Problem 9.10 on pages 293 to 295 had been based on real data for the late 1980s rather than the hypothetical graph on page 294, these figures would have answered parts (d), (f), and (g) of that problem.

One big reason why the cost to consumers is so great under price supports is that, as taxpayers, they finance the government's purchase of farm products that consumers do not want at the support price. To cut down on the amount that the government has to purchase (and store or dispose of), production controls frequently are imposed as well. These controls often take the form of quotas on the acreage used to grow the product. With such controls, the situation is shown in Figure 10.18, where OQ_3 is the total quota — in terms of output — for all farms. Because of the imposition of the production control, the government's expenditures are reduced from $OP' \times (OQ_1 - OQ_2)$ to $OP' \times (OQ_3 - OQ_2)$. The production controls tend to reduce the cost to consumers of farm price supports, but still consumers lose more than producers gain.

[8] H. McDowell and R. Fallert, "Gains and Losses in U.S. Dairy Programs," in Economic Research Service, *Economic Gains and Losses from Farm Commodity Programs* (Washington, D.C.: U.S. Department of Agriculture, forthcoming).

FIGURE 10.18 **Effect of Price Support and Production Control** If OQ_3 is the total production quota, and OP' is the support price, the government has to purchase an amount of the commodity equaling $(OQ_3 - OQ_2)$, which is less than $(OQ_1 - OQ_2)$.

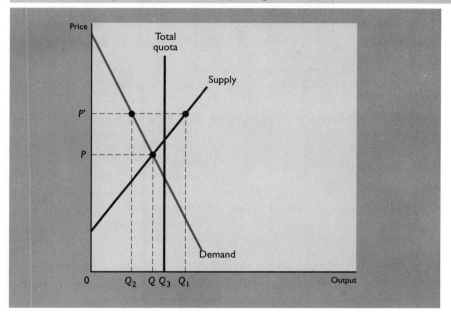

In 1996, Congress passed a major bill overhauling U.S. farm policies. Price supports for butter, powdered milk, and cheese would be phased out over four years. But not all farm price supports were eliminated; for example, peanuts, sugar, and tobacco retained their supports. Subsidy payments for crops like wheat, corn, and cotton would be altered.

SUMMARY

1. Perfect competition is defined by four conditions. No participant in the market can influence price, output must be homogeneous, resources must be mobile, and there must be perfect knowledge.
2. In the short run, the firm maximizes profit or minimizes losses by producing the output at which marginal cost equals price. However, if market

price is less than the firm's average variable costs at all levels of output, the firm will minimize losses by discontinuing production. The firm's short-run supply curve is the same as its marginal cost curve, as long as price exceeds average variable cost.

3. The short-run price of a product is determined by the interaction between the demand and supply sides of the market. As a rough approximation, the industry's short-run supply curve can be regarded as the horizontal summation of the short-run supply curves of the individual firms. However, this is not the case if the supply of inputs to the industry is not perfectly elastic.

4. The short-run equilibrium price level is the price at which the quantity demanded and the quantity supplied in the short run are equal. At the equilibrium price, price will equal marginal cost for all firms that choose to produce, rather than shut down their plants.

5. In the long run, firms can change their plant size and leave or enter the industry. The long-run equilibrium position of the firm is at the point at which its long-run average costs equal price. Moreover, firms must be operating at the minimum point on their long-run average cost curves.

6. Industries can be divided into three types: constant cost, increasing cost, and decreasing cost. Constant-cost industries have horizontal long-run supply curves, increasing-cost industries have positively sloped long-run supply curves, and decreasing-cost industries have negatively sloped long-run supply curves. Increasing-cost industries are generally regarded as being the most numerous of the three types.

7. Having presented this basic theory, we described the way in which resources are allocated in a perfectly competitive economy. In particular, we considered a case where, because of a shift in consumer demand from potatoes to corn, resources had to be shifted out of potato production and into corn production.

8. Producer surplus is the amount producers receive above and beyond the minimum price that would be required to get them to produce and sell a particular output. Total surplus, which is the sum of consumer and producer surplus, is a measure of the total net gain to consumers and producers from the production and sale of a particular number of units of a good. Total surplus is maximized when output is at the perfectly competitive level.

9. Finally, we used the theory to explain some of the characteristics of U.S. agriculture and to analyze government subsidy programs. For many farm products, the government has established a support price that exceeds the equilibrium price. The cost to consumers (reduced consumer surplus) has tended to exceed the benefit to producers (increased producer surplus). Recently, Congress passed legislation calling for the alteration of many of these programs.

QUESTIONS/PROBLEMS

1. Tom Kelly's dairy farm in Tyrone, Pennsylvania, has about 80 cows and 350 acres. Mr. Kelly has owned this farm for over 20 years and operates it with the help of some hired workers and his son. In October 1995, he received a price of 12.1 cents per pound for his milk. (a) If his farm can be regarded as perfectly competitive, describe the demand curve for Mr. Kelly's milk in October 1995. Is it downward sloping to the right? Why or why not? (b) In October 1995, what was Mr. Kelly's marginal revenue from an extra pound of milk sold? Can you answer this question without knowing how much milk his farm produced then? Why or why not? (c) According to the U.S. Department of Agriculture, the price elasticity of demand for fluid milk in the United States is about 0.26. Does this mean that Mr. Kelly, if he reduces the price of his milk by 10 percent, will experience a 2.6 percent increase in the quantity of his milk that is demanded? Why or why not? (d) The income elasticity of demand for fluid milk in the United States has been estimated to be less than 0.1. Does this mean that future increases in consumer incomes will have little or no effect on the price that Mr. Kelly can get for his milk?

2. In August 1992, the price of coffee fell to its lowest level in 17 years, about 51 cents per pound. According to one analyst, "At these prices, or close to them, it doesn't pay to sell. The price will not cover the costs of harvest and transportation." (a) Does this mean that price is below average variable cost? (b) If price is below average variable cost in one coffee-producing country but above it in another coffee-producing country, will the supply of coffee cease? Why or why not?

3. A perfectly competitive firm has the following total cost function:

Total output (units)	Total cost (dollars)
0	20
1	30
2	42
3	55
4	69
5	84
6	100
7	117

How much will the firm produce if the price is (a) $13? (b) $14? (c) $15? (d) $16? (e) $17?

4. If the textile industry is a constant-cost industry, and the demand curve for textiles shifts upward, what are the steps by which a competitive market insures an increased amount of textiles? What happens if the government will not allow textile prices to rise?

5. An economist estimates that, in the short run, the quantity of men's socks supplied at each price is as follows:

Price (dollars per pair)	Quantity supplied per year (millions of pairs)
1	5
2	6
3	7
4	8

Calculate the arc elasticity of supply when the price is between $3 and $4 per pair. (Review Chapter 1 if you do not recall the definition of the arc elasticity of supply.)

6. Suppose that there are 100 firms producing the good in Question 3, and that each firm has the total cost function shown there. If input prices remain constant (regardless of industry output), draw the industry supply curve.

7. According to D. Suits and S. Koizumi, the supply function for onions in the United States is $\log q = 0.134 + .0123t + 0.324 \log P - 0.512 \log C$, where q is the quantity supplied in a particular year, t is the year (less 1924), P is the price last season, and C is the cost index last season. Suppose that price is estimated by one forecaster to be 10 cents this season, whereas it is estimated to be 11 cents by another. Holding other factors constant, how much difference will this make in forecasting the quantity supplied next season?

8. Explain how it is possible for an industry to be a constant-cost industry even though each firm in the industry has increasing marginal costs.

9. In the period between the First and Second World Wars, the cotton textile industry was sometimes described as being closer to perfect competition than any other manufacturing industry in the United States. Considerable excess capacity existed in the cotton textile industry from about 1924 to 1936. Evidence of this overcapacity is presented in the table on page 335, which shows that the profit rate in cotton textiles was considerably below that in other manufacturing. For example, during 1924–28 and 1933–36, textile profits averaged less than 4 percent of the firms' capitalization, whereas profits as a percentage of capitalization in all manufacturing averaged 8 percent. Also, profit rates in cotton textiles were higher in the South than in the North, due to the fact that the prices of many inputs—like labor and raw cotton—were lower in the South.

	Profits as a percentage of capitalization	
Period	Cotton textiles	All manufacturing
1919–23	15.3	11.0
1924–28	4.7	11.0
1933–36	2.4	4.3

(a) Was the industry in long-run equilibrium? (b) What sorts of changes were required to make the industry approach long-run equilibrium? (c) In fact, did these changes occur — as our theory would predict?

10. "In long-run equilibrium, every firm in a competitive industry earns zero profit. Thus, if the price falls, all these firms will be unable to stay in business." Evaluate this statement.

11. Richard Webster is a Nebraska farmer who produces corn on 1,000 acres of land, 500 of which are rented and 500 of which are owned. In an interview reported in the *New York Times,* he estimated that his costs per acre for corn produced on his rented land were as shown on the following list:

Fertilizer	$ 41.84
Herbicides	2.76
Insecticides	5.50
Fuel	18.00
Seed	16.50
Electricity	15.00
Cost of services of plant and equipment	85.46
Labor	15.00
Insurance	10.00
Land rent	110.00
Total	$320.06

(a) Does this mean that the average cost of producing corn is $320.06? Why or why not? (b) On each acre of land that he owns, Mr. Webster does not have to pay a rent of $110, included above. Does this mean that the cost of using his own land is less than that of using rented land? (c) If each acre of land yields 120 bushels of corn, and if the price of a bushel of corn were expected to be 80 cents, should Mr. Webster produce any corn? (d) If the price were expected to be $1.50, should he produce any corn?

12. In Figure 10.17, suppose that the support price is $2 per ton, the equilibrium price is $1 per ton, the quantity demanded if the price is $2 is 100 million tons, the quantity supplied if the price is $2 is 200 million tons, and the equilibrium quantity is 150 million tons. (a) In dollar terms, how great is the loss to consumers due to the price support? (b) In dollar terms, how great is the gain to producers? (c) What is the effect on total surplus?

13. According to a 1978 study by Neil Ericsson and Peter Morgan, the supply curve for shale oil was as shown on the following page.

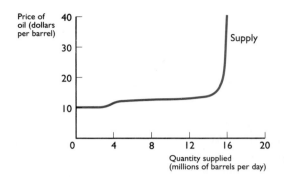

Two problems in producing shale oil are that the producer must dispose of the spent shale and that air pollution may occur. This supply curve assumes that the disposal of spent shale costs $5 per ton, and that federal air pollution standards are applied. (a) If the disposal of spent shale costs $10 per ton, would you expect the quantity supplied to be more or less than 16 million barrels per day if the price of oil were $40 per barrel? (b) Colorado air pollution standards are stricter than federal standards. If the Colorado standards are applied, would you expect the quantity supplied to be more or less than 16 million barrels per day if the price of oil were $40 per barrel? (c) Since no commercial-scale shale oil plants had been built, the above supply curve was based on engineering estimates. Do you think that this supply curve is very accurate? Why or why not? (d) A shale oil plant is estimated to cost over $1 billion. Would an investment in such a plant be risky? Why or why not? Would this influence the position and shape of the supply curve?

14. Studies indicate that the price elasticity of demand for rental housing in U.S. cities is 1.0 and that the price elasticity of supply of rental housing is 0.5 in the long run. (a) Suppose that a particular city's government decides that the level of rent should be pushed up in order to bring about a 2 percent increase in the supply of rental housing. How big an increase is required? (b) What will be the effect on the total amount of rental housing that is demanded?

15. Because New York City imposes ceilings on rents, there is a shortage of apartments. (Recall our discussion in Chapter 1.) As pointed out in the previous question, studies indicate that the price elasticity of demand for rental housing in U.S. cities is 1.0 and the price elasticity of supply of rental housing is 0.5 in the long run. If these elasticities are valid in New York City, and if its government pushes the level of rent down to a point that is 1 percent below its equilibrium value, how big will be the difference between the quantity demanded and the quantity supplied, as a percentage of the equilibrium quantity of rental housing?

16. Suppose that Figure 10.17 pertains to an agricultural commodity (but not milk) in 1997, that the support price (OP') equals $20 per ton, the equilibrium price (OP) equals $15 per ton, the equilibrium quantity (OQ) is 15 million tons, the quantity demanded if the support price prevails (OQ_2) is 10 million tons, and the quantity supplied if the support price prevails (OQ_1) is 23 million tons. (a) In dollar terms, what is the loss of consumer surplus due to the support price? (b) How big is the gain in producer surplus due to the support price? (c) What is the effect of the support price on total surplus? (d) In physical terms, how much of this commodity must the government buy? How great is the cost? (e) Can you suggest a way to make consumers better-off without making the producers of this commodity worse off?

17. The 1990 monthly production and inventories of distillate fuel oil, which is used for residential heating (and other purposes), are shown in the table below. (The figures are in millions of barrels.)

Month	Daily average Production (including imports)	Inventories at end of month
January	3.6	118
February	3.1	112
March	2.9	99
April	3.1	99
May	3.1	103
June	3.3	110
July	3.2	125
August	3.4	130
September	3.2	136
October	3.1	136
November	3.2	132
December	3.2	132

SOURCE: *Basic Petroleum Data Book.*

Unlike gasoline, which is consumed in greatest quantities during the summer, heating oil tends to be consumed most heavily during the cold winter months. As shown in this table, the oil companies produce distillate fuel oil at a relatively steady rate, the result being that inventories go down substantially in the winter, and build up gradually during the rest of the year. The price of heating oil tends to be somewhat higher in the winter than in other months. Based on data for a number of years, the quantity of heating oil consumed tends to be about 1.3 times as great in January as in May, and the price of heating oil tends to be about 4 percent higher in January than in May. Clearly, the demand curve for heating oil in January is to the right of its position in May. Can we represent the situation in January and May of any particular year by the following supply-and-demand diagram? Why or why not?

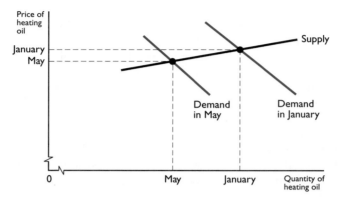

18. On July 22, 1995, the following editorial appeared in the *New York Times:* "New England senators and governors are pressuring Bob Dole, the Senate majority leader, to submit a pernicious bill to a hasty vote before it clears committee. The bill creates a compact among Maine, Vermont, New Hampshire, Connecticut, Rhode Island, and Massachusetts to raise milk prices above Federal levels. By some estimates the cost of a gallon of milk would rise from about $2.50 to between $2.85 and $3. Over all, the price increase would pump perhaps $500 million a year into the bank accounts of New England dairy farmers. But it would needlessly pummel poor parents by forcing them to spend up to 20 percent more to buy milk. Besides discouraging milk drinking, the compact sets an ugly precedent. New England cannot enforce artificially high prices unless it keeps milk produced outside New England from flowing into the region. That is why the bill imposes what amounts to a protective tariff on 'imported' milk." (a) Would this bill increase consumer surplus? (b) Would it increase producer surplus? (c) Would it increase total surplus?

Monopoly

11

INTRODUCTION

A. C. Neilsen's ratings of the size of the national audience for particular television shows are of great importance, since they guide advertisers' decisions (regarding over $10 billion of advertising) and are used to help determine whether individual shows live or die. Because Neilsen has been the only firm engaged in the measurement of such television audiences, it has sometimes been referred to as a monopolist. A monopoly is a situation where there is a single source of supply. And whether you live in the United States or Canada or Australia or the United Kingdom, you have probably encountered some firms that are monopolists, or close to it. Electric companies, telephone companies, and water companies often are examples.

In microeconomics, monopoly, like perfect competition, is a useful model. The conditions defining monopoly are easy to state: There must exist one and only one seller in a market. Monopoly, like perfect competition, does not correspond more than approximately to conditions in real industries. But, a model must be judged by its predictive ability, not the "realism" of its assumptions. The theory of monopoly has proved to be a very useful analytical device. Monopoly and perfect competition are opposites in the following sense: The firm in a perfectly competitive market has so many rivals that competition becomes impersonal in the extreme; the firm under monopoly has no rivals at all. Under monopoly, one firm is the sole supplier. There is no competition.

Having said this, it is important to add that the policies adopted by a monopolist are affected by certain indirect and potential forms of competition. Clearly, the monopolist is not completely insulated from the effects of actions taken in the rest of the economy. All commodities are rivals for the consumer's favor, as we saw in Chapter 3. Clearly this rivalry occurs among different products, as well as among the producers of a given commodity. For example, meat competes in this sense with butter, eggs, and even men's suits. Of course, the extent of the competition from other products depends on the extent to which other products are substitutes for the monopolist's product. For example, even if a firm somehow could obtain a monopoly on the supply of steel in a particular market, it would still face considerable competition from producers of aluminum, plastics, and other materials that are reasonably good substitutes for steel.

In addition, the threat of potential competition may act as a brake on the policies of the monopolist. The monopolist may be able to maintain its monopoly position only if it does not extract as much short-run profit as possible. If it sets prices above a certain point, other firms may enter its market and try to break its monopoly. If entry can occur, the monopolist must take this possibility into account. Failure to do so may make it an ex-monopolist.

Reasons for Monopoly

Why do monopolies arise? There are many reasons, but four seem particularly important. First, a single firm may control the entire supply of a basic input that is required to manufacture a given product. The example that is cited repeatedly to illustrate this situation is the pre-World War II aluminum industry. Bauxite is an input used to produce aluminum; and for some time, practically every source of bauxite in the United States was controlled by the Aluminum Company of America (Alcoa). For this reason (and others), Alcoa was, for a long time, the sole producer of aluminum in the United States.

Second, a firm may become a monopolist because the average cost of producing the product reaches a minimum at an output rate that is big enough to satisfy the entire market at a price that is profitable. In a situation of this sort, if there is more than one firm producing the product, each must be producing at a higher-than-minimum level of average cost. Each may be inclined to cut the price to increase its output rate and reduce its average costs. The result is likely to be economic warfare — and the survival of a single victor, the monopolist. Cases in which costs behave in this fashion are called *natural monopolies*. When an industry is a natural monopoly, the public often insists that its behavior be regulated by the government.

Natural monopoly

Third, a firm may acquire a monopoly over the production of a good by having patents on the product or on certain basic processes that are used in its production. The patent laws of the United States permit an inventor to get the exclusive control over the use of an invention for 20 years from initial filing. Patents can be very important in keeping competitors out. For example, Alcoa held important patents on basic production processes used to make aluminum. However, it is often possible to "invent around" another company's patents. That is, although a firm cannot use a product or process on which another firm has a patent (without the latter's permission), it may be able to develop a closely related product or process and obtain a patent on it.

Patents

Fourth, a firm may become a monopolist because it is awarded a market franchise by a government agency. The firm is granted the exclusive privilege to produce a given good or service in a particular area. In exchange for this right, the firm agrees to allow the government to regulate certain aspects of its behavior and operations. For example, as we shall see in a later section, the government may set limits on the firm's price. Regardless of the form of regulation, the important point is that the monopoly has been created by the government.

The Monopolist's Demand Curve

Since the monopolist is the only firm producing a product, it is obvious that the monopolist's demand curve is precisely the same as the market demand curve for the product. Consequently, the factors determining the shape of the monopolist's demand curve are the same factors that determine the shape of the demand curve for the product. As we saw in Chapter 5 these factors are the prices of other related products (substitutes and complements), incomes, and tastes. However, it should be noted that the monopolist sometimes can affect the prices of related products, as well as consumer tastes. To influence consumer tastes, monopolists often make considerable expenditures on advertising, the purpose being, of course, to shift the demand curve to the right.

Since the monopolist's demand curve is negatively sloped (because the demand curve for a product is negatively sloped, save for a few cases of little significance), average and marginal revenue are not the same. This is quite different from the case of perfect competition where average and marginal revenue were equal. To illustrate the situation faced by a monopolist, consider the hypothetical case in Table 11.1. The price at which each quantity (shown in column 1) can be sold is shown in column 2. The total revenue, the product of the first two columns, is shown in column 3. Obviously, the average revenue corresponding to each output is the price corresponding to that output.

Marginal revenue is of great importance to the profit-maximizing firm. How can we estimate marginal revenue from the figures in Table 11.1? Marginal revenue between q and $(q - 1)$ units of output is defined as $R(q) - R(q - 1)$, where $R(q)$ is the total revenue when the output equals q. The problem in Table 11.1 is that the data are not provided for each level of output; we only have data for $q = 3, 8, 15$, and so on. To cope with this problem, we assume that $R(q)$ is approximately a linear function of q between 3 and 8, 8 and 15, 15 and 21, and so on. If this is the case, the marginal revenue is ($640 - $300) ÷ 5 at an output of between 7 and 8, ($1,110 - $640) ÷ 7 at an output of between 14 and 15, and so forth. The results are shown in the last column of Table 11.1.

TABLE 11.1 Demand and Revenue of Monopolist			
Quantity sold	Price (dollars)	Total revenue (dollars)	Marginal revenue[a] (dollars)
3	100.00	300.00	—
8	80.00	640.00	68.00 $(=\frac{340}{5})$
15	74.00	1,110.00	67.14 $(=\frac{470}{7})$
21	70.00	1,470.00	60.00 $(=\frac{360}{6})$
26	67.50	1,755.00	57.00 $(=\frac{285}{5})$
30	65.50	1,965.00	52.50 $(=\frac{210}{4})$
33	62.00	2,046.00	27.00 $(=\frac{81}{3})$
35	60.00	2,100.00	27.00 $(=\frac{54}{2})$

[a]These figures pertain to the interval between the indicated quantity of output and 1 unit less than the indicated quantity of output.

The Monopolist's Costs

Although a firm is a monopolist in the product market, it may be a perfect competitor in the market for inputs, in which case it buys so small a proportion of the total supply of each input that it cannot affect input prices. If this is the case, there is no need to dwell further on the monopolist's costs, since the theory in Chapter 8 will apply without modification.

In many cases, however, the monopolist is not a perfect competitor in the input markets, because it buys a large proportion of certain specialized resources that have little use other than to produce the commodity in question. In a case of this sort, the price that the firm has to pay for this input depends on how much it buys. The more the firm wants of this resource, the more it will

TABLE 11.2 Costs of Monopolist

Output	Total variable cost (dollars)	Fixed cost (dollars)	Total cost (dollars)	Marginal cost[a] (dollars)
0	0	500	500	—
3	110	500	610	$36.67 \, (= \frac{110}{3})$
8	240	500	740	$26.00 \, (= \frac{130}{5})$
15	390	500	890	$21.43 \, (= \frac{150}{7})$
21	560	500	1,060	$28.33 \, (= \frac{170}{6})$
26	750	500	1,250	$38.00 \, (= \frac{190}{5})$
30	960	500	1,460	$52.50 \, (= \frac{210}{4})$
33	1,190	500	1,690	$76.67 \, (= \frac{230}{3})$
35	1,440	500	1,940	$125.00 \, (= \frac{250}{2})$

[a]These figures pertain to the interval between the indicated quantity of output and 1 unit less than the indicated quantity of output.

generally have to pay. Cases of this sort are discussed at some length in Chapter 15. In the present chapter we assume that the firm is a perfect competitor in the market for inputs.

Table 11.2 shows the costs of our hypothetical monopolist. Column 1 shows various output rates, column 2 shows the total variable cost at each output rate, and column 3 shows the firm's fixed costs. Finally, column 4 shows the firm's total cost at each output rate, and column 5 shows the firm's marginal costs.

SHORT-RUN EQUILIBRIUM PRICE AND OUTPUT

The monopolist, if unregulated and free to maximize profits, will, of course, choose the price and output at which the difference between total revenue and total cost is largest. For example, combining the data from Tables 11.1 and 11.2 into Table 11.3, we find that our hypothetical monopolist will choose an output rate of either 26 or 30 units per time period and a price of $65.50 or $67.50. Figure 11.1 shows the situation graphically.

Note that either of these optimal output rates is less than the output rate where price equals marginal cost. Under perfect competition, the profit-maximizing output was the one at which price equals marginal cost; indeed, this fact was used to derive the firm's supply curve. It is obvious from Tables 11.1 and 11.2 that this result is not true for monopoly.

TABLE 11.3 Revenue, Cost, and Profit of Monopolist

Output	Total revenue (dollars)	Total cost (dollars)	Total profit (dollars)
3	300	610	−310
8	640	740	−100
15	1,110	890	220
21	1,470	1,060	410
26	1,755	1,250	505
30	1,965	1,460	505
33	2,046	1,690	356
35	2,100	1,940	160

FIGURE 11.1 Total Revenue, Total Cost, and Total Profit of Monopolist To maximize profit, the monopolist will choose an output rate of 26 or 30 units per period and a price of $65.50 or $67.50.

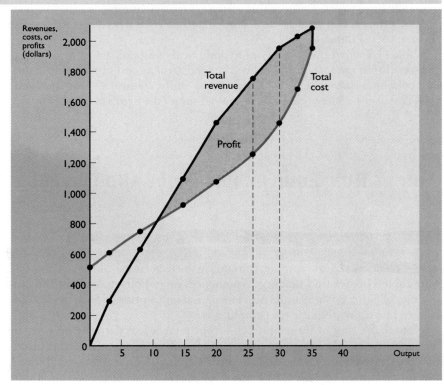

TABLE 11.4 Marginal Cost and Marginal Revenue of Monopolist			
Output	Marginal cost[a] (dollars)	Marginal revenue[a] (dollars)	Total profit (dollars)
3	36.7	—	−310
8	26.0	68.0	−100
15	21.4	67.1	220
21	28.3	60.0	410
26	38.0	57.0	505
30	52.5	52.5	505
33	76.7	27.0	356
35	125.0	27.0	160

[a] These figures pertain to the interval between the indicated quantity of output and 1 unit less than the indicated quantity of output.

Under monopoly, the firm will maximize profit if it sets its output rate at the point at which marginal cost equals marginal revenue. Table 11.4 and Figure 11.2 show that this is true in this example. It is easy to prove that this is generally a necessary condition for profit maximization. At any output rate at which marginal revenue exceeds marginal cost, profit can be increased by increasing output, since the extra revenue will exceed the extra cost. Thus profit will not be a maximum when marginal revenue exceeds marginal cost. At any output rate at which marginal cost exceeds marginal revenue, profit can be increased by reducing output, since the decrease in cost will exceed the decrease in revenue. Thus profit will not be a maximum when marginal cost exceeds marginal revenue. Since profit is not a maximum when marginal revenue exceeds marginal cost or when marginal cost exceeds marginal revenue, it must be a maximum only when marginal revenue equals marginal cost.[1]

Marginal cost= marginal revenue

---

[1] Suppose that the monopolist's demand function is $P = D(q)$, where P is price and q is output. Let $C(q)$ be the monopolist's total cost function. Then the monopolist's profit is

$$\pi = qD(q) - C(q),$$

and

$$\frac{d\pi}{dq} = D(q) + qD'(q) - C'(q).$$

Setting $d\pi/dq = 0$ to obtain the conditions under which profit is a maximum, we find that

$$D(q) + qD'(q) = C'(q).$$

Thus marginal revenue must equal marginal cost when profits are maximized, since the expression on the left-hand side is marginal revenue and the expression on the right-hand side is marginal cost. Of course, this is only the first-order condition for a local maximum. The second-order conditions must also be met, and the maximum may be only a local maximum.

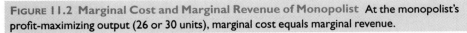

FIGURE 11.2 **Marginal Cost and Marginal Revenue of Monopolist** At the monopolist's profit-maximizing output (26 or 30 units), marginal cost equals marginal revenue.

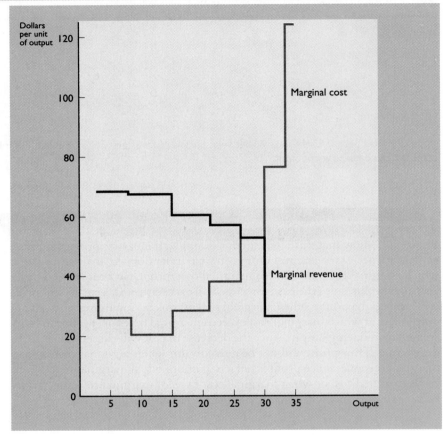

Using this result, it is also simple to represent graphically the short-run equilibrium of the monopolist. Figure 11.3 shows the demand curve, the marginal revenue curve, the marginal cost curve, and the average total cost curve faced by the firm. Short-run equilibrium will occur at the output OQ, where the marginal cost curve intersects the marginal revenue curve. If the monopolist produces OQ units, the demand curve shows that it must set a price of OP. Moreover, since the average cost curve shows that average costs are OC at an output of OQ units, the profit per unit of output is $(OP - OC)$, and the firm's total profit is $OQ(OP - OC)$.

In this case, the monopolist earns a profit, but this need not always be the case. It does not follow that a firm that holds a monopoly over the production

FIGURE 11.3 Equilibrium Position of Monopolist In equilibrium, the monopolist produces *OQ* units of output and sets a price of *OP*.

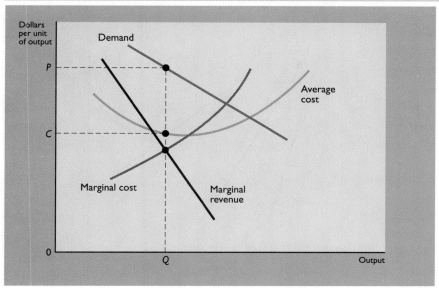

of a particular product must make a profit. The demand curve for the product may be such that, even when the firm produces at the point at which marginal revenue equals marginal cost, average cost exceeds price. For example, even if one could somehow obtain a monopoly on the sale of pearl-handled buggy whips, it might not be a profitable business to enter. Indeed, in the short run, a monopolist may not be able to cover its variable costs, in which case it will discontinue production.

Relationship between Price and Output

In perfect competition, one can define a unique relationship between the price of the product and the amount supplied. This is the industry's supply curve, which we discussed on pages 305 to 308 of Chapter 10. In monopoly, there is no such unique relationship between the product's price and the amount supplied. At first, this is likely to strike the reader as being extremely strange; indeed, one can be pardoned for questioning whether it really is so. The rest of this section is aimed at convincing the reader that it is true.

Figure 11.4 shows the marginal cost curve of the monopolist. It is assumed that the demand curve shifts from D_0 to D_1. When the demand curve is D_0, the firm produces OQ_0 units (since the marginal cost curve intersects the marginal revenue curve, R_0, at OQ_0) and the price must be *OP*. When the demand curve is D_1, the firm produces OQ_1 units (since the marginal cost curve intersects the

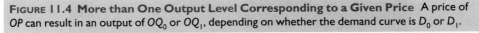

FIGURE 11.4 More than One Output Level Corresponding to a Given Price A price of OP can result in an output of OQ_0 or OQ_1, depending on whether the demand curve is D_0 or D_1.

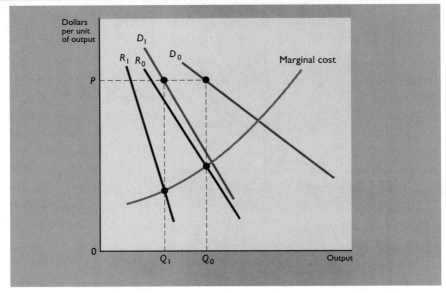

new marginal revenue curve, R_1, at OQ_1) and the price must be OP. This result shows that there is no unique relationship between price and quantity. A price of OP can result in an output of OQ_0 or OQ_1. Thus a particular price can result in a wide variety of output levels, depending on the shape and level of the demand curve.

LONG-RUN EQUILIBRIUM PRICE AND OUTPUT

In contrast to perfect competition, the long-run equilibrium of a monopolistic industry is not marked by the absence of economic profits or losses. If a monopolist earns a short-run economic profit, it will not be confronted in the long run with competitors, unless the industry is no longer a monopoly. (The entrance of additional firms into the industry is, of course, not compatible with the existence of monopoly.) Thus the long-run equilibrium of an industry under monopoly may be characterized by economic profits.

On the other hand, if the monopolist incurs a short-run economic loss, it will be forced to look for other, more profitable uses for its resources. One possibility is that its existing plant is not optimal and that it can earn economic profits if it alters the scale and characteristics of its plant appropriately. If this is the case, it will make these alterations in the long run and remain in the industry. However, if there is no scale of plant that will enable the monopolist to avoid economic losses, it will leave the industry in the long run.

Returning to the case in which the monopolist earns short-run profits, it must decide in the long run whether it can make even larger profits by altering its plant. For example, assume that the monopolist's demand curve, marginal revenue curve, long-run average cost curve, and long-run marginal cost curve are as shown in Figure 11.5. Suppose that the firm currently has a plant corresponding to short-run average cost curve, $A_0 A_0'$, and short-run marginal cost curve, $M_0 M_0'$. In the short run, it will produce OQ_0 units and set a price of OP_0. Since short-run average cost is OB, the firm's short-run profits will be OQ_0 $(OP_0 - OB)$.

However, the firm can adjust its plant in the long run so as to make bigger profits than $OQ_0 (OP_0 - OB)$. It is easy to show that the monopolist will maximize profit in the long run when it produces the output at which long-run marginal cost equals long-run marginal revenue. The reasoning behind this rule is precisely the same as that given in the section before last. Thus the firm

FIGURE 11.5 Long-Run Equilibrium for Monopolist In the long run, the monopolist will produce the output OQ_1, at which long-run marginal cost equals long-run marginal revenue.

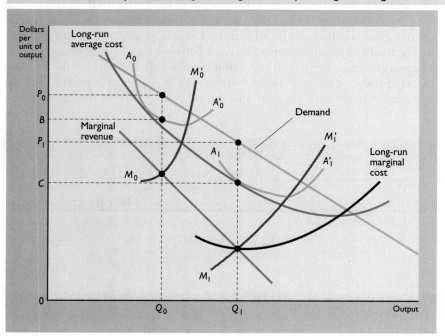

will produce OQ_1 units in the long run, since this is the point at which the long-run marginal cost curve intersects the marginal revenue curve. The long-run average cost will be OC, the price will be OP_1, and total profit will be $OQ_1 (OP_1 - OC)$. The resulting plant will have short-run average and marginal cost curves of $A_1 A_1'$ and $M_1 M_1'$, respectively.

MULTIPLANT MONOPOLY

In previous sections we have assumed that the monopolist operated only one plant. This, of course, is an unrealistic assumption in many industries. Even readers with the most superficial knowledge of the structure of various industries will recognize that many firms operate more than one plant and that cost conditions may vary among these plants. This section extends the analysis in previous sections to cover the case where the monopolist operates more than one plant.

An illustrative case is shown in Table 11.5, which assumes that the monopolist operates two plants with marginal cost curves shown in columns 2 and 3, output being shown in column 1. Judging from the figures in these columns, if the firm decides to produce only 1 unit of output, it should use plant A, since the marginal cost between 0 and 1 unit is lower in plant A than plant B. Thus, for the firm as a whole, the marginal cost between 0 and 1 unit of output is $5 (the marginal cost between 0 and 1 unit for plant A). Similarly, if the firm decides to produce 2 units of output, both should be produced in plant A, and the marginal cost between the first and second unit of output for the firm as a

| | Marginal cost[a] | | Marginal cost | | Marginal |
Output	Plant A (dollars)	Plant B (dollars)	for firm[a] (dollars)	Price (dollars)	revenue[a] (dollars)
1	5	7	5	20.00	—
2	6	9	6	15.00	10
3	7	11	7	13.00	9
4	10	13	7	11.50	7
5	12	15	9	8.00	-6

TABLE 11.5 Costs of Multiplant Monopoly

[a]These figures pertain to the interval between the indicated output and 1 unit less than the indicated output.

EXAMPLE 11.1

Playing the Slots at Foxwoods

Foxwoods, the largest casino in the United States, was established in 1992 when the state of Connecticut permitted the Mashantucket Pequot tribe to operate slot machines. In return, the Pequots agreed to pay the state 25 percent of the machines' revenues, or a minimum of $100 million per year. By 1994, Foxwoods, which extends over 7.6 acres, contained almost 4,000 slot machines, as well as about 200 table games (like blackjack and craps). For people from southern New England and many northern suburbs of New York, it was the only nearby casino of this kind.

(a) Was Foxwoods a monopoly? (b) Gross receipts at Foxwoods have been about $800 million a year, about 50 percent higher than at the Taj Mahal, the biggest of Atlantic City's 12 casinos. Given that there are 22 million people living within 150 miles of Foxwoods, as compared to 28 million people living within 150 miles of Atlantic City, are you surprised that Foxwoods's receipts are so much larger than those of the Taj Mahal? Why or why not? (c) Experts say that Foxwoods's profits (which are about $600 million per year, including the hotel and restaurants) are much higher than if it had many rivals nearby. Why? (d) A casino has been built by the Mohegan tribe in Montville, Connecticut, about 15 miles from Foxwoods. What is likely to be the effect on Foxwoods's receipts and profits?

SOLUTION: (a) Yes. For millions of people, it was the only nearby casino of this kind. (b) It is not surprising that Foxwoods's receipts are much large than those of the Taj Mahal. Whereas the Taj Mahal must share its 28 million potential customers (for day trips) with 11 other Atlantic City casinos, Foxwoods has no rivals for the 22 million potential customers that are nearby. (c) Based on pages 348 to 350, we would expect that a monopolist's profits would be higher than those of a perfectly competitive industry. (d) Foxwoods's receipts and profits would be expected to be lower than if this new casino were not built.*

---

*For further discussion, see the *New York Times,* August 8, 1994, February 20, 1995, and February 21, 1995.

---

whole is $6 (the marginal cost between the first and second unit in plant *A*). If the firm decides to produce 3 units of output, two should be produced in plant *A* and one in plant *B,* and the marginal cost between the second and third unit of output for the firm as a whole is $7 (the marginal cost between 0 and 1 unit of output for plant *B*). Alternatively, all three could be produced at plant *A*.

Continuing in this fashion, we can derive the marginal cost curve for the firm as a whole, shown in column 4 of Table 11.5. To maximize profits, the firm should find that output at which marginal revenue equals the marginal cost of the firm as a whole. This is the optimum output. In this case, it is 3 or 4 units: Suppose that the firm picks 4 units.[2] To find out what price to charge, the firm must see what price corresponds to this output on the demand curve. In this case, the answer is $11.50.

This solves most of the monopolist's problems, but not quite all. Given that it will produce 4 units of output per year, how should it divide this production

Allocation of output between plants

between the two plants? The answer is that it should set the marginal cost in plant *A* equal to the marginal cost in plant *B*. Table 11.5 shows that this means that plant *A* will produce 3 units per year and plant *B* will produce 1 unit per year. It should also be noted that the common value of the marginal costs of the two plants is also the marginal cost of the firm as a whole. Consequently, this common value must also be set equal to marginal revenue if the firm is maximizing profits.

In the long run the firm can vary the number and size of its plants. The monopolist can construct each plant of optimal size. In other words, in Figure 11.6, the short-run average cost, *AA′*, will equal the long-run average cost, and it will be at the minimum point on the long-run average cost curve. The firm will build plants, each of which produces *Oq* units of output at an average cost of *Ou* dollars per unit. Thus, once it has reached *Oq* units of output, further expansion of output will be accommodated by building more plants of opti-

---

[2] If the firm maximizes profit, it is a matter of indifference to the firm whether it produces 3 or 4 units since the profit is the same. Suppose that the firm flips a coin to determine which output it will choose and that 4 units is the winner.

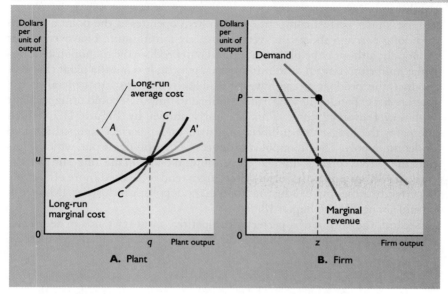

FIGURE 11.6 Equilibrium in the Long Run of a Multiplant Monopoly In the long run, the monopolist's total output will be *Oz*, it will charge a price of *OP*, and it will operate *Oz/Oq* plants. (Note that the scale in panel A is quite different from that in panel B; thus *Oz* will generally exceed *Oq*.)

mal size. Consequently the long-run marginal cost curve is a horizontal line at *Ou*. Since long-run marginal cost must equal marginal revenue, the firm's total output in the long run will be *Oz;* it will operate *Oz/Oq* plants; and it will charge a price of *OP*.[3]

COMPARISON OF MONOPOLY WITH PERFECT COMPETITION

It is important to note the differences between the long-run equilibrium of a monopoly and a perfectly competitive industry. Suppose that we could perform an experiment in which an industry was first operated under conditions

---

[3] Of course, we ignore here the problem that *Oz/Oq* may not be an integer. For simplicity we assume that it is an integer. Also, *Oz* will generally be bigger than *Oq*, the scale in panel A of Figure 11.6 being different from that in panel B.

of perfect competition and then under conditions of monopoly. Assuming that the demand curve for the industry's product and the industry's cost curves would be the same in either case, what would be the difference in the long-run equilibrium?[4]

Compar-
ison of
costs

First, under perfect competition, each firm operates at the point at which both long-run and short-run average costs are a minimum. However, under monopoly, although the plant that is used will produce the monopolist's long-run equilibrium output at minimum average cost, it is not the plant that will produce the product at the lowest possible average cost. In general, if the monopolist expanded its long-run equilibrium output, it could utilize a plant with lower average costs. This is clearly shown by Figure 11.7, which compares the long-run equilibria of a firm under perfect competition and under monopoly. The monopolist produces OQ_M units of output, which is less than the output corresponding to the minimum point on the long-run average cost curve. Consequently, society's resources tend to be used more effectively in perfectly competitive industries than in monopolistic industries.[5] More will be said about this in Chapter 18.

Second, the output of a perfectly competitive industry tends to be greater and price tends to be lower than under monopoly. The perfectly competitive

FIGURE 11.7 Comparison of Long-Run Equilibria In contrast to perfect competition, the long-run equilibrium output under monopoly (OQ_M) is less than the output corresponding to the minimum point on the long-run average cost curve.

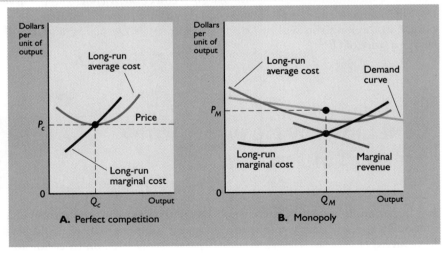

A. Perfect competition   **B.** Monopoly

[4] However, the cost and demand curves need not be the same, as we noted above.

[5] In multiplant monopoly the monopolist operates fewer plants than a competitive industry would.

firm operates at the point at which price equals marginal cost, whereas the monopolist operates at a point at which price exceeds marginal cost. Under various circumstances, as we shall see in Chapter 18, price is a good indicator of the marginal social value of the good. Consequently, under these conditions, a monopoly produces at a point at which the marginal social value of the good exceeds the good's marginal social cost. In a static sense, society would be better off if more resources were devoted to the production of the good, and if the marginal social value of the product were set equal to the marginal social cost of the product—as it is in perfect competition.

Because more will be said on this score in Chapter 18, it is sufficient for now to show that consumers lose more from monopoly than the monopolist gains. To see this, consider Figure 11.8, which compares the equilibrium price and output in monopoly and perfect competition. To maximize profit, the monopolist produces OQ_M units of output since this is where marginal cost equals marginal revenue; and to sell this number of units, the monopolist must set a price of OP_M. In contrast, since price must equal marginal cost in a perfectly competitive market, the output produced under perfect competition must be OQ_C, the only output at which price (given for each output by the demand curve) equals marginal cost. And if the perfectly competitive industry

FIGURE 11.8 Deadweight Loss from Monopoly If a perfectly competitive industry is transformed into a monopoly, price will be OP_M rather than OP_C, and output will be OQ_M rather than OQ_C. The loss of consumer surplus exceeds the gain of producer surplus by the area of triangle E plus triangle K, which is called the deadweight loss from monopoly.

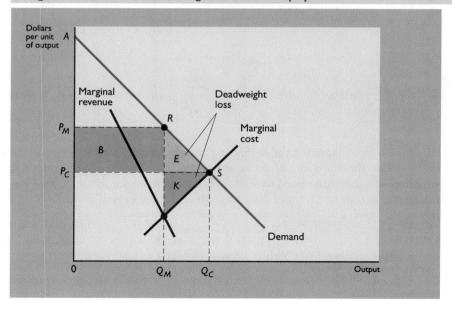

produces OQ_C units of output, the demand curve shows that the price must be OP_C so that this output will be sold.

If the perfectly competitive industry in Figure 11.8 is transformed into a monopoly, how much will consumers be hurt? In other words, what will be the loss of consumer surplus? Under perfect competition, consumer surplus equals the area of triangle $P_C SA$, while under monopoly it equals the area of triangle $P_M RA$. (Recall that consumer surplus is the area under the demand curve above the price, which is OP_M under monopoly and OP_C under perfect competition). Since the difference between these two areas is rectangle B plus triangle E, this is the loss of consumer surplus due to monopoly. How much does the monopolist gain from the monopolization of the industry? It gains the area of rectangle B by selling the product at a higher price (OP_M rather than OP_C), but loses the area of triangle K, the extra profit it would have made by selling ($OQ_C - OQ_M$) extra units of output at the competitive price. Thus, the increase in producer surplus due to monopoly is the area of rectangle B minus the area of triangle K.

Comparing the loss in consumer surplus (rectangle B plus triangle E) with the gain in producer surplus (rectangle B minus triangle K), we see that the former exceeds the latter by an amount equal to the area of triangle E plus triangle K. This total area, indicated in Figure 11.8, is often called the *deadweight loss from monopoly*. It equals the amount that consumers' losses exceed the producer's gains, and is thus the loss in total surplus (recall Chapter 10) due to monopoly rather than perfect competition. Even if the monopolist's profits were turned back to consumers, there would still be this deadweight loss. As pointed out above, much more will be said about the effects of monopoly on social welfare in Chapter 18.[6]

Dead-weight loss from monopoly

MONOPOLY POWER

Monopoly, as we stated at the beginning of this chapter, is relatively uncommon. While there are lots of situations where a few firms are the principal suppliers of a particular good or service, cases where only a single supplier exists are the exception far more often than the rule. But even if a firm is not the

[6] A. Harberger, "Monopoly and Resource Allocation," and H. Leibenstein, "Allocative Efficiency vs. X-Efficiency," both reprinted in Mansfield, *Microeconomics: Selected Readings,* 5th ed., and G. Tullock, "The Welfare Costs of Monopoly and Theft," *Western Economic Journal,* June 1967. Also, see K. Cowling and D. Mueller, "The Social Costs of Monopoly Power," *Economic Journal,* December 1978, and F. Fisher, "The Social Costs of Monopoly and Regulation: Posner Reconsidered," *Journal of Political Economy,* April 1985.

only supplier of a particular good or service, it may have a certain amount of monopoly power, in the sense that it, unlike a perfectly competitive firm, will find it profitable to raise its price above marginal cost. For example, suppose that a machine tool manufacturer charges $20,000 for a drilling machine, the marginal cost of which is $15,000. This firm has some monopoly power. If it did not, it, like any perfectly competitive firm, would have set price equal to marginal cost.

To measure the amount of monopoly power possessed by a firm, economists often use the *Lerner index* (named after Michigan State's Abba Lerner), which equals

Lerner index

$$L = (P - MC)/P,$$

where P is the firm's price and MC is its marginal cost. This index varies between 0 and 1. For a perfectly competitive firm, price equals marginal cost (recall Chapter 10), so the Lerner index equals 0. The higher L is, the higher the degree of monopoly power is. Another way to calculate the Lerner index is to obtain the reciprocal of the price elasticity of demand for the *firm's* product.[7] Note that this is not the same as the reciprocal of the price elasticity of demand for the *industry's* product. Instead, it is the reciprocal of the percentage increase in the quantity demanded of the firm's product if it cuts its price by 1 percent.

What factors influence the price elasticity of demand for a firm's product, and hence influence this firm's degree of monopoly power, as measured by the Lerner index? First, the higher the price elasticity of demand for the industry's product, the higher the price elasticity of demand is likely to be for any individual firm's product (and the lower the degree of monopoly power is likely to be). Second, the larger the number of firms in the industry and the more strongly they compete, the higher the price elasticity of demand is likely to be for any individual firm's product (and the lower the degree of monopoly power).

PRICE DISCRIMINATION

Price discrimination occurs when the same commodity is sold at more than one price. For example, an operation to cure a particular form of cancer may be

Price discrimination

---

[7] From Equation 5.3, we know that $MR = P(1 - 1/\eta)$, where MR equals marginal revenue, P equals price, and η equals the price elasticity of demand. If the firm maximizes profit, marginal revenue equals marginal cost. Thus, $MC = P(1 - 1/\eta)$, where MC equals marginal cost; this means that $MC/P = 1 - 1/\eta$, and $1/\eta = 1 - MC/P = (P - MC)/P$.

"sold" to a rich person for $5,000 and to a poor person for $1,000. Even if the commodities are not precisely the same, price discrimination is said to occur if very similar products are sold at prices that are in different ratios to marginal costs. For example, if a firm sells ballpoint pens with a label (cost of label: 1 cent) saying "Super Deluxe" in rich neighborhoods for $2 and sells the same ballpoint pens without this label in poor neighborhoods for $1, this is discrimination. Note that the mere fact that differences in price exist among similar goods is not evidence of discrimination. Only if these differences do not reflect cost differences is there evidence of this sort.

Under what conditions will a firm with monopoly power be able and willing to engage in price discrimination? The necessary conditions are that buyers fall into classes with considerable differences in the price elasticity of demand for the product, and that these classes can be identified and segregated at moderate cost. Also, it is important that buyers be unable to transfer the commodity easily from one class to another, since otherwise it would be possible for persons to make money by buying the commodity from the low-price classes and selling it to the high-price classes, thus making it difficult to maintain the price differentials between classes. The differences between classes of buyers in the price elasticity of demand may be due to differences between classes in income level, differences between classes in tastes, or differences between classes in the availability of substitutes. For example, the price elasticity of demand for a certain good may be lower for the rich than for the poor.

If a firm practices discrimination of this sort, it must decide two questions: How much output should it allocate to each class of buyer, and what price should it charge each class of buyer? To avoid unnecessary complications, let us assume that there are only two classes of buyers. Also, for the moment, assume that the firm has already decided on its total output, and consequently that the only real question is how it should be allocated between the two classes. In each class, there is a demand curve showing how many units of output would be bought by buyers in this class at various prices. In each class, there is also a marginal revenue curve that can be derived from the demand curve.

Given these marginal revenue curves, the firm will maximize its profits by allocating the total output between the two classes in such a way that marginal revenue in one class is equal to marginal revenue in the other class. The reason for this is clear. For example, if marginal revenue in the first class is $5 and marginal revenue in the second class is $3, the allocation is not optimal, since profits can be increased by allocating 1 less unit of output to the second class and 1 more unit of output to the first class. Only if the two marginal revenues are equal is the allocation optimal. And if the marginal revenues in the two classes are equal, the ratio of the price in the first class to the price in the

Setting marginal revenues equal

second class will equal

$$\left(1 - \frac{1}{\eta_2}\right) \div \left(1 - \frac{1}{\eta_1}\right),$$

where η_1 is the price elasticity of demand in the first class and η_2 is the price elasticity of demand in the second class. Thus it will not pay to discriminate if the two elasticities are equal. Moreover, if discrimination does pay, the price will be lower in the class in which demand is more elastic.

Next consider the more realistic case where the firm must also decide on its total output. In this case, the firm must look at its costs, as well as demand, in the two classes. It can be shown that the firm will choose the output where the **Optimal** marginal cost of its entire output is equal to the common value of the marginal **output** revenue in the two classes. To see this, consider Figure 11.9, which shows D_1, the demand curve in class 1; D_2, the demand curve in class 2; R_1, the marginal revenue curve in class 1; R_2, the marginal revenue curve in class 2; and the marginal cost curve. The firm begins to determine its total output by summing horizontally over the two marginal revenue curves, R_1 and R_2. The curve representing the horizontal summation of the two marginal revenue

FIGURE 11.9 Price Discrimination: Third Degree To maximize profit, the firm will produce a total output of OQ units, and set a price of OP_1 in the class 1 market and a price of OP_2 in the class 2 market.

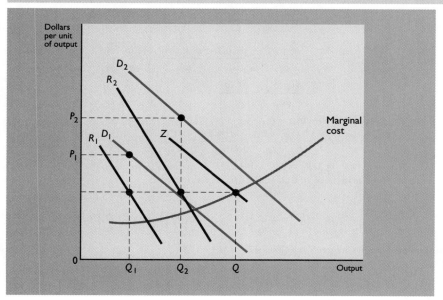

curves is Z. This curve shows, for each level of marginal revenue, the total output that is needed if marginal revenue in each class is to be maintained at this level. The optimal output is shown by the point where the Z curve intersects the marginal cost curve, since marginal cost must be equal to the common value of marginal revenue in each class. If this were not the case, profits could be increased by expanding output (if marginal cost were less than marginal revenue) or by contracting output (if marginal cost were greater than marginal revenue). Thus the firm will produce an output of OQ units and sell OQ_1 units in the class 1 market and OQ_2 units in the class 2 market. Price will be OP_1 in the class 1 market and OP_2 in the class 2 market.[8]

Other Types of Price Discrimination

Price discrimination can take a number of forms. The type discussed in the previous section is often called *third-degree price discrimination*. (This expres-

---

[8] Let p_1 be the price in the first class, p_2 the price in the second class, q_1 the quantity sold in the first class, and q_2 the quantity sold in the second class. If $C(q)$ is the firm's total cost, with q being equal to the sum of q_1 and q_2,

$$\pi = p_1 q_1 + p_2 q_2 - C(q),$$

where π is the firm's profits. Then

$$\frac{\partial \pi}{\partial q_1} = \frac{\partial (p_1 q_1)}{\partial q_1} - \frac{\partial C(q)}{\partial q_1} = \frac{d(p_1 q_1)}{dq_1} - \frac{dC(q)}{dq} \frac{\partial q}{\partial q_1}$$

$$= \frac{d(p_1 q_1)}{dq_1} - \frac{dC(q)}{dq} = 0.$$

and

$$\frac{\partial \pi}{\partial q_2} = \frac{\partial (p_2 q_2)}{\partial q_2} - \frac{\partial C(q)}{\partial q_2} = \frac{d(p_2 q_2)}{dq_2} - \frac{dC(q)}{dq} \frac{\partial q}{\partial q_2}$$

$$= \frac{d(p_2 q_2)}{dq_2} - \frac{dC(q)}{dq} = 0.$$

Thus, if π is to be a maximum,

$$\frac{d(p_1 q_1)}{dq_1} = \frac{d(p_2 q_2)}{dq_2} = \frac{dC(q)}{dq}.$$

In other words, $MR_1 = MR_2 = MC$, where MR_1 is marginal revenue in the first class, MR_2 is marginal revenue in the second class, and MC is marginal cost. Since

$$MR_1 = P_1\left(1 - \frac{1}{\eta_1}\right) \quad \text{and} \quad MR_2 = P_2\left(1 - \frac{1}{\eta_2}\right),$$

as pointed out in Chapter 5, it follows that, if $MR_1 = MR_2$,

$$P_1\left(1 - \frac{1}{\eta_1}\right) = P_2\left(1 - \frac{1}{\eta_2}\right)$$

and

$$\frac{P_1}{P_2} = \frac{1 - 1/\eta_2}{1 - 1/\eta_1}.$$

EXAMPLE 11.2

Why Should the Price of Bananas Be So Much Higher in Denmark Than in Ireland?

In the 1970s, the United Brands Company marketed its bananas in a variety of countries in Europe. The bananas were sold to wholesalers for distribution in individual national markets. They were all the same type and entered Europe either through Bremerhaven or Rotterdam. Although the cost of unloading them was essentially the same at these two ports, the prices that United Brands charged distributors differed considerably from country to country. The average difference in price per 20-kilogram box was about 11 to 18 percent, but some differences were much greater. For example, the price to Denmark was about 2.4 times the price to Ireland.*

Suppose that you are an adviser to the United Brands Company and that the company's president asks you whether its pricing policy resulted in maximum profit. After conversations with the company's marketing personnel, suppose you find that their studies indicate that the price elasticity of demand for the firm's bananas was about 2 in Denmark, about 2.5 in Germany, and about 4 in Ireland. Other company executives state that the marginal cost of shipping bananas to each of these countries (and marketing them) did not differ from country to country. What's the answer?

SOLUTION: To maximize profit, the price to Denmark divided by the price to Ireland should equal

$$\left(1 - \frac{1}{\eta_i}\right) \div \left(1 - \frac{1}{\eta_d}\right),$$

where η_i is the price elasticity of demand in Ireland and η_d is the price elasticity of demand in Denmark. (Recall page 359.) Thus, since $\eta_i = 4$ and $\eta_d = 2$, the price to Denmark divided by the price to Ireland should have equaled $(1 - \frac{1}{4}) \div (1 - \frac{1}{2}) = 1.5$, which is less than its actual value (2.4) in the 1970s. Based on the information you obtained, your conclusion should be that the firm's profits in the 1970s would have been greater if the price to Denmark had been lower relative to the price to Ireland.†

---

*S. Martin, *Industrial Economics* (New York: Macmillan Co, 1988).

†Of course, your conclusions depend on the price elasticities of demand that you are supposed to have obtained. If you somehow misinterpreted the results of the firm's marketing studies and if these elasticities are incorrect, your conclusions may be incorrect as well. Careful empirical research can be very important in cases of this sort.

sion was coined by A. C. Pigou, the English economist.)[9] Besides third-degree price discrimination, there are also first-degree and second-degree price discrimination. In *discrimination of the first degree,* the firm is aware of the maximum amount that each and every consumer will pay for each amount of the commodity. Since it is assumed that the product cannot be resold, the firm can charge each consumer a different price. And since the firm is assumed to be a profit maximizer, prices will be established so as to extract from each consumer the full value of his or her consumer surplus.

First-degree price discrimination

To illustrate this case, suppose that each consumer buys only 1 unit of the commodity. In this very simple case, the firm will establish a price for each consumer that is so high that the consumer is on the verge of refusing to buy the commodity. In the more realistic case, where each consumer can buy more than 1 unit of the commodity, it is assumed that the firm knows each consumer's demand curve for the commodity and that it adjusts its offer accordingly. For example, suppose that the maximum amount that a particular consumer would pay for 20 units of the commodity is $50 and that 20 units is the profit maximizing amount for the firm to sell to this consumer. Then the firm will make an all-or-nothing offer of 20 units of the commodity for $50.

Second-degree price discrimination

First-degree price discrimination is a limiting case that could occur only in the few cases when a firm has a small number of buyers and when it is able to guess the maximum prices they are willing to accept. *Second-degree price discrimination* is an intermediate case. In second-degree price discrimination, the firm takes part, but not all, of the buyers' consumer surplus. For example, consider the case of a gas company. Suppose that each of its consumers has the de-

---

[9] A. C. Pigou, *The Economics of Welfare* (4th ed.; London: Macmillan & Co., 1950).

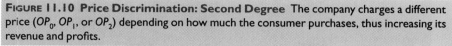

FIGURE 11.10 Price Discrimination: Second Degree The company charges a different price (OP_0, OP_1, or OP_2) depending on how much the consumer purchases, thus increasing its revenue and profits.

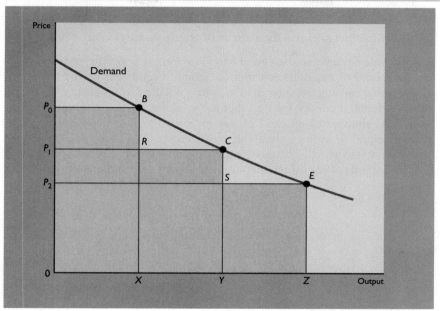

mand curve shown in Figure 11.10. The company charges a high price, OP_0, if the consumer purchases less than OX units of gas per month. For any amount beyond OX units per month, the company charges a medium price, OP_1. For purchases beyond OY, the company charges an even lower price, OP_2. Consequently, the company's total revenues from each consumer are equal to the shaded area in Figure 11.10, since the consumer will purchase OX units at a price of OP_0, $(OY - OX)$ units at a price of OP_1, and $(OZ - OY)$ units at a price of OP_2.[10]

It is obvious that the gas company, by charging different prices for various amounts of the commodity, is able to increase its revenue and profits considerably. After all, if it were permitted to charge only one price and if it wanted to sell OZ units, it would have to charge a price of OP_2. Thus the firm's total revenue would equal only the rectangle OP_2EZ, which is considerably less than

---

[10] Of course, this assumes for simplicity that each consumer purchases OZ units. Also, other simplifying assumptions (which need not concern us here) are made as well in this and the next paragraph.

the shaded area in Figure 11.10. By charging different prices, the firm is able to take part of the consumer surplus. According to some authorities, the schedules of rates charged by many public utilities — gas, water, electricity, and others—can be viewed as a type of second-degree price discrimination.[11]

Discrimination and the Existence of the Industry

Under some circumstances, a good or service cannot be produced without discrimination. For example, consider the case in Figure 11.11, where there are two types of consumers, their demand curves being $D_0 D'_0$ and $D_1 D'_1$. Adding the two demand curves, we find that the total demand for the commodity is $D_0 UV$. As shown in Figure 11.11, no output exists at which price is greater than or equal to average total cost if price discrimination is not practiced. However, with price discrimination, an output of OQ_0 can be sold at a price of OP_0 to one type of consumer; an output of OQ_1 can be sold at a price of OP_1 to

FIGURE 11.11 Discrimination Necessary for Existence of Industry With price discrimination, an output of OQ_2 can be sold at an average price of OP_2, which is greater than average total costs.

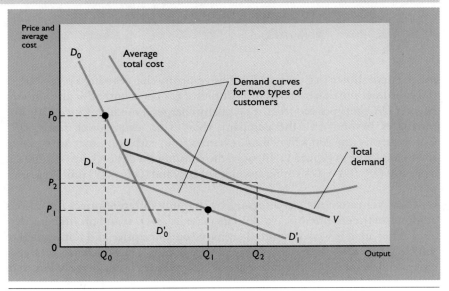

[11] Ralph Davidson, *Price Determination in Selling Gas and Electricity* (Baltimore: Johns Hopkins Press, 1975), and C. Cicchetti and J. Jurewitz, *Studies in Electric Utility Regulation* (Cambridge, Mass.: Ballinger, 1975).

the second type of consumer; and the total output (which equals OQ_2) brings an average price of OP_2, which is greater than average total costs.[12]

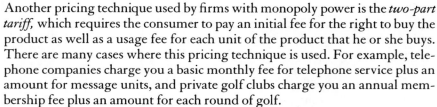

TWO-PART TARIFFS AND TYING

Another pricing technique used by firms with monopoly power is the *two-part*   Two-part
tariff, which requires the consumer to pay an initial fee for the right to buy the   tariff
product as well as a usage fee for each unit of the product that he or she buys.
There are many cases where this pricing technique is used. For example, telephone companies charge you a basic monthly fee for telephone service plus an
amount for message units, and private golf clubs charge you an annual mem-
bership fee plus an amount for each round of golf.

A firm that uses this pricing technique must determine how high the initial
fee must be, as well as the size of the usage fee. Clearly, the lower the initial fee,
the greater the number of consumers that will purchase the right to buy the
product. Thus lower initial fees are likely to result in greater profits from the
sales of the product. But this may not be best for the firm, since it also receives
profits from the initial fees it charges — and if it lowers the initial fee, these
profits will fall. Consequently, the firm would be expected to choose the initial
fee and usage fee so that its total profit — from both the sales of the product
and from initial fees — is a maximum. Example 11.3, about the use of a two-
part tariff at Disneyland, illustrates the relevant considerations.

If a firm produces a product that will function properly only if it is used in
conjunction with another product, it may require its customers to buy the
other product from it, rather than from alternative suppliers. This pricing
technique, called *tying,* has been used in the office equipment and computer   Tying
industries, among others. Several decades ago, the Xerox Corporation insisted
that firms or individuals that leased its copiers had to buy the copy paper from
Xerox, and the IBM Corporation insisted that those who leased its computers
had to use paper computer cards that it made. One reason why firms adopt
this pricing technique is that it allows them to charge higher prices to customers that use their products intensively than to those that make little use of
them. (Price discrimination of this sort often is difficult to carry out otherwise,

---

[12] This section assumes that there are no government subsidies for the product in question. If
such subsidies exist, it may be profitable to produce the product in Figure 11.11 even without
price discrimination.

EXAMPLE 11.3

A Two-Part Tariff at Disneyland

Firms, as we have seen, sometimes charge a two-part tariff, which consists of (1) a fee for the right to buy the product and (2) an additional fee for each unit of the product the consumer wants to consume. For example, Disneyland, the California amusement park, has charged each person a fee to enter the park and an additional amount for each ride he or she takes. An important problem facing the firm is: how big should the entrance fee be, and how big should the price per ride be?

(a) Suppose that each customer at Disneyland has the demand curve for rides shown below. If the price per ride is $3, how much will be the revenue per customer from the per-ride fees? (b) What is the maximum amount that each consumer would be willing to pay for the number of rides he or she will go on (if the price per ride is $3)? (c) To maximize Disneyland's profits, what entrance fee should be set (if the price per ride is $3)? (d) In the early 1980s, Disneyland eliminated the fee for individual rides and raised the entrance fee. In the graph below, suppose that there is no fee for individual rides. What is the maximum entrance fee that can be charged? (e) In this case, is it more profitable to eliminate the $3 price for individual rides, and raise the entrance fee? (For simplicity, assume that the marginal cost to Disneyland of providing a ride to any person is zero; that is, all costs are fixed costs.) (f) Is it always true that a firm will maximize its profit by relying entirely on a fee for the right to buy the product and by eliminating the fee for each unit of the product the consumer wants to consume?

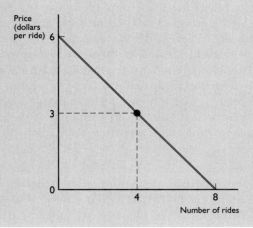

> SOLUTION: (a) If the price per ride is $3, each customer will go on 4 rides. Thus the revenue per customer will be 4× $3 = $12. (b) The area under the demand curve from zero to 4 rides equals the maximum amount that a customer would pay for the 4 rides. (Recall pages 111 to 116.) This area equals $18. (c) Since the maximum total amount that the customer will pay is $18, and since the amount he or she will pay for per-ride fees is $12, the maximum amount he or she will pay for an entrance fee is $18 − $12 = $6. (d) The area under the demand curve from 0 to 8 rides equals the maximum amount that a customer would pay for the 8 rides he or she would take if the price per ride were zero. This area equals $24. It is the maximum entrance fee that can be charged if the per-ride fee is zero. (e) Yes. Disneyland receives $24 per customer if the price per ride is zero (and the maximum entrance fee of $24 is charged), whereas it receives $18 per customer if the price per ride is $3 (and the maximum entrance fee of $6 is charged). (f) No. This is sometimes, but not always, true.*
>
> ─────────────────────────────
>
> *For further discussion, see W. Oi, "A Disneyland Dilemma: Two-Part Tariffs for a Mickey-Mouse Monopoly," *Quarterly Journal of Economics*, February 1971.

since a firm often does not know how intensively each customer uses its product.) Thus, by setting the price of its cards above their marginal cost, IBM could obtain a higher total price (from the computer and cards combined) from those that used its computers intensively than from those that used them infrequently. As we know from previous sections, price discrimination of this sort can (under the proper conditions) increase the firm's profits.[13]

BUNDLING: ANOTHER PRICING TECHNIQUE

Still another pricing technique that is sometimes used by firms with monopoly power is *bundling,* which occurs if a firm requires customers that buy one of its products to buy another of its products as well. This procedure can increase the firm's profits if customers have quite different tastes (and if the

─────────────────────────────

[13] Firms often argue that tying insures that their products will be used with the proper kind of complementary products so that good performance will result. See B. Klein and L. Salt, "The Law and Economics of Tying Contracts," *Journal of Law and Economics*, May 1985.

TABLE 11.6 Maximum Price That Each Theater Would Pay for Two Movies, Leased Separately or as a Bundle (Case Where Bundling Is Profitable)

Movie	Theater	
	Bijou	Rialto
A	$11,000	$ 8,000
B	7,000	9,000
Bundle (A and B combined)	$18,000	$17,000

firm cannot engage in price discrimination). To see why bundling can be profitable, consider a movie company that leases two movies, A and B. For simplicity, suppose that there are only two theaters, the Bijou and the Rialto, and that the maximum amount that each theater is willing to pay to lease each movie is as shown in Table 11.6.

If the movies are leased separately, the most that can be charged for movie A is $8,000, and the most that can be charged for movie B is $7,000. Why? Because if the movie company is foolish enough to set prices above these levels, it will not be able to lease its films to both theaters. Thus the most it can get from both films is $8,000 + $7,000 = $15,000. But what if the movie company insists that a theater must lease both movies? In this case, as shown in Table 11.6, the most that the Bijou is willing to pay for them both is $18,000, and the most that the Rialto is willing to pay is $17,000. Thus the movie company can charge $17,000 for both movies combined, which is more than the amount ($15,000) that it could obtain if it leased them separately.

The movie company will find it more profitable to lease them as a bundle than to lease them separately so long as there is an inverse relationship between the amount that a theater is willing to pay for one movie and the amount that it is willing to pay for the other movie. (Panel A of Figure 11.12 shows that the relationship in Table 11.6 is in fact inverse.) But if this relationship is direct, there will be no advantage to the movie company in bundling them. For example, if the maximum prices the theaters would pay are as shown in Table 11.7, the most that can be gotten for movie A (leased separately) is $8,000, and the most that can be gotten for movie B (leased separately) is $6,000. Thus, if they are leased separately, the most that can be gotten from them both is $8,000 + $6,000 = $14,000, which is the same as the amount that can be gotten if they are bundled. (Panel B of Figure 11.12 shows that there is in fact a direct relationship in Table 11.7 between the amount that a theater would be willing to pay for one movie and the amount it would be willing to pay for the other.)[14]

---

[14] For further discussion, see W. Adams and J. Yellen, "Commodity Bundling and the Burden of Monopoly," *Quarterly Journal of Economics,* August 1976, and R. Schmalensee, "Commodity Bundling by Single-Product Monopolies," *Journal of Law and Economics,* April 1982.

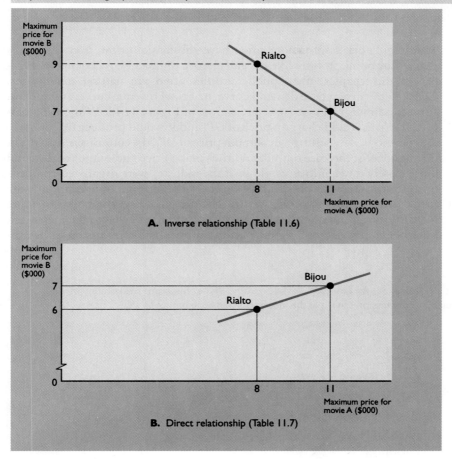

FIGURE 11.12 Alternative Relationships between the Maximum Amount a Theater Would Pay for Movie A and the Maximum Amount It Would Pay for Movie B
In panel A, bundling is profitable; in panel B, it is not profitable.

A. Inverse relationship (Table 11.6)

B. Direct relationship (Table 11.7)

TABLE 11.7 Maximum Price That Each Theater Would Pay for Two Movies, Leased Separately or as a Bundle (Case Where Bundling Is Not Profitable)

Movie	Theater	
	Bijou	Rialto
A	$11,000	$8,000
B	7,000	6,000
Bundle (A and B combined)	$18,000	$14,000

PUBLIC REGULATION OF MONOPOLY

State regulatory commissions often have substantial power over the prices charged by public utilities like gas and electric companies. As pointed out earlier in this chapter, these public utilities often are natural monopolies. Consider the firm whose demand curve, marginal revenue curve, average cost curve, and marginal cost curve are shown in Figure 11.13. Without regulation, the firm would charge a price of OP_0 and it would produce OQ_0 units of the commodity. By setting a maximum price of OP_1, the commission can make the monopolist increase output, and thus make price and output correspond more closely to what they would be if the industry were organized competitively. For instance, if the commission imposes a maximum price of OP_1, the firm's demand curve becomes P_1BD', its marginal revenue curve becomes P_1BCR', its optimum output becomes OQ_1, and it will charge the maximum price of OP_1. By establishing the maximum price, the commission helps con-

FIGURE 11.13 Regulation of Monopoly: Maximum Price By setting a maximum price of OP_1, a regulatory commission can make the monopolist increase output to OQ_1.

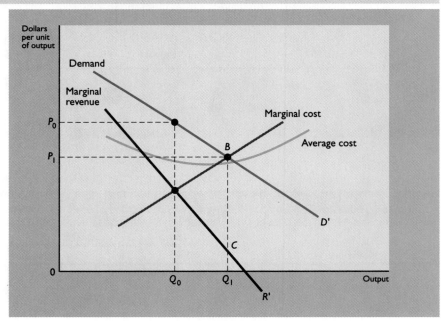

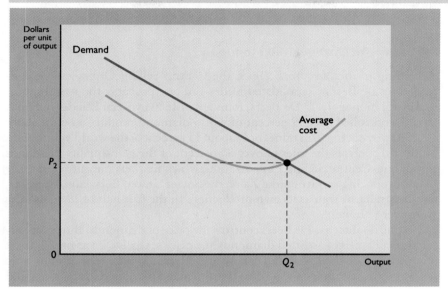

FIGURE 11.14 Regulation of Monopoly: Fair Rate of Return The regulated price is OP_2, where the demand curve intersects the average total cost curve which includes what the commission regards as a fair profit per unit of output.

sumers who pay a lower price for more of the good. By the same token, the commission deprives the monopolist of some of its monopoly power.

Commissions often set the price — or the maximum price — at the level at which it equals average total cost, including a "fair" rate of return on the company's investment. For example, in Figure 11.14, the price would be established by the commission at OP_2, where the demand curve intersects the average total cost curve. The latter curve includes what the commission regards as a fair profit per unit of output. Needless to say, there has been considerable controversy over what constitutes a fair rate of return. There has also been a good deal of controversy over what should be included in the company's investment on which the fair rate of return is to be earned.

Fair rate of return

The regulatory commissions also govern the extent to which price discrimination is used by the public utilities. Intricate systems of price discrimination exist in the rate structures of the electric and gas companies, the telephone companies, and so forth. Although some types of discrimination are prohibited, other types can be practiced if they are "reasonable." For example, a company may be permitted to charge a lower rate for a service where it must meet stiff competition. It should be noted that rate discrimination raises important questions of equity and of redistribution of income, as well as questions regarding economic efficiency. Particularly in transportation, some of the most nettlesome problems of rate regulation are concerned with questions of discrimination.

CASE STUDIES

De Beers: An Unregulated Monopoly

According to the *New York Times,* the Central Selling Organization, controlled by De Beers Consolidated Mines Ltd., is "probably the world's most successful monopoly."[15] De Beers, founded in 1880 by Cecil Rhodes in South Africa, controlled over 99 percent of world diamond production until about 1900. At present the firm mines only about 15 percent of the world's diamonds, but it still controls the sales of over 80 percent of the gem-quality diamonds through its Central Selling Organization, which markets the output of other major producing countries like Zaire, the Soviet Union, Botswana, Namibia, and Australia, as well as its own production. In the first half of 1989, its sales were over $2 billion.

No one doubts that De Beers controls the price of diamonds. Buyers are offered small boxes of assorted diamonds at a price set by De Beers on a "take it all or leave it" basis. Those that choose not to buy may have to wait some time before getting another opportunity. If the demand for diamonds falls, as it did during the early 1980s (when inflation slowed and diamonds as an investment lost much of their sparkle), De Beers stands ready to buy diamonds to support the price. (Between 1979 and 1984, its stockpile of diamonds increased from about $360 million to about $2 billion.) In the first half of 1992, its earnings fell by about 25 percent because the global recession had reduced the demand for diamonds.[16]

Besides limiting the quantity supplied, De Beers also works hard and cleverly to push the demand curve for diamonds to the right. An important part of its sales campaign has been to link diamonds and romance. (According to its 50-year-old slogan, "A Diamond Is Forever.") Of course, this has also been helpful in keeping diamonds, once sold, off the market. A good that is drenched with lasting sentiment is less likely to be sold when times get tough. De Beers's policies have paid off in very substantial profits, but the consumer has paid higher prices than if the diamond market were competitive.

---

[15] *New York Times,* September 7, 1986, p. 4F.

[16] Also, after Angola's civil war, thousands of prospectors there were digging for gems, mainly along the Cuango River. While the Angolan government normally cooperates with De Beers, the war left large parts of the country essentially ungoverned. Some observers claimed that De Beers might have to buy up $500 million worth of illicit Angolan diamonds in 1992.

The Michigan Telephone Industry: A Case Study of Regulation

The previous section described a case of unregulated monopoly. To illustrate the case of regulated monopoly, we turn to the telephone industry in Michigan. The two groups that have played a key role in the regulation of the telephone industry in Michigan are one firm, Michigan Bell (a subsidiary of Ameritech[17]), and one commission, the Public Service Commission in Michigan.[18] Although Michigan Bell is not the only telephone company in the state, it is the dominant firm, and there is no direct competition in the industry between firms. The commission, which is composed of three members appointed by the governor, has had authority over the telephone industry for about 50 years.

A general-rate case has been the common sort of regulatory "contest" in the Michigan telephone industry. Such cases have been initiated by the firms and have been based on company claims that earnings are deficient and a higher price level is required. It is generally assumed, though not proved, that demand is inelastic and that higher prices will mean greater revenues. The industry usually has received less than it asked for. Moreover, commission decisions have lagged behind the industry's revenue requests. However, it should be recognized that the fact that the commission has not approved all Bell requests does not mean that the company has been constrained much by the commission. The company may ask for more than it thinks it will get.

Nothing in public utility controls is more conventional, more securely established in regulatory methods, than the idea of a "reasonable return on the value of a firm's existing plant."[19] This is what the commission has been interested in establishing. Yet there are a host of questions, some obvious to the most naive schoolchild, others difficult for a trained engineer or accountant to understand, concerning what is a "reasonable return" and what is "the value of a firm's existing plant." The original cost or historical cost of the plant is the measure on which most commissions base their estimates of the value of the plant; but some allow firms to use replacement-cost valuations instead. In the early 1980s, regulated firms often sought a rate of return of about 10 to 15 percent; commissions in recent years have approved rates of return of about 6 to

---

[17] Ameritech (American Information Technologies Corporation) is one of seven regional holding companies resulting from the breakup of the American Telephone and Telegraph Company (AT&T). In 1982, a district court ordered AT&T to divest itself of the exchange telecommunications, exchange access, and Yellow Pages of its 22 wholly owned Bell operating telephone companies, one of which was Michigan Bell. This decision arose out of an antitrust case brought by the U.S. Department of Justice against AT&T.

[18] See C. E. Troxel, "Telephone Regulation in Michigan," in W. G. Shepherd and T. Gies, *Utility Regulation* (New York: Random House, 1966). Also, see M. Irwin, "The Telephone Industry," in W. Adams, *The Structure of American Industry* (5th ed.; New York: Macmillan Co., 1977).

[19] Ibid., p. 162.

10 percent.[20] There are lots of detailed and difficult questions in each case of this sort that provide employment for a great many lawyers, accountants, engineers, and economists.

In recent decades, considerable controversy has centered on the regulatory process, with many observers feeling that the commissions are lax and that they tend to be captured by the industries they are supposed to regulate. Also, in some cases, regulation, although effective, seems to have had unfortunate consequences. For example, the Civil Aeronautics Board, which was established in 1938, and which regulated the prices charged by the interstate scheduled airlines as well as entry into the industry, was criticized severely during the 1970s for preventing price competition among airlines and for permitting little new entry. After some experimentation with more active price competition in the late 1970s, Congress passed legislation that phased out CAB's powers. The power to regulate routes terminated at the end of 1981, and the power to regulate rates terminated at the end of 1982.[21]

The deregulation movement extended to a variety of other industries as well, including railroads and trucking, although the extent and nature of the changes varied from industry to industry. Without question, this movement has been important. But it is undeniable that many key industries, like the Michigan telephone industry, continue to be regulated.

SUMMARY

1. Monopoly exists when there is one and only one seller in a market. Monopolies arise because a single firm controls the entire supply of a basic input, because a firm has a patent on the product or on certain basic processes, because the average cost of producing the product reaches a minimum at an output rate that is big enough to satisfy the entire market at a price that is profitable, because the firm is awarded a franchise, or for other reasons.

---

[20] See W. Shepherd and C. Wilcox, *Public Policies Toward Business* (6th ed.; Homewood, Ill.: Irwin, 1979), and W. Shepherd, *Public Policies Toward Business: Readings and Cases* (Homewood, Ill.: Irwin, 1979).

[21] For an appraisal of the airlines' performance, and suggestions for improvement, see S. Morrison and C. Winston, "Enhancing the Performance of the Deregulated Air Transportation System," in M. Baily and C. Winston (eds.), *Brookings Papers on Economic Activity,* 1989.

2. The demand curve facing the monopolist is the demand for the product. The cost conditions facing a monopolist may be no different from those facing a perfectly competitive firm if the monopolist is a perfect competitor in the input markets.

3. Under monopoly, the firm will maximize profit if it sets its output rate at the point where marginal cost equals marginal revenue. It does not follow that a firm that holds a monopoly over the production of a particular product must make a profit. If the monopolist cannot cover its variable costs, it will shut down, even in the short run.

4. Under monopoly, there is no unique relationship between the product's price and the amount supplied. The long-run equilibrium of the industry is not necessarily marked by the absence of economic profits. If the monopolist has more than one plant, it should allocate production among its plants so that marginal costs are the same in each plant, and it should set its overall output rate so that this common marginal cost equals marginal revenue.

5. There are a number of important differences between the long-run equilibrium of a monopoly and of a perfectly competitive industry. Under perfect competition, each firm operates at the point where both long-run and short-run average costs are at a minimum; under monopoly, if the monopolist expanded its long-run equilibrium output, it could utilize a plant with lower average costs. The output of a perfectly competitive industry tends to be greater and price tends to be lower than under monopoly. The perfectly competitive firm operates at the point where price equals marginal cost, whereas the monopolist operates at a point where price exceeds marginal cost. The loss of consumer surplus due to monopoly exceeds the gain in producer surplus, the difference being called the deadweight loss due to monopoly.

6. Price discrimination occurs when the same commodity is sold at more than one price, or when similar products are sold at prices that are in different ratios to marginal costs. A firm will be able and willing to practice price discrimination if various classes of buyers with different price elasticities of demand can be identified and segregated, and if the commodity cannot be transferred easily from one class to another.

7. Another pricing technique used by firms with monopoly power is the two-part tariff, which requires the consumer to pay an initial fee for the right to buy the product, as well as a usage fee for each unit of the product that he or she buys. Also, if a firm produces a product that will function properly only if it is used in conjunction with another product, it may require its customers to buy the other product from it, rather than from alternative suppliers. This practice is called tying. Still another pricing technique is bundling.

8. Regulatory commissions frequently have the power to set the prices

charged by public utilities like gas or electric companies. They often set the price—or the maximum price—at the level at which it equals average total cost, including a "fair" rate of return on the company's investment. There has been considerable controversy over what constitutes a fair rate of return, and over what should be included in the company's investment.

QUESTIONS/PROBLEMS

1. Postal service, which since 1845 has been largely a government monopoly in the United States, has been the object of continual controversy. Suppose that the short-run demand and cost curves of the Philadelphia post office are as shown below:

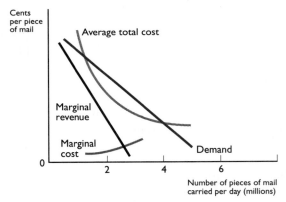

(a) Does the post office appear to be a natural monopoly, as some claim? (b) If the post office is a natural monopoly, must it be operated under government ownership? (c) If the Philadelphia post office wants to carry as many pieces of mail as it can without incurring a short-run deficit, how many should it carry per day? (d) The available evidence indicates that average revenue (per piece of mail) has exceeded average total cost and marginal cost for first-class mail, but not for third-class mail. Which type of mail is likely to attract private competitors? (e) What advantages might accrue if the post office were to face increased private competition?

2. A monopolist has two plants, with the following marginal cost functions:

$$MC_1 = 20 + 2Q_1$$

and
$$MC_2 = 10 + 5Q_2,$$

where MC_1 is marginal cost in the first plant, MC_2 is marginal cost in the second plant, Q_1 is output in the first plant, and Q_2 is output in the second plant. If the monopolist is minimizing its costs, and if it is producing 5 units of output at the first plant, how many units is it producing at the second plant?

3. One of the longest and most expensive antitrust cases in history began in 1969, when the government charged that IBM "has attempted to monopolize and has monopolized . . . interstate trade and commerce in general purpose computers in violation of Section 2 of the Sherman Act." According to IBM's economists, its share of revenue from the sale of electronic data processing products and services in the United States was as follows:

1952	90.1%
1961	56.4%
1968	54.0%
1972	40.7%

(a) Based on these figures, was IBM a monopolist? (b) Even if IBM did not have 100 percent of the market, could it have run afoul of the antitrust laws? (c) If a firm has a very large share of the market, does this mean that it should be prosecuted under the antitrust laws? (d) How should one define a market for these purposes? (e) Whereas IBM argued for a broad definition of the computer industry (including special purpose process control, message switching, and military computers and computer leasing and service activities), the government argued for a narrow definition (general electronic digital computer systems). Why? (f) What was the outcome of this case?

4. Prostatix, Inc., a hypothetical pharmaceutical manufacturer, is a monopolist. Its president says that its price at its profit-maximizing output is triple its marginal cost. What is the price elasticity of demand of its product?

5. A monopolist has the following total cost function and demand curve:

Price (dollars)	Output (units)	Total cost (dollars)
8	5	20
7	6	21
6	7	22
5	8	23
4	9	24
3	10	30

What price should it charge?

6. A. C. Harberger, in his study cited in footnote 6, found that the misallocation of resources due to monopoly was quite small. This conclusion stimulated considerable controversy. He assumed that the price elasticity of demand was unity everywhere. Will a rational monopolist operate at a point where the price elasticity of demand is unity? Can one be sure that monopoly gains are not included in the cost items that are reported by accountants?

7. Suppose that you are the owner of a metals-producing firm that is an unregulated monopoly. After considerable experimentation and research, you find that your marginal cost curve can be approximated by a straight line, $MC = 60 + 2Q$, where MC is marginal cost (in dollars) and Q is your output. Moreover, suppose that the demand curve for your product is $P = 100 - Q$, where P is the product price (in dollars) and Q is your output. If you want to maximize profit, what output should you choose? (Hint: To find the marginal revenue curve, use the material in footnote 9 on page 147.)

8. Authors customarily receive a royalty that is a fixed percentage of the price of the book. For this reason, economists have pointed out that an author has an interest in a book's price being lower than the price that maximizes the publisher's profits. Prove that this is true.

9. Suppose that you are hired as a consultant to a firm producing ball bearings. This firm sells in two distinct markets, one of which is completely sealed off from the other. The demand curve for the firm's output in the one market is $P_1 = 160 - 8Q_1$, where P_1 is the price of the product and Q_1 is the amount sold in the first market. The demand curve for the firm's output in the second market is $P_2 = 80 - 2Q_2$, where P_2 is the price of the product and Q_2 is the amount sold in the second market. The firm's marginal cost curve is $5 + Q$, where Q is the firm's entire output (destined for either market). The firm asks you to suggest what its pricing policy should be. How many units of output should it sell in the second market? How many units of output should it sell in the first market? What prices should it charge? (The hint given in problem 7 above may be useful here as well.)

10. The Errata Book Company is a monopolist that sells in two markets. The marginal revenue curve in the first market is

$$MR_1 = 20 - 2Q_1,$$

where MR_1 is the marginal revenue in the first market and Q_1 is the number of books sold per day in the first market. The marginal revenue curve in the second market is

$$MR_2 = 15 - 3Q_2,$$

where MR_2 is the marginal revenue in the second market and Q_2 is the number of books sold per day in the second market. If the marginal cost of a book is $6, how many books should the Errata Book Company sell in each market?

11. The past 25 years have seen a notable increase in the interest among economists in predatory behavior. Although definitions vary somewhat, a firm generally is said to engage in predatory pricing if it sets its price at a low level in an attempt to drive a rival firm out of business. For example, suppose that a monopolist is confronted with a competitor. The monopolist's average and marginal cost curves are shown below. (To avoid cumbersome language, we refer to the firm as "the monopolist," although it obviously is an ex-monopolist once the rival firm enters its market.)

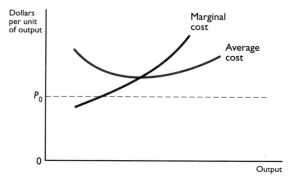

The monopolist sets a price of OP_0, which is below its average costs. Because this price is also below its rival's average cost, its rival experiences losses.

(a) Since both the monopolist and its rival will lose money if price equals OP_0, is it clear that the monopolist is well advised to set this price? (b) If the monopolist succeeds in driving its rival out of business, can it be sure that other entrants will not appear on the scene? (c) A large number of major lawsuits have alleged predatory behavior. For example, the government alleged that IBM's 360 line of computers was priced in a predatory fashion. To help solve the difficult problem of determining when predatory pricing takes place, Phillip Areeda and Donald Turner of Harvard University proposed that it be illegal for a dominant firm to set its price below both its average and marginal costs. What problems can you see in this rule?

12. In 1983, the Santa Fe and Southern Pacific railroads announced a plan to merge. The two railroads ran parallel to one another; they provided the only rail service between southern California and Texas (and the Gulf of Mexico ports). Legislation passed by Congress in 1980 reduced the amount of regulation in this industry. Nonetheless, the Interstate Commerce Commission, which has regulated the railroad industry since 1887, had to approve the merger application, and in 1986 it refused to do so on a 4-to-1 vote of the commissioners.

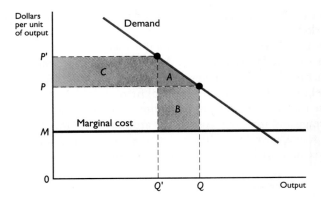

(a) According to analysts at the U.S. Department of Justice, the merger would have resulted in a substantial price increase by the railroads. In the graph above, the price would have increased from *OP* to *OP'*. (For the two firms combined, their demand curve and their marginal cost curve are shown in the graph. For simplicity, marginal cost is assumed to be constant.) These analysts estimated that the area of rectangle *C* equaled about $404 million. Is this the loss to shippers due to having to pay a price of *OP'* rather than *OP* for the *OQ'* units of railroad services they would buy after the merger? (b) With regard to rectangle *C*, do the railroads gain what the shippers lose? (c) These analysts estimated that the area of rectangle *B* equaled about $57 million. Is this the loss to the railroads from the reduction in their output (from *OQ* to *OQ'*) that was earning more than marginal cost? (d) These analysts estimated that the area of triangle *A* was about $22 million. Is this the loss to shippers of the consumer surplus from the railroad services they bought when the price was *OP* but would not buy when it is *OP'*? (e) On balance, are shippers hurt by the merger, according to these estimates? Do the railroads benefit? (f) If the merger reduces the firms' costs considerably, should the savings be deducted from the social costs of the merger?

Monopolistic Competition and Oligopoly

12

INTRODUCTION

What do Robert Crandall (head of American Airlines), Roberto Goizueta (head of Coca-Cola), and Eckhard Pfeiffer (head of Compaq, the computer maker) have in common? They are not in perfectly competitive or monopolized industries. This is not surprising because, while perfect competition and monopoly are useful models that shed a great deal of light on how markets work, they are polar cases. In this and the next chapter, we take up models that describe more realistically how many industries function. This chapter focuses attention on monopolistic competition and oligopoly. The theory of monopolistic competition is applicable to industries like retail trade, and oligopoly theory pertains to industries like automobiles, electrical equipment, and computers. In the following chapter, we continue our discussion of oligopoly, the primary focus being on game theory and strategic decision making.

MONOPOLISTIC COMPETITION

Product differentiation

Bergdorf Goodman has a monopoly on the sale of its dresses. However, other firms like Macy's and Bloomingdale's sell roughly similar dresses. Each firm has a monopoly over the sale of its own product, but the various brands are close substitutes. This is a case of *product differentiation*. In other words, there is no single, homogeneous commodity called a dress; instead, each seller differentiates its product from that of the next seller. This, of course, is a prevalent case in the modern economy. Each seller tries to make its product a little different, by altering the physical makeup of the product, the services it offers, and other such variables. Other differences—which may be spurious—are based on brand name, image-making, advertising claims, and so forth. In this way, each seller has some amount of monopoly power, but it usually is small, because the products of other firms are very similar.

Monopolistic competition

Monopolistic competition is a market structure where product differentiation exists and where there are elements of both monopoly and perfect competition. Under monopolistic competition, there is a large number of firms producing and selling goods that are close substitutes, but that are not completely homogeneous from one seller to another. For example, retail trade is often cited as an industry with many of the characteristics of monopolistic competition. Edward Chamberlin of Harvard University pioneered in the development of the theory of monopolistic competition.[1] While this theory has met with considerable criticism, it was a famous and noteworthy attempt to develop a model to handle the important middle ground between perfect competition and monopoly.[2]

To begin with, let's consider Chamberlin's concept of a product group. In perfect competition, the firms included in an industry are easy to determine,

---

[1] E. Chamberlin, *The Theory of Monopolistic Competition* (Cambridge, Mass.: Harvard University Press, 1933). Another very important work of the same period was J. Robinson, *The Economics of Imperfect Competition* (New York: Macmillan Co., 1933).

[2] Perfect competition and monopoly are two polar extremes. There is an extremely large number of firms (making the same good) in a perfectly competitive industry, but only one firm in a monopoly. Obviously, many industries in the real world fall between these two extremes.

because they all produce the same product. But if there is product differentiation, it is no longer easy to define an industry, since each firm produces a somewhat different product. Nevertheless, Chamberlin believes that it is useful to group together firms producing similar products and call them a *product group*. For example, we can formulate a product group called dresses. Of course, the process by which we combine firms into product groups is bound to be somewhat arbitrary, since there is no way to decide how close a pair of substitutes must be in order to be included in the same product group. However, Chamberlin asserts that meaningful product groups can be formulated.

Product group

The assumptions underlying Chamberlin's theory are as follows: First, he assumes that the product, which is differentiated, is produced by a large number of firms, with each firm's product being a fairly close substitute for the products of the other firms in the product group. Second, he assumes that the number of firms in the product group is sufficiently large so that each firm expects its actions to go unheeded by its rivals and to be unimpeded by any retaliatory measures on their part. Third, he assumes that both demand and cost curves are the same for all of the firms in the group. This, of course, is a very restrictive assumption since, if the products are dissimilar, one would ordinarily expect their demand and cost curves to be dissimilar, too.

EQUILIBRIUM PRICE AND OUTPUT IN THE SHORT AND LONG RUNS

Because each firm's product is somewhat different from that of its rivals, the demand curve for its product is downward sloping, as shown in Figure 12.1. This demand curve is for one firm's product, but its position depends on other firms' prices. (An increase in other firms' prices would cause this demand curve to shift to the right, while a decrease would cause it to shift to the left.) In the short run, an equilibrium will be reached when the situation is like that in Figure 12.1. The short-run equilibrium price and output of each firm are OP_1 and OQ_1, respectively. It can easily be verified that the firm has no incentive to change its price from OP_1. Since marginal revenue equals marginal cost at an output of OQ_1, the firm believes that it is maximizing profits by maintaining its price at OP_1.

Short run

In the case shown in Figure 12.1, the firm earns a short-run profit equal to the shaded area; but this need not always be the case in short-run equilibrium.

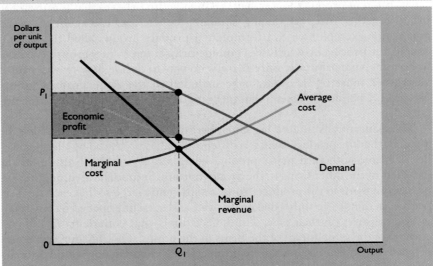

FIGURE 12.1 Short-Run Equilibrium under Monopolistic Competition The firm's price and output are OP_1 and OQ_1, respectively.

On the contrary, in some cases, firms may experience losses in short-run equilibrium. However, as long as OP_1 exceeds the firm's average variable costs, the firm will continue to produce in the short run.

Long run   As in perfect competition, firms in the long run are able to change the scale of their plant and to leave or enter the industry. The long-run equilibrium price and output of the representative firm are shown in Figure 12.2; the equilibrium price is OP_2 and the equilibrium output is OQ_2. Since there is free entry and exit in a monopolistically competitive industry, the long-run equilibrium is a situation in which all firms in the industry, although they are maximizing profits, have zero economic profits. This is similar to the long-run equilibrium in a perfectly competitive industry. Note that the cost curves in Figure 12.2 are long-run cost curves, not the short-run cost curves shown in Figure 12.1. The long-run equilibrium position is at the output where the long-run average cost curve is tangent to the demand curve and where the marginal cost curve intersects the marginal revenue curve. Because marginal revenue equals marginal cost, the firm is maximizing profit. Because average cost equals price, economic profits equal zero.

How is the long-run equilibrium position reached? The adjustments that take place can be described in terms of changes in the position of the demand curve facing the representative firm. The demand curve shifts in response to

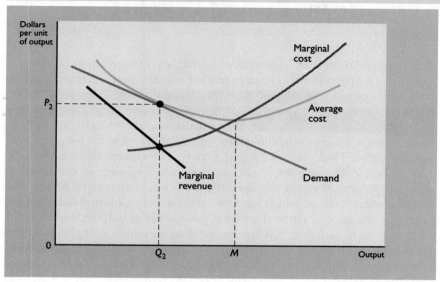

FIGURE 12.2 Long-Run Equilibrium under Monopolistic Competition The firm's price and output are OP_2 and OQ_2, respectively.

the entry of new firms and the exit of old firms. Increases in the number of firms in the industry shift the demand curve facing the representative firm to the left, because the market (which is relatively fixed) must be divided among more firms. Reductions in the number of firms shift the demand curve facing the representative firm to the right, because the market must be divided among fewer firms. As a result of entry and exit, the demand curve is pushed toward the equilibrium position, where it is tangent to the long-run average cost curve.

Consider Figure 12.1, which shows the short-run situation. This firm (and the others in the group) is making an economic profit since the current price is OP_1. The existence of profit encourages new firms to enter the group, and the demand curve facing the representative firm shifts to the left. As entry continues, this demand curve may shift further to the left. Only when at last the situation in Figure 12.2 is reached will a long-run equilibrium be established. In this situation, the demand curve is tangent to the long-run average cost curve, with the result that there is no incentive for entry or exit, since economic profits are nonexistent. Moreover, in this situation, the demand curve is always below the long-run average cost curve, except at the point where the firm is operating. Thus the firm has no incentive to change its price or output, since any such change appears to be unprofitable.

EXCESS CAPACITY AND PRODUCT DIVERSITY

A famous and controversial conclusion of the theory of monopolistic competition is that a firm under this form of market organization will tend to operate with excess capacity. In other words, it is alleged that the firm will construct a plant smaller than the minimum-cost size of plant and operate it at less than the minimum-cost rate of output. Why? Because, as shown in Figure 12.2, the demand curve must be tangent in long-run equilibrium to the long-run average cost curve. Thus, since the demand curve is downward sloping, the long-run average cost curve must also be downward sloping at the long-run equilibrium output rate. Consequently, the firm's output must be less than *OM*, the output rate at which long-run average cost is minimized, since the long-run average cost curve slopes downward only at outputs less than *OM*. Moreover, since each firm builds a smaller than minimum-cost plant and produces a smaller than minimum-cost output, more firms can exist under these circumstances than if there were no excess capacity. Thus it has been argued that there will be some "overcrowding" of monopolistically competitive industries.

    More recent research suggests that this argument may be somewhat myopic because, as pointed out by Avinash Dixit, Michael Spence, Joseph Stiglitz, and others, an important benefit to society of monopolistic competition is

Product diversity

product diversity. Like most consumers, you probably value the ability to choose among a wide variety of clothes, restaurant meals, and other styles and types of products and services. The social benefits from product diversity can be substantial, and may exceed the social costs cited in the previous paragraph.[3]

MARKUP PRICING

Empirical studies suggest that markup (or cost-plus) pricing is used by many monopolistically competitive (and other) firms. For example, many retail

---

[3] See A. Dixit and J. Stiglitz, "Monopolistic Competition and Optimum Product Diversity," *American Economic Review,* June 1977; M. Spence, "Product Selection, Fixed Costs, and Monopolistic Competition," *Review of Economic Studies,* June 1976; K. Lancaster, "Socially Optimal Product Differentiation," *American Economic Review,* September 1975; and H. Leland, "Quality Choices and Competition," *American Economic Review,* March 1977.

stores use markup pricing. There are two basic steps in this approach to pricing. First, the firm estimates the cost per unit of output of the product. Since this cost will generally vary with output, the firm must base this computation on some assumed output level. Usually, firms seem to use for this purpose some fraction, generally between two-thirds and three-quarters, of capacity. Second, the firm adds a *markup* (generally put in the form of a percentage) to the estimated average cost. This markup is meant to include certain costs that cannot be allocated to any specific product and to provide a return on the firm's investment. The size of the markup depends on the rate of profit that the firm believes it can earn. Some firms have set up a *target return* figure that they hope to earn, which determines the markup. For example, a firm may establish a target rate of return of 20 percent.

Markup
pricing

There has been considerable controversy over the extent to which markup pricing is compatible with profit maximization. At first glance, it seems extremely unlikely that this form of pricing can result in the maximization of profits. Indeed, this pricing technique seems naive, since it takes no account, explicitly at least, of the extent or elasticity of demand or of the size of marginal, rather than average, costs. Nevertheless, if marginal cost (not average cost) is really what is being marked up, and if the price elasticity of demand is used to determine the size of the markup, markup pricing can readily be used to maximize profit.

To see this, recall from Equation 5.3 that

$$MR = P(1 - 1/\eta),$$

where *MR* is the firm's marginal revenue, *P* is its price, and η is the price elasticity of demand of the firm's product. Solving this equation for *P*, and recognizing that marginal revenue will be equal to marginal cost if the firm is maximizing profit, we get

$$P = MC\left(\frac{1}{1 - 1/\eta}\right) = MC\left(1 + \frac{1/\eta}{1 - 1/\eta}\right). \qquad [12.1]$$

Thus, if marginal cost (rather than average cost) is what is being marked up, and if the markup (in absolute terms) equals $MC[1/\eta \div (1 - 1/\eta)]$, the firm can obtain the profit-maximizing price in this way.

From the point of view of a firm's managers, Equation 12.1 is a very useful result. Surprising as it may seem, this equation shows that, to determine the price that maximizes profit, all that a firm's managers need to know is their product's marginal cost and its price elasticity of demand, which can be inserted into Equation 12.1 to obtain the optimal price. As we saw in Chapters 5 and 8, even though very precise estimates of a product's marginal cost and price elasticity of demand may be hard to come by, rough estimates generally can be obtained. These estimates often are good enough to be helpful in guiding firms' pricing policies. For example, if marginal cost equals $10 and the price elasticity of demand is about 2, price should be established at about $10 $\left[\dfrac{1}{(1 - \frac{1}{2})}\right]$, or $20, if the firm wants to maximize profit. (It is also worth noting that Equation 12.1 can be useful for monopolists and other firms, as well as under monopolistic competition.)

COMPARISONS WITH PERFECT COMPETITION AND MONOPOLY

Frequently, attempts are made to compare the long-run equilibria that result from various market organizations. If we suppose that an industry were monopolistically competitive, rather than purely competitive or purely monopolistic, what difference would it make in the long-run behavior of the industry? It is difficult to interpret this question in a meaningful way, let alone answer it, since the output of the industry would be heterogeneous in one case and homogeneous in the other, and since the cost curves of the industry would probably vary with its organization. Nevertheless, many economists seem to believe that differences of the following kinds can be expected.

First, the firm under monopolistic competition is likely to produce less, and set a higher price, than under perfect competition. The demand curve confronting the monopolistic competitor is not perfectly elastic, as it is in perfect competition. Since marginal revenue is less than price in monopolistic competition, the firm will produce less than the amount at which price equals marginal cost, the consequence being that it will produce less than under perfect competition. However, the difference may not be very great, since the demand curve facing the firm under monopolistic competition may be close to perfectly elastic.

Second, relative to monopoly, monopolistically competitive firms are likely to have lower profits, greater output, and lower prices. The firms in a product group might obtain economic profits if they were to collude and behave as a monopolist. Of course, the increase in profit resulting from the monopoly would make the producers better off, but consumers would be worse off because of higher prices and a smaller output of goods.

Third, as noted in the section before last, firms in monopolistic competition are sometimes accused of being (somewhat) inefficient because they produce an output that is less than that which would minimize long-run average cost. However, if the differences among their products are real and are understood by consumers, the greater variety of alternatives available under monopolistic competition may be worth a great deal to consumers. Indeed, the social benefits from product diversity may outweigh these apparent inefficiencies.[4]

ADVERTISING EXPENDITURES: A SIMPLE MODEL

Industries with the characteristics of monopolistic competition spend very large amounts on advertising. Newspapers, which account for about 30 percent of total advertising expenditure in the United States, are full of advertisements by food stores, clothing stores, and other retailers. How much should a profit-maximizing firm spend on advertising? This is a very important question, and one that has occupied the attention of many economists in the 60 years since Chamberlin's work. In this section, we derive a simple rule that helps to answer this question.

For a particular firm, suppose that the quantity that it sells of its product is a function of the product's price and the level of the firm's advertising expenditure for the product. In particular, assume that there are diminishing marginal returns to advertising expenditures, which means that beyond some point successive increments of advertising outlays will yield smaller and smaller increases in additional sales. (Table 12.1 shows an illustrative case where successive increments of $100,000 in advertising outlays result in smaller and smaller increases in quantity sold. For example, the quantity sold increases by 2.0 million units when advertising expenditures rise from $800,000 to $900,000, but increases by only 1.5 million units when they rise from $900,000 to $1 million.)

We assume too that neither the price nor the marginal cost of producing an extra unit of the product will be altered by small changes in advertising expenditures. Letting P be the price of a unit of the product and MC be the marginal cost of production, the firm receives a gross profit of $(P - MC)$ from each addi-

---

[4] Many criticisms have been made of Chamberlin's theory. For example, Chicago's George Stigler and others have argued that the definition of the group of firms included in the product group is extremely ambiguous. It may contain only one firm or all of the firms in the economy. Moreover, in Stigler's view, the concept of the group is not salvaged by the assumption that each firm neglects the effects of its decisions on other firms in the group, and that each firm has essentially the same demand and cost curves. Indeed, according to Stigler, the firms in the group must be selling homogeneous commodities if the assumption of similar demand and cost curves for all firms in the group is to be at all realistic. But if the commodities are homogeneous, there is no reason why firms should have downward-sloping demand curves.

TABLE 12.1 Relationship between Advertising Expenditures and the Quantity Sold of the Firm's Product

Advertising expenditures (millions of dollars)	Quantity sold of product (millions of units)
0.8	5.0
0.9	7.0
1.0	8.5
1.1	9.5
1.2	10.0

tional unit of the product that it makes and sells. Why is this the *gross* profit of making and selling an additional unit of output? Because it takes no account of whatever additional advertising expenditures were required to sell this extra unit of output. To obtain the *net* profit, the firm must deduct these additional advertising outlays from the gross profit.

To maximize its total net profits, a firm must set its advertising expenditures at the level where an extra dollar of advertising results in extra gross profit equal to the extra dollar of advertising cost. Unless this is the case, the firm's total net profits can be increased by changing its advertising outlays. If an extra dollar of advertising results in more than a dollar increase in gross profit, the extra dollar should be spent on advertising (since this will raise total net profits). If an extra dollar (as well as the last dollar) of advertising results in less than a dollar increase in gross profit, advertising outlays should be cut.[5] Thus, if ΔQ is the number of extra units of output sold due to an extra dollar of advertising, the firm should set its advertising expenditures so that

$$\Delta Q(P - MC) = 1, \qquad [12.2]$$

because the right-hand side of this equation equals the extra dollar of advertising cost and the left-hand side equals the extra gross profit due to this advertising dollar.

Multiplying both sides of Equation 12.2 by $P/(P - MC)$, we obtain

$$P\Delta Q = \frac{P}{P - MC}. \qquad [12.3]$$

Since the firm is maximizing profit, it is producing an output where marginal cost (MC) equals marginal revenue (MR). Thus we can substitute MR for MC

---

[5] For simplicity, we assume that the gross profit due to an extra dollar spent on advertising is essentially equal to the gross profit due to the last dollar spent. This is an innocuous assumption.

in Equation 12.3, the result being

$$P \Delta Q = \frac{P}{P - MR}.$$ [12.4]

Using Equation 5.3, it can be shown that the right-hand side of Equation 12.4 equals η, the price elasticity of demand for the firm's product.[6] The left-hand side of Equation 12.4 is the *marginal revenue from an extra dollar of advertising* (since it equals the price times the extra number of units sold due to an extra dollar of advertising). Consequently, to maximize profit, the firm should set its advertising expenditure so that

Marginal revenue from an extra dollar of advertising = η.   [12.5]

> Marginal revenue from an extra dollar of advertising

This rule, derived by Harvard's Robert Dorfman and Michigan's Peter Steiner,[7] is interesting and useful. To illustrate its use, consider the Terratech Corporation, which knows that the price elasticity of demand for its product equals 1.5. If this firm maximizes profit, the rule in Equation 12.5 says that it must set the marginal revenue from an extra dollar of advertising equal to 1.5. Suppose that Terratech's managers believe that an extra $100,000 of advertising would increase the firm's sales by $180,000, which implies that the marginal revenue from an extra dollar of advertising is about $180,000 ÷ $100,000, or 1.8, rather than 1.5. Because the marginal revenue exceeds the price elasticity, Terratech will increase its profit if it does more advertising.[8] To maximize profit, it should increase its advertising up to the point where the marginal revenue from an extra dollar of advertising falls to 1.5, the value of the price elasticity of demand. (Since diminishing returns are assumed, marginal revenue falls as advertising increases.)[9]

---

[6] According to Equation 5.3, $MR = P(1 - 1/\eta)$. Thus $1 - 1/\eta = MR / P$, and $1/\eta = 1 - MR / P$, which means that

$$\eta = \frac{1}{1 - MR / P} = \frac{P}{P - MR},$$

which is the right-hand side of Equation 12.4.

[7] R. Dorfman and P. Steiner, "Optimal Advertising and Optimal Quality," *American Economic Review,* December 1954.

[8] Had Terratech's managers believed that the marginal revenue from an extra dollar of advertising was *less* than the price elasticity of demand, a *reduction* in the firm's advertising expenditures would increase profit.

[9] Of course, this analysis is highly simplified, and the rule in Equation 12.5 is by no means a full or adequate answer to the complex question of how much a firm should spend on advertising. Nonetheless, it is of interest. For a discussion of the game theoretic considerations involved, see pages 444 to 445.

OPTIMAL ADVERTISING EXPENDITURES: A GRAPHICAL ANALYSIS

Going a step further, we can use a simple graphical technique to see how much a firm, if it maximizes profit, will spend on advertising. Take the case of the Miller Electronics Company. Suppose that curve F in Figure 12.3 shows the relationship between the price elasticity of demand of this firm's product and the amount it spends on advertising. With little or no advertising, this firm's product would be regarded by consumers as similar to a host of other products; hence, its price elasticity of demand would be very high. However, because appropriate advertising can induce consumers to attach importance to this product's distinguishing features, increases in advertising expenditure reduce its price elasticity considerably.[10] At each level of advertising expen-

FIGURE 12.3 Optimal Advertising Expenditure The firm's optimal advertising expenditure is OV if the marginal revenue curve is G (or OW if the marginal revenue curve is G').

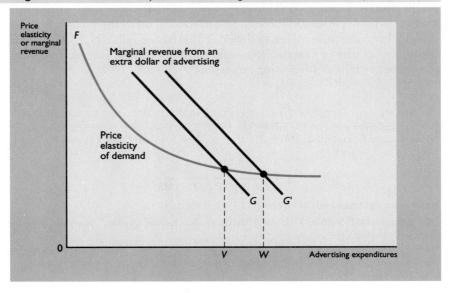

---

[10] In some cases, the price elasticity of demand is directly, not inversely, related to the amount spent on advertising. More is said later on this score.

diture, the G curve shows the marginal revenue from an extra dollar of advertising. Since the F curve intersects the G curve when Miller's advertising expenditure is OV dollars, this, based on Equation 12.5, is Miller's optimal level of advertising expenditure.

Clearly, a firm's optimal advertising expenditure depends on the position and shape of its G curve and its F curve. For example, suppose Miller's G curve shifts rightward to G', as shown in Figure 12.3. Such a shift might occur if the firm or its advertising agency found ways to increase the effectiveness of its advertisements. The result would be an increase in the optimal level of the firm's advertising expenditures (to OW dollars in Figure 12.3).

THE SOCIAL VALUE OF ADVERTISING

Thus far, we have considered advertising from the point of view of the firm, rather than of society as a whole. From society's point of view, there are obvious disadvantages stemming from certain kinds of advertising. To begin with, although private groups like the National Advertising Review Board and government agencies like the Federal Trade Commission try to stamp out blatantly deceptive advertising, some advertising misleads, rather than informs, consumers. Many consumers are properly skeptical about advertising claims, but the rest may be duped into making purchasing decisions that are far from optimal from their own point of view (but fine from the advertiser's perspective).

In addition, advertising may tend to augment the advertiser's monopoly power and may permit the advertiser more latitude to raise its price and profits. According to William Comanor and Thomas Wilson, the higher the ratio of advertising expenditures to sales in an industry, the higher the industry's profit rates.[11] If advertising makes customers recognize certain brands and if it encourages them to be loyal to these brands, sellers may have more power to raise prices without losing sales to competitors. In many retail establishments, advertised brands are priced higher than lesser-known brands. Advertising encourages customers to think that advertised brands are better than other brands, even though they may be essentially the same.

On the other hand, there also are advantages of advertising from a con-

Negative effects

---

[11] W. Comanor and T. Wilson, *Advertising and Monopoly Power* (Cambridge, Mass.: Harvard University Press, 1974).

sumer's point of view. As Nobel laureate George Stigler[12] and Phillip Nelson[13] have pointed out, the consumer frequently does not know the minimum price that he or she must pay for a commodity, and it is costly and time-consuming for the consumer to shop around in order to obtain this information. For example, it may cost a consumer $12 worth of time and travel expense to locate the store that offers a saving of $10 on the price of an item. If so, it is not worthwhile for the consumer to try to locate this store. On the other hand, if advertising (of various stores' prices) enables all consumers to identify and get to the lowest-price seller of this item at an additional cost of only $2, the identification of this lowest-price store is worthwhile—and the consumer will be better-off as a result of this advertising.

Also, if advertising is successful in enlarging the market for a firm's product, and if this product's average cost falls as more of it is produced, then the saving in production costs may more than offset the advertising cost. A case in point is the retailing of eyeglasses. (See Example 12.1.) Apparently, significant economies of scale can be realized by achieving a relatively large sales volume in an eyeglass retailing firm, but it is difficult to achieve that volume if sellers are constrained by bans on advertising and other restrictive provisions sometimes found in optometrists' codes of ethics.

In contrast to the view that advertising promotes monopoly power, both Stigler and Nelson conclude that advertising tends to increase the price elasticity of demand for products. According to their findings, the demand for goods that are not widely advertised tends to be price inelastic. The greater the advertising effort, the more price elastic the demand for a good becomes. And the more elastic the demand for a good, the more competitive is the market for that good—and frequently the lower is the price.

Based on the foregoing discussion, it is clear that advertising has a variety of social effects, some positive, some negative. To the extent that it provides trustworthy information to consumers about product quality and other matters, its effects may be positive, but if it is grossly misleading, they may be negative. To the extent that it enables consumers to shop around for lower prices more efficiently and at lower cost, its effects tend to be positive, but if it is used to increase the advertiser's monopoly power, they may be negative.

Because advertising is of so many kinds, it really is impossible to generalize about whether it is socially beneficial. The answer depends on the nature of the advertising and the circumstances under which it takes place.[14] Adver-

---

[12] G. Stigler, "The Economics of Information," *Journal of Political Economy,* June 1961.

[13] P. Nelson, "The Economic Consequences of Advertising," *Journal of Business,* April 1975.

[14] For some recent studies concerning advertising and its effects, see the papers by T. Bresnahan, R. Higgins and F. McChesney, Y. Kotowitz and F. Mathewson, and K. Lefler and R. Sauer in P. Ippolito and D. Scheffman (eds.), *Empirical Approaches to Consumer Protection Economics* (Washington, D.C.: Federal Trade Commission, 1986). Also, see G. Becker and K. Murphy, "A Simple Theory of Advertising as a Good," University of Chicago, 1990.

EXAMPLE 12.1

Advertising, Spectacles, and the FTC

The theory of monopolistic competition emphasizes the significance of selling expenses, including advertising. The market for eyeglasses in large cities has many of the characteristics of monopolistic competition, there being a large number of sellers of eyeglasses, each one's product being slightly different from the others. Some states have banned advertising of prices by sellers of eyeglasses. The following table shows the average price of eyeglasses in these states, as well as in states with no advertising restrictions:

	Average price	
Nature of state law	Eyeglasses	Eyeglasses and eye examinations
Ban on advertising	$33.04	$40.96
No ban on advertising	26.34	37.10

(a) Since advertising is a selling expense which requires the use of resources, is it reasonable to expect that a firm's costs would be lower if it didn't have to advertise? (b) If advertising increases costs, why did the price of eyeglasses tend to be lower in states with no ban on advertising? (c) In 1978, the Federal Trade Commission (FTC) declared restrictions on eyeglass advertising to be illegal. Why did the FTC take this action?

SOLUTION (a) Yes. Since advertising must be paid for, it increases a firm's costs. (b) In the markets studied, it appears that advertising improved the consumer's knowledge of the prices and services being offered by various sellers of eyeglasses. Without advertising, the cost to consumers of obtaining such knowledge is relatively high. Armed with such information, consumers were in a better position to seek out relatively low prices, and sellers were more likely to offer them. (Also, see page 394.) (c) Because the FTC felt that such restrictions impaired the effectiveness of the competitive process. In particular, as shown in the above table, consumers seem to pay higher prices when such restrictions exist. In fact, there tended to be a drop in eyeglass prices after this FTC ruling.*

*For further discussion, see L. Benham, "The Effects of Advertising on the Price of Eyeglasses," *Journal of Law and Economics,* October 1972.

tising by retail stores, which informs consumers of the price and availability of goods, is more likely to be socially beneficial than radio commercials consisting of mindless ditties. Advertising aimed at professional purchasers of equipment is more likely to be socially beneficial than television commercials that feature lots of movie stars and sports heroes but few facts.

OLIGOPOLY

Having sketched out the theory of monopolistic competition, and having discussed the firm's decision regarding advertising expenditures, we turn now to oligopoly. *Oligopoly* is a market structure characterized by a small number of firms and a great deal of interdependence, actual and perceived, among them. Unlike the case of monopolistic competition, oligopolies contain so few firms that each oligopolist formulates its policies with an eye to their effect on its rivals. Since an oligopoly contains a small number of firms, any change in the firm's price or output influences the sales and profits of competitors. Moreover, each firm must recognize that changes in its own policies are likely to elicit changes in the policies of its competitors as well.

Because of this interdependence, oligopolists face a situation where the optimal decision of one firm depends on what other firms decide to do, and where there is opportunity for both conflict and cooperation. A good example is the U.S. beer industry, in which a handful of firms, led by Anheuser-Busch, account for the bulk of the industry's sales. Each of the major beer producers must take account of the reaction of the others when it formulates its price and output policy, since its optimal strategy is likely to depend in part on how they are likely to respond. Thus, in a recent year, when Miller and Coors cut the prices of their beers by as much as 25 percent, they had to anticipate what the reactions of other firms, like Anheuser-Busch, would be. In fact, Anheuser-Busch met their price reductions.

Oligopoly
Oligopoly is a common market structure in the United States. The automobile industry contains relatively few major firms — General Motors, Ford, Chrysler, Toyota, Nissan, Honda, and a few others. Many parts of the electrical equipment industry have been dominated by General Electric and Westinghouse. The aerospace industry has been dominated by Boeing, General Dynamics, Lockheed Martin, McDonnell Douglas, United Technologies, and a few others. And these are only some highly visible examples. Not all oligopolists are large firms. If two grocery stores exist in an isolated community, they are oligopolists, too; the fact that they are small firms does not change this situation.

There are many reasons for oligopoly, one being economies of scale. In some industries, low costs cannot be achieved unless a firm is producing an output equal to a substantial percentage of the total available market, with the consequence that the number of firms will tend to be rather small. In addition, there may be economies of scale in sales promotion as well as in production, and this too may promote oligopoly. Further, there may be barriers (discussed below) that make it very difficult to enter the industry. Finally, of course, the number of firms in an industry may decrease in response to the desire to weaken competitive pressures.

NASH EQUILIBRIUM

When we studied perfect competition, monopoly, and monopolistic competition, we determined the price and quantity that would exist in the market in equilibrium. To do this for an oligopolistic market, we must recognize the interdependence among oligopolists stressed in the previous section. As pointed out there, any change in an oligopolist's price or output is likely to influence the sales and profits of its rivals, and thus induce changes in their price and output. Under these circumstances, it is difficult to determine what the equilibrium price and output of each firm will be, since each firm's behavior depends on what its rivals do (and on what it expects them to do) and their behavior depends in turn on what this firm does (and on what they expect it to do).

To resolve this problem, economists often assume that *each firm will do the best it can, given what its rivals decide to do.* This, of course, is consistent with our discussions of perfect competition, monopoly, and monopolistic competition: In these cases, we assumed that each firm maximized its profits. However, in these other cases, because each firm could regard the demand curve for its product as given, there was little or no reason for it to be much concerned about what its rivals would do. In oligopoly, on the other hand, each firm is forced to formulate its own price and output decisions based on its assumptions of what its rivals will do.

A Nash equilibrium is a situation where each firm is doing the best it can, given the behavior of its rivals. It was named after John F. Nash, a Princeton Nobel laureate who did pioneering studies of this type of equilibrium. Economists have made extensive use of the idea of a Nash equilibrium, and much more will be said on this topic in the following chapter, where we take up game theory and strategic behavior. The next section provides a more concrete and detailed discussion of the nature of a Nash equilibrium.

AN EXAMPLE OF NASH EQUILIBRIUM: THE COURNOT MODEL

Duopoly

To illustrate the concept of a Nash equilibrium, we consider a theory put forth by Augustin Cournot about 150 years ago.[15] Although this theory is too simple to capture much of the richness of the oligopolistic situation, it has attracted considerable attention and is still cited. Cournot considers the case in which there are two sellers, that is, the case of *duopoly;* but this model can easily be generalized to include the case of three or more sellers. To describe his model, it is convenient to assume that the two firms, firm I and firm II, produce the same product, have the same cost functions, and are perfectly aware of the demand curve for their product, which is supposed to be linear.

Turning to behavioral assumptions, both firms are supposed to maximize profits. Each assumes that, regardless of what output it produces, the other will hold its output constant at the existing level. Taking the other firm's output level as given, each firm chooses its own output level to maximize profit. Of course, the level of output that it chooses will depend on how much it thinks its rival will produce. For example, consider the situation in Figure 12.4, which shows the demand curve for firm I's product, based on three alternative assumptions by firm I concerning firm II's output:

1. *Firm I thinks that firm II will produce and sell nothing.* If this is what firm I thinks, the demand curve for firm I's product is believed to be the market demand curve, since firm I is expected to be the sole producer. Panel A of Figure 12.4 shows this demand curve and the corresponding marginal revenue curve. To maximize profit, firm I will choose the output where marginal revenue equals marginal cost, this output being 150 units per month. (For simplicity, we assume that marginal cost is constant in Figure 12.4.)

2. *Firm I thinks that firm II will produce and sell 100 units per month.* If this is what firm I thinks, the demand curve for firm I's product is believed to be the market demand curve *shifted to the left by 100 units.* Why? Because at each possible level of price, firm I expects to sell the total amount demanded less the 100 units that firm II is expected to produce and sell. Panel B of Figure 12.4 shows this demand curve, and the

---

[15] A. Cournot, *Recherches sur le Principes Mathématiques de la Théorie des Riches,* translated by Nathaniel Bacon (New York: Macmillan Co., 1897). He first published his model in 1838.

FIGURE 12.4 Optimal Output of Firm I if Firm II Produces 0, 100, or 200 Units of Output per Month Firm I will produce and sell 150, 100, or 50 units, depending on whether it believes that firm II will produce and sell 0, 100, or 200 units.

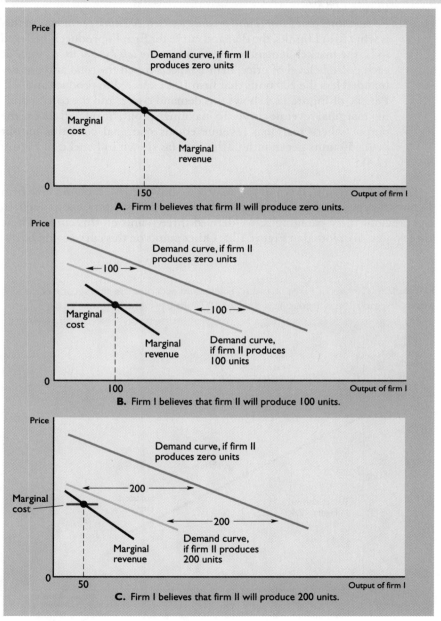

A. Firm I believes that firm II will produce zero units.

B. Firm I believes that firm II will produce 100 units.

C. Firm I believes that firm II will produce 200 units.

corresponding marginal revenue curve. To maximize profit, firm I will choose the output where marginal revenue equals marginal cost, this output being 100 units per month in this case. (See panel B of Figure 12.4.)

3. *Firm I thinks that Firm II will produce and sell 200 units per month.* If this is what firm I thinks, the demand curve for firm I's product is believed to be the market demand curve *shifted to the left by 200 units,* since at each possible level of price, firm I expects to sell the total amount demanded less the 200 units that firm II is expected to produce and sell. Panel C of Figure 12.4 shows this demand curve, and the corresponding marginal revenue curve. To maximize profit, firm I will choose the output where marginal revenue equals marginal cost, this output being 50 units per month in this case (as shown in panel C of Figure 12.4).

Using these results, it is a simple matter to draw a curve showing how firm I's output depends on how much it thinks that firm II will produce and sell. In the previous three paragraphs, we derived three points on this curve. These three points are plotted in Figure 12.5. Other points on this curve could be de-

FIGURE 12.5 Reaction Curves of Firms I and II Equilibrium occurs at the intersection of the reaction curves where each firm is producing and selling 100 units per month.

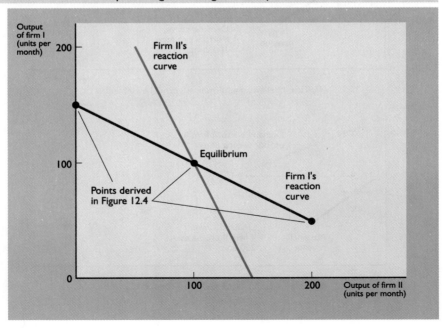

rived in the same way. This curve is called firm I's *reaction curve* because it shows how firm I will react, as a function of how much it thinks firm II will produce and sell. Firm II also has a reaction curve which is shown in Figure 12.5. Firm II's reaction curve shows how much firm II will produce, as a function of how much it thinks that firm I will produce and sell. It can be derived in precisely the same way that we derived firm I's reaction curve.

According to the Cournot model, an equilibrium will occur at the point where the firm's reaction curves intersect. Thus, in Figure 12.5, an equilibrium will occur if both firm I and firm II are producing and selling 100 units per month. Why is this a Nash equilibrium? Because each firm's expectation concerning the other's output is correct, and because each firm is maximizing its profit (given that its rival's output is what it is). To see that each firm's expectation concerning the other's output is correct at this intersection point, note that at this point firm I expects firm II to produce 100 units per month — and this in fact is what firm II produces. Similarly, at this point firm II expects firm I to produce 100 units per month — and this in fact is what firm I produces. Thus there are no surprises, and equally important, there are no incentives for either firm to alter its behavior. Each firm is maximizing its profit if (as is the case) the other produces 100 units per month.

Although the Cournot model is useful in illustrating the concept of a Nash equilibrium, its limitations should be noted. For one thing, it provides no satisfactory description or explanation of the way in which firms move toward this equilibrium. Cournot's own explanation is naive in many respects, and is rejected by most economists today. The lack of any explanation of the dynamic adjustment process is regarded as a serious problem by many economists. In later sections, as well as in the next chapter, we will take up models that pay more attention to dynamic considerations, and are far richer and more interesting.[16]

---

[16] Another way to describe the Cournot model is as follows: There is a demand curve for the industry's product, $p = f(q_1 + q_2)$, where q_1 is the output of firm I, q_2 is the output of firm II, and p is the price of the product. The total cost function of firm I is $C_1(q_1)$ and the total cost function of firm II is $C_2(q_2)$. Thus the profit of firm I is

$$\pi_1 = q_1 f(q_1 + q_2) - C_1(q_1),$$

and the profit of firm II is

$$\pi_2 = q_2 f(q_1 + q_2) - C_2(q_2).$$

If each firm takes the other firm's output as given and maximizes profit,

$$\frac{\partial \pi_1}{\partial q_1} = f(q_1 + q_2) + q_1 \frac{\partial f(q_1 + q_2)}{\partial q_1} - \frac{\partial C_1}{\partial q_1} = 0$$

and

$$\frac{\partial \pi_2}{\partial q_2} = f(q_1 + q_2) + q_2 \frac{\partial f(q_1 + q_2)}{\partial q_2} - \frac{\partial C_2}{\partial q_2} = 0.$$

Solving these two equations simultaneously, we obtain the equilibrium values of q_1 and q_2, which in turn tell us what the equilibrium value of p will be.

THE STACKELBERG MODEL

In the 1930s, Heinrich von Stackelberg, a German economist, took the Cournot model one step further. He studied the case where firm I knows that firm II will take firm I's output as given. Thus, firm I—the Stackelberg leader—enjoys a strategic advantage over firm I—the Stackelberg follower. Firm I can influence the behavior of firm II by altering its own output, and in choosing its own output, it will take account of the effects of its output on firm II's behavior. On the other hand, firm II naively takes firm I's output as given.

Under the circumstances in the previous section, firm II's reaction curve is:

$$q_2 = 150 - 0.5\,q_1, \tag{12.6}$$

where q_1 is the amount produced and sold by firm I and q_2 is the amount produced and sold by firm II. To convince yourself that this equation is correct, note that Figure 12.5 specifies that, according to form II's reaction curve, q_2 is 50 when q_1 is 200, q_2 is 100 when q_1 is 100, and q_2 is 150 when q_1 is 0. Clearly, this is in accord with Equation 12.6.

The central point to note is that firm I, knowing that Equation 12.6 links firm II's output to its own, can use this equation to determine how much output it should produce to maximize its profit. No longer will an equilibrium occur at the point where the firms' reaction curves intersect. Instead, firm I, taking into account that firm II will respond to its output decision according to Equation 12.6, will establish the output level that maximizes its own profit. In Figure 12.6, this is an output of q_1'. Firm I produces more than it would under the Cournot model.

The basic reason why an equilibrium no longer occurs at the intersection of the firms' reaction curves is that firm I no longer takes firm II's output as given. On the contrary, it recognizes that firm II's output will depend on its own, in accord with Equation 12.6. This recognition enables firm I to raise its profits above the level that it would have achieved under the Cournot model. The Stackelberg leader, by manipulating the output of the Stackelberg follower, increases both its output and its profits.

Suppose that firm I chooses its output level first, after which firm II sets its own output level. As shown in Figure 12.6, firm I maximizes its profit by choosing a larger output (q_1') than under the Cournot model (q_1). Because it goes first, it has a strategic advantage over firm II. It is able to establish its own output level; firm II must react as best it can. Given that firm I establishes the relatively high output of q_1', firm II, if it maximizes its own profit, must settle for the relatively low output level of q_2'. The advantage that firm I enjoys because it goes first is often called a *first-mover advantage*. More will be said about first-mover advantages in the next chapter.

FIGURE 12.6 Comparison of Stackelberg and Cournot Equilibria The Stackelberg leader (firm I) produces more than it would under the Cournot model, while the Stackelberg follower (firm II) produces less.

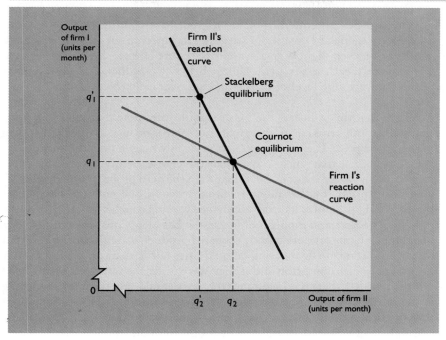

THE BERTRAND MODEL

In the previous two sections, we assumed that firms I and II focus on their outputs, rather than their prices. Suppose that each simultaneously chooses a price, rather than an output. This is the situation studied by Joseph Bertrand, a nineteenth-century French economist. To see what price each will charge, it is important to recognize that, since the product sold by both firms is the same, buyers will patronize only the firm charging the lower price. Thus, if firm I charges a lower price than firm II, firm I will have the entire market to itself and firm II's sales will be zero. If firms I and II set the same price, it is assumed that each would sell the same amount, presumably because buyers would not care which one they patronized.

Whereas this model may seem to be quite similar to those in the previous two sections, in fact it is very different. In contrast to the Cournot and

Stackelberg models, the Nash equilibrium here is the perfectly competitive outcome; that is, both firms set price equal to marginal cost, which means that both firms earn a profit of zero. This is an entirely different outcome than in the Cournot and Stackelberg models where both firms earn a positive profit.

Why is the Nash equilibrium so different here than in the Cournot and Stackelberg models? Because of each firm's incentive to cut price. If either one cuts its price, even slightly, it can supply the entire market and raise its profits. Consequently, each sets its price slightly below that of the other, until price is pushed down to the level of marginal cost (assumed to be the same for each firm).

To see that this is in fact the Nash equilibrium, note that, once the price charged by both firms equals marginal cost, there is no incentive for either firm to change its price. If either lowered its price, it would supply the entire market, but at a price that is below marginal cost. Consequently it would be worse off because it would incur a loss, rather than the zero profit it earned before it lowered its price. If either raised its price, it would sell nothing (because all buyers would patronize its rival) and hence would be no better-off.

While the Bertrand model is of interest, it has plenty of shortcomings. For one thing, if firms produce exactly the same product, it seems more likely that they would compete by focusing on quantities rather than prices. But even if they were to focus on price, and if they were to set the same price (in accord with the model), there is no assurance that they would split the market equally, as the model assumes. The big point that the Bertrand model drives home is that the firms' choice of strategic focus — price or output — can have a surprisingly major effect on the nature of equilibrium under oligopoly.

COLLUSION AND CARTELS

A Nash equilibrium is an equilibrium where firms do not cooperate or collude. If firms are able and willing to collude, they frequently can boost their profits. Thus, if firms I and II in the previous section set a common price to maximize their profits, they could make more money. For example, suppose that the demand curve for the product supplied by firms I and II is

$$P = a - bQ,$$

where Q is the total output of firms I and II. For simplicity, assume that each firm's costs are zero. (If this assumption is relaxed, the conclusions are essentially the same.) Table 12.2 shows the equilibrium outcome under (1) the

TABLE 12.2 Nature of Equilibrium under the Cournot Model, the Stackelberg Model, the Bertrand Model, and the Case in Which the Firms Collude and Act as a Monopolist (Where $P = a - bQ$ and Costs are Zero)

Model	Output			Profit			Price
	Firm I	Firm II	Total	Firm I	Firm II	Total	
Cournot	$a/3b$	$a/3b$	$2a/3b$	$a^2/9b$	$a^2/9b$	$2a^2/9b$	$a/3$
Stackelberg	$a/2b$	$a/4b$	$3a/4b$	$a^2/8b$	$a^2/16b$	$3a^2/16b$	$a/4$
Bertrand	$a/2b$	$a/2b$	a/b	0	0	0	0
Monopoly	$a/4b$	$a/4b$	$a/2b$	$a^2/8b$	$a^2/8b$	$a^2/4b$	$a/2$

Cournot model, (2) the Stackelberg model, (3) the Bertrand model, and (4) the case where the two firms collude and act as a monopoly.[17] Clearly, output is lowest and profits are highest when firms I and II collude and act as a monopoly.

Conditions in oligopolistic industries tend to promote collusion, since the number of firms is small and the firms recognize their interdependence. The advantages to the firms of collusion seem obvious: increased profits, decreased uncertainty, and a better opportunity to prevent entry. However, collusive arrangements are often hard to maintain, since once a collusive agreement is made, any of the firms can increase its profits by cheating on the agreement. Moreover, collusive arrangements generally are illegal, at least in the United States.

When a collusive arrangement is made openly and formally, it is called a *cartel*. In many countries in Europe, cartels have been common and legally acceptable. In the United States, most collusive agreements, whether secret or open cartels, were declared illegal by the Sherman Antitrust Act, which dates back to 1890. However, this does not mean that such agreements do not exist.

Cartel

---

[17] To derive the last row of Table 12.2, note that, if the two firms collude and act as a monopoly, they will set their total output at the level where marginal revenue equals marginal cost. Since marginal revenue equals $a - 2bQ$ (as pointed out in footnote 9 on page 147) and marginal cost equals zero, it follows that their total output equals $a/2b$, which is assumed to be split equally between them. If $Q = a/2b$, it follows from the demand curve that $P = a/2$. Since costs are zero, total profit equals PQ, or $(a/2)(a/2b)$, which is assumed to be split equally between them.

Turning to the Bertrand model, since marginal cost equals zero, equilibrium price will be zero. Thus, based on the demand curve, total output will be equal to $(a - P)/b$; and since $P = 0$, equilibrium total output will be a/b, which is assumed to be split equally between the two firms. Obviously, since price and costs are zero, profit must be zero.

Applying the analysis in footnote 16, one can obtain the row of figures pertaining to the Cournot model. With regard to the Stackelberg model, one can find firm I's output by maximizing its profit with recognition that Equation 12.6 holds. Then firm II's output can be obtained from its reaction curve. Given the output of both firms, the price can be determined from the demand curve, and the profit figures can be calculated.

For example, there was widespread collusion among U.S. electrical equipment manufacturers during the 1950s.[18] Moreover, trade associations and professional organizations may sometimes perform functions somewhat similar to a cartel. In addition, some types of cartels have the official sanction of the U.S. government.[19]

Suppose that a cartel is established to set a uniform price for a particular (homogenous) product. How will it go about determining what price to charge? To begin with, the cartel must estimate the marginal cost curve for the cartel as a whole. If input prices do not increase as the cartel expands, this marginal cost curve is the horizontal sum of the marginal cost curves of the individual firms. Suppose that the resulting marginal cost curve for the cartel is as shown in Figure 12.7. If the demand curve for the industry's product and the relevant marginal revenue curve are as shown there, the output that maximizes the total profit of the cartel members is OQ_0. Thus, if it maximizes cartel profits, the cartel will choose a price of OP_0. This, of course, is the monopoly price.

Another important task of a cartel is to distribute the industry's total sales among the firms belonging to the cartel. If the aim of the cartel is to maximize cartel profits, it will allocate sales to firms in such a way that the marginal cost of all firms is equal. Otherwise the cartel could make more money by reallocating output among firms so as to reduce the cost of producing the cartel's total output. For example, if the marginal cost at firm I was higher than at firm II, the cartel could increase its total profits by transferring some production from firm I to firm II.

Negotiation

However, this allocation of output—sometimes called the ideal allocation by economists—is unlikely to occur, since the allocation of output usually determines the allocation of cartel profits. For this reason, allocation decisions are the result of negotiation between firms with varying interests and varying capabilities. This is a political process in which various firms have different amounts of influence. Those with the most influence and the shrewdest nego-

---

[18] In early 1960 the U.S. Department of Justice charged that a large number of companies and individuals in the electrical equipment industry were guilty of fixing prices and dividing up the market for circuit breakers, switchgears, and other important products. Most of the defendants were found guilty; the companies, including General Electric and Westinghouse, received fines; and some of the guilty executives were sent to prison. The price-fixing agreements were reached in various ways. Many of the meetings occurred at conventions of the National Electrical Manufacturers Association and other trade groups. Some agreements were made through telephone calls and written memoranda transmitted from one sales executive to another. Efforts were made to keep the meetings and agreements secret. For example, codes were used, and the participants at meetings sometimes disguised their records and did not use their companies' names when registering at hotels. The executives recognized that these agreements were illegal.

[19] For example, airlines flying transatlantic routes have been members of the International Air Transport Association, which has been able to agree on uniform prices for transatlantic flights.

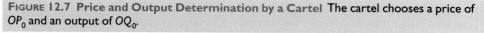

FIGURE 12.7 Price and Output Determination by a Cartel The cartel chooses a price of OP_0 and an output of OQ_0.

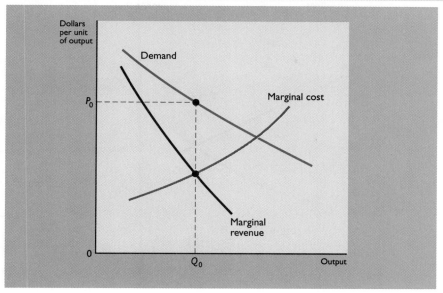

tiators are likely to receive the largest sales quotas, even though this increases total cartel costs. Moreover, high-cost firms are likely to receive larger sales quotas than cost minimization would dictate, since they would be unwilling to accept the small quotas dictated by cost minimization. In practice, there is some evidence that sales are often distributed in accord with a firm's level of sales in the past, or the extent of its productive capacity. Also, a cartel sometimes divides a market geographically, with some firms being given certain regions or countries and other firms being given other regions or countries.

THE INSTABILITY OF CARTELS

We have already noted that collusive agreements tend to break down. Of course, the difficulty in keeping a cartel from breaking down increases with the number of firms in the cartel. To see why firms are tempted to leave the cartel, consider the case of the firm in Figure 12.8. If this firm were to leave the

FIGURE 12.8 **The Instability of Cartels** If it leaves the cartel, the firm's profit equals $OQ_1 \times BP_1$, which is higher than if it adheres to the price and sales quota established by the cartel.

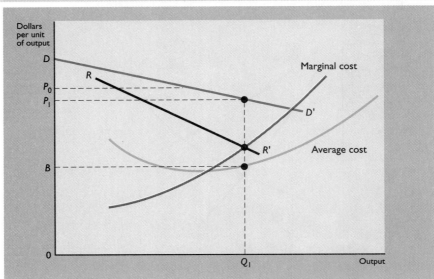

cartel, it would be faced with a demand curve of DD' as long as the other firms in the cartel maintain a price of OP_0. This demand curve is very elastic; the firm is able to expand its sales considerably by small reductions in price. Even if the firm were not to leave the cartel, but if it were to grant secret price concessions, the same sort of demand curve would be present.

Cheating

Under these circumstances the firm's maximum profit if it leaves the cartel or secretly lowers price will be attained if it sells an output of OQ_1, at a price of OP_1, since this is the output at which marginal cost equals marginal revenue. (RR' is the firm's marginal revenue curve.) This price would result in a profit of $OQ_1 \times BP_1$, which is higher than if the firm conforms to the price and sales quota dictated by the cartel. A firm that breaks away from a cartel—or secretly cheats—can increase its profits as long as other firms do not do the same thing and as long as the cartel does not punish it in some way. But if all firms do this, the cartel breaks down.

Consequently, as long as a cartel is not maintained by legal provisions, there is a constant threat to its existence. Its members have an incentive to cheat, and once a few do so, others may follow. Price concessions made secretly by a few "chiselers" or openly by a few malcontents cut into the sales of cooperative members of the cartel who are induced to match them. Thus the ranks of the unfaithful are expanded; and ultimately the cartel may break down completely.

EXAMPLE 12.2

The Retail Market for Tires

Some retail markets for automobile tires contain lots of sellers; others contain only one or two. For example, an isolated community in the Southwest or Mountain states may have only a single retailer selling tires; it is a monopoly. Other local markets contain two, three, four, or five such retailers; they are oligopolies. Timothy Bresnahan and Peter Reiss of Stanford University compared the average price of a tire in markets with varying numbers of sellers, the results being as follows:

Number of sellers	Average tire price (dollars)
1	54
2	55
3	53
4	51
5	50
Many	43

(a) Do these findings suggest that the average price exceeds the competitive level when there are five or fewer sellers? (b) Are these findings in accord with the Cournot model? Why or why not? (c) Are these findings in accord with the Bertrand model? Why or why not? (d) Do these findings suggest that duopolists often "cooperate" to promote higher profits? Why or why not?

SOLUTION: (a) Yes. (b) No. The Cournot model would lead us to believe that price would be lower if there were two sellers than if there were only one (a monopolist). For example, in Table

12.2, the price under the Cournot model with two sellers ($a/3$) is two-thirds of the price under monopoly ($a/2$). These data regarding tire prices indicate no such tendency. (c) No. The Bertrand model would predict that price would be at the competitive level (apparently about $43, since this is the average in markets where there are many sellers) when there are two sellers. No such tendency is found in these data. (d) If there is collusion in markets in which there are only two sellers, and if the sellers act as a monopolist, the average price in markets with two sellers may be about the same as in markets with one seller, which is what we find here.*

*For further discussion, see Timothy Bresnahan and Peter Reiss, "Entry and Competition in Concentrated Markets," *Journal of Political Economy,* October 1991.

THE OPEC OIL CARTEL: AN APPLICATION

To illustrate the nature and behavior of a cartel, consider the Organization of Petroleum Exporting Countries (OPEC) cartel. As pointed out in Chapter 6, this cartel first hit the headlines in late 1973 when its Arab members precipitated a crisis in the United States by announcing a cutback in oil exports to us. Then it attracted further attention by taking a series of actions resulting in very large increases in the price of crude oil. For example, the price of Saudi Arabian crude oil jumped from about $2.50 in 1972 to over $10 in early 1974. Again in 1979, in the wake of the Iranian revolution, OPEC raised the price enormously, to over $30 a barrel.

What is OPEC, and how has it functioned? As we saw in Chapter 6, OPEC consists of 12 major oil-producing countries, including Saudi Arabia, Iran, Venezuela, Libya, and Nigeria. The OPEC countries imposed an excise tax of so many cents per barrel on each barrel of oil produced in their countries. These taxes were well publicized and, like any excise tax, they were treated as a cost of production by any of the international oil companies operating in these countries. Thus, by increasing these taxes, the OPEC countries raised the price of crude oil, since no company can afford to sell oil for less than its production costs plus the tax. According to the model discussed on pages 404 to 407, one would expect the OPEC cartel to have pushed the crude oil price up toward the monopoly level, since this would have increased their tax revenues.

EXAMPLE 12.3

A Cartel in the Orange Groves

Cartels can occur in competitive, as well as oligopolistic, industries if the government creates the cartel. Since the 1930s, federal marketing orders have empowered producers in the California-Arizona orange industry (which supplies about two-thirds of the fresh oranges in the United States) to get together to determine how much of each year's crop will be sold for consumption in fresh form; the rest is sold in the processed market (where it is made into orange juice, among other things).* The price received by producers is much higher in the fresh market than in the processed market. Yet, according to the following estimates based on economic studies, the percentage of the orange crop that the cartel chooses to sell in the fresh market is much lower than would be the case if the cartel were disbanded:

	Percent sold in the fresh market	
	Valencia oranges	Navel oranges
Cartel	42	55
Without cartel	58	80

(a) The California-Arizona orange industry contains more than 4,000 growers and 100 packers. Is it an oligopoly? Why or why not? (b) Does the cartel have control over entry into the industry? (c) The price elasticity of demand for oranges in the fresh market is about 0.8 for Navel oranges and about 1.2 for Valencia oranges. In the processed market, the price elasticity for both types of oranges is more than 2.0. Does this help to explain why the cartel's price is higher in the fresh market than in the processed market? (d) Why does the cartel sell a smaller proportion of oranges in the fresh market than would be the case if the cartel were disbanded?

SOLUTION

(a) No. There are far more producers in the market than in an oligopoly. (b) No. (c) Yes. According to economists who have studied the situation, the cartel is engaging in price discrimination. To increase producers' profits, it is selling oranges at a higher price in the less price-elastic market (the fresh market) than in the more price-elastic market (the processed market). In accord with the discussion in Chapter 11, this is the way to maximize the profit from a given quantity of oranges supplied. (d) In effect, the cartel must divert some oranges from the fresh to the processed market in order to

> maintain the price in the fresh market at a substantially higher level
> than in the processed market. If the cartel did not exist, this diversion
> would not occur.[†]

---

* Congress has provided that these decisions operate with the force of law, and that the
antitrust laws do not apply in this area.

† For further discussion, see L. Shepard, "Cartelization of the California-Arizona
Orange Industry, 1934–1981," *Journal of Law and Economics,* April 1986.

In fact, this seems to have been exactly what occurred. Experts estimate that
hundreds of billions of dollars were transferred by this means from oil consumers to OPEC.

However, as described in Chapter 6, OPEC's economic power seemed to
wane in the 1980s, and the price of oil fell until it was below $15 per barrel. To
a considerable extent, the downward pressure on price was due to a continuing
shift away from the use of oil. For example, while national output in the
United States increased at a 5 percent annual rate in the first three quarters of
1983, oil consumption dropped nearly 2.5 percent. Because of conservation of
oil and competition from other fuels (due partly to the great increases in the oil
price in earlier years), there was a reduction in the quantity of oil demanded.
In addition, non-OPEC oil production (in Mexico and the North Sea, for example) has soared, thus putting additional pressure on OPEC.[20]

PRICE LEADERSHIP

Faced with the difficulties of forming an effective cartel, oligopolists may attempt to collude implicitly. In other words, they may attempt to cooperate
without actually making explicit agreements with one another. A useful
model of oligopolistic behavior is based on the supposition that one of the
firms in the industry is the price leader. This form of behavior seems to be
quite common in oligopolistic industries, where one or a few firms apparently
set the price and the rest follow their lead. Examples of industries that have

---

[20] For further discussion of OPEC, see J. Griffin and H. Steele, *Energy Economics and Policy*
(2d ed.; New York: Academic Press, 1985).

been characterized by price leadership, according to various studies, are steel, nonferrous alloys, and agricultural implements.

Let's assume that there is a single large dominant firm in the industry and a number of small firms (the "competitive fringe"). We assume too that the dominant firm sets the price for the industry, but that it lets the small firms sell all they want at that price. Whatever amount the small firms do not supply at that price is supplied by the dominant firm. If this model holds, it is easy to derive the price that the dominant firm will set if it maximizes profits. Since each small firm takes the price as given, it produces the output at which price equals marginal cost. Thus a supply curve for all small firms combined can be drawn by summing horizontally the marginal cost curves of the small firms. This supply curve is labeled S in Figure 12.9. The demand curve for the dominant firm can be derived by subtracting the amount supplied by the small firms at each price from the total amount demanded at that price. Consequently, if D is the demand curve for the industry's product, the demand curve for the output of the dominant firm, d, can be determined by finding the horizontal difference at each price between the D curve and the S curve.

To illustrate the derivation of d, suppose that the dominant firm sets a price of OP_0. The S curve shows that the small firms will supply OR_0, and the D

Price leader-ship

FiGURE 12.9 Price Leadership The dominant firm sets a price of OP_1, and supplies OQ_1 units of the product. Total industry output is OD_1.

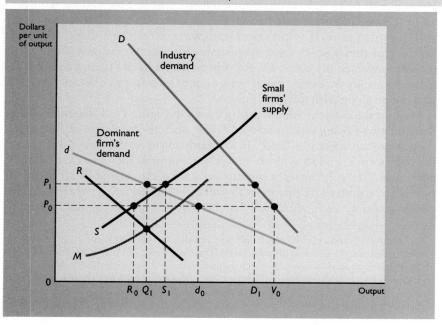

curve shows that the total amount demanded will be OV_0. Thus the amount to be supplied by the dominant firm is $(OV_0 - OR_0)$, which is the quantity on the d curve at price OP_0. In other words, Od_0 is set equal to $(OV_0 - OR_0)$. The process by which the other points on the d curve are determined is exactly the same; this procedure is repeated at various price levels.

Given the demand curve for the output of the dominant firm, d, and the dominant firm's marginal cost curve, M, it is a simple matter to determine the price and output that will maximize the profits of the dominant firm. The dominant firm's marginal revenue curve, R, can be derived from the dominant firm's demand curve, d, in the usual way. The optimal output for the dominant firm is the output OQ_1, where its marginal cost equals its marginal revenue. This output will be achieved if the dominant firm sets a price of OP_1. The total industry output will be OD_1, and the small firms will supply OS_1 $(= OD_1 - OQ_1)$.[21]

THE KINKED DEMAND CURVE

In many industries, there is no dominant firm of the sort we studied in the previous section, and firms may have a strong preference for stability, especially with regard to price. If a firm's costs go down or if the demand for its product falls, it may prefer not to lower its price because this might provoke its rivals into an unwanted price war. On the other hand, if its costs go up or if the demand for its product rises, it may prefer not to raise its price because its rivals may not go along with the price increase.

If this is the case, the situation is as shown in Figure 12.10, the oligopolist's demand curve being represented by DVD', and the current price being OP_0. As you can see, there is a "kink" in the demand curve: the demand curve for the oligopolist's product is much more elastic for price increases than for price decreases. This is because, as pointed out above, the oligopolist, if it cuts its price, can be pretty sure that its rivals will meet the reduction, whereas if it increases its price, it is likely to find that its rivals will not change their prices.

---

[21] If (as is often the case) a cartel controls only part, not all, of an industry's output, this model can be used to describe the behavior of such a cartel. Thus, in the case of OPEC (discussed on pages 410 to 412), this model has sometimes been applied, with OPEC playing the role of the "dominant firm." Obviously, the extent to which the cartel can push up the price depends on how price elastic the d curve in Figure 12.9 is. If it is very price elastic, perhaps because the output supplied by firms outside the cartel (which play the role of the "small firms") is highly price elastic, the cartel cannot push up the price very much.

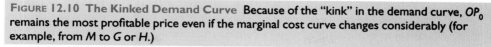

FIGURE 12.10 The Kinked Demand Curve Because of the "kink" in the demand curve, OP_0 remains the most profitable price even if the marginal cost curve changes considerably (for example, from M to G or H.)

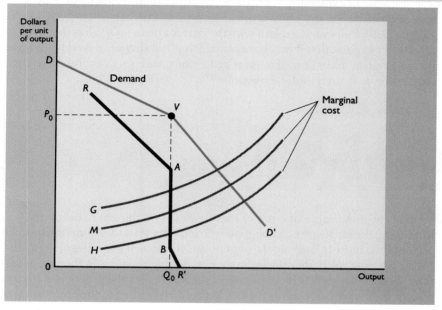

Because of the "kink" in the demand curve, the marginal revenue curve is not continuous: It consists of two segments, RA and BR'. Given that the firm's marginal cost curve is M, marginal revenue does not equal marginal cost at any level of output. But it can be shown that OQ_0 is the most profitable output of the firm.[22] Moreover, OQ_0 remains the most profitable output—and OP_0 the most profitable price—even if the marginal cost curve changes considerably. For example, it remains the most profitable output if the marginal cost curve shifts to G or H. Also, OQ_0 remains the most profitable output—and OP_0 the most profitable price—for some changes in demand as long as the kink remains at the same price level. Hence, under these circumstances, one might expect price to be quite rigid.

---

[22] To see that OQ_0 is the most profitable output, note that, if output is pushed above OQ_0, the increase in revenues (given by the marginal revenue curve) is less than the increase in cost (given by the marginal cost curve). On the other hand, if output falls below OQ_0, the loss in revenue (given by the marginal revenue curve) is greater than the reduction in cost (given by the marginal cost curve). Since profit decreases when output is pushed above, or falls below, OQ_0, it must be maximized when output equals OQ_0.

While this theory has received considerable attention, it is really not an explanation of oligopoly pricing. Although it may be helpful in some circumstances in explaining why price remains at a certain level (OP_0 in Figure 12.10), it is of no use in explaining why this level, rather than another, currently prevails. For example, it simply takes as given that the current price is OP_0 in Figure 12.10; it does not explain why the current price is OP_0. Further, tests of this theory suggest that it may have limited applicability since rival firms often do match price hikes as well as price reductions, and prices are no more rigid under oligopoly than under monopoly.[23]

ENTRY AND CONTESTABLE MARKETS

Finally, the importance of entry of new firms—and the exit of old firms—in modifying the structure of an oligopolistic industry should be emphasized. An oligopolistic industry may not be oligopolistic for long if every Tom, Dick, and Harry can enter. Whether the industry remains oligopolistic in the face of relatively easy entry depends on the size of the market for the product relative to the optimum size of a firm. If the market is small relative to the optimum size of a firm in this industry, the number of firms will remain sufficiently small so that the industry will still be an oligopoly.

There are a variety of barriers to entry. One is the requirement in some industries that a firm build and maintain a large, complicated, and expensive plant. The scale of the undertaking is likely to discourage many potential entrants. Also, the existence of patents may make entry difficult. Still another barrier to entry is the unavailability of raw materials. This factor is often cited in the case of nickel, sulfur, diamonds and bauxite. Also, the government is sometimes responsible for other barriers to entry. For example, taxicabs and buses must obtain franchises, and local licensing laws may be used to limit the number of plumbers, barbers, and so on.

---

[23] For further discussion of the kinked demand curve, see P. Sweezy, "Demand Under Conditions of Oligopoly," *Journal of Political Economy,* August 1939; G. Stigler, "The Kinky Oligopoly Demand Curve and and Rigid Prices," *Journal of Political Economy,* 1947; W. Primeaux, Jr., and W. Smith, "Pricing Patterns and the Kinky Demand Curve," *Journal of Law and Economics,* April 1976; J. Simon, "A Further Test of the Kinky Oligopoly Demand Curve," *American Economic Review,* December 1969; and D. Carlton, "The Rigidity of Price," *American Economic Review,* September 1986.

Although entry into some oligopolistic industries may be very difficult, this
is not always the case. A *contestable market* is one in which "entry is absolutely
free, and exit is absolutely costless."[24] In other words, firms can enter and leave
the market readily. For example, if the government permits, the owner of a
commercial jet aircraft can use it to fly passengers on a particular route and
then devote it to other uses. The essence of contestable markets is that they are
vulnerable to hit-and-run entry. "Even a very transient profit opportunity
need not be neglected by a potential entrant, for he can go in, and before prices
change, collect his gains and then depart without cost, should the climate grow
hostile."[25]

Despite the fact that a contestable market contains only a few firms (or perhaps only one), it will perform much like a perfectly competitive market.
Economic profit will tend to be zero. If it is positive, a new entrant can enter
the market, produce the same output (at the same cost) as a firm that is already
in the market, undercut the existing firm's price slightly, and make a profit.
Entrants will do this if economic profit is positive, and the price will be pushed
down to the point where economic profit is zero. In other words, if they like,
entrants can hit and run.

The firms in a contestable market, like those under competition, will produce at minimum cost. If they produce at more than minimum cost, firms will
enter the industry, produce at lower costs than the existing firms, undercut the
existing firms' price, and make a profit. Thus costs will be pushed down to the
minimum level. Also, in an oligopoly, price cannot exceed marginal cost. If existing firms are charging a price in excess of marginal cost, it is profitable for an
entrant to undercut the price of the existing firms. Thus, for an equilibrium to
occur, price cannot exceed marginal cost.

To illustrate the workings of a contestable market, suppose that an industry
contains three firms, each with the marginal and average cost curves shown in
Figure 12.11. If each firm produces Oq units of output, and charges a price of
OP, total output will be three times Oq, and all three firms will earn zero economic profit. Although they could attempt to collude and push up the price,
they do not do so because they know that new firms would enter the market
very quickly and undercut their price. Given that entrants could sell the product at a price of OP, each firm maximizes its profit by producing Oq units of
output and selling it at that price.

*Contest-
able
market*

---

[24] W. Baumol, "Contestable Markets: An Uprising in the Theory of Industry Structure,"
American Economic Review, March 1982, p. 3. Also see W. Baumol, J. Panzar, and R. Willig,
Contestable Markets and the Theory of Industry Structure (San Diego, Calif.: Harcourt Brace
Jovanovich, 1982).

[25] Ibid., p. 4. For criticism of this theory, see W. Shepherd, "Competition versus Contestability,"
American Economic Review, 1984.

FIGURE 12.11 A Contestable Market The threat of entry can lead oligopolists to behave more like perfectly competitive firms.

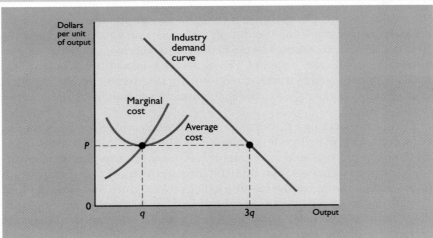

The theory of contestable markets, which is only about 15 years old, has provoked considerable controversy. Its critics charge that it is based on extremely unrealistic assumptions concerning entry and exit. (In reality, of course, entry is not free and exit is not costless.) However, models based on simplified assumptions can be very useful. At this point, it is too early to tell how important this relatively new theory will turn out to be, but without question it has had a noteworthy impact on many economists' views concerning oligopoly.

SUMMARY

1. Under monopolistic competition, there is a large number of firms producing and selling goods that are close substitutes, but that are not completely homogeneous from one seller to another. Each seller tries to make its product a little different, by altering the physical makeup of the product, the services it offers, and other such variables.

2. The firm under monopolistic competition is likely to produce less, and set a higher price, than under perfect competition. It is likely to operate with excess capacity, but the greater variety of alternatives available under monopolistic competition may be worth a great deal to consumers.

3. To maximize profit, a firm should set its advertising expenditures at the level where the marginal revenue from an extra dollar of advertising equals the price elasticity of demand for its product. If the marginal revenue is greater than the price elasticity, the firm should increase its advertising expenditures; if the marginal revenue is less than the price elasticity, it should decrease its advertising expenditures.

4. Whether or not advertising is socially beneficial depends on the nature of the advertising and the circumstances under which it takes place. From society's point of view, there are obvious disadvantages in advertising that misleads, rather than informs, consumers, and in advertising that augments the advertiser's monopoly power. On the other hand, advertising that enables sellers to take advantage of economies of scale in production, as well as advertising that allows consumers to shop around for lower prices more efficiently, can be socially beneficial.

5. Oligopoly is characterized by a small number of firms and a great deal of interdependence, actual and perceived, among them. A good example of an oligopoly is the U.S. beer industry, where a small number of firms accounts for the bulk of the industry's capacity.

6. A Nash equilibrium is a situation where each firm is doing the best it can, given the behavior of its rivals. To illustrate the concept of a Nash equilibrium, we considered the Cournot model, an early theory based on the supposition that each firm believes that the other firm will hold its output constant at the existing level. Also, we took up the Stackelberg and Bertrand models, two other early oligopoly models.

7. Conditions in oligopolistic industries tend to promote collusion, since the number of firms is small and firms recognize their interdependence. The advantages to be derived by the firms from collusion seem obvious: increased profits, decreased uncertainty, and a better opportunity to control the entry of new firms. However, collusive arrangements are often hard to maintain, since once a collusive agreement is made, any of the firms can increase its profits by "cheating" on the agreement. Also, such arrangements are illegal in the United States. An interesting example of collusion is the OPEC cartel, which has played so important a role in the oil markets.

8. Faced with the difficulties of forming an effective cartel, oligopolists may attempt to cooperate without making explicit agreements with one another. One useful model of oligopolistic behavior is based on the supposition that one of the firms in the industry is a price leader. A model based on the kinked demand curve is sometimes used to explain price rigidity.

9. In the 1980s, an interesting development was the theory of contestable markets, which assumed that entry is absolutely free and exit is absolutely costless. According to this theory, oligopolists will behave much like perfectly competitive firms, because of the threat of entry into their market. However, this theory remains controversial.

QUESTION/PROBLEMS

1. On June 1, 1992, American Coach Lines of Maryland sold its Washington, D.C., bus terminal to Peter Pan, the nation's largest privately owned bus company. On July 24, 1992, Peter Pan cut its one-way fare on the Washington–New York route from $25 to $9.95; Greyhound, its only rival on the route, responded by cutting its one-way fare to $7; Peter Pan answered with $6.95; Greyhound went to $5; and Peter Pan matched it. The operating cost of a bus which can carry 47 passengers traveling from New York to Washington is about $480. (a) Is this an example of a contestable market? Why or why not? (b) Is the $5 fare an equilibrium price? Why or why not?

2. A firm estimates its average total cost to be $10 per unit of output when it produces 10,000 units, which it regards as 80 percent of capacity. Its goal is to earn 20 percent on its total investment, which is $250,000. If it were sure that it could sell 10,000 units, what price should it set to achieve this goal? Can it be sure of selling 10,000 units if its sets this price?

3. In 1989, the top four firms—Anheuser-Busch, Miller, Coors, and Stroh's—accounted for over three-quarters of all beer produced in the United States. Anheuser-Busch alone had 42 percent of the market. (a) Do you think that the market for beer is a contestable market? (b) In the 1960s, the long-run average cost of producing beer was at a minimum when a firm produced about 2 million barrels per year. In the late 1970s, it was at a minimum when a firm's output was about 18 million barrels per year. Can you guess why this change occurred? (c) Do you think that this change in the long-run average cost curve helped to cause the decrease shown below in the number of firms in the brewing industry?

Year	Number of firms	Year	Number of firms
1963	171	1972	108
1967	125	1976	49

4. Explain in detail why you believe that each of the following industries can or cannot be represented by the theory of monopolistic competition: (a) copper, (b) outboard motors, (c) airlines, (d) cement. To answer this question, what characteristics of each industry should you look at? Why?

5. Suppose that you are on the board of directors of a firm which is the price leader in the industry. It lets all of the other firms sell all they want at the existing price. In other words, the other firms act as perfect competitors. Your firm, on the other hand, sets the price, which the other firms accept. The

demand curve for your industry's product is $P = 300 - Q$, where P is the product's price (in dollars per unit) and Q is the total quantity demanded. The total amount supplied by the other firms is equal to Q_r, where $Q_r = 49P$. If your firm's marginal cost curve is $2.96\,Q_b$, where Q_b is the output of your firm, at what output level should you operate to maximize profit? What price should you charge? How much will the industry as a whole produce at this price? (Q, Q_b, and Q_r are expressed in millions of units.)Is your firm the dominant firm in the industry? (Hint: To find the relevant marginal revenue curve, the material in footnote 9 on page 147 may be useful.)

6. In the United States agreements to fix prices and restrict output are illegal. Section 1 of the Sherman Antitrust Act says, "Every contract, combination . . . , or conspiracy in restraint of trade or commerce among the several states, or with foreign nations, is hereby declared to be illegal." (a) Does this mean that oligopoly is illegal? (b) Is any formal agreement among firms necessary to constitute an unlawful conspiracy? (c) For decades, the Big Three of the cigarette industry — American Tobacco, Liggett and Meyers, and Reynolds — followed a pattern of setting the same price. Even at the pit of the Great Depression, the other two firms matched a price increase by Reynolds. Also, they behaved in such a way as to make it likely that each would pay much the same price for tobacco. Can such parallel action be used in court as convincing circumstantial evidence of illegal collusion? (d) Is mere recognition of mutual interdependence and parallel behavior by a group of firms sufficient to make conspiracy charges against them stick?

7. There has been considerable criticism of the historically high price of milk in New York City. In 1986, Farmland Dairies, a New Jersey milk producer, began selling milk on Staten Island, one of New York City's five boroughs. Its low price drove down the retail price of milk by 40 cents per gallon. New York state law dictated that each milk producer like Farmland must get a license to sell milk, borough by borough. Existing dairies in New York City argued that the entry of Farmland into other parts of the city would not benefit consumers because it costs a great deal to distribute milk there. Further, they said that New York jobs should not go to New Jersey. In January 1987, a Federal judge ruled in favor of Farmland, saying that a state decision barring its expansion of sales in New York was unconstitutional. Evaluate in detail the above arguments of the existing New York dairies.

8. Suppose two firms are producers of spring water, which can be obtained at zero cost. The marginal revenue curve for their combined output is

$$MR = 10 - 2Q,$$

where MR is marginal revenue and Q is the number of gallons per hour of spring water sold by both together. (a) If the two producers collude to maximize their total profits, how much will be their combined output?

Why? (b) If the two firms behave according to the Bertrand model, what will be the equilibrium price?

9. Suppose that a cartel is formed by three firms. Their total cost functions are as shown below:

Units of output	Total cost		
	Firm 1	Firm 2	Firm 3
0	20	25	15
1	25	35	22
2	35	50	32
3	50	80	47
4	80	120	77
5	120	160	117

If the cartel decides to produce 11 units of output, how should the output be distributed among the three firms if they want to minimize cost?

10. The Sonora Software Company estimates that the price elasticity of demand for its product is 2 and that an extra $100,000 in advertising expenditure would increase its sales by $150,000. Is this firm maximizing profit? Why or why not? If not, should it increase or reduce its advertising expenditures? Why?

11. Describe in detail the social advantages and disadvantages of advertising. If a particular advertising campaign is profitable to the advertisers, does this mean that it is socially desirable? Why or why not?

12. Under what circumstances are increases in advertising likely to reduce a product's price elasticity of demand? Under what circumstances are they likely to increase it?

13. Suppose that a computer manufacturer's perceived demand curve is DVD', its marginal revenue curve is RAR', and its marginal cost curve is MM' in panel A below.*

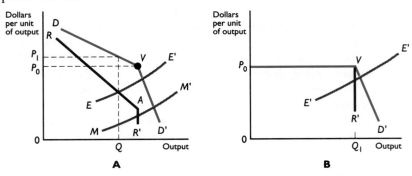

* In both panels of the graph, only parts of the marginal revenue curve are shown, but these parts are sufficient for present purposes.

Suppose further that, because of a jump in materials prices, the firm's costs increase sharply, with the result that the marginal cost curve rises from MM' to EE'. (a) An economist says that, because the firm's demand curve is kinked, this will not increase its price. Is he correct? (b) Fearful that the cost increase will result in a price hike, the government specifies that the firm's price must not exceed OP_0. What effect does this have on the firm's demand curve? Marginal revenue curve? Output?

14. According to the Senate Subcommittee on Antitrust and Monopoly, there has been a long history of international cartels that have controlled the price and output of quinine. What do you think the effects of the cartels have been? Do you think that such cartels should be broken up? If so, how can individual governments go about doing this?

15. Firms A and B are the only producers of a homogeneous good. Firm A's marginal revenue (in dollars) equals $100 - 8(Q_A + Q_B)$, where Q_A is firm A's monthly output and Q_B is firm B's monthly output. (Both Q_A and Q_B are expressed in units of output per month.) If firm A's marginal cost equals \$4 per unit of output, obtain the equation for firm A's reaction curve.

16. In the previous question, do each of the points on firm A's reaction curve represent a Nash equilibrium? Why or why not? If firm A is a Stackelberg leader and firm B is a Stackelberg follower, will the equilibrium be at the point where firm A's reaction curve intersects firm B's reaction curve? Why or why not?

17. Federal and state officials have found evidence that executives at large national and regional dairy firms have rigged bids on milk products sold to schools and military bases. For example, consider the bidding for the contract to supply milk for the school districts in Pinellas County, Florida. Before the bidding, a vice president of Pet Milk (now part of Land-O-Sun), the general manager of Borden's Tampa plant, and the manager of Pet's largest distributor in the area met at a restaurant in Tampa, Florida. They agreed that Borden would bid too high, so that Pet would get the Pinellas contract, and that Pet would give Borden part of the milk business in another county. A prosecutor said that the Pinellas schools paid about 14 percent more than they otherwise would have. Did this result in a decrease in consumer surplus? Did it result in an increase in producer surplus? Did it result in an increase in total surplus?[26]

---

[26] "Evidence Mounts of Bid-Rigging in Milk Industry," *New York Times*, May 23, 1993.

13

Game Theory and Strategic Behavior

INTRODUCTION

Since oligopolies abound in the modern economy, and since some of the most fundamental theories of oligopoly behavior have yet to be presented, we continue our treatment of oligopoly in this chapter. As we already know, a basic feature of oligopoly is that each firm must take account of its rivals' reactions to its own actions. For example, Peter Bijur, chairman of Texaco, cannot tell what effect an increase in Texaco's output will have on the price of gasoline and on its profits unless he understands how Texaco's rivals, like Exxon and Mobil, will respond to its output increase. Thus it seems clear that oligopolistic behavior has some of the characteristics of a game.

One of the most interesting developments in the theory of oligopoly in recent decades has been the appearance and elaboration of the theory of games, which has enriched oligopoly theory enormously.[1] In this chapter, we present a basic description of the objectives and concepts of game theory, and show how it sheds new light on some of the topics of the previous chapter, such as the firm's decision to cheat (or not cheat) on a cartel agreement and ways that a firm can deter entrants from invading its market, as well as on a variety of new topics. Finally, we discuss the effects of an oligopolistic market structure on price, output, and profits.

THE THEORY OF GAMES

Game theory attempts to study decision making in situations where there is a mixture of conflict and cooperation, as in oligopoly. A *game* is a competitive situation where two or more players pursue their own interests and no player can dictate the outcome. For example, poker is a game, and so is a situation in which two firms are engaged in competitive advertising campaigns. A game is described in terms of the players, the rules of the game, the payoffs of the game, and the information conditions that exist during the game. These elements, common to all conflict situations, are the fundamental characteristics of a game.

More specifically, a player, which may be a single person or an organization, is a decision-making unit. Each player has a certain amount of resources; the *rules of the game* describe how these resources can be used. For example, the rules of poker indicate how bets can be made and which hands are better than other hands. A *strategy* is a complete specification of what actions a player will take under each contingency in the playing of the game. For example, a corporation president might tell his subordinates how he wants an advertising campaign to start, and what should be done at subsequent points in time in response to various actions of competing firms.

The game's outcome clearly depends on the strategies used by each player. A player's *payoff* varies from game to game: It is win, lose, or draw in check-

---

[1] A seminal work on game theory was J. von Neumann and O. Morgenstern, *Theory of Games and Economic Behavior* (Princeton, N.J.: Princeton University Press, 1944). For more recent descriptions of game theory, see J. Tirole, "Noncooperative Game Theory: A User's Manual," in his *The Theory of Industrial Organization* (Cambridge, Mass.: MIT Press, 1988), and J. Eatwell, W. Milgate, and P. Newman (eds.), *Game Theory* (New York: Norton, 1989).

ers, and various sums of money in poker. For simplicity this section deals only with *two-person games,* games with only two players. The relevant features of a two-person game can be shown by constructing a *payoff matrix.* To illustrate, suppose that Coke and Pepsi are about to stage rival advertising campaigns and that each firm has a choice of emphasizing television ads or newspaper ads. The payoff, expressed in terms of profits for each firm, is shown in Table 13.1 for each combination of strategies. For example, if Coke emphasizes newspaper ads and Pepsi emphasizes television ads, Coke makes a profit of $300 million and Pepsi makes a profit of $200 million.

TABLE 13.1 Payoff Matrix: Advertising Campaigns		
	Possible strategies for Pepsi	
Possible strategies for Coke	Emphasize TV	Emphasize newspapers
Emphasize TV	Coke's profit: $200 million Pepsi's profit: $300 million	Coke's profit: $100 million Pepsi's profit: $200 million
Emphasize newspapers	Coke's profit: $300 million Pepsi's profit: $200 million	Coke's profit: $200 million Pepsi's profit: $100 million

This is an example of a game where the players move simultaneously. Each player selects a strategy before observing any action or strategy chosen by the other player. Not all games are of this type. As we shall see, in some games one of the players goes first, after which the other player responds.

In this game, there is a *dominant strategy* for each player. Regardless of whether Pepsi emphasizes television or newspaper ads, Coke will make more profit if it emphasizes newspaper rather than television ads. Thus, emphasizing newspaper ads is Coke's dominant strategy. Similarly, regardless of whether Coke emphasizes television or newspaper ads, Pepsi will make more profit if it emphasizes television rather than newspaper ads. Thus, emphasizing television ads is Pepsi's dominant strategy. The solution to this game is quite simple. Coke emphasizes newspaper ads, and Pepsi emphasizes television ads. Coke's profit is $300 million, and Pepsi's profit is $200 million. This is the best that either player — that is, either firm — can do.

One additional point should be noted regarding this game. The best strategies are the same regardless of whether the players choose their strategies simultaneously or whether one or the other player goes first. Thus Coke will choose the same strategy (emphasizing newspaper ads) regardless of whether it moves before, after, or at the same time as Pepsi. As we shall see, this is not always true. In some games, a player's best strategy depends on the timing of the player's move.

NASH EQUILIBRIUM: FURTHER DISCUSSION

Not all games have a dominant strategy for every player. For example, suppose that the payoff matrix for Coke and Pepsi is that shown in Table 13.2. (This is the same as the payoff matrix in Table 13.1 except that Pepsi's profit is $300 million, not $100 million, if both firms emphasize newspaper ads.) Under these circumstances, Coke still has a dominant strategy: to emphasize newspaper ads. Regardless of which strategy Pepsi adopts, this is Coke's best strategy. But Pepsi no longer has a dominant strategy, since its optimal strategy depends on what Coke decides to do. If Coke emphasizes television ads, Pepsi will make more profit if it emphasizes television ads rather than newspaper ads. If Coke emphasizes newspaper ads, Pepsi will make more profit if it emphasizes newspaper ads rather than television ads.

TABLE 13.2 Payoff Matrix: No Dominant Strategy for Pepsi

Possible strategies for Coke	Possible strategies for Pepsi	
	Emphasize TV	Emphasize newspapers
Emphasize TV	Coke's profit: $200 million Pepsi's profit: $300 million	Coke's profit: $100 million Pepsi's profit: $200 million
Emphasize newspapers	Coke's profit: $300 million Pepsi's profit: $200 million	Coke's profit: $200 million Pepsi's profit: $300 million

To figure out what to do, Pepsi must try to determine what action Coke is likely to take. In other words, Pepsi must put itself in Coke's place, and see whether emphasizing television ads or emphasizing newspaper ads is best for Coke. As pointed out in the previous paragraph, Coke's dominant strategy is to emphasize newspapers. Since Pepsi knows all the numbers in the payoff matrix, it can readily determine that this is the case. Thus, it will conclude that Coke will emphasize newspaper ads, and that it should therefore do the same (because this is Pepsi's optimal strategy if Coke emphasizes newspaper ads).

Consequently, Coke would be expected to emphasize newspaper ads, and Pepsi would be expected to do the same. This is the *Nash equilibrium* for this game. A Nash equilibrium occurs if each player's strategy is optimal, given the strategies chosen by the other player(s). Put differently, *a Nash equilibrium is a set of strategies (in this case, an emphasis on newspaper ads by both firms) such that each player believes (accurately) that it is doing the best it can given the strategy of the other player(s)*. Taking the other firm's decision as given, both Coke and

Pepsi are pursuing their own best interests by emphasizing newspaper ads. Neither regrets its own decision, or has any incentive to change it.

The idea of a Nash equilibrium is not new. On the contrary, we took up this concept in the previous chapter and used the Cournot model to illustrate it. But several new points should be noted. For one thing, it is important to recognize the difference between a Nash equilibrium and an equilibrium where each player has a dominant strategy (as in Table 13.1). If each player has a dominant strategy, this strategy is its best choice *regardless of what other players do*. In a Nash equilibrium, each player adopts a strategy that is its best choice *given what the other players do*. It is also important to recognize that some games do not have a Nash equilibrium, and that some games have more than one Nash equilibrium. Table 13.3 contains the payoff matrix for a game with two Nash equilibria. If firm I adopts strategy *A* and firm II adopts strategy 1, each is doing the best it can, given the other's choice of strategy. Also, if firm I adopts strategy *B* and firm II adopts strategy 2, each is doing the best it can, given the other's choice of strategy. Hence, there are two Nash equilibria in this game.

TABLE 13.3 Payoff Matrix: Two Nash Equilibria

Possible strategies for firm I	Possible strategies for firm II	
	1	2
A	Firm I's profit: $3 million Firm II's profit: $3 million	Firm I's profit: zero Firm II's profit: zero
B	Firm I's profit: zero Firm II's profit: zero	Firm I's profit: $3 million Firm II's profit: $3 million

MAXIMIN STRATEGIES

A Nash equilibrium is based on the rationality of the players. Pepsi's choice of strategy hinges on Coke's rationality as well as its own. Suppose that the payoff matrix is that in Table 13.4 rather than Table 13.2. Following the line of reasoning in the previous section, Pepsi will expect Coke to emphasize newspaper ads because this is Coke's dominant strategy. Thus, Pepsi will do the same since, if Coke emphasizes newspaper ads, Pepsi's optimal strategy is to follow suit.

But a careful inspection of Table 13.4 shows that Pepsi had better be sure that Coke is rational. If Coke decides for some reason to emphasize TV ads,

TABLE 13.4 Payoff Matrix: Maximin Strategy

Possible strategies for Coke	Possible strategies for Pepsi	
	Emphasize TV	Emphasize newspapers
Emphasize TV	Coke's profit: $200 million Pepsi's profit: $300 million	Coke's profit: $100 million Pepsi's profit: zero
Emphasize newspapers	Coke's profit: $300 million Pepsi's profit: $200 million	Coke's profit: $200 million Pepsi's profit: $300 million

Pepsi's strategy of emphasizing newspapers will be disastrous; its profits will be zero. Thus, if Pepsi has a cautious management that is concerned that Coke's managers may not be on top of the situation or rational (in the sense the word is used here), it may choose the strategy of emphasizing TV ads.

Economists call this a *maximin strategy* because it maximizes the minimum gain that can be achieved. Such a strategy is conservative, not profit maximizing. In effect, a player maximizes his or her payoff under the assumption that the other player will adopt the strategy most damaging to him or her. Many economists feel that this is an unnecessarily pessimistic outlook for the player who, by adopting a maximin strategy, is likely to forgo considerable extra profit. Nonetheless, strategies of this sort are sometimes used.

THE PRISONERS' DILEMMA

Having described the basic features of game theory, we turn our attention to an important type of game, known as the *prisoners' dilemma,* which has proved of use in oligopoly theory, as well as in many other areas of economics and behavioral (and political) science. Consider a situation where two persons, John Dillinger and Dutch Schultz, are arrested after committing a crime. The police lock each person in a separate room and offer each one the following deal: "If you confess, while your partner does not confess, you will get a 2-year jail term, while he will get 12 years." Each person knows that if they both confess, each will get 10 years (not 12 years because they cooperated with the police). If neither confesses, each will get only 3 years because the evidence against them is weak.

Both Dillinger and Schultz have two possible strategies: to confess or not to confess. The four possible outcomes, depending on which strategy each per-

Prisoners' dilemma

> ### EXAMPLE 13.1
>
> Should Amherst Buy All Its Steel from Duquesne?
>
> The Amherst Company must decide whether to buy all or part of its steel from the Duquesne Corporation. If Duquesne provides prompt delivery of the steel it sells Amherst, Amherst will make $2 million if it buys all its steel from Duquesne and $1 million if it buys only part from Duquesne. But if Duquesne does not provide prompt delivery, Amherst will lose $50 million if it buys all its steel from Duquesne and $1 million if it buys only part from Duquesne. If it receives an order for all of Amherst's steel requirements, Duquesne will make $3 million if it provides prompt delivery and $2 million if it does not do so. If it receives an order for part of Amherst's steel requirements, Duquesne will make $2 million if it provides prompt delivery and $1 million if it does not do so.
>
> (a) Amherst must decide whether to buy all or part of its steel from Duquesne, and Duquesne must decide whether or not to provide prompt delivery. What is the payoff matrix for this game? (b) Does each player have a dominant strategy? If so, what is it? (c) Does this game have a Nash equilibrium? If so, what is it? (d) Suppose that Duquesne's managers are known to be inefficient and not much interested in how much money their firm makes. Do you think that Amherst will act in accord with the Nash equilibrium? Why or why not?
>
> | SOLUTION: | (a) The payoff matrix is as follows: |
>
> | Possible strategies for Amherst | Possible strategies for Duquesne | |
> |---|---|---|
> | | Provide prompt delivery | Do not provide prompt delivery |
> | Buy all steel from Duquesne | Amherst's profit: $2 million
Duquesne's profit: $3 million | Amherst's profit: −$50 million
Duquesne's profit: $ 2 million |
> | Buy part of steel from Duquesne | Amherst's profit: $1 million
Duquesne's profit: $2 million | Amherst's profit: −$ 1 million
Duquesne's profit: $ 1 million |
>
> (b) Duquesne has a dominant strategy, which is to provide prompt delivery. Regardless of which strategy is chosen by Amherst, Duquesne makes more money if it provides prompt delivery than if it does not do so. Amherst does not have a dominant strategy, since its optimal strategy depends on whether or not Duquesne provides prompt delivery. (c) Yes. The Nash equilibrium is for Amherst to buy all its steel from Duquesne and for Duquesne to provide prompt delivery. Each firm is doing the best it can, given the other firm's strategy. (d) Probably not. A

> Nash equilibrium assumes that all players are "rational" in the sense that they will adopt whatever strategy results in maximum profit. If Duquesne is not "rational" in this sense, it might not provide prompt delivery even though its failure to do so would reduce its profit, the result being that Amherst would lose $50 million if it bought all its steel from Duquesne. If Amherst has strong enough doubts about Duquesne's "rationality" (or is uncertain about what Duquesne's true payoffs are), it may buy only part of its steel from Duquesne, thus cutting its potential loss (if Duquesne does not provide prompt delivery) from $50 million to $1 million. In other words, it may adopt a maximin strategy.*
>
> ------
>
> *For further relevant discussion, see Tirole, *The Theory of Industrial Organization.*

son chooses, are shown in the payoff matrix in Table 13.5. What strategy will Schultz choose? If Dillinger does not confess, the better strategy for Schultz is to confess, since Schultz will serve less time (2 years) than if he does not confess (3 years). If Dillinger confesses, the better strategy for Schultz is to confess, since Schultz will serve less time (10 years) than if he does not confess (12 years). Thus Schultz will confess, since regardless of which strategy Dillinger adopts, Schultz is better off to confess than not to confess.

Similarly, Dillinger too will confess since, regardless of which strategy Schultz adopts, Dillinger is better off to confess than not to confess. To see this, note that, if Schultz does not confess, the better strategy for Dillinger is to confess, since Dillinger will serve less time (2 years) than if he does not confess (3 years). Also, if Schultz confesses, the better strategy for Dillinger is to confess, since Dillinger will serve less time (10 years) than if he does not confess (12 years).

Thus, in this situation, it appears that both Dillinger and Schultz will confess. This is the dominant strategy for each player. (Prove to yourself that it is

TABLE 13.5 Payoff Matrix: Dillinger and Schultz		
Possible strategies for John Dillinger	Possible strategies for Dutch Schultz	
	Confess	Do not confess
Confess	Both get 10-year jail terms.	Dillinger gets 2 years; Schultz gets 12 years.
Do not Confess	Dillinger gets 12 years; Schultz gets 2 years.	Both get 3-year jail terms.

also the maximin strategy for each player.) But it is important to recognize that each is doing worse than if neither of them confessed. If they could trust each other not to confess, or if they were able to communicate with one another (and thus if each could assure himself that the other would not confess), each could serve 3 years rather than 10 years. However, because there is no way for them to coordinate their decisions (and to trust each other), they serve the longer prison term.

CHEATING ON A CARTEL AGREEMENT

The type of game discussed in the previous section — the so-called prisoners' dilemma — is useful in analyzing oligopoly behavior. For example, it can help to indicate the circumstances under which firms will tend to cheat (that is, secretly cut price) on a cartel agreement. As we stressed in the previous chapter, there frequently is a temptation for cartel members to cheat in this way.

Suppose that the only two producers of lasers — Ambler, Inc., and the Elysian Company — form a cartel. Each firm has two possible strategies: to stick by the cartel agreement or to cheat. There are four possible outcomes, depending on which strategy each firm pursues. They are shown in Table 13.6.

What should Ambler do? If Elysian sticks by the agreement, it appears that the better strategy for Ambler is to cheat, since Ambler's profits will be greater than if it sticks by the agreement. If Elysian cheats, the better strategy for Ambler seems to be to cheat as well, since Ambler's profits will be higher than if it sticks by the agreement. Thus it appears that *Ambler will choose the strategy of cheating since regardless of which strategy Elysian adopts, Ambler seems better-off by cheating than by sticking by the agreement.*

What should Elysian do? If Ambler sticks by the agreement, the better strategy for Elysian appears to be to cheat, since Elysian's profits will be greater than if it sticks by the agreement. If Ambler cheats, the better strategy for

Possible strategies for Ambler	**Possible strategies for Elysian**	
	Stick by agreement	Cheat
Stick by agreement	Ambler's profit: $4 million Elysian's profit: $4 million	Ambler's profit: $1 million Elysian's profit: $5 million
Cheat	Ambler's profit: $5 million Elysian's profit: $1 million	Ambler's profit: $3 million Elysian's profit: $3 million

TABLE 13.6 Payoff Matrix: Ambler and Elysian

Elysian appears to be to cheat as well, since Elysian's profits will be higher than if it sticks by the agreement. Thus it seems that *Elysian will choose the strategy of cheating, since regardless of which strategy Ambler adopts, Elysian is better-off by cheating than by sticking by the agreement.*

Consequently, in this situation it appears that both firms will cheat. Like the game in Table 13.5 involving John Dillinger and Dutch Schultz, this is an example of the prisoners' dilemma. Recall that, because neither Dillinger nor Schultz could trust the other not to confess, both wound up serving more time in jail (10 years versus 3 years) than if they had trusted each other. Similarly, Ambler and Elysian, because they do not trust each other to stick by their agreement, wind up with lower profits than if they both were to stick by the agreement ($3 million versus $4 million).

REPEATED PRISONERS' DILEMMA AND TIT FOR TAT

At this point, it is essential to recognize that there is an important difference between the situation facing Ambler and Elysian and that facing Dillinger and Schultz. In the case of Dillinger and Schultz, if this was the only crime they performed together and if they did not intend to work together again, it may have been reasonable for each of them to assume that they would play this game only once. But for Ambler and Elysian, such an assumption would not be reasonable. At every point in time, each of these firms must decide whether it will cheat or not. Since they are continually dealing with customers, they must continually decide whether or not to secretly cut price.

Repeated prisoners' dilemma

Because Ambler and Elysian play this game repeatedly, the analysis in the previous section may not be correct. To see this, suppose that Ambler refuses to cheat the first time it must make a decision and that it continues to stick by the agreement so long as Elysian does so. But if Elysian fails even once to cooperate, Ambler will revert forever to the safe policy of cheating. If Elysian adopts the same sort of policy, then each can reap profits of $4 million. If either one cheats, it will raise its profit to $5 million for a brief period of time, but subsequently its profit will fall permanently to $3 million. Thus it will not be in the interest of either firm to cheat.[2]

---

[2] This assumes that the game is repeated indefinitely. If it is repeated only a finite number of times, there may, of course, be a tendency to cheat in the final periods. Indeed, in an effort to be the first to start cheating, players may cause the situation to unravel, and cheating may begin im-

It is important to recognize that Ambler and Elysian can achieve this outcome even if they do not collude or make any binding agreements. If each presumes that the other will have the intelligence to maintain the monopoly price, their presumptions will tend to be correct. As David Hume, the eighteenth-century British economist, put it over 200 years ago,

> I learn to do a service to another, without bearing him any real kindness; because I foresee that he will return my service, in expectation of another of the same kind, and in order to maintain the same correspondence of good offices with me or with others. And accordingly, after I have served him, and he is in possession of the advantage arising from my action, he is induced to perform his part, as foreseeing the consequences of his refusal.[3]

Tit for tat According to Robert Axelrod of the University of Michigan, a good strategy for each player is *tit for tat,* which means that each player should do on this round whatever the other player did on the previous round. If Ambler pursues a tit-for-tat strategy, it should abide by the agreement on the first round. If Elysian also abides by it, Ambler should continue to do so, but once Elysian cheats, Ambler should retaliate by cheating as well. Robert Axelrod's experimental results, based on a computer analysis of the results of various strategies, suggest that this is a very effective approach.[4]

In accord with Axelrod's findings, some cartels seem to have adopted tit-for-tat strategies in the past. For example, the cartel that set the price of railroad freight in the United States in the 1880s (prior to the Sherman Antitrust Act) retaliated against member firms that cut price to increase their market shares. When such cheating occurred, the other members of the cartel would cut their own price as well, inflicting economic damage on the price cutters.[5]

---

mediately. However, if firms have doubts about the rationality (in the narrow sense of the word used here) of their rivals, they may not cheat even if the game is played only a finite number of times. See D. Kreps, P. Milgrom, J. Roberts, and R. Wilson, "Rational Cooperation in the Finitely Repeated Prisoners' Dilemma," *Journal of Economic Theory,* 1982.

[3] J. Friedman, *Game Theory with Applications to Economics* (New York: Oxford University Press, 1986), p. 70. Of course, this assumes that each firm can quickly detect whether the other firm is cheating. In fact, this may not be so easy. In some cases, trade associations have been authorized to collect detailed information concerning each firm's transactions. In this way, an attempt has been made to detect cheating quickly. Of course, the quicker cheating is detected, the less profitable it tends to be.

[4] R. Axelrod, *The Evolution of Cooperation* (New York: Basic Books, 1984).

[5] R. Porter, "A Study of Cartel Stability," *Bell Journal of Economics,* Autumn 1983.

STRATEGIC MOVES

In previous sections of this chapter, we have emphasized that oligopolists must recognize that their own profits depend on the decisions and behavior of their rivals, as well as on their own decisions and behavior. Given that this is the case, each oligopolist must decide on which strategic moves to make. According to Maryland's Thomas Schelling, who has made important contributions to the theory of strategic decision making, "A strategic move is one that influences the other person's choice in a manner favorable to one's self, by affecting the other person's expectations on how one's self will behave."[6] For example, if DuPont reacts to a rival's price cut by reducing its own price to a level that imposes losses on its rival, this is a strategic move. It influences how other firms can expect DuPont to behave.

Firms can engage in a variety of types of strategic moves. Some moves are not in any sense threatening to a firm's rivals. Thus Hewlett Packard may raise its price, hoping that its rivals will go along with the price increase. The problem with such a move is that other firms may not cooperate. For example, Hewlett Packard's rivals may not go along with the price increase. If such a move can be rescinded quickly and cheaply, this problem may not be very important, but if this is not the case, such a move can be very risky. *Nonthreatening moves*

Other moves are threatening to a firm's rivals. For example, the American Hospital Supply Corporation developed a new container for intravenous solutions, which it began to market. This move threatened Baxter Travenol Laboratories, which already sold products of this type. In weighing the pros and cons of making such a move, a firm must try to estimate how likely it is that there will be retaliation, and how quick and effective this retaliation will be. In the case of the American Hospital Supply Corporation, it met substantial retaliation from Baxter, which cut its prices considerably and tried hard to wrest business away from American Hospital Supply Corporation.[7] *Threatening moves*

To prevent its rivals from carrying out threatening moves, a firm often behaves in such a way as to lead its rivals to believe that they can expect rapid and effective retaliation if they carry out such a move. For example, firms often en-

---

[6] T. Schelling, *The Strategy of Conflict* (New York: Oxford University Press, 1960). Another important book in this area is M. Porter, *Competitive Strategy* (New York: Free Press, 1980). Many of the concepts and results discussed in this chapter are treated in more detail in these two books.

[7] Ibid.

gage in vicious price cutting to drive out a firm that enters their market, the idea being that this will teach other potential entrants that it does not pay to threaten or challenge them.

**Commit-
ment**
　　　An important element of a firm's strategic planning is *commitment*. If a firm can convince its rivals that it is unequivocally committed to a particular move that it is making, they may back down without retaliating, since they may be convinced that they would lose more than they would gain from a protracted struggle. If a firm can convince its rivals that it is unequivocally committed to retaliate if a rival makes particular moves, no rival may make such a move. And if a firm can convince its rivals that it is unequivocally committed to take no (threatening) actions of a particular type, they may eventually begin to trust this firm not to do so.

　　　A commitment tends to be more persuasive if it seems binding and irreversible. For example, suppose that a firm commits itself to enter a particular market. If this firm buys a plant rather than leases it, or if it signs a long-term, rather than a short-term, contract for raw materials, this is an indication that this firm is irreversibly committed to entering the market in question. Or suppose that a firm commits itself to meet price reductions by its rivals. If this firm makes written or verbal agreements with customers to meet price cuts, these agreements can make such a commitment irreversible — and hence more persuasive. On the other hand, if a firm's rivals feel that it can easily renounce or ignore a particular commitment that it makes (much as politicians frequently do), they are not likely to pay as much attention to this commitment.

　　　To be credible, a firm's commitments must be backed up with the assets and expertise required to carry out the commitment. Thus, if a firm commits itself to invade another firm's market if the latter firm invades its market, it must have the financial and technological power and skills needed to carry out this commitment. Also, a firm's commitments are more credible if it has a long history of adherence to past commitments. Here, as in other aspects of life, a firm's (and its managers') reputation counts. If a firm has a well-deserved reputation for honoring its past commitments, its rivals are likely to pay careful attention to whatever new commitments it makes.

THREATS: EMPTY AND CREDIBLE

Firms frequently send signals to one another indicating their intentions, motives, and objectives. Some signals are threats. For example, suppose that the Smith Company learns that the Jones Corporation, its principal rival, intends to lower its price. Smith may announce its intention of lowering its own price

TABLE 13.7 Payoff Matrix: Smith and Jones

Possible strategies for Smith	Possible strategies for Jones	
	Low price	High price
Low price	Smith's profit: $ 1 million Jones's profit: $ 2 million	Smith's profit: $ 2 million Jones's profit: − $ 1 million
High price	Smith's profit: $ 6 million Jones's profit: $10 million	Smith's profit: $10 million Jones's profit: $ 7 million

significantly, signaling to Jones that it is willing to engage in a price war if Jones goes ahead with its price reduction. Indeed, some of Smith's executives may see to it that this message gets transmitted indirectly to some of Jones's executives.

But not all threats are credible. If, for example, the payoff matrix is as shown in Table 13.7, Smith's threat is not very credible. To see why, let's compare Smith's profits if it sets a low price with its profits if it sets a high price. (For simplicity, we assume that price can be set at only two levels.) If Jones sets a high price, Smith makes $10 million if it sets a high price and $2 million if it sets a low price. If Jones sets a low price, Smith makes $6 million if it sets a high price and $1 million if it sets a low price. Thus, regardless of whether Jones sets a high or low price, Smith will do better if it sets a high price than a low price.

Given that this is the case, it certainly seems unlikely that Smith will carry out its threat to cut its price to the low level. After all, as we've just seen, if Jones does cut its price to the low level, Smith will earn higher profits by keeping its price at the high level. Consequently, if Jones can be sure that Smith will take the course of action that maximizes Smith's profit, it can dismiss Smith's threat as no more than an empty gesture.

However, if Smith can convince Jones that it is *not* going to take the course of action that maximizes its profit, it can make its threat credible. Specifically, if it can convince Jones that, if Jones sets the low price, it will match it, *even though this lowers Smith's own profits,* Jones may decide not to set the low price. After all, Jones's profits are higher ($7 million versus $2 million) if it maintains a high price (and Smith does the same) than if Jones sets a low price (and Smith does the same).

How can Smith convince Jones that it will lower its price, even though this seems to be irrational? One way is for Smith's managers to develop a reputation for doing what they say, "regardless of the costs." They may have a well-publicized taste for facing down opponents and for refusing to back down, regardless of how crazy they may seem. Faced with the "irrational" Smith Company, the Jones Corporation may decide not to cut price. But if Smith cannot convince Jones if its "irrationality," Jones will rightly regard Smith's threat to lower price as not being credible.

THE DETERRENCE OF ENTRY

Firms, like countries and politicians, try to discourage entrants from invading their turf. As we saw in the previous chapter, the entry of new firms tends to reduce the profits of existing firms. To illustrate the situation, consider the Mason Company, which faces the threat of entry by the Newton Company. Table 13.8 shows the profits of each firm, depending on whether Newton enters the market and on whether Mason resists Newton's entry (for example, by cutting price and increasing output).[8]

TABLE 13.8 Payoff Matrix, before Mason Makes Credible Its Threat to Resist

Possible strategies for Mason Company	Possible strategies for Newton Company	
	Enter	Do not enter[a]
Resist entry	Mason's profit: $ 2 million Newton's profit: $ 5 million	Mason's profit: $12 million Newton's profit: $ 8 million
Do not resist entry	Mason's profit: $ 3 million Newton's profit: $11 million	Mason's profit: $12 million Newton's profit: $ 8 million

[a]See footnote 8.

In this game, the first move is up to Newton, which must decide whether to enter. If it enters, Mason must decide whether to resist. Based on the payoff matrix in Table 13. 8, Mason, if it is "rational," will not resist because its profits will be $1 million less (that is, $2 million rather than $3 million) if it resists than if it does not resist. Knowing this, Newton will enter because its profits will be $3 million higher (that is, $11 million rather than $8 million) if it enters than if it does not enter. Of course, Mason may well threaten to resist, but given the nature of the payoff matrix in Table 13.8, this threat is not credible (if Mason is "rational") because resistance by Mason would lower profits.

What can Mason do to deter Newton's entry into the market? It can alter the payoff matrix. For example, suppose that it builds excess production capacity — capacity that is unnecessary if Newton does not enter, but that will be used to increase output (and lower price) if Newton enters. Because it costs money to keep excess capacity on hand, Mason's profits are reduced by $2 million if it does not resist entry or if Newton does not enter; the new payoff ma-

Making resistance credible

---

[8] If Newton does not enter the market, there is no difference between Mason's resisting and not resisting, so the profit figures are the same, regardless of which strategy Mason is assumed to adopt.

| Possible strategies | Possible strategies for Newton Company | |
for Mason Company	Enter	Do not enter
Resist entry	Mason's profit: $ 2 million Newton's profit: $ 5 million	Mason's profit: $10 million Newton's profit: $ 8 million
Do not resist entry	Mason's profit: $ 1 million Newton's profit: $11 million	Mason's profit: $10 million Newton's profit: $ 8 million

TABLE 13.9 Payoff Matrix, after Mason Makes Credible Its Threat to Resist

trix is as shown in Table 13.9.[9] Mason's profits are now greater ($2 million versus $1 million) if it resists Newton's entry than if it does not resist. Thus Mason's threat to resist becomes credible, and Newton will not enter because its profits will be $3 million lower (that is, $5 million rather than $8 million) if it enters than if it does not enter.

Paradoxical as it may seem, Mason has succeeded in convincing Newton not to enter *by reducing its own profits if it does not resist entry.* This is an irrevocable commitment by Mason to fight. If Newton enters, Mason is ready to fight (by increasing output and driving price down), and has an incentive to fight (since its profits are higher than if it does not fight). It has gained an advantage by committing itself in this way to resist entry.

But harking back to the previous section, this is not the only way for Mason to convince Newton not to enter. If Mason has imposed huge losses on every firm that has tried to enter in the past, and it has a reputation for "irrational" resistance to entry, Newton may decide that Mason is too tough an opponent to challenge. Thus it may be in Mason's interests to foster such a reputation by declaring total war on every entrant that appears, since the short-term losses from these wars may be more than offset by the longer-term gains from the prevention of entry.

LIMIT PRICING

A *limit price* is a price that discourages or prevents entry. Economists often have asserted that a firm can deter entry by keeping its price relatively low. In recent years, Stanford's Paul Milgrom and John Roberts have provided an in-

---

[9] For simplicity, we assume that these are the only changes in the payoff matrix due to Mason's construction of excess production capacity. In fact, there may be other changes, but from a pedagogical point of view, it is convenient to assume that they do not exist.

teresting explanation, based on game theory, of why this may be true.[10] Suppose that the Moran Manufacturing Company is a very low-cost producer of hardware. If potential entrants knew how low its costs really are, they would not be foolish enough to enter the industry (because they would recognize that they have no chance to survive). But they have no reliable way of telling what Moran's costs are, since hardware is only one of its products, and its accounting statements are useless for this purpose.

Price as a signal
To signal potential entrants that it is a very low-cost producer, Moran may find it worthwhile and effective to set a relatively low price. Of course, this will lower Moran's profits in the short run, but it may result in bigger profits over the long run because of the reduced likelihood that Moran will have to compete with entrants. Why can't Moran simply announce that its costs are very low? Because potential entrants are smart (and suspicious) enough to recognize that such announcements may be lies aimed at discouraging entry. However, under the proper circumstances, a relatively low price may be reasonably convincing evidence that Moran really is a very low-cost producer — and that entry would be unwise.

FIRST-MOVER ADVANTAGES

In many situations, the firm that makes the first move has a substantial advantage. (As Andrew Carnegie, the steel magnate, put it, "The first person gets the oyster, the second person gets the shell.") For example, suppose that two firms, *A* and *B*, are about to introduce a new product, and that each must choose whether to tailor its product for the civilian or military market. Table 13.10

TABLE 13.10 Payoff Matrix: Firms A and B

Possible strategies for firm *A*	Possible strategies for firm *B*	
	Tailor product for civilian market	Tailor product for military market
Tailor product for civilian market	Firm *A*'s profit: − $10 million Firm *B*'s profit: − $10 million	Firm *A*'s profit: $30 million Firm *B*'s profit: $15 million
Tailor product for military market	Firm *A*'s profit: $15 million Firm *B*'s profit: $30 million	Firm *A*'s profit: − $10 million Firm *B*'s profit: − $10 million

---

[10] Paul Milgrom and John Roberts, "Limit Pricing and Entry under Incomplete Information: An Equilibrium Analysis," *Econometrica,* March 1982.

shows the relevant payoff matrix. If both firms tailor their products for the same market (civilian or military), both will lose $10 million because these markets are too small to support two (profitable) producers. If one firm tailors its products for the civilian market while the other firm focuses on the military market, it will make $30 million, and its rival will make $15 million, since the civilian market for this product is more profitable than the military market.

If each firm must make this choice independently and without any information concerning what the other firm will do, it is likely that both will tailor their products to the civilian market. After all, this is the more profitable market. But the result (as Table 13.10 shows) will be that both will lose $10 million.

On the other hand, if one of these firms — say firm *A* — can introduce its product before the other firm does so, it enjoys a great advantage. It can tailor its product to the civilian market, since this market is more profitable than the military market. Of course, if the other firm — firm *B* — enters the civilian market too, both will lose money. But given that firm *A* has already entered the civilian market, firm *B* is unlikely to enter it too. Why? Because this would result in a substantial loss for firm *B*, whereas if firm *B* enters the military market, it will earn a tidy profit — not as big a profit as if it had made the first move (and thus could have been the sole producer in the civilian market), but a tidy profit nonetheless. Hence, it seems likely that, if one of these firms has the first move, it will tailor its product to the civilian market, and that the other firm will tailor its product to the military market.

Frequently, firms try to commit themselves first to a particular move, even if they cannot be first to actually carry out this move. For example, suppose that neither of the above firms can introduce its product before the introduction of the other firm's product. Firm *A* may announce that it is about to introduce a new product tailored for the civilian market. It may engage in an expensive advertising campaign, and begin to order the sorts of materials needed to produce a civilian version of the new product. It may even go so far as to begin seeking orders from civilian customers. In this way, firm *A* tries to persuade firm *B* that it is committed to entering the civilian market and that there is nothing that firm *B* can do to prevent it. Firm *A*'s intention is to convince firm *B* to settle for the military market and offer no resistance to firm *A*'s entry into the civilian market.

First-mover advantages

CAPACITY EXPANSION AND PREEMPTION

The decision of whether — and if so, how much — to expand production capacity is one of the most important strategic decisions made by a firm. Some firms adopt a preemptive strategy; that is, they try to expand before their rivals

EXAMPLE 13.2

The Role of Incentives and Contracts

Suppose the Intel Corporation and the Microsoft Corporation are considering engaging in a joint venture. Each will have to invest $10 million in assets that are of no use or value outside this project. If both firms act in accord with their promises, the annual economic profit to each firm is $2.5 million. If one or both do not act in this way, the annual economic profit to each is as shown below:

Possible strategies for Intel	Possible strategies for Microsoft			
	Act in accord with promises		Do not act in accord with promises	
Act in accord with promises	Intel's profit:	$2.5 million	Intel's's profit:	−$1 million
	Microsoft's profit:	$2.5 million	Microsoft's profit:	$5 million
Do not act in accord with promises	Intel's profit:	$5 million	Intel's profit:	zero
	Microsoft's profit:	−$1 million	Microsoft's profit:	zero

(a) If a contract can be formulated that will ensure that both firms will act in accord with their promises, will this contract be drawn up and signed by both firms (if the attorneys' fees are nominal)? Why or why not? (b) If such a contract cannot be formulated, will either firm enter into the joint venture? Why or why not? (c) Why may it be very difficult to formulate an effective contract of this sort? (d) Is this an ordinary prisoners' dilemma game? If not, why not?

SOLUTION: (a) Yes, because both firms will make an economic profit of $2.5 million (before deducting the attorneys' fees). Recall that an economic profit is profit above what could have been earned from alternative ways of investing the $10 million. (b) Without such a contract, each firm would have an incentive not to act in accord with its promises once both had invested in the joint venture. To see this, note that, whether or not Intel acts in accord with its promises, Microsoft would make more money by not acting in accord with its promises than by doing so. Similarly, whether or not Microsoft acts in accord with its promises, Intel would make more money by not acting in accord with its promises than by doing so. Perhaps both nonetheless would trust each other, but if they did so and one did not keep its promises, the relevant managers of the other firm might be vulnerable to criticism, perhaps dismissal. Thus, the relevant managers of

one or both firms may not be willing to take the risks. (c) It is very difficult to foresee the full range of circumstances that may prevail in the future and to specify in a contract completely and unambiguously what
action each firm is to take under each possible set of circumstances.
Often it is impractical to attempt to formulate such a contract. (d) No.
In this case both firms have the option of not playing the game.*

---

*For further discussion, see P. Milgrom and J. Roberts, *Economics, Organization, and
Management* (Englewood Cliffs, N.J.: Prentice-Hall, 1992); F. Joskow, "Vertical
Integration and Long-Term Contracts," *Journal of Law, Economics, and Organization,*
Spring 1985; and B. Klein, R. Crawford, and A. Alchian, "Vertical Integration,
Appropriate Rents, and the Competitive Contracting Process," *Journal of Law and
Economics,* 1978.

do, and thus discourage their rivals from building extra capacity of their own.
If the future growth of demand for a particular product is known with reasonable precision, such a strategy can be effective.

Suppose that two firms, Monroe Company and the Madison Corporation,
are the only producers and sellers of a particular kind of machine tool. Since
the demand for this type of machine tool is growing substantially, each firm is
considering the construction of an additional plant. The payoff matrix is
shown in Table 13.11. If only one of the firms builds an additional plant, it will
make $10 million, but if both firms build an additional plant, both will lose $5
million, since there will be too much capacity. If neither firm builds an additional plant, both will earn zero profits.

Preemptive strategy

In this game, there are two Nash equilibria — one where Madison alone
builds an additional plant, and one where Monroe alone builds an additional
plant. Which equilibrium takes place is dependent on which firm moves

TABLE 13.11 Payoff Matrix: Monroe and Madison		
Possible strategies for Monroe	**Possible strategies for Madison**	
	Build additional plant	Do not build additional plant
Build additional plant	Monroe's profit: − $ 5 million Madison's profit: − $ 5 million	Monroe's profit: $10 million Madison's profit: zero
Do not build additional plant	Monroe's profit: zero Madison's profit: $10 million	Monroe's profit: zero Madison's profit: zero

first. If Madison moves first, it will choose to build an additional plant, since the rational response of Monroe is not to build an additional plant too (because if it did so, it would lose $5 million). Similarly, if Monroe moves first, it will choose to build an additional plant, since Madison's rational response is not to build an additional plant too.

However, such a preemptive strategy can be risky. For example, if the demand for the product grows more slowly than expected (or not at all), a firm that pursues this strategy may be stuck with a plant that is an unprofitable white elephant. Also, if a firm pursues this strategy, it must be careful to insure (as best it can) that its rival will respond "rationally." If its rival refuses to yield to this preemptive strategy, and builds its own additional plant, the industry is plunged into a war that may do serious harm to both firms. A firm that adopts a preemptive strategy of this sort could regret it.

NONPRICE COMPETITION

In many oligopolistic industries, firms tend to use nonprice competition, like advertising and variation in product characteristics, more than price, as strategic weapons. They seem to view price-cutting as a dangerous tactic, since it can start a price war that may have grave consequences. On the other hand, advertising and product variation are viewed as less-risky ways of wooing customers away from competitors.

When a firm advertises, it attempts to shift the demand curve for its product to the right. An effective advertising campaign will make it possible for a firm to sell more at the same price. (Recall page 389.) Firms use advertising to differentiate their product from those of their competitors. In this way customers may be induced to stick with a particular brand name, even though the products of all firms in the industry are much the same. For example, various brands of beer are quite similar, although not identical. The beer industry has spent hundreds of millions of dollars a year on advertising to impress their brand names, and whatever differences exist among brands, on the consumer.[11]

Sometimes advertising expenditures only have the effect of raising the costs of the entire industry, since one firm's advertising campaign causes other firms

---

[11] Other industries that spend very heavily on advertising are department stores, retail food stores, drugs and medicines, and cigarettes. See L. Telser, "Advertising and Cigarettes," *Journal of Business,* 1963, and W. Comanor and T. Wilson, *Advertising and Market Power* (Cambridge, Mass.: Harvard University Press, 1974), for historical material and analysis.

to increase their advertising. The total market for the industry's product may not increase in response to the increased advertising, and the effects on the sales of individual forms may be small, since the effects of the advertising may cancel out. However, once every firm has increased its advertising expenditures, no single firm can reduce them to their former size without losing sales. Thus the cost curves — including both production and selling costs — of the firms in the industry are pushed upward.

To see why an individual firm may spend a large amount on advertising even though its profits might have been higher with a smaller advertising budget, recall the prisoners' dilemma. If each firm believes that its profits will fall if its rival spends more on advertising, it may feel that a large advertising budget is in its own interest, although its profits, as well as those of its rival, would be greater if both it and its rival agreed to spend less on advertising. Consider the situation in Table 13.12. Both firms X and Y may adopt large advertising budgets (since this is the dominant strategy for each firm), even though both would enjoy higher profits ($4 million rather than $1 million) if they both adopted small advertising budgets.

Prisoners' dilemma revisited

TABLE 13.12 Payoff Matrix: Firms X and Y		
Possible strategies for firm Y	**Possible strategies for firm X**	
	Large advertising budget	Small advertising budget
Large advertising budget	Firm Y's profit: $1 million Firm X's profit: $1 million	Firm Y's profit: $5 million Firm X's profit: zero
Small advertising budget	Firm Y's profit: zero Firm X's profit: $5 million	Firm Y's profit: $4 million Firm X's profit: $4 million

Frequently a firm varies the characteristics of its product as well as advertises in order to differentiate its product from those of its competitors. Like advertising, one purpose of varying the firm's product is to manipulate the firm's demand curve. Of course, changes in product, like other competitive tactics, often result in retaliatory moves by competitors. Successful changes in product design or product quality tend to be imitated by competitors, although with a lag of varying lengths. The costs of competition through style and quality of product can be very great. For example, the automobile industry has been engaged for many years in intense competition of this sort; the annual cost of model changes has sometimes been $5 billion or more.[12]

---

[12] See L. White, *The Automobile Industry Since 1945* (Cambridge, Mass.: Harvard University Press, 1971), and F. Fisher, Z. Griliches, and C. Kaysen, "The Cost of Automobile Model Changes since 1949," *Journal of Political Economy,* October 1962, for historical data.

GAME TREES

Before leaving the topic of game theory, some attention should be devoted to game trees, which are often used to represent games. Suppose that firms A and B each must decide whether to expand its productive capacity and that firm A must make this decision first. The small square (with "Firm A" above it) on the left-hand side of Figure 13.1 is used to represent firm A's decision. From this square, firm A can take one of two branches, one labeled "Expand" (which means that firm A expands its capacity), the other labeled "Don't expand" (which means that firm A does not expand its capacity).

FIGURE 13.1   **A Game Tree** This game tree indicates that firm A will expand and firm B will not.

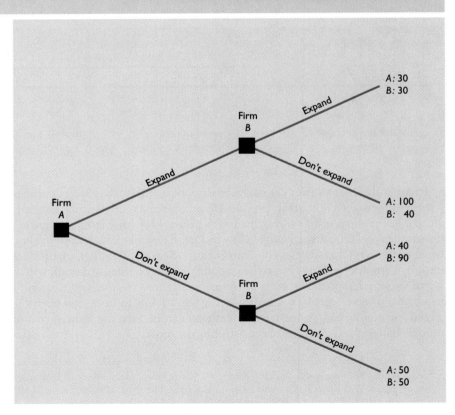

A: 30
B: 30

A: 100
B: 40

A: 40
B: 90

A: 50
B: 50

If firm A takes the upward branch (labeled "Expand"), the next decision is firm B's, represented by the small square (with "Firm B" above it) that this branch leads to. From this small square, firm B can take one of two branches, one labeled "Expand" (which means that firm B expands its productive capacity), the other labeled "Don't expand" (which means that firm B does not expand its productive capacity). The payoffs for each possible outcome (combination of actions) are shown at the end of each final branch. If both firms choose to expand, firm A's profit is $30 million and firm B's profit is $30 million. If firm A expands and firm B does not expand, firm A's profit is $100 million and firm B's profit is $40 million.

If firm A takes the lower branch (labeled "Don't expand"), this branch leads to a small square (with "Firm B" above it) which represents firm B's subsequent decision. From this small square, firm B can take one of two branches, one labeled "Expand" (which means that firm B expands its capacity), the other labeled "Don't expand" (which means that firm B does not expand its capacity). Here too the payoffs are at the end of each final branch. If firm A does not expand but firm B does, firm A's profit is $40 million and firm B's profit is $90 million. If neither firm expands, firm A's profit is $50 million and firm B's profit is $50 million.

The game tree in Figure 13.1 enables us to determine each firm's optimal strategy. If firm A expands, it is clear that firm B will not expand, since firm B's profit is $30 million if it expands and $40 million if it does not do so. If firm A does not expand, firm B will do so because firm B's profit is $90 million if it expands and $50 million if it does not do so. Thus, firm A will expand because its profit will be $100 million if it expands (since firm B will not expand) and $40 million if it does not expand (since firm B will expand). In sum, the game tree indicates that firm A will expand and firm B will not.

EFFECTS OF OLIGOPOLY

Finally, having completed our discussion of game theory, let's return to the general topic of oligopoly. In this and the last chapter, we have taken up some of the oligopoly models that economists have built. Since there is no agreement that any of these models is an adequate general representation of oligopolistic behavior, it is hard to gauge the effects of an oligopolistic market structure on price, output, and profits. Nevertheless, a few things can be said.

First, the models we have discussed usually indicate that price will be higher than under perfect competition. The difference between the oligopoly price and the perfectly competitive price will depend, of course, on the number of firms in the industry and the ease of entry. The larger the number of firms and the easier it is to enter the industry, the closer the oligopoly price will be to the perfectly competitive level.

Second, if the demand curve is the same under oligopoly as under perfect competition, it also follows that output will be less under oligopoly than under perfect competition. However, it is not always reasonable to assume that the demand curve is the same under oligopoly as under perfect competition, since the large expenditures for advertising and product variation that are incurred by some oligopolies may tend to shift the demand curve to the right. Consequently, in some cases both price and output may tend to be higher under oligopoly than under perfect competition.

Third, oligopolistic industries tend to spend large amounts on advertising and product differentiation. The use of some resources for these purposes is certainly worthwhile since advertising provides buyers with information, and product differentiation allows greater freedom of choice. Whether oligopolies spend too much for these purposes is by no means obvious, although it is sometimes claimed that in some oligopolistic industries such expenditures have been expanded beyond the levels that are socially optimal.[13]

Fourth, one would expect on the basis of most oligopoly models that the profits earned by oligopolists should be higher, on the average, than the profits earned by competitive firms. About 45 years ago, a seminal study by Berkeley's Joe Bain found that firms in industries in which the few largest firms had a high proportion of total sales tended to have higher rates of return than firms in industries in which the few largest firms had a small proportion of total sales. However, there has been considerable disagreement over the interpretation of such evidence. According to some economists, these results are due in considerable part to the largest firms' superior efficiency in oligopolistic industries.[14]

---

[13] Note that we are not talking here about expenditures on relatively fundamental research and development, when we talk about product differentiation. A great deal of existing product differentiation is based on relatively superfical differences among products.

[14] See J. Bain, "Relation of Profit Rate to Industry Concentration: American Manufacturing 1936–1940," *Quarterly Journal of Economics,* August 1951; H. Demsetz, "Industry Structure, Market Rivalry, and Public Policy," *Journal of Law and Economics,* April 1973; L. Weiss, "The Concentration-Profits Relationship and Antitrust," in H. Goldschmid, H. M. Mann, and J. F. Weston (eds.), *Industrial Concentration: The New Learning* (Boston: Little, Brown, 1974); and J. Kwoka, "The Effect of Market Share Distribution on Industry Performance," *Review of Economics and Statistics,* February 1979.

SUMMARY

1. A game is a competitive situation where two or more players pursue their own interests and no player can dictate the outcome. The relevant features of a two-person game can be shown by constructing a payoff matrix. In some games, each player has a dominant strategy — a strategy that is best regardless of what strategy the other player chooses. A game tree is often used to represent a game.

2. The prisoners' dilemma is a type of game that has proved very useful in analyzing oligopoly behavior. In particular, it helps to explain why firms have a tendency to cheat on cartel agreements. However, if this game is played repeatedly, firms may not cheat; for example, they may adopt a tit-for-tat strategy.

3. A firm can engage in a variety of types of strategic moves. Some are threatening to its rivals; others are not. An important element of a firm's strategic planning is commitment. For example, if a firm can convince its rivals that it is unequivocally committed to a particular move that it is making, they may back down without retaliating, since they may be convinced that they would lose more than they would gain from a protracted struggle.

4. Although firms frequently threaten their rivals, not all threats are credible. One way for a firm to make its threats credible is to develop a reputation for doing what it says, "regardless of the costs." Also, the firm can alter the payoff matrix to make its threat credible. For example, this can be effective in deterring entry.

5. The firm that makes the first move often has an advantage. For instance, with regard to capacity expansion, some firms adopt a preemptive strategy; that is, they try to expand before their rivals do.

6. The effects of oligopoly are difficult to predict, but most models suggest that price and profits will tend to be higher than under perfect competition. Also, oligopolists frequently engage in nonprice competition; advertising and product differentiation can be very important.

QUESTIONS/PROBLEMS

1. Two firms, A and B, exist in a particular market. Each has two strategies, the payoff matrix being as follows:

Possible strategies for firm B	Possible strategies for firm A	
	1	2
I	Firm A's profit: − $ 6 million Firm B's profit: − $ 5 million	Firm A's profit: $10 million Firm B's profit: $ 5 million
II	Firm A's profit: $ 5 million Firm B's profit: $10 million	Firm A's profit: − $ 5 million Firm B's profit: − $ 6 million

(a) If firm A has the first move, what strategy is it likely to choose? What strategy is firm B likely to choose?

(b) If firm B has the first move, what strategy is it likely to choose? What strategy is firm A likely to choose?

(c) Construct the game tree in part (a).

2. The industrial robot is one of the most important technological innovations of this century. In 1985, about 50 U.S. firms produced robots, with the following 6 firms accounting for about 70 percent of total sales:

	Sales (millions of dollars)		Sales (millions of dollars)
GMF Robotics	180	ASEA	39
Cincinnati Milacron	59	GCA	35
Westinghouse	45	DeVilbiss	33

(a) Robotics firms devoted about 17 percent of their sales to research and development in 1983. Is nonprice competition important in this industry?

(b) During 1979 to 1982, the robotics industry experienced substantial losses, although its sales increased at a relatively rapid rate. Why did firms stay in this industry in the face of these losses? (c) Does the fact that they stayed in the industry mean that they were "irrational"? (d) In 1992, General Motors sold its interest in GMF Robotics. Some other U.S. firms had already left the industry. Does it appear that robotics firms were overly optimistic in the 1980s? If so, did this optimism cause them to estimate incorrectly some of the figures in the payoff matrix (that is, the profits they would receive if they adopted particular strategies and their rivals adopted the same or other strategies)?

3. Two firms, C and D, exist in a particular market. Each has two strategies, the payoff matrix being as follows:

Possible strategies for firm D	Possible strategies for firm C	
	1	2
I	Firm C's profit: $8 million Firm D's profit: $5 million	Firm C's profit: $4 million Firm D's profit: $7 million
II	Firm C's profit: $6 million Firm D's profit: $9 million	Firm C's profit: $3 million Firm D's profit: $8 million

(a) Does firm *C* have a dominant strategy? If so, what is it? (b) Does firm *D* have a dominant strategy? If so, what is it? (c) What is the solution to this game?

4. The Brooks Company's managers begin to sense that the Harris Corporation may attempt to enter their market. (a) What steps might they take to dissuade Harris from doing so? (b) What factors are likely to determine whether they will succeed? (c) What actions that they have taken (or not taken) in the past may play an important role in influencing whether or not Harris tries to enter?

5. The Ewe Company and the Zee Company are the only firms in a particular market. The payoff matrix is as follows:

	Possible strategies for Ewe	
Possible strategies for Zee	Build plant on East Coast	Build plant on West Coast
Build plant on East Coast	Ewe's profit: − $50 million Zee's profit: − $60 million	Ewe's profit: $60 million Zee's profit: $30 million
Build plant on West Coast	Ewe's profit: $40 million Zee's profit: $70 million	Ewe's profit: − $30 million Zee's profit: − $40 million

(a) Is there a Nash equilibrium? (b) If so, what is it? (c) Are there more than one?

6. Suppose the payoff matrix is as given below. What strategy will firm I choose? What strategy will firm II choose?

Possible strategies for firm I	Possible strategies for firm II		
	1	2	3
	(Profits for firm I, or losses for firm II, in millions of dollars)		
A	10	9	11
B	8	7	10

7. In the previous question, the game is a zero-sum game; that is, the amount that one player wins is exactly equal to the amount that the other player loses. Is this realistic in the case of duopoly? Why or why not?

8. The Miller Company must decide whether to advertise its product or not. If its rival, the Morgan Corporation, decides to advertise its product, Miller will make $4 million if it advertises and $2 million if it does not advertise. If Morgan does not advertise, Miller will make $5 million if it advertises and $3 million if it does not. (a) Is it possible to determine the payoff matrix? Why or why not? (b) Can you tell whether Miller has a dominant strategy? If so, what is it?

9. The Morgan Company, introduced in the previous question, must decide whether to advertise its product. If its rival, the Miller Company, decides to advertise, Morgan will make $2.5 million if it advertises and $2 million if it does not advertise. If Miller does not advertise, Morgan will make $2 million if it advertises and $2.5 million if it does not advertise. (a) Based on the data in this and the previous question, is it possible to determine the payoff matrix? If so, what is it? (b) Do both firms have dominant strategies? If so, what are they? (c) Is there a Nash equilibrium? If so, what is it?

10. (a) Is the game in Question 1 an example of the prisoners' dilemma? Why or why not? (b) Is the game in Question 3 an example of the prisoners' dilemma? Why or why not? (b) Is the game in Question 6 an example of the prisoners' dilemma? Why or why not?

Applying Microeconomic Theory: The Case of Carmike Cinemas, Inc.

INTRODUCTION

Carmike Cinemas, which operates a chain of movie theaters, is the second largest movie exhibitor (in terms of the number of movie screens it operates) in North America (Table 14.1). In 1994, it had total revenues of about $300 million. Headquartered in Columbus, Georgia, it has theaters in over 200 markets, predominantly in southern and western states like Georgia, Tennessee, Oklahoma, Texas, and Alabama. These theaters tend to be in markets with populations of less than 150,000, like Ponca City, Oklahoma, and Nacogdoches, Texas.[1] Carmike dates back to 1912, when Roy Martin founded the

---

[1] M. Bounds, "Impresario of America's Hometowns," *New York Times,* November 28, 1991.

Theater chain	Headquarters	Number of screens
United Artists Communications	Denver, Colorado	2,236
Carmike Cinemas	Columbus, Georgia	1,906
Cineplex Odeon	Toronto, Canada	1,625
American Multi-Cinema	Kansas City, Missouri	1,623
General Cinema	Chestnut Hill, Massachusetts	1,226

SOURCE: *New York Times,* March 3, 1995.

Martin Theatres chain in Georgia. In 1945, Carl Patrick, Sr., went to work for Martin as a trainee; within 3 years, he was general manager and director. Under his leadership, the chain grew substantially in the next two decades. In 1969, Fuqua Industries purchased Martin, and Patrick subsequently became president (and later vice chairman) of Fuqua Industries. During the 13 years that Martin was a subsidiary of Fuqua, it generated a substantial stream of profit, but by 1980 this was no longer the case.[2]

Carmike Headquarters

In 1982, the Patrick family and a limited number of investors acquired Martin Theatres in a leveraged buyout. (A *leveraged buyout* allows the managers of a firm, ordinarily in conjunction with other investors, to purchase the firm from the stockholders; the takeover group borrows practically all of the money needed for the buyout.) The company was named Carmike after Carl Patrick, Sr.'s sons, Carl and Michael. From 1982 to 1986, the firm's operations

---

[2] M. L. Taylor, "Martin Theatres," *Case Research Journal,* Summer 1991.

grew rapidly, from 265 screens at 128 theaters to 415 screens at 156 theaters. In 1986, Carmike issued stock to the general public. By 1991, the Patrick family held 19 percent of Carmike's stock and controlled 70 percent of its voting shares. Throughout this period, Carmike's president was Michael Patrick, who began working for Martin Theatres while in high school and college (Georgia State University and Columbus College, where he majored in economics). He has had experience in most aspects of the movie theater business. His brother, Carl, a certified public accountant and lawyer, who is chairman of Summit Bank Corporation, has been a member of the firm's board of directors. His father, Carl Patrick, Sr., has been chairman of the board.[3]

THE DEMAND FOR ADMISSION AT A CINEMA

By 1994, Carmike had about 1,900 screens in 445 theaters. At any theater, the quantity of tickets demanded depends on the following factors, among others:

1. *The popular appeal of the film.* Without question, attendance at a theater depends heavily on the popular appeal of the film (or films, if there is more than one screen at this particular theater) that is shown. For example, there was a box-office slump in 1991 that many observers attributed to the dearth of top-notch films. In 1982, on the other hand, there was one of the biggest box office hits of all time —*E.T. the Extra-Terrestrial,* which grossed hundreds of millions of dollars. The booking for the entire chain of Carmike theaters is done by computer from the desk of the president, who feels that "The market

---

[3] M. L. Taylor, "Carmike Cinemas, Inc.: Industry and Company Perspectives," *Case Research Journal,* Spring 1992.

Carl and Michael Patrick   E.T. The Extra-Terrestrial

rules what we play."[4] An attempt is made to tailor the movie shown in a particular market to the tastes of the population there.

2. *Population per screen.* Ticket demand depends on the number of people per movie screen in the geographical area in which the theater is located. Clearly, if there is a large population and few movie screens, a theater's potential market tends to be greater than if there is a small population and lots of screens. In 1980, when Fuqua was considering the sale of Martin Theatres, it commissioned some reports by consultants to analyze Martin's operations. The consultants compared the numbers of people per screen in various areas. For example, in the Columbus, Georgia market, the number of people per screen was relatively high (about 18,000), whereas in some other areas it was much lower (about 5,000). The consultants recommended that Martin close some of its theaters in the latter areas to increase the number of people per screen there and raise ticket demand at its remaining theaters.[5]

3. *Ticket price and consumer income.* A major statistical study concluded that the price elasticity of demand for movie tickets is about 0.9 in the short run and over 3 in the long run. This study did not differentiate between first-run movies and older movies. According to theater experts, demand for tickets to first-run movies backed by positive word-of-mouth advertising and strong reviewer support tends to be price inelastic. However, this may not be the case for older movies shown at very low prices, which attract retired and unemployed people, among others. Also, this is the price elasticity of market demand, not the price elasticity for a particular theater. The income elasticity of demand for movie tickets is often claimed to be negative: during recessions,

---

[4] Bounds, "Impresario of America's Hometowns," p. D4.

[5] Taylor, "Martin Theatres."

people seek escape in movie theaters, according to this hypothesis. But the evidence on this score seems to be mixed.[6]

4. *Theater location.* The number of tickets demanded depends on the location of the theater. There are obvious advantages if prospective moviegoers regard the location as convenient and safe. Since the 1960s, movie exhibitors have tended to consolidate into big chains operating theaters located near or in shopping malls. Older movie theaters in run-down center-city locations often have experienced financial hard times.

5. *Advertising expenditure.* Obviously, the quantity of tickets demanded depends on how much advertising the theater does. According to the consulting reports cited above, more advertising could be expected to increase net box-office receipts until receipts per screen reached about $400,000; further increases in advertising would result in sharply diminishing returns.[7]

COST STRUCTURE OF A CINEMA

Table 14.2 shows the weekly revenues and costs of a movie theater. (Industry experts have published these figures as illustrative.[8]) The ticket sales are $4,500, and the revenues from concessions (candy, beverages, and popcorn) is $675; thus, total gross revenues are $5,175 per week. The costs of the movie theater are of five types:

---

[6] H. L. Vogel, *Entertainment Industry Economics* (Cambridge: Cambridge University Press, 1986), pp. 37–40.

[7] Taylor, "Martin Theatres."

[8] The original data appear in Vogel, *Entertainment Industry Economics,* p. 109. See the source of Table 14.2 for adjustments that have been made.

TABLE 14.2 Weekly Revenues and Costs of a Movie Theater: An Example

Revenues:		
Weekly ticket sales (box office)		$4,500
Concession sales		675
Total gross revenues		$5,175
Costs:		
Film rental		$2,250
Labor costs (including manager)		970
Rent		675
Advertising		450
Miscellaneous		600
Total costs		$4,945

SOURCE: P. M. Lowe, "Refreshment Sales and Theater Profits," in J. Squire (ed.), *The Movie Business Book* (Englewood Cliffs, N.J.: Prentice-Hall, 1983). The figures were adjusted roughly for inflation and simplified for pedagogical purposes.

1. *Film rental.* One of the biggest costs is the rental of the film from the distributor. (Distributors are firms like Twentieth Century Fox, Paramount, and Warner Brothers, all of which distribute their films to theaters.) Ordinarily, the distributor receives a certain percentage of the theater's gross ticket sales ("box office") after deducting an allowance for the theater's expenses (rent, telephone, electricity, insurance, mortgage payments, and so on). For the first week, the percentage may be 70 percent; for the second week, it may be 60 percent; and for subsequent weeks, it may be lower.[9] In Table 14.2, the movie theater pays the distributor $2,250 to rent the film.

2. *Labor costs.* Any theater must hire people to sell tickets and to run the concession stand, as well as to manage the theater. Carmike, which is totally nonunion, prefers to allow theater managers to hire members of their own family because it reduces theft, which obviously can be a problem in movie theaters. In its experience, people are less likely to steal if it will endanger the reputation and livelihood of their parents or other senior relatives. Many of Carmike's 8,000 employees were paid (approximately) the minimum wage.[10] In Table 14.2, the movie theater incurs labor costs of $970 per week.

3. *Rent.* Movie theaters are sometimes owned, sometimes leased; and the land is sometimes owned, sometimes leased. The cost of constructing new facilities in many areas has increased substantially; in areas like New York or

[9] Ibid., p. 78.

[10] Taylor, "Carmike Cinemas, Inc."

Los Angeles the average construction cost now comes to over $1 million per screen.[11] In Table 14.2, the theater is rented, and the weekly rent is $675.

4. *Advertising.* Movie theaters generally advertise in local newspapers and elsewhere. The costs of advertising are often split between the movie theater and the distributor.[12] In Table 14.2, advertising costs are $450 per week.

5. *Miscellaneous.* In addition, there are costs of utilities (heat, light, water, and so on), insurance, repairs, maintenance, popcorn, candy, soft drinks, and a variety of other items. In Table 14.2, these miscellaneous costs are $600 per week.

MARKET STRUCTURE AND PRICING

According to the federal government's 1948 Consent Decree, the major film studios like Paramount, Warner Brothers, and Twentieth Century Fox had to get rid of either their studios and film exchanges or their movie theaters. They chose to sell the movie theaters. But in 1984 the Justice Department offered advance support to any studio that sued to reenter the movie theater business. MCA, owner of Universal Studios (which made films like *E.T. the Extra-*

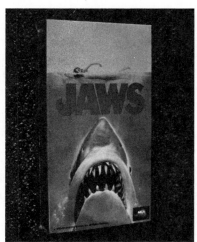

[11] H. L. Vogel, "Theatrical Exhibition: Consolidation Continues," in W. R. Green (ed.), *The 1987 Encyclopaedia of Exhibition* (New York: National Association of Theater Owners, 1988), p. 62.

[12] Vogel, *Entertainment Industry Economics.*

Terrestrial and *Jaws*) bought 49.7 percent of Cineplex Odeon, the third largest movie chain (Table 14.1). Gulf and Western, owner of Paramount Studios (which made films like *Raiders of the Lost Ark* and *Beverly Hills Cop*) bought Trans-Lux, Mann Theaters, and Festival Enterprises. By about 1990, the top six movie theater chains owned about 40 percent of the United States's screens — a considerable increase in concentration.[13]

There seem to be considerable economies of scale in movie theater operation. For example, in metropolitan areas, one omnibus newspaper ad can cover all a chain's theaters. According to John Duffy, an Atlanta theater owner, "There's no way the small, independent operator can compete against the large screen owners these days."[14] Also, as the studios have reduced their wholesaling operations, it has become more difficult for smaller operators to get the films they want on the terms they want. As Michael Patrick, president of Carmike, has put it, "The ability of smaller exhibitors to negotiate bookings is diluted relative to the buying power of the larger circuits."[15]

As pointed out above, Carmike has established theaters in relatively small cities and towns. In many of its markets, it owns the only movie theater. This continues the philosophy of Carl Patrick, Sr., Carmike's chairman, who in the 1960s concentrated the attention of Martin Theatres on smaller cities and towns. As he has stated, "The proper niche for our company was in medium-sized towns such as Columbus, Georgia and Nashville, Tennessee where it was not so competitive and you could have some semblance of control over your destiny."[16]

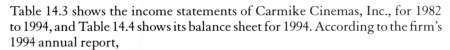

THE PROFITABILITY OF CARMIKE CINEMAS, INC.

Table 14.3 shows the income statements of Carmike Cinemas, Inc., for 1982 to 1994, and Table 14.4 shows its balance sheet for 1994. According to the firm's 1994 annual report,

> We are delighted to report that 1994 was the best year in Carmike's history in all categories — revenues, net income, and

---

[13] J. Wolfe, "Cineplex Odeon Corporation," in E. Mansfield, *Study Guide and Casebook in Applied Microeconomics* (2d ed.; New York: Norton, 1997).

[14] *Wall Street Journal,* February 9, 1989, p. B1.

[15] M. Patrick, "Trends in Exhibition," in Green, *The 1987 Encyclopaedia of Exhibition,* p. 109.

[16] Taylor, "Martin Theatres," p. 138.

TABLE 14.3 Income Statements, Carmike Cinemas, Inc., 1982–1994 (millions of dollars)*

	1994	1993	1992	1991	1990
Revenues					
Admissions	232	167	119	99	86
Concessions and other	95	75	53	47	41
Total revenues	328	242	172	146	127
Costs and expenses					
Cost of operations	254	187	135	113	98
General and administrative	5	5	4	4	4
Depreciation	23	16	11	9	8
	282	208	150	126	109
Operating income	45	34	22	20	18
Interest expense	17	14	12	10	8
Income before income taxes	28	20	10	10	10
Income taxes	11	8	4	4	4
Net income	17	12	6	6	6

	1989	1988	1986	1984	1982
Revenues					
Admissions	65	55	43	44	34
Concessions and other	34	30	18	17	14
Total revenues	99	85	61	61	47
Costs and expenses					
Cost of operations	73	64	49	48	39
General and administrative	3	3	3	3	3
Depreciation	5	6	3	3	2
	82	73	55	54	44
Operating income	17	12	6	7	3
Interest expense	7	6	2	3	0
Income before income taxes	10	5	4	4	3
Income taxes	4	2	2	2	1
Net income	6	3	2	3	2

[a] Because of rounding errors, figures may not sum to totals.
SOURCE: Company annual reports.

cash flow. We are aware this did not happen by accident or plain luck. It happened first by good planning, second by hard work and third by the enthusiastic efforts of Carmike's management team. While the nature of our business creates fluctuations in the short term due to the availability of popular pictures, we believe that proper planning and management skills will insure that the pace-setting accomplishments of the past will continue into the future.

TABLE 14.4 Balance Sheet, Carmike Cinemas, Inc., December 31, 1994 (millions of dollars)[a]

Assets	
Current assets	
Cash	17.9
Short-term investments	4.8
Accounts receivable	3.8
Inventories	1.9
Prepaid expenses	5.0
Other assets	
Investments in partnerships	4.6
Other	2.4
Property and Equipment	
Land	31.8
Buildings and improvements	88.5
Leasehold improvements and interests	149.7
Equipment	111.8
Accumulated depreciation and amortization	−87.9
Excess of purchase price over net assets of businesses acquired	43.2
Total	377.6
Liabilities and shareholders' equity	
Current liabilities	
Accounts payable	23.5
Accrued expenses	11.3
Maturities of obligations	9.4
Long-Term Liabilities	
Debt	3.5
Notes	118.2
Lease obligations and subordinate debt	22.3
Deferred income taxes	17.5
Shareholders' equity	
Stock and paid-in capital	100.1
Retained earnings	71.9
Total	377.6

[a] Because of rounding errors, figures may not sum to totals.
SOURCE: 1994 Company Annual Report.

The management of Carmike is optimistic about the future of the industry and about continuing Carmike's strategy of growth through acquisition and construction of new screens. We are just as eager to grow today as we were ten years ago.[17]

---

[17] 1994 Annual Report, Carmike Cinemas, Inc., p. 1.

DEMAND FOR ADMISSION: CAN YOU APPLY THE THEORY?

The following two problems are concerned with the demand for admission at movie theaters, a topic of major concern to theater owners.

PROBLEM 14.1 During the 1980s, there was considerable worry that cable television and videocassette recorders (VCRs) would make a big dent in the movie theaters' business. As Carl Patrick, Sr., Carmike's chairman, put it, "There was a real downbeat in the news and the financial reports about the future of motion picture theaters. . . ." One of the producers in California said, 'In six months all of the theaters are going to close and films are going to be on cable.' "[18] Whereas 1984 was a record year for admissions and gross revenues in movie theaters, there was a big drop in 1985, which fueled these worries, as the use of VCRs and cable TV grew rapidly.

(a) Is there a significant difference between the experience of seeing a movie in a theater and that of seeing the same movie at home? Put differently, is a movie seen at home a perfect substitute for a movie seen in a theater? Why or why not?

(b) What effect, if any, did the growing use of VCRs and cable TV have on the demand curve for tickets at a typical movie theater, if the worries expressed above accorded with the facts? Table 14.5 shows recent and projected changes in the age distribution of the U.S. population. About 54 percent of movie tickets are sold to people from 12 to 24 years old.[19] What effects have recent and prospective changes in the age distribution had on the demand for movie tickets? Why?

(c) In 1985, a major study of the effects of VCR ownership on theater attendance indicated that, during the first year of VCR ownership, movie attendance decreased by about 10 percent, on the average, but that the drop was less than 3 percent by the third year and even less thereafter.[20] How can you account for this finding? What implications does it have for the demand curve for tickets at a typical movie theater?

---

[18] Taylor, "Martin Theatres," p. 145.

[19] Vogel, *Entertainment Industry Economics,* p. 367.

[20] F. Segers, "'Say VCR Effect on Tax Sales Peaking' Study Suggests Homevid a Phase," *Variety,* January 15, 1986.

TABLE 14.5 U.S. Population by Age Group for 1980, 1990, and 2000

Age (years)	Percent of total population		
	1980	1990	2000
5–17	20.7	18.1	18.6
18–24	13.2	10.3	9.2
25–44	27.9	32.6	29.9
45–64	19.5	18.6	22.7
65 and over	11.3	12.8	13.0

SOURCE: Wolfe, "Cineplex Odeon Corporation."

(d) According to some people like Michael Patrick, president of Carmike, the growth of VCRs and cable TV will be a positive factor for movie theaters. He has said, "I love it because the revenues [from cable TV and VCRs] help create more good movies."[21] In his view, will VCRs and cable TV shift the demand curve for tickets at a typical movie theater to the left or the right? Why?

(e) Was there any way in 1985 to forecast the effect of VCRs and cable TV on the demand curve for tickets at a typical movie theater? If so, how would you go about doing so? (For some relevant basic data available in 1985, see Table 14.6.)

PROBLEM 14.2 According to the report of the consultants that Fuqua Industries hired in 1980, only 7.2 percent of the population in the Columbus, Georgia market attended a movie each week as compared to the national average of 11 percent.[22] The consultants attributed this to the low advertising intensity in this market. Suppose that the relationship between the amount that Martin Theatres spent on advertising in this market and its total revenues in this market was as follows:

Advertising (thousands of dollars)	Total revenue (millions of dollars)	Advertising (thousands of dollars)	Total revenue (millions of dollars)
100	1.000	180	1.095
120	1.030	200	1.111
140	1.054	220	1.125
160	1.075	240	1.135

[21] Taylor, "Carmike Cinemas, Inc.," p. 12.

[22] Taylor, "Martin Theatres."

	Movie theater box office revenues ($ millions)	Movie theater admissions (millions)	Average movie ticket price (dollars)	Number of movie screens (thousands)	Subscribers to cable TV (millions)	Percent of TV households with VCRs
	TABLE 14.6 Basic Statistics Regarding Movie Theaters, Cable TV, and VCRs, United States, 1965–1984					
1984	4,031	1,199	3.36	20.2	30.0	20
1983	3,766	1,197	3.15	18.9	25.0	11
1982	3,453	1,175	2.94	18.3	21.0	6
1981	2,966	1,067	2.78	18.1	18.3	4
1980	2,749	1,022	2.69	17.7	16.0	2
1979	2,821	1,121	2.52	17.1	14.1	1
1978	2,643	1,128	2.34	16.8	13.0	1
1977	2,372	1,063	2.23	16.6	11.9	0
1976	2,036	957	2.13	16.0	10.8	0
1975	2,115	1,033	2.05	16.0	9.8	0
1974	1,909	1,011	1.89	15.4	8.7	0
1973	1,524	865	1.76	14.6	7.3	0
1972	1,583	934	1.70	14.4	6.0	0
1971	1,350	820	1.65	14.1	5.3	0
1970	1,429	921	1.55	13.8	4.5	0
1969	1,294	912	1.42	13.5	3.6	0
1968	1,282	979	1.31	13.2	2.8	0
1967	1,110	927	1.20	13.0	2.1	0
1966	1,067	975	1.09	12.9	1.6	0
1965	1,042	1,032	1.01	12.8	1.3	0

SOURCE: Vogel, *Entertainment Industry Economics.*

(a) If the price elasticity of demand for tickets at Martin Theatres in this market was 0.80, how much should Martin have spent on advertising, according to the model in Chapter 12? Why?

(b) If the price elasticity of demand was 1.2, how much should it have spent on advertising? Why?

(c) Suppose that Martin Theatres had hired you to estimate the price elasticity of demand for tickets at its theaters in Columbus, Georgia. How would you have proceeded? How accurate do you think your results would have been?

CINEMA COSTS AND TAXES:
CAN YOU APPLY THE THEORY?

The following three problems deal with important aspects of Carmike's cost structure, as well as multiplexing and the amusement tax on movie tickets.

PROBLEM 14.3   Carmike prides itself on its cost control techniques. Using a computer system he helped to develop, Michael Patrick, Carmike's president, can tell quickly how many tickets were sold at each of his theaters — and when the janitors checked in and out last night.[23] Each department of the firm receives weekly reports showing all individual expenditures and, where necessary, there are requests for explanations of these expenditures. To help reduce costs, Carmike has adopted various forms of new technology. For example, projectionists have been displaced by automated projection booths. In one city which required that all projectionists be certified by a city board, the projectionists went to the City Council in an attempt to preserve their jobs. Michael Patrick responded by asking his theater managers to become certified. "I told our managers that once the automated projection booth was in operation and the job of projectionist eliminated, I would give them a raise consisting of 40 percent of whatever the projectionists had made. All of a sudden the managers went from being against the program of converting to automated projection booths to where I got a flood of letters from managers saying, 'I passed the projectionist test. I am now certified by the electrical board. Fire my projectionist.' "[24]

(a) In a given week, which of the costs of a movie theater in Table 14.2 are fixed costs? Which are variable costs? If a movie theater does not have a concession stand, and if it pays half of the price of each ticket it sells to the distributor to rent the film, do increases in the number of tickets sold (up to the capacity of the theater) result in decreases in average cost? Why or why not? (Assume that the ticket price is $4, regardless of the number of tickets sold.)

(b) If the typical projectionist made $250 per week, did the adoption of automated projection booths shift the total cost curve for a Carmike

---

[23] Bounds, "Impresario of America's Hometowns."

[24] Taylor, "Carmike Cinemas, Inc.," p. 6.

movie theater downward by .6 × $250 = $150 per week? Why or why not? By how much did it shift the marginal cost curve pertaining to a 1-week period?

(c) When Michael Patrick wanted to fire the projectionists, did he encounter a principal-agent problem? If so, how did he solve it?

(d) During periods when the supply of films is small relative to the total capacity of movie theaters, the percentage of the theaters' box office going to distributors tends to go up.[25] Why? According to Michael Patrick, during a period when there were a lot of bad movies, rival theaters in a particular town "beat each other up during the period bidding up what pictures were available. [One] went under."[26] Would this be a good reason for a company to place its theaters in areas where there are no other movie theaters? Why or why not?

PROBLEM 14.4   One of the most important developments during recent decades in the exhibition segment of the motion picture industry has been the growth of *multiplexes*— multiscreen theaters. A pioneer in this development was Sumner Redstone, a New England theater owner who subsequently became chairman of Viacom (owner of Paramount Pictures).[27] In 1975, only 5 of Martin's 162 theaters and, in 1981, only 27 of its 167 theaters had three or more screens. The consultants hired by Fuqua Industries criticized Martin for being slow to operate theaters with six, eight, or more screens. (Theater exhibitors suggested at that time that efficient operations required at least four screens per theater.) A big advantage of multiplexes was that labor and related costs per screen tended to decline with the number of screens per theater. Also, as the number of screens increased, the construction cost per screen fell, and the percentage of total seats filled increased.[28] Since Carmike took over Martin's theaters, the number and average size of multiplexes have grown substantially. In 1986, over 20 percent of its screens were in theaters with six or more screens.

(a) Why do increases in the number of screens per theater tend to reduce the labor cost per ticket sold? Suppose that a doubling of the number of screens results in only 10 percent more labor-hours required. Does this mean that it is always optimal for a theater to have a dozen or more screens? Why or why not?

---

[25] Vogel, *Entertainment Industry Economics,* p. 83.

[26] Taylor, "Carmike Cinemas, Inc.," p. 10.

[27] *Business Week*, September 21, 1992.

[28] Wolfe, "Cineplex Odeon Corporation."

A Multiplex Theater

(b) According to many observers, an important advantage of multiplexes is that the theater is not so dependent on only one film, which may not be a success. Does this mean that multiplexes allow the theater owner to diversify in much the same sense that a large portfolio of stocks allows an investor to diversify? If so, on a particular day, should a theater exhibit films that are likely to appeal to quite different audiences?

PROBLEM 14.5   Movie theaters, like other firms, have to pay taxes. Between 1942 and 1953, there was an amusement tax on movie tickets; in 1953, it equaled 10 cents. In a market where there are lots of competing movie theaters, suppose that, in the absence of the tax, the demand and supply curves for movie tickets in 1953 would have been as follows:

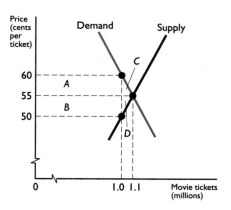

(a) By how much did this 10-cent tax raise the price to the consumer of a movie ticket?

(b) How great was the loss of consumer surplus due to this tax?

(c) How great was the loss in producer surplus due to this tax?

(d) How much did the government earn in revenue from this tax?

(e) Did consumers and suppliers of movies lose more than the government gained from this tax? In other words, was there a deadweight loss due to this tax? If so, how big was it?

(f) If the price elasticity of demand were to increase and the price elasticity of supply were to decrease, would more of the burden of the tax fall on consumers and less fall on suppliers of movies? Why or why not?

(g) If the price elasticity of demand were to decrease and the price elasticity of supply were to increase, would more of the burden of the tax fall on suppliers of movies and less fall on consumers? Why or why not?

PRICING AND STRATEGY: CAN YOU APPLY THE THEORY

The following two problems are concerned with Carmike's pricing policies, as well as with its strategic moves in particular markets.

PROBLEM 14.6 When Carmike took over Martin Theatres, Michael Patrick, president of Carmike, cut ticket prices substantially in a number of theaters that were "off the beaten track." In his words, "Phenix City is a perfect example. I took the admission price from $3.75 to 99 cents. Everybody said I was a fool. The first year that theater made $70,000 which I thought was a great increase over the $26,000 it had been making. . . . The people in Phenix City are poor, very poor blue collar workers, but the theater is as nice as anything I have over here (in Columbus). So as word of mouth got going, that theater kept getting better and better. Now it almost sells out every Friday, Saturday, and Sunday. And I still charge 99 cents. That theater will make over $200,000 this year."[29]

---

[29] Taylor, "Carmike Cinemas, Inc.," p. 6.

(a) It has been estimated that only 23 percent of a theater's revenue from concession sales (popcorn, soft drinks, candy) are needed to cover the cost of the relevant goods sold.[30] If each of the people attending the Phenix City theater spent 30 cents, on the average, at the concession stand, how much of the increase in profit (from $26,000 to $70,000 per year) could be accounted for by enhanced concession sales if the price elasticity of demand for tickets at this theater equaled 1 at all relevant prices? (Assume that 1,000 tickets were sold per week before the price cut.)

(b) As more and more time elapsed after the price cut, would you expect this price elasticity of demand to increase? Why or why not? Would this help to explain the increasing profits from this theater? Also, if Carmike maintained the price at this theater at 99 cents, was this really a price reduction? If so, would this too help to explain the increased profits even if the price elasticity remained equal to 1?

(c) In the short run, suppose that all the costs (other than the costs of film rental and of popcorn, soft drinks, and candy) at one of Carmike's theaters are fixed, and that this theater can seat 500 people per day, no more. The demand curve for tickets at this theater is

$$P = 8 - .01Q,$$

and the marginal revenue curve is

$$MR = 8 - .02Q,$$

where P is price (in dollars per ticket), MR is marginal revenue from ticket sales (in dollars per ticket), and Q is the number of people who buy tickets per day. If each person who buys a ticket to this theater spends 50 cents at the concession stand for items that cost the theater 10 cents, if the theater must pay half of its ticket sales to rent the film, and if the theater's fixed costs are $1,200 per day, what price should Carmike charge for a ticket if it wants to maximize profit? How big will its profit be?

(d) When *Superman, Annie,* and some Disney films were released, distributors sometimes insisted that movie theaters charge at least a certain minimum amount for admission in order to prevent children's prices from being too low.[31] Suppose that each child who comes to such a movie has been given a total of $3, which is to cover admission, popcorn, soda, and candy combined. If the theater keeps 50 cents of every dollar spent on ticket sales (the rest goes to the distributor) and 77 cents of every dollar

---

[30] Lowe, "Refreshment Sales and Theater Profits." This percentage may be lower for Carmike, but for simplicity, we assume here that this figure applies to Carmike. About 40 percent of refreshment-stand sales are from popcorn, about 40 percent from soft drinks, and about 20 percent from candy. See Vogel, *Entertainment Industry Economics,* pp. 78, 108, and 412.

[31] Ibid., p. 78.

spent on popcorn, soda, and candy (the rest goes to the firms that supply them), derive an equation showing how the theater's profit per child varies with the price it charges. If you owned the only theater in an area where all the children will see a new hit movie, what price would you charge under the above circumstances? If you were the distributor, what price would you like the theater to charge? (Assume that each child spends the entire $3 in the theater.)

PROBLEM 14.7   Carmike expanded at a rapid rate from 1988 to 1991 (when its number of screens doubled), as well as in the early 1980s. To illustrate its aggressiveness, consider a particular metropolitan area where a rival built a multiplex with 6 screens (a "sixplex") in a shopping center near a Carmike theater. Carmike responded by building a sixplex nearby and by adding screens to two of its existing theaters in the area. Thus, it had a total of 12 screens in its three theaters in the area, which was about as large a number of screens as the population in this area could support, in the judgment of its top executives.[32]

(a) If you had been president of a theater chain competing with Carmike, would you have been discouraged from building a new theater in the area by Carmike's expansion? Why or why not?

(b) Many small towns can support no more than a single movie theater. Suppose that both Carmike and a rival chain are considering the construction of a theater in a small town with no theater, the payoff matrix being as follows:

Possible strategies for Carmike	Possible strategies for Carmike's rival	
	Construct theater	Do not construct theater
Construct theater	Carmike's Profit: −$300,000 Rival's profit: −$300,000	Carmike's profit: $500,000 Rival's profit: zero
Do not construct theater	Carmike's profit: zero Rival's profit: $500,000	Carmike's profit: zero Rival's profit: zero

Does Carmike have a dominant strategy? If so, what is it? Is there a Nash equilibrium? If so, is there more than one? If Carmike has the first move, what is likely to be the outcome?

(c) Carmike buys or builds theaters that can be expanded to as many as 14 screens.[33] If you were president of a rival theater chain, would you regard this as an indication that Carmike would be likely to resist your entry into one of its markets? Why or why not?

---

[32] Taylor, "Carmike Cinemas, Inc."

[33] Bounds, "Impresario of America's Hometowns."

PROFITABILITY AND MARKET STRUCTURE: CAN YOU APPLY THE THEORY?

The remaining three problems take up factors influencing the profitability of movie theaters; analyze the profitability of Carmike Cinemas and of another movie theater chain, Cineplex Odeon Corporation; and look at the effects of market structure in this industry.

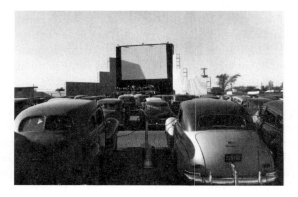

PROBLEM 14.8   According to Carmike's balance sheet in Table 14.4, it owned land valued at $31.8 million. During the 1940s drive-in movies were established in many areas. Theater owners would purchase 15 or 20 acres right outside a town and construct a drive-in. According to Carl Patrick, Sr., chairman of Carmike, they often were attended by young couples who would take their children: the children would go to sleep and the couple would watch the movie. By the 1970s, the advent of television had eaten into the drive-in business, and many towns had expanded to the point where the land on which the drive-in movie theaters were located was desirable as a site for office buildings or parking lots.[34]

(a) Suppose that the land on which a drive-in movie theater is located can be sold for $500,000 as a site for office buildings and parking lots. The theater produces an annual profit of $25,000. Since the theater owner bought the theater (including the land) for $125,000, he or she is earning a 20 percent return on the original investment. If the theater owner can obtain a 10 percent return (no more) on alternative investments, he or she be-

---

[34] Taylor, "Martin Theatres."

lieves that it would be foolish to sell such a lucrative investment. Is this correct? Why or why not?

(b) During the 1970s, Martin Theatres sold the land underlying many of its drive-in movies at a spectacular profit. For example, land in Nashville, Tennessee bought in 1948 for $50,000 was sold for $1,400,000.[35] Suppose that this land was rented by the new owners to a firm that constructed a complex of buildings on it, the rent being $150,000 per year. If 10 percent was the highest rate of return that the new owners could get from alternative investments, was this a profitable deal for them?

| **PROBLEM 14.9** | In one of Carmike's largest markets, suppose that the population is big enough to support a large number of |

movie theaters and that, if competition prevailed, the demand and supply curves for movie tickets would be as shown below.

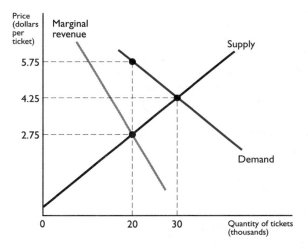

(a) If all of these movie theaters were bought up by the same movie chain, and if the marginal cost curve of this chain (now a monopolist) were the same as the competitive supply curve, what would be the effect on the price of a movie ticket and the number of tickets sold?

(b) How big would be the loss of consumer surplus due to the monopolization of this market?

(c) How big would be the gain of producer surplus due to this monopolization?

(d) What would be the dollar magnitude of the deadweight loss due to monopoly?

---

[35] Ibid.

(e) Does this analysis show that social welfare would be promoted if Carmike's operations were replaced with several smaller theaters in each of its markets? Why or why not?

PROBLEM 14.10 In 1990, Carmike's total revenues per screen were $140,000, less than half the industry average of $310,000. Its operating profits of $33,846 per screen were comparable with those of its rivals.[36] The equity (in millions of dollars) of the common stockholders in the firm was as follows:[37]

1983: 2.8	1987: 23	1990: 63	1993: 94
1985: 9.2	1989: 33	1991: 69	1994: 172

(a) How is it possible for Carmike's operating profits per screen to have been about equal to those of its rivals, whereas its total revenues per screen were less than half of those of its rivals? Can these figures be reconciled? If so, how?

(b) In 1991, Carmike's average admission price for first-run features was $3.76 versus the industry average of $4.75 for all showings.[38] Why would a firm with so many monopoly theaters set a lower price than its rivals? Is this an indication of irrational or incompetent management?

(c) Can you determine the rate of return that Carmike's stockholders have been earning on their investment in the firm? Has it been relatively high?

(d) Whereas Carmike specializes in relatively low-price second-run multiplexed theaters in smaller towns, the Cineplex Odeon Corporation, the third largest movie theater chain in North America (Table 14.1), has specialized in high-price, extravagantly built theaters in metropolitan areas. As Garth Drabinski, the Canadian head of the firm (and subsequently the producer of *Show Boat, Kiss of the Spider Woman,* and other Broadway shows), put it, "We've introduced the majesty back to picturegoing."[39] The rate of return that Cineplex Odeon earned on equity during 1984 to 1989 was as follows:[40]

1984: 31%	1987: 11%
1985: 41%	1988: 10%
1986: 18%	1989: 10%

---

[36] Bounds, "Impresario of America's Hometowns."

[37] Annual reports, Carmike Cinemas, Inc.

[38] Bounds, "Impresario of America's Hometowns."

[39] *U.S. News and World Report,* January 25, 1988, p. 58.

[40] Wolfe, "Cineplex Odeon Corporation."

According to some observers, Cineplex Odeon, with its luxurious theaters, was trying to cater to the aging baby boomers. Given the prospective changes in the age distribution in Table 14.5, did it appear likely that the demand for luxurious moviegoing would increase? Why or why not?

(e) At a time when New York City's movie theaters charged no more than $6, Cineplex Odeon raised its price to $7. When then-Mayor Ed Koch expressed his anger at this price hike, Garth Drabinski replied that the alternative was "to continue to expose New Yorkers to filthy, rat-infested environments. We don't intend to do that."[41] If Cineplex Odeon's marginal cost was the same as that of any theater charging $6, and if each of the latter theaters felt that the price elasticity of demand for admission at its theater was 2, what must Mr. Drabinski have estimated the price elasticity of demand to have been at Cineplex Odeon? (Assume that he and the other theater owners were maximizing profit, and ignore profits from concessions, which are taken up in the next part of this problem.)

Former Mayor
Ed Koch

(f) According to Mr. Drabinski, "People don't just like coming to our theaters. They linger afterward. They have another cup of *cappucino* in the cafe or sit and read the paper."[42] Over a dozen blends of tea, as well as croissant sandwiches, fudge brownies, freshly popped popcorn (served with real butter), *cappucino,* and a variety of other such items were sold in his theaters. Suppose that each person who buys a ticket to a particular theater of his spends $4 for such items (which cost the theater $1), that the demand curve for tickets at this theater is

$$P = 20 - .02Q,$$

and that the marginal revenue curve (from ticket sales) is

$$MR = 20 - .04Q,$$

---

[41] *Time,* January 25, 1988, pp. 60–61.

[42] *Forbes,* June 2, 1986, p. 93.

where P is price (in dollars per ticket), MR is marginal revenue from ticket sales (in dollars per ticket), and Q is the number of people who buy tickets per day. The theater, which can seat 1,000 people per day, pays half of its ticket revenue to the distributor to rent the film. In the short run, all the theater's costs (other than for film rental and for tea, brownies, popcorn, and such items) are fixed, the total being $3,200 per day. Does the relatively high expenditure ($4) of each ticket buyer on tea, brownies, and other such items result in the ticket price's being higher or lower than it otherwise would be? To find out, calculate the profit-maximizing ticket price if (1) each ticket buyer spends $4 on these items and (2) if each ticket buyer spends nothing on these items. Is the former price higher or lower than the latter? How big is the difference?

CONCLUSION

Returning from the world of entertainment to the halls of academe, it should be obvious from this chapter that simple microeconomic models are of great use in understanding the strategies and tactics of firms' top managers, and in competing with them if they head rival firms. Carmike's pricing policies and investment strategies can be analyzed effectively and evaluated with the help of theories of imperfect competition, game theory, and other concepts and models taken up in previous chapters. However, it is important to recognize that it is impossible to confine our attention solely to the past few chapters and ignore topics like market demand that were taken up earlier. The top managers of Carmike must constantly be concerned with market demand, costs, pricing, and their interactions with their rivals, and we too must consider them all simultaneously if we are really to understand and evaluate the behavior and performance of these managers.

SELECTED SUPPLEMENTARY READINGS

1. H. L. Vogel, *Entertainment Industry Economics* (Cambridge, Eng.: Cambridge University Press, 1986).
2. M. Taylor, "Carmike Cinemas," *Case Research Journal,* Spring 1992.

3. M. Bounds, "Impresario of America's Hometowns," *New York Times,* November 28, 1991.

4. P. Waldman, "Silver Screens Lose Some of Their Luster," *Wall Street Journal,* February 9, 1989.

5. M. Fischer, "They're Putting Glitz Back into Movie Houses," *U.S. News and World Report,* January 25, 1988.

6. *1994 Annual Report* (Columbus, Ga.: Carmike Cinemas, 1995).

PART FIVE

Markets for Inputs

Price and Employment of Inputs

15

INTRODUCTION

Why is the wage rate for major executives frequently in the neighborhood of $100 an hour, while the wage rate for secretaries is only about $10 per hour? To answer this question, you must understand the determinants of input prices, since the wage that a worker (either an executive or a secretary) receives is an input price from the viewpoint of the firm. The previous five chapters were concerned with the analysis of the pricing and output of consumer goods. We turn now to the determinants of the price and employment of inputs.

At the outset, two points should be noted. First, a good deal of the theory presented in Chapters 10 to 13 is applicable to inputs as well as commodities;

for example, the price of inputs as well as commodities is determined by the interaction of supply and demand. However, the demand for inputs differs in important respects from the demand for commodities, and the supply of inputs differs in important respects from the supply of commodities. These differences stem largely from the fact that inputs are demanded by firms, not consumers; and that some important inputs, like labor, are supplied by consumers, not firms.

Second, in the nineteenth century it was customary for economists to classify inputs into three categories: land, labor, and capital.[1] The theory of input pricing was therefore a theory of the distribution of income among landowners, wage earners, and capitalists, three important economic and social classes. (The incomes of these classes were rent, wages, and profits, respectively.) A disadvantage of this simple classification of inputs is that each category contains such an enormous amount of variation. For example, labor includes the services of a Nobel Prize-winning biochemist and the services of her secretary whose typing is strictly hunt-and-peck. In this chapter we shall seldom use this tripartite classification; instead we ordinarily present our results in general terms so that the user of the model can classify inputs to fit any particular problem.

PROFIT MAXIMIZATION AND INPUT EMPLOYMENT

Fortunately, we do not have to start from scratch in constructing a model of input pricing and utilization under perfect competition. We learned a great deal that is relevant and useful in Chapters 7 and 8 when we analyzed the firm's decisions concerning input combinations and output level. A moment's reflection should convince you that, when we determined how much the firm would produce and the input combination it would use to produce this output, we in effect determined how much of each input the firm would demand under various sets of circumstances. This, of course, is an important beginning.

To make sure that the implications of our findings in Chapter 7 are clear, we shall review a few of these findings. In particular, recall the way in which a firm combines inputs in order to minimize costs. We showed that the firm will pick a combination of inputs where the ratio of each input's marginal product

---

[1] Toward the end of the nineteenth century, a fourth "factor of production"— or type of input —was recognized: entrepreneurship. Then profits were viewed as the return to the entrepreneur, and interest was viewed as the return to the owner of capital.

to its price is equal. That is, it will set

$$\frac{MP_x}{P_x} = \frac{MP_y}{P_y} = \cdots = \frac{MP_z}{P_z}, \qquad [15.1]$$

where MP_x is the marginal product of input x, P_x is the price of input x, MP_y is the marginal product of input y, P_y is the price of input y, and so on. If Equation 15.1 does not hold, the firm can always reduce costs by changing the utilization of certain inputs. For example, if the marginal product of a unit of input x is 2 units of output, the price of a unit of input x is \$1, the marginal product of a unit of input y is 6 units of output, and the price of a unit of input y is \$2, the firm can reduce its costs by using 1 unit less of input x—which reduces output by 2 units and cost by \$1—and by using 1/3 unit more of input y—which increases output by 2 units and cost by \$.67. This substitution of input y for input x has no effect on output but reduces the cost by \$.33.

Going a step further, it can be shown that, if a firm minimizes cost, each of the ratios in Equation 15.1 equals the reciprocal of the firm's marginal cost. In other words,

$$\frac{P_x}{MP_x} = \frac{P_y}{MP_y} = \cdots = \frac{P_z}{MP_z} = MC, \qquad [15.2]$$

where MC is its marginal cost. To prove this, consider input x. What is the cost of producing an extra unit of output if this extra unit of output is achieved by increasing the utilization of input x while holding constant the utilization of other inputs? Since an extra unit of input x results in MP_x extra units of output, $1/MP_x$ units of input x will result in 1 unit of extra output. Since $1/MP_x$ units of input x will cost $(1/MP_x)P_x$, P_x/MP_x equals marginal cost. This same type of reasoning can be used for any input, not just input x, with the consequence that Equation 15.2 holds.[2]

---

[2] Let $Q = f(X_1, \ldots, X_n)$, where Q is the firm's output, X_1 is the amount of the first input used by the firm, X_2 is the amount of the second input used by the firm, and so on. To minimize cost subject to the constraint that output equals Q^*, we form the Lagrangian function:

$$L = \sum_{i=1}^{n} P_i X_i - \lambda [f(X_1, \ldots, X_n) - Q^*],$$

where P_i is the price of the ith input and λ is a Lagrangian multiplier. Setting $\partial L / \partial X_i = 0$, we have

$$P_i - \frac{\lambda \partial f}{\partial X_i} = 0, \qquad \text{where } i = 1, \ldots, n.$$

Thus,
$$P_i \div \frac{\partial f}{\partial X_i} = \lambda, \qquad \text{where } i = 1, \ldots, n. \qquad \textit{(Cont.)}$$

As an illustration, suppose that there are only two inputs, input x and input y. Suppose that the marginal product of a unit of input x is 2 units of output, the price of a unit of input x is \$1, the marginal product of a unit of input y is 4 units of output, and the price of a unit of input y is \$2. The extra cost of producing an extra unit of output, if the extra production occurs by increasing the use of input x, is \$.50, since an extra 1/2 unit of input x — at \$1 a unit — will result in an extra unit of output. Similarly, the extra cost of producing an extra unit of output, if the extra production comes about by increasing the use of input y, is \$.50, since an extra 1/4 unit of input y — at \$2 a unit — will result in an extra unit of output. Thus the ratio of the price of each input to its marginal product equals marginal cost, which is \$.50.

Going a step further, the firm, if it maximizes profit, must be operating at a point at which marginal cost equals marginal revenue. Thus it follows that

$$\frac{P_x}{MP_x} = \frac{P_y}{MP_y} = \cdots = \frac{P_z}{MP_z} = MR, \qquad [15.3]$$

where MR is the firm's marginal revenue. Rearranging terms,

$$MP_x \cdot MR = P_x \qquad [15.4a]$$

$$MP_y \cdot MR = P_y \qquad [15.4b]$$

$$\cdot$$
$$\cdot$$
$$\cdot$$

$$MP_z \cdot MR = P_z \qquad [15.4c]$$

Thus we conclude that the profit-maximizing firm employs each input in an amount such that the input's marginal product multiplied by the firm's marginal revenue equals the input's price. This result, as we shall see in the following section, provides the basis for the firm's demand curve for an input.

The point in the text is that λ equals marginal cost. To prove this, note that

$$dC = \sum_{i=1}^{n} P_i dX_i$$

and
$$dQ = \sum_{i=1}^{n} \frac{\partial f}{\partial X_i} dX_i,$$

where dC is a small change in cost, dQ is a small change in output, and dX_i is a small change in X_i. Since marginal cost equals dC/dQ, it follows that marginal cost equals

$$\frac{\sum_{i=1}^{n} P_i dX_i}{\sum_{i=1}^{n} (\partial f / \partial X_i) dX_i} = \sum_{i=1}^{n} \lambda \frac{(\partial f / \partial X_i) dX_i}{\sum_{i=1}^{n} (\partial f / \partial X_i) dX_i} = \lambda.$$

This proves the point in the text.

THE FIRM'S DEMAND CURVE: THE CASE OF ONE VARIABLE INPUT

Our first step in analyzing the demand for an input is to consider the demand curve of an individual firm for an input, assuming that this input is the only variable input in the firm's production process. In other words, the quantities of all other inputs are fixed. This assumption is relaxed in the next section. The demand curve of a firm for this input — call it input x— shows the quantity of input x that the firm will demand at each possible price of input x. Assuming that the firm maximizes its profits, it will demand that amount of input x at which the value of the extra output produced by an extra unit of input x is equal to the price of input x. This is the meaning of Equation 15.4a.

To make this more concrete, suppose that we know the firm's production function, from which we deduce that the marginal product of input x (at each level of utilization of input x) is as shown in Table 15.1. Suppose that the price of the product is \$3. Since the product market is perfectly competitive, the marginal revenue is also \$3. The value to the firm of the extra output resulting from its increasing its utilization of input x by 1 unit is shown in the last column of Table 15.1. This is called the *value of the marginal product* of input x, and equals $MP_x \cdot P$, where P is the price of the product. Since $P = MR$ in perfect competition, the value of the marginal product is the left-hand side of Equation 15.4a.

Value of the marginal product

How many units of input x should the firm use if input x costs \$10 a unit? A 1-unit increase in the utilization of input x adds to the firm's revenues the amount shown in the last column of Table 15.1, and it adds \$10 to the firm's

TABLE 15.1 Value of Marginal Product of Input x

Quantity of x	Marginal product[a]	Value of marginal product[a] (dollars)
3	8	24
4	7	21
5	6	18
6	5	15
7	4	12
8	3	9
9	2	6

[a] The figures pertain to the interval between the indicated quantity of input x and 1 unit less than the indicated quantity of input x.

costs. (Since the input markets are perfectly competitive, the firm cannot influence the price of any input.) Thus the firm should increase its utilization of input x as long as the increase in revenue exceeds the increase in costs, that is, as long as the figure in the last column of Table 15.1 exceeds $10. For example, if the firm is using 5 units of input x, the use of an extra unit will increase revenues by $15 and increase costs by $10; consequently, the extra unit should be used. What about adding still another unit? If the firm is using 6 units of input x, the use of an extra unit will increase revenue by $12 and increase costs by $10; thus it too should be added. Increases in the utilization of input x are profitable up to 7 units; beyond this point, an extra unit of input x increases costs more than revenues. Thus the firm should use 7 units of input x.

The optimal number of units of input x is the number at which the value of the marginal product of input x equals the price of input x. This, of course, is just another way of stating the result in Equation 15.4a, since under these circumstances the value of the marginal product of input x is equal to the left-hand side of the equation and the price of input x is the right-hand side of the equation.[3]

If the firm demands the optimal amount of input x at each price of input x, its demand schedule for input x must be the value-of-marginal-product schedule in the last column of Table 15.1. For example, if the price of input x is between $6 and $9, the firm will demand 8 units of input x; if the price of input x is between $9 and $12, the firm will demand 7 units of input x. Thus the firm's demand curve for input x is the value-of-marginal-product curve, which shows the value of input x's marginal product at each quantity of input x used. This curve will slope downward and to the right, because it is proportional to the curve showing the input's marginal productivity.

THE FIRM'S DEMAND CURVE:
THE CASE OF SEVERAL VARIABLE INPUTS

Suppose now that the firm uses a number of inputs that can be varied in quantity and input x is only one of them. Under these circumstances, the firm's demand curve for input x is no longer the value-of-marginal-product curve. This

---

[3] This assumes that the quantity of the input can be varied continuously, which is often the case. However, it is not the case in Table 15.1. Since only integer values can be used, according to Table 15.1, this rule must be changed somewhat here. In this case, the optimal number of units of input x is the largest integer at which the value of the marginal product of input x is greater than or equal to the price of input x.

is because a change in the price of input x will result in a change in the quantities of the other variable inputs used, and these changes in the quantities of the other variable inputs will affect the quantity of input x used.

As an example, suppose that the price of input x is initially \$10 and the quantity of input x used is 100 units. Holding constant the use of other inputs, suppose that the value-of-marginal-product curve is V_1 in Figure 15.1. If none of the other inputs were variable, this would be the demand curve for input x. In fact, however, a number of other inputs are variable. Suppose that the price of input x falls to \$6. What will happen to the quantity of input x demanded by the firm? Since the value of its marginal product exceeds its new price, the firm will tend to expand its use. But the increase in its use will shift the value-of-marginal-product curves of other inputs. For example, if another variable input is complementary to input x, its value-of-marginal-product curve will shift to the right. These shifts in the value-of-marginal-product curves of other variable inputs will result in changes in the amounts used of them. And the changes in the amounts used of other inputs will in turn shift the value-of-marginal-product curve of input x.

When all of these effects have occurred, the firm will be on another value-of-marginal-product curve for input x, say V_2 in Figure 15.1. And the amount demanded of input x will be such that the value of its marginal product will be equal to its new price. Thus the firm will demand 200 units of input x. Points

FIGURE 15.1 Demand Curve of the Firm for Input x Points A and B are on the firm's demand curve for input x. (V_1 and V_2 are value-of-marginal-product curves.)

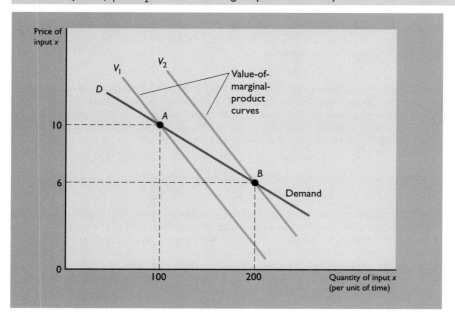

A and *B* are both on the firm's demand curve for input *x*. Other points can be determined in a similar fashion; the complete demand curve is *D*. It can be shown that all demand curves of this type slope down and to the right, as would be expected.[4]

THE MARKET DEMAND CURVE

When we derived a market demand curve for a commodity in Chapter 5, we summed horizontally over the demand curves of individual consumers of the commodity. At first glance it may seem that we can derive the market demand curve for an input by simply summing horizontally over the demand curves of individual firms for the input. Although this would provide a first approximation, it would not yield the correct result because it neglects the effect of changes in the input price on the product price.

---

[4] In passing, we should note that economists of the past were bothered by the question of whether, if each input was paid the value of its marginal product, the total amount paid by firms for inputs would be equal to the firm's revenues. Much of the discussion of this question was beside the point, and need not concern us here (see P. Samuelson, *Foundations of Economic Analysis* [Cambridge, Mass.: Harvard University Press, 1947], pp. 81–87). However, it may be worth noting that, if the production function exhibits constant returns to scale, Euler's theorem states that the total physical output of a firm will be identically equal to the sum of the amount of each input used multiplied by the input's marginal product:

$$Q = X_1 MP_1 + X_2 MP_2 + \cdots + X_n MP_n, \qquad [15.5]$$

where Q is the firm's output level, X_1 is the amount of the first input used by the firm, X_2 is the amount of the second input used by the firm, X_n is the amount of the nth input used by the firm, MP_1 is the marginal product of the first input, MP_2 is the marginal product of the second input, MP_n is the marginal product of the nth input, and n is the number of inputs used by the firm. Thus, multiplying both sides of Equation 15.5 by P, the price of the product, we have

$$PQ = X_1 P(MP_1) + X_2 P(MP_2) + \cdots + X_n P(MP_n). \qquad [15.6]$$

If each input is paid the value of its marginal product, it follows that

$$PQ = X_1 P_1 + X_2 P_2 + \cdots + X_n P_n, \qquad [15.7]$$

where P_1 is the price of the first input, P_2 is the price of the second input, and P_n is the price of the nth input. The left-hand side of Equation 15.7 is the firm's receipts. The right-hand side of Equation 15.7 is the total amount paid by the firm to inputs. Thus, if there are constant returns to scale, the firm's total receipts will be identically equal to the amount necessary to pay all inputs the value of their marginal products. Finally, note that Equation 15.7 is an identity under these circumstances. In general, Equation 15.7 holds as a condition of long-run competitive equilibrium (see Samuelson, *Foundations of Economic Analysis*).

EXAMPLE 15.1

The Value of the Marginal Product of Irrigation Water

Under the auspices of the U.S. Department of Agriculture, controlled experiments have been carried out to determine the production functions for a variety of crops. One such experiment estimated the effects of various amounts of irrigation water on the output of cotton in medium-textured soil in Arizona. Based on this experiment, the value of the marginal product of irrigation water in the production of Arizona cotton (if the cotton price is 76¢ or 51¢ per pound of lint) is as follows:

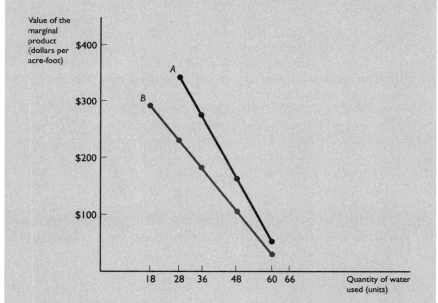

(a) Which of these curves is based on the cotton price of 76¢? Which is based on the cotton price of 51¢? (b) If the price of water is $50 per acre-foot, about how much water will be demanded for irrigation purposes, if the price of cotton is 76¢? (c) Most studies indicate that the demand for irrigation water is price inelastic. Is this in accord with the above curves if the price of water is $50 per acre-foot? (d) If substantial increases occur in the price of irrigation water, farmers can respond by installing a completely different type of irrigation apparatus which conserves water. If this were to occur, would the above curves still show the demand curve for water? Why or why not?

SOLUTION: (a) The higher curve, *A*, is based on the higher price; the lower curve, *B*, is based on the lower price. The value of the marginal product at any quantity of water equals the marginal product of water times the price of cotton. Thus the higher the price of cotton, the higher the value of the marginal product. (b) About 60 units of water. (c) Yes. For example, if the price of water increases from $50 to $100, the quantity of water demanded is reduced from about 60 to about 55 units of water, based on curve *A* in the graph on page 487. Thus the arc elasticity of demand is about

$$\frac{-(55 - 60)}{57.5} \div \frac{100 - 50}{75} = 0.13.$$

(d) No. The value-of-marginal-product curve is the demand curve for water only if the amount used of all other inputs remains constant. If a different apparatus were used, the quantity (and perhaps the type) of other inputs used would change.*

---

*For further discussion, see D. Gibbons, *The Economic Value of Water* (Washington, D.C.: Resources for the Future, 1986). Much more will be said about the demand and supply of water in Chapter 19.

Each firm's demand curve for the input is based on the supposition that the firm's decisions cannot affect the price of its output. For example, in Table 15.1, the firm assumes that the price of its product will be $3, regardless of how it alters its utilization of input x in response to changes in the price of input x. This is a perfectly reasonable assumption for the firm to make, because it is only a very small portion of the industry. But this is not the situation underlying the market demand curve. The market demand curve shows the total amount of the input demanded at various possible prices of the input. Thus it shows the effect of changes in input price on the utilization of the input *when all firms in the industry respond at the same time.*

Suppose that the price of input x decreases substantially. This will result in increased utilization of input x by all firms in the industry and in increased output by all members of the industry. Although the increased output by any single firm cannot affect the price of the industry's product, the combined expansion of output by all firms results in a decrease in the price of the product. This decrease in the price of the product shifts each firm's value-of-marginal-product curve, and consequently it shifts each firm's demand curve for input x.

Market demand curve

To derive the market demand curve for input x, suppose that its initial price is \$8 and that each firm in the market is in equilibrium, with its demand curve for input x being d in Figure 15.2. Each firm uses Oq units of input x. Multiplying Oq by the number of firms in the market, we get OQ, the total amount taken off the market at a price of \$8. Thus A is a point on the market demand curve.

Suppose that the price of input x falls to \$6. Each firm will increase its use of input x and increase output, with the consequence that the price of the product will fall and the individual firm demand curves for input x will shift toward e. When all adjustments have been made, each firm will be using Or units of input x. This is less than the Os units that each would have used if it had re-

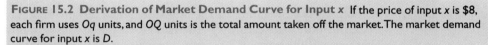

FIGURE 15.2 Derivation of Market Demand Curve for Input x If the price of input x is \$8, each firm uses Oq units, and OQ units is the total amount taken off the market. The market demand curve for input x is D.

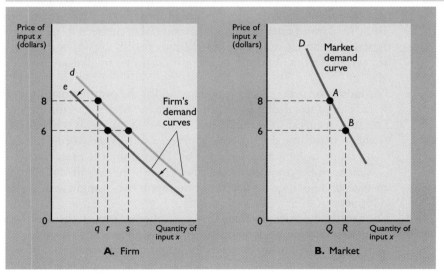

mained on the demand curve, *d*. Multiplying *Or* by the number of firms in the market, we get *OR,* the total amount taken off the market at a price of $6. Thus *B* is another point on the market demand curve. Other points on the market demand curve can be obtained in similar fashion; the complete market demand curve for input *x* is *D*.

DETERMINANTS OF THE PRICE ELASTICITY OF DEMAND FOR AN INPUT

In Chapter 5 we pointed out that, in the case of commodities, the price elasticity of market demand varies enormously, the quantity demanded of some commodities being very sensitive to price changes, and the quantity demanded of other commodities being quite insensitive to price changes. This is true of inputs as well. The quantity demanded of some inputs is very sensitive to price changes, whereas the quantity demanded of other inputs is not at all sensitive to price changes. Why is this the case? What determines whether the price elasticity of demand for a particular input will be high or low? Several rules are important.

1. The more easily other inputs can be substituted for a certain input, say input *x,* the more price elastic is the demand for input *x*. This certainly makes sense. If the technologies of the firms using input *x* allow these firms to substitute other inputs readily for input *x,* a small increase in the price of input *x* may result in a substantial decrease in its use. But if these firms cannot substitute other inputs readily for input *x,* a large increase in the price of input *x* may result in only a small decrease in its use.

2. The larger the price elasticity of demand for the product that input *x* helps to produce, the larger the price elasticity of demand for input *x*. This, too, seems clear enough. The demand for an input is prompted by the demand for the product it produces; in other words, the demand for an input is a *derived demand*. The greater the price elasticity of demand of the product, the more sensitive is the output of the product to changes in its price that occur in response to changes in the price of input *x*.

Derived demand

3. The greater the price elasticity of supply of other inputs, the greater is the price elasticity of demand for input *x*. The supply curve for an input is the relationship between the amount of the input that is supplied and the input's price. The price elasticity of supply of an input is

the percentage increase in the quantity supplied of the input resulting from a 1 percent increase in the price of the input.[5] Thus, if small increases in price bring forth large increases in the quantity of other inputs supplied, this will mean that the demand for input x will be more price elastic than if large increases in price are required to bring forth small increases in the quantity supplied of other inputs.

4. The price elasticity of demand for an input is likely to be greater in the long run than in the short run. The reasoning here is like that underlying the similar proposition in Chapter 5 concerning the demand for commodities. Basically, the point is that it takes time to adjust fully to a price change. For example, if the price of skilled labor increases, it may not be possible for many plants to reduce very greatly the quantity of skilled labor demanded in the short run, since their plants are built to use fairly rigidly defined amounts of this input. But in the long run, firms can build new plants to reduce their utilization of skilled labor.[6]

THE MARKET SUPPLY CURVE

Under perfect competition, the supply of an input to an individual firm is infinitely elastic. In other words, the firm can buy all it wants without influencing the price of the input. When we consider the market supply curve, which is the relationship between the price of the input and the total amount of the input supplied in the entire market, it is often untrue that the supply is infinitely elastic. In many cases, the total amount of the input supplied in the entire market will increase only if the price of the input is increased. Indeed, in some cases it is alleged that the market supply curve is perfectly inelastic, that is, the total amount of the input supplied in the entire market is fixed and unresponsive to the price of the input.

Market supply curve

There is, of course, no contradiction between the assertion that the supply of an input *to an individual firm* is perfectly elastic under perfect competition and the assertion that the *market* supply curve may not be perfectly elastic under perfect competition. For example, arable land might be available to any one

---

[5] More accurately, the price elasticity of supply is $dQ/dP \div Q/P$, where Q is the quantity supplied of the input and P is its price.

[6] For durable inputs, this proposition may not hold. See footnote 2 on page 138.

Another frequently advanced proposition is that the demand for an input will be less elastic if the payments to this input are a small, rather than a large, proportion of the total cost of the product. There may be a good deal of truth in this proposition, but it does not always hold.

farmer in as great an amount as he could possibly use at a given price; yet the aggregate amount of arable land available to all farmers may increase little with increases in the price per acre. The situation is similar to the sale of commodities: We saw in Chapter 10 that any firm under perfect competition believes that it can sell all it wants at the existing price; yet the total amount of a commodity sold in a given market can usually be increased only by reducing price.

There is sometimes a tendency to underestimate the extent to which the market supply of an input will be increased in response to an increase in the price of the input. For example, it is sometimes argued that the country is provided with a certain amount of land and mineral resources, and that there is no way to change these amounts. For this reason, it is assumed that their market supply is perfectly inelastic, the available supply being completely unresponsive to price. But this can be quite wrong. For present purposes, what is important is the amount of land and mineral resources that is used, not the amount in existence. A large increase in price generally will increase the amount of these resources in use. This will occur because a higher price will result in more exploration for resources, in the reopening of high-cost mines and farms, and in the irrigation and upgrading of poorer land.

Labor Inputs and the Backward-Bending Supply Curve

Most inputs are *intermediate goods,* goods that are bought from other business firms. For example, an important input in the electric power industry is coal, which is bought from the coal industry. The supply curve for inputs of this kind is already familiar, and there is no need to discuss once again the determinants of the nature and shape of the market supply curve in these cases.

However, not all inputs are supplied by business firms. One of the most significant inputs — labor — is provided by individuals. (In addition, individuals provide other inputs like savings.) When individuals supply an input like labor, they are supplying something that they themselves can use, since the time that they do not work can be used for leisure activities. Thus sellers of these inputs want to keep some of them for themselves. And the amount of these inputs that is supplied to firms depends on the quantities of these inputs that are produced and the quantities that the suppliers want to keep for themselves.

In Chapter 10, we saw that the market supply curve for inputs supplied by business firms will generally slope upward and to the right. In other words higher prices generally are required to bring forth an increased supply. An interesting feature of the market supply function for inputs supplied by individ-

Backward-bending supply curve uals is that it, unlike the supply function for inputs supplied by business firms, may be *backward-bending*. That is, increases in price may result in smaller amounts of the input being supplied. An example of a backward-bending supply curve is *SS'* in Figure 15.3.

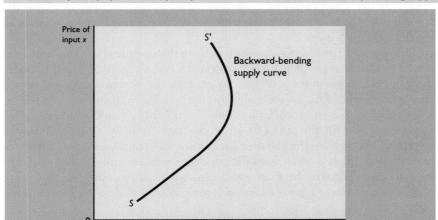

FIGURE 15.3 Backward-Bending Supply Curve If the supply curve is backward-bending, increases in price (beyond some point) result in smaller amounts of the input being supplied.

To see how such a case can occur, consider the labor time supplied by a single worker, Bill Jones. Jones has 24 hours a day to allocate between work and leisure. To him leisure time is a commodity he desires, and its price is the hourly wage rate — the amount of money he gives up to enjoy an hour of leisure time. What will be the effect of an increase in the wage rate on the amount of leisure time that Jones will demand? Clearly, this is a problem of consumer choice, since the question can be restated: What is the effect of an increase in the price of leisure time on the quantity of leisure time that Jones demands? The theoretical tools discussed in Chapter 4 can help us to answer this question.

As we learned in Chapter 4, we can divide the effect of the price increase into two parts: the substitution effect and the income effect. The substitution effect is the effect of the increase in the cost of leisure relative to other commodities. Since other consumer goods will become relatively less expensive, the substitution effect will result in his reducing his leisure time and increasing his purchase of other consumer goods. Thus the substitution effect will result in his increasing the amount of labor time he puts forth. **Substitution effect**

In addition, there is an income effect, which is quite different from the income effect in the case of the purchase of most consumer products. In the first place, the income effect here works in the opposite direction from the income effect in the case of the purchase of the typical consumer product. As we saw in Chapter 4, the income effect of a price increase of a good is generally to reduce the consumption of the good, since the price increase reduces the con- **Income effect** sumer's real purchasing power. But this is not the case here. An increase in the price of his leisure time due to an increase in his wage makes Jones more affluent and better able to afford the things he wants, including leisure. Thus the income effect of an increase in the price of leisure is likely to be an increase in the demand for leisure.

The income effect in this case differs from the income effect for most consumer products in another important respect: It is likely to be much stronger than for most consumer products. In general, the consumer spends only a small percentage of his or her budget on the product in question, with the result that an increase in its price has only a small impact on his or her real income. However, in the case of leisure, an increase in its price will almost certainly have a great effect on the consumer's real income, since most of his or her income is likely to stem from the sale of labor. (Remember that the price of leisure time is equal to the wage rate.) Thus an increase in the price of leisure time is likely to have a great effect on Jones's income and on his consumption pattern.

The income effect may offset the substitution effect, with the result that an increase in the wage rate may reduce the supply of labor. In other words, an increase in the price of leisure time may increase the quantity demanded of leisure time. Of course, institutional constraints often prevent workers from choosing their own working hours; for example, the 40-hour week is commonly worked in industry. But the typical, or average, work week responds to the shape of the supply curve for labor. Thus, in the United States, as workers have become more affluent the average work week has tended to decrease. For example, the average work week in 1850 was almost 70 hours, as contrasted with about 40 hours at present.

EQUILIBRIUM PRICE AND EMPLOYMENT OF AN INPUT

Equilibrium price

The market demand and supply curves for an input determine the input's equilibrium price. The price of the input will tend in equilibrium to the level at which the quantity of the input demanded equals the quantity of the input supplied. Thus, in Figure 15.4, the equilibrium price of the input is OP_0. If the price were higher than OP_0, the quantity supplied would exceed the quantity demanded, and there would be downward pressure on the price. If the price were lower than OP_0, the quantity supplied would fall short of the quantity demanded, and there would be upward pressure on the price.

The equilibrium amount of the input that is employed is also given by the intersection of the market demand and supply curves. For example, in Figure

FIGURE 15.4 Determination of Equilibrium Price and Quantity The equilibrium price is OP_0, and the equilibrium quantity is OQ_0.

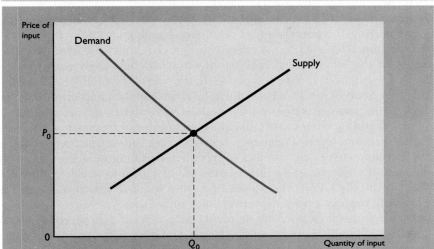

15.4, OQ_0 units of the input will be employed in equilibrium. In equilibrium the value of the marginal product of an input will be equal in each and every place where the input is used. In all uses the value of the marginal product of an input will equal the price of the input — and the price of the input will, of course, be the same to all firms under perfect competition.

Equilibrium employment

The Market for Engineers: An Application

At this point, it is advisable to pause for a moment and illustrate how the theory we have been discussing has been put to use. During much of the period since World War II, top government policymakers have been concerned with the adequacy of the national supply of engineers. During the late 1960s and early 1970s, there was a feeling that too many engineers were being turned out by the country's colleges and universities. The situation turned around in the late 1980s, when the National Science Board worried that a 23 percent decline in the college-age population between 1980 and 1985 "may impose restraints on the supply of newly trained scientists and engineers."[7] Both during the period of apparent surplus and that of apparent shortage, questions were repeatedly raised by knowledgeable people concerning the workings of the market for engineers. In particular, it was asked whether the sort of model described

---

[7] National Science Board, *Science and Engineering Indicators —1987* (Washington, D.C.: Government Printing Office, 1988), p. 69.

in previous sections of this chapter really explained the quantity of engineers graduated in a particular period and the level of their salaries.

To help answer this question, Richard Freeman of Harvard University gathered detailed data concerning the annual number of freshmen enrolling in engineering, the annual number of engineers graduating and seeking work, and the annual level of starting salaries of engineers (with a bachelor's degree). Based on careful statistical analysis, he estimated the supply and demand curves for engineers during this period. In the case of the supply curve, he divided the analysis into two parts. First, he estimated the effect of the level of engineering starting salaries on the number of freshmen enrolling in engineering. Holding other factors (like the total number of freshmen in all fields and the previous levels of salaries and enrollments) constant, he found that the relationship between the number of freshmen enrolling in engineering and the level of engineering starting salaries was as shown in panel A of Figure 15.5. Specifically, a 1 percent increase in starting salaries results in a 2.9 percent increase in freshman enrollment in engineering.

Next, taking the freshman enrollment in engineering as given, he estimated the effect of the level of engineering starting salaries on the number of engineers graduating 4 years later and seeking work. Holding the freshman enrollment (and other factors) constant, he found that the relationship between the number of engineers graduating (and seeking work) and the level of starting salaries was as shown in panel B of Figure 15.5.[8] Specifically, a

FIGURE 15.5 Estimated Relationship between Number of People Going into Engineering and the Level of Engineering Salaries, United States An increase in starting engineering salaries results in a substantial increase in freshman engineering enrollments, as well as an increase in the number of engineers graduating from college.

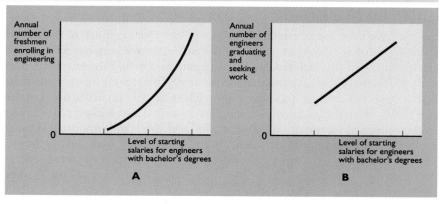

[8] Starting salaries here refer to a couple of years before graduation.

1 percent increase in starting salaries results in about a 1 percent increase in the number of graduate engineers. In other words, more students switched to engineering or stayed in engineering when engineering salaries were relatively high than when they were relatively low. But as one would expect, the quantitative impact of salaries was smaller here than on freshman enrollment in engineering.

Together, the two panels of Figure 15.5 provide some interesting insights concerning the supply curve for engineers in the United States. To government policymakers, information of this sort is of great importance. For example, if national goals seem to require a certain number of engineers, such information can be used to help indicate the level of starting salaries that, in the absence of other measures, would be required to call them forth. Further, Freeman's results shed valuable light on the extent to which the theory presented in previous sections can explain the workings of the market for engineers. He concludes that "traditional market forces—shifts in supply and demand — explain changes in engineering starting salaries, though with a lag due to sluggish adjustment to unexpected supply conditions."[9]

THE CONCEPT OF RENT

Earlier in this chapter we stated that there is sometimes a tendency to underestimate the extent to which the market supply of an input will be increased in response to an increase in the price of the input. Nevertheless, some inputs, like certain types of land, may be in relatively fixed supply. Suppose that the supply of an input is completely fixed: Increases in its price will not increase its supply and decreases in its price will not decrease its supply. Following the terminology of the classical economists of the nineteenth century, the price of such an input is rent. This use of the word *rent* is quite different from everyday usage, according to which *rent* is the price of using an apartment or a car or some other object owned by someone else.

Rent

If the supply of an input is fixed, its supply curve is a vertical line, as shown in Figure 15.6. Thus the price of this input, that is, its rent, is determined entirely by the demand curve for the input. For example, if the demand curve is

---

[9] In panel B of Figure 15.5, the annual number of engineers graduating and seeking work is estimated holding constant the number of freshmen enrolled in engineering 4 years earlier.

FIGURE 15.6 An Input in Completely Fixed Supply The price of an input in fixed supply is called a rent. If the demand curve is D, the rent is OP.

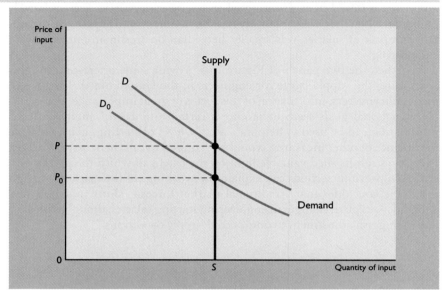

D, the rent is OP; if the demand curve is D_0, the rent is OP_0. Since the supply of the input is fixed, the price of the input can be lowered without influencing the amount of the input that is supplied. Thus a rent is a payment above the minimum necessary to attract this amount of the input.[10]

In recent years, there has been a tendency among economists to extend the use of the word *rent* to encompass all payments to inputs that are above the minimum required to make these inputs available to the industry or to the economy. To a great extent these payments are costs to individual firms, since these firms must make such payments in order to attract and keep these inputs, which are useful to other firms in the industry. But, if the inputs have no use in other industries, these payments are not costs to the industry as a whole (or to the economy as a whole) because the inputs would be available to the industry whether or not these payments are made.

Why is it important to know whether or not a certain payment for inputs is a rent? Because a reduction of the payment will not influence the availability

---

[10] Note that whether rent is or is not price-determined depends on whether we are looking at the matter from the point of view of a firm, a small industry, a large industry, or the whole economy. Although a payment to an input that is in fixed supply to the whole society or a large industry may be a rent from the point of view of the society or the industry, it may appear to be a price-determining cost to an individual small firm or a small industry.

and use of the inputs if the payment is a rent; whereas, if it is not a rent, a reduction of the payment is likely to change the allocation of resources. For example, if the government imposes a tax on rents, there will be no effect on the
supply of resources to the economy.

Quasi-rents

The payment to any input in temporarily fixed supply is called a quasi-rent. In
previous chapters, we have seen that many inputs are in fixed supply to a firm
in the short run. For example, a firm's plant cannot be changed appreciably. In
the short run, fixed inputs cannot be withdrawn from their current use and
transferred to a use where the returns are higher. Also, fixed inputs cannot be
supplemented with other similar inputs in the short run. Thus the payments
to the fixed inputs are determined differently from the payments to the variable inputs. Whereas inputs that are variable in quantity are free to move
where the returns are highest, fixed inputs are stuck where they are, at least in
the short run. Consequently, firms must pay the variable inputs as much as
they can earn in alternative uses, and the fixed inputs receive whatever is
left over.

The return to the fixed inputs is a *quasi-rent*. It is a residual. To understand
its nature, it is useful to consider the diagram in Figure 15.7, which shows a
firm's short-run cost curves. Suppose that the price is OP_0, with the result that

**Quasi-
rent**

FIGURE 15.7 Quasi-rent A quasi-rent is the payment to any input in temporarily fixed supply. The
amount received by the fixed inputs, which equals GP_0CB, is a quasi-rent.

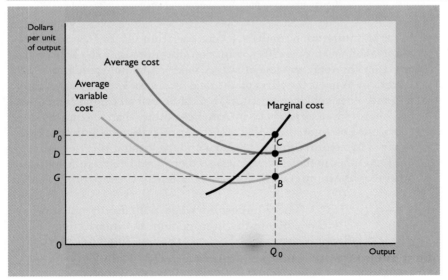

EXAMPLE 15.2

Does Immigration Benefit the United States?

On June 11, 1995, the *New York Times* editorialized that "Immigration . . . promises to become an incendiary issue in the 1996 elections". Current levels of immigration to the United States, about 900,000 a year, are regarded as excessive by some observers. While this is only partly an economic issue, the concepts provided here are relevant. Suppose that the economy is competitive (with constant returns to scale) and that the value-of-marginal-product curve for labor is shown below.

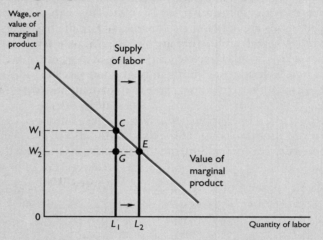

(a) If immigration results in an increase from OL_1 to OL_2 in the supply of labor, what is the effect on the equilibrium wage? (b) What is the effect on the total amount of wages received by nonimmigrant U.S. labor? (c) What is the effect on the total income of U.S. owners of capital (and other nonlabor resources)? Assume that all capital (and other nonlabor resources) is owned by Americans other than the immigrants. (d) Taking account of the effects of the immigration on both the wages received by nonimmigrant U.S. labor and the income of owners of capital (and other nonlabor resources), is there a net benefit to Americans other than the immigrants? If so, how big is it?

SOLUTION: (a) The equilibrium wage will drop from OW_1 to OW_2. Before the immigration, the intersection of the demand and supply curves for labor was at point C; after the shift in the supply curve for labor, it is at point E. (b) The quantity of nonimmigrant U.S. labor is OL_1. Since the wage rate was OW_1 before the immigration, nonimmigrant U.S. labor received total wages amounting to OW_1 times OL_1, which equals area OW_1CL_1. After immigration, nonimmigrant U.S. labor received total wages amounting to OW_2 times OL_1, which equals area OW_2GL_1. Thus the immigration reduced the total wages to nonimmigrant U.S. labor by an amount equal to area W_2W_1CG. (c) The value of the total output produced by n workers is the sum of the values of the marginal products of the first, second, . . . , and mth workers.* Thus, since OL_1 workers were hired before the immigration, the value of the total output at that time equaled the sum of the values of the marginal products of the OL_1 workers — which amounts to area $OACL_1$. Since wages equaled area OW_1CL_1, owners of capital (and other nonlabor resources) received an amount equal to W_1AC (the difference between area $OACL_1$ and area OW_1CL_1). After the immigration, the value of the total output produced by the OL_2 workers is the sum of the values of their marginal products, which equals $OAEL_2$. Subtracting total wages, owners of capital (and other nonlabor resources) received an amount equal to area W_2AE (the difference between area $OAEL_2$ and area OW_2EL_2). Thus owners of capital (and other nonlabor resources) received an increase in income amounting to the area W_2W_1CE (the difference between area W_2AE and area W_1AC). (d) The increase in the total income of U.S. owners of capital and other nonlabor resources (area W_2W_1CE) exceeds the loss to nonimmigrant U.S. labor (area W_2W_1CG), the difference equaling triangle CGE.†

---

*To see this, let the value of total output be $V(n)$ when n workers are hired. Since the value of the marginal product of the first worker is $V(1) - V(0)$, the value of the marginal product of the second worker is $V(2) - V(1)$, . . . , and the value of the marginal product of the nth worker is $V(n) - V(n-1)$, it follows that the sum of the values of the marginal products of the n workers equals

$$[V(1) - V(0)] + [V(2) - V(1)] + \cdots + [V(n) - V(n-1)].$$

Since $V(1), V(2), \ldots V(n-1)$ appear with both positive and negative signs, they cancel out; and since $V(0) = 0$, this sum must equal $V(n)$.

†For further discussion, see G. Borjas, "The Economic Benefits from Immigration", R. Friedberg and J. Hunt, "The Impact of Immigrants on Host Country Wages, Employment, and Growth", and K. Zimmerman, "Tackling the European Migration Problem", all in the *The Journal of Economic Perspectives,* Spring 1995.

---

the firm will produce OQ_0 units and its total variable costs will be $OGBQ_0$ (since OG equals its average variable cost). This area, $OGBQ_0$ represents the amount that the firm must pay in order to attract and keep the amount of variable inputs corresponding to an output of OQ_0. It cannot pay less and expect to keep them. The fixed inputs get the residual, which is GP_0CB. This is the quasi-rent.

The short-run average total cost curve includes both the average variable costs and the average fixed costs. To determine the average fixed costs, we see what the returns on the firm's fixed assets would be if the rate of return were equal to that available elsewhere in the economy. Thus, since the firm's average total cost curve is as shown in Figure 15.7, the total fixed costs of the firm are equal to $GDEB$. Consequently, this amount of the quasi-rent is not pure economic profit; only DP_0CE is economic profit. Needless to say, quasi-rent need not be greater than total fixed costs. Firms with pure economic losses do not have quasi-rents that are large enough to cover total fixed costs.

IMPERFECTLY COMPETITIVE OUTPUT MARKETS

Suppose that there is perfect competition in the market for the input, but imperfect competition (that is, monopoly, oligopoly, or monopolistic competition) in the relevant product markets. In other words, let's allow some of the firms that are potential buyers of the input to have some monopoly power in the sale of their products. Under these circumstances, what determines the price and employment of the input?

Suppose that the only variable input is input x. Assuming that a firm maximizes its profits, it will hire that amount of input x at which the value of the extra output produced by an extra unit of input x is equal to the price of a unit of input x. (Recall Equation 15.4a) To be more specific, suppose that the marginal product of input x at various levels of utilization of input x is that shown in Table 15.2; the total amount of output that can be derived from each number of units of input x is shown in the third column of Table 15.2. Because the firm is an imperfect competitor, the price of its product will vary with the amount it sells; the fourth column of Table 15.2 provides the price that corresponds to each output in the third column. Multiplying the output in the third column by the price in the fourth column, we get the total revenue corresponding to each number of units of input x used; this is shown in column 5.

Finally, in column 6 of Table 15.2, we show the increase in total revenue that stems from the use of each additional unit of input x. For example, the fifth unit of input x (that is, going from 4 to 5 units of input x) increases the firm's total revenue by $131. Similarly, the seventh unit of input x (that is, going from 6 to 7 units of input x) increases the firm's total revenue by $79.50. The increase in total revenue due to the use of an additional unit of input x is called the *mar-*

TABLE 15.2 Marginal Revenue Product of Input x

Quantity of x	Marginal product of x[a]	Total output	Price of good (dollars)	Total revenue (dollars)	Marginal revenue product of x[a] (dollars)
3	10	33	20.00	660.00	—
4	9	42	19.50	819.00	159.00
5	8	50	19.00	950.00	131.00
6	7	57	18.50	1,054.50	104.50
7	6	63	18.00	1,134.00	79.50
8	5	68	17.50	1,190.00	56.00
9	4	72	17.00	1,224.00	34.00

[a] These figures pertain to the interval between the indicated amount of input x and 1 unit less than the indicated amount of input x.

ginal revenue product of input x, which explains the heading of column 6. The marginal revenue product of input x is equal to the marginal physical product of input x times the firm's marginal revenue.[11] Thus it is equal to the left-hand side of Equation 15.4a.

Marginal revenue product

If the firm maximizes profit, it sets the marginal revenue product of input x equal to the price of input x. This is the meaning of Equation 15.4a. Thus the firm's demand schedule for input x must be the marginal-revenue-product schedule in Table 15.2. For example, suppose that the price of input x is $56. Then according to Equation 15.4a the firm will set the marginal revenue product of input x equal to $56; this means that it will demand 8 units of input x. Or suppose that the price of input x is $34. Then the firm will set the marginal revenue product of input x equal to $34; this means that it will demand 9 units of input x. Thus the number of units of input x that the firm will demand at any price is given by the marginal-revenue-product curve, which shows the marginal revenue product of input x at various quantities of input x used. This curve is shown in Figure 15.8.

---

[11] It is easy to prove that the marginal revenue product is the product of the marginal product (MP) and marginal revenue (MR). By definition,

$$MRP = \frac{\Delta R}{\Delta I},$$

where ΔR is the change in total revenue and ΔI is the change in the quantity of the input. Since $MR = \Delta R/\Delta Q$, where ΔQ is the change in output, it follows that

$$MRP = \frac{MR\Delta Q}{\Delta I}.$$

But since $MP = \Delta Q/\Delta I$, it also follows that $MRP = MR \times MP$, as we set out to prove.

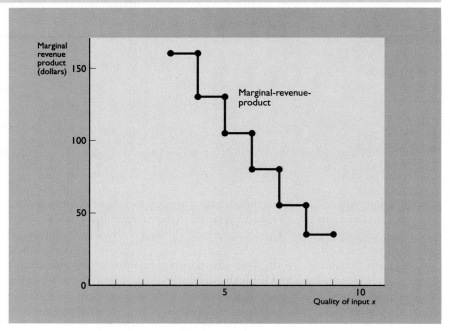

FIGURE 15.8 Marginal-Revenue-Product Curve for Input x The marginal revenue product of input *x* is the increase in the total revenue due to the use of an additional unit of input *x*. The data come from the last column of Table 15.2.

Two points should be noted concerning the marginal-revenue-product curve. First, it will slope downward and to the right (as a demand curve should for an input) for two reasons: the input's marginal product will decrease as more of it is used, and the firm's marginal revenue will decrease as its output increases. Since the marginal revenue product is the product of the input's marginal product and the firm's marginal revenue, it will decrease for both reasons as more of the input is used. Second, the value-of-marginal-product schedule, which played a major role in early sections of this chapter, can be regarded as a special case of the marginal-revenue-product schedule. If marginal revenue is equal to price (as it is in perfect competition), the marginal-revenue-product schedule becomes precisely the same as the value-of-marginal-product schedule.

To find the equilibrium price of input *x*, the demand curves of the individual firms in the market (for the input) must be combined into a single market demand curve for the input. This step can be accomplished in essentially the same way as described earlier (pages 486 to 490) in this chapter. Give the market demand curve for the input, the equilibrium price of the input will be the price at which this demand curve intersects the input's market supply curve. Moreover, the total amount of the input that will be used in equilibrium in this market is also determined in the usual way by the intersection of this demand curve and this supply curve. The nature and determinants of an input's market supply curve, discussed earlier in this chapter, need not be altered by the existence of imperfect competition in the product market.

MONOPSONY

Up to this point we have assumed that there is perfect competition in the input market. Now we change this assumption. We begin by considering the case of monopsony. *Monopsony* is a situation in which there is a single buyer. For example, a group of small firms may be set up to provide tooling, supplies, or materials for a single large manufacturing firm, and because this large firm is the only one of its type in the area and its requirements are highly specialized, this large firm may be the only buyer for the products of the small firms. This is a case of monopsony.

Note the difference between monopsony and monopoly: Monopsony is a case of a single buyer; monopoly is a case of a single seller. Other market situations that could also be studied are oligopsony (where there are a few buyers) and monopsonistic competition (where there are many buyers but the inputs are not homogeneous and some buyers prefer some sellers' inputs to other sellers' inputs). However, it is sufficient for present purposes to limit our attention to monopsony.

Monopsony can occur for various reasons. In some cases, a particular type of input is much more productive in one kind of use than in others. For example, some land that is rich in iron ore may be much more profitably devoted to iron mining than to any other use. Or a person with certain specialized skills may be much more profitably employed using these skills than working at other jobs. If there is only one firm that rents such land or hires such labor, the result is a monopsonistic situation.

The classic case of monopsony is the company town in which a single firm is the sole buyer of labor services. Many "mill towns" and "mining towns" have been dominated by a single firm. As long as workers are unable or unwilling to move elsewhere to work, this firm is a monopsonist. If the mobility of labor can be increased, the monopsony can be broken, at least partially. However, the difficulties in increasing the mobility of labor should not be underesti-

Monopsony

mated: Workers become emotionally attached to a particular area and to their friends and family located there; they often are ignorant of opportunities elsewhere; and they sometimes lack the money and skills that are required to move.

Input Supply Curves and Expenditure Curves

The supply curve of the input facing the monopsonist is the market supply curve: This is the key feature of monopsony. The reason why the monopsonist faces the market supply curve of the input is that the monopsonist is the entire market for the input: It is the sole buyer. Since the market supply curve of an input is generally upward sloping, as we saw in the previous chapter, this means that the supply curve for the input that the monopsonist faces is upward sloping. In other words, the monopsonist is forced to increase the price of the input if it wishes to use more of it, and it can reduce the input's price if it chooses to use less of it.

The contrast between this situation and the situation under perfect competition in the input market should be noted. In the case of perfect competition in the input market, each firm buys only a very small proportion of the total supply of any input, the consequence being that each firm faces a perfectly elastic supply curve for the input. In other words, each firm can buy all it wants of an input without affecting the input's price.

The situation under monopsony is illustrated by the case in Table 15.3. Suppose that a firm is a monopsonist with respect to input x. Suppose that the market supply schedule for input x is that shown in columns 1 and 2. For example, 8 units of input x will be supplied if the price of input x is $10.00, 9 units of input x will be supplied if the price of input x is $10.50, and so forth. Column 3 shows the total cost to the firm of buying the quantities of input x in column 1. For example, the total cost of 8 units of input x is $80.00, and the total cost of

TABLE 15.3 Marginal Expenditure for Input x			
Quantity of x	Price of x (dollars)	Total cost of x (dollars)	Marginal expenditure for x[a] (dollars)
8	10.00	80.00	—
9	10.50	94.50	14.50
10	11.00	110.00	15.50
11	11.50	126.50	16.50
12	12.00	144.00	17.50
13	12.50	162.50	18.50
14	13.00	182.00	19.50

[a] Each figure pertains to the interval between the indicated amount of input x and 1 unit less than the indicated amount of input x.

9 units of input *x* is $94.50. Of course, column 3 is simply the product of the figures in columns 1 and 2.

Column 4 shows the additional cost to the firm of increasing its utilization of input *x* by 1 unit. This is called the *marginal expenditure* for input *x*. For example, the marginal expenditure for the ninth unit of input *x* is $14.50, and the marginal expenditure for the tenth unit of input *x* is $15.50. When the market supply curve for the input is upward sloping, the marginal expenditure for the input will be greater than the input price. The reason for this is simple. Suppose, for example, that the firm in Table 15.3 increases its use of input *x* from 8 to 9 units. If it did not have to increase the price of input *x* in order to expand the supply of the input, it would have to pay only the price, $10, of another unit. But because the supply curve *is* upward sloping, the firm *will* have to increase the price of input *x* in order to increase the supply. *Moreover, this will mean paying all 9 units the higher price, not just paying more for the ninth unit.* Consequently, the marginal expenditure will exceed the input's price.

Marginal expenditure for an input

Figure 15.9 shows input *x*'s supply curve, *SS'*. If the input is bought by a single buyer, the monopsonist's marginal expenditure curve, which shows the

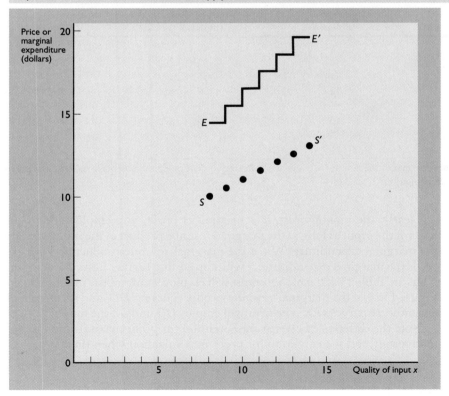

FIGURE 15.9 Supply Curve and Marginal Expenditure Curve for Input x The marginal expenditure curve, *EE'*, lies above the supply curve, *SS'*. The data come from Table 15.3.

marginal expenditure for the input at various quantities used of the input, is *EE'*. Since the supply curve is upward sloping, the marginal expenditure curve lies above it.

Price and Employment: A Single Variable Input

Suppose that there is only one variable input. If the monopsonist maximizes profit, it will purchase larger amounts of the input as long as the extra revenues derived from the additional quantity of input are at least as large as the extra cost of the additional quantity of input. When this is no longer the case, the monopsonist will no longer increase its employment of the input.

More specifically, consider the case in Table 15.4. Column 3 shows the marginal revenue product of the input, that is, the additional revenue derived from an additional unit of the input. For example, the addition of the sixth unit of the input results in $38 of additional revenue. Column 4 shows the marginal expenditure for the input, that is, the additional cost of an additional unit of the input. For example, the addition of the sixth unit of the input results in $15 of additional costs.

TABLE 15.4 Optimal Employment of Input *x*: Monopsony

Quantity of input *x* used by monopsonist	Price of *x* (dollars)	Marginal revenue product of *x*[a] (dollars)	Marginal expenditure for input *x*[a] (dollars)
5	9	40	—
6	10	38	15
7	11	35	17
8	12	30	19
9	13	24	21
10	14	18	23
11	15	10	25
12	16	2	27

[a] These figures pertain to the interval between the indicated amount of input *x* and 1 unit less than the indicated amount of input *x*.

Clearly, the monopsonist, if it maximizes profit, will employ additional units of the input as long as the marginal revenue product of the input exceeds the marginal expenditure. When the marginal revenue product no longer exceeds the marginal expenditure, it will stop adding further units of the input. Thus, in Table 15.4, the monopsonist will employ 9 units of the input. Also, in Figure 15.10, if the marginal-revenue-product curve is *DD'* and the marginal expenditure curve is *EE'*, the firm will employ *OQ* units of the input.

Note the difference between the condition for profit maximization under monopsony and the condition for profit maximization when there is perfect

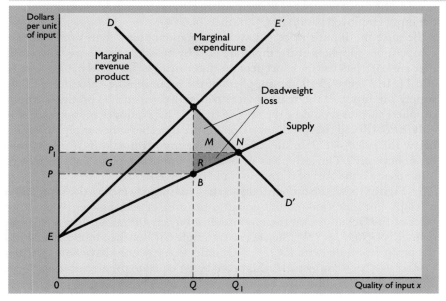

FIGURE 15.10 **Monopsony** The monopsonist sets a price of *OP* and employs *OQ* units of the input. Relative to perfect competition, the loss in producer (input supplier) surplus exceeds the gain in consumer (monopsonist) surplus by the area of triangle *M* plus triangle *R*, which is called the deadweight loss from monopsony.

competition in the input market. Under perfect competition in the input markets, we saw in Equation 15.4a of this chapter that the firm must set

$$MP_x \times MR = P_x.$$

However, if the firm is a monopsonist, it must set

$$MP_x \times MR = ME_x, \qquad [15.8]$$

where ME_x is the marginal expenditure for input x.

The difference between Equations 15.4a and 15.8 lies in the quantities on the right-hand side: P_x in one case and ME_x in the other. Since ME_x is greater than P_x if the input's supply curve is upward sloping (see page 507) and since the marginal revenue product of input x (which equals $MP_x \times MR$) decreases as more of input x is used, it follows that less of input x is used if Equation 15.8 is met than if Equation 15.4a is met. Thus the monopsonist will employ less of the input than would be used if the input market were perfectly competitive.

The monopsonist sets the input's price at the level at which the quantity it demands—the quantity at which marginal revenue product equals marginal expenditure—will be supplied. Thus, in Table 15.4, it sets a price of \$13. And

Monop-
sony
price
in Figure 15.10 it sets a price of OP if the supply curve for input x is as shown there.[12] Note that the price set by the monopsonist is lower than would be set in a competitive market for the input. For example, in Figure 15.10, if DD' were the demand curve for the input in a competitive market, the equilibrium price of the input would be OP_1 rather than OP and the equilibrium amount of the input employed would be OQ_1 rather than OQ.

Because the input's price is lower under monopsony than under perfect competition, suppliers of the input are hurt by monopsony. To see how much they are hurt, let's use the concept of producer surplus discussed in Chapters 10 and 11. In Figure 15.10, the suppliers of the input are the "producers"; they supply the input. If the market were perfectly competitive, producer (input supplier) surplus would be the area of triangle EP_1N; under monopsony, it is only EPB. (Recall that producer surplus is the area above the supply curve and below the price — OP_1 in the case of perfect competition and OP in the case of monopsony.) Thus, the loss in producer (input supplier) surplus due to monopsony is the area of rectangle G plus triangle R.

In Figure 15.10, the monopsonist is the "consumer"; it buys the input. The monopsonist gains an amount equal to the area of rectangle G because the price of the OQ units that the monopsonist buys is OP rather than OP_1. [The savings is $OQ(OP_1 - OP)$, the area of rectangle G.] But the monopsonist loses the profit from the extra $(OQ_1 - OQ)$ units that it would have bought if the market had been competitive, this profit being equal to the area of triangle M. Thus, the gain in consumer (monopsonist) surplus is the area of rectangle G minus triangle M.

Comparing the loss in producer (input supplier) surplus (rectangle G plus triangle R) with the gain in consumer (monopsonist) surplus (rectangle G minus triangle M), we see that the former exceeds the latter by an amount equal to the area of triangle R plus triangle M. This total area, indicated in Figure 15.10, is often called the *deadweight loss from monopsony*. It tells us how much the input suppliers' losses exceed the monopsonist's gains. Even if the monopsonist's gains were turned over to the input suppliers, there would still be this deadweight loss because less of the input is being used than under perfect competition.

Dead-
weight
loss from
monop-
sony

Baseball: A Case Study

Before leaving the subject of monopsony, sports fans (and others) may be interested to note that the labor market in professional baseball has had many monopsonistic characteristics. There has been a tight set of rules governing

---

[12] Because the amount of the input used does not vary continuously in Table 15.4, the marginal revenue product does not exactly equal the marginal expenditure when profit is maximized. But in Figure 15.10, where it does vary continuously, the marginal revenue product does exactly equal the marginal expenditure when profit is maximized.

contractual arrangements between players and teams. Until the mid-1970s, once a player signed his first contract, the club could renew his contract for the following year at a price that the club could set (as long as it was not less than about 75 percent of his current salary). Another stipulation was that the team had exclusive right to the use of the player's services. He could not play baseball for anyone else without the team's consent.

Consequently, once a player had signed his first contract in organized baseball, he was no longer able to sell his services in any way he chose. He could not move freely from one team to another. He could, of course, drop out of organized baseball and take up some other occupation. But if he stayed in organized baseball, he had to do what the team with his contract said. If the team assigned his contract to another team, the player had to work for the assignee team. No other team in organized baseball could hire him.

Given these rules, one would expect, on the basis of the analysis in the previous three sections, that baseball players would receive less than they would if the labor market for baseball players were perfectly competitive. It may seem hard to believe that baseball stars making very large salaries were being exploited—in the sense that their salaries were less than they would have received in a free labor market. But leading labor economists reached this conclusion after careful study of the market for baseball players.

According to some observers, the situation could be represented (in simplified form) by Figure 15.11, which shows the club owners' demand curve for baseball players and the supply curve for baseball players. Assuming that the club owners did not compete among themselves for players, but acted as a monopsonist, they would hire players up to the point where the marginal expenditure curve (EE') intersected the demand curve. That is, they would hire OU players and pay a wage of OX thousands of dollars per year. On the other hand, if the market for players were competitive, the club owners would hire OV players and pay a wage of OY thousands of dollars per year. In this highly simplified situation, it is clear that the wage was lower in the former case than in the latter.[13]

A number of reasons were given for the restrictive rules built into contracts for professional athletes. For example, it was frequently asserted that they

---

[13] For an early, influential study, see S. Rottenberg, "The Baseball Players' Labor Market," *Journal of Political Economy*, June 1956. Note that Figure 15.11 is highly simplified. For one thing, it assumes that the players do not band together to try to counteract the monopsony power of the club owners. In fact, the players have formed an association and have carried out strikes on occasion. For further discussion, see R. Noll and B. Okner, *The Economics of Professional Baseball* (Washington, D.C.: Brookings Institution, 1973); J. Quirk and M. El Hodiri, "Model of a Professional Sports League," *Journal of Political Economy*, December 1971; and G. Scully, "Pay and Performance in Major League Baseball," *American Economic Review*, December 1974. I am indebted to Professor Edward D. Mansfield for sharing his extensive knowledge of this subject with me, and for doing his best to keep me from error.

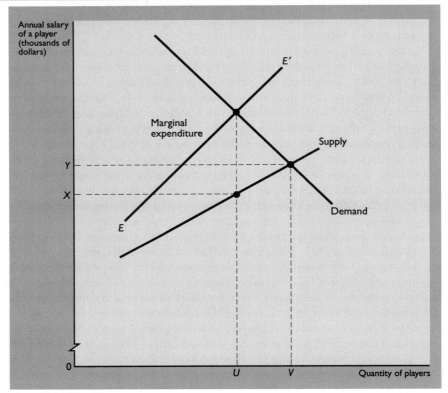

were necessary to maintain a relatively equal distribution of playing talent among the various teams. Without these rules, it was claimed that the wealthier clubs would buy up most of the best players, with the result that games would be uneven and attendance would drop. This argument was challenged by many observers who argued that a free market for players would produce better results: "It appears that free markets would give as good aggregate results as any other kind of market for industries, like the baseball industry, in which all firms must be nearly equal if each is to prosper. On welfare criteria, ... the free market is superior to the others, for in such a market each worker receives the full values of his services and exploitation does not occur."[14]

In the mid-1970s, after protracted legal battles, the rules governing the hiring of baseball players were changed. Players were allowed to declare them-

---

[14] Rottenberg, "The Baseball Players' Labor Market."

selves free agents, and other teams were allowed to bid for their services. These and other such changes (some of which were factors in the baseball strike of 1981) meant a reduction in the monopsonistic power of the baseball clubs.[15] But peace and harmony were not guaranteed on the baseball diamond, as shown by the long (and costly) baseball strike of 1994, which produced the first autumn in 89 years without a World Series.

LABOR UNIONS

One of the most important inputs is, of course, labor, and an important feature of the labor market is the existence of unions. About one in six nonfarm workers in the United States belongs to a union. The four largest unions are the Teamsters, the Food and Commercial Workers, the Automobile, Aerospace, and Agricultural Implement Workers, and the State, County, and Municipal Employees. Until the 1930s, there was strong opposition to unions, but since the passage of the Wagner Act in 1935, many manufacturing industries have become unionized. In the remainder of this chapter, we discuss briefly the ways in which unions can try to increase wages, the nature of union objectives, and the economic effects of unions.

How unions increase wages

For the moment, let us suppose that a union wants to increase the wage rate paid its members. How might it go about accomplishing this objective? First, the union might try to shift the supply curve from S to S_0 in the top panel of Figure 15.12, with the result that the price of labor will rise from OP to OP_0. To cause this shift in the supply curve, the union might restrict entry into the union, it might not let nonunion workers obtain jobs, or it might restrict the labor supply in other ways.

Second, the union might try to get the employers to pay a higher wage, while allowing some of the supply of labor forthcoming at this higher wage to find no opportunity for work. For example, in the middle panel of Figure 15.12, the union might exert pressure on the employers to get them to raise the price of labor from OP to OP_0. At OP_0, not all the available supply of labor can find jobs, because the quantity of labor supplied is OQ_1, while the amount of

---

[15] However, in 1989, an arbitrator awarded about $10 million to players he said were financially damaged during the 1986 season due to the owners' collusion. According to the arbitrator, "In the place of competition among the clubs the owners substituted a common understanding that no club would bid on the services of a free agent until and unless his former club no longer desired to sign that free agent." See "Collusion Award Exceeds $10 Million," *New York Times,* September 1, 1989.

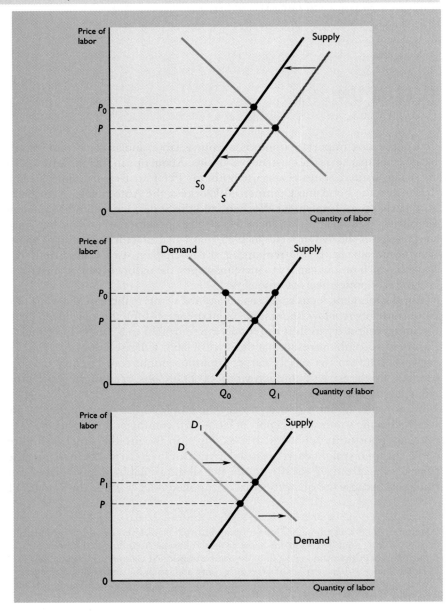

EXAMPLE 15.3

Increasing the Minimum Wage: Controversy over the Effects

In 1996, the minimum hourly wage was raised to $4.75, and in 1997 it rose to $5.15. Among economists, there is considerable controversy over the effects of such an increase. On the one hand, David Card and Alan Krueger of Princeton University challenge the accepted view that a higher minimum wage tends to increase unemployment. On the other hand, Donald Deere and Finis Welch of Texas A and M University and Kevin Murphy of the University of Chicago insist that the accepted view is correct.

(a) If the labor market is perfectly competitive and if the minimum wage exceeds the equilibrium wage, would you expect that increases in the minimum wage would increase unemployment? Why or why not? (b) Card and Krueger suggest that there may be monopsonistic features in the labor market. In the absence of a minimum wage, suppose that the supply curve for labor, the marginal-revenue-product curve for labor, and the marginal expenditure curve for labor are as shown below:

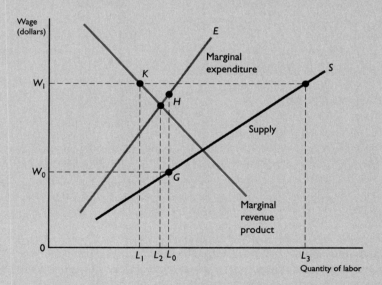

If the minimum wage is set at OW_0, how much labor will the monopsonist hire? Will there be unemployment? If so, how much? (c) If the minimum wage is set at OW_1, how much labor will the monopsonist hire? Will there be unemployment? If so, how much? (d) Under monopsony, does a minimum wage reduce unemployment? (e) If an increase in the minimum wage affects unemployment in the long run but has a much smaller effect in the short run, can this help to explain why Card and Krueger found little relationship between the minimum wage and unemployment?

SOLUTION: (a) Yes. Increases in the minimum wage would result in a bigger gap between the quantity of labor supplied and the quantity demanded. (b) If the minimum wage is set at OW_0, the effective supply curve of labor to the monopsonist is $W_0 GS$. Thus the marginal expenditure curve is $W_0 GHE$. The monopsonist will hire OL_0 units of labor, since this is the point where the marginal expenditure curve ($W_0 GHE$) intersects the marginal-revenue-product curve. There is no unemployment perceived. (c) If the minimum wage is set at OW_1, the effective supply curve of labor to the monopsonist is $W_1 K$. Since this effective supply curve is horizontal, it is also the marginal expenditure curve; this means that the monopsonist will hire OL_1 units of labor. Since OL_3 units of labor will be supplied at this wage, there will be ($OL_3 - OL_1$) units of labor trying to find jobs but not succeeding. (d) A minimum wage of OW_0 will increase, not decrease, employment. Without the minimum wage, employment would be OL_2; with it, employment is OL_0. However, if the minimum wage is high enough (OW_1, for example), it will reduce employment. A minimum wage of OW_1 would result in employment of OL_1, which is less than OL_2, the level of employment without a minimum wage. (e) Yes. As they point out, their findings may change if a longer period of time is considered.*

*For further discussion, see D. Card and A. Krueger, *Myth and Measurement* (Princeton, N.J.: Princeton University Press, 1995); D. Deere, K. Murphy, and F. Welch, "Employment and the 1990–1991 Minimum-Wage Hike," *American Economic Review,* May 1995; and C. Brown, C. Gilroy, and A. Kohen, "The Effect of the Minimum Wage on Employment and Unemployment," *Journal of Economic Literature,* June 1982.

labor demanded is OQ_0. The effect is the same as in the top panel, but in this case the union does not limit the supply directly: It lets the higher wage reduce the opportunity for work.

Third, the union might try to shift the demand for labor upward and to the right. For example, in the bottom panel of Figure 15.12, it might shift the demand curve from D to D_1, with the result that the price of labor will increase from OP to OP_1. To cause this shift in the demand curve for labor, the union might help the employers advertise their products, it might help them to be more efficient and better able to compete against other industries, or it might try to get Congress to pass legislation to protect the employers from foreign competition. Also, it might try to force employers to hire more workers than are needed for particular jobs.

The Nature of Union Objectives

What are the objectives of unions? This is a difficult matter to settle, since unions, like firms, have diverse goals that are not easy to encapsulate and measure. Indeed, the problem is even more difficult for unions than for firms, because there is less agreement that any relatively simple objective like profits is a reasonable approximation. Nevertheless, it is worthwhile discussing the implications of some simple hypotheses concerning union motivation that have been put forth. Three possible union objectives that are often considered are: (1) The union wants to keep its members fully employed, (2) the union wants to maximize the aggregate income of its members, and (3) the union wants to maximize the wage rate subject to the condition that a certain minimum number of its members be employed. All three hypotheses concerning union motivation have a certain amount of plausibility. It is easy to show, however, that they lead to quite different conclusions regarding union behavior.

Possible union objectives

Suppose that the demand curve for labor that faces the union is as shown in Figure 15.13. If the union has objective 1 and if it contains OM_1 members, it will have to accept a wage of OP_1, since this is the highest wage that will enable all its members to find work.

But suppose that it has objective 2. Then it will choose OP_2, since this is the wage that maximizes the total wage bill of the union. To prove this, note that the wage bill is the union's total revenue from its product, labor, and that consequently the wage bill is maximized when the union's marginal revenue is zero. Since the union's marginal revenue curve is RR', and since this marginal revenue curve intersects the horizontal axis at OM_2, the union's wage bill is maximized when OM_2 workers are employed; this means that the wage must be OP_2. Note that, if the union has objective 2, it must be prepared to see a great many of its members out of work.[16]

On the other hand, suppose that the union has objective 3. Specifically, suppose that it wants to maximize the wage rate subject to the condition that OM_3 of its members are employed, these members being perhaps those with considerable seniority. If this is its objective, it will choose a wage of OP_3, since this is the highest wage at which the employment level is at least OM_3.

It is clear that the wage desired by the union—and the supply of labor—will vary considerably, depending on which of these objectives is pursued. After all, OP_1, OP_2, and OP_3 are quite different wage levels, and OM_1, OM_2, and OM_3 are quite different labor supplies. Moreover, it is also perfectly

---

[16] And there is the difficult question of which members should be unemployed and which members should work.

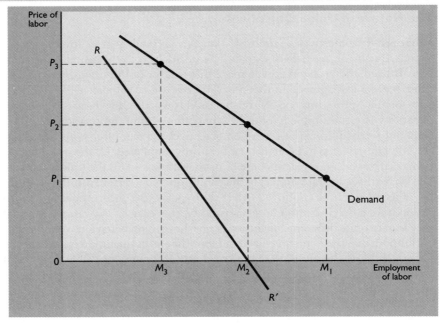

FIGURE 15.13 Three Types of Union Behavior If the union wants to keep its members fully employed, it will have to accept a wage of OP_1. If it wants to maximize the aggregate income of its members, it will choose OP_2. If it wants the employment level to equal OM_3, it will choose OP_3.

clear that the three objectives stated above are only three possibilities out of a very large number. For example, the union leadership obviously has as one objective the maintenance of its own position in the union.

SUMMARY

1. Under perfect competition, if there is only one variable input, the firm's demand curve for the input is the same as the value-of-marginal-product schedule. The market demand curve for the input can be derived from the demand curves of the individual firms in the market; however, it cannot be derived by simply taking their horizontal sum.

2. Under perfect competition, the supply of an input to an individual firm is infinitely elastic. However, when we consider the market supply curve, which is the relationship between the price of the input and the amount of

EXAMPLE 15.4

Economic Effects of Unions

Suppose that the economy can be divided into a unionized sector and a nonunion sector. The demand curve for labor in the union sector is D_u, the demand curve for labor in the nonunion sector is D_n, and the demand curve for labor in both sectors combined is D_c. The supply curve for labor in the economy as a whole is shown below.

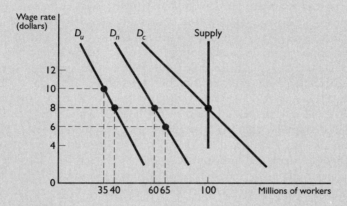

(a) Before the entry of the union, what will be the wage rate? (b) If the union raises the wage rate to $10 in the unionized sector, how many workers will the union sector lay off? (c) If all of these workers get jobs in the nonunion sector, what will be the effect on the wage rate in the nonunion sector? (d) Unions sometimes engage in featherbedding, which requires employers to hire more workers than they would otherwise. For example, railroads often have been required to hire more operating employees per train than they deemed necessary (or profitable). In the short run, such practices often increase the employment of union members. Does this effect persist in the long run as well?

SOLUTION: (a) $8, since this is where the combined curve, D_c, intersects the supply curve. (b) Its employment will fall from 40 million to 35 million, so 5 million will be laid off. (c) The wage rate in the nonunion sector will have to fall to $6 if an additional 5 million workers are to be hired there. (d) In the long run, the effect is unpredictable since the increase in the labor costs may accelerate types of substitution that the union cannot block. For example, new technologies utilizing fewer or other types of labor may be developed more quickly,

> or the product (made more expensive by featherbedding) may lose
> some of its markets to competing products or to imports.*
>
> ---
>
> *For further discussion, see A. Rees, *The Economics of Work and Pay,* (2d ed. New York:
> Harper & Row, 1979).

the input supplied in the entire market, it is often not true that supply is infinitely elastic.

3. Many inputs are supplied by business firms, and the factors influencing
   their supply have been discussed in previous chapters. But other inputs —
   notably labor — are supplied by individuals, not business firms. For inputs
   supplied by individuals, the supply curve may be backward bending; that
   is, increases in input price may result in a smaller supply of the input, at
   least over some range of variation of input price.

4. Given the market demand and supply curves for an input, the price of the
   input will tend in equilibrium to the level at which the quantity of the
   input demanded equals the quantity of the input supplied. The equilibrium amount of the input that is utilized is also given by the intersection of
   the market demand and supply curves.

5. The payment to an input that is completely fixed in supply is called a rent;
   and the payment to an input in temporarily fixed supply is a quasi-rent.

6. If there is imperfect competition in product markets but perfect competition in the market for an input, and if there is only one variable input, the
   firm's demand curve for the input is the same as the marginal-revenue-
   product curve.

7. Monopsony is a situation in which there is a single buyer. The supply curve
   of the input facing the monopsonist is the market supply curve. If the
   monopsonist maximizes profit, it sets the marginal expenditure for the
   input equal to the marginal revenue product of the input.

8. The mŏnopsonist will employ less of the input than would be used if the
   input market were perfectly competitive. Also, the monopsonist will set a
   lower price for the input than if the input market were perfectly competitive. If monopsony is compared with perfect competition, we find that
   there is a deadweight loss due to monopsony. This deadweight loss tells us
   how much the input suppliers' losses exceed the monopsonist's gains.

9. An important feature of the market for labor is the existence of labor
   unions. To some extent, unions can be viewed as labor monopolies.
   However, it is difficult to know what the objectives of the union are. Under
   certain circumstances the union might want to keep its members fully employed. Under other circumstances, a union might want to maximize the
   aggregate income of its members. And these two objectives are only two
   possibilities out of a very large number.

1. There have been many complaints of a shortage of nurses. In 1993, most of the 10,000 nurses in a survey by the Service Employees union reported chronic short staffing. Suppose that you are an adviser to a U.S. senator who asks you to estimate how much of an effect a 1 percent increase in the wage for nurses would have on the size of the shortage. He claims that the quantity of nurses demanded currently exceeds the quantity supplied by 14 percent, that the price elasticity of demand for nurses is 0.3, and that the price elasticity of supply for nurses is 0.1. If these estimates are correct, what is the answer?

2. Studies by John Landon and Robert Baird indicate that, when other factors are held equal, the level of teachers' salaries in a school district depends on the number of other school districts in the county containing the district in question. (a) If there are a relatively large number of other districts in the county containing a particular school district, would you expect the salary level of teachers in this district to be relatively high or relatively low? Why? (b) Suppose that teachers could move costlessly to school districts outside the county. Would this influence your answer to part (a)? (c) In recent years, there has been a tendency for large metropolitan school districts to decentralize into a number of autonomous districts, each of which makes its own hiring and firing decisions. What effect, if any, do you think that such decentralization will have on teachers' salaries? (d) What are some of the arguments put forth by those who favor such decentralization?

3. A perfectly competitive firm can hire labor at $30 per day. The firm's production function is as follows:

Number of days of labor	Number of units of output
0	0
1	8
2	15
3	21
4	26
5	30

If each unit of output sells for $5, how many days of labor should the firm hire?

4. A firm sells its product for $10 per unit. It produces 100 units per month, and its average variable cost is $5. What is its quasi-rent? If its average fixed cost is $4, does its quasi-rent equal its economic profit?

5. (Advanced) Suppose that a chemical firm's production function is $Q = L^{.8}K^{.2}$, where Q is output, L is the amount of labor used, and K is the amount of capital used. If the firm takes the product price and the input prices as given, show that total wages paid by the firm will equal 80 percent of its revenues.

6. A firm's demand curve for its product is given in the table below:

Output	Price of good (dollars)
23	5.00
32	4.00
40	3.50
47	3.00
53	2.00

Also, suppose that the marginal product and total product of labor (the only variable input) is:

Amount of labor	Marginal product of labor	Total output
2	10	23
3	9	32
4	8	40
5	7	47
6	6	53

(Note that the figures regarding marginal product pertain to the interval between the indicated amount of labor and 1 unit less than the indicated amount of labor.) Given these data, how much labor should the firm employ if labor costs $12 a unit?

7. Martin Feldstein estimated that physicians have a backward-bending supply curve for labor. He found that the price elasticity of supply of physicians' services was about − 0.91. (a) Draw a graph where hours per week devoted to leisure are plotted along the horizontal axis, and income derived from working is plotted along the vertical axis. Letting leisure be one good and income derived from working be the other, construct an individual physician's budget line and indifference curves. (b) Using the graph constructed in part (a), show how the physician's desired amount of leisure is influenced by a decrease in his or her wage rate if his or her supply curve for labor is backward-bending. (c) The American Medical Association has argued that any legislation that reduces the fees that physicians can charge will cut the supply of physicians' services. Based on Feldstein's results, does this appear to be true?[17]

---

[17] Note that Feldstein's study, while very influential, is not the only one bearing on this topic, and that results vary from study to study.

8. Several hundred colleges and universities belong to the National Collegiate Athletic Association (NCAA), which investigates and enforces the rules pertaining to over twenty sports. The NCAA rules prohibit bidding for college athletes in an open manner, and the NCAA regulates the number of student athletes, as well as the prices, wages, and conditions under which colleges can hire them. Is the NCAA a monopsonist? Why or why not? Do colleges tend to cheat on the NCAA rules? If so, how?

9. The Davis-Bacon Act, passed by Congress during the Great Depression of the 1930s, has required that an area's "prevailing wage" be paid to workers on construction projects receiving some federal funding. The original purpose of this law was to make sure that northern contractors could not import relatively cheap southern workers unless they were willing to pay them the relatively high wage received by northerners. More recently, the Department of Labor has had the task of specifying what the "prevailing wage" is in a particular area. According to many studies, the department often specifies that it is the union wage, even in areas where the bulk of workers do not belong to unions. Many observers have criticized this law; indeed, the U.S. General Accounting Office recommended its repeal. Suppose that you are an adviser to a U.S. senator who asks you to indicate the economic effects of this law and why it has been criticized. What answer would you give?

10. The market for a particular input is a monopsony. For this input:

$$MRP = 8 - 2Q_D,$$
$$P = 2Q_S,$$
and
$$ME = 4Q_S,$$

where MRP is this input's marginal revenue product, P is its price, ME is marginal expenditure for this input, Q_D is the quantity demanded of this input, and Q_S is the quantity supplied of this input. (MRP, P, and ME are expressed in dollars per unit of input; Q_D and Q_S are expressed in thousands of units per day.) How large is the deadweight loss due to monopsony? Interpret your result.

Investment Decisions and Risk

16

INTRODUCTION

The previous chapter looked in detail at firms' decisions concerning how much of various inputs to employ and at the factors governing input prices. But it did not provide a full treatment of a very important topic — firms' investment decisions. When a firm like Exxon or IBM invests, it increases its stock of capital, which consists of durable items like plant and equipment. As we know from previous chapters, capital is a very important input, and one of its salient characteristics is that it lasts a long time. Thus, when a firm is faced with the problem of whether it should invest in a particular factory or piece of equipment, it must consider more than the present time period: both the present and the future must be taken into account. In the first part of this chapter, we indicate how firms should make investment decisions. Discussions of the interest rate and the central concept of present value play an important role in our analysis.

In the second half of this chapter, we take up the important and related topic of risk. As we saw in Chapter 6, Standard Oil of Ohio spent about $1.7 billion between 1980 and 1985 looking for oil at Mukluk, 14 miles off the north coast of Alaska. It was a very risky gamble which did not pay off: no oil was found. Risk is involved in a great many business decisions, not just oil exploration. Our discussion in this chapter will analyze how people make decisions under conditions of risk. While this analysis can shed light on investment decisions by managers, it is equally applicable to many other types of decisions, as we shall see.

INTERTEMPORAL CHOICE: CONSUMPTION AND SAVING

Since interest rates have an important impact on firms' investment decisions, we begin by discussing their effects, but before taking up their effects on firms, we see how they affect consumers' saving decisions. People try to maintain a desired balance between consumption in the present and consumption in the future. For example, if Shirley Morrison receives a lump-sum payment of $50,000 on retirement, she is likely to save much of it to tide her over the subsequent years. In this section, we take up the consumer's intertemporal choice with regard to consumption, and to keep things simple, we consider only two periods: this year and next year. The consumer's income is $30,000 this year and only $11,000 next year. If the consumer can borrow or lend at an annual rate of interest of 10 percent, how much will he or she consume this year. How much next year?[1]

The consumer's choice between the amount consumed this year and the amount consumed next year can be analyzed by the simple model of consumer behavior presented in Chapter 3. The consumer has preferences between consumption this year and consumption next year, just as he or she has preferences between meat and potatoes in a particular time period. (Recall Figure 3.1.)

---

[1] We assume that prices of goods and services next year are the same as this year: that is, there is no inflation. Note too that, since there are only two periods, this year and next year, the consumer is assumed to have no reason to leave part of his or her receipts unspent at the end of the second year.

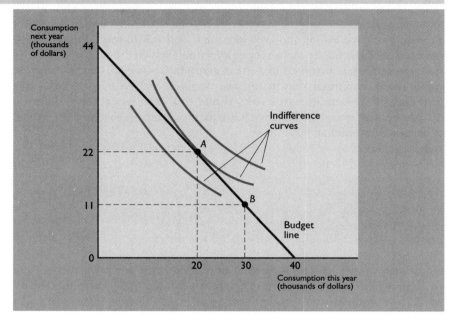

FIGURE 16.1 The Consumer's Choice of Consumption Level: This Year and Next Year
To maximize his or her satisfaction, the consumer should consume $20,000 worth of goods and services this year and $22,000 next year. Since the consumer receives $30,000 in income this year, he or she should save $10,000 then.

These preferences are represented by an indifference map like that shown in Figure 16.1. In addition, the consumer is confronted by a budget line, also shown in Figure 16.1, which indicates the alternative combinations of present and future consumption that he or she can attain. The optimal choice for the consumer is represented by the point on the budget line that is on the highest indifference curve. In Figure 16.1, this optimal point is *A*, where he or she consumes $20,000 worth of goods and services this year and $22,000 next year.

The slope of the budget line indicates the terms on which the consumer can borrow or lend. More specifically, it equals −1 times the extra amount that can be consumed next year if the consumer lends a dollar for a year. Since the *rate of interest* is the premium received by the consumer 1 year hence if he or she lends a dollar for a year, the slope of the budget line in Figure 16.1 must equal $-(1 + r)$, where r is the interest rate. More specifically, because $r = .10$, the slope equals -1.10. Note that *the interest rate can be viewed as a price,* since $(1 + r)$ is the price of a dollar today in terms of dollars a year hence. For example, if the interest rate equals .10, a dollar today is worth $1.10 a year hence.

The position of the consumer's budget line is determined by the consumer's *endowment position,* which is his or her income each year. In Figure 16.1, the

Rate of interest

consumer's endowment position is represented by point *B,* since his or her income is $30,000 this year and $11,000 next year. Of course, the consumer does not have to consume this amount each year. By borrowing or lending, he or she can move to other points on the budget line. If the consumer moves upward from *B* along the budget line, this represents *lending* (because less is consumed this year, and more is consumed next year). If the consumer moves downward from *B* along the budget line, this represents *borrowing* (because more is consumed this year, and less is consumed next year). By *saving,* we mean refraining from consumption. Thus, the consumer saves $10,000 this year; this amount is lent out, and together with the interest of $1,000 that is earned, supplements next year's income of $11,000.

Endow-
ment
position

Saving

The choices made by consumers are influenced by the rate of interest. To see that this is the case, suppose that the consumer in Figure 16.1 is confronted with a higher rate of interest. As shown in Figure 16.2, the increase in the interest rate will shift the budget line. Specifically, the budget line will be steeper after the increase in the interest rate, since the slope of the budget line equals $-(1 + r)$, as we know from page 526. Thus, with the higher interest rate, the consumer will choose a different amount to consume each year than with the lower interest rate. Specifically, the consumer's new optimal point is *D.*

FIGURE 16.2 Effect of Increase in the Interest Rate on the Equilibrium of the Consumer
With the higher interest rate, the consumer saves $11,000. With the lower interest rate, he or she saves $10,000.

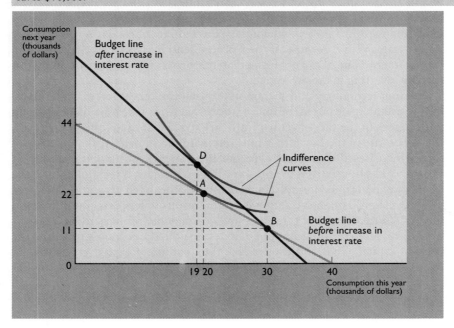

Clearly, the increase in the interest rate affects the amount the consumer saves this year. With the higher interest rate, the consumer saves $11,000. (Recall from page 525 that the consumer receives an income of $30,000 this year. Since he or she decides to consume only $19,000 this year, it follows that $30,000 − $19,000 must be saved.) With the lower interest rate the consumer saves $10,000. (Since he or she consumes $20,000 this year, it follows that $30,000 − $20,000 is saved.) Clearly, the higher interest rate results in a greater amount saved than does the lower interest rate.

THE INTEREST RATE AND INVESTMENT

Producers, like consumers, are influenced by rates of interest. They must decide whether to expand their productive capacity by investing in new buildings and factories, new equipment, and increases in inventory. Unless the rate of return they can earn from an investment exceeds the interest rate they must pay to borrow the funds to finance the investment, they will not carry out the investment. For example, if a firm invests in a project with an 8 percent rate of return and borrows the money to finance the project at 9 percent interest, it will incur an annual loss of 1 cent (9 cents minus 8 cents) per dollar invested. Even if the firm does not borrow money to finance the project, it will be unlikely to invest in a project where the expected rate of return is less than the interest rate. Why? Because, if the firm can lend money to others at the prevailing interest rate, it can obtain a greater return from its money by doing this than by investing in the project.

Holding technology and the amount of noncapital resources in the economy constant, increases in the total amount that firms invest are likely to result in decreases in the rate of return from an extra dollar of investment. In part, this is because of the law of diminishing marginal returns. If the quantity of capital increases (due to increases in total investment), the marginal product of capital would be expected to fall, according to this law, if technology and the quantity of noncapital inputs remain constant. Since a fall in capital's marginal product means that an extra unit of capital results in less extra output, it will tend to reduce the rate of return from an extra dollar of investment. In addition, increases in the total amount of investment in the economy may raise the price of capital goods and thus reduce the quantity of capital goods that an extra dollar can purchase; this will also reduce the return from an extra dollar of investment.

Suppose that the relationship between the total amount of investment and

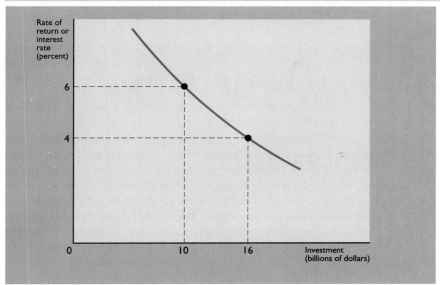

FIGURE 16.3 Investment Demand Curve If the interest rate is 6 percent, firms want to invest $10 billion; if it is 4 percent, they want to invest $16 billion.

the rate of return from an extra dollar of investment is shown by the curve in Figure 16.3, which (in accord with the previous paragraph) slopes downward and to the right. For present purposes, the important thing to note is that this curve, often called the *investment demand curve,* can tell us how much firms would like to invest at various interest rates. For example, if the interest rate is 6 percent, they would like to invest $10 billion, the amount where the rate of return from an extra dollar of investment is 6 percent.

Invest-
ment
demand
curve

Why would they like to invest $10 billion? Because if they invest less than $10 billion, the rate of return from an extra dollar of investment exceeds the interest rate; this means that they can make money by increasing investment. Thus, if the rate of return from an extra dollar of investment is 8 percent while the interest rate is 6 percent, firms can make money by borrowing an extra dollar at 6 percent interest and investing it to obtain an 8 percent return. On the other hand, if they invest more than $10 billion, the rate of return from an extra dollar of investment is less than the interest rate; this means that they can make money by reducing investment. Thus, if the rate of return from an extra dollar of investment is 4 percent while the interest rate is 6 percent, firms can make money by reducing investment by a dollar (the rate of return from it being only 4 percent) and lending this dollar out at 6 percent interest.

Given that the investment demand curve in Figure 16.3 slopes downward and to the right, hikes in the interest rate tend to reduce investment, and cuts in the interest rate tend to raise investment. For example, in Figure 16.3, a reduction of the interest rate from 6 to 4 percent would increase investment from $10 billion to $16 billion.

THE EQUILIBRIUM LEVEL OF INTEREST RATES

The interest rate is a price, the price that borrowers pay lenders to use their funds. Thus, it should come as no surprise that interest rates are determined by supply and demand — specifically, the supply and demand of loanable funds.

    The supply curve for loanable funds, shown in Figure 16.4, is the relationship between the quantity of loanable funds supplied and the interest rate. **Supply curve for loanable funds** The supply of loanable funds comes from households and firms that find the available rate of interest sufficiently attractive to induce them to save. (For example, the consumer in Figure 16.1 contributed $10,000 to the supply of loanable funds this year by saving this amount.) Since the incentive to save is generally thought to be greater when interest rates are high, the supply curve slopes upward to the right, as shown in Figure 16.4.

FIGURE 16.4 Equilibrium Level of the Interest Rate The equlibrium level of the interest rate is OR, the level at which the quantity of loanable funds supplied equals the quantity demanded.

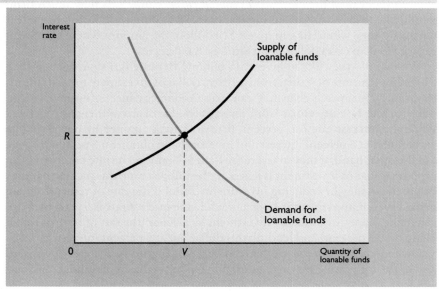

The demand curve for loanable funds, also shown in Figure 16.4, is the relationship between the quantity of loanable funds demanded and the interest
rate. As indicated in the previous section, a large demand for loanable funds
stems from firms that want to borrow money to invest in capital goods like machine tools and buildings. Large demands are also made by consumers (to buy
houses, cars, and other items) and government (to finance the building of
schools, highways, and many other types of public projects). Since the quantity
of loanable funds demanded tends to decline as the rate of interest rises, the demand curve slopes downward to the right, as shown in Figure 16.4.

The equilibrium level of the interest rate is the level where the quantity of
loanable funds demanded equals the quantity of loanable funds supplied —
OR in Figure 16.4.

As it stands, Figure 16.4 seems to imply that there is only one interest rate in
the economy, which is by no means true. Loans vary greatly, some being for 50
years, others for 50 days. Some borrowers are extremely likely to repay the
loan; others are not. For each type of loan, there is a demand curve and supply
curve of the sort shown in Figure 16.4, and the equilibrium interest rate varies
from one type of loan to another. In general, interest rates for more risky
loans — loans where the probability is relatively great that the borrower will
not pay in full and on time — tend to be higher than for less risky loans. Thus,
small, financially rickety firms have to pay higher interest rates than large blue-
chip firms, and the large, well-known firms have to pay higher interest rates
than the federal government.

PRESENT VALUE

Having looked briefly at the nature and determinants of interest rates, we
must now indicate how interest rates enable firms (and individuals) to put
amounts of money gained or lost at different points in time on a comparable
footing. This is something firms (and individuals) must do in making investment decisions. Take the case of the IBM Corporation. Clearly, IBM regards a
dollar received today as worth more than a dollar received a year from today.
Why? Because IBM can always invest money that is available now and obtain
interest on it. If the interest rate is 6 percent, a dollar received now is equivalent
to $1.06 received a year hence. Why? Because if IBM invests the dollar now, it
will have $1.06 in a year. Similarly, a dollar received now is equivalent to $(1.06)^2$
dollars 2 years hence. Why? Because if IBM invests the dollar now, it will have
1.06 dollars in a year, and if it reinvests this amount for another year at 6 percent, it will have $(1.06)^2$ dollars.

More generally, suppose that IBM can invest at a compound rate of r percent per year. What is the *present* value — that is, the value *today* — of a dollar received n years hence? Based on the foregoing argument, its present value (sometimes called *present discounted value*) is

Present value

$$\frac{1}{(1 + r)^n}. \qquad\qquad [16.1]$$

Thus, if the interest rate is .10 and if $n = 4$ (which means that the dollar is received in 4 years), the present value of a dollar equals

$$\frac{1}{(1 + .10)^4} = \frac{1}{1.4641} = \$.683.$$

In other words, the present value of the dollar is 68.3 cents.

To see that this answer is correct, let's see what would happen if IBM invested 68.3 cents today. As shown in Table 16.1, this investment would be worth 75.1 cents after 1 year, 82.6 cents after 2 years, 90.9 cents after 3 years, and 1 dollar after 4 years. Thus, 68.3 cents is the present value of a dollar received 4 years hence, because if IBM invests 68.3 cents today, it will have exactly 1 dollar in 4 years.

TABLE 16.1 Value of 68.3 Cents Invested at 10 Percent Interest		
Number of years hence	**Return received**	**Value of investment**
1	68.3(.10) = 6.830¢	68.3+6.830 = 75.13¢
2	75.13(.10) = 7.513¢	75.13+7.513 = 82.64¢
3	82.643(.10) = 8.264¢	82.643+8.264 = 90.91¢
4	90.907(.10) = 9.091¢	90.907+9.091 = 100.00¢

Table 16.2 shows the value of $1 \div (1 + r)^n$, for various values of r and n. For example, according to this table, the present value of a dollar received 10 years hence is 46.3 cents if the interest rate is .08. To see this, note that the figure in Table 16.2 corresponding to $n = 10$ and $r = .08$ is .46319.

Using this table, you can readily determine the present value of any amount received n years hence, not just $1. If IBM (or any other firm or individual) receives X dollars n years hence, the present value of this amount is

$$\frac{X}{(1 + r)^n}. \qquad\qquad [16.2]$$

Thus, to determine the present value of X dollars, all that you have to do is multiply X by $1/(1 + r)^n$. Since Table 16.2 provides us with the value of $1/(1 + r)^n$, this is a simple calculation.

TABLE 16.2 Present Value of a Dollar Received *n* Years Hence If the Interest Rate Is *r*

					Value of *r*				
n	.01	.02	.03	.04	.06	.08	.10	.15	.20
1	.99010	.98039	.97007	.96154	94340	.92593	.90909	.86957	.83333
2	.98030	.96117	.94260	.92456	.89000	.85734	.82645	.75614	.69444
3	.97069	.94232	.91514	.88900	.83962	.79383	.75131	.65752	.57870
4	.96098	.92385	.88849	.85480	.79209	.73503	.68301	.57175	.48225
5	.95147	.90573	.86261	.82193	.74726	.68058	.62092	.49718	.40188
6	.94204	.88797	.83748	.79031	.70496	.63017	.56447	.43233	.33490
7	.93272	.87056	.81309	.75992	.66506	.58349	.51316	.37594	.27908
8	.92348	.85349	.78941	.73069	.62741	.54027	.46651	.32690	.23257
9	.91434	.83675	.76642	.70259	.59190	.50025	.42410	.28426	.19381
10	.90529	.82035	.74409	.67556	.55839	.46319	.38554	.24718	.16151
11	.89632	.80426	.72242	.64958	.52679	.42888	.35049	.21494	.13459
12	.88745	.78849	.70138	.62460	.49697	.39711	.31683	.18691	.11216
13	.87866	.77303	.68095	.60057	.46884	.36770	.28966	.16253	.09346
14	.86996	.75787	.66112	.57747	.44230	.34046	.26333	.14133	.07789
15	.86135	.74301	.64186	.55526	.41726	.31524	.23939	.12289	.06491
16	.85282	.72845	.62317	.53391	.39365	.29189	.21763	.10686	.05409
17	.84436	.71416	.60502	.51337	.37136	.27027	.19784	.09293	.04507
18	.83602	.70016	.58739	.49363	.35034	.25025	.17986	.08080	.03756
19	.82774	.68643	.57029	.47464	.33051	.23171	.16354	.07026	.03130
20	.81954	.67297	.55367	.45639	.31180	.21455	.14864	.06110	.02608
21	.81143	.65978	.53755	.44883	.29415	.19866	.13513	.05313	.02174
22	.80340	.64684	.52189	.42195	.27750	.18394	.12285	.04620	.01811
23	.79544	.63414	.50669	.40573	.26180	.17031	.11168	.04017	.01509
24	.78757	.62172	.49193	.39012	.24698	.15770	.10153	.03493	.01258
25	.77977	.60953	.47760	.37512	.23300	.14602	.09230	.03038	.01048

To illustrate, suppose that IBM will receive $10,000 ten years hence, and that the interest rate is .15. According to Equation 16.2, the present value of this amount equals $10,000 \times 1/(1 + r)^n$. Since Table 16.2 shows that $1/(1 + r)^n = .24718$ when $n = 10$ and $r = .15$, the present value of this amount is $10,000(.24718) = $2,471.80.

VALUING A STREAM OF PAYMENTS

Frequently, an individual or firm will receive a stream of payments at various points in time, not just a single payment. For example, suppose that a firm leases a warehouse to another firm, and that it will receive $100,000 per year in payment for 5 years. What is the present value of this stream of payments? To

EXAMPLE 16.1

Can Increases in the Interest Rate Reduce Saving?

Newspapers like the *Wall Street Journal* frequently run articles discussing the effects of changes in the interest rate on savers. Clearly, the interest rate influences how much people save. In Figure 16.2, the individual was induced to save more by an increase in the interest rate. To see that this need not always be true, consider John Green, whose budget lines before and after an increase in the interest rate are as shown below:

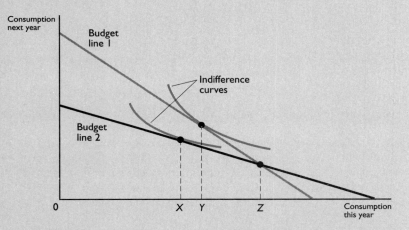

(a) Which budget line pertains to the period before the increase in the interest rate? Which pertains to the period after it? Why? (b) How much will Mr. Green save before this increase in the interest rate? (c) How much will he save after this increase in the interest rate? (d) Suppose that Mr. Green is saving for only one reason: to pay for an around-the-world trip he wants to take next year. If the trip will cost $10,000 and has to be paid for entirely from his savings this year, will an increase in the interest rate result in his saving more or less? Why? (e) In Chapter 15, we saw that there can be a backward-bending supply curve for labor. Can there be a backward-bending relationship between the interest rate and the quantity of saving?

SOLUTION   (a) Budget line 2 pertains to the period before the increase in the interest rate; budget line 1 pertains to the period after it. Since the slope of the budget line equals $-(1 + r)$, a higher value of r results in a steeper budget line. (b) ($OZ - OX$) dollars will be saved. (c) $(OZ - OY)$ dollars will be saved. (d) An increase in the interest rate will result in his saving less because he will have to save less this year to result in his having $10,000 next year. For example, if the interest rate is 5 percent, he will have to save $10,000/1.05 = $9,524 this year to obtain $10,000 next year, whereas if the interest rate is 10 percent, he will only have to save $10,000/1.10 = $9,091 this year to achieve the same result. (e) Yes. As the interest rate is increased, beyond a point the quantity of saving might decrease, not increase. As the case of Mr. Green demonstrates, it is possible for increases in the interest rate to reduce the quantity of saving.

see how questions of this sort can be answered, it is convenient to begin by considering the simple case where you receive $1 per year for n years, the interest rate being r. More specifically, the n receipts of $1 occur 1 year from now, 2 years from now, . . . , and n years from now. The present value of this stream of $1 receipts is

$$\frac{1}{1 + r} + \frac{1}{(1 + r)^2} + \cdots + \frac{1}{(1 + r)^n}. \qquad [16.3]$$

For example, the present value of $1 to be received at the end of each of the next 5 years, if the interest rate is .10, is

$$\frac{1}{1 + .10} + \frac{1}{(1 + .10)^2} + \frac{1}{(1 + .10)^3} + \frac{1}{(1 + .10)^4} + \frac{1}{(1 + .10)^5}$$
$$= .90909 + .82645 + .75131 + .68301 + .62092 = \$3.79. \qquad [16.4]$$

To obtain each of the terms on the right-hand side of Equation 16.4, we use Table 16.2. For example, the final term on the right is .62092, which is the present value of a dollar received 5 years hence (if the interest rate is .10), according to Table 16.2. Table 16.3 shows that $3.79 is indeed the present value of $1 to be

TABLE 16.3 Demonstration That $3.79 (Invested at 10 Percent Interest) Provides Exactly $1 at the End of Each of the Next 5 Years			
Number of years hence	Return received	Amount withdrawn	Net value of investment
1	$3.79 (.10) = .379	$1.00	$3.79 + .379 − 1.00 = 3.169
2	$3.169(.10) = .3169	$1.00	$3.169 + .3169 − 1.00 = 2.486
3	$2.486(.10) = .2486	$1.00	$2.486 + .2486 − 1.00 = 1.735
4	$1.735(.10) = .1735	$1.00	$1.735 + .1735 − 1.00 = 0.909
5	$0.909(.10) = .0909	$1.00	$0.909 + .0909 − 1.00 = 0

received at the end of each of the next 5 years if the interest rate is .10. As you can see, if you invest $3.79 at 10 percent interest, you will be able to withdraw $1 at the end of each year, with nothing left over or lacking.

In general, of course, annual payments will differ from $1. Suppose that a payment is received at the end of each of the next n years, that the interest rate is r, that the amount received at the end of the first year is X_1, the amount received at the end of the second year is X_2, and so on. The present value of this series of unequal payments is

$$\frac{X_1}{1+r} + \frac{X_2}{(1+r)^2} + \cdots + \frac{X_n}{(1+r)^n}. \qquad [16.5]$$

Table 16.2 can be used to help carry out this computation. For example, suppose that $r = .10$, that $n = 3$, and that the amount received at the end of the first year is $3,000, the amount received at the end of the second year is $2,000, and the amount received at the end of the third year is $1,000. Table 16.2 shows that $1/(1 + .10) = .90909$, $1/(1 + .10)^2 = .82645$, and $1/(1 + .10)^3 = .75131$. Thus, the present value of this stream of payments is

$$\frac{\$3,000}{1+.10} + \frac{\$2,000}{(1+.10)^2} + \frac{\$1,000}{(1+.10)^3}$$
$$= \$3,000(.90909) + \$2,000(.82645) + \$1,000(.75131) = \$5,131.48.$$

THE NET-PRESENT-VALUE RULE FOR INVESTMENT DECISIONS

One of the most important applications of the foregoing results regarding the valuation of a payments stream is to investment decisions. Once again, take the case of the IBM Corporation. IBM's manufacturing engineers propose the building of new plant and equipment to reduce costs. IBM's marketing executives propose investments in new warehouses and marketing facilities. IBM's research directors propose the purchase of additional instrumentation and the construction of new laboratories. Which of these investment proposals should IBM accept?

For IBM or any other firm, the answer is: *accept an investment proposal if the present value of the expected future cash flows from the investment is greater than the investment's cost.* For example, suppose that an investment costs $100 today and that it results in profits of $60 a year hence and $60 two years hence. The **Net-present-value** net present value of the investment is the present value of the future cash flows minus the investment's cost. In this case, the net present value equals

$$-\$100 + \frac{\$60}{1 + r} + \frac{\$60}{(1 + r)^2},$$

where r is the discount rate. When an interest rate is used to calculate the net **Discount rate** present value of an investment, it is called the *discount rate.*

In general, if an investment costs C dollars now and if it is expected to yield cash flows of X_1 dollars a year hence, X_2 dollars 2 years hence, . . . , and X_n dollars n years hence, the net present value of the investment equals

$$-C + \frac{X_1}{1 + r} + \frac{X_2}{(1 + r)^2} + \cdots + \frac{X_n}{(1 + r)^n}. \qquad [16.6]$$

The net present value is a measure of the benefits minus the costs of the investment. Clearly, *a firm should accept an investment project only if its net present* **Net-present-value rule** *value is positive.* This is the so-called net-present-value rule.

To evaluate the net present value, the firm must choose a value for r, the discount rate. What value should it choose? To answer this question, the firm must estimate the rate of return that it could obtain if it used the money it would spend on this investment in alternative ways. Typically, a firm has a variety of investment projects that it could carry out. For example, as we have seen, if IBM does not invest in new plant and equipment to reduce costs, it can invest in new warehouses and marketing facilities or in additional instrumentation and new research laboratories — or in stocks and bonds, for that matter. *The firm should use as a discount rate its opportunity cost of capital, which is defined as the rate of return it can obtain if it invests its money in some other, comparable investment project.*

But what do we mean by a "comparable" investment project? In general, investors require higher rates of return on more-risky investments than on less-risky ones. This, of course, is why interest rates tend to be higher on more-risky than less-risky loans. (If lenders have doubts about getting their money back, they will charge a higher interest rate than if they are sure of being repaid.) A "comparable" investment project is one that is as risky as the investment project under consideration. *The firm should use as a discount rate the rate of return it can obtain from other, equally risky investment projects.*[2]

---

[2] For detailed information regarding ways to estimate the rate of return that can be obtained from other, equally risky investment projects, see E. Mansfield, *Managerial Economics* (3d ed.; New York: Norton, 1996).

THE INVESTMENT DECISION: AN EXAMPLE

The net-present-value rule, described in the previous section, has found wide-spread application. To illustrate its use, consider a firm that had to decide whether to purchase a machine that would reduce the firm's labor requirements. The machine had a price of $25,000 and an anticipated life of 5 years with no salvage value at the end of that time. If the firm bought the machine, it would incur savings of labor costs in subsequent years, as shown in Table 16.4. Since the firm regarded these savings as certain, the appropriate discount rate was 10 percent, the rate of interest at that time on government bonds. Should the firm have bought the machine? According to the net-present-value rule, the answer depends on whether the net present value of the

TABLE 16.4 Effects of Machine on Firm's Stream of Cash Inflows

Number of years hence	Effect on cash inflow[a] (dollars)
0	− 25,000
1	2,000
2	6,000
3	8,000
4	14,000
5	12,000

[a] Positive numbers indicate cash inflows; negative numbers indicate cash outflows.

investment is positive. Using Equation 16.6, the net present value of this investment was

$$-\$25{,}000 + \frac{\$2{,}000}{1 + .10} + \frac{\$6{,}000}{(1 + .10)^2} + \frac{\$8{,}000}{(1 + .10)^3}$$
$$+ \frac{\$14{,}000}{(1 + .10)^4} + \frac{\$12{,}000}{(1 + .10)^5} = \$4{,}800,$$

because $C = \$25{,}000$, $X_1 = \$2{,}000$, $X_2 = \$6{,}000$, $X_3 = \$8{,}000$, $X_4 = \$14{,}000$, $X_5 = \$12{,}000$, and $r = .10$. Since the net present value of the investment was positive, the firm should have bought the machine.

FIGURE 16.5 Net Present Value of Investment in Machine in Table 16.4

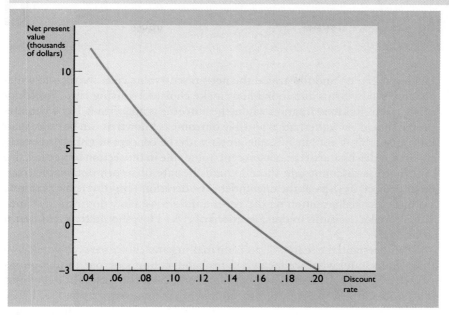

Note two things. First, the net present value of this investment depends on the value of the discount rate. In particular, the net present value equals

$$-\$25{,}000 + \frac{\$2{,}000}{1+r} + \frac{\$6{,}000}{(1+r)^2} + \frac{\$8{,}000}{(1+r)^3} + \frac{\$14{,}000}{(1+r)^4} + \frac{\$12{,}000}{(1+r)^5},$$

where r is the discount rate. Figure 16.5 shows that the net present value decreases as the discount rate increases. This is true of many investments, not just this one. For discount rates below about .16, the net present value is positive, and the firm should invest in this project. For discount rates above about .16, the net present value is negative, and the firm should not invest in this project.

Second, in Equation 16.6, there is no reason why all the Xs have to be positive. Recall that the Xs are the future cash flows. In some cases, in the first year after an investment is made in a new plant, the firm loses money because of startup costs and "teething" problems; in such cases, X_1 — the cash flow during the year following the investment — is negative. This causes no problems in calculating the net present value of the investment, since X_1 can be either positive or negative. Similarly, $X_2, X_3, \ldots, X_n$ can be positive or negative. The validity and usefulness of Equation 16.6 are unaffected.

CHOICES INVOLVING RISK[3]

Having taken up and illustrated the net-present-value rule, we turn to a discussion of how firms and individuals make choices involving risk. To economists, risk refers to a situation where the outcome is not certain, but where the probability of each alternative possible outcome is known or can be estimated. Of course, this is not our first encounter with the concept of risk. (For example, in our discussion of the net-present-value rule in the section before last, we said that the discount rate should equal the rate of return obtainable from other projects as risky as the one under consideration.) But this is the first time we have focused attention on the general questions: How do firms and individuals make decisions under conditions of risk? How should they make such decisions?

Proba-
bility

To understand the theory of decision making and choice involving risk, you must understand what we mean by a probability. Suppose that a situation exists where one of a number of possible outcomes can take place. For example, if a gambler throws a single die, the number that comes up may be 1, 2, 3, 4, 5, or 6. A probability is a number that is attached to each outcome. It is the proportion of times that this outcome results over the long run if the situation occurs over and over again. Thus the probability that a particular die will come up a 1 is the proportion of times this will occur if the die is thrown many, many times, and the probability that the same die will come up a 2 is the proportion of times this will occur if the die is thrown many, many times; and so on.

Similarly, the probability that a U.S. male just turning 45 will die before his forty-sixth birthday is the proportion of times that this outcome occurs. Detailed statistics are available concerning the proportion of people in a particular age group who die each year. On the basis of such statistics, one can calculate the proportion of 45-year-old U.S. males who die before their forty-sixth birthdays. This proportion equals the probability in question.

In general, if a situation exists a very large number of times M, and if outcome U occurs m times, the probability of U is

$$P(U) = \frac{m}{M}. \qquad [16.7]$$

Thus, if a die is "true" (meaning that each of its sides is equally likely to come

---

[3] Some instructors may want to take up the material on choices involving risk (on pages 540 to 557) after Chapter 5. This can readily be done because this material is self-contained.

EXAMPLE 16.2

Neil Simon Goes Off-Broadway

When Neil Simon, the hugely successful playwright, decided in late 1994 to open his play *London Suite* in an Off-Broadway theater, alarm bells rang all along Broadway. According to Mr. Simon's producer, Emanuel Azenberg, the reason for abandoning Broadway was simple economics. He estimated that the investment required to open the play at a Broadway theater would be about $1.3 million, while the required investment at an Off-Broadway theater would be only about $440,000. If the play were to run for a year, its receipts and operating expenses at a Broadway and Off-Broadway theater would be as follows:

	Broadway	Off-Broadway
Receipts	$13,000,000	$5,668,000
Expenses		
Rent and house crew	2,340,000	624,000
Salaries	2,808,000	1,040,000
Advertising	1,560,000	780,000
Lights and sound rental	312,000	182,000
Administration	1,664,000	572,000
Royalties	1,222,000	728,000
Other	832,000	338,000
Profit	$2,262,000	$1,404,000

(a) To simplify the analysis, suppose that the play runs for 1 year and that all the profit is received 1 year after the investment is made. If the play were produced at a Broadway theater, what would be the net present value of the investment? (Assume that the discount rate equals 10 percent.) (b) If the play were produced at an Off-Broadway theater, what would be the net present value of the investment? (Again, assume that the discount rate equals 10 percent.) (c) Comparing the net present values in parts (a) and (b), does it appear that Mr. Simon made the right decision? Why or why not? (d) If the play were a flop (which in fact it was not), would the loss be greater if it were produced at a Broadway theater than Off-Broadway? Why or why not? (e) If the investment was riskier if the play was produced on Broadway rather than Off-Broadway, is it correct to use the same discount rate (of 10 percent)? Why or why not?

SOLUTION (a) The net present value would equal

$$-\$1,300,000 + \frac{\$2,262,000}{1 + .10} = \$756,364.$$

(b) The net present value would equal

$$-\$440{,}000 + \frac{\$1{,}404{,}000}{1 + .10} = \$836{,}364.$$

(c) The net present value of the investment is higher if the play opens Off-Broadway than at a Broadway theater. [To see this, compare the answers to parts (a) and (b).] Thus, based on this highly simplified analysis, it appears that Mr. Simon's decision was correct. (d) Yes. Suppose, for example, that the play closed before any performances, but after the investment required to open had been made. If the play were at a Broadway theater, the loss would be \$1.3 million; if it were at an Off-Broadway theater, the loss would only be \$440,000. (e) No. For reasons discussed on page 537, the discount rate should be higher for more-risky investments.*

---

*For further discussion, see the *New York Times,* November 21, 1994.

up when the die is rolled), the probability of its coming up a 1 is 1/6, or 0.167, because if it is rolled many, many times, this will occur 1/6 of the time. Moreover, even if the die is not true, this definition can be applied. Suppose, for instance, that a local mobster injects some loaded dice into a crap game, and that one of the players (who is suspicious) asks to examine one of them. If he rolls the die, what is the probability that it will come up a 1? To answer this question, we must imagine the die in question being rolled again and again. After many thousands of rolls, if the proportion of times that it has come up a 1 is .195, then this is the probability of its coming up a 1.

The foregoing is the so-called *frequency definition of probability.* In some situations, this concept of probability may be difficult to apply because these situations cannot be repeated over and over. Consider, for example, the probability that George Johnson will pass all his college courses. If he decides to attend the University of California at Los Angeles (UCLA) in 1997, this is an "experiment" that cannot be repeated over and over again under essentially the same set of circumstances. If he decides to attend UCLA in 1999 instead, his knowledge and attitude, the identity of the professors, and a host of other relevant factors may be quite different.

In dealing with cases of this sort, economists and statisticians sometimes use a *subjective* or *personal definition of probability.* According to this definition, the probability of an event is the degree of confidence or belief on the part of the decision maker that the event will occur. For example, if the decision maker believes that outcome *A* is more likely to occur than outcome *B*, the probability of *A* is higher than the probability of *B*. If the decision maker believes that it is equally likely that a particular outcome will or will not occur, the probability attached to the occurrence of this outcome equals .50. The important factor in this concept of probability is what the decision maker believes.

EXPECTED MONETARY VALUE

Having defined what probabilities are, let's make some use of them. Specifically, take the case of Cecile Miller, a stockbroker, who is thinking of buying some stock in Eli Lilly, the big drug firm. Based on her estimates, she will gain $20,000 from the stock purchase if Eli Lilly gets approval from the Food and Drug Administration to market a new drug it has developed. On the other hand, if it does not get approval, she figures that she will lose $12,000. In her judgment, there is a .5 probability that Eli Lilly will get approval, and a .5 probability that it will not get approval. Ms. Miller must decide whether to accept the gamble. That is, she must decide whether to buy the stock.

In such a situation, it frequently is useful to calculate the *expected monetary value* of the gamble. The expected monetary value is the sum of the amount of money gained (or lost) if each outcome occurs times the probability of occurrence of the outcome. In the case of Cecile Miller, the expected monetary value equals

Expected monetary value

$$.5 (\$20,000) + .5(-\$12,000) = \$4,000.$$

To see why this is the expected monetary value, note that there are two possible outcomes: (1) Eli Lilly gets approval to market its new drug, or (2) it does not get approval to do so. If we multiply the amount of money gained (or lost) if the first outcome occurs times its probability of occurrence, the result is .5($20,000). If we multiply the amount of money gained (or lost) if the second outcome occurs times its probability of occurrence, the result is .5(−$12,000). Summing these two results, we obtain $4,000, which is the expected monetary value if she buys this stock.

The expected monetary value is important because it is the mean amount that a decision maker would gain (or lose) if he or she were to accept a gamble over and over again. For example, if Cecile Miller were to buy Eli Lilly stock (under the above circumstances) repeatedly, sometimes the Food and Drug Administration would grant approval, and sometimes it would not. Over the long run, given the above probabilities, it would do so in half of the cases and not do so in half of them. Thus the mean amount that she would make (per purchase) would be $4,000.

What would be the expected monetary value if Cecile Miller did not buy this stock? If it were certain that she would experience neither a gain nor a loss if she did not buy it, the expected monetary value under these circumstances would be zero. [Since it would be certain that there would be neither a gain nor a loss, the expected monetary value would equal the amount of money gained if this outcome occurs (zero) times its probability of occurrence (one).] That is, the mean amount that she would make (per decision not to buy) would be zero.

Under certain conditions, it is rational to choose the action or gamble that has the largest expected monetary value. If these condition exist, Cecile Miller should buy the stock in Eli Lilly, because the expected monetary value if she does so equals $4,000, whereas the expected monetary value if she does not do so equals zero. Later on in this chapter we shall discuss at length the circumstances under which it is rational to maximize expected monetary value — and how to proceed if it is not rational to do so.

INVESTING IN AN OIL VENTURE: A CASE STUDY

To illustrate further the concept of expected monetary value, consider the case of William Beard, an actual investor.[4] Suppose that Mr. Beard must decide whether to invest in drilling an oil well in a particular location. He has information concerning the cost of drilling and the price of oil, as well as geologists' reports concerning the likelihood of striking oil. Based on the geologists' reports, he believes that, if the well is drilled, there is a .80 probability that no oil will be found, a .12 probability that 100,000 barrels will be found, and .08 probability that 1 million barrels will be found.

Based on these probabilities alone, he cannot decide whether to invest in drilling the well. In addition, information is needed concerning the gain (or loss) that will accrue to him if each of these outcomes occurs. Suppose that he believes that, if he makes the investment, he will incur a $50,000 loss if no oil is found, a $50,000 gain if 100,000 barrels are found, and a $500,000 gain if 1 million barrels are found. On the basis of this information, should he make this investment? (For simplicity, assume all these gains or losses occur immediately after the well is drilled.)

If he wants to maximize the expected monetary value, he can answer this

---

[4] Mr. Beard was included in C. Jackson Grayson, *Decisions Under Uncertainty: Drilling Decisions by Oil and Gas Operators* (Boston: Harvard Business School, 1960). This was an early (and classic) study. Many of the details have been altered here for pedagogical reasons.

question by comparing the expected monetary value if he makes the investment with the expected monetary value if he does not make it. Based on the above estimates, the expected monetary value if he makes the investment is

$$.80(-\$50,000) + .12(+\$50,000) + .08(+\$500,000) = +\$6,000.$$

If he does not make the investment, the expected monetary value is zero (because it is certain that he will gain nothing). Thus, if he wants to maximize the expected monetary value, Mr. Beard should invest in drilling the well.

THE EXPECTED VALUE OF PERFECT INFORMATION

In many cases, the decision maker can obtain information that will dispel (at least some of) the relevant risk. If the decision maker can get perfect information, how much is it worth? To answer this question, we define the expected value of perfect information as the increase in expected monetary value if the decision maker could obtain completely accurate information concerning the outcome of the relevant situation (but if he or she does not yet know what this information will be). Thus, in the case of Cecile Miller (the stockbroker cited above who must decide whether or not to buy some Eli Lilly stock), the expected value of perfect information is the increase in expected monetary value if she could obtain perfectly accurate information indicating whether the Food and Drug Administration will approve the marketing of Eli Lilly's new drug.

To see how one can compute the expected value of perfect information, let's consider Ms. Miller's case. To determine the expected value of perfect information, we carry out two steps. First, we evaluate the expected monetary value to Ms. Miller if she can obtain access to perfectly accurate information of this sort. Then we calculate the extent to which this expected monetary value exceeds the expected monetary value based on the information actually available to her.

Step 1: If Ms. Miller obtains perfect information, she will be able to make the correct decision, regardless of whether or not the Food and Drug Administration approves the marketing of Eli Lilly's new drug. If it will do so, she will be aware of this fact, and will buy the stock. If it will not do so, she will be aware of this fact also, and will not buy it. Thus, given that she has access to perfect information, the expected monetary value is

$$.5(\$20,000) + .5(0) = \$10,000.$$

To see why this is the expected monetary value if she has access to perfect information, it is important to recognize that although it is assumed that she has access to perfect information, *she does not yet know what this information will be.* There is a .5 probability that this information will show that the Food and Drug Administration will grant approval, in which case she will buy the stock and the gain will be $20,000. There is also a .5 probability that the information will show that the Food and Drug Administration will not grant approval, in which case she will not buy the stock and the gain will be zero. Thus, as shown above, the expected monetary value if she has access to perfect information (that is not yet revealed to her) is $10,000.

Step 2: The expected monetary value if she bases her decision on existing information is $4,000 (as we saw on pages 543 to 544), not $10,000. The difference between these two figures —$10,000 minus $4,000, or $6,000— is the expected value of perfect information. It is a measure of the worth of perfect information. *It shows the amount by which the expected monetary value increases as a consequence of Ms. Miller's having access to perfect information.* Put differently, *it is the maximum amount that she should pay to obtain perfect information.*

In many situations, it is very important that a person knows how much perfect information would be worth. People are continually being offered information by testing services, research organizations, news bureaus, and a variety of other organizations. Unless they know how much particular types of information are worth, they will not be able to tell whether the information's worth exceeds its cost. Thus they will find it difficult to decide rationally whether various types of information should be bought. The sort of analysis presented in this section is useful to guide such decisions.[5]

HOW MUCH ARE ACCURATE WEATHER FORECASTS WORTH TO RAISIN PRODUCERS?

To illustrate how the expected value of perfect information can be employed, consider the California raisin industry, which produces raisins by sun-drying grapes in the early autumn. If a farmer chooses to produce raisins, but rain

---

[5] In this section, we have dealt only with the relatively simple case where information is perfect. If the only available information is less than perfect (that is, if it contains errors), can we determine whether its expected worth exceeds its cost? Under many circumstances, the answer is yes. To see how, consult the sections on preposterior analysis in any statistics text.

occurs, he or she takes a considerable loss because the grapes are no longer of much use to a winery. Thus, if rain is expected, the grapes are likely to be crushed to make wine, even though this may not be as profitable as using them to produce raisins (if weather permitted). Clearly, weather forecasting is very important to the California raisin industry, as it is to many other parts of agriculture, as well as to summer and winter resorts, outdoor concerts, and other weather-dependent industries.

Several decades ago, Lester Lave of Carnegie-Mellon University calculated the expected value of perfect information concerning the likelihood of rain over a 3-week period to California raisin producers.[6] His results indicated that perfect 3-week forecasts would raise the raisin producers' profits by about $90 per acre; this means that the value of such forecasts to the California raisin industry would have been over $20 million per year, which is a substantial amount, particularly since the raisin industry is relatively small. (However, as Lave points out, this industry figure should be adjusted for a variety of reasons that need not concern us here.) Results of this sort have played an important role in quantifying the economic benefits from improved weather forecasting techniques.

SHOULD A DECISION MAKER MAXIMIZE EXPECTED MONETARY VALUE?

Returning to Cecile Miller's stock decision and William Beard's investment decision, we have assumed in both cases that the decision maker wants to maximize the expected monetary value. In this and the following sections we will discuss how a more realistic criterion can be formulated. To understand why a decision maker may not want to maximize the expected monetary value, consider a situation where you are given a choice between (1) receiving $1,000,000 for certain and (2) a gamble in which a fair coin is tossed, and you will receive $2,100,000 if it comes up heads or you will lose $50,000 if it comes up tails. The expected monetary value for the gamble is

$$.5(\$2,100,000) + .5(-\$50,000) = \$1,025,000,$$

so you should choose the gamble over the certainty of $1,000,000 if you want to maximize the expected monetary value. However, it seems likely that many

---

[6] L. Lave, "The Value of Better Weather Information to the Raisin Industry," *Econometrica,* January 1963.

persons would prefer the certainty of $1,000,000 since the gamble entails a 50 percent chance that you will lose $50,000, a very substantial sum. Moreover, many people may feel that they can do almost as much with $1,000,000 as with $2,100,000, and therefore the extra amount is not worth the risk of losing $50,000.

Clearly, whether you will want to maximize the expected monetary value in this situation depends on your attitude toward risk. If you are a person of modest means, you will probably be overwhelmed at the thought of taking a 50 percent chance of losing $50,000. On the other hand, if you are a wealthy speculator, the prospect of a $50,000 loss may not be the least bit unsettling, and you may prefer the gamble to the certainty of a mere $1,000,000 profit. And if you are the sort of person who enjoys danger and risk, you may prefer to gamble even though a $50,000 loss may wipe you out completely.

Fortunately, there is no need to assume that the decision maker wants to maximize the expected monetary value. Instead, we can construct a so-called *von Neumann-Morgenstern utility function* for the decision maker, which is based on his or her attitudes toward risk.[7] From this, we can then go on to find the alternative that is best for the decision maker, given his or her attitude toward risk. The von Neumann-Morgenstern utility function was named after John von Neumann, a famous mathematician at the Institute for Advanced Study, and Oskar Morgenstern, an economist at Princeton University. A utility function of this sort should not be confused with the utility functions discussed in Chapter 3. As we shall see, it is quite a different sort of concept.

MAXIMIZING EXPECTED UTILITY

According to the theory put forth by von Neumann and Morgenstern, *a rational decision maker will maximize expected utility.* In other words, the decision maker should choose the course of action with the highest expected utility. But what (in this context) is a *utility?* It is a number that is attached to a possible outcome of the decision. Each outcome has a utility. The decision

---

[7] John von Neumann and Oskar Morgenstern, *Theory of Games and Economic Behavior* (Princeton, N.J.: Princeton University Press, 1944). For some alternative approaches, see M. Machina, "Dynamic Consistency and Non-Expected Utility Models of Choice Under Uncertainty," *Journal of Economic Literature,* December 1989.

maker's von Neumann-Morgenstern utility function shows the utility that he or she attaches to each possible outcome. The utility function, as we shall see, shows the decision maker's preferences with respect to risk. What is *expected utility?* It is the sum of the utility if each outcome occurs times the probability of occurrence of the outcome. For example, if a situation has two possible outcomes, S and T, if the utility of outcome S is 5 and the utility of outcome T is 10, and if the probability of each outcome is .5, the expected utility equals

Expected utility

$$.5(5) + .5(10) = 7.5.$$

To take a more complicated and realistic case, what is the expected utility if William Beard invests in drilling the well under the circumstances described on pages 544 to 545? It equals

$$.80U(-50) + .12U(50) + .08U(500),$$

where $U(-50)$ is the utility he attaches to a monetary loss of \$50,000, $U(50)$ is the utility he attaches to a gain of \$50,000, and $U(500)$ is the utility he attaches to a gain of \$500,000. Since there is a .80 probability of a \$50,000 loss, a .12 probability of a \$50,000 gain, and a .08 probability of a \$500,000 gain, this is the expected utility. What is the expected utility if he does not make this investment? It equals one times $U(0)$, where $U(0)$ is the utility he attaches to a zero gain, since under these circumstances the probability is 1 that the gain will be zero (since this is certain).

The point of attaching a utility to each monetary value is that many people do not regard each and every dollar as being of equal weight and importance to them. For example, you may regard a \$10,000 loss as being more undesirable than a \$10,000 gain is desirable. By attaching utilities to each monetary value, we can recognize this fact, and use it to help indicate how you should choose among various risky alternatives — and to help predict what choices you in fact will make.

SHOULD MR. BEARD INVEST IN THE OIL VENTURE?

To determine the utility that the decision maker attaches to each possible outcome, he or she must respond to a series of questions that indicate his or her preferences with regard to risk. The specific questions that must be asked are described in the chapter appendix. The decision maker's utility function is the relationship between his or her utility and the amount of his or her monetary gain (or loss). The chapter appendix shows how one can determine the utility function for a given decision maker.

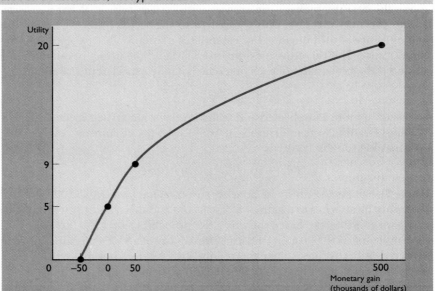

FIGURE 16.6 William Beard's von Neumann-Morgenstern Utility Function This utility function is based on an actual case, not hypothetical data.

Once a decision maker's von Neumann-Morgenstern utility function has been constructed, it can be used to indicate whether he or she should accept or reject particular gambles. To illustrate, consider the actual case of William Beard, whose utility function (measured in the chapter appendix) is shown in Figure 16.6.[8] Suppose that Mr. Beard must decide whether to invest in drilling the well described on page 544. According to the theory put forth by von Neumann and Morgenstern, he should maximize expected utility. Thus he should invest in drilling the well if his expected utility if the investment is made exceeds his expected utility if it is not made. As pointed out in the previous section, his expected utility if the investment is made equals

$$.80U(-50) + .12U(50) + .08U(500).$$

According to Figure 16.6, $U(-50)$ equals 0, $U(50)$ equals 9, and $U(500)$ equals 20. Thus, if the investment is made, his expected utility is

$$.80(0) + .12(9) + .08(20) = 2.68.$$

---

[8] The utility function derived in the chapter appendix and presented in Figure 16.6 is based on an actual case, and its general shape is correct, but the numbers have been simplified for pedagogical reasons.

As pointed out in the previous section, if the investment is not made, Mr. Beard's expected utility is $U(0)$, which equals 5, according to Figure 16.6. Thus he should not invest in drilling the well. Why? Because if he does not invest, his expected utility is 5, whereas if he invests, his expected utility is 2.68. Since he should maximize expected utility, he should choose the action with the higher expected utility, which is not to invest. Note that this is not the decision that maximizes the expected monetary value. As we saw on page 545, if Mr. Beard wants to maximize the expected monetary value, he should invest. But because of Mr. Beard's preferences with respect to risk, as shown by his utility function, this is not the best decision for him.

Besides being useful in indicating the sorts of decisions that people *should* make, utility functions can also be useful in predicting the decisions that they *actually will* make. To the extent that they conform to the theory put forth by von Neumann and Morgenstern, decision-makers will choose the course of action that maximizes expected utility. Thus, if we have a decision maker's utility function, we can predict which course of action he or she will choose by comparing the expected utilities. For example, suppose that William Beard is confronted with a choice between (1) the certainty of a $50,000 gain and (2) a gamble where there is a .25 probability that he will gain $500,000 and a .75 probability that he will lose $50,000. Which will he choose?

Using Mr. Beard's utility function in Figure 16.6, we can readily determine the utility he attaches to $-$50,000, $+$50,000, and $+$500,000. These utilities are 0, 9, and 20, respectively. Thus the expected utility from the certainty of a $50,000 gain equals 9. And the expected utility from the gamble equals

$$.75(0) + .25(20) = 5.$$

Since the expected utility from the certain gain of $50,000 exceeds that from the gamble, we would predict that Mr. Beard will choose the certainty of a $50,000 gain over the gamble.[9]

PREFERENCES REGARDING RISK

Not all utility functions look like the one in Figure 16.6. Although one can expect that utility increases with the decision maker's income, the shape of the

---

[9] Of course, decision makers sometimes are inconsistent and, like all of us, they make mistakes. Thus it would be foolish to expect that predictions of this sort would always be correct, even if the theory were basically correct.

utility function can vary greatly, depending on the person's attitude toward risk. Figure 16.7 shows three general types of utility functions, each of which is discussed below.

Risk averters

Risk averters. The utility function in the top panel of Figure 16.7 is like that in Figure 16.6 in the sense that utility increases with the person's income, but *at a decreasing rate.* In other words, an increase in income of $1 is associated with *smaller and smaller* increases in utility as the person's income increases in size.[10] People with utility functions of this sort are *risk averters.* That is, when confronted with gambles with equal expected monetary values, they prefer a gamble with a more-certain outcome to one with a less-certain outcome.

For example, suppose that the top panel of Figure 16.7 pertains to Roland Staid, who must choose between two job offers which are basically the same except for income. If he chooses the first job, he is certain to receive $40,000 a year. If he chooses the second job, his income depends heavily on a variety of uncertain factors, and there would be a .50 probability that it would be $20,000 a year and a .50 probability that it would be $60,000 a year. According to the top panel of Figure 16.7, the utilities of incomes of $20,000, $40,000, and $60,000 are 20, 28, and 30, respectively. Thus, the utility he attaches to the certainty of a $40,000 income is 28, and the expected utility he attaches to a gamble where there is a .5 probability of a $20,000 income and .5 probability of a $60,000 income is .5(20) + .5(30) = 25. The consequence is that he will choose the first job since its expected utility is higher. As will always be the case for a risk averter, he chooses a gamble with a more-certain outcome in preference to one with a less-certain outcome, given that the expected monetary values of the gambles are the same. (Note that the expected monetary value of both jobs is $40,000.)[11]

Risk lovers

Risk lovers. The utility function in the middle panel of Figure 16.7 is one where utility increases with the person's income, but *at an increasing rate.* In other words, an increase in income of $1 is associated with *larger and larger* increases in utility as the person's income increases in size. People with utility functions of this sort are *risk lovers.* That is, when confronted with gambles with equal expected monetary values, they prefer a gamble with a less-certain outcome to one with a more-certain outcome.

To see that this is true, suppose that the middle panel of Figure 16.7 pertains to Mary Wager, who faces the same choice of jobs as Roland Staid. In her case, the utilities of incomes of $20,000, $40,000, and $60,000 are 5, 15, and 30, respectively. Thus, the utility she attaches to the $40,000 (with certainty) job is

---

[10]   Using the concepts in the appendix to Chapter 3, this amounts to saying that there is diminishing marginal utility of income. That is, the additional (or marginal) utility resulting from an extra dollar of income declines as income goes up.

[11]   The two jobs can be regarded as "gambles"; the outcome (that is, salary) of the first job is more certain than that of the second job. Indeed it is completely certain.

FIGURE 16.7 Utility Functions of Risk-Averse, Risk-Loving, and Risk-Neutral Individuals

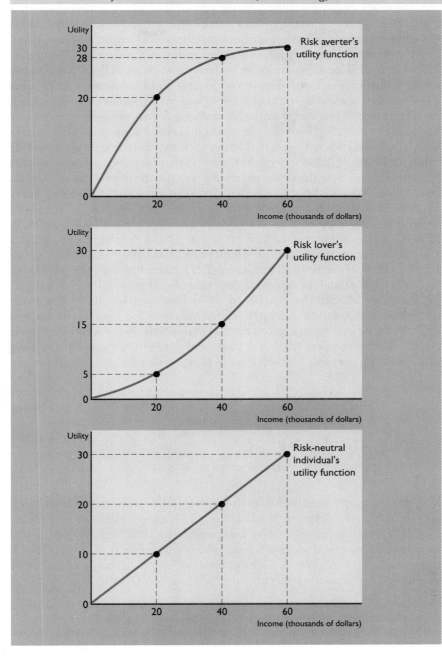

15, and the expected utility of the second job is .5(5) + .5(30) = 17.5. In contrast to Mr. Staid, she will choose the second job since its expected utility is higher. As will always be the case for a risk lover, she chooses a gamble with a less certain outcome in preference to one with a more-certain outcome, given that the expected monetary values of the gambles are the same.

**Risk
neutral**

Risk neutral. The utility function in the bottom panel of Figure 16.7 is one where utility increases with the person's income and *at a constant rate.* In other words, an increase in income of $1 is associated with a *constant* increase in utility as the person's income grows larger and larger. Put still another way, there is a *linear* relationship between income and utility. People with utility functions of this sort are *risk neutral.* That is, they maximize expected monetary value regardless of risk. On page 544, we said that under some circumstances it is rational to choose the action or gamble that has the largest expected monetary value. Now we know what these circumstances are: *the decision maker must be risk neutral.*

To illustrate, suppose that the bottom panel of Figure 16.7 pertains to Milton Canute, who faces the same choice of jobs as Roland Staid and Mary Wager. In his case, the utilities of incomes of $20,000, $40,000, and $60,000 are 10, 20, and 30, respectively. Thus, the utility he attaches to the $40,000 (with certainty) job is 20, and the expected utility of the second job is .5(10) + .5(30) = 20. In contrast to Mr. Staid or Ms. Wager, he is indifferent between the two jobs since the expected utility attached to each is the same (20). Like all risk-neutral individuals, he isn't influenced by the fact that income in the second job is less certain than in the first job. He is interested only in the expected monetary value, which is the same for both jobs. In his eyes, risk doesn't matter.[12]

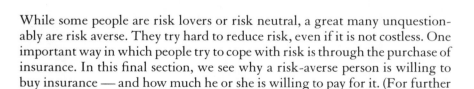

WHY PEOPLE BUY INSURANCE

While some people are risk lovers or risk neutral, a great many unquestionably are risk averse. They try hard to reduce risk, even if it is not costless. One important way in which people try to cope with risk is through the purchase of insurance. In this final section, we see why a risk-averse person is willing to buy insurance — and how much he or she is willing to pay for it. (For further discussion of insurance markets, see pages 564 to 568 of the chapter appendix.)

---

[12] It is important to recognize that a person can be a risk averter under some circumstances, a risk lover under other circumstances, and risk neutral under still other circumstances. The utility functions in Figure 16.7 are "pure" cases where the person is always only one of these types, at least in the range covered by the graphs.

EXAMPLE 16.3

Who Buys State Lottery Tickets?

Many states, like Connecticut, Massachusetts, Michigan, New Jersey, and Pennsylvania, run lotteries that provide them with revenues. In 1986, the average adult living in a state with lotteries spent about $110 on lottery tickets. According to Charles Clotfelter and Philip Cook, betting is heaviest among males, Hispanics, African Americans, the middle-aged, Catholics, laborers, and those with less than a college degree. In an earlier year, the total sales of lottery tickets and the total prize money in six states were as follows (in millions of dollars):

	Ticket sales	Prize money		Ticket sales	Prize money
Connecticut	34.7	15.6	Michigan	135.7	61.1
Maryland	40.1	16.0	New Jersey	112.7	51.8
Massachusetts	70.6	30.5	Pennsylvania	124.4	54.4

(a) Is the expected monetary value of a lottery ticket positive or negative in these states? (b) On the average, about how much do these state lotteries pay out per dollar bet? (c) Will a risk averter buy a lottery ticket in any of these states? (d) Will one of these lottery tickets be bought by a person who is risk neutral?

SOLUTION (a) Negative, because the prize money is much less in each state than the ticket sales. (b) The amount paid out in prizes per dollar bet ranged from 40 cents in Maryland to 46 cents in New Jersey. Thus the expected amount that a buyer of a 1 dollar ticket will win is only 40 to 46 cents, which is considerably less than the price of the ticket. (c) The expected monetary value of *not* buying a lottery ticket is zero, and there is no risk if he or she does not buy the ticket. A risk averter would prefer not buying the ticket to buying it *even if the ticket's expected monetary value were zero* (because the risk would be less if it were not bought than if it was bought, and the expected monetary value would be the same). Consequently, he or she would certainly not buy it if its expected monetary value is *negative,* as it is here. (d) People who are risk neutral maximize expected monetary value, regardless of risk. Since the expected monetary value of not buying the ticket (zero) is higher than that of buying the ticket (negative), such people will not buy the ticket.*

---

* For further discussion, see R. Brinner and C. Clotfelter, "An Economic Appraisal of State Lotteries," *National Tax Journal,* 1975, and C. Clotfelter and P. Cook, "The Demand for Lottery Products," National Bureau of Economic Research, 1989.

Suppose that Roland Staid, who suffers from arthritis of the hip, believes that there is a .5 probability that he will need a hip replacement operation next year, the cost of the operation being $20,000. Since his income is $40,000 (recall that he took the first job in the previous section), there is therefore a .5 probability that his income net of the cost of the operation will be $20,000 and a .5 probability that it will be $40,000 (because no operation will be needed). According to Figure 16.8, which shows his utility function, the utility that he attaches to an income of $20,000 is 20, and the utility that he attaches to an income of $40,000 is 28. Thus, his expected utility equals[13]

$$.5(20) + .5(28) = 24.$$

Suppose that an insurance company offers to sell Mr. Staid a policy which will pay for his operation (if he needs it) for $10,000. In that case, he can be sure that his income less his insurance costs will be $40,000 − $10,000 = $30,000. As shown in Figure 16.8, the utility he attaches to a $30,000 net income equals

FIGURE 16.8 Willingness of a Risk-Averse Individual to Buy Insurance Mr. Staid will be willing to pay up to $14,000 for insurance to pay for an operation if he needs it.

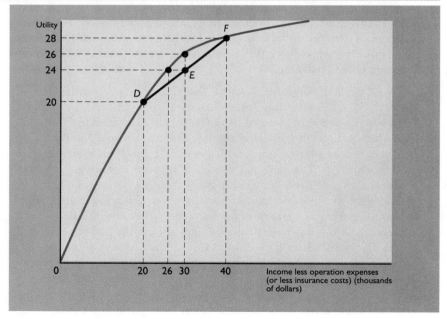

---

[13] Geometrically, his expected utility can be determined by drawing the chord between point D and point F in Figure 16.8, and finding the midpoint of that chord, which is point E. The vertical coordinate of point E is clearly his expected utility since it equals 1/2 times the utility of $20,000 plus 1/2 times the utility of $40,000. As shown in Figure 16.8, the vertical coordinate of this point is 24, which agrees with the algebraic result in the equation in the text on this page.

26, which exceeds his expected utility (24) without insurance. Thus, he will be quite willing to buy the insurance. Indeed, he will be willing to pay up to $14,000 for insurance of this kind. To see that this is true, note that, if his income less his insurance costs equals $26,000 (which means that his insurance costs equal $14,000), his utility, which equals 24, is no lower than if he has no insurance.

SUMMARY

1. The consumer has preferences between consumption this year and consumption next year, and these preferences can be represented by a set of indifference curves. The consumer is confronted by a budget line which indicates the combination of present and future consumption that he or she can attain. The slope of the budget line is $-(1+r)$, where r is the interest rate. The optimal choice between the amount consumed this year and the amount consumed next year is represented by the point on the budget line that is on the highest indifference curve.

2. A higher interest rate often leads to more saving than a lower interest rate does. The investment demand curve shows that a higher interest rate tends to reduce total investment by firms. For equilibrium to occur, the quantity demanded of loanable funds must equal the quantity supplied. The equilibrium level of the interest rate is the level at which this equality occurs.

3. If you receive X dollars n years from now, the present value of this amount is $X/(1+r)^n$, where r is the rate of interest. If you receive X_1 dollars a year from now, X_2 dollars two years from now, . . . , and X_n dollars n years from now, the present value of this series of payments is $X_1/(1+r) + X_2/(1+r)^2 + \cdots + X_n/(1+r)^n$.

4. If an investment costs C dollars now and if it is expected to yield cash flows of X_1 dollars a year hence, X_2 dollars two years hence, . . . , and X_n dollars n years hence, the net present value of the investment equals

$$-C + \frac{X_1}{1+r} + \frac{X_2}{(1+r)^2} + \cdots + \frac{X_n}{(1+r)^n},$$

where r is the discount rate. The net present value is a measure of the benefits minus the costs of the investment.

5. A firm should accept an investment project only if its net present value is positive. In calculating the net present value of an investment project, a

firm should use the rate of return that it can obtain from other, equally risky investment projects as the value of r, the discount rate.

6. The probability of a particular outcome is the proportion of times that this outcome results over the long run if this situation were to occur over and over again. The expected monetary value of a gamble is the sum of the amount of money gained (or lost) if each outcome occurs times the probability of occurrence of the outcome. The expected monetary value is important because it is the average amount that the decision maker would gain (or lose) if he or she were to accept this gamble repeatedly.

7. The expected value of perfect information is the increase in expected monetary value if the decision maker could obtain completely accurate information concerning the outcome of the relevant situation (but he or she does not yet know what this information will be). This is the maximum amount that the decision maker should pay to obtain such information. Using methods described in this chapter, one can calculate the expected value of perfect information.

8. Whether a decision maker wants to maximize expected monetary value depends on his or her attitude toward risk, which can be measured by his or her von Neumann-Morgenstern utility function (and which should not be confused with the utility function described in Chapter 3). The von Neumann-Morgenstern utility function is useful in indicating the courses of action that the decision maker should choose, and in predicting those that he or she will choose.

9. Risk averters, when confronted with gambles with equal expected monetary values, prefer a gamble with a more-certain outcome to one with a less-certain outcome. The reverse is true for risk lovers. People who are risk neutral maximize expected monetary value; in their eyes, risk doesn't matter.

QUESTIONS/PROBLEMS

1. A major oil company evaluated a proposed investment in improvements in visbreakers, a particular type of petroleum-refining equipment. According to the company's analysts, such improvements would require an investment of $15 million and would result in a saving of $2 million per year for the following 9 years. Thus, if the investment were made in 1998, the effect on the firm's cash flow would be as shown on the next page:

Year	Effect on cash flow (millions of dollars)	Year	Effect on cash flow (millions of dollars)
1998	−15	2003	2
1999	2	2004	2
2000	2	2005	2
2001	2	2006	2
2002	2	2007	2

(a) If the interest rate was 10 percent, what was the net present value of this investment? (b) If cost overruns resulted in the investment being $20 million rather than $15 million, what would be the net present value of the investment? (c) In fact, the oil company decided not to carry out this investment project. Was this a wise decision? Why or why not?

2. An investment will have the following effect on a firm's annual cash inflow:

1995	−$5,000
1996	+$2,000
1997	+$2,000
1998	+$1,000
1999	+$1,000

If the interest rate is 10 percent, should this firm carry out this investment?

3. Government agencies, as well as business firms, use the net-present-value rule to determine whether investments should be carried out. In 1977, there was a famous controversy at the highest levels of government over water projects (such as dams). President Jimmy Carter objected to 18 water projects that had been approved when interest rates were lower. He said, "A more realistic interest rate must be used in calculating the costs and benefits of projects." (a) Suppose that a project costs $1.5 billion in 1997 and $3 billion in 1998 and that it results in the following benefits (in billions of dollars) in subsequent years:

1999	1	2001	1	2003	1
2000	1	2002	1	2004	1

If the interest rate is .10, what is the net present value of the costs and benefits? Should the project be carried out? (b) If the interest rate really is .05 rather than .10, should the project be carried out? (c) Why do reductions in the interest rate tend to increase a project's chances of being accepted? (d) What value of the interest rate should government agencies use for this purpose?

4. Suppose that Mary Brown's situation is as follows, where AB is her budget line:

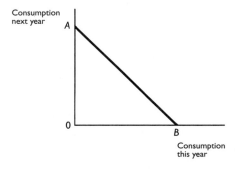

If $OA = \$40,000$, and the interest rate equals .08, what does OB equal?

5. A firm developed and introduced a new product used in connection with the drilling of wells. The product results in lower drilling costs because the drilling goes faster. This is an actual (not hypothetical) case. The effect of the investment in this new product on the firm's cash flow is shown below. (These figures, which were provided by the firm, have been rounded to make the computations simpler.)

Year	Effect on cash flow (dollars)	Year	Effect on cash flow (dollars)
1980	−100,000	1990	15,000
1981	−100,000	1991	200,000
1982	−100,000	1992	700,000
1983	−100,000	1993	700,000
1984	−100,000	1994	700,000
1985	−100,000	1995	700,000
1986	−100,000	1996	700,000
1987	15,000	1997	700,000
1988	15,000	1998	700,000
1989	15,000	1999	700,000

(a) Was the firm wise to make this investment if the interest rate was 10 percent? (b) If the effect of this investment on the firm's cash flow was zero in 1987 to 1991 (but the figures for the other years in the above table are correct), would the firm have been wise to make this investment?

6. John Murphy must decide whether to go forward with an investment project. If the project is successful, he will gain $5 million. If it is not successful, he will lose $1 million. He believes that the probability is .2 that it will be successful and .8 that it will not be successful. What is the expected value of perfect information concerning whether it will be successful?

7. Mary Wilkens is considering the purchase of stock in a firm that produces tools and dies. She feels that there is a 50-50 chance, if she buys the stock, that she can make $6,000, and a 50-50 chance that she will lose $12,000. What is the expected monetary value to her of buying the stock? If she maximizes expected monetary value, should she purchase the stock?

8. In Problem 7, Mary Wilkens attaches a utility of −20 to a $12,000 loss, a utility of 0 to a zero gain, and a utility of 5 to a $6,000 gain. What is the expected utility of buying the stock? Should she purchase the stock? Why or why not? If in fact Mary Wilkens decides to purchase the stock described in Problem 7, does this mean that she is (a) risk neutral or (b) risk averse?

9. Ms. Cherrytree's von Neumann-Morgenstern utility function can be represented by

$$U = 10 + 2M,$$

where U is utility and M is monetary gain (in thousands of dollars). She has the opportunity to invest $25,000 in Archie Dallas's Bar and Grill. She believes that there is a .5 probability that she will lose her entire investment and a .5 probability that she will gain $32,000. (a) If she makes the investment, what is her expected utility? (b) Should she make the investment?

10. Nobel laureate Milton Friedman and L. J. Savage hypothesized that a person's von Neumann-Morgenstern utility function for income typically has the shape indicated below.

   (a) If John Jones has this utility function, will he prefer the certainty of an income of B to a gamble in which there is a .5 probability that his income is A and a .5 probability that his income is C? (Note that B is the average of A and C.) (b) Will he prefer the certainty of an income of D to a gamble where there is a .5 probability that his income is C and a .5 probability that his income is E? (Note that D is the average of C and E.)

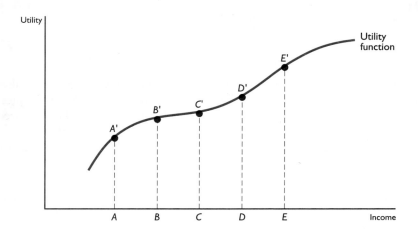

11. The Carborundum Corporation had to decide whether to expand its production capacity for Ceramax, a high-porosity ceramic material it manufactured. Sales for this material had been growing rapidly, and its only manufacturing plant had reached capacity. The firm could expand its existing plant at Lockport, New York, or build a new plant in Birmingham, Alabama. Carborundum's staff calculated the net present value of each of these investments, the results being as follows:[14]

	Net present value (millions of dollars)
Expand Lockport plant	−.163
Build new plant	−.153

(a) Based on these results, does it appear that Carborundum should expand the Lockport plant? (b) Does it appear that it should build a new plant? (c) In calculating the net present value of the investment in the new plant, Carborundum's staff considered only the first 5 years after its construction. Does that seem to be the relevant period? (d) In calculating the above net present values, Carborundum's staff used a discount rate of 15 percent, although the firm's return on comparable investments during the previous decade appeared to have averaged less than 10 percent. Does this figure of 15 percent seem too high? (e) If the discount rate that is used is too high, will this bias the net present values upward or downward? Why?

APPENDIX

How to Construct a Utility Function

To determine the von Neumann-Morgenstern utility that the decision maker attaches to each possible outcome, he or she must respond to a series of questions which indicate his or her preferences with regard to risk. The required utilities can be found in two steps. The first step is simple: *We set the utility attached to two monetary values arbitrarily.* The utility of the better consequence

---

[14] R. Hayes, S. Wheelwright, and K. Clark, *Dynamic Manufacturing* (New York: Free Press, 1988).

is set higher than the utility of the worse one. In the case of Mr. Beard, we might set $U(-50)$ equal to 0 and $U(500)$ equal to 20. It turns out that the ultimate results of the analysis do not depend on which two numbers we choose, as long as the utility of the better consequence is set higher than the utility of the worse one. Thus we could set $U(-50)$ equal to 1 and $U(500)$ equal to 10. It would make no difference to the ultimate outcome of the analysis.[15]

The second step is somewhat more complicated: *In this step we present the decision maker with a choice between the certainty of one of the other monetary values and a gamble where the possible outcomes are the two monetary values whose utilities we set arbitrarily.* For example, in the case of Mr. Beard, suppose that we want to find $U(0)$, which is the utility that he attaches to a zero gain. To do so, we ask whether he would prefer the certainty of a zero gain to a gamble where there is a probability of P that the gain is \$500,000 and a probability of $(1-P)$ that the loss is \$50,000. We then try various values of P until we find the one where he is indifferent between the certainty of a zero gain and this gamble. Suppose that this value of P is 1/4.

If he is indifferent between the certainty of a zero gain and this gamble, it must be that the expected utility of the certainty of a zero gain equals the expected utility of the gamble. (Why? Because he maximizes expected utility.) Thus

$$U(0) = \tfrac{1}{4}U(500) + \tfrac{3}{4}U(-50).$$

And since we set $U(500)$ equal to 20 and $U(-50)$ equal to zero, it follows that

$$U(0) = \tfrac{1}{4}(20) + \tfrac{3}{4}(0) = 5.$$

In other words, the utility attached to a zero gain is 5.

To obtain $U(50)$, we ask Mr. Beard whether he would prefer the certainty of a \$50,000 gain to a gamble where there is a probability of P that the gain is \$500,000 and a probability of $(1-P)$ that the loss is \$50,000. Then we try various values of P until we find the one where he is indifferent between the certainty of a \$50,000 gain and this gamble. Suppose that this value of P is 9/20. Then the expected utility of a certain gain of \$50,000 must equal the expected utility of this gamble, which means that

$$U(50) = \tfrac{9}{20}U(500) + \tfrac{11}{20}U(-50).$$

And since $U(500)$ equals 20 and $U(-50)$ equals zero, $U(50)$ must equal 9.

---

[15]It is important to note that the utility function that we construct is not unique. Since we set two utilities arbitrarily, the results will vary, depending on the values of the utilities that are chosen. If $X_1, X_2, \ldots, X_n$ are the utilities attached to n possible monetary values, $(\alpha + \beta X_1)$, $(\alpha + \beta X_2)$, $\ldots$, $(\alpha + \beta X_n)$ can also be utilities attached to them (where α and β are constants, and $\beta > 0$).

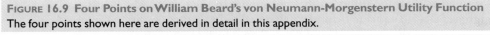

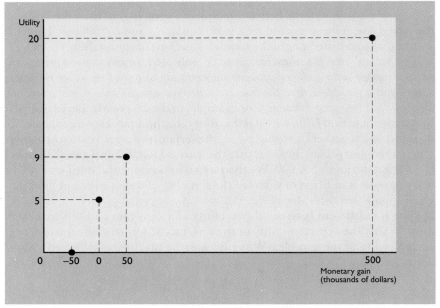

The decision-maker's utility function is the relationship between his or her utility and the amount of his or her monetary gain (or loss). Based on our evaluation of $U(-50)$, $U(0)$, $U(50)$, and $U(500)$ in previous paragraphs, we can identify four points on Mr. Beard's utility function, as shown in Figure 16.9. Through the repeated use of the procedure described above, we can obtain as many such points as we like — or as the decision-maker's patience permits. In this way, we can trace out Mr. Beard's entire utility function, shown in Figure 16.6.

Adverse Selection and Moral Hazard

On pages 554 to 557 we looked at insurance decisions from the point of view of the individual consumer like Roland Staid. Now let's consider insurance markets from the point of view of the insurance company. To begin with, let's suppose that there is a .01 probability that any individual house will burn down, and that an insurance company sells policies stipulating that it will pay each person $100,000 if his or her house burns down. (For simplicity, we assume that all houses are worth $100,000.) If the insurance company sells a large number of policies, it can be reasonably sure that about 1 percent of the policyholders will have houses that burn down, and hence will receive $100,000 each from the company. For example, if it sells 100,000 policies, it can be reasonably sure that about 1,000 of them will have to be paid off. Thus, ignoring its administrative and marketing costs, the company can afford to sell such a policy at a price of about $1,000, since it will sell about 100 policies for every one that has to be paid off.

In this case, $1,000 is the price (the so-called premium) that is *actuarially fair.* If the market for insurance is competitive, the price will be pushed down to somewhat more than this level. (Why somewhat more? Because the insurance company incurs a variety of costs, such as the wages of employees who sell the insurance and process claims; and to remain solvent, the company must cover these costs, as well as have enough in premiums to pay off the claims.) As stressed above, many consumers are risk averse, which means that they prefer the certainty of a $1,000 loss to a gamble where there is a .01 probability of losing $100,000 (the value of their house), and a .99 probability of losing nothing. These consumers are willing to pay more than $1,000 for this insurance. Consequently, the conditions exist under which a market can develop: firms can offer insurance policies at a price that (some) consumers find acceptable.

In fact, everyone does not have the same probability of having his or her house burn down, and while the insurance company can use historical data to estimate the average probability that a house in a particular area will burn down, it often finds it difficult, if not impossible, to determine how this probability varies from one homeowner to another. Under these circumstances, consumers with a relatively high risk of a fire (and who know their risk is high) will find the price of $1,000 very attractive. Since their probability of a fire exceeds .01, the expected amount that they will receive exceeds $1,000, the price of the insurance. On the other hand, consumers with a relatively low risk of a fire (and who know that their risk is low) will not find this price attractive. Consequently, the insurance company will find that a disproportionately large share of their customers will come from the high-risk group. In other words, it will obtain an *adverse selection* from the total group of potential customers. The customers who are bad risks are more likely to want to buy this insurance, and the insurance company finds it very difficult to tell whether a particular customer is high risk or low risk when it sells the insurance policy.

Adverse selection

Consequences of Adverse Selection

Who cares whether adverse selection occurs? Lots of people do. Because so many high-risk customers buy the insurance, the insurance company must pay off on a larger percentage of its policies than it expected. Thus, to remain solvent, it must raise the price of its insurance, which discourages even more low-risk customers from buying insurance. Consequently, the proportion of insurance buyers who are high-risk becomes even higher, and the insurance company must raise the price further. Eventually, only high-risk customers may be willing to buy this insurance, even though low-risk customers would be happy to buy it if its price were in keeping with their own actual low-risk status.

Note two things. First, if the insurance company could somehow obtain full information concerning a customer's risk status, it could deal with this situation by simply charging a higher price to high-risk than to low-risk customers. This higher price would reflect the fact that high-risk customers are more likely to have a fire and collect $100,000 from the company. Second, the problem facing the insurance company is essentially the same as the problem facing the buyer of a used car, discussed in Chapter 1. Recall that, since used-car buyers could not distinguish between a good used car and a "lemon" (a defective used car), there was an adverse selection from the total potential supply of used cars. "Lemons" constituted a disproportionately large proportion of the used cars offered for sale.

This problem of adverse selection occurs in many insurance markets, not just the market for fire insurance. For example, in the case of health insurance, some customers may be much more likely than others to have serious illnesses, and it may be very difficult for the insurance company to determine whether this is the case. Here, as in the case of fire insurance, low-risk customers may be driven from the market because of increases in the price of health insurance due to the disproportionately large percentage of insurance buyers who are high-risk customers.

To help deal with this problem, insurance companies have devised a number of responses. (1) Insurance companies often require physical examinations to obtain better information as to whether or not a person is high-risk or low-risk. (2) They often offer lower prices for health insurance to members of group plans, such as *all* employees of a large firm, than to individuals. In such group plans, since insurance is mandatory for *all* employees, there is little or no problem of adverse selection. (3) They often set insurance rates that differ from one segment of the population to another. To take an example from the automobile insurance market, since young women tend to be better drivers than young men, companies tend to sell auto insurance to young women at a considerably lower price than to young men.

In recent years, some people have argued that such gender-based discrimination is unfair. Others have retorted that banning gender-based insurance rates would discriminate against young women (in the case of auto insurance) because it would ignore the basic actuarial facts. Whatever your position on this question, it is easy to see why insurance companies would respond as they have to the adverse selection problem.

Moral Hazard

Moral hazard

Another difficulty faced by insurance companies is the moral hazard problem, which occurs when a buyer of insurance alters his or her behavior so as to increase the probability that the company will have to pay off a claim. To illustrate, consider Ms. Hamilton, who insures her diamond against theft. Suppose that she buys enough insurance so that the value of her assets will be the same regardless of whether her diamond is stolen or not. Feeling that she has nothing to lose if her diamond is stolen, she does not take many precautions to prevent its theft. Thus the probability of its theft is greater than if she had bought less or no insurance. Why? Because if she had bought less or no insurance, she would lose more if the diamond were stolen, and consequently she would take greater precautions.

Whenever the insurance company cannot ascertain what actions people take that may influence the likelihood of the unfavorable event that is being insured against, the moral hazard problem may arise. This problem exists for various kinds of insurance, not for theft insurance alone. For example, people who buy lots of accident insurance may drive less carefully because they are well insured, the result being that they are more likely to have an accident than if they had less insurance. Similarly, people with lots of medical insurance may spend less on preventive health care, and if they get sick, they may make more visits to the physician and incur more expensive treatments than if they had less insurance.

Consider the extreme case where a health insurance policy reimburses the policyholder for all medical costs. In this case, if a person gets sick, he or she really pays nothing for extra treatment. Clearly, the patient under these circumstances is likely to consume medical services in excess of what he or she would consume if the extra services were not free. Any drug or treatment, whatever its price, may be prescribed by physicians who know that the insurance company, not the patient, will pay for it. The result, of course, is that medical costs increase and the price of insurance goes up commensurately.

Responding to this problem, insurance companies frequently impose limits on the amount of medical services that an insurance policy will cover. For example, a particular policy may pay for no more than 4 days in the hospital for a person undergoing a gallbladder operation. In addition, many insurance policies have a feature called *co-insurance,* which means that the insurance company pays for less than 100 percent of the total bill, and the policyholder pays the balance. For example, health insurance policies often have a 20 percent co-insurance rate, which implies that the insurance company pays 80 percent and the policyholder pays 20 percent. (Recall Example 3.2.) Thus, if someone incurs a medical bill of $500, he or she must pay $.20 \times \$500$, or $100 of it. The point of co-insurance is that the policyholder is given more incentive to hold down medical bills and take preventative care.

Still another way that insurance companies respond to the moral hazard problem is by inserting a *deductible* into the insurance policy. With a deductible, the policyholder has to bear the loss (which is insured against) up to some limit. For example, a medical insurance policy may stipulate that the patient must pay the first $200 of medical expenses that he or she incurs per year.

(Recall Example 3.2.) Thus, if you have such a policy and if you incur $1,000 in medical bills in 1997, you must pay $200 of them. This provides patients with an incentive to consider the full costs in the case of minor treatments or injuries.

In summary, the problems of adverse selection and moral hazard — both of which stem from the fact that there is asymmetric information in the marketplace — play an important role in insurance markets. To understand many of the practices in these markets, you have to know what these problems are and how insurance companies try to reduce their effects.

Applying Microeconomic Theory: The Case of Jetliners

17

INTRODUCTION

Robert Crandall, chairman and chief executive officer of American Airlines, the nation's largest carrier, is widely regarded as one of the hardest-driving top executives in the United States. As he himself has said, "My friends call me Mr. Crandall. My enemies call me Fang."[1] After graduating from the University of Pennsylvania's Wharton School in 1960, he held jobs in finance at Eastman Kodak, Hallmark Cards, Trans World Airlines, and

---

[1] *New York Times Magazine,* September 23, 1990, p. 25.

Bloomingdale's before joining American Airlines as senior vice president of finance in 1972. His frugality is legendary. (He once eliminated a single olive from American's salads and saved the airline $40,000 per year.) Also legendary are his 12- and 18-hour workdays, which helped him rise to president in 1980 and chairman in 1985.

In 1992, his picture hit the front pages when he dramatically simplified and reduced American's fares. Subsequently, a price war erupted among major U.S. airlines, as air tickets were sold at half their previous price. According to Crandall, "The half-price sale was a monstrous stupidity. A monstrous stupidity perpetuated by Northwest." The head of Northwest Airlines, the country's fourth largest airline, replied "What American Airlines did was predatory and very damaging."[2] Regardless of who is right, the major U.S. airlines reported losses from the half-price sale, while travelers beamed.

When he assumed the presidency, one of Crandall's first problems was that American had an aging fleet of planes. To the airlines, an airplane is an input, one form of capital. The demand for large transport aircraft is a derived demand, stemming from the demand for air travel.[3] As the public demands more air travel, the airlines demand more aircraft. Besides the demand for aircraft to satisfy the growth in demand, the airlines also demand aircraft to replace the older planes that are being retired. In 1980, Crandall had to obtain some new aircraft to replace an earlier generation of jets as well as to expand his fleet. Of course, he was not the only airline executive shopping for new aircraft. Every major airline must constantly try to figure out whether it should purchase new planes, and if so, how many and of what type.

SUPPLIERS OF JETLINERS

In the 1990s, there have been three principal manufacturers of large commercial aircraft — Boeing, McDonnell Douglas, and Airbus. Boeing, the world's

---

[2] *New York Times,* September 12, 1992. Crandall has not always been a price-cutter. On February 21, 1982, he called the chairman of Braniff Airline and suggested that they raise their prices. The call was secretly taped, and the Justice Department threatened to ban him from the airline industry for 2 years, but eventually settled for his promise not to do such a thing again.

[3] Large transport aircraft are planes that can carry 50 or more passengers or large amounts of cargo. In contrast, general aviation aircraft for personal and business use include transports that can carry fewer than 50 passengers, cropdusters, and so forth. Since the revenues from large transports far exceed those of general aviation aircraft, we focus attention here solely on large transports.

Boeing Headquarters

largest producer of commercial aircraft, is the industry leader. With the stated goal of dominating every part of the commercial transport market, it has committed itself to technological preeminence, and is regarded as a low-cost producer. It has developed a basic aircraft for each segment of the market — the Boeing 737 (115 seats with about a 2,000 mile range), the Boeing 757 (180 seats with about a 3,500 mile range), the Boeing 767 (211 seats with about a 4,000 mile range), the Boeing 777 (350 seats with about a 5,000 mile range), and the Boeing 747 (440 seats with about a 6,000 mile range).[4] In recent years, it has been the United States's biggest exporter, a highly visible symbol that in many areas this country's ability to compete in an increasingly competitive world marketplace is vital and strong.

McDonnell Douglas, headquartered in St. Louis, Missouri, is the leading military contractor in the United States. Among its products have been the F-15 Eagle fighter plane (used for bombing and air-to-air combat), which saw extensive action in the Persian Gulf War. Product of a 1967 merger between McDonnell Aircraft Corporation and Douglas Aircraft Corporation (which made large civilian transports), its facilities to produce commercial aircraft have employed about 36,000 people in Long Beach, California. In 1995, its commercial aircraft division received some bad news. Scandinavian Airlines canceled a major order for McDonnell's proposed MD-95, a new twin-engine

---

[4] 1994 Annual Report, Boeing Company, and D. Yoffie, *International Trade and Competition* (New York: McGraw-Hill, 1990). Of course, the number of seats can be varied somewhat. Thus, the numbers given in Table 17.3 by Bailey, Graham, and Kaplan for the Boeing 737 and 747 differ somewhat from those given here by Yoffie.

Airbus Industries Headquarters

aircraft. Subsequently, the firm felt compelled to issue a denial of rumors that its inability to obtain orders for the MD-95 would induce it to take on the Chinese government as a partner.[5]

Airbus Industries is a consortium of French, British, German, and Spanish aerospace firms, all supported and/or owned by their governments. Established in 1970, Airbus was an attempt by the European partners to compete with the dominant U.S. firms. By the early 1990s, Airbus had developed and launched five aircraft. It started with two wide-body medium-range aircraft, the A300 (260 seats with a range of about 3,000 miles) and the A310 (210 seats with a range of about 4,000 miles); later it introduced the A320 (150 seats, with a range of about 1,800 miles), which competes with the Boeing 737. In 1992, deliveries began of its long-range jets, the A330 and A340. Airbus has emphasized technological innovations in airframe design, advanced digital avionics, airfoil design, engine technology, and new materials. A big victory for Airbus occurred in 1987 when Northwest Airlines ordered more than 100 of its planes. According to Lawrence Kahn, Northwest's director of fleet planning, "We were attracted to Airbus because it offers a new generation of technology."[6]

---

[5] *Business Week,* October 9, 1995; *New York Times,* June 16, 1992 and June 18, 1992; and S. Zahra, G. Nalepa, and J. Pearce, "McDonnell Douglas Corporation," in J. Pearce and R. Robinson (eds.), *Cases in Strategic Management;* (2d ed.; Homewood, Ill.: Irwin, 1991).

[6] *New York Times,* June 23, 1991, p. F6, and S. Zahra, D. Hurley, and J. Pearce, "Airbus Industries: A Wave of the Future," in Mansfield, *Study Guide and Casebook in Applied Microeconomics.*

THE COSTS OF PRODUCING A JETLINER

Since airline executives like American's Robert Crandall are continually looking for ways to provide better, cheaper, and faster air travel, the aircraft manufacturers have an incentive to develop and introduce new types of aircraft,
which is an extraordinarily expensive process. To begin with, there are the
costs of developing the new aircraft. Designs are formulated to demonstrate
the new technologies incorporated in the aircraft and to obtain reactions from
key airlines, which, it is hoped, will guarantee a minimum number of orders
and thus signal that the new plane will be a success. Once sufficient orders
have been received, the full-scale development process begins, including flight
tests and prototype construction and assembly. About 40 percent of the total
investment in launching a new aircraft is included in this development phase
of the process.

In addition, there are big tooling costs, largely associated with building
expensive construction jigs. Also, a considerable number (perhaps 40) of the
aircraft must be produced before the airplane is certified to enable the manufacturer to deliver the aircraft promptly, rather than a year or two after certifi-
cation. The total investment in launching a new aircraft may be about $20
million per seat. For Airbus's A-320, the launch investment was $2.5 billion
and for Boeing's 757 and 767 aircraft, the combined launch investment exceeded the firm's net worth.[7]

THE MARKET FOR JETLINERS

As we have seen, Robert Crandall and his fellow airline executives are the
principal players on the demand side of the market for commercial aircraft,
while Boeing, McDonnell Douglas, and Airbus are the principal players on
the supply side. In recent years, there have been notable shifts in the fortunes
of these suppliers. According to the *New York Times,* in 1990 Boeing had about
45 percent of the passenger jet market (based on orders), whereas McDonnell
Douglas had 15 percent and Airbus had 34 percent. This was a substantial

---

[7] Yoffie, *International Trade and Competition.*

change from 1988 when Boeing had 59 percent, and McDonnell Douglas and Airbus had 22 percent and 15 percent, respectively.[8] Clearly, Airbus was on the move, while the fortunes of McDonnell Douglas, which in 1982 was urged by some top advisors to quit the commercial aircraft business, seemed to be waning. Even John McDonnell, former chairman of McDonnell Douglas, characterized his firm's position in commercial aircraft in 1992 as "No. 3 and fading."[9] In 1996, Boeing announced it would acquire McDonnell Douglas.

Top officials of Boeing and McDonnell Douglas complain bitterly that the governments of France, Germany, Britain, and Spain have poured about $26 billion of subsidies into Airbus. They say that there has been $13 billion in development aid to Airbus since its founding — or $26 billion including interest. Airbus officials reply that this aid was more a loan than a subsidy, since Airbus repays the governments a predetermined amount for each plane it sells. U.S. aircraft manufacturers retort that the payments should be made in accord with ordinary commercial conditions: over 15 years and at market interest rates.[10]

THE BOEING COMPANY

In 1996, Philip Condit, who was appointed president and a member of Boeing's board of directors in 1992, was promoted to chief executive officer. He had played a very important role in the development of the Boeing 777. According to Wolfgang Demisch, a prominent Wall Street analyst, Mr. Condit had contributed greatly to making Boeing more efficient and cost conscious. "The old Boeing would never have gone to learn from Toyota, but Phil Condit did."[11]

Condit presided over a firm that is one of the biggest spenders on research and development (R&D) in the United States (Table 17.1). Historically, the development of commercial aircraft has benefited considerably from government support of R&D aimed at improving military aircraft. For example, the Boeing 707, which put Boeing on the map as a producer of commercial aircraft, was very similar to the KC-135, a jet tanker that Boeing had sold to the Air

---

[8]   *New York Times,* June 23, 1991, pp. F1–F6.

[9]   *Business Week,* July 6, 1992, p. 72.

[10]   *New York Times,* June 23, 1991.

[11]   *New York Times,* February 27, 1996, p. D5.

Philip Condit

Force. "The 707 airframe design followed that of the KC-135 quite closely, so closely, in fact, that the first prototype 707 to be 'rolled out' of the Seattle factory did not have windows in the fuselage."[12] But this takes nothing away from Boeing's prowess as a developer of high-tech aircraft; without question, Boeing has been a U.S. success story.

TABLE 17.1 U.S. Firms with Largest R&D Expenditures, 1994

Firm	R&D expenditures (billions of dollars)
General Motors	7.0
Ford	5.2
IBM	3.4
AT&T	3.1
Hewlett-Packard	2.0
Motorola	1.9
Boeing	1.7
Digital Equipment	1.3
Chrysler	1.3
Johnson and Johnson	1.3

SOURCE: *Business Week*, July 3, 1995.

---

[12] D. Mowery and N. Rosenberg, "The Commercial Aircraft Industry," in R. Nelson (ed.), *Government and Technical Progress* (New York: Pergamon, 1982), p. 131.

THE DEMAND FOR JETLINERS: CAN YOU APPLY THE THEORY?

The following two problems are concerned with the demand for jetliners.

PROBLEM 17.1   In 1985, the three manufacturers of large transport aircraft, Boeing, McDonnell Douglas, and Airbus, made separate forecasts of the total number of such aircraft that would be sold between 1986 and 2005. Their forecasts were as follows:

	Boeing[13]	McDonnell Douglas[14]	Airbus[15]
Average annual world passenger traffic growth (%)	5.1	6.4	5.5
New aircraft required for growth	3,913	5,327	3,659
Aircraft retirements	3,869	4,437	4,499
	7,782	9,764	8,158

As you can see, Boeing and Airbus forecasted that about 8,000 aircraft would be demanded during the period 1986 to 2005, whereas McDonnell Douglas was more optimistic, its forecast being well over 9,000.

(a) In 1985, there were about 6,000 large commercial aircraft.[16] Assuming for simplicity that there were 200 seats, on the average, in a plane, the total seating capacity was $6,000 \times 200 = 1.2$ million seats. Suppose that the income elasticity of demand for air travel is 1.75, which is close to some industry estimates.[17] If seating capacity must be proportional to the quantity demanded of air travel, by what percentage will seating capacity have to increase per year (during 1985 to 2005) if consumer income goes up by 2 percent annually?

---

[13] "Current Market Outlook—World Travel Demand and Airplane Economic Requirements," Boeing Commercial Airplane Company, 1986. The figures have been adjusted to a 1986 to 2005 basis.

[14] "1985–99 Outlook for Commercial Jet Aircraft," Douglas Aircraft Company, September 1985. The figures have been adjusted to a 1986 to 2005 basis.

[15] "Global Market Forecast," Airbus Industries, March 1986.

[16] Yoffie, *International Trade and Competition.*

[17] J. M. Cigliano, "Price and Income Elasticities for Airline Travel: The North Atlantic Market," *Business Economics,* September 1980.

(b) According to various studies, the price elasticity of demand for air travel is about 1.2.[18] Holding consumer incomes constant, if the price of air travel falls by 1 percent per year (in real terms) because of productivity increases in air transportation, by what percentage will seating capacity have to go up each year, if seating capacity must be proportional to the quantity demanded of air travel?[19]

(c) If *both* consumer income goes up by $2\frac{1}{2}$ percent per year *and* the price of air travel goes down by 1 percent per year, by what percentage will the quantity of air travel increase each year? Is this figure close to the rate of growth of world passenger traffic forecasted by Boeing, McDonnell Douglas, and Airbus? If so, how close is it?

(d) In absolute terms, how great would the annual increase in seating capacity have had to be in 1985, under the above assumptions? If each aircraft has 200 seats, on the average, how many aircraft would have had to be added each year to accommodate the growth in air travel?

(e) Suppose that a recession occurs, with the result that consumer income declines by 5 percent. What will be the percentage change in the quantity demanded of air travel, based on the foregoing assumptions?

(f) In previous parts of this problem, we have constructed a simple model to forecast how many aircraft will have to be added each year to accommodate the growth in air travel. What are the limitations of this model? What central factors, if any, does it ignore? How does it differ from the models presented in previous chapters to explain the amount of an input that will be employed?

PROBLEM 17.2   As pointed out above, there were about 6,000 large commercial aircraft in 1985. Suppose that the year when each was purchased was as follows:

Year	Number purchased
1966–70	1,000
1971–75	1,200
1976–80	1,800
1981	530
1982	400
1983	350
1984	300
1985	420
Total	6,000

[18] Ibid. and G. Douglas and J. Miller, *Economic Regulation of Domestic Air Transport* (Washington, D.C.: Brookings Institution, 1974).

[19] That is, we assume that, when adjusted for overall inflation, the price falls by 1 percent per year.

(a) On the average, an aircraft's normal service life is over 20 years.[20] Suppose for simplicity that all aircraft have a length of life of 25 years (no more, no less). How many aircraft will be retired from operation in the period from 1986 to 2005?

(b) Under these circumstances, which firm — Boeing, McDonnell Douglas, or Airbus — will be the most accurate forecaster of aircraft retirements during the period 1986 to 2005?

(c) Obviously, the assumption that all aircraft have a life of 25 years is a simplification. What determines how long a particular aircraft remains in operation? Are airlines always in control of the longevity of their aircraft? If not, why not?

(d) Part (a) of this problem presents what is in effect a rudimentary model to explain how many aircraft will be retired, and presumably replaced. If you were hired to evaluate this model, what criticisms would you direct at it?

JETLINER PRODUCTION COSTS: CAN YOU APPLY THE THEORY?

The following three problems deal with aircraft production costs, and show how present values play a major role in managerial decisions.

PROBLEM 17.3   In recent years, Boeing has launched the Boeing 777, a wide-bodied 350- to 400-passenger jet delivered in 1995 and later. The total launch costs for this airplane have been estimated to be about $10 billion. Generally, it takes about 12 years before a manufacturer begins to make money on a new aircraft. Besides all the money spent on development and manufacturing capability, a manufacturer ordinarily requires 2 or 3 years to correct design flaws and eliminate production mistakes. In the case of the 777, Boeing tried to use a new computer-aided design system to save time and money. According to Joseph W. Ozimek, a chief engineer at Boeing, "The [computer-aided] design program visually assembles all the parts of the plane at once . . . [Ordinarily] you find problems only after you've started building. . . . If we can get this to work, we can make a leap forward in quality you won't believe."[21]

---

[20] Yoffie, *International Trade and Competition.*

[21] *Philadelphia Inquirer,* April 5, 1992, p. D5.

(a) Wolfgang Demisch has reported that by using this new design system, "Boeing hopes to move up the start of profitable production by two years. . . ."[22] Suppose that the cash flows (in billions of dollars) for the Boeing 777 would have been as follows, with or without the use of the new design system:

	Cash flow	
Year	Without the new system	With the new system
1991	−1	−1
1992	−2	−2
1993	−3	−3
1994	−3	−2
1995	−1	0
1996	0	0
1997	0	1
1998	1	1
1999	2	2
2000	2	3
2001	3	3
2002	4	4

If the cash inflows in years after 2002 are the same whether the new system is used or not, what was the total value of the new system, based on the differences during 1991 to 2002 in the cash flows? Specifically, in 1994, what was the present value of those differences? (Suppose the interest rate is .08.)

(b) For a new airplane's total revenue (less total variable cost) to equal its launch costs, the manufacturer often has to sell about 400 units of the

---

[22] Ibid.

aircraft.[23] If this is true of the Boeing 777, what is the difference between the price of the aircraft and its average variable cost if it produces and sells 400 units of this aircraft? (Assume that the launch costs are all fixed costs, and that there are no fixed costs other than launch costs.)

(c) If Boeing were to sell enough units (no more, no less) of the 777 in the late 1990s so that the total revenue from this aircraft minus its total variable cost would equal the cost of launching the aircraft, would it really break even? Why or why not?

(d) If Boeing is the only buyer of a product supplied by a competitive industry, and if the demand, supply, and marginal expenditure curves for this product (which is an input from Boeing's point of view) are as shown below, how large is the deadweight loss from monopsony?

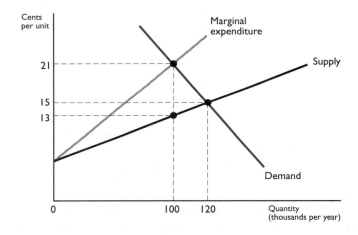

PROBLEM 17.4 The learning curve is very important in aircraft manufacture. Indeed, the first paper, published in 1936, dealing with the learning curve was based on experience in the aircraft industry.[24] Figure 17.1 shows how the number of direct labor-hours required to assemble an advanced jet aircraft decreased as experience was gained in its production. This is typical of aircraft manufacture.

(a) According to many empirical studies, a doubling of cumulative output results in about a 20 percent reduction in variable cost.[25] If the variable cost of the 40th unit produced of a particular aircraft is $10 million, what is the variable cost of the 80th unit produced? Of the 160th unit produced?

---

[23] Yoffie, *International Trade and Competition.*

[24] T. P. Wright, *Journal of Aeronautical Science,* 1936.

[25] L. Argote and D. Epple, "Learning Curves in Manufacturing," *Science,* February 23, 1990.

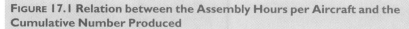

FIGURE 17.1 Relation between the Assembly Hours per Aircraft and the Cumulative Number Produced

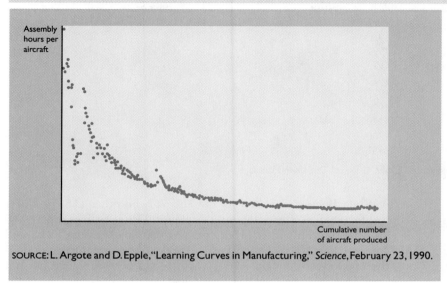

Assembly hours per aircraft

Cumulative number of aircraft produced

SOURCE: L. Argote and D. Epple, "Learning Curves in Manufacturing," *Science*, February 23, 1990.

(b) During the early 1970s, Lockheed Corporation (which has since left the commercial aircraft business) manufactured a commercial aircraft, the L-1011. On the basis of the learning curve, Lockheed estimated that its costs would fall below a certain level when the fiftieth plane was built, in 1973. The data suggest that this in fact occurred, but in the late 1970s, the airplane's costs (corrected for inflation) began to increase.[26] Was this in accord with the learning curve? Why or why not? On the basis of the data in Table 17.2, can you guess why this happened?

PROBLEM 17.5 According to McDonnell Douglas, the average cost of producing an aircraft generally falls in response to increases in the number of units of the aircraft produced and sold, as shown in Figure 17.2.[27] In part, this is because the huge costs of launching the aircraft are spread over a larger number of units. In part, it is also because of the learning curve discussed in the previous problem.

(a) If a manufacturer were to sell 500 units of a particular aircraft, by what percentage would its average costs exceed what they would have been if it had sold 700 units?

---

[26] Ibid.

[27] National Research Council, *The Competitive Status of the U.S. Civil Aviation Manufacturing Industry* (Washington, D.C.: National Academy Press, 1985).

TABLE 17.2 Number of Units of L-1011 Produced per Year

Year	Annual units	Cumulative units
1972	17	17
1973	39	56
1974	41	97
1975	25	122
1976	16	138
1977	6	144
1978	8	152
1979	24	176
1980	25	201
1981	18	219

SOURCE: Argote and Epple, "Learning Curves in Manufacturing."

(b) When Boeing launched its 757 and 767, no other U.S. producer stepped forward to offer competing airplanes. Delta Airlines ordered 60 Boeing 757s, but only after protracted negotiations between Delta and McDonnell Douglas. Although Delta expressed a strong interest in buying the McDonnell Douglas DC-11, which had been designed but not launched, McDonnell Douglas was reluctant to go forward with the launch of this new aircraft without additional orders from other airlines.

FIGURE 17.2 Relationship between the Average Cost of Producing an Aircraft and the Number of Units of the Aircraft Produced and Sold

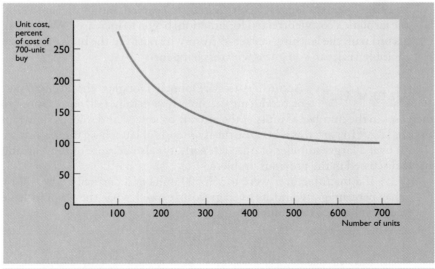

SOURCE: National Research Council, *The Competitive Status of the U.S. Civil Aviation Manufacturing Industry.*

According to *Business Week,* "Delta wanted the DC-11 in order to make certain that McDonnell Douglas would keep building airliners, thus preventing a Boeing monopoly in commercial aircraft. But when it came to making a commitment, McDonnell Douglas was timid. Soured by a profitless decade for its commercial planes, the DC-9 and DC-10, McDonnell Douglas insisted on finding a second carrier [that was willing to place an order] before launching the DC-11."[28] Why was McDonnell Douglas so reluctant to proceed without an order from a second airline?

(c) If McDonnell Douglas had to sell 400 units of the DC-11 at a particular price to break even, and if in reality it sold 200 units at this price, by what percentage would its total costs exceed its total revenues from this airplane if Figure 17.2 is assumed to be a valid representation of the relationship between its average total costs and the number of units sold?

THE MARKET FOR JETLINERS: CAN YOU APPLY THE THEORY?

The following three problems deal with the market for jetliners and the subsidies to Airbus that U.S. firms object to.

PROBLEM 17.6 Some types of aircraft have more seats than others; some can fly longer distances than others; and some are cheaper to operate than others. For example, the operating cost per passenger mile of a Boeing 747 is somewhat higher than for a DC-10 for

Boeing 747

---

[28] *Business Week,* December 1, 1980.

TABLE 17.3 Operating Cost (in cents) per Passenger Mile, Domestic Airlines, 1981

	Aircraft type				
	DC-9	B-737	B-727	DC-10	B-747
Number of seats	115	121	164	371	500
Mileage					
200	12.0	11.7	12.1	12.5	15.4
400	8.3	8.1	8.1	7.8	9.0
600	7.1	6.9	6.8	6.2	6.9
800	6.5	6.3	6.2	5.5	5.9
1,000	6.1	6.0	5.8	5.0	5.2
1,250	—	—	5.5	4.6	4.7
1,500	—	—	5.2	4.4	4.4
1,750	—	—	—	4.2	4.1
2,000	—	—	—	4.0	4.0
2,250	—	—	—	3.9	3.8
2,500	—	—	—	3.9	3.7

SOURCE: E. Bailey, D. Graham, and D. Kaplan, *Deregulating the Airlines* (Cambridge, Mass.: MIT Press, 1985), p. 51. Note that these figures pertain to 1981, whereas the figures regarding the B-747 in Example 8.2 pertain to 1975.

distances less than 1,500 miles but lower than the DC-10 for longer distances; however, the Boeing 747 can carry about a third more passengers (Table 17.3). Because of such differences among types of aircraft, some types are demanded in much greater quantities than others. The biggest seller to date is the Boeing 737, the smallest of Boeing's jetliners, of which more than 2,500 have been purchased since 1967.[29]

(a) Is the market for aircraft a perfectly competitive market? Why or why not?

(b) Will an airline obtain additional aircraft up to the point where the value of the marginal product of an airplane equals the airplane's price?

(c) In recent years, Boeing has had the capacity to produce 400 aircraft per year; this means that it alone could meet all or most of the world's demand for large commercial aircraft. Does this mean that Boeing is a monopsonist? Why or why not?

(d) According to industry observers, each airline tends to feel that it would be inefficient to mix directly competitive types of aircraft or engines in its fleet.[30] Does this put great pressure on aircraft producers to get an initial order from an airline?

(e) Suppose that American Airlines is considering the purchase of 10 aircraft from Boeing, and that the price of each plane is $20 million. If

[29] 1993 Boeing Annual Report.

[30] Yoffie, *International Trade and Competition.*

American Airlines expects that each plane will result in cash inflows of $2 million per year for the next 20 years, should it purchase these aircraft if the discount rate is 10 percent? What factors determine whether 10 percent is the appropriate discount rate?

(f) Airplanes obviously are only one type of input used by the airlines; another is labor—pilots, cabin attendants, and others. When Robert Crandall became president of American Airlines, he convinced the firm's union members to accept a two-tier wage system in which workers employed at the time received a higher wage than newcomers. According to Crandall, "We went to the union and said, 'If you will agree with us to let us hire new people at market rates, we will double the size of the airline, and everyone will move up fast.' "[31] Was this an example of the use of efficiency wages? Why or why not?

PROBLEM 17.7   The market for commercial aircraft is international in scope. Many of the jetliners produced in the United States are bought by foreign airlines. (Between 1982 and 1985, 60 percent of Boeing's orders were from non-U.S. airlines.) In June 1984, Boeing received an order from India Airlines for 12 Boeing 757 aircraft and the option to buy 13 more. In October 1984, Airbus managed to reopen the negotiations, and offered its new A-320 aircraft to India Airlines for $24 million a plane. Boeing responded by lowering its price from $42 million to $27 million per plane. Nonetheless, India Airlines bought the aircraft from Airbus.[32]

(a) The Airbus A-320 has about 162 seats; the Boeing 757 has about 208 seats. On a per-seat basis, which aircraft—the Airbus A-320 or the Boeing 757—was cheaper?

(b) In choosing between aircraft, should an airline look solely at the cost per seat? If not, what else should it consider?

Airbus A-320

[31] *New York Times Magazine,* September 23, 1990, p. 25.

[32] Yoffie, *International Trade and Competition.*

(c) The Boeing 757 was available immediately, whereas the Airbus A-320 would not be available for 5 years and even then would be untested.[33] Would this be expected to influence India Airlines' decision? If so, how?

(d) The Boeing 757 required a more powerful engine, which would have resulted in a bigger fuel cost per seat than the Airbus A-320. According to expert observers, whereas the Boeing 757 offered an $18,000 saving per seat in investment cost, it would have cost $3,000 per seat more in fuel (and other such) costs per year than the Airbus A-320.[34] If India Airlines could have obtained a 25 percent rate of return on comparable investments, was the additional fuel cost of $3,000 per year sufficient to outweigh the $18,000 saving in investment cost? Why or why not?

(e) Responding to the decision by India Airlines to buy the aircraft from Airbus, the U.S. embassy in New Delhi, acting on instructions from Washington, made a formal complaint to the Indian Ministry of Aviation. India Airline officials said that "the decision was made at the highest levels of Indian government," and claimed that the decision to switch from Boeing to Airbus was made by Rajiv Gandhi, then India's Prime Minister.[35] Do you think that the purchase of aircraft by a country's airlines is often influenced by political factors? Do you think that the national airlines of particular countries have been pressured at times to buy planes made (partly or largely) within their own countries?

| PROBLEM 17.8 | One of the major issues in the aircraft industry is the subsidies that European governments are giving Airbus. |

Suppose that Boeing and Airbus are the only two companies capable of producing a new 150-seat passenger aircraft. Each firm has the choice of producing or not producing this aircraft, but Boeing has a headstart that permits it to commit itself to produce before Airbus's decision. In the absence of government intervention, suppose that the payoff matrix is:

Possible strategies for Boeing	Possible strategies for Airbus	
	Produce the aircraft	Do not produce it
Produce the aircraft	Boeing's profit: −$100 million Airbus's profit: −$100 million	Boeing's profit: $1 billion Airbus's profit: zero
Do not produce it	Boeing's profit: zero Airbus's profit: $1 billion	Boeing's profit: zero Airbus's profit: zero

---

[33] Ibid.

[34] Ibid.

[35] Ibid.

(a) Without government intervention, will Airbus produce this aircraft? Will Boeing produce this aircraft? Why or why not?

(b) If the European governments commit themselves in advance to pay a subsidy of $200 million to Airbus if it produces the plane, will this alter the payoff matrix? If so, how?

(c) With this subsidy, will Airbus produce this aircraft? Will Boeing produce this aircraft? Will the profits of Airbus increase by more than the amount of the subsidy?

(d) According to Lawrence Clarkson, Boeing's senior vice president, "If they continue these subsidies, then there may be no one left in the business except Airbus in 15 years. It doesn't take a lot to imagine a scenario where Boeing could not afford to bring out new aircraft. And if your product line becomes obsolete, you're out of business."[36] Does this mean that the United States should subsidize Boeing? Why or why not?

Jean Pierson

(e) The United States has threatened to slap higher tariffs on European products if the subsidies continue. (A tariff is a tax that the government imposes on imports.) Airbus's president, Jean Pierson, an engineering whiz kid who became a factory manager at the age of 36, has said, "Whoever starts a war is going to find himself in a war. If the Americans take some action, I can assure you the Europeans will respond."[37] What are the hazards if the United States were to take such actions?[38]

(f) Suppose that the United States imposes a tariff of $10 on a good it imports from Europe. If the world price of the good is $20, and if the demand and supply curves for the good in the United States are as shown in

---

[36] *New York Times,* June 23, 1991, p. F1.

[37] Ibid., p. F6.

[38] For further analysis, see P. Krugman, *The Age of Diminished Expectations* (Rev. ed.; Cambridge, Mass.: MIT Press, 1995), and J. Brander and B. Spencer, "International R and D Rivalry and Industrial Strategy," *Review of Economic Studies,* 1983.

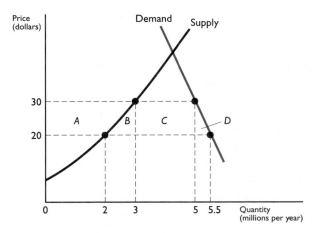

the graph above, it is clear that the United States imports 3.5 million units of the good before the tariff is imposed. (Why? Because if the world price is $20, we demand 5.5 million units, but supply only 2 million units.) Given that the tariff raises the price of the good in the United States to $30, the United States will import 2 million units of the good after the tariff is imposed. (Why? Because if the price is $30, we demand 5 million units and supply 3 million units.) How big is the loss in consumer surplus due to the tariff? How much is the increase in producer surplus due to the tariff? How great are the government's revenues from the tariff? Is there a deadweight loss due to the tariff? If so, how big is it?

R&D AND PROFITS: CAN YOU APPLY THE THEORY?

The remaining two problems are concerned with research and development in the aircraft industry and with Boeing's profitability.

PROBLEM 17.9 In the late 1960s, a federal program, administered by the Federal Aviation Agency, was established to develop the SST, or supersonic transport plane. This program was a response to the fear that U.S. dominance of commercial aircraft sales might be threatened by the Concorde, an airplane which was being developed jointly by the British and the French. The federal government set in mo-

FAA
Headquarters

tion a design competition and proposed to finance the development activities of the winning firm. The prototype development contract was awarded to Boeing.

(a) There was considerable opposition to the development of the SST among environmental groups, who objected to its noise and other characteristics. Also, many economists questioned whether it was a good use of resources. The Institute for Defense Analysis presented estimates to Congress of the present value of the net benefits from developing the SST. Do the results, shown in Table 17.4, indicate that the program should have been carried out?

(b) While the SST program was eventually ended in the United States in 1971, due to the objections of environmentalists, economists, and others, the British and French stuck by their guns and went ahead with the development of the Concorde. In 1979, after spending many billions of dollars (according to some accounts, $500 for every man, woman, and child in the two countries), Britain and France stopped producing the Concorde. They had not been able to sell one of the planes commercially. Because its operating costs were several times as high as a Boeing 747, the Concorde's services could not be priced low enough to attract sufficient

TABLE 17.4 Present Value of Estimated Net Benefits from the Supersonic Transport Program	
Interest rate (percent)	Present value (millions of dollars)
5	−344
10	−528
15	−579

Concorde Airplane

demand. Does it appear that the United States was smart to abandon the SST program when it did? Why or why not?

(c) According to Berkeley's David Mowery and Stanford's Nathan Rosenberg, "It is clear that the early phases of the SST design paid no attention to prospective operating costs. That was, of course, also true of the Concorde...."[39] What was emphasized was the technical feasibility of the aircraft (whether it could fly safely), not the commercial feasibility (whether it could be sold at a profit). What problems, if any, are likely to occur if this attitude is dominant?

(d) The idea of a U.S. supersonic transport plane is by no means dead; Frank Shrontz, Boeing's former CEO, has said that "we could maybe expect a supersonic by the year 2010."[40] Suppose that there are two possible approaches to developing such a plane. If either one is adopted, there is a .5 probability that the development cost will turn out to be $20 billion, and a .5 probability that it will turn out to be $10 billion. If Boeing chooses one of the approaches and carries it to completion, what is the expected cost of developing the plane? If the two approaches are run in parallel and if the true cost of development using each approach can be determined after $100 million has been spent on each approach, what is the expected cost of developing the plane? (Note that the total cost figure for each approach, if adopted, includes the $100 million.) Should parallel approaches be adopted?

PROBLEM 17.10   In 1990, Boeing's Frank Shrontz said his principal mission was to raise the firm's return on equity from its previous level of about 12 percent. In his view, "We've got to enhance our earnings."[41] According to some critics, he had tended to be too cau-

---

[39] Mowery and Rosenberg, "The Commercial Aircraft Industry," p. 146.

[40] "The Future of the Aviation Industry," p. 38.

[41] *Business Week,* July 9, 1990, p. 49.

Year	Total revenues	Earnings after taxes	Assets	Stockholders' equity
1994	21.9	0.9	21.5	9.7
1993	25.4	1.2	20.5	9.0
1992	30.2	1.6	18.1	8.1
1991	29.6	1.6	15.8	8.1
1990	28.0	1.4	14.6	7.0
1989	20.6	1.0	13.3	6.1
1988	17.3	0.6	12.6	5.4
1987	15.8	0.5	12.6	5.0

TABLE 17.5 Revenues, Earnings, Assets, and Stockholders' Equity, Boeing Company, 1987–1994 (billions of dollars)

SOURCE: *Annual Reports*, Boeing Company.

tious. As one analyst put it, Boeing's "been a company that has been prepared to take huge risks. The challenge is to keep taking them."[42] Shrontz's reply has been: "You can't be in this business and not take risks. But we need to be reflective before we take risks."[43]

(a) Table 17.5 shows Boeing's revenues, earnings, assets, and stockholders' equity during the period 1987 to 1994. As a percentage of its stockholders' equity, how large have Boeing's earnings been? Have they been increasing or declining? Do you think that Boeing has been earning economic profits? Why or why not?

(b) Airbus's financial statements are confidential, so outsiders do not know exactly how much money it is making or losing, but industry officials estimate that it made about $350 million in 1994, its total revenues being about $8.5 billion.[44] As a percent of total revenues, did its 1994 earnings seem to be as large as Boeing's?

(c) By early 1995, Boeing had accumulated orders from 16 customers on four continents for 150 units of the Boeing 777 (with options for 108 more). If the probability was .6 that Boeing would gain $10 billion from launching the Boeing 777 and .4 that it would lose $5 billion from doing so, should its managers have launched the plane if they were risk neutral? How much should Boeing have been willing to pay for perfect information regarding the gain (plus $10 billion or minus $5 billion) from launching the plane? Philip Condit allowed representatives of United and other airlines to sit in with the teams designing the aircraft.[45] Why did he do this?

---

[42] Ibid.

[43] Ibid.

[44] *New York Times,* April 13, 1995.

[45] *Business Week,* September 14, 1992.

(d) The huge wide-bodied Boeing 747 cost so much to develop that Boeing was almost pushed into bankruptcy. To survive, it reduced its work force from 101,000 in 1968 to 37,000 in 1971. If the probability was .3 that Boeing would gain $12 billion, .3 that it would break even, and .4 that it would lose $10 billion by launching the Boeing 747, were Boeing's managers risk averse, risk loving, or risk neutral? Why?

(e) Turning from Boeing's top managers to its junior executives, consider a young marketing manager who believes that there is a .5 probability that she will have to undergo surgery next year, the cost being $30,000. If her income is $50,000 per year, and her von Neumann-Morgenstern utility function is as shown below, what is the maximum amount that she will be willing to pay for an insurance policy that will pay for this operation if she needs it?

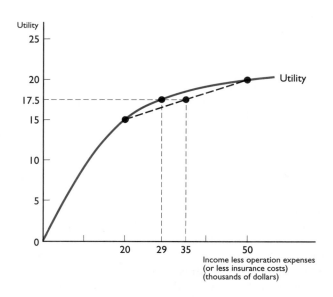

CONCLUSION

Few inputs have the power and grace of a jetliner, and few are more expensive to launch or buy. The aircraft industry and the airlines have a popular appeal, much as the entertainment industry does. But regardless of how Robert Crandall's plans for American Airlines turn out (and how many olives he deletes), and regardless of how the fascinating economic brawl between Airbus and Philip Condit's Boeing is resolved, one thing is clear: To understand the market for inputs, whether they be aircraft, pilots, jet fuel, or olives, you have to understand the microeconomic concepts and models discussed in previous chapters. Without a basic knowledge of the theory of input pricing, present value, the theory of decision making under risk, learning curves, and game theory, among other things, you would be like a person with poor vision who is fortunate enough to have gotten tickets to the tennis championships at Wimbledon, but unfortunate enough to have forgotten to bring his or her eyeglasses.

SELECTED SUPPLEMENTARY READINGS

1. "The Hint of an Updraft," *Business Week,* June 20, 1994.
2. D. Mowery and N. Rosenberg, "The Commercial Aircraft Industry", in R. Nelson (ed.), *Government and Technical Progress* (New York: Pergamon, 1982).
3. D. Yoffie and B. Gomes-Casseres, *International Trade and Competition* (New York: McGraw-Hill, 1994).
4. J. M. Cigliano, "Price and Income Elasticities for Airline Travel: The North Atlantic Market," *Business Economics,* September 1980.
5. L. Argote and D. Epple, "Learning Curves in Manufacturing," *Science,* February 23, 1990.
6. "Can Boeing's New Baby Fly Financially?" *New York Times,* March 27, 1994.
7. "Booming Boeing," *Business Week,* September 30, 1996.

PART SIX

Economic Efficiency

18

Economic Efficiency, Externalities, and Public Goods

INTRODUCTION

At the beginning of this book, we made the claim that microeconomics is of use in clarifying public policy issues. Having made this claim, we hastened to add that microeconomics alone is seldom able to provide a clear-cut solution to such issues, but that, in combination with other relevant disciplines, it frequently can provide useful ways of structuring and analyzing these issues. The purpose of this chapter is to describe and discuss the nature of the policy recommendations that economists can make to promote economic efficiency. As we shall see, economists consider resources to be allocated efficiently when it is impossible to make one person better-off without making another person worse off.

More specifically, we begin by defining general equilibrium analysis and showing how the Edgeworth box diagram can be used to determine the efficient allocation of resources under highly simplified conditions. Then we describe the conditions for efficient resource allocation under more realistic circumstances, and demonstrate that these conditions are met under perfect competition. Next, we take up the effects of external economies and diseconomies, including a treatment of environmental pollution, property rights, and Coase's theorem. Finally, we discuss the efficient allocation of resources to public goods.

PARTIAL EQUILIBRIUM ANALYSIS VERSUS GENERAL EQUILIBRIUM ANALYSIS

Before discussing the efficient allocation of resources, we must indicate how partial equilibrium analysis differs from general equilibrium analysis. In previous chapters, we have focused on a single market, viewed in isolation. According to the models we have used, the price and quantity in each such market are determined by supply and demand curves, and these supply and demand curves are drawn on the assumption that other prices are given. Each market is regarded as independent and self-contained for all practical purposes. In particular, it is assumed that changes in price in this market do not have significant repercussions on the prices existing in other markets.

But this assumption in reality may be seriously wrong. No market can adjust to a change in conditions without there being a change in other markets, and in some cases the change in other markets may be substantial. For example, suppose that a shift to the left occurs in the demand for pork. In previous chapters, it was assumed that when the price and output of pork changed in response to this change in conditions, the prices of other products would remain fixed. However, the market for pork is not sealed off from the markets for lamb, beef, and other meats.[1] (For that matter, it is not completely sealed off from the markets for other food products or from the markets for other less similar products, like washing machines and autos.) Thus the market for pork

---

[1] Quantitative evidence on this point was presented in Table 5.4, where the cross elasticity of demand for beef with respect to the price of pork was given.

EXAMPLE 18.1

The Deregulation of Railroads and Trucks

During the 1980s, steps were taken toward the deregulation of both the railroad and trucking industries. In 1981, Ann Friedlander and Richard Spady of Massachusetts Institute of Technology published a study attempting to forecast the effects of the deregulation of both industries. Before deregulation, they found that the demand curve for rail services for bulk commodities in the South and West was as shown below.

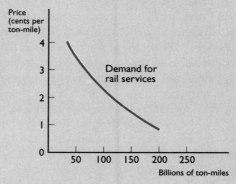

(a) If deregulation would result in a cut in the price of rail service from 2 cents to 1 cent per ton-mile, what would be the effect on the number of ton-miles carried by the railroads in the South and West, based on the above graph? (b) Could the market for rail service adjust to deregulation without disturbing the equilibrium in the market for trucking service? (c) Would the disturbances in the market for trucking service (due to railroad deregulation of this sort) have an impact on the market for rail services? (d) In trying to estimate the effects on each industry of the simultaneous deregulation of them both, what were the advantages of general equilibrium analysis over partial equilibrium analysis? (e) Friedlander and Spady estimated that, when all the reverberations of deregulation from one market to the other (and vice versa) had worked themselves out, the prices of some (but by no means all) types of rail service were likely to rise. Did this mean that deregulation would not be a success?

SOLUTION: (a) The number of ton-miles carried by the railroads would increase from about 120 billion to about 180 billion. (b) No. The lower price of railroad services would push the demand curve for trucking services to the left since railroad and trucking services were substitutes. Consequently, the price of trucking services was likely to fall. (c) Yes. The fall in the price of trucking services described in the answer to part (b) was likely to shift the demand curve for railroad services to the left, causing a change in the price and quantity of rail service. (d) Since the demand for rail service depended on the price of truck service, a change in the price of truck service due to deregulation would have an effect on the demand curve for rail service. Similarly, the demand for truck service depended on the price of rail service. Further, each industry's costs depended on the way in which traffic was divided between them. When both the prices of rail service and of truck service changed due to deregulation, it was very hazardous to carry out a partial equilibrium analysis of either the market for rail service or the market for truck service, since such an analysis would disregard many of the interdependencies between the two markets. In fact, Friedlander and Spady carried out a general equilibrium analysis. (e) No. In these cases, the price before deregulation was below marginal cost; this meant that railroads were losing money on these services. The test of the success of deregulation was whether economic efficiency and equity were promoted, not the direction in which particular prices moved.*

---

*See A. Friedlander and R. Spady, *Freight Transport Regulation* (Cambridge, Mass.: MIT Press, 1981).

cannot adjust without disturbing the equilibrium of other markets *and without having these disturbances feed back on itself.*

Partial equilibrium analysis

An analysis that assumes that changes in price can occur without causing significant changes in price in other markets is called a *partial equilibrium analysis.* This is the kind of analysis we carried out in previous chapters. An analysis that takes account of the interrelationships among prices is called a *general equilibrium analysis.* Both kinds of analyses are very useful, each being valuable in its own way. Partial equilibrium analysis is perfectly adequate in cases in which the effect of a change in market conditions in one market has *little* repercussion on prices in other markets. For example, in studying the effects of a proposed excise tax on the production of a certain commodity, the assumption that prices of other commodities are fixed may be a good approximation to the truth. However, if the effects of a change in market conditions in one market result in *important* repercussions on other prices, a general equilibrium analysis may be required.

General equilibrium analysis

In subsequent sections of this chapter, we frequently will be concerned with general equilibrium analyses, because to determine the efficient allocation of resources we will need to look at more than one market, not the market for a single product or input alone.

RESOURCE ALLOCATION AND THE EDGEWORTH BOX DIAGRAM

In the simple models that we shall take up, the Edgeworth box diagram finds extensive use. The Edgeworth box diagram shows the interaction between two economic activities when the total amount of commodities consumed or inputs used by these activities is fixed in quantity. To see how the Edgeworth box diagram is constructed, and how it should be interpreted, see Figure 18.1. We assume that there are two goods, food and medicine, and two consumers, Tom and Harry. The total amount of food that they have is *OF* and the total amount of medicine that they have is *OM*.

**Edge-
worth box
diagram**

FIGURE 18.1 Edgeworth Box Diagram Point P indicates that Tom consumes *OR* of food and *OS* of medicine, while Harry consumes (*OF* − *OR*) of food and (*OM* − *OS*) of medicine.

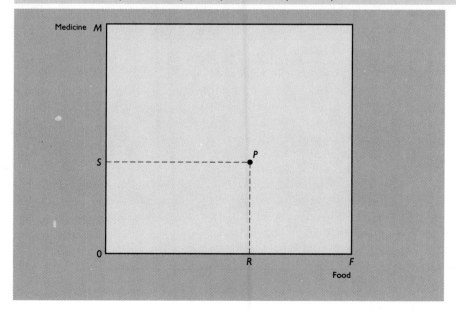

The amount of food that Tom has is measured horizontally from the origin at O. The amount of medicine that Tom has is measured vertically from O. Thus any point in the box diagram indicates a certain amount of food and a certain amount of medicine consumed by Tom. For example, the point P indicates that Tom consumes OR of food and OS of medicine. The amount of food that Harry consumes is measured by the horizontal distance to the left of the upper right-hand corner of the box diagram. And the amount of medicine that Harry consumes is measured by the vertical distance downward from the upper right-hand corner of the box diagram. Thus every point in the diagram indicates an amount of food and medicine consumed by Harry. For example, the point P indicates that Harry consumes $(OF-OR)$ of food and $(OM-OS)$ of medicine.

The important points to remember about the Edgeworth box diagram are that its length and width represent the total amounts of the two commodities that both consumers together have, and that each point in the box represents an allocation of the total supplies of the two goods between the two consumers.

The Edgeworth box diagram can be used for production problems, as well as consumption problems. For example, suppose that there are two industries, industry A and industry B, and that there are two inputs, labor and capital. Suppose that the total amount of labor available to the two industries is OL and the total amount of capital available to the two industries is OK. Figure 18.2 shows the relevant Edgeworth box diagram, the height of which equals

FIGURE 18.2 Edgeworth Box Diagram: Production   Point Q indicates that industry A has OU of labor and OV of capital, while industry B receives $(OL-OU)$ of labor and $(OK-OV)$ of capital.

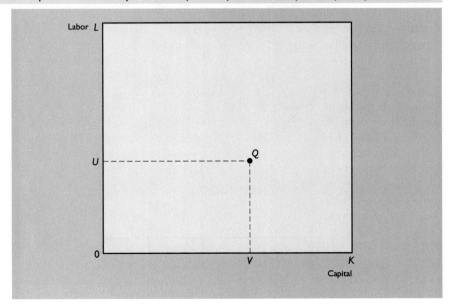

the total amount of labor, *OL,* and the width of which equals the total amount of capital, *OK.*

Any point in the box represents an allocation of this total supply of labor and total supply of capital between the two industries. The amount of labor allocated to industry *A* is represented by the vertical distance upward from the origin, and the amount of capital allocated to industry *A* is represented by the horizontal distance to the right of the origin. For example, point *Q* indicates that industry *A* has *OU* of labor and *OV* of capital. The amount of labor allocated to industry *B* is represented by the distance downward from the upper right-hand corner of the box diagram, and the amount of capital allocated to industry *B* is represented by the distance leftward from the upper right-hand corner of the box diagram. Thus point *Q* indicates that industry *B* receives $(OL - OU)$ of labor and $(OK - OV)$ of capital.

EXCHANGE

Let's return now from production to consumption, and discuss the process of exchange. To begin with, consider an economy of the simplest sort. There are only two consumers, Tom and Harry, and only two commodities, food and medicine. There is no production; the only economic problem is the allocation of a given amount of food and medicine between the two consumers. If it helps, you may regard Tom and Harry as two shipwrecked sailors marooned on a desert island with a certain amount of food and medicine that they rescued from their ship.

The amount of food and medicine brought by Tom to the island is indicated in the Edgeworth box diagram in Figure 18.3: He arrives with *OH* units of food and *OI* units of medicine. The amount of food and medicine brought by Harry to the island is also indicated in Figure 18.3: He arrives with $(OF - OH)$ units of food and $(OM - OI)$ units of medicine. The total amount of food brought to the island by both men is *OF,* and the total amount of medicine brought to the island by both men is *OM.*

If the two men are free to trade with one another, what sort of trading will take place? What can be said about the efficient allocation of the commodities between the two men? To find out, we must insert the indifference curves of Tom and Harry into the Edgeworth box diagram in Figure 18.3. Three of Tom's indifference curves are T_1, T_2, and T_3. The highest indifference curve is T_3; the lowest is T_1. Three of Harry's indifference curves are H_1, H_2, and H_3. The highest indifference curve is H_3; the lowest is H_1. In general, Tom's satisfaction is increased as we move from points close to the origin to points close to

Efficient allocation of goods

FIGURE 18.3 Exchange Points P_0, P_1, and P_2 are on the contract curve, which includes all points where the marginal rates of substitution are the same for both consumers.

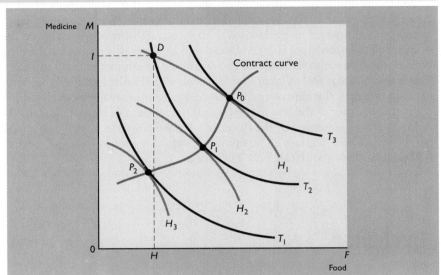

the upper right-hand corner of the box. Conversely, Harry's satisfaction is increased as we move from points close to the upper right-hand corner of the box to points close to the origin.

Given the initial allocation of food and medicine, we find that Tom is on indifference curve T_2 and Harry is on indifference curve H_1. At this point, Tom's marginal rate of substitution of food for medicine is much higher than Harry's, as shown by a comparison of the slope of T_2 with the slope of H_1 at this point. Thus, if both men are free to trade, Tom will trade some medicine to Harry in exchange for some food. The exact point to which they will move cannot be predicted, however. If Tom is the more astute bargainer, he may get Harry to accept the allocation at point P_0, where Harry is no better off than before (since he is still on indifference curve H_1) but Tom is better off (since he has moved to indifference curve T_3). On the other hand, if Harry is the better negotiator, he may be able to get Tom to accept the allocation at point P_1, where Tom is no better-off than before (since he is still on indifference curve T_2) but Harry is better-off (since he has moved to indifference curve H_2). The ultimate point of equilibrium is very likely to be between P_0 and P_1.

One thing is certain. If the object is to make the men as well-off as possible, an efficient allocation of the commodities is one in which the marginal rate of substitution of food for medicine will be the same for both men. Otherwise one man can be made better-off without making the other worse off. In other words, an efficient allocation is a point at which Tom's indifference curve is tangent to Harry's. The locus of points at which such a tangency occurs is called the *contract curve*. This curve, shown in Figure 18.3, includes all points, like P_0, P_1, P_2, where the marginal rates of substitution are equal for both consumers. The contract curve is an efficient set of points in the sense that, if the consumers are at a point *off* the contract curve, it is always preferable for them to move to a point *on* the contract curve, since one or both can gain from the move while neither incurs a loss.

Contract curve: exchange

PRODUCTION

In the previous section we discussed the case in which consumers exchange quantities of commodities, when there is no production. In this section and the next, we take up a simple case in which there is production but no consumption.

Consider a simple economy in which only two goods are being produced, the production sector of the economy being composed of a food industry and a medicine industry. Suppose that there are two inputs, labor and capital, and that the total amount of labor to be allocated between the two industries is OL and the total amount of capital to be allocated between the two industries is OK. Suppose that the initial allocation of labor and capital is that represented by point Z in the Edgeworth box diagram in Figure 18.4. That is, the food industry has OA units of labor and OB units of capital, and the medicine industry has $(OL - OA)$ units of labor and $(OK - OB)$ units of capital.

On the basis of the production functions for food and medicine one can insert isoquants for both food production and medicine production in Figure 18.4. Three isoquants for food production are F_1, F_2, and F_3. The isoquant pertaining to the highest output level is F_3; the isoquant pertaining to the lowest output is F_1. Three isoquants for medicine production are M_1, M_2, and M_3. The isoquant pertaining to the highest output level is M_3; the isoquant pertaining to the lowest output level is M_1.

What will be an efficient allocation of inputs between the two industries? At the original allocation at point Z, the marginal rate of technical substitution of capital for labor in producing food is higher than in producing medicine. This is indicated by the fact that the slope of F_1 is steeper than the slope of M_2 at point Z. The fact that the marginal rates of technical substitution are unequal means that the inputs are not being allocated efficiently. For example, suppose that at point Z the food industry can substitute 2 units of labor for 1

Efficient allocation of inputs

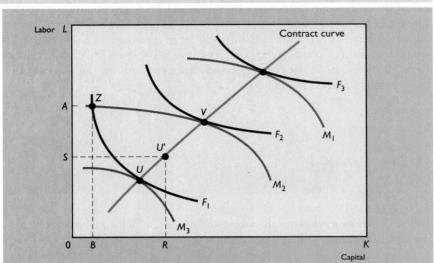

unit of capital without changing its output level, while the medicine industry must substitute 1 unit of labor for 2 units of capital to maintain its output level. In this case, if the medicine industry uses more labor and less capital and if the food industry uses less labor and more capital, it will be possible for one industry to expand its output without any reduction in the other industry's output. Specifically, it is possible to move to point *U*, where the output of food is the same as at *Z* but the output of medicine is at the level corresponding to M_3. It is also possible to move to point *V*, where the output of medicine is the same as at *Z* but the output of food is at the level corresponding to F_2. Or it is possible to move to a point between *U* and *V*.

Regardless of which point is chosen, production should occur at a point at which the marginal rate of technical substitution between inputs is the same for all producers, if the allocation of inputs is to be efficient in the sense that an increase in the output of one commodity can be achieved only by reducing the output of the other commodity. Thus an efficient allocation of inputs will lie along the locus of points where the marginal rates of technical substitution are equal — and consequently where a food isoquant is tangent to a medicine isoquant. This locus of points, like the analogous set in the previous section, is called the *contract curve*, and is shown in Figure 18.4. This curve is an efficient set of points in the sense that, if producers are at a point *off* the contract curve and if society is interested in producing as much as possible of each good, it is

Contract curve: production

EXAMPLE 18.2

The Allocation of Fissionable Material

Although the 1990s have witnessed the apparent end of the cold war, it is still important that our military establishment be efficient. A classic illustration of the application of Edgeworth box diagrams occurred in the 1950s, when a key U.S. defense problem was how to allocate fissionable material between our tactical and strategic forces. There were a fixed total number of aircraft (OA) and a fixed supply of fissionable materials (OM) in the short run. Every point in the Edgeworth box diagram shown below indicates an allocation of fissionable material and airplanes to the tactical and strategic forces. For example, point P represents a case where our strategic forces get OU units of aircraft and OV units of fissionable material, and our tactical forces get ($OA-OU$) units of aircraft and ($OM-OV$) units of fissionable material. Within limits, it was possible to substitute airplanes for fissionable material and vice versa. For example, fewer aircraft would be required to destroy a certain number of targets if atomic weapons, rather than conventional weapons, were used. Curve T_1 contains combinations of aircraft and fissionable material that result in equal effectiveness of the tactical forces. Curve T_0 also contains combinations that result in equal effectiveness of the tactical forces — but at a lower level than curve T_1. Curve S_2 contains combinations of aircraft and fissionable material that result in equal effectiveness of the strategic forces. Curve S_3 also contains combinations that result in equal effectiveness of the strategic forces — but at a higher level than curve S_2. The allocation at the time was represented by point W. Was this an efficient choice?

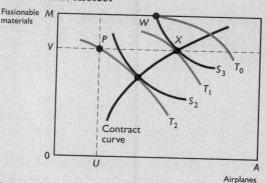

SOLUTION: No, because point W is not on the contract curve. The Defense Department could increase the effectiveness of either the tactical or the strategic forces without reducing the effectiveness of the other by moving to a point on the contract curve. For example, point X results in the same effectiveness of our strategic forces as point W, since both points are on curve S_3. But point X results in more effectiveness of our tactical forces than point W. In fact, this simple kind of economic analysis was used to help solve this important policy problem.*

_____

* For further discussion, see S. Enke, "Using Costs to Select Weapons," _American Economic Review,_ May 1965, and "Some Economic Aspects of Fissionable Materials," _Quarterly Journal of Economics,_ May 1964.

always socially desirable for them to move to a point _on_ the contract curve, since output in one industry or the other can be increased without a reduction in the other's output.

Note that this analysis of production is entirely analogous to the analysis of exchange in the previous section. The total amounts of the two inputs determine the dimensions of the Edgeworth box in this section; the analogous quantities in the previous section are the total amounts of the two commodities. The isoquant maps play an analogous role to the indifference maps in the previous section.

Necessary Conditions for Efficient Resource Allocation

Condition #1

In the previous three sections, we took up a case where there were only two consumers and two goods. Now let's consider the more realistic case where there are more than two consumers and more than two goods. Fundamentally, there are three necessary conditions for efficient resource allocation. The first pertains to the efficient allocation of commodities among consumers. It states that _the marginal rate of substitution between any two commodities must be the same for any two consumers._ The proof that this condition is necessary to maximize consumer satisfaction is quite simple. All that needs to be noted is that, if the marginal rates of substitution were unequal, both consumers could benefit by trading. For example, suppose that the first consumer regards an additional unit of product A as having the same utility as 2 extra units of product B, whereas the second consumer regards an additional unit of product A as having the same utility as 3 extra units of product B. Then, if the first consumer trades 1 unit of product A for 2.5 units of product B from the second consumer, both consumers are better-off.

This condition implies that commodities should be distributed in such a way that consumers are on their contract curve, since the contract curve is composed of points where the marginal rates of substitution are equal for the consumers. In the case of only two commodities and two consumers, we showed in the section before last that this condition must be met if consumer satisfaction is to be maximized. We are now stating the more general proposition that this condition must also be met in the more realistic case in which there are more than two commodities and two consumers.

The second condition pertains to the efficient allocation of inputs among producers. It states that *the marginal rate of technical substitution between any two inputs must be the same for any pair of producers.* If this condition does not **Condition** hold, it is possible to increase total production merely by reallocating inputs **#2** among producers. For example, suppose that, for the first producer, the marginal product of input 1 is twice that of input 2, whereas for the second producer the marginal product of input 1 is three times that of input 2. Then, if the first producer gives 1 unit of input 1 to the second producer in exchange for 2.5 units of input 2, both firms can expand their output.

To see this, suppose that the marginal product of input 1 is M_1 for the first producer and M_2 for the second producer. Then the output of the first producer is reduced by M_1 units because of its loss of the unit of input 1, but it is increased by $2.5 \times M_1/2$ units because of its gain of the 2.5 units of input 2, with the consequence that, on balance, its output increases by $M_1/4$ units because of the trade. Similarly, the output of the second producer is increased by M_2 units because of its gain of the 1 unit of input 1, but it is decreased by $2.5 \times M_2/3$ units because of its loss of the 2.5 units of input 2, with the consequence that, on balance, its output increases by $M_2/6$ units because of the trade.

This condition implies that inputs should be allocated so that producers are on their contract curve, since the contract curve is made up of points at which the marginal rates of technical substitution are equal for producers. In the case of only two inputs and two producers, we showed in the previous section that this condition must be met if the output of each producer is maximized, holding constant the output of the other producer. We are now stating the more general proposition that this condition must also be met in the more realistic case in which there are more than two inputs and two producers.

The third condition pertains to both the efficient allocation of inputs among industries and the efficient allocation of commodities among consumers. It states that *the marginal rate of substitution between any two commodities must be* **Condition** *the same as the marginal rate of product transformation between these two com-* **#3**

FIGURE 18.5 **Production Possibilities Curve and Indifference Curves** To maximize consumer satisfaction, production must take place at point *T*.

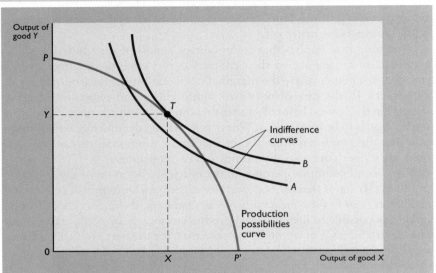

modities for any producer. The production possibilities curve shows the maximum amount of one good that can be produced, given various output levels of another good. For example, *PP'* in Figure 18.5 is a production possibilities curve showing the maximum amount of good *X* that can be produced, given various output levels for good *Y*. The marginal rate of product transformation is the negative of the slope of the production possibilities curve; it shows the number of units of good *Y* that society must give up in order to get an additional unit of good *X*.

Suppose that curves *A* and *B* in Figure 18.5 represent the indifference curves of a consumer who, for simplicity, is assumed to be the only consumer in the economy. To maximize the consumer's satisfaction, production must take place at point *T,* where the output of good *X* is *OX* and the output of good *Y* is *OY.* Clearly, *T* is the point on the production possibilities curve that is on the consumer's highest indifference curve. Since the production possibilities curve is tangent to the indifference curve at point *T*, it follows that the marginal rate of product transformation equals the marginal rate of substitution at point *T.* Thus the marginal rate of product transformation equals the marginal rate of substitution if consumer satisfaction is maximized. This result will hold for any number of consumers, not just for one.

AGRICULTURAL PRICE SUPPORTS: AN APPLICATION

We can use these three conditions for efficient resource allocation to analyze many interesting questions, such as the choice among alternative agricultural price support schemes. From Chapter 10 it will be recalled that in the past such schemes have commonly specified that each farm can produce a certain quota, represented by OX in panel A of Figure 18.6. The total quota for the entire industry is OY in panel B of Figure 18.6. Also, a support price has frequently been set by the government, which is OP in this case. Since the demand curve for the product is as shown in panel B of Figure 18.6, consumers will purchase OQ_1 units of the product, and the government will buy $(OY - OQ_1)$ units of the product. This is in contrast to the situation that would prevail if there were no quotas and price supports; under these circumstances, price would be OP_1 and the total output of the product would be OQ_2. The purpose of the quotas and price supports is to increase the income of farmers.

FIGURE 18.6 **Agricultural Price Supports** If OP is the support price and OX is the quota for each farm, the industry's total output will be produced inefficiently. Consumers will buy OQ_1 units of the product, and the government will buy $(OY - OQ_1)$ units.

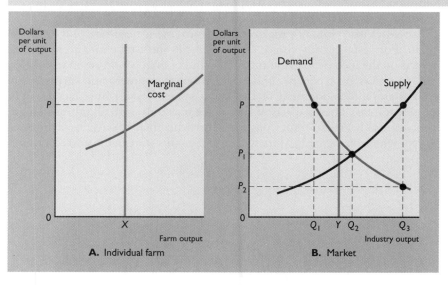

A. Individual farm

B. Market

Unfortunately, this type of support scheme leads to inefficiencies of various kinds in the use of resources. First, because the marginal cost at OX will certainly vary from farm to farm, the industry's total output will be produced inefficiently. That is, the total cost of producing the total output could be decreased by reducing the output of farms with high marginal cost at OX and increasing the output of farms with low marginal cost at OX. Since the industry's total output is being produced inefficiently, it is clear that the second condition in the previous section is being violated. Second, part of the industry's output is unnecessary, and is taken off the market by the government. Third, since price is above marginal cost for this product (see panel A of Figure 18.6), the third condition in the previous section is also violated, if the prices of other goods equal marginal cost (as they would in a perfectly competitive economy). The reasoning underlying this statement is explained in some detail in the section after next. For the moment, it is sufficient to accept it on faith.

On the other hand, suppose that the government adopts a different sort of scheme, one closer to that adopted in 1973. Suppose that the government guarantees each farmer a price of OP, with the result that the industry produces OQ_3 units of the product. But then suppose that it lets the free market alone, with the result that the OQ_3 units of the agricultural product command a price of only OP_2 in the market and the government pays each farmer $(OP - OP_2)$ per unit. The first type of inefficiency would be eliminated because each farmer would set marginal cost equal to OP, with the result that the marginal cost for each farm would be the same. The second type of inefficiency would be eliminated because the government no longer would take part of the industry's output off the market. The third type of inefficiency remains, since the price to consumers would be less than marginal cost.

However, this does not mean that this scheme is necessarily an improvement. For instance, any choice among policies must take into account their effects on the income distribution. This kind of plan would result in a different distribution of benefits and costs among consumers and farmers. For example, the abandonment of the quota system would hurt farmers who possess quotas. These aspects of the choice may outweigh all others in many people's minds. (Members of Congress in particular may be sensitive to the question of whose ox is gored.) More will be said on this score in the next section.[2]

---

[2] In Chapter 19, we shall take up this topic further, when we look in detail at the effects of California water pricing on farmers and urbanites.

ECONOMIC EFFICIENCY AND EQUITY

Practically all economists accept the proposition that a change that harms no one and improves the lot of some people (in their own eyes) is an improvement. This criterion, put forth by Vilfredo Pareto at about the turn of the century, is often called the *Pareto criterion.*[3] If a change benefits one group of people and harms another group, the criterion is not applicable. Nonetheless, this criterion is by no means useless, and most economists would agree that all changes that satisfy this criterion should be carried out. That is, they believe that society should make any change that harms no one and improves the lot of some people. If all such changes are carried out — and thus no opportunity to make such changes remains — the situation is termed *economically efficient.* On pages 606 to 608 we described and discussed three necessary conditions for an efficient allocation of resources.

Pareto criterion

Economic efficiency

Having described these conditions for efficient resource allocation, we must recognize that more than one pattern of resource allocation will satisfy these conditions. In other words, these conditions do not determine a single best pattern of resource allocation. Instead, they result in many patterns of resource allocation, and which one is regarded as best depends on what one regards as an optimal distribution of income. There is no purely scientific way of telling whether one distribution of income is better than another because there is no scientifically meaningful way to compare the utility level of various individuals. No one can state scientifically that a piece of Aunt Mary's apple pie will bring you more satisfaction than it will me, or that your headache is worse than mine. Thus, if you receive twice as much income as I do, economics cannot tell us whether this is a better distribution of income than if I receive twice as much income as you do. This is a value judgment, pure and simple.

While there is no scientifically valid way of making interpersonal comparisons of utility, this does not mean that people cannot and should not have views as to what constitutes an equitable distribution of income. Some argue that each person should receive the same amount of goods and services (that is, the same income). This is the egalitarian view of equity. According to others, like Harvard philosopher John Rawls, income inequality is justified only to the context that it benefits the least advantaged.[4] Still others believe that the most

---

[3] V. Pareto, *Manuel d'Economie Politique* (1909).

[4] In *A Theory of Justice* (Cambridge, Mass.: Harvard University Press, 1971), Rawls argues that "all social values . . . are to be distributed equally unless an unequal distribution . . . is to everyone's advantage." Needless to say, this proposition has aroused much controversy.

equitable allocation is that which results from the workings of competitive markets; in their view, this rewards the ablest and most diligent persons.

Even if an allocation of resources is efficient, it may be regarded as less socially desirable than an inefficient allocation of resources if it results in a very inequitable distribution of income. For example, suppose that the choice is between points D and P_2 in Figure 18.3. At point D, the allocation of resources is inefficient. (We know this because point D is not on the contract curve; this means that either Tom or Harry could be made better off without making the other worse off.) Yet this allocation of resources may be regarded as socially preferable to the allocation of resources at point P_2 where the allocation of resources is efficient. Why? Because at point P_2 Tom's standard of living may be very low; his consumption of food and medicine may be so low that he may be only barely able to survive.

Thus, while economic efficiency is a reasonable goal, it is not the only goal: the distribution of income is important too. Recognizing this fact, economists do not claim that all changes that result in economic efficiency should necessarily be carried out. To achieve equity objectives, society has established tax systems and government expenditure programs to help the poor, even though devices of this sort — which redistribute income — tend to reduce economic efficiency. (For example, taxes may dull incentives to work and to produce.)

PERFECT COMPETITION AND ECONOMIC EFFICIENCY

One of the most important, and most fundamental, findings of microeconomics is that a perfectly competitive economy satisfies the three conditions for economic efficiency set forth on pages 606 to 608. The argument for competition can be made in various ways. For example, some people favor competition simply because it prevents the undue concentration of power and the exploitation of consumers. But to the economic theorist, the basic argument for a perfectly competitive economy is the fact that such an economy satisfies these conditions. In this section we prove that this is indeed a fact. In the next two sections, we discuss how prices might be used in planned economies and by regulated industries to achieve the same kind of results.

The first condition for economic efficiency is that the marginal rate of substitution between any pair of commodities must be the same for all consumers. To see that this condition is met under perfect competition, we must recall from Chapter 4 that under perfect competition consumers choose their purchases so that the marginal rate of substitution between any pair of commodities is equal to the ratio of the prices of the pair of commodities. Since prices, and thus price ratios, are the same for all buyers under perfect competition, it follows that the marginal rate of substitution between any pair of commodities must be the same for all consumers. For example, if every consumer can buy bread at 50¢ a loaf and butter at $1 a pound, each one will arrange his or her purchases so that the marginal rate of substitution of butter for bread is 2. Thus the marginal rate of substitution will be the same for all consumers: 2 for everyone.

The second condition for economic efficiency is that the marginal rate of technical substitution between any pair of inputs must be the same for all producers. To see that this condition is met under perfect competition, we must recall from Chapter 8 that, under perfect competition, producers will choose the quantity of each input so that the marginal rate of technical substitution between any pair of inputs is equal to the ratio of the prices of the pair of inputs. Since input prices, and thus price ratios, are the same for all producers under perfect competition, it follows that the marginal rate of technical substitution must be the same for all producers. For example, if every producer can buy labor services at $8 an hour and machine tool services at $16 an hour, each one will arrange the quantity of its inputs so that the marginal rate of technical substitution of machine tool services for labor is 2. Thus the marginal rate of technical substitution will be the same for all producers: 2 for each of them.

The third condition for economic efficiency is that the marginal rate of product transformation must equal the marginal rate of substitution for each pair of goods. The proof that this condition is met under perfect competition is somewhat lengthier than in the case of the other conditions. To begin with, we must note that the marginal rate of product transformation is the number of units of good A that must be given up to produce an additional unit of good B. The additional cost of producing the extra unit of good B is, of course, the marginal cost of good B. To see how many units of good A must be given up to get this extra unit of good B, we must divide the marginal cost of good B by the marginal cost of good A. This will tell us how many extra units of good A cost as much as 1 extra unit of good B. Thus the marginal rate of product transformation under perfect competition equals the ratio of the marginal cost of good B to the marginal cost of good A.

From Chapter 10 it will be recalled that price equals marginal cost under perfect competition. Consequently, the ratio of the marginal cost of good B to the marginal cost of good A equals the ratio of the price of good B to the price of good A under perfect competition. Coupled with the result of the previous paragraph, this means that the marginal rate of product transformation is equal to the ratio of the price of good B to the price of good A under perfect competition. But, as we noted in connection with our discussion of the first condition, the marginal rate of substitution is equal to the ratio of the price of good B to the price of good A under perfect competition. Consequently, it follows that the marginal rate of product transformation equals the marginal rate of substitution for any pair of products under perfect competition.

Referring back to our earlier discussion of agricultural price supports in this chapter, it is obvious now why these price supports violate the third condition for efficiency. Since the price of the agricultural good does not equal marginal cost (see Figure 18.6), the third condition must be violated if the prices of other goods equal marginal cost. For example, take some other good with marginal cost, MC_X, and price, P_X. The marginal rate of product transformation between this good and the agricultural product is $MC_A \div MC_X$, where MC_A is the marginal cost of the agricultural good. Moreover, if consumers maximize satisfaction, the marginal rate of substitution between the two goods is $P_A \div P_X$, where P_A is the price of the agricultural product. However, since $P_X = MC_X$ and $MC_A \neq P_A$, it follows that the marginal rate of substitution does not equal the marginal rate of product transformation.

Case for perfect competition Returning to the original topic of this section, we find that all three conditions for economic efficiency are satisfied under perfect competition. This is one of the principal reasons why economists are so enamored of perfect competition and so wary of monopoly. If a formerly competitive economy is restructured so that some industries become monopolies, these conditions for economic efficiency are no longer met. As we know from Chapter 11, each monopolist produces less than the perfectly competitive industry that it replaces would have produced. Thus too few resources are devoted to the industries that are monopolized, and too many resources are devoted to the industries that remain perfectly competitive. This is one of the economist's chief charges against monopoly. It wastes resources because its actions result in an overallocation of resources to competitive industries and an underallocation of resources to monopolistic industries. Society is then less well off.[5]

ECONOMIC PLANNING AND MARGINAL COST PRICING

The previous section showed that the three conditions for economic efficiency are satisfied under perfect competition. Economists interested in the function-

[5] In evaluating this result and judging its practical relevance, it is important to note that it stems from a very simple model that ignores such things as technological change and other dynamic considerations, risk and uncertainty, and externalities. The reader should be very careful to note the qualifications and assumptions that must be made. Sometimes the argument for perfect competition is made without full recognition of these qualifications. Of course, the moral of this section is entirely in keeping with our discussion of the maximization of total surplus on pages 323 to 325 of Chapter 10.

ing of planned, or socialist, economies have argued that a price system could be used in a similar way to increase social welfare in such economies. According to these economists, rational economic organization could be achieved in a socialist economy that is decentralized, as well as under perfect competition.[6] For example, the government might try to solve the system of equations that is solved automatically in a perfectly competitive economy, and obtain the prices that would prevail under perfect competition. Then the government might publish this price list, together with instructions for consumers to maximize their satisfaction and for producers to maximize profit. (Of course, the wording of the instructions to consumers might be a bit less heavy-handed than "Maximize your satisfaction!")

An important advantage claimed for planning and control of this sort is that the government does not have to become involved in the intricate and detailed business of setting production targets for each plant. It need only compute the proper set of prices. As long as plant managers maximize "profits," the proper production levels will be chosen by them. Thus decentralized decision making, rather than detailed centralized direction, could be used, with the result that administrative costs and bureaucratic disadvantages might be reduced.

The prices that the government would publish, like those prevailing in a perfectly competitive economy, would equal marginal cost. Many economists have recommended that government-owned enterprises in basically capitalist economies also adopt *marginal cost pricing,* that is, that they set price equal to marginal cost. For example, Harold Hotelling argued that this should be the case.[7] Taking the case of a bridge where the marginal cost (the extra cost involved in allowing an additional vehicle to cross) is zero, he argued that the socially optimal price for crossing the bridge is zero and that its cost should be defrayed by general taxation. If a toll is charged, the conditions for economic efficiency are violated.

Marginal cost pricing

Marginal cost pricing has fascinated economists during the more than 50 years that have elapsed since Hotelling's article.[8] But there are a number of important problems in the application of this idea. One of the most important is that, if (as is frequently the case in public utilities) the firm's average costs

---

[6] A. Lerner, *The Economics of Control* (New York: Macmillan Co., 1944). For many years, a fascinating economic debate took place in the Soviet Union and Eastern Europe. Many influential economists argued that a decentralized, market-oriented economic system would be more efficient than the existing system of economic planning, which eventually was altered drastically as these countries moved toward capitalism.

[7] See H. Hotelling, "The General Welfare in Relation to Problems of Taxation and of Railway and Utility Rates," *Econometrica,* July 1938.

[8] See the papers by M. Boiteux and others in J. Nelson (ed.), *Marginal Cost Pricing in Practice* (Englewood Cliffs, N.J.: Prentice-Hall, 1964); Nobel laureate W. Vickrey, "Some Implications of Marginal Cost Pricing for Public Utilities," reprinted in Mansfield, *Microeconomics: Selected Readings,* 5th ed.; and A. Kahn, *The Economics of Regulation* (New York: Wiley, 1970).

decrease with increases in its scale of output, it follows from the discussion in Chapter 8 that marginal cost must be less than average cost, with the consequence that the firm will not cover its costs if price is set equal to marginal cost. This means that marginal cost pricing must be accompanied by some form of subsidy if the firm is to stay in operation. However, the collection of the funds required for the payment of the subsidy may also violate the conditions for economic efficiency. Moreover, this subsidy means that there is a change in the income distribution favoring users of the firm's output and penalizing nonusers of its output. Whether marginal cost pricing results in improved economic welfare depends on how one views this change in the income distribution.

Marginal Cost Pricing: A Case Study

During the midfifties, Électricité de France, the French nationalized electricity industry, introduced marginal cost pricing for its high-tension service. The ultimate goal of the new pricing scheme was that the price paid for a kilowatt-hour of electricity at a given time of day in a given season of the year in a given region was to approximate the cost of an additional kilowatt-hour at this time in this season in this region.

Of course, a great many simplifications had to be made in computing the new price schedule. First, consider price differences at various times of day. In the winter, the day is divided into three periods: the peak daytime hours, the other daytime hours, and the night. In the summer, it is divided into two periods: day and night. A consumer in a given region must pay a different price for kilowatt-hours in each period, with the differences reflecting differences in marginal costs. Next, consider price differences among regions. To estimate the marginal costs in each region, a pattern of movements of electricity from generating stations to consumption areas is derived that meets estimated demands at minimum total cost given present capacity. The marginal costs corresponding to this pattern are used to determine prices in various regions.

Finally, consider price differences among seasons. Differences among seasons in demand curves, as well as differences in hydroelectric reservoir levels and river flows, are responsible for these differences in price. The seasonal differences in demand are assumed by the industry to be like those observed in the past. Average snow and rainfall levels in each season can be used in the calculations. Since water tends to be less abundant in the winter, peak demands for electricity have to be satisfied by using less efficient thermal plants than have to be used in the summer. Also, demand for electricity tends to be higher in the winter. Both of these factors clearly influence the level of the marginal cost of electricity.

What has this pricing scheme achieved? According to Berkeley's Thomas Marschak, who made a careful study of the French experience, Électricité de France's marginal cost pricing had a number of important beneficial results. In his view, a "clear improvement over the [old] pricing scheme is very plausibly claimed. Preliminary observation suggests that a leveling of consumption between the daytime and the nighttime periods may be expected. One immediate result is a reduction by 5 percent in the capacity required to meet peak demands. . . . Another is a substantial saving of imported (American) coal in winter, since the flattening of peaks eliminates the need for some of the inefficient thermal output previously required."[9]

EXTERNAL ECONOMIES AND DISECONOMIES

Up to this point, we have generally assumed implicitly that there is no difference between private and social benefits, or between private and social costs. For example, costs to producers have been assumed to be costs to society, and costs to society have been assumed to be costs to producers; benefits to producers have been assumed to be benefits to society, and benefits to society have been assumed to be benefits to producers. In fact, however, there are many instances in which these assumptions do not hold. Instead, producers sometimes confer benefits on other members of the economy but are unable to obtain payment for these benefits, and they sometimes act in such a way as to harm others without having to pay the full costs. In these cases, the pursuit of private gain will not promote the social welfare. The purpose of this section is to describe how differences between private and social returns are likely to arise and the ways in which these differences influence our results. The following sections show how this theory can illuminate public policies toward basic research and toward environmental pollution.

It is convenient, and customary, to classify these divergences into four types. First, there are *external economies of production.* An external economy occurs when an action taken by an economic unit results in uncompensated benefits to others; when such benefits are due to an increase in a firm's production, they are called external economies of production. The firm may benefit others directly. For example, it may train workers that eventually go to work for other firms that do not have to pay the training costs. Or the firm may benefit other firms indirectly because its increased output may make it more economical for firms outside the industry to provide services to other firms in the industry. For example, a great expansion in an aircraft firm may make it possible for aluminum producers to take advantage of economies of scale, with the

External economies of production

---

[9] T. Marschak, "Capital Budgeting and Pricing in the French Nationalized Industries," *Journal of Business,* January 1960, p. 151.

result that other metal fabricating firms can also get cheaper aluminum. In either case, there is a difference between private and social returns; the gains to society are greater than the gains to the firm.

Second, there are *external economies of consumption,* which occur when an action taken by a consumer, rather than a producer, results in an uncompen-

External economies of consumption

sated benefit to others. For example, if I maintain my house and lawn, this benefits my neighbors as well as myself. If I educate my children and make them more responsible citizens, this too benefits my neighbors as well as myself. The list of external economies from consumption could easily be extended, but the idea should be clear at this point.

Third, there are *external diseconomies of production.* An external diseconomy occurs when an action taken by an economic unit results in uncompensated

External diseconomies of production

costs to others; when such costs are due to increases in a firm's production, they are called external diseconomies of production. For example, a firm may pollute a stream by pumping out waste materials, or it may pollute the air with smoke or materials. Such actions result in costs to others; for instance, Chesapeake Bay's oyster beds and Long Island's clam beds continually are being threatened by water pollution. Moreover, the private costs do not reflect the full social costs, since the firms and cities responsible for the pollution are not charged for their contribution to poorer quality water and their harm to industries dependent on good water. There are many cases of external diseconomies of production, such as traffic congestion and the defacement of scenery.

External diseconomies of consumption

Fourth, there are *external diseconomies of consumption,* which occur when an action taken by a consumer results in an uncompensated cost to others. Some external diseconomies of consumption can be fairly subtle. For example, Mrs. White may be trying hard to keep up with the social leader in town, Mrs. Brown. If Mrs. Brown obtains a new mink coat, this may make Mrs. White worse off, since she may become dissatisfied with her old mink coat. Similarly, a family that feels that a 3-year old Chevrolet is perfectly adequate may become dissatisfied with it after moving to a community where everyone drives a new Cadillac.

The foregoing are some of the most important cases where social and private costs and benefits differ. At first glance, these cases may not seem very important. But when all these types of external economies and diseconomies are considered, their aggregate significance can be substantial. For example, the fact that environmental pollution of various kinds resulting from industrial output is important has been stressed repeatedly in the United States in recent years. The importance of various types of external economies of production is undeniable, and the fact that consumer tastes and well-being are determined by the tastes and well-being of other members of society is obvious as well.

How do these external economies and diseconomies alter the efficiency of the allocation of resources under perfect competition? If a person takes an action that contributes to society's welfare but receives no payment for it, he or she is likely to take this action less frequently than would be socially desirable. The same holds true for firms. Thus, if the production of a certain good, say beryllium, is responsible for external economies, less than the socially efficient amount of beryllium is likely to be produced under perfect competition, since the producers are unlikely to increase output simply because it reduces the costs of other companies. By the same token, if a person takes an action that results in costs borne by others, he or she is likely to take this action more frequently than is socially desirable. The same holds true for firms. Thus, if the production of a certain good is responsible for external diseconomies, more of this good is likely to be produced under perfect competition than is socially efficient.

Public Policy toward Basic Research: An Application

To illustrate how the theory of external economies and diseconomies, together with the other principles discussed in this chapter, can be used to throw light on problems of public policy, consider the nature of social policy toward basic research. One of the most fundamental questions in this area is: Why should the government support basic research? Why not rely on private enterprise to support sufficient basic research?

To answer this question, it is important to recognize that basic scientific research is likely to generate substantial external economies. Important additions to fundamental knowledge often have an impact on a great many fields. If a firm produces an important scientific breakthrough, it generally cannot hope to capture the full value of the new knowledge it creates. It cannot go into the full range of activities in which the knowledge has use, and it is seldom able to capture through patent rights the full social value of the new knowledge. Indeed, fundamental discoveries, such as natural laws, cannot be patented at all.

Because of these external economies, there is likely to be a divergence between the private and social benefits from basic research, with the result that a perfectly competitive economy would be expected to devote fewer resources to basic research than is socially efficient. Consequently, there seems to be a good case on purely economic grounds for the government (or some other agency not motivated by profit) to support basic research. As pointed out in the 1987 report of the Council of Economic Advisers, "the Federal Government has an important role in funding basic scientific research. Such research can contribute to technological advance in the longer term. However, its benefits are often too diffuse and difficult to profit from for it to be undertaken by private business."[10]

---

[10] *Economic Report of the President* (Washington, D.C.: U.S. Government Printing Office, 1987), p. 49.

EXAMPLE 18.3

External Diseconomies on the Highways

Each morning, thousands of motorists travel the route from Philadelphia's western suburbs to the central business district where they work or shop. Suppose that the full cost of this auto trip — including both the money costs (of fuel, oil, tire wear, and so on) and *the value of the drivers' (and passengers') time* — is measured along the vertical axis of the graph below, and that the number of vehicles attempting this trip between 7 A.M. and 8 A.M. on a particular day is measured along the horizontal axis. The relationship between the full cost of this trip to a motorist and the number of vehicles attempting this trip is *CC'*. The demand curve shows at each price of this trip (including both money and time costs) the number of vehicles that will set out on this route.

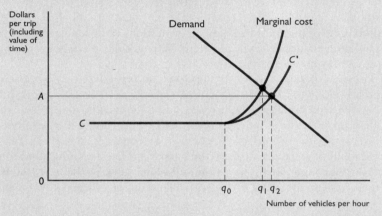

(a) If more than Oq_0 vehicles attempt this trip, the cost of the trip increases as more and more vehicles per hour set out on this route. Why? Is this due to external diseconomies? (b) How many autos per hour will travel along this route? (c) Is this the economically efficient number? (d) What measures might be taken to push the actual number closer to the efficient number?

SOLUTION: (a) If more than Oq_0 vehicles per hour travel this route, the highway becomes congested. Traffic becomes tied up, it takes longer to make the trip, and the full cost (including time) increases. As more and more vehicles travel this route, the congestion gets worse. Each extra vehicle, by delaying other vehicles taking this route, is responsible for external diseconomies. (b) Oq_2 vehicles per hour. If less than Oq_2 vehicles per hour travel this route, the full cost of the trip (indicated by the CC' curve) is less than the value of the trip to the motorist (indicated by the demand curve), and more vehicles will make the trip. If more than Oq_2 vehicles per hour travel this route, the full cost of the trip exceeds the value of the trip to the motorist, and less vehicles will make the trip. (c) No. The economically efficient number is Oq_1 vehicles per hour. If more than Oq_0 vehicles per hour travel this route, the marginal cost to society of an extra vehicle's traveling this route (shown by the colored line in the graph) exceeds the cost to the motorist driving this extra vehicle because the extra vehicle delays other motorists. Up to Oq_1 vehicles per hour, the marginal cost to society of an extra vehicle (shown by the colored line) is less than the marginal benefit (shown by the demand curve), and society gains if more vehicles per hour take this route. But above Oq_1 vehicles per hour, this is no longer true. (d) Some economists have suggested that a tax be imposed on motorists that travel congested highways.* In this way, the private costs would be brought closer to the true social costs. Tolls also can be used, at least under some circumstances.

---

*See A. Walters, "The Theory and Measurement of Private and Social Costs of Highway Congestion," *Econometrica*, October 1961.

Based on similar considerations, there is a strong argument for government support of fundamental research to extend the technological underpinnings of broad industrial areas. For example, the National Advisory Committee on Aeronautics carried out research and development concerning wind tunnels, aircraft fuels, aircraft design, and other fundamental matters regarding aviation. No individual firm had much incentive to do such work because it could appropriate only a small share of the benefits. But because the benefits to the economy as a whole were substantial, the government intervened to finance work of this sort. The simple principles of microeconomics help to indicate why such a policy was justified.

EFFICIENT POLLUTION CONTROL

In recent decades, the U.S. public has become much more concerned about environmental pollution. External diseconomies result in considerable air and water pollution. When firms (and governments and households) dispose of their wastes by pumping them into the air and water, this often means that others must incur costs to put the environment back into a usable condition. Thus the polluters tend to pay less than the full social costs of using the environment in this way, with the result that they engage in an undesirably high level of pollution. Given that this is the case, an important question facing policymakers is: What is the economically efficient level of pollution control? In other words, how much pollution ought we to allow an industry to discharge?

Figure 18.7 shows the total social cost of each level of discharge of an industry's wastes, holding constant the industry's output. Clearly, the more untreated waste the industry dumps into the environment, the greater the total costs. Figure 18.7 also shows the costs of pollution control of each level of discharge of the industry's wastes. Clearly, the more the industry cuts down on the amount of wastes it discharges, the higher are the costs of pollution control. Finally, the sum of these two costs — the cost of pollution and the cost of pollution control — at each level of discharge of the industry's wastes is also shown in Figure 18.7.

From the point of view of society as a whole, the industry should reduce its discharge of pollution to the point where the sum of these two costs — the cost of pollution and the cost of pollution control — is a minimum. Specifically, the efficient level of pollution in the industry is *OR* in Figure 18.7. Why is this the efficient level? Because if the industry discharges *less* than this amount of

FIGURE 18.7 Sum of Pollution Cost and Pollution Control Cost From the point of view of society as a whole, the efficient level of pollution in this industry is *OR*.

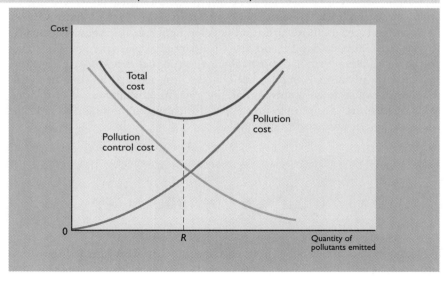

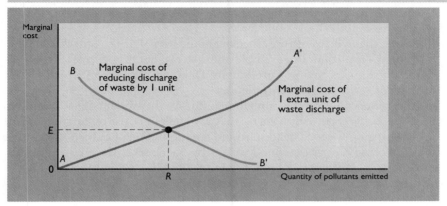

FIGURE 18.8 **Marginal Costs of Pollution and of Pollution Control** At the economically efficient level of pollution, *OR*, the cost of an extra unit of pollution is equal to the cost of reducing pollution by an extra unit.

pollution, a 1-unit increase in pollution will reduce the cost of pollution control by more than it will increase the cost of pollution, whereas if the industry discharges *more* than this amount of pollution, a 1-unit reduction in pollution will reduce the cost of pollution by more than it will increase the cost of pollution control.

To make this more evident, Figure 18.8 shows the marginal cost of an extra unit of discharge of waste, at each level of discharge of the industry's wastes: This is designated by *AA′*. Figure 18.8 also shows the marginal cost of reducing the industry's discharge of waste by 1 unit: This is designated by *BB′*. The economically efficient level of pollution for the industry is at the point where the two curves intersect. At this point, the cost of an extra unit of pollution is just equal to the cost of reducing pollution by an extra unit. Regardless of whether we look at Figure 18.7 or 18.8, the answer is the same: *OR* is the economically efficient level of pollution.

Efficient level of pollution

It is important to note that the optimal level of pollution is generally not zero. Despite the fact that some observers seem to believe that zero is the optimal level, our analysis shows clearly that this simply is not true. Why isn't it true? Because beyond some point, the cost of reducing pollution exceeds the benefits. In Figures 18.7 and 18.8, this point is reached at a pollution level of *OR*.[11]

---

[11] For further discussion, see R. and N. Dorfman, *Economics of the Environment* (3d ed.; New York: Norton, 1993), and A. Freeman, R. Haveman, and A. Kneese, *The Economics of Environmental Policy* (New York: Wiley, 1973).

Direct Regulation, Effluent Fees, and Transferable Emission Permits

Left to its own devices, the industry in Figure 18.8 will not reduce its pollution level to OR, because it does not pay all the social costs of its pollution. This, as we have seen, is the heart of the problem. How can the government establish incentives that will lead to the efficient amount of pollution control? One way is by direct regulation. For example, the government may decree that this industry is to limit its pollution to OR units. Direct regulation of this sort is relied on in many sectors of the U.S. economy.

Another way for the government to influence the amount of pollution is to impose an *effluent fee,* which is a fee that a polluter must pay to the government for discharging waste. The idea behind the imposition of effluent fees is that they can bring the private cost of waste disposal closer to the true social costs. For example, in Figure 18.8, an effluent fee of OE per unit of pollution discharge might be charged. If so, the marginal cost of an additional unit of pollution discharge to the industry is OE, with the result that it will cut back its pollution to the efficient level, OR units. Why? Because it will be profitable to cut back pollution so long as the marginal cost of reducing pollution by a unit is less than OE — and, as you can see from Figure 18.8, this is the case so long as the pollution discharge exceeds OR. Thus, to maximize their profits, the firms in the industry will reduce pollution to OR units.[12]

Effluent fees often have at least two advantages over direct regulation. First, it obviously is socially desirable to use the cheapest way to achieve any given reduction in pollution. A system of effluent fees is more likely to accomplish this result than direct regulation. To see why this is the case, consider a particular polluter. Faced with an effluent fee — that is, a price it must pay for each unit of waste it discharges — the polluter will find it profitable to reduce its discharge of waste to the point where the cost of reducing waste discharges by 1 unit equals the effluent fee. (Recall our discussion in the previous paragraph.)

It follows that, since the effluent fee is the same for all polluters, the cost of reducing waste discharges by 1 extra unit is then the same for all polluters. But if this is so, the total cost of achieving the resulting decrease in pollution must be a minimum. To see this, suppose that the cost of reducing waste discharges by an additional unit is *not* the same for all polluters. Then there is a cheaper way to reduce pollution to its existing level — by getting polluters whose cost of reducing waste discharges by an additional unit is low to reduce their waste

---

[12] Another way for the government to intervene is to establish tax credits for firms that introduce pollution control equipment. Such subsidies may not be very effective, since it still may be cheaper for the firms to continue polluting. Also, they may not be very efficient, since pollution control equipment may not be the most economical means of reducing some kinds of pollution. Further, they are frequently attacked on the grounds that they are not equitable. Nonetheless, such subsidies are sometimes used.

disposal by an additional unit, and by allowing polluters whose cost of reducing waste discharges by an additional unit is high to increase their pollution commensurately.

Second, economists tend to favor effluent fees because this approach requires far less information in the hands of the relevant government agencies than does direct regulation. After all, when effluent fees are used, all the government has to do is meter the amount of pollution a firm or household produces (which admittedly is sometimes not easy) and charge accordingly. It is left to the firms and households to figure out the most ingenious and effective ways to cut down on their pollution and save on effluent fees.

Still another way that the government can curb the amount of pollution is to issue *transferable emissions permits,* which are permits to generate a certain amount of pollution. These permits, which are limited in total number so that the aggregate amount of pollution equals (approximately) the economically efficient amount, are allocated among firms. They can be bought and sold. Firms that find it very expensive to reduce pollution are likely to buy these permits; firms that find it cheap to do so are likely to sell them.

Transferable emissions permits

To illustrate how market mechanisms can be used to curb pollution, consider the Clean Air Act of 1990, which gave electric companies the right to meet sulfur dioxide standards by buying and selling pollution emissions permits issued by the Environmental Protection Agency. The act establishes a limit on total emissions of sulfur dioxide from 110 electric companies. In the year 2,000, this limit will be reduced substantially. One object of this program is to reduce acid rain.

PROPERTY RIGHTS AND COASE'S THEOREM

Under certain circumstances, a perfectly competitive economy will allocate resources efficiently, even in the face of seemingly important external benefits or costs. For example, consider a firm that pollutes a stream by pumping out waste materials. Suppose that the downstream water users have well-defined property rights to water of a specified quality level, which means that they can sue the firm for damages if it passes water on to them that is below this quality level. In such a case, the firm can be required to pay for the pollution costs it imposes on others. Or consider a firm that upgrades the water in a stream, and thus benefits downstream water users. If this firm raises the water quality above the legally required level, it can seek compensation from the water users if property rights of this sort are well defined.

If the costs of negotiating are not too large, the parties responsible for an external benefit or cost can negotiate with the parties affected by this externality. For example, if downstream water users are entitled to water of a particular quality, a firm may purchase from them the right to pollute the stream to a certain extent. Or the downstream users may purchase from the firm the right to water of better quality than they would otherwise be entitled to. In this way, the externality is brought into the calculations of the interested parties. Thus there is no divergence between social and private costs because a firm or individual that harms others must pay for this right, and a firm or individual that benefits others receives compensation.

Coase's theorem

According to Nobel laureate Ronald Coase of the University of Chicago, a competitive economy will allocate resources efficiently, even in the face of seemingly important external effects, if it is possible to carry out such negotiations at little or no cost. In the course of these negotiations, the relevant parties will be led to take proper account of the effects of their actions on others. For example, if downstream water users are endowed with a property right to obtain water of a particular quality, a firm that wants to pollute a stream will be led to offer compensation to them, and, pursuing its own interest, it will not find it worthwhile to pollute beyond the economically efficient point. Moreover, Coase has shown that, *regardless of which party is endowed with the relevant property rights,* the outcome will be the same. That is, regardless of whether the downstream users are endowed with the right to obtain water of a particular quality or the firm is endowed with the right to emit a certain amount of pollutants into the stream, the parties will be led to buy or sell these rights so that the economically efficient amount of pollution results.[13]

This theorem, often referred to as Coase's theorem, is of considerable interest and importance. However, it is important to recognize that it assumes that the costs of negotiating and contracting by the interested parties are relatively small. For example, it assumes that the downstream water users can get together with the polluting firm and that they can negotiate effectively without prohibitive expense. In fact, however, when there are more than a relatively small number of interested parties, the costs of such negotiations may be so high that they are not feasible. Indeed, even if the costs are moderate, negotiations of this sort may not be practical. If the number of interested parties is large, it may not be possible to get the unanimity required to make the negotiations effective. And if the number of interested parties is small, the fact that mutually advantageous deals are possible does not mean that they will necessarily be consummated.

Nonetheless, Coase's theorem suggests that the assignment of well-defined property rights might help to promote economic efficiency. For example, to

---

[13] R. Coase, "The Problem of Social Cost," *Journal of Law and Economics,* October 1960, reprinted in Mansfield, *Microeconomics: Selected Readings,* 5th ed.

EXAMPLE 18.4

The Optimal Response to Global Warming

According to many scientists, the accumulation of carbon dioxide and other so-called greenhouse gases is likely to produce global warming and other climatic changes over the next century. While it is difficult to predict the economic consequences of such climatic changes, agriculture and coastal areas, as well as the construction, energy, and recreation sectors of the economy, may be affected. Thus, many observers have argued that governments should adopt policies to reduce the emission of greenhouse gases. William Nordhaus of Yale University has estimated that the marginal cost (that is, the forgone world output) of reducing the emission of greenhouse gases by a ton is as shown below:

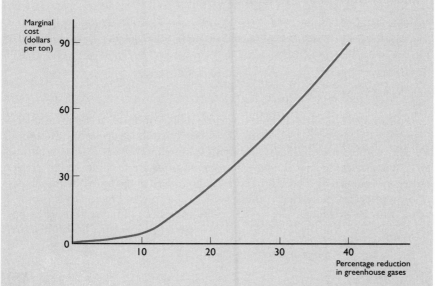

(a) If these estimates are correct, and if the emission of greenhouse gases is reduced by 20 percent, how much output must the world give up to reduce their emission by an extra ton? (b) In Nordhaus's view, a reasonable estimate of the marginal damage to society of an extra ton of greenhouse gases emitted is about $7 per ton. If so, by what percentage should the emission of such gases be reduced? (c) What policies might governments use to reduce the emission of greenhouse gases? (d) In the absence of international agreements, are individual governments likely to reduce emissions by the optimal amount? Why or why not?

SOLUTION: (a) According to the graph, the marginal cost of reducing the emission of greenhouse gases by a ton is about $27 if the emission of such gases has already been cut by 20 percent. (b) As emphasized in Figure 18.8, the emission of pollutants should be reduced to the point where the marginal cost of pollution equals the marginal cost of pollution control. If the marginal cost of an extra ton of greenhouse gases emitted is about $7 per ton, such emissions should be reduced to the point where the marginal cost of reducing them by an extra ton is also about $7 per ton. According to the graph, this point is reached when such emissions are reduced by about 11 percent. (c) Economists have proposed fees or systems of transferable emissions permits which would lead firms and individuals to consider the social cost of greenhouse gas emissions in their private decisions. (d) If each government cannot be reasonably sure that others will reduce emissions, it will be unlikely to do so by itself, since little might be achieved.*

---

*For further discussion, see W. Nordhaus, "A Sketch of the Economics of the Greenhouse Effect," *American Economic Review,* May 1991, and the *Economic Report of the President,* 1990.

get around the difficulties caused by external diseconomies arising from waste disposal, society might find it useful to try to establish more unambiguous property rights for individuals and firms with respect to environmental quality. Then, assuming that the relevant negotiations are feasible, the interested parties in a particular area might try to negotiate to determine how much pollution will occur. Note that if these negotiations are to be effective, property rights must be exchangeable, as well as unambiguous. That is, it must be possible for a person (or firm) to buy or sell his or her property rights of this sort.

PUBLIC GOODS

In an earlier section, we learned that under the specified conditions (and with the proper qualifications), a perfectly competitive economy results in an efficient allocation of resources. However, it was assumed that the goods being produced were not public goods. A public good has two characteristics: it is

Nonrival   nonrival and nonexclusive. By *nonrival* we mean that the marginal cost of providing the good to an additional consumer is zero. Thus a public good can be enjoyed by an extra person without reducing the enjoyment it gives others. Consider the case of national defense. If a baby is born in the United States at this moment, he or she can enjoy the protection of our military establishment without reducing the protection it affords the rest of us. Thus national defense is a nonrival good.

By *nonexclusive,* we mean that people cannot be excluded from consuming the good. Ordinarily, whether a person consumes a good depends on whether he or she pays the price. Those who pay for the good can consume it, while those who do not pay cannot consume it. But this is not always the case, as illustrated again by national defense. Once a country has created a military establishment, all citizens enjoy its protection. Since there is no practical way of excluding citizens from its protection, national defense is a nonexclusive good. **Non-exclusive**

A public good is defined here as a good that is *both* nonrival and nonexclusive. Not all nonrival goods are nonexclusive goods (and not all nonexclusive goods are nonrival goods). Consider an uncrowded bridge. If Mr. Smith crosses the bridge, this does not interfere with Mr. Jones's crossing it, which indicates that the use of this bridge is a nonrival good. But it is not a nonexclusive good, as shown by the fact that it is perfectly feasible to charge a fee for crossing the bridge and to prevent people who do not pay from crossing it.

Public goods will not be provided in the right amounts by the market mechanism, which operates on the principle that those who do not pay for a good cannot consume it. As we have just seen, it is impossible to prevent people from consuming a public good whether or not they pay for it. For example, there is no way to prevent someone from benefitting from national defense, regardless of whether or not he or she helps pay for it. Thus, in many cases, the market mechanism simply is not applicable.

THE EFFICIENT OUTPUT OF A PUBLIC GOOD

If resources are to be allocated efficiently, how much should be produced of a public good? In this section, we analyze this question from the point of view of partial equilibrium analysis. Suppose for simplicity that there are only two consumers, the Adams family and the Brown family. Suppose that D_A is the Adams family's demand curve for a good, D_B is the Brown family's demand curve for the same good, and the supply curve for the good is as shown in Figure 18.9.

FIGURE 18.9 Determination of Efficient Output: Private Good and Public Good For a private good, the efficient output is *OQ* in panel A. For a public good, the efficient output is *OR* in panel B.

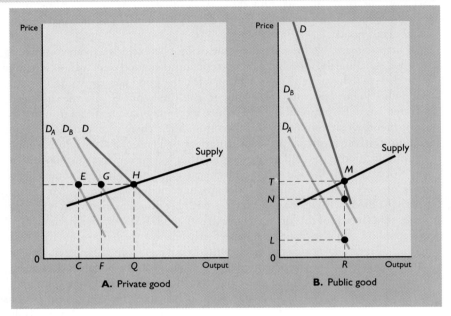

A. Private good

B. Public good

Efficient output of private good   The left-hand panel of Figure 18.9 shows the efficient output of this good, assuming that it is a *private* good produced under perfect competition. Summing horizontally the demand curves of the two consumers, we obtain the market demand curve for the good, *D*. The efficient output is *OQ*, where this market demand curve intersects the market supply curve. Why is this efficient? Because at this output, the marginal benefit each consumer would obtain from an extra unit of the good equals its marginal cost. Assuming that the marginal benefit can be measured by the maximum amount that each family will pay for the extra unit, the marginal benefit for the Adams family would be *CE,* and the marginal benefit for the Brown family would be *FG*. The marginal cost of the extra unit is *QH* at an output of *OQ*. (Recall from Chapter 10 that the supply curve shows the marginal cost at each level of output.) Since *CE = FG = QH,* it follows that the marginal benefit to each consumer equals the marginal cost.

If, on the other hand, the good is a *public* good, the efficient output is shown in the right-hand panel of Figure 18.9. In this case, the market demand curve is obtained by summing the individual demand curves *vertically,* not horizontally.[14] This fundamental difference stems from the fact that both consumers consume the *total* amount of the good and that the combined price paid by the two consumers is the sum of the prices paid by each one. The efficient output of the good is now *OR,* and the total price (the sum of the prices paid by each consumer) is *OT.*

To see why *OR* is the efficient output, recall (from page 355 of Chapter 11) that the efficient output is the one where marginal social benefit equals marginal social cost. Next, note that the marginal social benefit from an extra unit of output of a public good is obtained by adding vertically the distances under every consumer's demand curve. This is because all consumers share entirely in the consumption of whatever quantity of the good is available and because the marginal social benefit is the sum of the marginal benefits to each consumer. (Also, if an extra unit of the good is worth to an individual the maximum amount that he or she is willing to pay for it, the marginal benefit to each consumer is the distance under his or her demand curve.) Thus, if output is *OR,* the marginal social benefit from an extra unit of output is the vertical sum of *OL* and *ON,* which equals *OT.* Since the marginal social cost of an extra unit of output is *RM* (as in the case of a private good), and since the efficient output is where marginal social benefit equals marginal social cost, it follows that *OR* must be the efficient output, since marginal social benefit (*OT*) and marginal social cost (*RM*) are equal at this output.

This analysis is illuminating. For example, Figure 18.9 shows the important fact that, whereas economic efficiency requires that each consumer's marginal benefit equals marginal cost for a private good, it requires that the *sum* of the marginal benefits of all consumers equals marginal cost for a public good. But despite its good points, this kind of analysis can take us only so far. For one thing, the demand curves in Figure 18.9 will not be revealed voluntarily if citizens believe that the amount they pay will be related to the preferences they reveal. Consumers will find it worthwhile to be *free riders.* In other words, when consumers feel that the total output of the good will not be affected significantly by the action of any single person, they are likely to make no contribution to supporting the good, although they will use whatever output of the good is forthcoming.[15]

---

[14] These demand curves are sometimes called pseudo-demand curves or willingness-to-pay curves. See Dorfman, *Economics of the Environment.*

[15] In addition, a partial equilibrium analysis of this problem has obvious limitations. For a general equilibrium analysis, see P. Samuelson, "Diagrammatic Exposition of a Theory of Public Expenditure," *Review of Economics and Statistics,* November, 1955, reprinted in Mansfield, *Microeconomics: Selected Readings,* 5th ed.

THE PROVISION OF PUBLIC GOODS

If the number of people in a society is quite small, it may be worthwhile for people acting individually to provide some quantity of public goods. For example, consider a case where there are two families on an island that is infested with poisonous snakes. The reduction of the number of such snakes is a public good, if there is no way of preventing the snakes from moving from one family's land to the other's, and if providing enhanced protection against the snakes for one family automatically provides it for the other family at no additional cost. Under these conditions, one of the families may well deem it worthwhile to engage in some activities to kill the snakes, even though this benefits the other family as well. Thus, when numbers are small, it is a mistake to say that no public goods will be produced unless the government does so. However, this does not mean that the proper amount of public goods will be produced, and that brings us to the next point.

Output too small

Even if there are few people in the society, there is a tendency for the provision of a public good to be too small, if its provision is left entirely up to the people acting individually in their own self-interest. To see why, suppose that a family lives alone for some time on the island cited above, and then is joined by a family that formerly lived alone on another island. Once the second family arrives, the first family will reduce its efforts to kill poisonous snakes because it will count on the other family to do some such work. Similarly, the other family will do less work of this sort than when they lived alone on the other island, for the same reasons. Both will cut back too much on their efforts because, whereas each family pays the full cost of devoting its time to this activity, it receives only part of the benefits, some of which accrue to the other family. Thus less will be produced of this public good than is economically efficient.

If there are few people in the society, there is a tendency for those who have the biggest interest in the outcome, or the biggest share of the resources, to provide a disproportionately large share of the amount of a public good that is supplied. For example, suppose that the first family in the previous paragraph owns 90 percent of the land (and other resources) on the island, and the second family owns 10 percent. Then the first family will recognize that whatever attempts are made to control the snake nuisance will rest largely on its shoulders, and it will act almost as if it were by itself on the island. On the other hand, the second family, recognizing that the first family has an incentive to do an effective job of this sort, is likely to reduce its efforts to a minimal level. Consequently, the first family is likely to do more than 90 percent of the snake control work, and the second family is likely to do less than 10 percent.

EXAMPLE 18.5

Economics of a Lighthouse

A lighthouse warns fishing boats away from a treacherous rock. Different levels of service can be provided by the lighthouse, resulting in different probabilities that a boat will be warned of its nearness to the rock. For example, the more powerful the beacon or signal emitted by the lighthouse, the higher the probability that a boat will receive the warning. The marginal cost of attaining various probabilities that a boat will be warned is as shown in the graph below. There are three boats in the area, owned by Captains Amos, Barnaby, and Columbus. The price that each captain is willing to pay for each level of service (that is, each probability that a boat will be warned) is shown by the individual demand curves in the graph below.

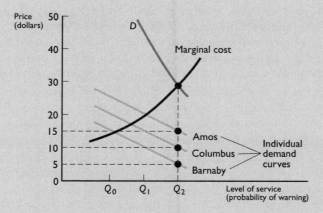

(a) Is the service provided by the lighthouse a nonrival good? (b) Is it a nonexclusive good? (c) What is the efficient level of service (if it is a public good)? That is, what should be the probability that a boat will be warned? (d) Is it impossible for a lighthouse to be privately owned and operated?

SOLUTION (a) It is a nonrival good because, if the service is provided for any fishing boat, it is available to all other boats at no extra cost. (b) It is a nonexclusive good because the light can be used by all boats that see it. (c) To obtain the market demand curve for the service, we must sum the three individual demand curves vertically, the result being D. The efficient level of service is at the point where the marginal cost curve intersects the *D* curve; that is, the efficient level of service is OQ_2. (d) No. In England lighthouses were private for many years. They assessed the shipowners at the docks. Ordinarily only one ship was in sight of the lighthouse at a particular point in time. The light would not be shown if the ship (which was identified by its flag) had not paid.*

---

* For further discussion, see N. Singer, *Public Microeconomics* (Boston: Little, Brown, 1976), and R. Coase, "The Lighthouse in Economics," *Journal of Law and Economics,* October 1974.

The larger the number of people in the society, the farther it will fall short of producing an efficient amount of a public good. Thus, in large societies like the United States, the government intervenes in an attempt to ensure the proper amount of public goods. There is general agreement that the government must provide public goods like national defense, and the provision of such goods unquestionably accounts for a significant portion of the government's expenditure. In democratic societies, the ballot box is used to determine the amount spent on various public goods. Each person votes for candidates that represent (often imperfectly) the set of public expenditures and taxes that is closest to his or her own preferences.[16]

SUMMARY

1. Previous chapters have been concerned with partial equilibrium analysis, which assumes that changes in price can occur in whatever market is being studied without causing significant changes in price in other markets, which in turn affect the market being studied. An analysis that takes account of the interrelationships among prices in various markets is called a general equilibrium analysis.
2. Microeconomics is concerned with the policy recommendations that economists can make. An important limitation of microeconomics is that there

---

[16] To a considerable extent, this section is based on M. Olson, *The Logic of Collective Choice* (Rev. ed.; New York: Shocken, 1971). Also, see M. Olson and R. Zeckhauser, "An Economic Theory of Alliances," *Review of Economics and Statistics,* August 1966.

is no scientifically meaningful way to compare the utility levels of different individuals, with the result that we cannot tell whether one distribution of income is better than another.

3. Putting aside the question of income distribution, there are three conditions for an efficient allocation of resources: (1) The marginal rate of substitution between any two commodities must be the same for any two consumers; (2) the marginal rate of technical substitution between any two inputs must be the same for any pair of producers; and (3) the marginal rate of substitution between any two commodities must be the same as the marginal rate of transformation between these two commodities for any producer.

4. One of the most fundamental findings of microeconomics is that a perfectly competitive economy satisfies these three sets of conditions for economic efficiency. To the economic theorist, this is one of the basic arguments for a perfectly competitive economy. Economists interested in the functioning of planned, or socialist, economies have argued that a price system could be used in a similar way to increase welfare in such economies. The prices that would be set would equal marginal cost.

5. If social costs differ from private costs and/or social benefits differ from private benefits, perfect competition will not lead to an efficient allocation of resources. If the production of a certain good is responsible for external economies, less than the efficient amount of this good is likely to be produced under perfect competition. If the production of a certain good is responsible for external diseconomies, more of this good is likely to be produced under perfect competition than is economically efficient. To a large extent, undesirably high levels of pollution are due to external diseconomies in waste disposal.

6. A public good has two characteristics: it is nonrival and nonexclusive. By nonrival, we mean that the marginal cost of providing the good to an additional consumer is zero. By nonexclusive, we mean that people cannot be excluded from consuming the good (whether or not they pay for it).

7. Whereas economic efficiency requires that each consumer's marginal benefit equal marginal cost for a private good, it requires that the sum of the marginal benefits of all consumers equal marginal cost for a public good. An important problem is to get people to reveal their true preferences since, if they can avoid paying, they can get the benefits from public goods anyway.

8. If the number of people in a society is quite small, it may be worthwhile for people acting individually to provide some quantity of public goods. However, there is a tendency for the provision of a public good to be too small; the larger the number of people in the society, the farther it will fall short of providing an efficient amount of a public good. Thus the government tends to intervene in an attempt to ensure the proper amount of such goods.

QUESTIONS/PROBLEMS

1. The Times Mirror Company wanted to complete the $120 million expansion of a papermaking plant near Portland, Oregon. State and federal officials were concerned about the effects on air quality. Eventually, the firm bought the right to emit about 150 tons of extra hydrocarbons into the air per year from a wood-coating plant that had gone out of business, the price being $50,000. If the firm had not bought this right, it would not have been able to get permission from the state and federal regulators to make this expansion, according to the firm's manager of environmental and energy services.

   One way that government agencies can reduce pollution is to issue transferable emissions permits, as we saw on page 625. These permits can be bought and sold, much as the Times Mirror Company did. Suppose that you are an adviser to the Environmental Protection Agency and that you are asked to tell the agency's officials what determines the price of a permit. What's the answer? (For simplicity, assume that there are many buyers and sellers of such permits, so the market for them is competitive, and that each permit allows its owner to emit 1 ton of pollutants.)

2. According to Milton Friedman, significant external economies are gained from the education of children: "The gain from the education of a child accrues not only to the child or its parents but also to other members of the society." Moreover, "It is not feasible to identify the particular individuals (or families) benefited and so to charge for the services rendered." What kind of government action is justified by these considerations?

3. Gasohol is a blend of 10 percent ethanol and 90 percent regular gasoline. Ethanol can be made from corn. In late 1979, the cost of a gallon of ethanol made from corn was estimated at $1.20. The refinery price of regular gasoline was $.85 per gallon. To encourage the production of gasohol, the federal government exempted gasohol from the federal gasoline tax, worth $.40 on the 10 percent ethanol content of gasohol. And many states exempted it from their motor fuel taxes, worth another $.40 to $1 per gallon of ethanol. (a) Does each gallon of ethanol used in gasohol result in a 1-gallon reduction in the amount of regular gasoline (or other fuels) used in the United States? (b) Given the above tax incentives, was it profitable to produce gasohol? If so, was it likely that gasohol would displace regular gasoline completely? (c) What are the effects of these tax exemptions on corn prices? On the value of corn-producing land? Can a partial equilibrium analysis answer those questions?

4. Martin Cantine leaves an estate consisting of 200 acres of land and 50 paintings. In his will, he states that his estate should be divided equally between his two children, Mary and John. (That is, each child should receive half

the land and half the paintings.) (a) Construct an Edgeworth box diagram showing the various ways in which the estate might be divided. (b) Show the point in this diagram that represents the division of the estate according to the will. (c) Can we be sure that this point is on the contract curve?

5. Suppose that two consumers, after swapping goods back and forth, have arrived at a point on the contract curve. In other words, neither can be made better-off without making the other worse off. Does this mean that neither of them can find a point *off* the contract curve that is preferable to the point at which they have arrived? If it does not mean this, why do economists claim that points on the contract curve are to be preferred?

6. In 1986, Congress passed a bill making business entertainment expenses partly, but not wholly, tax deductible. (Previously they had been completely deductible.) What segments of the population did this hurt? What segments did it help? Is there any way to tell whether, on balance, it was good or bad for society?

7. A small private jet lands at Kennedy Airport in New York at the busiest time of day. It pays a nominal landing fee. What divergences may exist between the private and social costs of this plane's landing there at that time? What policies might help to eliminate such divergences?

8. Microeconomics is concerned in part with the determination of ways to satisfy human wants as best we can. But is this really a sensible goal? For example, suppose that people want the wrong things. Is it still sensible to try to satisfy these wants as completely as possible? Shouldn't microeconomics be concerned, too, with how wants are created?

9. Suppose that the market for videocassette recorders is in disequilibrium; that is, the actual price does not equal the equilibrium price. If all industries in the economy are perfectly competitive (including videocassette recorders), will the necessary conditions for efficient resource allocation be met?

10. In judging various social mechanisms and policies, microeconomics tends to emphasize the outcomes of these mechanisms and policies, as measured by the extent to which various human wants are satisfied. But shouldn't microeconomics be concerned with *means* as well as *ends*? For example, suppose that a particular policy resulted in an ideal allocation of resources, but that it was achieved by trickery or coercion. Doesn't this matter?

11. Suppose that there are only three citizens of a (very small) country and that the amount of national defense each would demand (at various prices) is as follows:

Price of a unit of national defense (dollars)	Number of units demanded		
	Citizen A	Citizen B	Citizen C
1	10	8	12
2	9	7	9
3	8	6	7
4	7	5	5

If the marginal cost of a unit of national defense is $9, what is the efficient amount of national defense for this country?

12. The paper industry has been a notable source of water pollution. Suppose that every ton of paper that is produced imposes costs on others (for example, on people using local rivers for recreation and fishing) of $5. The supply and demand curves for paper are given below.

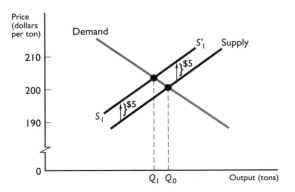

What will be the output of the paper industry? What is the efficient output of the paper industry?

APPENDIX

Economic Benefits from Free Trade

Countries gain considerably from trade with other countries, as well as from commerce carried out within their borders. To understand these gains, you must be familiar with the concept of *comparative advantage.* Suppose that Germany can produce 2 computers or 6,000 pounds of textiles with 1 unit of resources, and England can produce 1 computer or 4,000 pounds of textiles with 1 unit of resources. Under these circumstances, Germany is a more-productive and less-costly supplier of both computers and textiles than England, since it produces more of each good from a unit of resources than England does. Thus, economists say that Germany has an *absolute advantage* over England in the production of both of these goods.

But comparative advantage is not the same as absolute advantage. A country has a comparative advantage over another country in the production of a particular good if the cost of making this good, *compared with the cost of mak-*

ing other goods, is lower in this country than in the other country. Under the above circumstances, Germany has a comparative advantage over England in the production of computers. Why? Because the cost of a computer in Germany is the same as the cost of 3,000 pounds of textiles (since both require 1/2 unit of resources), whereas in England it is the same as the cost of 4,000 pounds of textiles (since both require 1 unit of resources). Thus, relative to the cost of producing other goods (in this case, textiles), computers are cheaper to produce in Germany than England.

If a country has a comparative advantage in the production of a particular commodity, and if it can trade freely with other countries, it is likely to find that it can improve its economic lot by specializing in the production of this commodity and by importing those commodities in which it does not have a comparative advantage. For example, consider Germany under the above circumstances. Figure 18.10 shows Germany's production possibilities curve. If Germany cannot trade with England, perhaps because of protectionist measures (tariffs, quotas, and the like) in both countries, consumer satisfaction in Germany will be maximized by choosing point G, where the marginal rate of substitution between the two commodities equals the marginal rate of transformation between them.

FIGURE 18.10 Economic Benefits from Free Trade Without trade, production and consumption are at point G, where indifference curve 1 is tangent to the production possibilities curve. With trade, Germany can move from point H along the trading possibilities curve to point M, and reach indifference curve 2 (higher than indifference curve 1.)

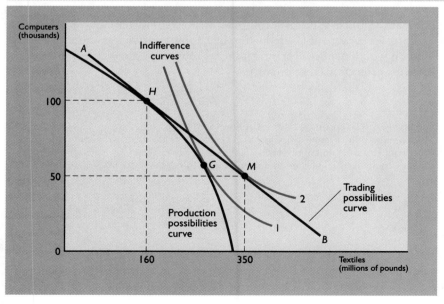

Suppose now that free trade is permitted and that Germany is able to trade the commodity in which it has a comparative advantage — computers — for English textiles. (Note that England has a comparative advantage in textile production.[17]) The line AB in Figure 18.10, called Germany's trading possibilities curve, shows the various amounts of computers and textiles that Germany can end up with if it chooses point H on its production possibilities curve — where it produces 100,000 computers and 160 million pounds of textiles — and exports various amounts of its computers to England. The slope of line AB equals (in absolute value) the number of computers Germany must give up to get 1,000 pounds of English textiles.

Clearly, Germany will increase consumer satisfaction if it moves along line AB from point H to point M, where line AB is tangent to indifference curve 2. In this way, it reaches a higher indifference curve. At point M, Germany is exporting $100,000 - 50,000 = 50,000$ computers, and importing 350 million $- 160$ million $= 190$ million pounds of textiles. Since indifference curve 2 is considerably higher than indifference curve 1, Germany's consumers are much better-off than in the days when trade was not permitted.

At the same time, England will increase consumer satisfaction if it specializes in the production of textiles (where it has a comparative advantage) and exports them to Germany, while cutting back its production of computers and importing them from Germany. Thus, both countries will specialize in the production of those goods in which they have a comparative advantage and export them to the other country.

Whereas free trade of this sort provides many benefits to people in both countries, not everyone gains from it. In particular, German textile producers (and textile workers) may be hurt considerably by the cut in textile output in Germany. Similarly, English computer makers (and computer workers) may incur losses because of the reduction in computer production in that country. Thus, it would not be surprising if these groups were to oppose free trade and press for protection from imports.

---

[17] The cost of 4,000 pounds of textiles in England is the same as the cost of 1 computer (since both require 1 unit of resources), whereas in Germany it is the same as the cost of $1\frac{1}{3}$ computers (since both requires $\frac{2}{3}$ unit of resources). Thus, relative to the cost of producing other goods (in this case, computers), textiles are cheaper to produce in England than in Germany.

Applying Microeconomic Theory: The Case of California Water

INTRODUCTION

One of the leading movies of the 1970s was *Chinatown,* starring Jack Nicholson and John Huston. According to the movie's plot, water is being diverted from public reservoirs in Los Angeles for use in irrigating orange groves. Huston, a superrich mover-and-shaker in the area, clashes with the water commissioner and others over who should own the water and how it should be distributed. Eventually he kills the water commissioner, but is apprehended by Jack Nicholson. Why this exercise in summarizing old movies? Because it illustrates the critical role of water in the California economy. As one character in the movie says, "Los Angeles is a desert community."

California uses about 40 million acre-feet of water per year. (An acre-foot is the quantity of water required to cover 1 acre to a depth of 1 foot, or about 300,000 gallons.) Agriculture has accounted for about 85 percent of the state's water use. In particular, irrigated pasture (grass and hay), alfalfa, cotton, and rice have been heavy users of water; together they have accounted for 42 percent of the state's total water use. California's agriculture is very important to the country, as suggested by the total value of its crops (over $15 billion per year). Over 90 percent of the country's grapes, broccoli, artichokes, almonds, and walnuts, and over half of the country's lettuce, tomatoes, plums, lemons, celery, peaches, melons, carrots, and asparagus are grown in the state.[1]

CRITICISMS OF CALIFORNIA'S WATER ALLOCATION SYSTEM

Bill Bradley, former basketball star of Princeton University and the New York Knicks and former Rhodes Scholar, seems about as far removed from California water as Newark is from Sacramento. But having twice been elected U.S. Senator from New Jersey, he was chairman of the Senate's Subcommittee on Water and Power in the early 1990s and was deeply concerned with the nation's water problems. He introduced federal legislation, discussed below, to try to influence the use and allocation of water in California.

Bill Bradley

According to Bradley, a variety of severe problems would have occurred unless California's water allocation system was drastically changed.

---

[1] Memorandum of Tom Jensen, Counsel of U.S. Senate Committee on Energy and Natural Resources, March 13, 1991, and J. Gomez-Ibanez and J. Kalt, *Cases in Microeconomics* (Englewood Cliffs, N.J.: Prentice-Hall, 1990).

> The Bureau of Reclamation and . . . agribusiness will continue to sit on 20 percent of the State's water supply and run it for their own interests. . . . California cities, unable to secure ready access to new water through voluntary transfers, will be left with no obvious choice but to spend billions of dollars on energy-intensive, polluting, and expensive desalinization plants. . . . During the next drought, urban residents . . . , who pay hundreds of dollars for every acre-foot of water they use, will watch gardens . . . die, while just over the hill . . . , hundreds of thousands of acres of taxpayer-subsidized cotton and rice will flourish in the desert. Numerous species will become extinct, not the least of which will be California's fishermen.[2]

The state's farmers, who receive the bulk of its water, have been understandably inclined to drag their feet in response to proposals for radical change. As Calvin Dooley, a member of Congress from California put it,

> I represent the 17th congressional district . . . , I have many communities which are almost totally reliant on agriculture. Critics . . . , even well-intentioned, thoughtful critics, have been so successful in demonizing irrigated agriculture that it is difficult for many people to think of the [water users] as anything but big, rich, corporate villains. . . . How can we most effectively meet the environmental objectives [and other worthwhile aims of the critics of the existing system] and still ensure that we are going to maintain the long-term viability of this region?[3]

WATER PRICING, RESOURCE ALLOCATION, AND MARGINAL COST PRICING

In the United States, there are two different doctrines of water law. In the western states, the *doctrine of appropriation* is the primary basis of the law, whereas in the eastern states, the *riparian doctrine* plays this role. According to

---

[2] Senate Committee on Energy and Natural Resources, *Reclamation Projects Authorization and Adjustment Act of 1992* (Washington, D.C.: Government Printing Office, 1992), pp. 205–06.

[3] Subcommittee on Water and Power, *Central Valley Project Improvement Act* (Washington, D.C.: Government Printing Office, 1992), pp. 189–91.

the riparian doctrine, an owner of land bordering a lake or stream has the right to take water for use on his or her property. In contrast, according to the doctrine of appropriation, landowners have no preferred status; instead, the water right is acquired by use. The earliest water right on a given body of water has preference over later users. That is, "first in time means first in right."[4]

California's water laws were based at first on the riparian doctrine, then on the doctrine of appropriation. Eventually, a system of state control of water evolved. Most of the state's water has been delivered by about 2,000 local water agencies. These retailers have received their water from wholesalers who in turn have bought it from federal, state, and local sources. Federal water has been cheap, perhaps $10 per acre-foot; water from state reservoirs has often sold for $30 to $60 per acre-foot; and underground water may have cost $100 per acre-foot. Retailers have been charged a weighted average of the prices paid by the wholesaler for water. The retailers — the local water agencies — frequently have charged agricultural users a lower price than residential or industrial users. Particularly in areas where farmers have lots of political clout, the price of water for agriculture may have been one-tenth or less of the price to residential users.[5]

The Rand Corporation Headquarters

Many economists and others have argued that marginal cost pricing should be used for California water. The Rand Corporation, a think tank in Santa Monica, California, has expressed the case for marginal cost pricing in the following simple terms:

---

[4] Hirshleifer, DeHaven, and Milliman, *Water Supply* (Chicago: University of Chicago, 1969), p. 318.

[5] Gomez-Ibanez and Kalt, *Cases in Microeconomics*.

> Suppose that at a certain moment of time [the price of water] is $30 per unit. Then, if the community as a whole can acquire and transport another unit of water for, say $20, it would clearly be desirable to do so; in fact, any of the individual customers to whom the unit of water is worth $30 would be happy to pay the $20 cost, and none of the other members of society is made worse off thereby. We may say that, on efficiency grounds, additional units should be made available so long as any members of the community are willing to pay the additional or marginal costs incurred. So the . . . rule is to make the price equal to the marginal cost. . . .[6]

In 1982, the voters of California were asked whether local water districts should be encouraged to use marginal cost pricing. The proposal was turned down, the no vote being particularly heavy in agricultural parts of the state.[7]

"THE FEDERAL WATER SCANDAL"

In 1902, Congress set up the Bureau of Reclamation to promote the development of irrigation in the western United States, the idea being to spur rural development by helping small family farms. According to President Theodore Roosevelt, "Our people as a whole will profit, for successful home-making is but another name for upbuilding of the Nation."[8] At first, it was required that the irrigators repay the capital costs of the projects in 10 years, but without interest. In 1914, the period was lengthened to 20 years, in 1926 to 40 years, and in 1939 to 50 years. In 1955, the Hoover Commission — a high-level commission established to analyze the performance of the executive branch of the federal government — felt that the government had granted excessive subsidies:

> Water users in irrigation projects are required to pay back a portion of the irrigation capital costs which is judged to be within their capacity, but they pay no interest. The portion they are judged capable of repaying rarely is the full cost . . . of the project. Recently

---

[6] Hirshleifer, DeHaven, and Milliman, *Water Supply*, pp. 40–41.

[7] Gomez-Ibanez and Kalt, *Cases in Microeconomics*.

[8] Quoted in *The Report of the President's Water Resources Policy Commission,* Vol. III (Washington, D.C.: Government Printing Office, 1950), p. 183.

the general range has been between one-quarter and one-third of the capital costs, and a few are as low as 10 percent. Thus, even in projects classed as reimbursable, there is a considerable element of subsidy. Over and above the portion of the construction costs that water users do not pay, the forgoing of interest alone usually provides an additional subsidy equal to the total costs of construction. Thus, in some cases, the federal subsidy amounts to some 95 percent of capital costs plus interest.[9]

The Department of the Interior

According to the Rand study cited above,

> Federal water programs have been referred to in the less scholarly analyses as the "federal water scandal"—with justice, we believe. . . . From the point of view of rational decision-making, improvement in the record of public investment in water-resource development is urgently needed. If the projects engaged in are, as is almost always claimed, efficient ones, then the benefits will exceed the costs and subsidy should not be required. It is possible, of course, to subsidize a project that is economically efficient. In this case, the question of subsidy relates to the desirability of redistributing income from the taxpayers to the project beneficiaries. The more typical situation currently is one where subsidies are required to finance projects that cannot be justified on economic

---

[9] Task Force on Water Resources and Power for the Commission on the Organization of the Executive Branch of the Government, *Report on Water Resources and Power* (Washington, D.C.: 1951), p. 15.

grounds. In such cases, the subsidy leads not merely to a changed distribution of income but to a lower level of overall economic production.[10]

NORTHERN CALIFORNIA: WATER SUPPLIER TO THE SOUTH

The snow that falls during the winter on the mountains of northeastern California generally provides an enormous yearly water runoff. For centuries, most of this runoff "would flow into the Pacific Ocean via the rivers draining into the Central Valley, through the delta of the Sacramento River, and into San Francisco Bay. This runoff, diverted by dams, reservoirs, aqueducts, and pipelines, [now] provides most of the water used by farms, residents, and in-

The Feather River Dam

dustry throughout California. Although 75 percent of the state's water is located in the northern part of the state, 75 percent of the population is in the southern part."[11]

Southern California, including the cities of Los Angeles and San Diego, has experienced enormous population and industrial growth. Since it is an arid

[10] Hirshleifer, DeHaven, and Milliman, *Water Supply,* pp. 228, 230.

[11] P. Milgrom and J. Roberts, *Economics, Organization, and Management* (Englewood Cliffs, N.J.: Prentice-Hall, 1992), p. 298.

area, water has always been very important to its existence and vitality. Its annual average precipitation is about 18 inches, much lower than the national average of 30 inches. Rainfall occurs largely in the winter. The quantity of water entering the area by precipitation or from mountain runoff water is both seasonal and highly variable from year to year. The amount of rainfall in a typical "dry" year may be only one-fifth of that in a typical "wet" year.

In 1960, the voters of California were asked to decide whether the Feather River Project should be initiated. This project, with expected capital costs of about $3 billion, was the central component of the California State Water Plan, a huge scheme to reallocate California's waters from areas of "surplus" to areas of "deficiency." The major purposes of the project were: (1) flood control in the area north of Sacramento, (2) water supply for irrigation purposes in the San Joaquin Valley, (3) water supply for urban purposes in southern California, and (4) hydropower development in northern California. To achieve these purposes, an enormous dam and reservoir were built on the Feather River in north-central California, together with a variety of aqueducts. In 1960, the voters of California, by a narrow margin, approved a bond issue of almost $2 billion to go ahead with this project.[12]

Irrigation Ditch

PROPERTY RIGHTS

Water rights have varied depending on where the water comes from. For example, as we shall see, some farmers have had lucrative rights to obtain large amounts of cheap water delivered to them by the federal government. In 1982, the California Water Code was changed to permit the temporary sale of "con-

[12] Hirshleifer, DeHaven, and Milliman, *Water Supply.*

served" water without the loss of the water rights. Previously this had not been allowed. California metropolitan water districts (wholesalers of water for largely urban areas) have often tried to purchase additional water from water authorities in farm areas on a medium- and long-term basis. However, the farmers have often been unwilling to share their low-priced water with the metropolitan water districts.

In many cases, the farmers' water rights have not been entirely transferrable.[13] During the late 1980s and early 1990s, there were many proposals by Californians and others that individuals and water districts be given the right to charge what they liked for water without danger of forfeiting future rights. For example, in 1986 Ron Khachigian, senior vice president of Blackwell Land Company, one of the biggest corporate farms in California, said, "I'm sitting at a witness table with the Environmental Defense Fund, and here I am a real conservative farmer, and we're both espousing the marketing of water."[14] In Washington, there was also considerable interest in expanding the role of market forces. According to the *New York Times* of February 5, 1992, Congress was likely to increase the price of federal water, and in return, "irrigation districts would gain the clear legal right to sell water to urbanites."[15]

WATER PRICING AND RESOURCE ALLOCATION: CAN YOU APPLY THE THEORY?

The following two problems are concerned with the allocation of water in California and whether it has been efficient, as well as with the value of the marginal product of water in the production of various California crops.

PROBLEM 19.1: In California, suppose that farmers pay $10 per acre-foot for water and that manufacturing industry pays $50 per acre-foot. If the total amount of water to be divided between agriculture and manufacturing is 36 million acre-feet per year, and if the total amount of nonwater inputs to be divided between them is *OG,* the following diagram shows the Edgeworth box diagram and isoquants of each in-

---

[13] *New York Times,* September 14, 1992.

[14] *Sacramento Bee,* August 10, 1986, pp. D1–2.

[15] *New York Times,* February 5, 1992, p. D2. Also see R. Wahl, *Markets for Federal Water* (Washington, D.C.: Resources for the Future, 1989).

dustry. Three isoquants for agriculture are A_1, A_2, and A_3. The isoquant corresponding to the highest output is A_3; that pertaining to the lowest output is A_1. Three isoquants for manufacturing are M_1, M_2, and M_3. The isoquant corresponding to the highest output is M_3; that pertaining to the lowest output is M_1.

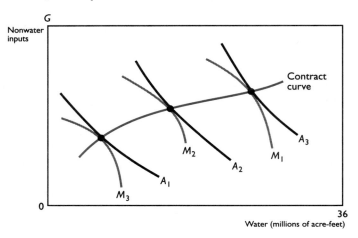

(a) If farmers minimize cost, and if the price of a unit of nonwater inputs is $1, what will be the marginal rate of technical substitution of water for nonwater inputs in agriculture? If manufacturers minimize costs, and if they too pay $1 for a unit of nonwater inputs, what will be the marginal rate of technical substitution of water for nonwater inputs in manufacturing?

(b) Under the above conditions, will the agricultural and manufacturing industries be on or off the contract curve? Will the allocation of resources be efficient? If not, should farmers use less water and manufacturers use more, or should farmers use more water and manufacturers use less?

(c) Some urban households in California have paid over $200 per acre-foot for water; indeed, in some nonfarm coastal communities, desalinization plants have been constructed to get potable water from the ocean at about $3,000 per acre-foot. Does it appear that an extra acre-foot of water has been more valuable to these urban households than to farmers for irrigation? Why or why not?

(d) Suppose that the urban households that are willing to pay over $200 for an extra acre-foot want to use the extra water in their swimming pools, whereas the farmers that can get water for $10 per acre-foot use it to produce cotton and rice. Is it economically efficient for the farmers to use less water and for urban households to use more? Aren't cotton and rice more important than swimming in the back yard?

PROBLEM 19.2: According to available studies, the value of the marginal product of water in the production of various crops has been as shown in Table 19.1. Specifically, this table shows the estimated value of the increased output of each crop that would result if an extra acre-foot of water was devoted to its production.

(a) If an acre-foot of water could have been diverted (at no cost) from artichoke production to cotton production, would this have increased the total value of California agricultural output? If so, by how much?

(b) If farmers were maximizing their profits, why wasn't the value of the marginal product of water the same for all crops? Why didn't competition ensure that the value of the extra output resulting from an extra acre-foot of water was the same on one farm as another?

TABLE 19.1 Value of Marginal Product of Water in Producing Various California Crops

Crop	Value of marginal product (dollars per acre-foot)	Crop	Value of marginal product (dollars per acre-foot)
Lemons	62	Prunes/plums	28
Cotton	56	Celery	21
Onions	52	Asparagus	17
Oranges	47	Rice	17
Grapes	40	Lettuce	17
Barley	37	Peaches	11
Alfalfa hay	36	Artichokes	10
Tomatoes	33	Broccoli	10
Almonds	32	Apricots	9
Grain hay	31	Lima beans	9

SOURCE: Gomez-Ibanez and Kalt, *Cases in Microeconomics.*

MARGINAL COST PRICING: CAN YOU APPLY THE THEORY?

The following problem looks at the effects of marginal cost pricing on producers of various California crops.

PROBLEM 19.3: If marginal cost pricing had been adopted in California, the price of water would have gone up more for the producers of some crops than for the producers of others.

This is due in part to the fact that some crops have tended to be grown in one area, while other crops have been grown in other areas. Thus, since the ratio of the price to the marginal cost of the water has been much lower in some areas (like the North San Joaquin basin) than in others (like the Sacramento Valley), producers of crops grown in areas where this ratio has been low would have been confronted with bigger water-price increases than producers of other crops.

(a) According to available estimates, if marginal cost pricing had been adopted, producers of each of the following crops would have been confronted by the following average price increase for water (in dollars per

acre-foot): lettuce, 80; grapes, 70; cotton, 60; alfalfa hay, 40; and rice, 30.[16] Does this mean that producers of lettuce or grapes would have been affected more drastically by the adoption of marginal cost pricing of water than would producers of alfalfa hay or rice? Why or why not?

(b) Suppose that the table on page 653 shows how the cost function of a particular farm would have been changed if marginal cost pricing of water had been adopted:

If the price of the crop produced by this farm was $160 per ton, what effect would marginal cost pricing of water have had on this farm's output? (For simplicity, assume that this farm can produce only an integer number of tons per day.)

---

[16] D. Robyn, "California Water Pricing," in E. Mansfield, *Study Guide and Casebook for Applied Microeconomics* (2d ed.; New York: Norton, 1997).

Daily output (tons)	Total daily cost (dollars)	
	Without marginal cost pricing	With marginal cost pricing
5	1,020	1,060
6	1,040	1,090
7	1,100	1,160
8	1,250	1,330
9	1,500	1,600

(c) If there are 10,000 farms producing the crop in part (b), all with the cost function shown there (and all in California), draw the market supply curve, with and without marginal cost pricing of water, in the graph below. If the demand curve for this crop is

$$P = 2,400 - 30Q,$$

where P is the price (in dollars per ton) and Q is the quantity demanded (in thousands of tons per day), what will be the equilibrium price, with and without marginal cost pricing of water? (Continue to assume that a farm can produce only an integer number of tons per day.)

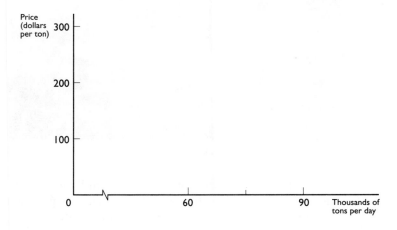

(d) California accounts for about a quarter of U.S. rice production. Suppose we regard California rice and non-California rice as two different goods. Can we predict the effect of marginal cost pricing of water on the price and output of California rice by looking at the demand and supply of California rice alone? Or must we look at the demand and supply of both California and non-California rice? In other words, should a partial equilibrium analysis or a general equilibrium analysis be used?

"THE FEDERAL WATER SCANDAL": CAN YOU APPLY THE THEORY?

The following three problems are concerned with the nature and size of the federal subsidies for California water projects, changes that have been proposed in the pricing of water from federal projects, and environmental damage due to such projects.

PROBLEM 19.4: As we have seen, the Hoover Commission stressed that the forgoing of interest on the construction costs provides a substantial subsidy. Suppose that the federal government spends $1 billion in 1998 to construct a dam and aqueducts, and that the

Shasta Dam

people receiving the water pay the government $40 million a year for 25 years (that is, from 1999 to 2023), the result being that they pay back the government for the construction costs, but without interest.

(a) In 1998, what is the present value of the payments to be made (from 1999 to 2023) to the government by the water users? (Assume that the interest rate is .06.)

(b) How big is the federal subsidy, if any?

(c) According to the Hoover Commission, water users generally reimburse the federal government for only between one-quarter and one-third of the capital costs. Suppose that, rather than paying $40 million a year, water users pay $12 million a year in this case. If they pay this amount each year from 1999 to 2023, what is the present value in 1998 of their payments? (Again assume that the interest rate is .06.)

(d) Under the circumstances in part (c) of this problem, how big is the federal subsidy?

PROBLEM 19.5: The Central Valley Project is one of the world's biggest irrigation projects. Begun in the 1930s and expanded in subsequent decades at a cost to the federal government of about $4 billion, it collects and distributes water from rivers north of the Sacramento–San Joaquin River delta to irrigated farmland and communities in the Central Valley and San Francisco Bay areas. (See Figure 19.1.) In all, it supplies about 7 million acre-feet per year, or about 20 percent of California's water supply.[17]

FIGURE 19.1 Major Components of the Central Valley Project in California

SOURCE: U.S. General Accounting Office, *Reclamation Law: Changes Needed Before Water Service Contracts Are Renewed* (Washington, D.C.: Government Printing Office, 1991).

---

[17] Jensen, Memorandum.

(a) The present value of expected payments by water users for the construction costs of the Central Valley Project are estimated to be about $200 million. How big is the federal subsidy?

(b) Suppose that, because the Central Valley Project has provided cheap water to California farmers, the supply curve for agricultural products has shifted to the right, as shown in the graph below. How big has been the gain in consumer surplus to consumers of agricultural products? How big has been the gain in producer surplus to California farmers? (Note: The area of *ABCF* is $0.925 billion; the area of triangle *CBD*— as well as that of triangle *DBE* and triangle *KDE*— is $0.025 billion; and the area of *GCDKH* is $1.875 billion.)

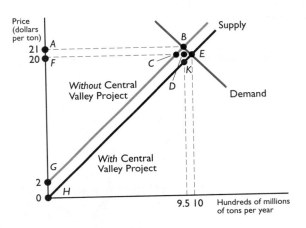

(c) Prove that the increase in total surplus from the rightward shift of the supply curve in the above graph equals the area of *GBEH*.

(d) According to a 1992 statement by Senator Paul Wellstone of Minnesota, "Congress has received considerable evidence from the General Accounting Office and others demonstrating that some of the nation's largest agricultural corporations are still receiving substantial amounts of subsidized water, in clear violation of the spirit and letter of our reclamation laws."[18] The Rand study (quoted on page 645) points out that a federal subsidy can sometimes be justified if it is felt that the resulting redistribution of income is fair or just. Do you feel that the subsidies cited by Senator Wellstone are justifiable on these grounds?

(e) Many of the original 40-year water contracts in the Central Valley Project came up for renewal in the next 10 years or so. Many observers,

[18] Senate Committee on Energy and National Resources, *Reclamations Projects Authorization and Adjustment Act of 1992*, p. 207.

like Worldwatch's Sandra Postel, have felt that the price of water should be raised closer to its true marginal cost. According to the *New York Times* on February 5, 1992, "A best guess now is that roughly half the water will be guaranteed with subsidies-as-usual, with the rest going at sharply higher prices that are closer to the real cost of delivery."[19] Can one use the Pareto criterion to determine whether these changes should have been made?

(f) The Metropolitan Water District of Southern California, water wholesaler for about half of California's population, has agreed to pay for the lining of the canals and other conservation projects in an irrigation district near the Mexican border, and receive in return the water saved.[20] If its customers value the water they obtain in this way more than the amount it costs them for the lining and other conservation measures, is this a desirable action, on the basis of the Pareto criterion? Why or why not?

(g) Senator Wellstone has pointed out that: "Through the Bureau [of Reclamation] the federal government provides subsidized water to thousands of farms, encouraging and enabling them to grow more crops on their irrigated land. At the same time, through the Department of Agriculture, it pays farms (and sometimes the same farms) to set aside acreage so they do not grow some of the same crops."[21] Are these federal agencies working at cross purposes? If so, how would you resolve whatever conflict may exist?

PROBLEM 19.6: The farms receiving water from the Central Valley Project have had an unfortunate effect on the environment. According to the *Sacramento Bee,* "As with atomic power, the federal government promoted the development of a vast agricultural industry within the Central Valley knowing full well that it had no means of disposing of the hazardous wastes that industry produces. Today, the largest and richest of California's agricultural districts, Westlands, is facing the consequences of that short-sightedness."[22] Reports have indicated that irrigation drainage water containing high concentrations of selenium and other toxins has caused deaths and deformities among waterfowl, and threatens the drinking water of over a million residents of the San Joaquin Valley.[23]

[19] *New York Times,* February 5, 1992, p. D2.

[20] S. Postel, "California's Liquid Deficit," *New York Times,* February 27, 1991.

[21] Senate Committee on Energy and Natural Resources, *Reclamations Projects Authorization and Adjustment Act of 1992,* p. 208.

[22] W. Kahrl, "The Poison Also Rises: Westlands' Unresolved Waste-Water Dilemma," *Sacramento Bee,* July 21, 1985. Also see U.S. General Accounting Office, *Reclamation Law.*

[23] E. P. LeVeen and L. King, *Turning Off the Tap on Federal Water Subsidies,* Vol. I (San Francisco: National Resources Defense Council, 1985).

(a) Are there external diseconomies of producing crops in the Central Valley? If so, what are some of them?

(b) If the marginal cost of pollution and the marginal cost of pollution control are as shown below and if direct regulation is used to control pollution, what level of pollution should the regulations permit?

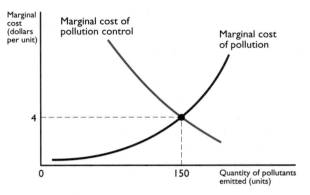

(c) If an effluent fee were used to control pollution, what is the optimal value of this fee?

(d) Could transferable emissions permits be used to control pollution in this case? If so, how?

(e) By diverting so much water from its natural pattern of flow, government water projects have permitted salt water from the Pacific Ocean to go further inland, and have harmed the environment of the San Francisco Bay. According to Tom Bradley, former mayor of Los Angeles, "Our long-term goal would be elimination of water price subsidies."[24] If this goal were achieved, would the private and social costs of water delivery to the Central Valley still differ? Why or why not?

Former Mayor
Tom Bradley

---

[24] Subcommittee on Water and Power, *Central Valley Project Improvement Act,* p. 45.

THE CALIFORNIA STATE WATER PLAN: CAN YOU APPLY THE THEORY?

The following problem is concerned with the economic rationale for the California State Water Plan, the huge project that the voters of California approved in 1960.

PROBLEM 19.7: The California State Water Plan was based on the idea that there were reasonably well-defined water requirements that had to be met. Since the total amount of water received by the state through precipitation and through imports from other states exceeded the total state requirements (estimated by state officials), the problem seemed to be relatively simple: transport the water from where it is abundant to where it is needed. The water requirements of southern California (more specifically, the south coastal area) during the period 1950 to 2020, as estimated by the state officials, are shown in Table 19.2.

(a) For the purpose of constructing these estimates, the relevant state officials assumed that the price of water would be $30 per acre-foot. According to estimates made by the Rand Corporation, the marginal cost

TABLE 19.2 Estimated Water Requirements in Southern California,[a] 1950–2020

Year	Population projection (millions)	Per capita use per day (gallons)[b]	Requirements (millions of acre-feet per year)		
			Urban	Irrigation	Total[c]
1950	5.4	140	0.9	1.0	1.8
1960	8.7	160	1.6	0.7	2.3
1970	12.0	170	2.3	0.7	3.0
1980	15.0	176	3.0	0.6	3.6
1990	17.3	186	3.6	0.6	4.2
2000	19.4	199	4.3	0.6	4.9
2010	21.2	207	4.9	0.5	5.4
2020	22.7	210	5.3	0.5	5.8

SOURCE: Hirshleifer, DeHaven, and Milliman, *Water Supply*, pp. 311, 313.

[a]For present purposes, southern California is defined as the coastal plains of Ventura, Los Angeles, Orange, San Bernardino, Riverside, and San Diego counties and the large metropolitan areas of Los Angeles and San Diego.

[b]This is an average figure, but not the one used by the state planners. See the source cited.

[c]Because of rounding errors, the urban figure plus the irrigation figure may not equal the total figure.

of providing water from the Feather River would be about $60 per acre-foot.[25] If the Rand estimates were correct, should the officials have based their estimates on the assumption that the price would be $60, not $30? Why or why not? If, in fact, water users are charged $30 per acre-foot, but the marginal cost is $60, is the quantity of water demanded at an efficient level?

(b) The Rand study questioned whether a new supply of water was needed for California, at least in the immediate future. According to Rand,

> The most obvious alternative is to raise the price to water-users as the capacity limit [of the existing water supply system] is approached, so that efficient use tends to be insured. Only when the price . . . comes to equal the incremental cost of the new supply is that new supply economically justified. It seems clear that a period of rising water prices should intervene before incremental supplies costing at least $60 an acre-foot . . . are introduced to this area — if, indeed, importation of Feather River water is the best new source, and accepting the official cost estimate.[26]

Do you agree? If so, why should the price of water be raised?

(c) Using official estimates, the Rand economists calculated the present value of the Feather River project's costs and receipts, as well as the net present value. Also, they calculated an adjusted net present value, which takes account of the project's flood-control benefits and salvage value. Do the results, shown in Table 19.3, indicate that the project was economically justified? Why or why not?

TABLE 19.3 Estimated Present Values of Receipts and Costs, Feather River Project

	Discount Rate	
	2.7 percent	5 percent
	(millions of dollars)	
Present value of receipts	1,079	515
Present value of costs	1,241	1,035
Net present value	−162	−520
Adjusted net present value	−97	−502

SOURCE: Hirshleifer, DeHaven, and Milliman, *Water Supply*, p. 340.

---

[25] Hirshleifer, DeHaven, and Milliman, *Water Supply*.

[26] Ibid., p. 318.

PROPERTY RIGHTS: CAN YOU APPLY THE THEORY?

The final three problems pertain to the nature and effects of property rights regarding water, to suggested solutions of California's water crisis, and to 1992 federal legislation to change water policy in California.

PROBLEM 19.8: The California rice farmers have been the water guzzlers that everyone in the state has seemed to like to hate, particularly during droughts. Surprising as it may be, they have used more water than all the households in Los Angeles and San Francisco combined. In 1988, over 200,000 acres of the state were used to grow rice, which many people feel is more appropriate for the soggy fields of Southeast Asia than for the California desert. The ancestors of these rice farmers were the first settlers on the banks of the Sacramento River, and under the existing system of property rights, they owned the land and the water that went by it. In the 1930s, the federal government, wanting to build the Shasta Dam (see Figure 19.1), asked whether the rice farmers would be willing to give the federal government their water and then buy it back. They said yes, if their water would forever be the lowest priced and most plentiful in the state, even during droughts.

(a) In 1990, the state of California offered the rice farmers $125 per acre-foot for their federal water. Said Al Driver, who owns a 2,400-acre ranch on which 1,046 acres of rice are grown, "None of us here want to be knot-headed about it. But we don't care for it, and we're not going to do it."[27] As Tim Leathers, the manager of a water district near Grimes, California, put it, "We don't trust the system."[28] Why is it that they were overwhelmingly opposed to accepting what was seemingly a generous offer?

Governor Pete Wilson

(b) Droughts have been a recurring problem in California. When California experienced a series of droughts from 1975 to 1977, many communities adopted water conservation programs which ruled out washing cars and watering lawns. In May 1991, after 5 consecutive dry years, residents of Los Angeles were required by city ordinance to cut back water usage by 15 percent. During a recent drought, Governor Pete Wilson announced that he might have to invoke emergency powers if the drought got worse. George Miller, a member of Congress from California, asked state and federal authorities to seize the rice farmers' water rather than permit them to "shake down" taxpayers by buying water for a pittance and selling it at high prices.[29] Do you think that the state or federal government should be empowered to seize water if someone other than the present recipient is willing to pay more for it than it costs the present recipient? Why or why not?

(c) The federal government supports the price of rice, and federal subsidies account for about one-third of the rice farmers' income. According to the *New York Times,* rice farmers have been afraid that, if they idled their land, they would lose federal subsidies.[30] Richard Howitt of the

---

[27] *New York Times,* April 7, 1991, p. 20.

[28] Ibid.

[29] Ibid.

[30] Ibid.

University of California at Davis has estimated that a rice farmer who lost his or her subsidy of $260 per acre would need to get $200 for an acre-foot of water to break even. If you were a rice farmer who felt that there was a .5 probability that your federal subsidy would be lost if you sold your water and idled the land (and that there was a .5 probability that it would not be lost if you did so), what would be the expected profit from selling an acre-foot of water for $125? (Assume that the profit from selling it at this price is $110 if your federal subsidy is not lost.) How large would this probability have to be to induce a risk-neutral farmer to refuse to sell water for this reason alone?

PROBLEM 19.9: In 1991, Senators Bill Bradley of New Jersey and Alan Cranston of California introduced the Central Valley Project Improvement Act, legislation aimed at dealing with California's water problems. Among other things, this proposed legislation called for a ban on renewal of federal water contracts for longer than 1 year until specified fish and wildlife and water quality improvements were met. However, if a contractor would agree to cut back the amount of water received by 20 percent, then 20-year renewals were available.

(a) Calvin Dooley, the California representative cited above, commented as follows on the provision of the proposed legislation: "You know, I am a farmer myself, as my family has been for about four generations. And I guess one of the issues that is of great concern to me and a lot of other farmers . . . is the one-year contract renewal process . . ."[31] If federal water contracts could not be renewed for more than a year, what problems might arise for farmers who need to obtain financing for their operations? For a reallocation of water to occur, is it necessary for the 1 year contract renewal process to be accepted?

(b) The reaction of former Los Angeles Mayor Tom Bradley, also cited above, to the proposed legislation was: "It is time for overhaul of the federal government's water policies as relate to the Central Valley Project. We need a fair resource balance to serve the needs of the urban areas of our state, the agricultural needs as well as the wildlife regions of California. I do not regard this bill as an effort to impose the will of Washington on Californians. There is no consensus in California, unfortunately."[32] How can one determine what a fair resource balance is? If farmers and city dwellers cannot agree on this, is it impossible to be sure that any change is really desirable?

(c) Responding to the Los Angeles mayor, Senator Bill Bradley said,

---

[31] Subcommittee on Water and Power, *Central Valley Project Improvement Act,* p. 190.
[32] Ibid., p. 43.

It has often occurred to me what if there was, in the Los Angeles Basin somewhere, one of the largest oil refineries in the world that was built by the federal government prior to World War II and at that time had entered into contracts with certain motorists for 20¢-a-gallon gasoline and those contracts were good for 40 years. They are up now. The question is: Should we renew those contracts again for 20¢ a gallon of gasoline? It is not an exact parallel, but there are some real parallels between that . . . circumstance and what prevails today in California water. I am sure that you would want to make sure that people who were paying $1.60 or $1.70 were now given the opportunity to get some of that 20¢-a-gallon gasoline or at least see that the 20¢-a-gallon gasoline people pay a little bit more or have the right to sell it when they get it.[33] Would the rice farmers agree that this is a close parallel? Why or why not?

PROBLEM 19.10: On October 30, 1992, President George Bush signed into law a bill sponsored by Representative George Miller and Senator Bill Bradley that allowed farmers to sell their water from the Central Valley Project and that increased the amount of water available for fisheries and environmental purposes.[34] Under this bill, the first 800,000 acre-feet of water from the Central Valley Project are devoted to keeping wetlands wet. Farmers are permitted to renew their contracts for the remaining 6 or 7 million acre-feet and can sell their water for whatever price it will bring. However, they will be charged much higher prices for the last 20 percent of the water delivered, and a fee will be imposed to support a $50 million-a-year program to limit environmental damage.

Farmers have objected strenuously to this bill. Pete Wilson, governor of California, has called it "a vicious economic blow to California."[35] After its passage, farm leaders said they would try to minimize its effects. According to Stephen Hall, executive director of the California Farm Water Coalition, "If it's implemented in a way that farmers don't feel is just, they will litigate."[36]

(a) Do you think that economic efficiency will be promoted if farmers' water rights are entirely transferable and if they charge whatever price they want for their water? Why or why not? Will the marginal rate of

---

[33] Ibid., pp. 47–48.

[34] *New York Times,* November 1, 1992, p. 39.

[35] *New York Times,* October 29, 1992, p. D2.

[36] *New York Times,* November 1, 1992, p. 39. Also see R. Smith, "Sinking or Swimming in Water Policy," *Regulation,* No. 3, 1994.

technical substitution of water for nonwater inputs be the same for all firms, whether agricultural or manufacturing? Why or why not? Will the opportunity cost of continuing to apply an acre-foot of water to agricultural uses equal the price that urban communities are willing to pay for an extra acre-foot? Why or why not? Will urbanites no longer value an extra acre-foot of water more highly than farmers? Why or why not?

(b) Farmers getting water from the Central Valley Project worried in the past that, if they saved a portion of their water, they might lose their future rights to the saved quantity of water. (This was sometimes called "use it or lose it.") Was this likely to result in wasteful use of water? If so, is the same sort of waste likely to occur if water rights are entirely transferable and if farmers charge what they like for their water? Why or why not?

(c) In contrast to the above scheme, suppose that urbanites, not farmers, were given the water rights and that they could charge the farmers whatever price they wanted for their water. (In this scheme, the farmers would buy water from urbanites, not the other way around.) Whether or not it is equitable, would this scheme promote economic efficiency? Why or why not?

(d) Has the previous lack of clear, transferable property rights made it difficult to achieve economic efficiency? Why or why not?

(e) Is economic efficiency the only consideration in trying to solve California's water problems? If not, what other considerations are important?

(f) What measures, if any, would you favor to improve the allocation of water in California?

CONCLUSION

Whatever your political views, and whether you are a farmer or an apartment dweller, it should be clear at this point that the concepts and models discussed in the previous chapter are of great importance in trying to formulate a feasible and sensible solution to California's water problems. Concepts and models related to the Pareto criterion, economic efficiency, the Edgeworth box diagram, marginal cost pricing, external diseconomies, and other topics discussed in the previous chapter are valuable tools that help us to analyze important public policy issues like this one. To understand the arguments advanced by various interested parties and to be an effective analyst and advocate of whatever policy you come to favor, the tools of microeconomics are essential.

SELECTED SUPPLEMENTARY READINGS

1. R. Smith, "Sinking or Swimming in Water Policy," *Regulation,* no. 3, 1994.
2. "As Drought Looms, Farmers in California Blame Politics," *New York Times,* June 24, 1994.
3. R. Wahl, *Markets for Federal Water* (Washington, D.C.: Resources for the Future, 1989).
4. E. P. LeVeen and L. King, *Turning Off the Tap on Federal Water Subsidies,* Vol. 1 (San Francisco: National Resources Defense Council, 1985).
5. J. Hirshleifer, J. DeHaven, and J. Milliman, *Water Supply* (Chicago: University of Chicago, 1969).
6. Subcommittee on Water and Power, *Central Valley Project Improvement Act* (Washington, D.C.: Government Printing Office, 1992).

Appendix

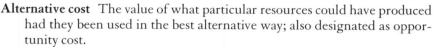

GLOSSARY OF TERMS

Alternative cost The value of what particular resources could have produced had they been used in the best alternative way; also designated as opportunity cost.

Arc elasticity of demand If P_1 and Q_1 are the first values of price and quantity demanded, and P_2 and Q_2 are the second set, the arc elasticity equals $-(Q_1 - Q_2)(P_1 + P_2) \div (P_1 - P_2)(Q_1 + Q_2)$.

Asymmetric information In some markets, all participants do not have the same information. For example, in the market for used cars, sellers frequently have better information regarding the quality of a used car than prospective buyers do.

Average cost Total cost divided by output. It is also called average total cost.

Average fixed cost Total fixed cost divided by output.

Average product Total output divided by the quantity of input.

Average variable cost Total variable cost divided by output.

Break-even chart A chart showing how both total revenue and total cost vary with changes in the total number of units of a product that is sold. The break-even point is the minimum number that must be sold to avoid loss.

Budget line A line showing all combinations of quantities of good X and good Y the consumer can buy. Its slope equals -1 times the price of good X divided by the price of good Y.

Bundling A marketing technique whereby a firm that sells two products requires customers who buy one of them to buy the other as well.

Capital Equipment, buildings, inventories, raw materials, and other non-human producible resources that contribute to the production, marketing, and distribution of goods and services.

Capitalism A type of economic system that depends on the price system to answer the basic economic questions: What is produced? How is it produced? Who gets how much? What should be the rate of economic growth?

Cardinal utility Utility that is measurable in a cardinal sense, like a person's weight or height (which means that the difference between two utilities, that is, marginal utility, is meaningful). This is in contrast to ordinal utility, which is measurable in only an ordinal sense.

Cartel A form of market structure in which there is an open and formal agreement among firms to collude.

Cobb-Douglas production function A production function where $Q = AL^{\alpha_1}K^{\alpha_2}M^{\alpha_3}$. In this equation, Q is the output rate, L is the quantity of labor, K is the quantity of capital, M is the quantity of raw materials, A, α_1, α_2, and α_3 are constants.

Collusion Agreements by firms with others in their industry with regard to price, output, and other matters.

Complements If goods X and Y are complements, the quantity demanded of X is inversely related to the price of Y.

Constant-cost industry An industry with a horizontal long-run supply curve; its expansion does not result in an increase or decrease in input prices.

Constant returns to scale If the quantities of all inputs are increased by the same percentage, and if as a result output increases by the same percentage, there are constant returns to scale.

Consumer surplus The maximum amount that the consumer would pay for a particular good or service less the amount that he or she actually pays for it.

Contestable market A market in which entry is absolutely free and exit is absolutely costless. The essence of contestable markets is that they are vulnerable to hit-and-run entry.

Contract curve The locus of points where the marginal rates of substitution are the same for both consumers (in exchange between consumers) or the locus of points where the marginal rates of technical substitution are the same for both products (in exchange between producers).

Corner solution Case in which the budget line reaches the highest achievable indifference curve at a point along an axis. (Analogous cases occur in the theory of production too.)

Cross elasticity of demand The percentage change in the quantity demanded of good X resulting from a 1 percent change in the price of good Y.

Deadweight loss from monopoly If a perfectly competitive market is transformed into a monopoly, the deadweight loss is the reduction in total surplus resulting from this transformation.

Deadweight loss from monopsony If a perfectly competitive market is transformed into a monopsony, the deadweight loss is the reduction in total surplus resulting from this transformation.

Decreasing-cost industry An industry with a negatively sloped long-run supply curve; its expansion results in a decrease in its average cost.

Decreasing returns to scale If the quantities of all inputs are increased by the same percentage, and if as a result output increases by less than this percentage, there are decreasing returns to scale.

Demand curve A curve showing the amount of a product demanded at each price.

Demand curve for loanable funds Relationship between the quantity of loanable funds demanded and the interest rate.

Discount rate When an interest rate is used to calculate the net present value of an investment, the interest rate is called the discount rate.

Dominant firm In an oligopolistic industry, a single large firm that sets the price, but lets the small firms in the industry sell all they want at that price.

Dominant strategy A strategy that is best for a player regardless of what the other player's strategy may be.

Duopoly A form of market structure in which there are two sellers. The Cournot model, among others, is concerned with duopoly.

Economic efficiency A situation in which all changes that harm no one and improve the well-being of some people have been carried out. Such a situation is economically efficient (or Pareto efficient or Pareto optimal).

Economic profit The difference between a firm's revenues and its costs, where the latter include the returns that could be gotten from the most lucrative alternative use of the firm's resources.

Economic region of production The input combinations for which isoquants are negatively sloped. No profit-maximizing firm will operate at a point where the isoquant has a positive slope, since the marginal product of one or the other input must be negative.

Economic resource A scarce resource, which commands a nonzero price.

Economies of scope Economies resulting from the scope rather than the scale of the enterprise. They exist where it is less costly to combine two or more product lines in one firm than to produce them separately.

Endowment position The consumer's income each year.

Engel curve The relationship between the equilibrium quantity purchased of a good and the consumer's level of income. It was named after Ernst Engel, a nineteenth-century German statistician.

Equilibrium A situation in which there is no tendency for change. For example, an equilibrium price is a price that can be maintained.

Excess capacity The difference between the minimum-cost output and the actual output in a long-run equilibrium. A famous and controversial conclusion of the theory of monopolistic competition is that firms under this form of market structure will tend to operate with excess capacity.

Expansion path The locus of points where the isoquants corresponding to various outputs are tangent to the isocost curves. (No inputs are fixed.)

Expected monetary value To determine the expected monetary value of a gamble, calculate the sum of the amount of money gained (or lost) if each outcome occurs times the probability of occurrence of the outcome.

Expected value of perfect information The amount by which the expected monetary value increases as a consequence of the decision maker's having access to perfect information. It is the maximum amount that the decision maker should pay to obtain perfect information.

Explicit costs The ordinary expenses of the firm that accountants include, such as payroll costs and payments for raw materials.

External diseconomy An uncompensated cost to one person or firm resulting from the consumption or output of another person or firm.

External economy An uncompensated benefit to one person or firm resulting from the consumption or output of another person or firm.

First-mover advantages The advantages that accrue to the player who makes the first move in a game.

Fixed cost The total cost per period of time of the fixed inputs.

Fixed input A resource used in the production process (such as plant and equipment) whose quantity cannot be changed during the period under consideration.

Free resource A resource that is so abundant that it can be had for a zero price.

General equilibrium analysis An analysis that (in contrast to a partial equilibrium analysis) takes account of the interrelationships among various markets and prices.

Giffen's paradox A situation in which the quantity demanded of a good is directly related to its price. This occurs when the substitution effect of a price change is not strong enough to offset an inferior good's income effect.

Implicit costs The alternative costs of using the resources owned by the firm's owner, such as his or her time and capital.

Income-consumption curve A curve connecting points representing equilibrium market baskets corresponding to all possible levels of the consumer's money income. Curves of this sort can be used to derive Engel curves.

Income effect The change in the quantity demanded of good X due entirely to a change in the consumer's level of satisfaction, all prices being held constant.

Income elasticity of demand The percentage change in quantity demanded resulting from a 1 percent change in consumer income, when prices are held constant.

Increasing-cost industry An industry with a positively sloped long-run supply curve; its expansion results in an increase in input prices.

Increasing returns to scale If the quantities of all inputs are increased by the same percentage, and if as a result output increases by more than this percentage, there are increasing returns to scale.

Indifference curve The locus of points representing market baskets among which the consumer is indifferent.

Inferior good A good where the income effect is such that increases in real income result in decreases in the quantity demanded.

Input Any resource used in the production process.

Interest rate The premium received by the lender 1 year hence if he or she lends a dollar for a year. If the interest rate equals r, he or she receives $(1+r)$ dollars a year hence.

Intermediate good A good that is used to produce other goods and services.

Investment The process of creating new capital assets.

Investment demand curve The relationship between the total amount of investment and the rate of return from an extra dollar of investment.

Isocost curve A curve showing the combinations of inputs that can be obtained for a fixed total outlay.

Isoquant A curve showing all possible (efficient) combinations of inputs that are capable of producing a certain quantity of output.

Kinked demand curve A demand curve facing an oligopolist on which there is a kink at the existing price, demand being more elastic for price increases than for price decreases.

Labor Human effort, physical or mental, used to produce goods and services.

Land Natural resources, including both minerals and plots of ground, used to produce goods and services.

Law of diminishing marginal returns According to this law, if equal increments of an input are added (and if the quantities of other inputs are held constant), the resulting increments of product will decrease beyond some point; that is, the marginal product of the input will diminish.

Law of diminishing marginal utility According to this law, as a person consumes more and more of a given commodity (the consumption of other commodities being held constant), the marginal utility of the commodity eventually will tend to decline.

Lerner index A measure of the amount of monopoly power possessed by a firm. Specifically, it equals $(P-MC)/P$, where P is the firm's price and MC is its marginal cost.

Limit pricing A form of pricing in which price is set so as to bar entry. A limit price is one that discourages or prevents entry.

Long run The period of time in which all inputs are variable. The firm can change completely the resources it uses in the long run.

Marginal cost The addition to total cost resulting from the addition of the last unit of output.

Marginal cost pricing A pricing rule whereby firms or government-owned enterprises set price equal to marginal cost.

Marginal expenditure curve A curve showing the additional cost to the firm of increasing its utilization of input X by 1 unit.

Marginal product The addition to total output due to the addition of the last unit of an input (when the quantity of other inputs is held constant).

Marginal rate of product transformation The negative of the slope of the production possibilities curve.

Marginal rate of substitution The number of units of good Y that must be given up if the consumer, after receiving an extra unit of good X, is to maintain a constant level of satisfaction.

Marginal revenue The addition to total revenue due to selling 1 more unit of the product.

Marginal revenue product The increase in total revenue due to the use of an additional unit of input X. It equals the marginal product of input X times the firm's marginal revenue.

Marginal utility The additional satisfaction (that is, utility) derived from an additional unit of a commodity (when the levels of consumption of all other commodities are held constant).

Market A group of firms and individuals in touch with each other in order to buy or sell some good.

Market demand curve A curve that shows the relationship between a product's price and the quantity of it demanded in the entire market.

Market demand schedule A table that shows the relationship between a product's price and the quantity of it demanded in the entire market.

Market structure Four general types of market structure are perfect competition, monopoly, monopolistic competition, and oligopoly. The structure of a market depends on the number of buyers and sellers, as well as the extent of product differentiation and other factors.

Market supply schedule A table showing the quantity of a good that would be supplied at various prices.

Markup A percentage (or absolute) amount added to a product's estimated average (or marginal) cost to obtain its price; this amount is meant to include costs that cannot be allocated to any specific product and to provide a return on the firm's investment.

Maximin strategy A strategy in which the player maximizes the minimum gain that can be achieved.

Microeconomics The part of economics dealing with the economic behavior of individual units such as consumers, firms, and resource owners (in contrast to macroeconomics, which deals with the behavior of economic aggregates like gross domestic product).

Minimum efficient size of plant The smallest size of plant for which long-run average cost is at or close to its minimum value.

Model A theory based on assumptions that simplify and abstract from reality, from which predictions or conclusions about the real world are deduced.

Money income　Income of the consumer measured in actual dollar amounts per period of time.

Monopolistic competition　A market structure in which there are many sellers of differentiated products, entry is easy, and there is no collusion among sellers.

Monopoly　A market structure in which there is only one seller of a product. Public utilities often are examples.

Monopsony　A market structure in which there is only a single buyer. A firm that hires all the labor in a company town is an example.

Multinational firm　A firm that invests in other countries, and produces and markets its products abroad.

Multiplant monopoly　A monopolist that owns and operates more than one plant, and that must determine the output for each of its plants.

Multiproduct firm　A firm that produces more than one product. For example, DuPont produces a wide variety of chemical, oil, and other products.

Nash equilibrium　An equilibrium in game theory where, given that every other player's strategy is what it is, each player has no reason to change his or her own strategy.

Natural monopoly　An industry in which the average cost of production reaches a minimum at an output rate large enough to satisfy the entire market; thus competition cannot be sustained and one firm becomes the monopolist.

Nonprice competition　Rivalry among firms based on the use of advertising and other marketing weapons, as well as on the variation in product characteristics due to research and development and styling changes.

Normal goods　Goods that experience increases in quantity demanded in response to increases in the consumer's real income.

Oligopoly　A market structure in which there are only a few sellers of products that can be identical or differentiated. Examples are the markets for computers or petroleum.

Oligopsony　A market structure in which there are a few buyers.

Opportunity cost　The value of what particular resources could have produced if they had been used in the best alternative way; also designated as alternative cost.

Optimal input combination　The combination of inputs that is economically efficient or that maximizes profit (that is, that is optimal from a profit-maximizing firm's point of view).

Ordinal utility　Utility that is measurable in an ordinal sense, which means that a consumer can only rank various market baskets with respect to the satisfaction they give him or her.

Pareto criterion A criterion to determine whether a particular change is an improvement; according to this criterion, a change that harms no one and improves the lot of some people (in their own eyes) is an improvement.

Partial equilibrium analysis An analysis assuming (in contrast to a general equilibrium analysis) that changes in price in a particular market can occur without causing significant changes in price in other markets.

Perfect competition A market structure in which there are many sellers of identical products, no one buyer or seller has control over price, entry is easy, and resources can switch readily from one use to another. Examples having many of the characteristics of perfectly competitive markets include many agricultural markets.

Predatory pricing The practice of setting price at a low level in order to drive a rival firm out of business.

Present value The value today of a payment, or stream of payments, now and in the future (or in the past).

Price ceiling A government-imposed maximum for the price of a particular good. For example, New York City's rent controls impose a ceiling on rents.

Price-consumption curve A curve connecting the various equilibrium points corresponding to market baskets chosen by the consumer at various prices of a commodity.

Price discrimination The practice whereby one buyer is charged more than another buyer for the same product.

Price elastic The demand for a product if its price elasticity of demand exceeds 1.

Price elasticity of demand The percentage change in quantity demanded resulting from a 1 percent change in price (by convention, always expressed as a positive number).

Price elasticity of supply The percentage change in quantity supplied resulting from a 1 percent change in price.

Price floor A government-imposed minimum for the price of a particular good. For example, federal farm programs have imposed floors for the prices of wheat and corn.

Price inelastic The demand for a product if its price elasticity of demand is less than 1.

Price leader A firm in an oligopolistic industry that sets a price that other firms are willing to follow.

Price system A system whereby each good and service has a price, and which in a purely capitalistic economy carries out the basic functions of an economic system (determining what will be produced, how it will be produced, how much of it each person will get, and what the country's growth of per capita output will be).

Principal-agent problem The problem that arises because managers or workers may pursue their own objectives, even though this reduces the profits of the owners of the firm. The managers or workers are agents who work for the owners, who are the principals.

Prisoners' dilemma A situation in which two persons (or firms) would both do better to cooperate than not to cooperate, but where each feels it is in his or her interests not to do so; thus each fares worse than if they cooperated.

Private cost The expense incurred by the individual user to obtain the use of a resource.

Probability The proportion of times that a particular outcome occurs over the long run. For example, if a die is thrown many, many times, and if it comes up a 1 on 1/6 of the times, the probability of its coming up a 1 is 1/6.

Producer surplus Includes the aggregate profits of firms producing the good, plus the amount that owners of inputs (used to make the good) are compensated above and beyond the minimum they would insist on. Geometrically, it equals the area above the supply curve and below the price.

Production possibilities curve A curve showing the various combinations of quantities of two products that can be produced with a given amount of resources.

Production function The relationship between the quantities of various inputs used per period of time and the maximum amount of output that can be produced per period of time.

Profit The difference between a firm's revenue and its costs

Public good A good that is nonrival and nonexclusive. By nonrival, we mean that the marginal cost of providing the good to an additional consumer is zero. By nonexclusive, we mean that people cannot be excluded from consuming the good (whether or not they pay for it).

Quasi-rent A payment to an input in temporarily fixed supply. For example, in the short run, a firm's plant cannot be altered, and the payments to this and other fixed inputs are quasi-rents.

Ray A line that starts from some point and goes off into space. If capital is on one axis, and labor is on the other, a ray from the origin describes all input combinations where the capital-labor ratio is constant.

Reaction curve A curve showing how much one duopolist will produce and sell, depending on how much it thinks the other duopolist will produce and sell.

Rent The return paid to an input that is fixed in supply.

Ridge lines Lines (on a graph with capital on one axis and labor on the other axis) between which are included all input combinations that would be chosen by a profit-maximizing firm.

Risk averters When confronted with gambles with equal expected monetary values, risk averters prefer a gamble with a more-certain outcome to one with a less-certain outcome.

Risk lovers When confronted with gambles with equal expected monetary values, risk lovers prefer a gamble with a less-certain outcome to one with a more-certain outcome.

Risk neutral Risk neutral individuals do not care whether a gamble has a less-certain or more-certain outcome. They choose among gambles on the basis of expected monetary value alone; specifically, they maximize expected monetary value.

Saving When a consumer refrains from consuming part of the income he or she receives, this is saving.

Second-degree price discrimination A monopolist charges a different price, depending on how much the consumer purchases, thus increasing its revenue and profit.

Selling expenses The expenses of advertising and distributing a product and of trying to convince potential customers that they should buy it.

Short run A period of time in which some of the firm's inputs (generally its plant and equipment) are fixed in quantity.

Social cost The cost to society of producing a given commodity or taking a particular action. This cost may not equal the private cost.

Static efficiency Efficiency when technology and tastes are fixed. If departures from static efficiency result in a faster rate of technological change and productivity increase, they may lead to a higher level of consumer satisfaction than if the conditions for static efficiency are met.

Strategic move A move that influences the other person's choice in a manner favorable to one's self, by affecting the other person's expectations of how one will behave.

Substitutes If goods X and Y are substitutes, the quantity demanded of X is directly related to the price of Y.

Substitution effect The change in the quantity demanded of a good resulting from a price change when the level of satisfaction of the consumer is held constant.

Supply curve A curve that shows how much of a product will be supplied at each level of the product's price.

Supply curve of loanable funds The relationship between the quantity of loanable funds supplied and the interest rate.

Target return A desired rate of return that a firm hopes to achieve by means of markup pricing.

Technological change New ways of producing existing products, new designs enabling the production of new products, and new techniques of organization, marketing, and management.

Technology Society's pool of knowledge regarding how goods and services can be produced from a given amount of resources.

Third-degree price discrimination A situation in which a monopolist sells a good in more than one market, the good cannot be transferred from one market and resold in another, and the monopolist can set different prices in different markets.

Tit for tat A strategy in game theory in which each player does on this round what the other player did on the previous round.

Total cost The sum of a firm's total fixed cost and total variable cost.

Total cost function Relationship between a firm's total cost and its output.

Total fixed cost A firm's total expenditure on fixed inputs per period of time.

Total revenue A firm's total dollar sales volume per period of time.

Total surplus The sum of consumer and producer surpluses.

Total utility A number representing the level of satisfaction that a consumer derives from a particular market basket.

Total variable cost A firm's total expenditure on variable inputs per period of time.

Transferable emissions permits Permits to generate a certain amount of pollution, limited in number, that are allocated among firms and that can be bought or sold.

Two-part tariff A pricing technique whereby the consumer pays an initial fee for the right to buy the product as well as a usage fee for each unit of the product that he or she buys.

Tying A marketing technique whereby a firm producing a product that will function only if used in conjunction with another product requires its customers to buy the latter product from it, rather than from alternative suppliers.

Unitary elasticity A price elasticity of demand equal to 1.

Utility A number that represents the level of satisfaction that the consumer derives from a particular market basket is the utility attached by the consumer to this market basket.

Utility-possibility curve A curve showing the maximum utility that one person can achieve, given the utility achieved by another person.

Value of marginal product The marginal product of an input (that is, the extra output resulting from an extra unit of the input) multiplied by the product's price.

Variable cost The total cost per period of time of the variable inputs.

Variable input A resource used in the production process whose quantity can be changed during the particular period under consideration.

von Neumann-Morgenstern utility function A function showing the utility that a decision maker attaches to each possible outcome of a gamble; it shows the decision maker's preferences with regard to risk.

Winner's curse If a number of bids are made for a particular piece of land (or other good or asset), and if the bidders' estimates of the land's value are approximately correct, on the average, the highest bidder is likely to pay more for the land than it is worth, if each bidder bids what he or she thinks the land is worth.

BRIEF ANSWERS TO ODD-NUMBERED QUESTIONS AND PROBLEMS

CHAPTER 1

1. (a) Let P_1 be the "bargain" price of $19.92, P_2 be the preconvention price of $29, Q_{D1} be the quantity of lunches demanded at the "bargain" price, and Q_{D2} be the quantity demanded at the preconvention price. Then the arc elasticity of demand equals

$$\eta = -\frac{\Delta Q_D}{(Q_{D1} + Q_{D2})/2} \div \frac{\Delta P}{(P_1 + P_2)/2}$$

$$= -\frac{150 - 40}{(150 + 40)/2} \div \frac{19.92 - 29}{(19.92 + 29)/2} = 3.1.$$

Thus, the price elasticity of demand equals 3.1. (b) Yes. Le Perigord reduced its price by ($29 − $19.92) ÷ $29 = 31 percent; the other restaurant reduced its price by ($24 − $19.92) ÷ $24 = 17 percent since its preconvention price was $29 − $5 = $24. Given that the price elasticity of demand is the same at both restaurants, the percentage increase in quantity demanded must be greater at Le Perigord than at the other restaurant because Le Perigord reduced its price by a greater percentage that the other restaurant did. (c) Yes. Yes. Daily expenditure on lunches was 40 × $29 = $1,160 before the price reduction and 150 × $19.92 = $2,988 afterward. This is consistent with our finding in part (a) that the price elasticity of demand is 3.1. As pointed out on page 10, if the price elasticity of demand exceeds 1, a price reduction must lead to an increase in expenditure. (d) Le Perigord increased its daily revenue from lunches by $2,988 − $1,160 = $1,828. If the extra cost of serving the 150 − 40 = 110 extra lunches exceeded $1,828, it lost money.

3. (a) According to the economic consultant's demand curve, about 60,000 tickets will be purchased if the price of a ticket is $400; about 70,000 will be purchased if the price is $200. Thus the arc elasticity of demand is

$$\frac{-(70,000 - 60,000)}{(70,000 + 60,000)/2} \div \frac{200 - 400}{(200 + 400)/2} = 0.23.$$

This is quite different from Verleger's finding (that the price elasticity is 0.67). (b) Such an increase in price would reduce the *quantity of tickets demanded*, but it would *not* shift the demand curve. In other words, there would be a *movement along* the demand curve from a point corresponding to the old price to a point corresponding to the new price, but no *shift* in the demand curve. (c) Yes, it may shift it to the left, because fewer people will travel between these two cities for vacations and recreation, and because business travel may also be curtailed. (d) No, but it does affect the supply curve, which is shifted to the left.

5. Since the quantity supplied (Q_S) must equal the quantity demanded (Q_D), we have two equations to be solved simultaneously:

$$120 - 3Q_D = 5Q_S$$
$$Q_D = Q_S.$$

Letting quantity equal Q, it follows that

$$120 - 3Q = 5Q$$
$$120 = 8Q$$
$$15 = Q.$$

Since $P = 5Q$, it follows that $P = 75$. Thus the equilibrium price is 75 cents and the equilibrium quantity is 15 million pounds per year.

7.

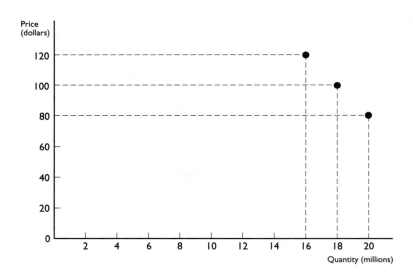

(a) $\eta = -\dfrac{20 - 18}{(20 + 18)/2} \div \dfrac{80 - 100}{(80 + 100)/2} = 0.47.$

(b) $\eta = -\dfrac{18 - 16}{(18 + 16)/2} \div \dfrac{100 - 120}{(100 + 120)/2} = 0.65.$

9. $100. Excess demand. Excess supply.

11. With the excise tax, the supply curve is

Price (dollars)	Quantity supplied (millions)
100	14
120	16
140	18
160	19

Thus the equilibrium price of a camera is $120, since at this price the quantity supplied equals the quantity demanded. If the government sets a price ceiling of $100, there will be a shortage of 4 million cameras per year, since the quantity demanded will equal 18 million while the quantity supplied will equal 14 million.

13. From Question 5,

$$P = 120 - 3Q_D,$$
$$3Q_D = 120 - P$$

or
$$Q_D = 40 - \tfrac{1}{3}P.$$

Also, $Q_S = \tfrac{1}{5}P$. Thus, if $P = 80$, $Q_D = 40 - 80/3 = 13\tfrac{1}{3}$, and $Q_S = 80/5 = 16$. Consequently, $Q_S - Q_D = 16 - 13\tfrac{1}{3} = 2\tfrac{2}{3}$, which means that the resulting surplus equals $2\tfrac{2}{3}$ million pounds per year. To reduce this surplus, the government could attempt to reduce the amount of cantaloupes produced by farmers or expand the demand for cantaloupes.

15. No. One.

CHAPTER 2

Problem 2.1:

(a) A regional market. Yes.

(b) Let X be the number of cases sold if the price had been $6.50 for six bottles. Since the arc price elasticity of demand equals 0.8,

$$-\frac{100,000 - X}{(100,000 + X)/2} \div \frac{5.99 - 6.50}{(5.99 + 6.50)/2} = 0.8.$$

Thus,

$$\frac{100,000 - X}{(100,000 + X)/2} = \left(\frac{1}{12.245}\right)(0.8) = .06533,$$

$$100,000 - X = \frac{.06533}{2}(100,000 + X)$$

$$96,734 = 1.03266X$$

$$93,675 = X.$$

(c) If Red Brick Ale is the only microbrew in Georgia, the demand curve for Red Brick Ale is the same as the demand curve for all microbrews in Georgia. Otherwise it is not.

(d) The demand curve for microbrews should shift to the left because mass-produced beer is a substitute for microbrews.

(e) Yes. If the demand curve were the same for both types of beer, the price would be higher for the type of beer with the supply curve that is farther to the left.

Problem 2.3:

(a) Many people feel that the consumption of alcoholic beverages should be discouraged.

(b) The price of beer will rise from $90 to $110 per barrel, and the quantity consumed will fall from 200 to 180 millions of barrels. This is because the supply curve shifts upward to position A below.

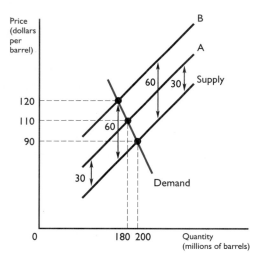

(c) No. The price to the consumer will go up by $20, which is less than the amount of the tax ($30).

(d) The amount spent on beer is 200 million × $90 = $18 billion before the tax; it is 180 million × $110 = $19.8 billion after the tax. Thus, it increases by $1.8 billion.

(e) As shown in the graph in the answer to part (b), the supply curve must have risen to position B if the price rose to $120 per barrel. Thus, the tax must have been increased by $30, from $30 to $60 per barrel.

(f) The lower tax rate provides the microbreweries with a competitive edge, because their outlay per barrel for taxes is lower than that of the big firms. However, if their outlay per barrel for labor, materials, and other inputs is higher than that of the big firms, this may more than off-set this tax advantage.

Problem 2.5:
(a) Because of the costs incurred by suppliers due to government seizures of their product and their assets, as well as the high wages that must be paid workers for the risk of arrest and imprisonment. Also, consumers in the United States are willing and able to pay more than in many South American markets.

(b) Yes. If cocaine were legal, the costs incurred to avoid arrest and impris-onment, as well as the costs due to government seizures, would not have to be incurred. Thus, the supply curve would shift downward and to the right, with the result that the price of cocaine would fall.

(c) Yes, they are designed to shift it to the left.

(d) Yes. The percentage reduction in cocaine consumption due to a 2 per-cent increase in the price of cocaine equals two times the price elasticity of demand for cocaine (since the price elasticity of demand equals the percentage reduction in quantity demanded resulting from a 1 percent increase in price).

(e) Annual cocaine consumption will fall by $2 \times .5 = 1$ percent.

Problem 2.7:
(a) Yes, for the reasons given in Chapter 1, pages 31 to 33.

(b) Yes, for the reasons given in Chapter 1, pages 31 to 33.

(c) Because they are aware of the bids already made by other bidders. If they make a bid that is only slightly higher than that of some previous bidder, they can be confident that their evaluation of the item being auctioned off is not greatly above that of other bidders.

(d) It would be likely to be greater if buyers acted independently than if they colluded. For reasons given on page 33, if collusion occurs, the price received by the seller may be significantly less than if the buyers act independently.

(e) In a sealed-bid auction, no bidder can be sure that other bidders are act-ing in accord with whatever collusive agreement is made among them. Thus, it is harder to collude effectively than in an open auction in which every bidder knows what the others have bid, and whether they are conforming to the collusive agreement.

Problem 2.9:
(a) Yes, although there may be more heterogeneity among radio stations than among certain types of wheat, corn, or lamb chops.

(b) Yes. By approving over a thousand new radio stations, the FCC shifted the supply curve for radio stations to the right: this tended to reduce the price of a radio station.

(c) No, because the quantity of radio stations supplied would exceed the quantity demanded, since the price of a radio station would be above its equilibrium level.

(d) Yes, for the reasons given in the answer to part (c).

CHAPTER 3

1. $1,000 since the budget line intersects the vertical axis at 20. $Q_A = 20 - 0.5Q_B$, where Q_A is the quantity consumed of good A and Q_B is the quantity consumed of good B. $- 0.5$. It must be $1,000 ÷ 40, or $25. 0.5.

3. 1. It does not vary at all, at least in this range. No.

5. Martin will be better-off and will consume less bread. Because the $50 gift enables him, despite the price increase, to buy as much bread (and the other good) as he did before the price increase, the new budget line (after the price increase and gift) goes through point A, which corresponds to the old market basket Martin purchased. (See the figure below.) The new equilibrium market basket (point B) is on a higher indifference curve than point A, and contains less bread than point A.

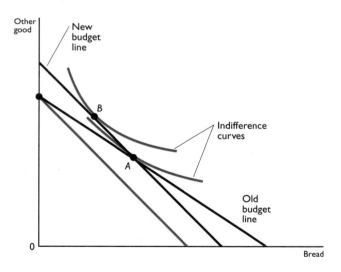

7. No. Los Angeles, because the price of a pear divided by the price of an apple is higher in Los Angeles.

9. He should set the ratio of the marginal utility of good X to its price equal to the ratio of the marginal utility of good Y to its price. If he buys 5 units

of good X and 1 unit of good Y, the total amount spent is $1,000, and this condition is met, since for each good this ratio equals 1 util $\div$ 10.

CHAPTER 4

1. (a) According to the diagram, a decrease in the price of good X from P_1 to P_2 results in an increase (from OA to OB) in the amount not spent on good X but spent on all other goods. This means that the consumer's expenditure on good X must have declined with a decrease in price, which implies that the consumer's demand for good X is price inelastic. (Recall page 10.) (b) If this price-consumption curve were downward sloping, a decrease in the price of good X would result in a decrease in the amount not spent on good X. Thus the consumer's expenditure on good X must be increased with a decrease in price; this implies that the consumer's demand for good X is price elastic. (Recall page 10.)

3. (a) The loss is the area under the demand curve from 5 to 10 trips, which equals $6+$4+$3+$2+$1, or $16. (b) Once a family buys the permit, a trip to the lake is free. Thus, if it buys the permit, it will make 10 trips per year, as shown by the demand curve. The maximum amount that each family would pay for these 10 trips is the area under the demand curve from 0 to 10 trips, which is $20+$16+$12+$10+$8+$6+$4+$3+$2+$1, or $82. Since the maximum amount exceeds $75, each family would find it worthwhile to buy the permit. (c) The calculations assume that these indifference curves are parallel. That is, if we measure the number of trips along the horizontal axis and the amount of money for all other goods along the vertical axis, the vertical distance between any two indifference curves is assumed to be the same regardless of where along the horizontal axis one measures this distance. (Recall footnote 8 in Chapter 4.)

5. (a) Yes. (b) If all consumers are maximizing utility (and if the optimal point is a tangency point, not a corner solution), the marginal rate of substitution of telephone calls for newspapers must equal the price of a telephone call divided by the price of a newspaper. (c) Yes, it equals $25 \div 25$, or 1.

7. Both part (b) and part (c) are true.

9. 3. Price elastic. Decrease.

CHAPTER 5

1. (a) A 1 percent increase in the price of electricity would cut electricity consumption by about 1.2 percent, because the price elasticity of demand is 1.2. A 6 percent increase in the price of natural gas would raise electricity consumption by about 1.2 percent, because the cross elasticity of demand is 0.2.

Thus, if the price of natural gas were to increase by about 6 percent, this would offset the effect of the increase in electricity's price. (b) On the basis of the data in the table given on page 159, a 10 percent increase in income seems to result in about a 1 percent increase in electricity consumption. Thus the income elasticity seems to be about 0.1, not 0.2, as reported by Chapman, Tyrell, and Mount. This discrepancy could be due to the fact that the inhabitants of this suburb regard electricity to be more of a necessity than all Americans do. (c) Both would be expected to be lower in the short run because consumers have less time to adapt to changes in income or price. In fact, Chapman, Tyrell, and Mount found both to be about 0.02 in the short run.

   3. (a) There are a considerable number of important substitutes, notably plastics, aluminum, and concrete. For example, buildings and bridges formerly requiring structural steel can now use prestressed concrete. (b) No, because the demand curve for the output of a single firm (Bethlehem) is not the same as the demand curve for the output of the steel industry as a whole. In general, we would expect the demand curve for the output of a single firm to be more price elastic than the industry's demand curve, because the output of other firms in the industry can be substituted for the output of the firm in question. (c) If the demand for a firm's product is inelastic, this means that its price elasticity of demand, η is less than 1. On the basis of Equation 5.3, it follows that, if η is less than 1, the firm's marginal revenue must be *negative*. Since marginal revenue is the change in total revenue attributable to the increase of one unit to sales, it follows that a *reduction* in the amount produced and sold by the firm would *increase* total revenue (because price would be raised enough to more than offset the smaller number of units sold). In a case of this sort, the firm could increase its profit by reducing its output (and raising its price). Why? Because profit equals total revenue minus total cost, and a reduction in output would increase total revenue and reduce total cost (since it would cost less to produce fewer units). Consequently, a reduction in output would increase profit; this means that the firm is not currently maximizing its profit. (d) The cross elasticity of demand is positive because Bethlehem's steel and imported Japanese steel are substitutes.

   5. Holding his income constant, the total amount he spends on Geritol is constant too; that is,

$$PQ = I,$$

where P is the price of Geritol, Q is the quantity demanded by the consumer, and I is his income. Thus

$$Q = \frac{I}{P}.$$

Since I is held constant, this demand curve is a rectangular hyperbola, and the price elasticity of demand equals 1. Since $Q = I/P$, it follows that a 1 percent increase in I will result in a 1 percent increase in Q when P is held constant. Thus the income elasticity of demand equals 1. Since Q does not depend on the price of any other good, the cross elasticity of demand equals 0.

7. Substitutes have a positive cross elasticity of demand. Therefore, cases (b) and (e) are likely to have a positive cross elasticity of demand.

9. It would indicate the extent to which fare increases would decrease subway travel. For example, if demand is price inelastic, fare increases would increase total revenue. Obviously this is an important fact.

11. Other factors—notably the general level of prices and incomes and the quality of the students—have not been held constant. Holding these factors—and the tuition rates at other universities—constant, it is almost surely untrue that large increases in tuition at this university would not cut down on the number of students demanding admission to the university.

13. The Engel curve shows the relationship between money income and the amount consumed of a particular commodity. If this relationship is a straight line through the origin, it follows that the amount consumed of this commodity is *proportional* to the consumer's money income. Thus a 1 percent increase in the consumer's money income results in a 1 percent increase in the amount consumed of this commodity. Consequently, the income elasticity of demand for this commodity equals 1.

15. If the price (monetary and nonmonetary) of using marijuana is pushed up enough, teenagers may turn to alcohol.

CHAPTER 6

Problem 6.1:

(a) Yes. Foreign oil could be produced and supplied for about $1.75 per barrel, whereas U.S. suppliers, if they produced more than 3.4 billion barrels per year, would require more than $1.75 per barrel to produce and supply an extra barrel.

(b) $1.75 per barrel. 2.1 billion barrels per year.

(c) $3.00 per barrel.

(d) The loss in consumer surplus equals the area to the left of the demand curve above $1.75 and below $3.00. This area equals ($3.00 − $1.75) (4.9 billion) + $\frac{1}{2}$($3.00 − $1.75) (5.5 billion − 4.9 billion) = $6.125 billion + $.375 billion = $6.5 billion per year.

Problem 6.3:

(a) By increasing the price of gasoline. This, of course, is what would happen in a free market.

(b) Increases in price of about 182 percent would be required. To see this, let Q_{D2} be the quantity demanded after the increase in price (from P_1 to P_2), Q_{D1} be the quantity demanded before the increase in price, η be the price elasticity of demand, $\Delta P = P_2 - P_1$, and $\Delta Q_D = Q_{D2} - Q_{D1}$. It follows from Equation 2.2 that $-\Delta Q_D (P_1 + P_2) \div \Delta P (Q_{D1} + Q_{D2}) = \eta$. If consumption is to be cut by 25 percent, Q_{D2} equals $0.75 Q_{D1}$, and $\Delta Q_D = -.25 Q_{D1}$. Thus, $.25\, Q_{D1}\,(P_1 + P_2) \div 1.75 Q_{D1} \Delta P = \eta$, or

$$\frac{\Delta P}{P_1 + P_2} = \frac{.25}{1.75\eta} = \frac{1}{7\eta}.$$

Consequently, if $\eta = 0.3$,

$$\frac{\Delta P}{P_1 + P_2} = \frac{1}{7 \times .3} = \frac{1}{2.1} = 0.476,$$

and (since $\Delta P = P_2 - P_1$),

$$\frac{P_2 - P_1}{P_1 + P_2} = 0.476.$$

Solving for P_2 in terms of P_1,[*]

$$P_2 = 2.82 P_1.$$

That is, the price must increase by 182 percent.

(c) Fortunately, subsequent analysis indicated that gasoline consumption did not have to be cut so severely, and it was possible to avoid both rationing and the enormous price increase set forth in the answer to part (b). However, there were substantial price increases.

Problem 6.5:

(a) 50¢ per gallon. The supply curve is shifted vertically by the amount of the tax. As you can see from the diagram, it must be raised by 50¢ per gallon to raise the price from $1 to $1.25. (To verify that this is true, note that the vertical distance from point M to point N equals 50¢.) Thus, the tax must equal 50¢.

(b) The loss in consumer surplus can be calculated from the diagram on page 176. It equals ($1.25 − $1.00)(90 billion) + $\frac{1}{2}$($1.25 − $1.00) (100 billion − 90 billion) = $23.75 billion.

(c) Yes. 25¢ per gallon less (since the tax is 50¢ but the increase in the price to the consumer is only 25¢).

(d) 50¢ × 90 billion gallons = $45 billion per year.

(e) KE. While she could still purchase OK units of goods other than gasoline if she spent her entire income on such goods, she could buy only 24 thousand gallons of gasoline if she spent her entire income on gasoline. To see this, note that her income equals $30,000, since she could buy a maximum of 30,000 gallons of gasoline when the price was $1 per gallon. Thus, when the price is $1.25, she can buy no more than 24,000 gallons.

---

[*] Since $(P_2 - P_1)/(P_1 + P_2) = 0.476$, it follows that $P_2 - P_1 = 0.476(P_1 + P_2)$, which means that $0.524 P_2 = 1.476 P_1$, or $P_2 = 2.82 P_1$.

(f) 4,000 gallons per year. 3,000 gallons per year. Yes. It would have reduced her consumption by 1,000 gallons per year.

(g) Because the rebate increases the amount of money she has to spend, but does not affect the price of gasoline or the price of goods other than gasoline. Thus, it raises the budget line, but does not affect its slope.

(h) $1,250, since it was big enough to allow her to increase her gasoline consumption by 1,000 gallons per year if she purchased only gasoline. Because the price of gasoline was $1.25 per gallon, her income must have gone up by $1,250.

(i) Yes. She would reduce her gasoline consumption by 500 gallons, from 4,000 to 3,500 gallons per year.

(j) Based on the case of Ms. Muller, it certainly could have this effect.

Problem 6.7:

(a) No, because this price elasticity of demand refers to the effect of a price change in the entire market on the quantity demanded in the entire market. This is quite different from the effect of a price change in Washington, D.C. on the quantity demanded in Washington, D.C. when gas stations immediately outside Washington, D.C. in Maryland and Virginia do not change their prices.

(b) No, one reason being that Tennessee is a much larger geographical unit than Washington, D.C. For many residents of Tennessee, it would be very time-consuming and expensive to go outside Tennessee to obtain lower prices. But because Washington, D.C. is relatively small, it is not much trouble for many of its residents to go outside its borders to get cheaper gasoline.

(c) If P is the pretax price and Q is the pretax quantity, the arc elasticity equals

$$-\frac{.67Q - Q}{(.67Q + Q)/2} \div \frac{1.06P - P}{(1.06P + P)/2} = -\frac{.67 - 1}{(.67 + 1)/2} \div \frac{1.06 - 1}{(1.06 + 1)/2} = 6.8$$

Thus, the price elasticity of demand seemed to have been about 6.8, a high figure.

(d) Because Washington, D.C. is a relatively small area, when the tax was imposed, many of its residents bought their gasoline outside its limits.

(e) Gas stations in neighboring Virginia and Maryland benefited because of the increase in their sales to people from Washington, D.C.

Problem 6.9:

The profit from producing a barrel of oil is much less than the price of the barrel of oil because the firm must incur various costs to produce and transport it. On the other hand, Sohio had many assets besides the oil alone. The central point is that one cannot value a firm by simply multiplying its reserves by the price of oil.

CHAPTER 7

1. (a) Up to some point, increases in the firm's output result in increases in profit; beyond this point, they result in decreases in profit. Thus, since the entrepreneur's days of work are assumed to be proportional to the firm's output, up to some point, increases in the number of days he or she works result in increases in profit; beyond this point, they result in decreases in profit. Finally, since the entrepreneur's number of days of leisure equals the total time during the year minus his or her number of days of work, it follows that, up to some point, increases in his or her number of days of leisure are associated with increases in profit; beyond that point (indicated by e in the graph), they are associated with decreases in profit. (b) No. He or she maximizes utility by choosing point C, where there are Of days of leisure, and profit is below the maximum that could be achieved. (c) Yes. He or she would choose point B, where profits are a maximum.

3. The complete table is:

Number of units of variable input	Total output	Marginal product	Average product
3	90	Unknown	30
4	110	20	$27\frac{1}{2}$
5	130	20	26
6	135	5	$22\frac{1}{2}$
7	$136\frac{1}{2}$	$1\frac{1}{2}$	$19\frac{1}{2}$

5. Because of the law of diminishing marginal returns, the marginal product begins to decline at some point. If the marginal product exceeds the average product at that point, the marginal product can fall to some extent without reducing the average product. Only when it falls below the average product will the average product begin to decrease. The marginal product can continue to fall without reducing the total product. Only when it falls below zero will the total product begin to decrease.

7. 1.04 percent.

9. Yes.

11. (a) Yes, since it seems to reduce the amount of grain and protein that must be used to produce 150 pounds of pork. However, this assumes that it has no negative effect on the quality of the pork and that it does not increase the amount of other inputs that must be used. (b) At each quantity of protein, curve B is steeper than curve A. In other words, the absolute value of its slope is greater. Thus the marginal rate of technical substitution of protein for grain is greater when Aureomycin is added than when it is not (when the quantity of protein is held constant).

13. (a) Yes. (b) No.

CHAPTER 8

1. (a) The marginal cost was the extra cost of an additional flight in 1989. The fuel, wages, and other extra costs were included. (b) No, because some of these costs would be incurred regardless of whether the extra flight occurred. (c) There probably would be additional costs to raise safety levels.

3. The table is as follows:

Total fixed cost (dollars)	Total variable cost (dollars)	Average fixed cost (dollars)	Average variable cost (dollars)
50	0	—	—
50	20	50	20
50	50	25	25
50	70	$16\frac{2}{3}$	$23\frac{1}{3}$
50	100	$12\frac{1}{2}$	25
50	150	10	30

Each value of marginal cost would increase by 50 percent.

5. (a) Its fixed cost equaled $182.1 million, because, when $Q = 0, C = 182.1$, according to the equation. (b) If U.S. Steel produced 10 million tons of steel, $Q = 10$. Thus $C = 182.1 + 55.73(10) = 739.4$. This is total cost, not total variable cost. To obtain total variable cost, we subtract the fixed cost, 182.1, from 739.4, the result being $557.3 million. Since 10 million tons were produced, average variable cost was $557.3 million divided by 10 million, or $55.73 per ton. (c) If output increased by 1 ton, the equation indicates that total cost increased by $55.73. Thus marginal cost was $55.73 per ton. (d) No. Beyond some point, as output increased, marginal cost was bound to increase, because of the law of diminishing marginal returns. (See page 262 for further discussion of this point.) (e) This equation is not appropriate for present conditions, because it is based on the input prices and technology of the 1930s, not those of today. (f) No, because it is based on input prices and technology in the United States in the 1930s, not on those in Japan now.

7. (a) No, since no information is given concerning the way in which cost varies with output when capacity is held constant. (b) The steam reforming process using natural gas, since its cost is lowest. (c) Yes, because costs tend to fall as the scale of a plant increases. (d) Yes, the function shifted downward. In the early 1960s, it was not possible to produce ammonia for $16 a ton, as is evident from the graph.

9. 1,000 copies sold.

CHAPTER 9

Problem 9.1:

(a) One of the most obvious effects of this plan is that Connecticut consumers would be hurt if the price they paid for milk were to rise. But unless milk from other states could be kept out of Connecticut, it would be difficult to maintain the price support. If Connecticut supported the price of milk at a higher level than in other states, milk from other states would tend to be bought by the residents of Connecticut because it would be cheaper than Connecticut milk. (For further discussion, see Problem 18 on page 338.)

(b) No. His land could be used for other than agricultural purposes.

(c) Yes, the alternative cost has increased because the land has become more and more valuable for weekend homes and for other nonfarm uses. When land prices (and other input prices) become so high that dairy farming is no longer profitable, the price system is emitting signals that the land can be used more efficiently for purposes other than dairy farming.

(d) Yes. Many communities are concerned about the loss of dairy farms because they provide open spaces and beauty to areas that are becoming increasingly suburban and urban.

Problem 9.3:

(a) Because this cost does not vary with the amount of milk produced.

(b) By estimating the alternative (or opportunity) cost of the time devoted by the family members to work on the farm.

(c) To produce 7,600 pounds of milk, 5,700 pounds of feed must be consumed by a cow, according to Problem 9.2. Since there are 50 cows, $50 \times 5,700 = 285,000$ pounds of feed must be consumed. At 6 cents per pound, this amounts to $17,100, so total cost equals $17,100 + $40,000 = $57,100. To produce 10,000 pounds of milk, 7,900 pounds of feed must be consumed by a cow, according to Problem 9.2. Since there are 50 cows, $50 \times 7,900 = 395,000$ pounds of feed must be consumed. At 6¢ per pound, this amounts to $23,700, so total cost equals $23,700 + $40,000 = $63,700.

(d) Since feed is the only variable input, total variable cost equals $17,100 if each cow produces 7,600 pounds of milk. [See the answer to part (c)]. Because total output is $50 \times 7,600 = 380,000$ pounds of milk, average variable cost equals $17,100 \div 380,000 = 4.5$¢ per pound of milk. Total variable cost equals $23,700 if each cow produces 10,000 pounds of milk. [See the answer to part (c).] Because total output is $50 \times 10,000 = 500,000$ pounds of milk, average variable cost equals $23,700 \div 500,000 = 4.7$¢ per pound of milk.

(e) $\$40,000 \div (50 \times 7,600) = \$40,000 \div 380,000 = 10.5\cent$ per pound of milk.
$\$40,000 \div (50 \times 10,000) = \$40,000 \div 500,000 = 8\cent$ per pound of milk.

(f) If each cow produces 9,800 pounds of milk (which means that total output is $50 \times 9,800 = 490,000$ pounds of milk), total cost equals $(6\cent)$ (50) $(7,500) + \$40,000 = \$22,500 + \$40,000 = \$62,500$. If each cow produces 10,000 pounds of milk (which means that total output is $50 \times 10,000 = 500,000$ pounds of milk), total cost equals $\$63,700$, as we know from the answer to part (c). Thus, the marginal cost of an extra pound of milk is

$$\frac{\$63,700 - \$62,500}{500,000 - 490,000} = \frac{\$1,200}{10,000} = 12\cent.$$

(g) The average total cost of a pound of milk is as follows if each amount of feed is consumed per cow:

Pounds of feed consumed	Average total cost of a pound of milk		
5,700	$\dfrac{(6\cent)(50)(5,700) + \$40,000}{50(7,600)}$	$= \dfrac{\$57,100}{380,000}$	$= 15.0\cent$ per lb.
6,100	$\dfrac{(6\cent)(50)(6,100) + \$40,000}{50(8,200)}$	$= \dfrac{\$58,300}{410,000}$	$= 14.2\cent$ per lb.
6,600	$\dfrac{(6\cent)(50)(6,600) + \$40,000}{50(8,800)}$	$= \dfrac{\$59,800}{440,000}$	$= 13.6\cent$ per lb.
7,100	$\dfrac{(6\cent)(50)(7,100) + \$40,000}{50(9,400)}$	$= \dfrac{\$61,300}{470,000}$	$= 13.0\cent$ per lb.
7,500	$\dfrac{(6\cent)(50)(7,500) + \$40,000}{50(9,800)}$	$= \dfrac{\$62,500}{490,000}$	$= 12.8\cent$ per lb.
7,900	$\dfrac{(6\cent)(50)(7,900) + \$40,000}{50(10,000)}$	$= \dfrac{\$63,700}{500,000}$	$= 12.7\cent$ per lb.

Thus, the amount of feed per cow (among those considered here) that would minimize the farm's average total cost is 7,900 pounds, not 7,500 pounds. However, this is not really the optimal amount to feed each cow because it generally will not maximize profit, as we shall see in subsequent chapters.

Problem 9.5:

(a) About 18 cents per pound. About 13 cents per pound. Yes.

(b) About 12.5 cents per pound. About 12 cents per pound. Yes.

(c) Because of climatic and other differences, one would not expect the production function to be the same in California as in Wisconsin. It seems unlikely that California's lower costs can be attributed entirely to low wages; for example, economies of scale may be partly responsible.

(d) No. His level of utility seems to be a function of his profits and the amount of time he spends farming (which he enjoys). He seems to maximize utility, not profits.

Problem 9.7:

(a) No. Because the milk output goes up by 1,200 pounds at each and every amount of feed consumed, the marginal product of a pound of feed is unaffected. For example, if between 5,700 and 6,100 pounds of feed are consumed, the marginal product equals $(9,400-8,800) \div (6,100-5,700) = 1.5$ pounds of milk per pound of feed, which is the same as without bST. No, for the reason given in the second sentence of this paragraph.

(b) $11,000 \div 7,500 = 1.47$ pounds of milk per pound of feed. Yes.

(c) It would require 6,600 pounds of feed per cow, which would cost $6¢ \times 6,600 \times 50 = \$19,800$. In addition, there are fixed costs of $40,000 and $60 \times 50 = \$3,000$ for the bST. Thus, total cost equals $19,800 + \$40,000 + \$3,000 = \$62,800$. Without bST, it would require 7,900 pounds of feed per cow, so the total cost would be $6¢ \times 7,900 \times 50 + \$40,000 = \$63,700$. Consequently, total cost would be lower than if bST were not adopted. Total cost would be reduced by $63,700 - \$62,800 = \$900$.

(d) If the number of cows is fixed in the short run and if it has been decided to adopt bST, the cost of the bST is a fixed cost; it does not vary with output per cow, which depends only on the amount each cow is fed. Average total cost would be $62,800 \div (50 \times 10,000) = 12.6¢$ per pound; average variable cost would be $19,800 \div (50 \times 10,000) = 4.0¢$ per pound; and average fixed cost would be $43,000 \div (50 \times 10,000) = 8.6¢$ per pound. No. Average fixed cost rises because of the cost of the bST.

(e) The total cost of producing 50 times 11,200 pounds of milk would be $6¢ \times 7,900 \times 50 + \$40,000 + \$3,000 = \$66,700$. The total cost of producing 50 times 11,000 pounds of milk would be $6¢ \times 7,500 \times 50 + \$40,000 + \$3,000 = \$65,500$. Thus, marginal cost equals $(\$66,700 - \$65,500) \div (560,000 - 550,000) = 12¢$ per pound of milk. Yes, because the output resulting from each level of total variable cost increases by $50 \times 1,200 = 60,000$ pounds. For example, as shown in part (f) of Problem 9.3, marginal cost also equals 12¢ when each of the farm's cows produces between 9,800 and 10,000 pounds of milk before the introduction of bST.

(f) The total cost curve (after the adoption of bST) and the total revenue curve are shown below. As you can see, the break-even point is 530,000 pounds of milk. No, the total cost function is not linear.

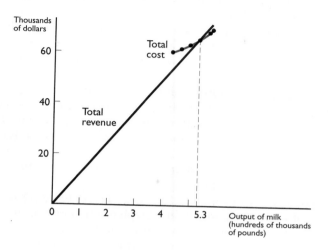

(g) On the basis of the above data, the use of bST will lower the Cox Dairy Farm's costs, so long as the farm produces more than 470,000 pounds of milk. Thus, if it will operate in this range, the use of bST seems profitable.

Problem 9.9:

(a) When corrected for inflation, the price of cheese went down. To see this, note that

$$P_{90} = 1.48 P_{80},$$

where P_{90} is the price of cheese in 1990 and P_{80} is the price of cheese in 1980. Since a dollar in 1980 could buy as much as 1.59 1990 dollars, we must divide the price of cheese in 1990 by 1.59 to obtain its price then in 1980 dollars. The result is

$$\frac{P_{90}}{1.59} = \frac{1.48}{1.59} P_{80} = 0.93 P_{80}.$$

Thus, in 1980 dollars, the price of cheese in 1990 was 7 percent below its 1980 level.

(b) Since the price elasticity is reported to be about 0.30, we would expect an increase of 7 percent $\times 0.30 = 2.1$ percent in the quantity of cheese demanded between 1980 and 1990, based on the change in price alone.

Note that the percentage change in the price adjusted for inflation is what is relevant here.

(c) If the income elasticity of demand is 0.45, this increase in income would have been expected to result in a $0.45 \times 18 = 8.1$ percent increase in quantity demanded.

(d) No. Changes in price and income account for only about a $2.1 + 8.1 = 10.2$ percent increase in per capita cheese consumption, whereas the actual increase was about 39 percent between 1980 and 1990.

(e) There has been an enormous increase in the demand for pizza and fast foods. This suggests that one of the major factors explaining the growth in cheese consumption has been a change in consumer tastes: people have become much fonder of pizzas and fast foods than in the past.

(f) Perhaps it is because cheese and beef are used together to make cheese-burgers, which are popular.

(g) As pointed out in Problem 1 on page 126, if the price-consumption curve is downward sloping in a graph of this sort, the consumer's demand for the good in question is price elastic. Thus, Mr. Lee's demand for cheese is price elastic, which is atypical because the price elasticity of demand for cheese in the United States is about 0.30.

CHAPTER 10

1. (a) No, because the demand curve for the product of a perfectly competitive firm is horizontal. Recall pages 147 to 150.

(b) 12.1 cents. Under perfect competition, price equals marginal revenue, regardless of how much milk his farm produces.

(c) No, because this price elasticity refers to the effect of changes in market price on the total amount of milk demanded.

(d) Increases in consumer incomes are likely to have a very small effect on the market demand curve for milk. Thus, milk prices are not likely to rise appreciably for this reason.

3. The firm's marginal cost curve is:

Output	Marginal cost (dollars)
0 to 1	10
1 to 2	12
2 to 3	13
3 to 4	14
4 to 5	15
5 to 6	16
6 to 7	17

(a) If the price is $13, the firm will produce 2 or 3 units. (b) 3 or 4 units. (c) 4 or 5 units. (d) 5 or 6 units. (e) 6 or 7 units.

5.
$$\eta s = \frac{8 - 7}{(8 + 7)/2} \div \frac{4 - 3}{(4 + 3)/2} = 0.47.$$

7. A difference of about 3.24 percent.

9. (a) No. (b) Firms had to leave the textile industry, so that eventually the profit rate in cotton textiles would increase to the point where it approximated the profit rate in other industries. Also, the industry had to become more concentrated in the South, the exit rate being higher in the North than in the South. (c) Yes.

11. (a) No. This is the cost per acre, not the cost per bushel of corn produced. (b) If Mr. Webster could rent the land that he owns for $110 per acre, the alternative cost of using an acre of land he owns is $110. Thus, based on the concept of alternative cost, the cost of using his own land is the same as that of using rented land. (c) If each acre of land yields 120 bushels of corn, the cost per bushel of corn of fertilizers, herbicides, insecticides, fuel, seed, electricity, and labor equals ($41.84+2.76+5.50+18.00+16.50+15.00+15.00)÷120, or 95.5¢. Assuming that these inputs (and no others) are variable, average variable cost is 95.5¢ per bushel. Since the price of 80¢ is less than the average variable cost, he should not produce any corn (unless, of course, he can somehow reduce his average variable cost by altering his output or by taking some other measures). (d) Since the price of $1.50 per bushel exceeds the average variable cost of 95.5¢ per bushel, he should produce corn, even though the price is less than average total cost.

13. (a) Less. The supply curve will be to the left of the one shown on page 336. (b) Less. The supply curve will be to the left of the one shown on page 336. (c) There commonly are substantial errors in estimates of this sort if they are based on no actual operating experience. Many unanticipated problems can arise in operating new types of plants. (d) Because of the uncertainties cited in part (c), such an investment would clearly be risky. Thus less shale oil is likely to be produced than under riskless conditions.

15. Suppose that the equilibrium rent and quantity are P and Q respectively. If the rent is reduced by 1 percent, the quantity demanded will increase by 1 percent; this means that it will increase by $.01Q$. At the same time, the quantity supplied will fall by .5 percent, which means that it will fall by $.005Q$. Thus the difference between the quantity supplied and the quantity demanded will equal $.01Q+.005Q$, or $.015Q$. In other words, it will equal 1.5 percent of the equilibrium quantity.

17. No. Because of changes from month to month in inventories of heating oil (and other factors), the supply curve shifts from month to month. Suppose that the supply curve in January is to the right of the supply curve in May.

Then the situation is as follows:

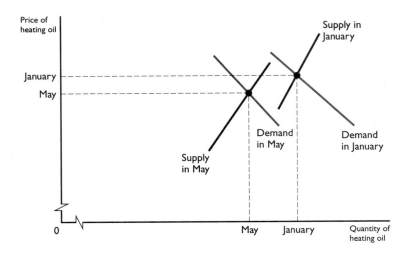

CHAPTER 11

1. (a) One cannot tell, because the answer depends on the long-run (not the short-run) average cost curve. A firm is a natural monopolist if its long-run average cost reaches a minimum at an output rate that is big enough to satisfy the market at a price that is profitable. (b) Many natural monopolies—for example, telephone companies and electric-power producers—are privately owned, so it is by no means clear that government ownership is implied. (c) 4 million pieces, since this is the point where the average total cost curve intersects the demand curve. (d) First class mail, because it earns a profit. With respect to parcels, there is already considerable competition (from United Parcel Service, in particular). (e) More competition might prod the post office to increase its own efficiency.

3. (a) In the early 1950s, IBM seems to have been close to a monopoly, since it sold over 90 percent of the electronic data processing products and services in the United States. But during the 1960s and 1970s, its share of the market fell to about 50 percent and then to about 40 percent, according to its economists. On the basis of these data, they argued that IBM was not a monopolist. (b) Yes. If a firm has a large share (say 60 percent or more) of the market, and if there is evidence that the firm's dominant position resulted from its own policies (and particularly if some form of abuse can be shown), past experience indicates that it may be challenged under Section 2 of the Sherman Act. (c) Not necessarily. If the firm's large market share has been achieved by its own "su-

perior skill, foresight, and industry," this can be an effective defense. (In fact, this was one of IBM's defenses.) The firm may argue that, if it were broken up, this would result in a slower rate of innovation and less efficiency. (d) One of the most important considerations is the cross elasticity of demand among products. One wants to include products that are closely substitutable (that is, that have high cross elasticities of demand). (e) The narrower the definition of the market, the larger IBM's share is likely to be. On the basis of the government's definition, IBM's market share exceeded those shown in the table on page 377. Clearly, it was consistent with the government's case to show that IBM's market share was high. (f) In 1981, the Justice Department ended the case on the grounds that it was "without merit."

5. The monopolist's total revenue, total cost, and total profit at each level of output are as follows:

Output	Total revenue (dollars)	Total cost (dollars)	Total profit (dollars)
5	40	20	20
6	42	21	21
7	42	22	20
8	40	23	17
9	36	24	12
10	30	30	0

Thus the optimal output is 6; this means that price should be $7.

7. Marginal revenue $= 100 - 2Q$.
Marginal cost $= 60 + 2Q$.
Consequently, $100 - 2Q = 60 + 2Q$
$$40 = 4Q$$
$$10 = Q.$$

That is, you should choose an output of 10 units.

9. $MR_1 = 160 - 16Q_1$.
$MR_2 = 80 - 4Q_2$.
$MC = 5 + (Q_1 + Q_2)$.

Therefore $160 - 16Q_1 = 5 + Q_1 + Q_2$
and $80 - 4Q_2 = 5 + Q_1 + Q_2$.
Or $155 + 17Q_1 = Q_2$
and $75 + 5Q_2 = Q_1$.

Thus $155 - 17(75 - 5Q_2) = Q_2$
$$155 - 1275 + 85Q_2 = Q_2$$
$$84Q_2 = 1120$$
$$Q_2 = 13\tfrac{1}{3}.$$

It should sell $13\frac{1}{3}$ units in the second market, and the price in this market should be $53\frac{1}{3}$.

$$Q_1 = 75 - 5Q_2$$
$$= 75 - 5(1120/84)$$
$$= 75 - 5600/84$$
$$= 75 - 66\frac{2}{3}$$
$$= 8\frac{1}{3}.$$

It should sell $8\frac{1}{3}$ units in the first market, and the price in this market should be $93\frac{1}{3}$.

11. (a) Whether the monopolist is well advised to set this price depends on the likelihood that the rival will be driven out of business. Given the monopolist's larger output, it will lose more money than the rival. However, the monopolist may have larger financial resources and may be in a better position to withstand such losses. (b) No. However, if it manages to impose heavy losses on its rival, this may teach other potential entrants the lesson that it does not pay to challenge the monopolist. (c) Perhaps the most fundamental criticism of the Areeda-Turner test is that the comparison of price with marginal (and average) cost may not be related to predatory pricing. The price set by the monopolist can be viewed as a signal to the entrant. The monopolist may be able to use this signal to convince the entrant that it should withdraw from the industry (to avoid losses), even if its price exceeds marginal (and average) cost. For reasons of this sort, the Areeda-Turner rule has received considerable criticism. Nonetheless, this rule has been used (or at least considered) by many courts.

CHAPTER 12

1. (a) No, it is a temporary price war that pushed the price below average cost, so both firms were losing money. (b) No. Both firms are losing money.

3. (a) No. Entry does not seem to be free, and exit does not seem to be costless. (b) This shift in the long-run average cost curve occurred as a consequence of technological change. For example, on the closing line, 900 cans could be moved per minute in 1965, whereas about 1,500 cans per minute could be moved in the late 1970s. (c) Certainly, this shift in the long-run average cost curve was one of the factors responsible for the decrease in the number of firms. Because breweries had to get so much bigger, fewer of them were required.

5. Since $Q = 300 - P$, and the demand for the firm's output is $Q - Q_r$, it follows that the firm's demand curve is

$$Q_b = Q - Q_r = (300 - P) - 49P$$
$$= 300 - 50P,$$
$$P = 6 - 0.02Q_b.$$

or

Thus the firm's marginal revenue curve is $MR = 6 - 0.04\,Q_b$. And since its marginal cost curve is $2.96Q_b$,

$$6 - 0.04Q_b = 2.96\,Q_b$$
$$Q_b = 2.$$

That is, your output level should be 2 million units.
Since $P = 6 - 0.02\,Q_b$, and $Q_b = 2$, it follows that $P = 6 - 0.02(2) = 5.96$. That is, the price should be $5.96 per unit.
Since $Q = 300 - P$, and $P = 5.96$, it follows that $Q = 300 - 5.96 = 294.04$. Your firm is not a dominant firm in terms of its output. It accounts for only a small percentage of industry output.

7. Whether or not it costs a great deal to distribute milk in other parts of New York, the competition from Farmland is likely to reduce prices, and thus benefit consumers. New York consumers should be able to buy goods (including milk) produced by workers outside New York.

9. They should set the marginal cost at one firm equal to the marginal cost at each other firm. If firm 1 produces 4 units, firm 2 produces 3 units, and firm 3 produces 4 units, the marginal cost at each firm equals $30. Thus this seems to be the optimal distribution of output.

11. See pages 393 to 396. No; it might, for example, induce consumers to buy the advertiser's product by means of misleading or erroneous claims.

13. (a) No. As shown in panel A in Question 13, the new marginal cost curve (EE') intersects the marginal revenue curve at an output of OQ; this means that the profit-maximizing price is OP_1, not OP_0. Thus, if the firm maximizes profit, it will increase its price to OP_1. (b) Its demand curve now is P_0VD', as shown in panel B in Question 13. In contrast to the situation before Congress acted, the firm now cannot sell anything at a price exceeding OP_0. Its marginal revenue curve now is P_0VR'. Since its demand curve is horizontal for outputs less than OQ_1, so is its marginal revenue curve. Its output now is OQ_1, since this is the output where the marginal revenue curve (P_0VR') intersects the new marginal cost curve (EE').

15. If firm A believes that firm B will produce Q_B units of output per month, its marginal revenue equals

$$100 - 8Q_A - 8Q_B.$$

To maximize its profit firm A will set its marginal revenue equal to its marginal cost, which is $4. Thus

$$100 - 8Q_A - 8Q_B = 4,$$

or

$$Q_A = 12 - Q_B.$$

17. Yes. Yes. No.

CHAPTER 13

1. (a) Strategy 2. Strategy I. (b) Strategy II. Strategy 1.

(c)

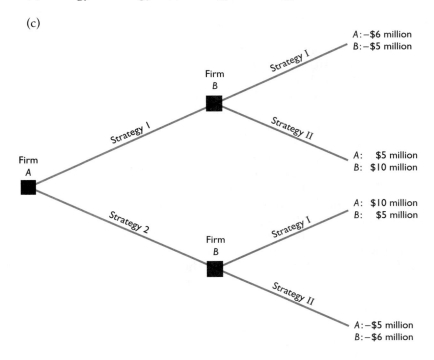

3. (a) Yes. Strategy 1. (b) Yes. Strategy II. (c) Firm *C* will choose strategy 1, and firm *D* will choose strategy II.

5. (a) Yes. (b) There are two Nash equilibria. One occurs if Ewe builds a plant on the East Coast and Zee builds a plant on the West Coast. The other occurs if Ewe builds a plant on the West Coast and Zee builds a plant on the East Coast.

7. No. One firm often can increase its profit without decreasing its rival's profit by the amount of its profit gain.

9. (a) The payoff matrix is as follows:

Possible strategies for the Miller Company	Possible strategies for the Morgan Company	
	Advertise	Do not advertise
Advertise	Morgan's profit: $2.5 million Miller's profit: $4 million	Morgan's profit: $2 million Miller's profit: $5 million
Do not advertise	Morgan's profit: $2 million Miller's profit: $2 million	Morgan's profit: $2.5 million Miller's profit: $3 million

(b) Miller has a dominant strategy (to advertise), but Morgan does not have a dominant strategy. (c) Yes. Both Miller and Morgan will advertise.

CHAPTER 14

Problem 14.1:

(a) Yes. No. A movie seen at home is not a perfect substitute for a movie seen in a theater. On the one hand, some viewers want to get out of the house; on the other hand, some viewers like the informality, comfort, and ease of staying at home. Also, the big-screen effect in a theater is different from the small picture at home.

(b) The demand curve for tickets at a typical movie theater would be shifted to the left by the growing use of VCRs and cable TV. The percentage of the population that is 18 to 24 years old has declined and will continue to decline. The percentage that is 5 to 17 years old decreased from 1980 to 1990 and will increase only slightly from 1990 to 2000. Overall, the shifts in the age distribution seem to be shifting the demand curve to the left.

(c) Apparently, VCR ownership reduces movie attendance, but the effects taper off over time. After a few years, VCR owners do not continue to reduce their movie attendance appreciably.

(d) He believes that VCRs and cable television will shift the demand curve for tickets at a typical movie theater to the right because the revenues from VCRs and cable TV help to stimulate the production of more good films, which results in a bigger demand for movie theater tickets.

(e) You might construct a model in which the quantity of movie tickets demanded depends on the average price of a movie ticket, the level of consumer income, the size of the population, the number of subscribers to cable TV, the number of households with VCRs, and other variables. Using data like those in Table 14.6, you might use statistical techniques to estimate the parameters of this equation.

Problem 14.3:

(a) Basically, all the costs are fixed costs, except the cost of film rental and the cost of popcorn, candy, and soft drinks sold. Labor costs (for selling tickets, running the concession stand, and managing the theater) do not vary with the number of people buying tickets to the theater. Neither do theater rental costs nor advertising costs nor the costs of utilities, insurance, repairs, or maintenance. If a movie theater has no concession stand, the amount paid for film rental is the only variable cost. Increases in the number of tickets sold result in decreases in average cost because average fixed cost declines while average variable cost (the amount paid for film rental per ticket sold) remains constant (at $2) as increases occur in the number of tickets sold.

(b) No. If a projectionist cost Carmike $250 per week, the gross saving was .6 × $250 per week, since the managers received a raise of .4 × $250 per week. But the net saving was lower because the automated projection booth was not free; its introduction increased Carmike's costs, and this increase should be deducted from the gross saving. The marginal cost curve did not change because the wages of both the projectionists and the managers, as well as the costs of introducing the automated projection booths, were fixed costs, for a 1-week period.

(c) Yes, he encountered such a problem. Although the automated projection booths would promote the firm's interests, the managers felt initially that the booths would not promote their own interests. By changing the incentives of the managers, he induced them to introduce automated projection booths.

(d) When the supply of films is small, the distributors have more bargaining power vis-à-vis the theater owners, and the theater owners tend to compete more intensely for the limited supply of films. By putting its theaters in areas where there are no rivals, a company can cut down on such competition.

Problem 14.5:

(a) The 10¢ tax shifted the supply curve upward by 10¢, so the posttax supply curve intersected the demand curve at 60¢. Thus, the price to the consumer rose by 5¢, from 55¢ to 60¢.

(b) The loss in consumer surplus because the ticket price to the consumer rose from 55 to 60¢ is rectangle A plus triangle C, which equals $(60¢ - 55¢)(1 \text{ million}) + \frac{1}{2}(60¢ - 55¢)(1.1 \text{ million} - 1.0 \text{ million}) = \$50,000 + \$2,500 = \$52,500$.

(c) Theaters paid the tax of 10¢ per ticket to the government. After paying this tax, the price per ticket received by the theater was $60¢ - 10¢ = 50¢$. Thus, the loss in producer surplus because the net price received by the producer (that is, the theater) was 50¢ rather than 55¢ was rectangle B plus triangle D, which equals $(55¢ - 50¢)(1 \text{ million}) + \frac{1}{2}(55¢ - 50¢)(1.1 \text{ million} - 1.0 \text{ million}) = \$52,500$.

(d) 1 million × 10¢ = $100,000.

(e) Yes. Yes. $52,500 + $52,500 − $100,000 = $5,000.

(f) No. See page 26.

(g) No. See page 26.

Problem 14.7:

(a) Yes, because Carmike had plenty of unutilized capacity and the area seemed to have more screens than the population could support.

(b) No, Carmike does not have a dominant strategy. There are two Nash equilibria: (1) Carmike constructs a theater, and its rival does not con-

struct a theater; (2) Carmike does not construct a theater, and its rival does construct a theater. If Carmike has the first move, it would be expected to build a theater, and its rival would not be expected to do so.
(c) Yes. Carmike seems to be positioned to expand its capacity quickly and at relatively low cost and to cut prices, if necessary, to resist entry.

Problem 14.9:

(a) The price of a movie ticket would increase from $4.25 to $5.75, and the number of tickets sold would fall from 30,000 to 20,000 tickets per period of time.
(b) ($5.75 − $4.25) (20,000) + $\frac{1}{2}$($5.75 − $4.25) (30,000 − 20,000) = $30,000 + $7,500 = $37,500.
(c) ($5.75 − $4.25) (20,000) − $\frac{1}{2}$($4.25 − $2.75) (30,000 − 20,000) = $30,000 − $7,500 = $22,500.
(d) $15,000.
(e) No. For one thing, according to various accounts, Carmike has significantly lower costs than a variety of smaller theaters would have. (See Problem 14.10.)

CHAPTER 15

1. If it is true that the quantity of nurses demanded currently exceeds the quantity supplied by 14 percent, the current shortage equals

$$H = Q_D - Q_S = 1.14Q_S - Q_S = .14Q_S,$$

where Q_D is the quantity of nurses demanded and Q_S is the quantity supplied. Letting ΔH be the change in the size of the shortage due to the wage increase, it follows that:

$$\Delta H = \Delta Q_D - \Delta Q_S$$

where ΔQ_D is the change in the quantity of nurses demanded and ΔQ_S is the change in the quantity supplied. On the basis of the elasticities provided by the senator, a 1 percent increase in the wage for nurses would result in a 0.3 percent reduction in the quantity demanded and a 0.1 percent increase in the quantity supplied; this means that $\Delta Q_D = -.003Q_D$ and $\Delta Q_S = .001 Q_S$. Thus

$$\Delta H = -.003Q_D - .001Q_S.$$

Recalling that $Q_D = 1.14Q_S$,

$$\Delta H = -.003(1.14Q_S) - .001Q_S$$
$$= -.00442Q_S.$$

Since the shortage currently equals $.14Q_S$, the percentage change in the size of the shortage would be

$$\frac{\Delta H}{H} = \frac{-.00442Q_S}{.14Q_S} = -3.2 \text{ percent.}$$

In other words, based on the senator's estimates, the answer is that a 1 percent increase in the wage for nurses would reduce the shortage by about 3.2 percent. However, before putting any confidence in this result, you would do well to check the senator's estimates against the results of studies carried out by economists and others.

3. The value of the marginal product is shown in the following table.

Number of days of labor	Output	Marginal product	Value of marginal product (dollars)
0	0	8	40
1	8	7	35
2	15	6	30
3	21	5	25
4	26	4	20
5	30		

Thus, if the daily wage of labor is $30, the firm should hire 2 or 3 days of labor.

5. The wage, P_L, will equal the price of the product, P, times the marginal product of labor, which equals

$$\frac{\delta Q}{\delta L} = 0.8L^{-.2}K^{.2} = \frac{0.8Q}{L}.$$

Thus
$$P_L = \frac{0.8Q}{L} P, \quad \text{or} \quad \frac{P_L L}{PQ} = 0.8.$$

Since $P_L L$ equals the total wages paid by the firm and PQ equals its revenues, this completes the proof.

7. (a) Such a graph is shown in panel A on p. A43. The budget line is CD. To derive this budget line, note that a physician who devoted every hour in the week to leisure would receive no income from working. That there are 168 hours in a week explains why the budget line passes through point D. If the physician devotes no time to leisure, the amount of income received from working is OC (which equals $168W$, where W is the physician's hourly wage rate). This explains why the budget line passes through point C. Note that the

slope of the budget line equals -1 times the physician's hourly wage rate, because every extra hour devoted to leisure reduces the amount of income received from working by an amount equal to the hourly wage rate. Panel A also shows the physician's indifference curves. Given these indifference curves and the budget line, the physician will maximize utility by choosing OX hours of leisure and by obtaining OY dollars of income from working.

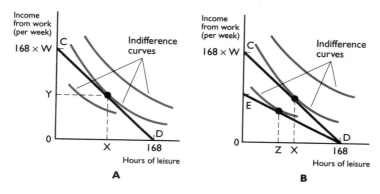

(b) A decrease in the physician's hourly wage rate reduces the amount that he or she can earn if no time is devoted to leisure from OC to OE in panel B. Thus, the budget line is no longer CD, but ED, and the physician will maximize utility by choosing OZ rather than OX hours of leisure. Since he or she is in the backward-bending portion of the supply curve, OZ is less than OX. (c) If the price elasticity of supply for physicians' services is negative, this does not appear to be true.

9. This law helps to push wages above competitive levels. The general public loses because the cost of federal construction projects is increased.

CHAPTER 16

1. (a) The present value (in millions of dollars) was

$$-15+\frac{2}{1.10}+\frac{2}{(1.10)^2}+\frac{2}{(1.10)^3}+\frac{2}{(1.10)^4}+\frac{2}{(1.10)^5}+\frac{2}{(1.10)^6}+\frac{2}{(1.10)^7}+\frac{2}{(1.10)^8}+\frac{2}{(1.10)^9}.$$

This is equal to $-15+2(.9091+.8264+.7513+.6830+.6209+.5645+.5132+.4665+.4241) = -15+2(5.7590) = -3.482$ millions of dollars.

(b) The present value would be

$$-20+\frac{2}{1.10}+\frac{2}{(1.10)^2}+\frac{2}{(1.10)^3}+\frac{2}{(1.10)^4}+\frac{2}{(1.10)^5}+\frac{2}{(1.10)^6}+\frac{2}{(1.10)^7}+\frac{2}{(1.10)^8}+\frac{2}{(1.10)^9}.$$

This is equal to $-20+2(.9091+.8264+.7513+.6830+.6209+.5645+.5132+.4665+.4241) = -20+2(5.7590) = -8.482$ millions of dollars.

(c) Yes. Since its present value was negative, the investment was not worth while. (It decreased the firm's wealth.) The firm's analysts carried out the above calculations and recommended that the project be turned down.

3. (a) The present value of the costs and benefits is

$$-1.5 - \frac{3}{1.10} + \frac{1}{(1.10)^2} + \frac{1}{(1.10)^3} + \frac{1}{(1.10)^4} + \frac{1}{(1.10)^5} + \frac{1}{(1.10)^6} + \frac{1}{(1.10)^7},$$

which equals –.27 billion dollars. Since the present value is negative, it should not be carried out.

(b) If the interest rate is .05, the present value is

$$-1.5 - \frac{3}{1.05} + \frac{1}{(1.05)^2} + \frac{1}{(1.05)^3} + \frac{1}{(1.05)^4} + \frac{1}{(1.10)^5} + \frac{1}{(1.05)^6} + \frac{1}{(1.05)^7},$$

which equals .48 billion dollars. Since the present value is positive, it should be carried out.

(c) Because net costs occur early and net benefits occur late in the life of water projects.

(d) The interest rate should be based on the alternative cost of public funds. That is, it should reflect the value of private alternatives forgone by the expenditure of public funds for water projects.

5. (a) If the interest rate is 10 percent, the present value of the investment is

$$-\$100{,}000 - \frac{\$100{,}000}{1.10} - \frac{\$100{,}000}{(1.10)^2} - \frac{\$100{,}000}{(1.10)^3} - \frac{\$100{,}000}{(1.10)^4}$$

$$- \frac{\$100{,}000}{(1.10)^5} - \frac{\$100{,}000}{(1.10)^6} + \frac{\$15{,}000}{(1.10)^7} + \frac{\$15{,}000}{(1.10)^8}$$

$$+ \frac{\$15{,}000}{(1.10)^9} + \frac{\$15{,}000}{(1.10)^{10}} + \frac{\$200{,}000}{(1.10)^{11}} + \frac{\$700{,}000}{(1.10)^{12}}$$

$$+ \frac{\$700{,}000}{(1.10)^{13}} + \frac{\$700{,}000}{(1.10)^{14}} + \frac{\$700{,}000}{(1.10)^{15}} + \frac{\$700{,}000}{(1.10)^{16}}$$

$$+ \frac{\$700{,}000}{(1.10)^{17}} + \frac{\$700{,}000}{(1.10)^{18}} + \frac{\$700{,}000}{(1.10)^{19}}.$$

This is equal to $-\$100{,}000(1 + .9091 + .8264 + .7513 + .6830 + .6209 + .5645) + \$15{,}000(.5132 + .4664 + .4241 + .3855) + \$200{,}000(.3505) + \$700{,}000 (.3186 + .2897 + .2633 + .2394 + .2176 + .1978 + .1799 + .1635),$ or $-\$100{,}000(5.3552) + \$15{,}000(1.7893) + \$200{,}000(.3505) + \$700{,}000 (1.8698).$ Thus the answer is

$-\$535,520 + \$26,840 + \$70,100 + \$1,308,860 = \$870,280$. Since its present value is positive, the investment is worthwhile. It increases the firm's wealth. (b) If the effect on the firm's cash flow is zero in 1987–91, the present value is $-\$100,000(5.3552) + \$700,000(1.8698)$, or $\$773,340$. Since it is positive, the investment is still worthwhile.

7. The expected monetary value equals

$$.5(\$6,000) + .5(-\$12,000) = -\$3,000.$$

No, because the expected monetary value is less if she buys the stock than if she does not buy it, in which case it equals zero (since she makes or loses nothing).

9. (a) The utility of zero equals $10 + 2(0) = 10$. The utility of $-\$25,000$ equals $10 + 2(-25) = -40$. The utility of $+\$32,000$ equals $10 + 2(32) = 74$. Her expected utility equals $.5(-40) + .5(74) = 17$. (b) Since the expected utility if she makes the investment (17) exceeds the expected utility if she does not make it (10), she should make it.

11. (a) No, since the net present value of such an investment is negative. (b) No, since the net present value of this investment is negative too. (c) If the new plant is expected to operate for as long as many plants do, a 5-year period seems rather short because the new plant's effects on profits are likely to extend for much longer than 5 years. (d) If the firm can only obtain 10 percent or less on comparable alternative investment possibilities, the figure of 15 percent seems too high. (e) It will tend to bias the net present values downward because net costs occur early and net benefits occur late in the life of such investment projects.

CHAPTER 17

Problem 17.1:
(a) 2.5 percent $\times 1.75 = 4.375$ percent.
(b) 1.2 percent.
(c) About $4.375 + 1.2 = 5.575$ percent. Yes. The average of the estimates by the three aircraft manufacturers is $(5.1 + 6.4 + 5.5) \div 3 = 5.67$ percent, which differs by only one-tenth of a percentage point from this estimate.
(d) If there were about 1.2 million seats in 1985 [see part (a)], a 5.575 percent increase amounts to about $.05575 \times 1.2$ million $= 66,900$ extra seats. If each aircraft has about 200 seats, this means an increase of about 335 airplanes per year.
(e) Since the income elasticity of demand for air travel is assumed to be 1.75 in part (a), this reduction in consumer income would result in about a $5 \times 1.75 = 8.75$ percent reduction in the quantity demanded of air travel.

(f) This model assumes that the quantity demanded of air travel is a function of only consumer income and the price of air travel, whereas other factors are very important. For example, because much air travel is for business purposes, the marginal revenue product of air travel—and the firms' demand for air travel—should be considered. Also, this model assumes that the number of aircraft is proportional to the amount of air travel. However, this is a very rough approximation, because there can be substantial variation in the proportion of seats that are filled. Further, this model ignores the fact that the price of aircraft, the interest rate that airlines have to pay to finance their investment in aircraft, and the rate of technological change in aircraft influence how profitable an airline's investment in new aircraft will be, and hence how many planes will be bought. Factors of this sort have been stressed in previous chapters.

Problem 17.3:
(a) The difference each year in cash flow between the situation with and without the new system is given below:

$$1991: -1-(-1) = 0 \quad 1995: 0-(-1) = 1 \quad 1999: 2-2 = 0$$
$$1992: -2-(-2) = 0 \quad 1996: 0-0 = 0 \quad 2000: 3-2 = 1$$
$$1993: -3-(-3) = 0 \quad 1997: 1-0 = 1 \quad 2001: 3-3 = 0$$
$$1994: -2-(-3) = 1 \quad 1998: 1-1 = 0 \quad 2002: 4-4 = 0$$

If the interest rate is 8 percent, the present value (in 1994) of these differences is

$$1 + \left(\frac{1}{(1+.08)}\right)1 + \left(\frac{1}{(1+.08)^3}\right)1 + \left(\frac{1}{(1+.08)^6}\right)1 = 1 + .92593$$

$$+ .79383 + .63017 = 3.34993 \text{ billion dollars.}$$

(b) If total revenue (less total variable cost) equals $10 billion (the total launch costs, according to page 578) if Boeing sells 400 units of this aircraft, the price must exceed average variable cost by $10 billion ÷ 400, or $25 million. (This assumes that the launch costs are all fixed costs and there are no fixed costs other than the launch costs.)

(c) No. It would have earned no accounting profit on its $10 billion investment. Thus, it would have incurred an economic loss, since it could have obtained an accounting profit from this investment if the money had been invested differently.

(d) The deadweight loss from monopsony is equal to $\frac{1}{2}(21¢ - 15¢)$ $(120,000 - 100,000) + \frac{1}{2}(15¢ - 13¢)(120,000 - 100,000) = \$600 + \$200$ $= \$800$ per year.

Problem 17.5:

(a) The vertical axis in Figure 17.2 shows unit cost as a percent of a 700-unit buy. According to the relationship, the value on the vertical axis is about 120 when the value on the horizontal axis is 500. Thus, it appears that average cost if 500 units were sold would exceed average cost if 700 units were sold by about 20 percent.

(b) Because the launch costs are very high. Unless there are reasonably clear signals that a substantial number of units will be sold, the aircraft manufacturer is taking a very big risk by launching a new aircraft.

(c) According to Figure 17.2, the average cost if 400 units are sold is about 130 percent of the average cost if 700 units are sold; and the average cost if 200 units are sold is about 180 percent of the average cost if 700 units are sold. Thus, the average cost if 200 units are sold is about $180 \div 130 = 1.38$ times as great as the average cost if 400 units are sold. The average cost if 400 units are sold equals the price of the plane, since McDonnell Douglas just breaks even if it sells 400 units. Consequently, the average cost if 200 units are sold is about 1.38 times the plane's price; this means that, if McDonnell Douglas sells 200 units, its total costs exceed its total revenues by about 38 percent.

Problem 17.7:

(a) On a per-seat basis, the Airbus A-320 cost $24 million $\div$ 162 = $148,000 per seat, while the Boeing 757 cost $27 million $\div$ 208 = $130,000 per seat. Thus, the Boeing 757 was cheaper.

(b) No. Obviously, it should look at operating costs, among other things.

(c) Yes. One would expect that the Boeing 757's immediate availability would weigh in its favor.

(d) By buying the Airbus A-320, Air India was investing $18,000 per seat more than if it bought the Boeing 757. In return for this investment, Air India received an annual $3,000 saving in fuel cost per seat. Assuming for simplicity that this saving would go on forever, Air India was obtaining a return on its investment of 3 $\div$ 18 = 17 percent per year. (In reality, it was somewhat lower because the savings really would not go on forever.) Since this rate of return was less than the 25 percent rate of return that we assume Air India could have obtained from alternative comparable investments, the difference in annual fuel cost was not sufficient to outweigh the difference in investment cost.

(e) Yes. It seems likely.

Problem 17.9:

(a) No. The present value of the estimated net benefits is negative, whether the discount rate is 5, 10, or 15 percent.

(b) Yes, since it avoided the sorts of losses the British and French experienced.

(c) The airplane is designed without proper regard for the commercial and economic considerations that will determine whether it will be a success.

(d) If Boeing chooses one of the approaches and carries it to completion, the expected cost is

$$.5(\$20 \text{ billion}) + .5(\$10 \text{ billion}) = \$15 \text{ billion}.$$

If the two approaches are run in parallel and if the true cost of development using each approach can be determined after $100 million has been spent on each approach, the expected cost is

$$.25(\$20 \text{ billion}) + .75(\$10 \text{ billion}) + \$100 \text{ million} = \$12.6 \text{ billion}.$$

(Note that the total cost figure for each approach, if adopted, includes the $100 million.) Why is this expression correct? Because there is a .25 probability that total costs with the better of the two approaches will be $20 billion and a .75 probability that they will be $10 billion. In addition, there is the certainty that a cost of $100 million will be incurred for the approach that is dropped. (The reason why there is a .25 chance that total costs with the better of the two approaches is $20 billion is that this will occur only when the total cost of both approaches turns out to be $20 billion, and the probability that this will occur is .5 times .5, or .25.) Comparing the above results, it is obvious that the expected total cost of development is lower with two parallel approaches than with a single approach. With two parallel approaches, the expected cost is $12.6 billion; with a single approach, it is $15 billion.

CHAPTER 18

1. If there is a sufficiently large number of firms and permits, a competitive market for the permits will develop. The price of a permit will tend to equal the marginal cost of reducing pollution by 1 ton, which will tend to be equalized among firms.

3. (a) No, because fuel must be used to produce and transport the corn required to produce the ethanol. (b) Yes. Although the cost of a gallon of ethanol was 35¢ higher (that is, $1.20 minus 85¢) than a gallon of gasoline, exemption from the federal gasoline tax was worth 40¢ per gallon and exemption from state taxes was often worth at least 40¢ more per gallon. Thus the tax exemptions more than offset the higher cost of production of ethanol. However, some very optimistic forecasts in the late 1970s of gasohol sales were not achieved. Gasohol would never displace regular gasoline completely, because as more and more gasohol is produced, the price of corn would be bid up, and eventually, despite the tax exemptions, it would no longer be prof-

itable to substitute more gasohol for regular gasoline. (c) Corn prices and the value of corn-producing land tend to rise. A general equilibrium analysis can handle these questions more adequately than a partial equilibrium analysis.

5. No. Because, if the two consumers arrive at any point off the contract curve, they can find a superior point on the contract curve, in the sense that one of them can be made better off without making the other worse off.

7. The plane's landing at that time may delay large commercial jets and impose substantial costs (in terms of delay and inconvenience) on the passengers carried by these commercial aircraft. Increases in the landing fees paid by small private aircraft could help to eliminate such divergences.

9. No.

11. 7 units of national defense.

CHAPTER 19

Problem 19.1:

(a) To minimize cost, farmers will set the marginal rate of technical substitution equal to the ratio of the price of an acre-foot of water to the price of a unit of nonwater inputs; this ratio is $10 ÷ $1 = 10$. To minimize cost, manufacturers will set the marginal rate of technical substitution equal to the ratio of the price of an acre-foot of water to the price of a unit of nonwater inputs; this ratio is $50 ÷ $1 = 50$.

(b) They will be off the contract curve. No, the allocation will not be efficient because the marginal rate of technical substitution between water and nonwater inputs will not be the same in farming as in manufacturing. Farmers should use less water, and manufacturers should use more.

(c) Yes, since they are willing to pay much more for an extra acre-foot of water than farmers do.

(d) Yes, it is economically efficient for farmers to use less water and for urban households to use more. Cotton and rice are not necessarily more important. People may value additional swimming in their backyards more highly than additional cotton or rice.

Problem 19.3:

(a) Not necessarily. How much effect a water price increase has on a crop's average cost depends on how much water is used, as well as on the increase in the water price.

(b) Without marginal cost pricing of water, this farm would have produced 8 tons per day. With marginal cost pricing of water, this farm would have produced 7 tons per day.

(c) The market supply curve, with and without marginal cost pricing of water, is as shown on page A50:

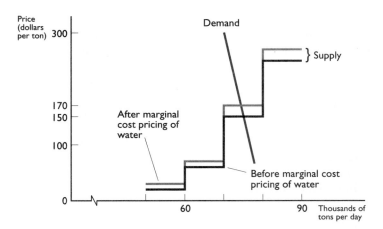

Before marginal cost pricing of water, the equilibrium price of this crop is $150 per ton; after marginal cost pricing of water, it is $170 per ton.
(d) No, we must look at the demand and supply of both California and non-California rice. A general equilibrium analysis should be used.

Problem 19.5:
(a) About $4 billion − $200 million = $3.8 billion.
(b) The gain in consumer surplus is area $ABEF$ = ($21 − $20) (950 million) + $\frac{1}{2}$ ($21 − $20) (1 billion − 950 million) = $950 million + $25 million $\overset{.}{=}$ $975 million. The gain in producer surplus is area HFE minus area GAB, or area $GCEH$ minus area $ABCF$. Since area $GCEH$ equals area $GCDKH$ (which is $1.875 billion) plus area KDE (which is $.025 billion), and area $ABCF$ equals $.925 billion, the gain in producer surplus equals $1.875 billion + $.025 billion − $.925 billion = $975 million. (In this particular case, the gain in consumer surplus equals the gain in producer surplus. This, of course, will not generally be true.)
(c) The increase in total surplus equals the increase in consumer surplus plus the increase in producer surplus. The increase in consumer surplus equals area $ABCF$ plus area CBD plus area DBE. The gain in producer surplus equals area $GCDKH$ plus area KDE minus area $ABCF$. [Recall the answer to part (b).] Thus, the increase in total surplus equals

$$\text{area } ABCF + \text{area } CBD + \text{area } DBE$$
$$+ \text{area } GCDKH + \text{area } KDE - \text{area } ABCF$$
$$= \text{area } CBD + \text{area } DBE + \text{area } GCDKH + \text{area } KDE$$
$$= \text{area } GBEH.$$

(d) It is by no means obvious that large agricultural corporations should be subsidized in this way.

(e) For the Pareto criterion to be applicable, a change must benefit some people without harming others. In this case, the farmers whose water prices would be raised would be hurt. Thus, the Pareto criterion cannot be applied.

(f) Yes. This seems to be a case where the customers of the Metropolitan Water District are better-off, since they value the extra water they obtain more highly than the amount it costs them, and no one else is worse off because the irrigation district near the Mexican border receives full compensation for the canal lining and other conservation measures.

(g) These federal agencies do seem to be working at cross purposes. Many economists would recommend that both water subsidies and government intervention in agriculture be reduced.

Problem 19.7:

(a) The officials should have based their estimates on the assumption that the price would be $60 if this in fact was the marginal cost. See page 615. For the provision of the water to be economically efficient, price should equal marginal cost. Since this would not be the case if the price were $30, the quantity demanded would not be at an efficient level.

(b) Yes. The price must be raised to ration the existing supplies of water.

(c) No. The present value of the net benefits is negative, whether the discount rate is 2.7 or 5 percent.

Problem 19.9:

(a) Many farmers might find it difficult to obtain loans if they could not demonstrate that they had reasonably long-term access to water. For a reallocation of water to occur, it does not seem necessary for the 1-year contract renewal process to be accepted.

(b) There is no scientific, purely objective way to determine what a "fair" resource balance is, but this does not mean that policymakers and analysts should not try to figure out whether (and if so, how) improvements can be made, on the basis of rough judgments of what is "fair" or "equitable."

(c) The rice farmers would almost certainly argue against the proposed changes for reasons discussed above.

PHOTOGRAPH CREDITS

INDEX

List of Real-World Applications
(other than in Chapters 2, 6, 9, 14, 17, and 19)

1. Coffee bars invade Manhattan
2. The price of cotton: highest since the Civil War
3. Air travel between Los Angeles and New York
4. Drought and beef prices
5. Lunch at Le Perigord
6. A tax on white wine?
7. Rent control in New York City
8. Rent control California-style
9. Floods and the price of lettuce
10. Determination of indifference curves
11. Sickness and health insurance
12. The food-stamp program
13. New York state budget
14. Medical insurance
15. Sugar import quotas
16. The Consumer Price Index
17. New York City's water crisis
18. Calculating a cost-of-living index
19. Prescription drug prices in New York
20. Lewis and Clark Lake
21. Residential demand for water
22. Fur sales take a hit
23. Animal experiments
24. Free public transit
25. Not a cough in a carload?
26. Demand for electricity
27. Steel demand
28. Demand for cellophane
29. Cigarette demand
30. Substitution between alcohol and marijuana
31. Is a CEO worth $26 million per year?
32. Producing broilers
33. The cotton industry in India
34. Pork production
35. Corn production
36. Rice milling
37. Enforcement of laws
38. Costs of a Boeing 747
39. Antibiotic's production costs
40. Costs of IBM
41. Costs of hosiery mill
42. Hospital costs
43. Space shuttle costs
44. Costs of steel
45. Ammonia costs
46. Auctions
47. National dental insurance
48. Rent and total surplus
49. Farm programs
50. Tom Kelly's farm
51. Coffee price
52. Onion price
53. Cotton textile industry
54. Webster farm
55. Shale oil supply
56. Rental housing
57. Output of heating oil
58. New England milk prices
59. Playing the slots at Foxwood
60. Banana prices
61. Prices at Disneyland
62. De Beers
63. Michigan Bell